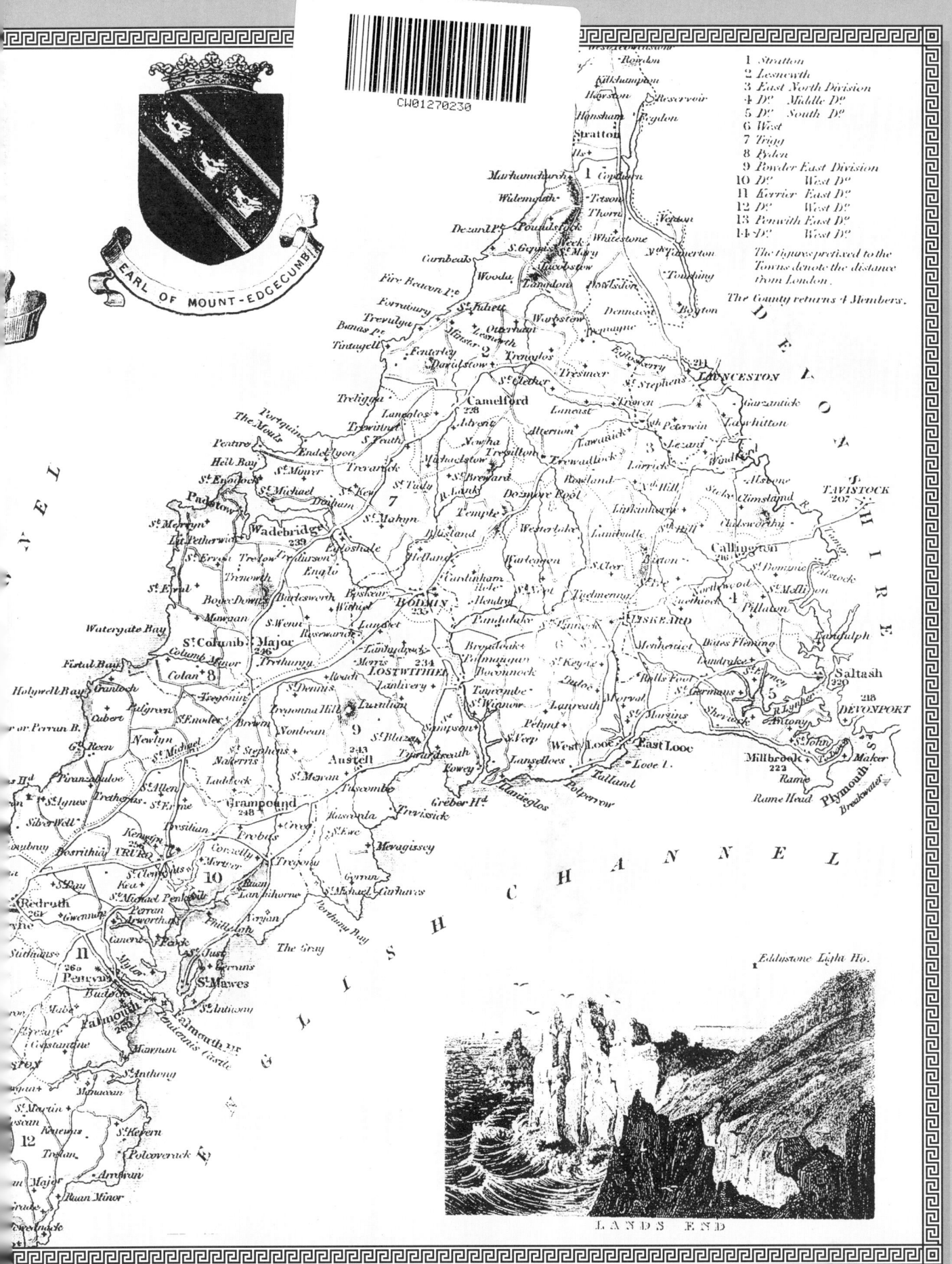

The Parks and Gardens of Cornwall

Werrington Park. The Triumphal Arch, serpentine lake and White Bridge. The Duchess's Bridge was at the other end of the lake. (Gilbert 1820: ii. 522)

The Parks and Gardens of Cornwall:

A Companion Guide arranged to correspond with the Ordnance Survey Landranger maps

by

DOUGLAS ELLORY PETT

with a foreword by
HRH the Prince of Wales

ALISON HODGE

First published in 1998 by

Alison Hodge, Bosulval, Newmill, Penzance, Cornwall TR20 8XA.

This edition © Alison Hodge 1998.

© Douglas Ellory Pett 1998.

Reprinted, with corrections, 1999.

The right of Douglas Ellory Pett to be identified as author of this work has been asserted by him in accordance with the Copyright, Designs and Patents Act 1988.

All rights reserved. Apart from any fair dealing for the purpose of private study, research, criticism or review, as permitted under the Copyright, Designs and Patents Act 1988, no part of this work may be photocopied, stored in a retrieval system, published, performed in public, adapted, broadcast, transmitted, recorded or reproduced in any form or by any means, without the prior permission in writing of the copyright owner. Enquiries should be addressed to Alison Hodge.

ISBN 0 906720 27 3

British Library Cataloguing-in-Publication Data
A catalogue record for this book is available from the British Library.

Edited, designed and originated in house.

Dustjacket design by Christopher Laughton.

Reprographics by Input Words & Graphics.

Printed and bound in the UK by Short Run Press Ltd., Bittern Road, Sowton, Exeter EX2 7LN.

Contents

Foreword	7
Preface	9
Introduction	11
Geology and soil	11
Climate	14
Garden history	16
How to Use the Topography	26
Explanatory notes	
1 The Isles of Scilly (*OS. Explorer 101*)	29
2 Land's End and The Lizard (*OS. Landranger 203*)	36
1. Penzance and St Ives	36
2. Hayle and Helston	57
3. Camborne and Redruth	75
3 Truro and Falmouth (*OS. Landranger 204*)	86
1. Truro	86
2. Falmouth	109
3. Grampound, St Mawes and Mevagissey	134
4 Newquay and Bodmin (*OS. Landranger 200*)	150
1. St Austell, Lostwithiel and Fowey	150
2. Newquay, Padstow and Wadebridge	171
3. Bodmin	185
5 Bude and Launceston (*OS. Landranger 190 & 201*)	200
1. Bude and North-East Cornwall	200
2. Launceston	205
3. South-East Cornwall	218
6 Deer Parks in Cornwall	254
The Bibliographies	263
Pre-Seventeenth Century: Early Site References, 1086-1699	264
Eighteenth Century: Topographical References, 1716-1824	268
Nineteenth Century: Horticultural and General References, 1792-1899	274
Twentieth-Century References	283
Historic Illustrations, 1690-1874	291
Plant Records	295
Indexes	300
Garden Types and Features	300
Biographical Notes	314
Index of Places	332

ST. JAMES'S PALACE

"The Parks and Gardens of Cornwall" is the most comprehensive survey of such sites to have been made so far in any county in England. It traces those who pioneered settlement, in one way or another, often in adverse conditions; who experimented with the re-forestation of a treeless and wind-swept terrain; who were able eventually to plant up and beautify the landscape and who supported, or themselves travelled, on expeditions to foreign parts to enhance our native flora. In all of these ways Cornwall has made a unique contribution to the introduction and acclimatisation of beautiful and exotic plants which not only give us great pleasure, but place upon us the obligation to conserve and enrich the heritage which has been left to us.

I hope that this book will not only be of interest to Cornish men and women and those who visit their countryside, but will inspire others to study, preserve and enhance the treasures of our past which the best of our man-made landscapes represent.

It is perhaps somewhat questionable, if there be any department in literature in which a writer has less hope, or more fear, than in local history. As every man is an historian of his own parish, town, or village, the peasant is frequently much better acquainted with the facts which exist in his own neighbourhood, than the man who has prosecuted his inquiries with diligence, devoted his time to profound researches, and who finally sits down to arrange his thoughts in philosophical retirement.

There is, however, unhappily in the human mind, a stronger propensity to detect faults, than to relish excellencies; and the former are frequently recollected with pleasure, when all traces of the latter are obliterated from the memory. An error, thus discovered, is but rarely suffered to perish from the want of propagation; and a tale, which begins in an audible whisper, having awakened attention, furnishes sagacity with employment and continues to circulate, until suspicion takes the place of confidence, and the writer receives his condemnation from persons who are totally incompetent to form any judgment of the facts which he has stated. To escape censure, is therefore a privilege which no writer of provincial history has any just reason to expect.

Samuel Drew, in the Preface to
The History of Cornwall, 1824.

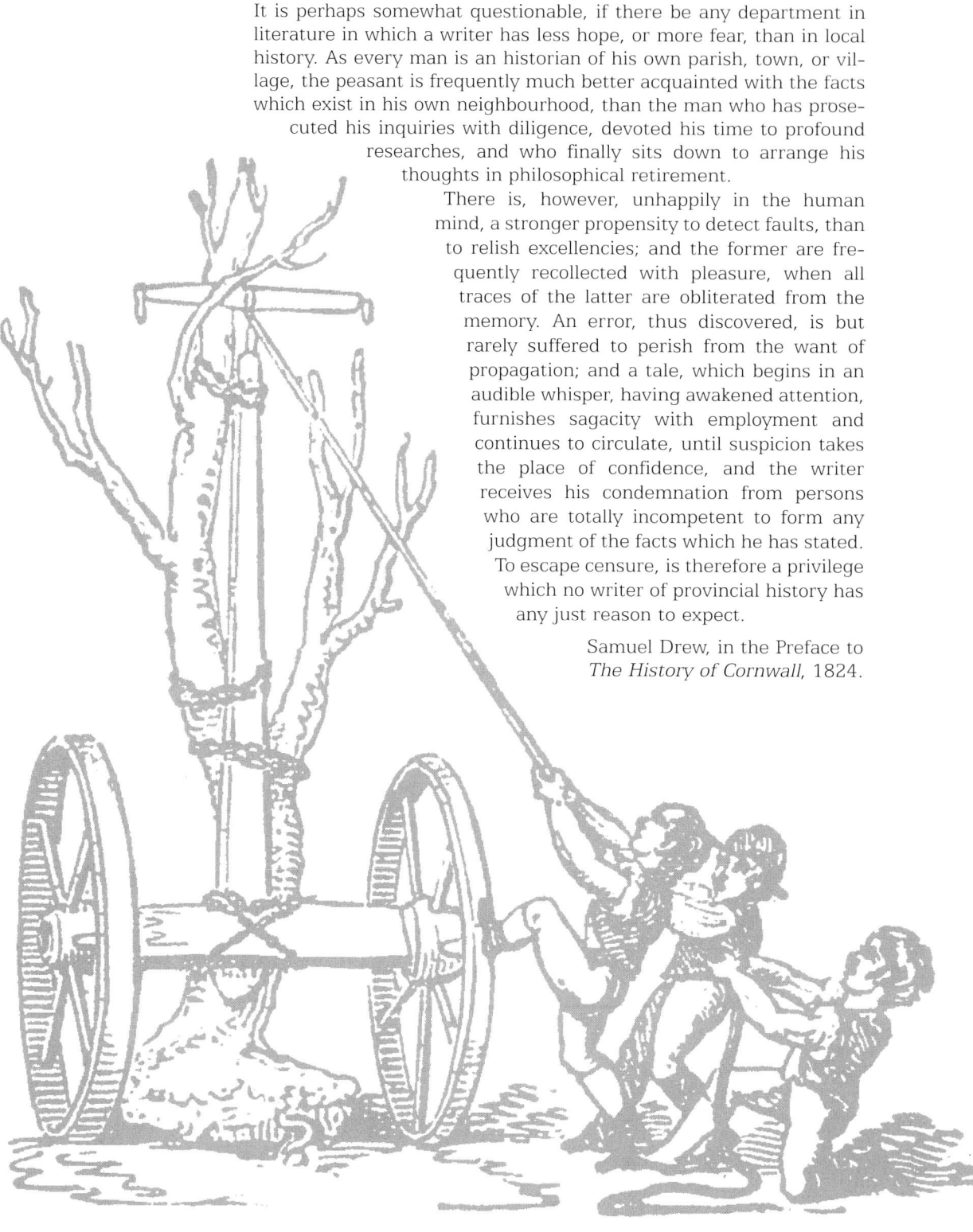

Preface

Over the last twenty years gardens have increasingly been arousing interest among a wide spectrum of people, from the observant traveller to the serious social or garden historian. This book is addressed to both ends of this spectrum. At first sight, such a task might appear impossible, but in the present infancy of the subject, the information which might interest the casual tourist will tend in the first instance to be the same as that needed by the research worker setting out on a new course of enquiry.

The material here gathered together has its origins in the writer's response to an appeal in 1985 by the late Fred Shepherd from the local branch of the National Council for the Conservation of Plants and Gardens for a 'bibliography of horticulture and horticulturists'. In particular it was suggested that the Cornish references in the great nineteenth-century horticultural journals needed to be investigated. As the work proceeded a list of significant gardens in the county was built up, having as its criterion for inclusion that the grounds had been noticed in print, even if only by such a word as 'improved'. As the list developed into a topography this proved to be a workable criterion, since such brief and rudimentary notices in the great majority of cases pointed in the right direction, and were filled out as more sources were examined. What follows is, then, essentially based upon published material; surveys, such as that made by Norden (1597), county histories such as that by Charles Gilbert (1817-20), parochial histories such as that published by Lake (1867-72) and, of course, a wide spread of horticultural journals. Documents in manuscript were consulted only incidentally, not through unwitting neglect, still less because their importance had not been recognized, but because in a first essay it seemed wiser to concentrate upon ploughing one field of enquiry, thereby opening up the ground so others could delve more deeply later.

In 1991 a survey, *Historic Gardens in Cornwall*, was published in association with Dr David Hunt, as a first stage in his updating of Edgar Thurston's *Trees and Shrubs in Cornwall* (1930). Shortly after this, Dominic Cole, of Land Use Consultants, was independently engaged to draw up a plan for a professional survey of all the parks and gardens throughout Cornwall, for submission to the Lottery Fund. The present writer who, by that time, had already set up a database and individual garden files, was invited to act as one of the advisors in this enterprise. In the event a grant was not awarded, which seemed to make it imperative that the mass of material already collected should as soon as possible be made available, not only to research workers, but also to the public at large. This, then, is the genesis of the present volume, which is designed on a broad basis. For convenience, the entries are listed under thirteen districts, grouped around the principal towns, and arranged in chapters to correspond with the Ordnance Survey *Landranger* maps. The descriptions are printed more prominently than the technical preliminary matter and the references, which are chiefly pointers to the much fuller synoptic bibliographies at the back of the book. The object has been to produce a readable text, without sacrificing the requirements of scholarship and research. The survey of parks and gardens is followed by a gazetteer of the historic deer parks of the county, and an appendix which, after discussing plant lists, is followed by indexes of garden features and persons. Throughout, the text is illustrated from the rich treasury of old prints and plans, many of which have never before been reproduced.

In general, the purpose of this study has been, not simply to present information in an undigested form, but to relate the estates described to their geographical, historical, social and family context, in the hope that this may illuminate, and open up avenues for further topical or thematic research.

ACKNOWLEDGEMENTS

The ensuing work is the result of solitary researches, based upon a principal advocated by Elizabeth Banks when reviewing her inventory of gardens in Scotland, that a regional survey should be reported by one single person, so that, as well as the virtues, so also the inconsistencies and prejudices would be recognizably uniform. For this reason the book has been written independently, without reference to garden owners. In this connection I should perhaps emphasize that all of the information that follows is openly observable without trespass, or is contained in sources freely available to those who care to look for them.

Nevertheless, it would be ungracious not to admit that a work of this nature could not have been brought to a conclusion without the help of many specialists. Among these I must thank the Librarian and assistants at the Lindley Library of the Royal Horticultural Society, who have patiently and uncomplainingly shepherded me through their vast collection of books and horticultural journals; Angela Broome of the Courtney Library of the Royal Institution of Cornwall, who has been uncannily ready with an answer almost before the question has been asked, and Elizabeth Jackson at the Institute of Cornish Studies, who was ready with advice from the outset. I am especially grateful to the Planning Department of the Cornwall County Council, who were never too busy to make their English Heritage listings and maps accessible to me. The Cornwall Record Office, and County Library, as well as that of the RIBA, I used less often, but found their staff always ready with help. More personally, I have valued the opportunities for discussion and exchange of material with Sue Pring, who has contributed two sketch plans to this book, and the helpful guidance of Dr S.J. Daniels and John Phibbs on the Repton gardens.

There have been many others - among them the numberless, and often inevitably nameless casual acquaintances, who have pointed me in a direction, identified a site, given their reminiscences of past times, mouthed the correct pronunciations, or provided countless titbits of valuable information which could have been obtained in no other way. To these and many others to whom anyone who has undertaken a work of this dimension must be indebted, I would like to express my gratitude. Those who have provided or assisted me with the illustrations will receive their acknowledgement in a later section.

Although by way of conclusion, I must express my appreciation to Alison Hodge for greatly easing the path of this work to publication, and especially to an independent sponsor, without whose generosity this book could never have seen the light of day. I must pay equal credit to the contribution of my wife, Mary, who has not only without complaint borne the burden of the many household and horticultural tasks which I have neglected, but entered into the spirit of the composition, taking the driving seat in our forays into remote and forgotten places. Finally I cannot omit to thank Esther Mary Page, who joined us on these expeditions, and insisted that I should look at churches as well as gardens, which, since this is my own vocation, I am well aware have been the social and spiritual centre of the communities in which so many Adams and Eves have sought to regain Paradise, by creating their own little Eden out of a wasteland.

DOUGLAS ELLORY PETT
TRESILLIAN, TRURO 1998

Introduction

The first impression of an observant visitor to Cornwall is that it is quite un-English. Crossing the bridge over the Tamar at once induces a sense of isolation. Here there are no large towns acting as regional centres, such as Plymouth or Exeter. Villages are scattered, clustering around crossroads or along a highway, often with the church standing apart. The windswept plateaux, out of which rise great granite bosses, are covered with a tapestry of small, squarish fields, surrounded by stone or slate-walled hedges, dotted at surprisingly regular distances with isolated farmsteads. Everywhere there are the relics of antiquity, and the wastes of mining and quarrying.

It is out of this historic landscape that the manor houses and mansions, set in their luxuriant gardens and parks, sprang up, both influenced by, and utilizing the unique features of the terrain. So before passing on to a history of the development of these estates, we will look briefly at the physical characteristics of the county which moulded their shape.

GEOLOGY AND SOIL

Cornwall forms the western projection of what is known as 'Highland Britain', to distinguish it from the lowlands of the central and eastern mainland. The peninsula runs in a south-west, north-east direction, narrowing from about fifty miles at its widest point in the east, to an average of twenty miles, so that most of the county is within five to eight miles of the coast or a tidal estuary, thus everywhere experiencing to a greater or lesser extent a maritime climate.

The geological history[1] began with a long period of elevation during which aerial erosion exposed several granite domes, principally on Bodmin Moor, St Austell Moor, Carnmenellis near Camborne, and the Land's End peninsula, becoming drowned at the western extremity to form the Isles of Scilly. In geologically more recent times there followed what are believed to have been a sequence of marine submergences, which resulted in a series of flattenings, at about 1,000 feet (305m.) on Bodmin Moor, at 750-800 feet (239-244m.) on the Penwith peninsula, at 550-675 feet (168-205m.) around Bodmin and St Austell Moors, and an extensive 300-400 foot (92-122m.) plateau which fringes much of the coast, merging into a lower surface from about 200 to 250 feet (61-76m.). This step-like transition needs to be borne in mind when considering the altitudes given for gardens in the Topography. The general southward tilting of the land has caused the rivers to cut V-shaped valleys, which at their estuaries have become submerged to form a 'rias', or drowned valley, among which Helford, the Fal, Fowey and the Tamar are the best examples. This, as we shall see, was to influence the distribution of parks and gardens throughout the county. The north-south trend of these valleys has created problems for communication from east to west, so that the main line of travel has tended to be well inland, along the backbone of the central watershed, which roughly follows the route of the A30, joining the principal towns.

The underlying formations fall into two types – granite, and what is known locally as 'killas', that is various slates, with some sand- or mud-stones, and grits. The soil over the granite typically is peaty and acid, so that very few of the gardens by choice are found there. Between the granite and the surrounding killas, the rock became heated up at the time of the igneous extrusions to create changed or 'metamorphic' forms, and it is in these regions that, at a late stage, minerals were deposited which brought into being the great mining areas of St Just, Camborne/Redruth and Callington. It was in these mineral resources that the great wealth of the county lay, making it possible, at first for the building of manor houses, such as that of the Godolphins,[2] whose mines seemed for a time

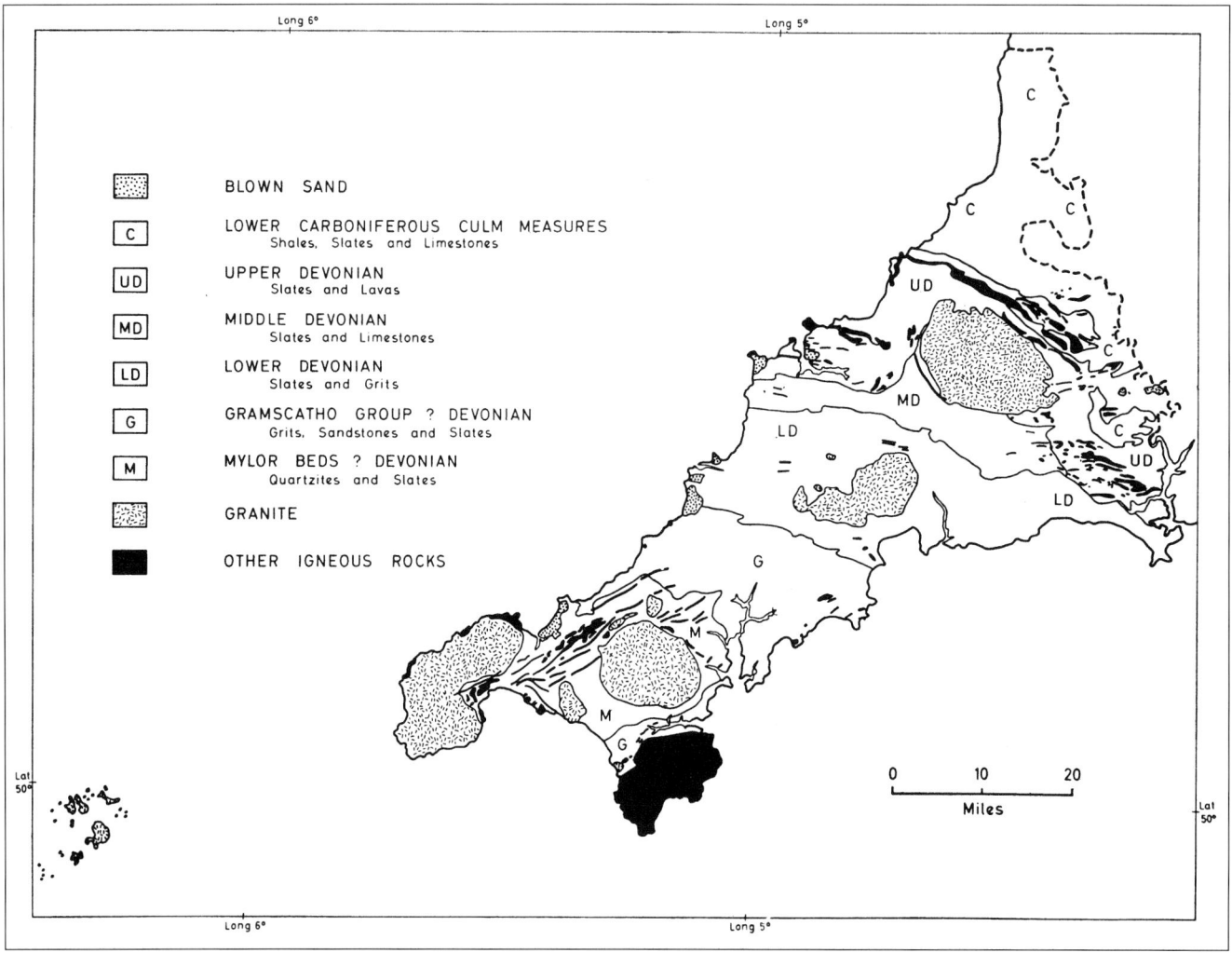

1. The geology of Cornwall, based mainly on the quarter-inch maps of the Geological Survey.

inexhaustible, or enabling others like William Lemon to afford to purchase *Carclew*, or as the Williamses of *Burncoose* and *Scorrier* to build themselves grand mansions close to their sources of income.

Two other types of alteration in the granite were of equal economic importance: the decomposition or 'kaolinisation' of the feldspar produced china-clay, and the introduction of fluorspar formed china-stone. These occurred most abundantly in the region of the St Austell Moors, leading to the growth of a prosperous town, around which sprang up the estates of those who benefited from the industry. During the eighteenth and nineteenth centuries many new gardens were created around the fringes of the granite, in these regions of changed sedimentary rocks, or the 'metamorphic aureole' as it is termed.

Not all of the killas, however, was as fertile as the Devonian series, which comprises the greater part of mid-Cornwall. The Carboniferous rocks of the Culm Measures to the north-east, so described because they did not contain usable coal, resulted in a sticky clay which, combined with the strong winds along the north coast, was not conducive to horticulture. Here mansions are thin on the ground, and found only on the more favourable sites.

The serpentines of the Lizard peninsula to the south form another area, where an excess of manganese produced a soil unfavourable to cultivation. The most significant gardens here, such as *Bochym*, *Bonython* and *Lanarth*, lie to the north and off the serpentine, whereas *Erisey*, whose very name in Cornish is thought to mean 'a dry field', was established upon an island of granite isolated from the surrounding boggy serpentine moorland where only the Cornish heath, *Erica vagans*, thrived.

The highest quality soils in the county are to be found in three areas. The first is a triangle running from Lelant to Perranuthnoe and Penzance, which encompasses the gardens of *Treloyhan*, *Trewidden*, *Trengwainton* and *Ludgvan*, as well as the former daffodil fields of the Gulval 'Golden Mile'. At the other end of the county, on the south-facing slopes of the Tamar Valley, between Callington and Saltash, celebrated for its strawberries and other fruit crops, are to be found *Cotehele* and *Pentillie Castle*. But it is in the central area, along the western side of the Fal estuary up to Truro, that the highest density of Cornish gardens is found, among which are *Carclew*, the three Fox gardens at *Trebah*, *Glendurgan* and *Penjerrick*, and the oldest of them all at *Enys*.

Even so, it was as much the topography of these gardens as their soil which led to their success. *Trebah* and *Glendurgan*, as well as *Bosahan* and the more recent *Trelean* on the other side of the river, and other gardens on the Helford estuary, are all 'ravine' or valley gardens. Farther west, *Boskenna*, and *Penberth*, even though near Land's End, and without benefit from the soil around Penzance, could flourish against the odds because they were in south-facing valleys. Hence it should cause no surprise that if the Fowey and Looe rivers are traced to their sources, concentrations similar to those on the Fal and Tamar are found, even though the soil may be classified as no more than medium grade. Indeed, a census of estates in proximity to the Hayle, Fal, Fowey, Looe and Tamar estuaries embraces the majority of the chief parks and gardens in Cornwall.

The maps of the Geological Survey, to which references are given in each entry, provide a

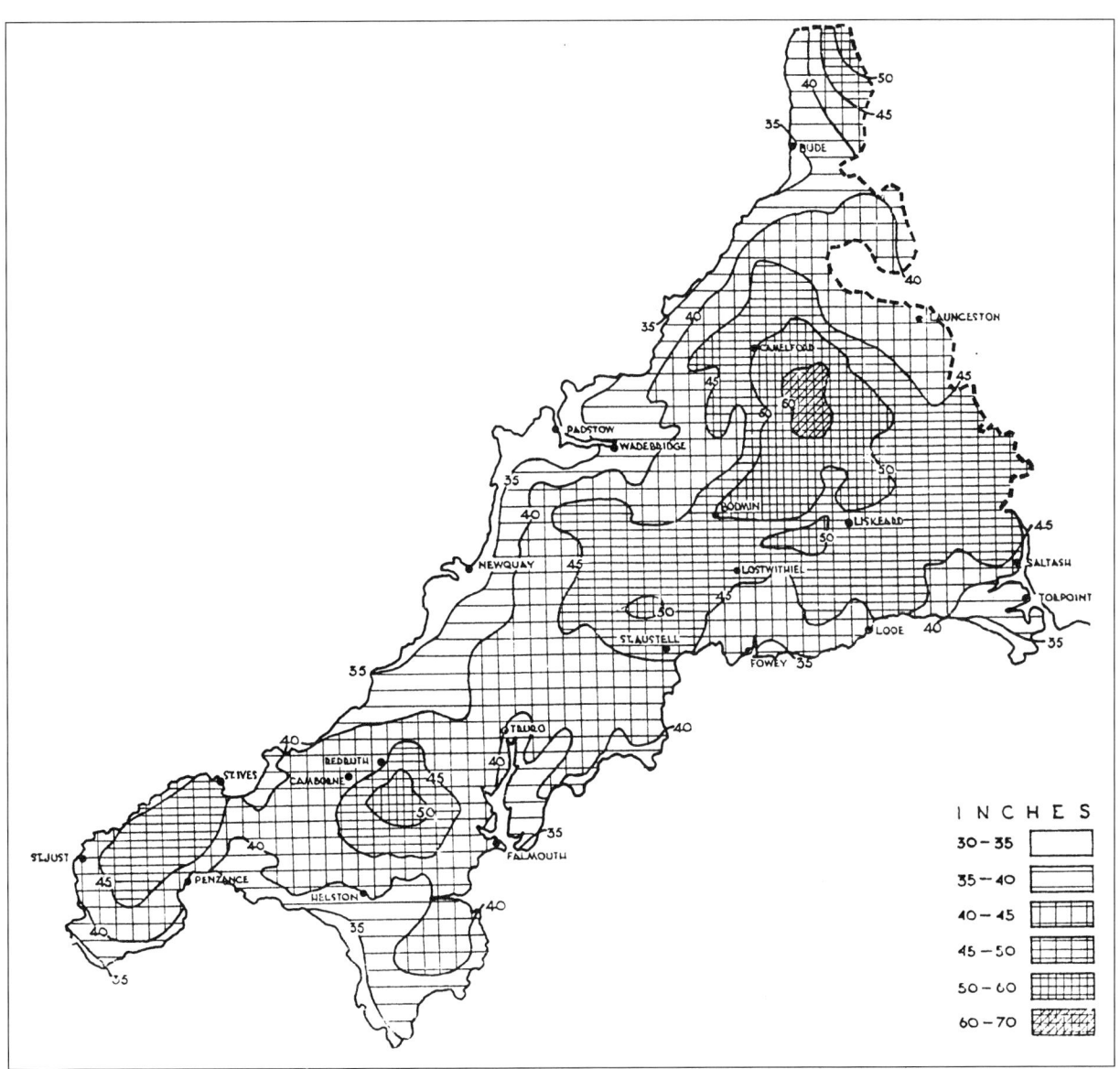

2. *Rainfall, 1881-1915.*

detailed outline of the substrate of the county, but soil maps exist for only three limited areas. Even were these available, nothing can replace the detailed and intimate knowledge of those who actually till their own ground, a medium which is infinitely variable, even within a single garden. In the ensuing topography, local observations have been recorded wherever they were found, but for the rest, the generalisations presented must suffice for the present.

CLIMATE

If it is not possible to offer more than generalisations upon the subject of soil, this is even more true for climate, for meteorology in the widest sense is a study of generalisations. The successful gardener needs to gain a knowledge of his own 'micro-climates', for even the tiniest garden has its frost-pockets and hot-spots.

The primary factors which are of importance to the horticulturist are rainfall, temperature and wind, in which Cornwall exhibits unique features. It is to these that we shall now turn.

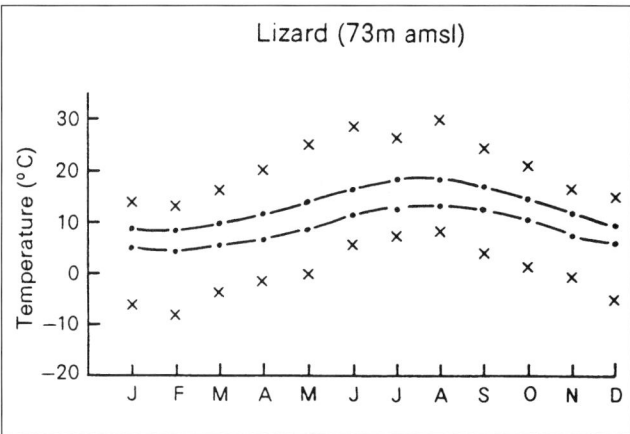

3. Average variation of maximum and minimum temperature over the period 1941-1970.

Rainfall and humidity

The accompanying map[3] summarizes records during the period when the great gardens were at their zenith. Here the rainfall can be seen to reflect closely the topography, although the south-west, north-east alignment of the peninsula results in some 10 inches (25.5cm.) less annual rainfall from rain-bearing winds along the western slopes of elevated land than in Dartmoor, Wales and other similar areas. Below 400 feet (122m.) the average rainfall was generally less than 45 inches (115cm.), the lowest being experienced along the margins of the north coast. Since the information to be gleaned from this map offers at least some guidance as to what might be expected in individual gardens, the rainfall figures are recorded in the entries to the major sites. The warning that, 'Annual deviations from the long period mean are considerable', should be observed, coupled with an awareness that in the short term local variations are frequent. Despite Bishop Hunkin's remark that rain fell in Cornwall 'every day and twice on Sundays', sunshine is certainly no less, and often more than in other parts, and rainfall is generally well distributed throughout the year, though with extremes in autumn and winter.

Perhaps of equal importance for the growth of plants is the humidity, which in Cornwall is unusually high. While this may be beneficial for certain species such as camellias, rhododendrons and conifers, for which the county is celebrated, it causes damping off in other varieties which originate in drier climes. Relative humidity 'averages around 80% over the year with higher values occurring in winter and at night'. Indeed, 'relative humidities equal or exceed 95% for around 20-30% of the time in the area, and humidities of 100% can be reached in fog', which occurs most commonly along the coast and on high ground, although it is soon dispersed by the prevailing winds.

Temperature

In general terms the climate of Cornwall can be described as 'warmer and more equable' than anywhere else in Britain, but such a statement is commonly misunderstood by those who have little experience of the county. The frequent use of the expression 'sub-tropical' conjures up an imaginary land of hot summers, with palm trees, and frost-free winters. A glance at Fig. 3 will at once dispel this illusion.[4] The dotted lines indicating the mean maximum and minimum temperatures more precisely define the meaning of an 'equable' climate, namely a climate which has a narrow range between its high and low average temperatures, which in Cornwall is the narrowest in the country. The crosses signifying the extreme maxima and minima, again emphasize, not only that Cornwall, though mild, is certainly not 'frost-free', but also that it is never very hot. This has important consequences for vegetation, for though the temperature for much of the year does not fall below that required for growth, it is rarely hot enough to provide the roasting needed by some quite hardy plants to ripen and flower.

Nevertheless, it is probably the lower end of the scale which is of most interest to the Cornish gardener who experiments with plants on the margin of hardiness. Fig. 4 summarizes the average number of days in the year with air and ground frost at an inland site.[5] The maps published by the Meteorological Office make it possible to add more detail to this picture. The mean annual number of days with a temperature less than 0°C from 1956 to 1970, for instance, are shown to be 10-20 days in Penwith, 20-40 days from Penwith along the coastal areas both north and south, and 40-60 days in the central area from roughly around the western side of Bodmin Moor and eastwards. From the point of view of the cultivation of tender plants, however, it is often the depth of frost, and occasional extremes which will cause the practical gardener his greatest anguish. The mean annual minima from 1941 to 1970 have been -2°C in West Penwith, and from -4° to -6°C from there to the border, but the prediction for a projected exceptional lowest temperature over a fifty-year period, based on the evidence of these years, drops to around -8°C from Land's End to the Lizard and south Fal estuary, to between -8° and -10°C over most of Cornwall, and from -10° to -12°C on the Devon border.

It needs to be pointed out that these figures are 'means', that is mid-points, and that all have been reduced to mean sea level, whereas in Cornwall the land rises quite quickly from the coast to the first of a series of plateaux, with a consequent fall in temperature. It will, therefore, be realized that accurate statements about garden climates can only come from scrupulously kept local records, of which, considering the busy life of gardeners, there are naturally few. Nevertheless, it was felt that at least some general indication of climate should be given in the major entries of the gazetteer, for which purpose the map in Fig. 5, showing the mean daily minimum from 1941 to 1970 for February - the coldest month in Cornwall - has been chosen to mark out certain broad zones for the county.[6] However, it must be remembered that this can provide no more than a basis for comparison between sites, and must not be thought of in terms of absolute values.

Borlase confirmed the remarks of Carew in his *Survey* of 1602, that the procession of seasons in Cornwall differs from that in other parts - spring being early, summer late, autumn long and winter short. He had made observations from 1753 to 1772 at his Rectory at *Ludgvan*, set in the warmest district in the country, and was the first to keep detailed records here.[7] During this period there was an average of sixteen days of frost each year, which may be directly compared with the number of days for Penwith, in the 1956-70

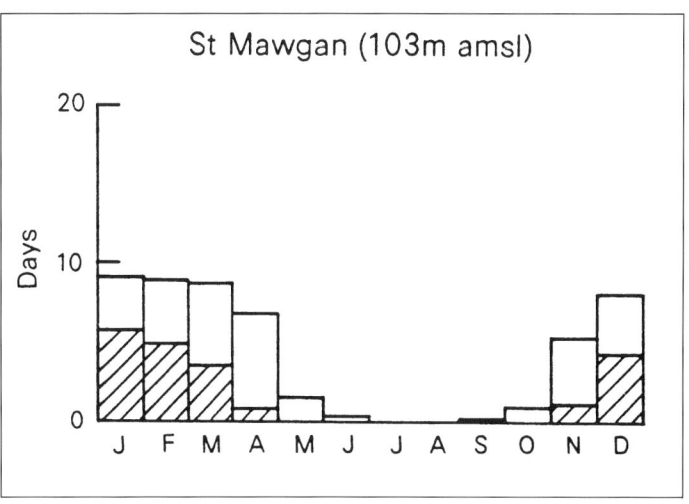

4. *Average number of days with air frost (hatched areas) and ground frost (whole column) over the period 1961-1980.*

map already referred to, where Ludgvan lies at approximately the mid-point between the 10- to 20-day lines. His notes also exposed two perennial hazards of this unusual seasonal climate - late spring and early autumn frosts, often preceded or followed by long frost-free periods. In 1757, for instance, he records that the last frost came on 30 May, after a frost-free March and April. Typically the first frost of winter would arrive in November, but in 1763 there was a frost on 22 September, followed by only one day in October, and three in December. Those who garden in Cornwall will know the disastrous effect of May frosts on even hardy plants encouraged into growth by an early spring, and the calamitous consequences for the experimenter

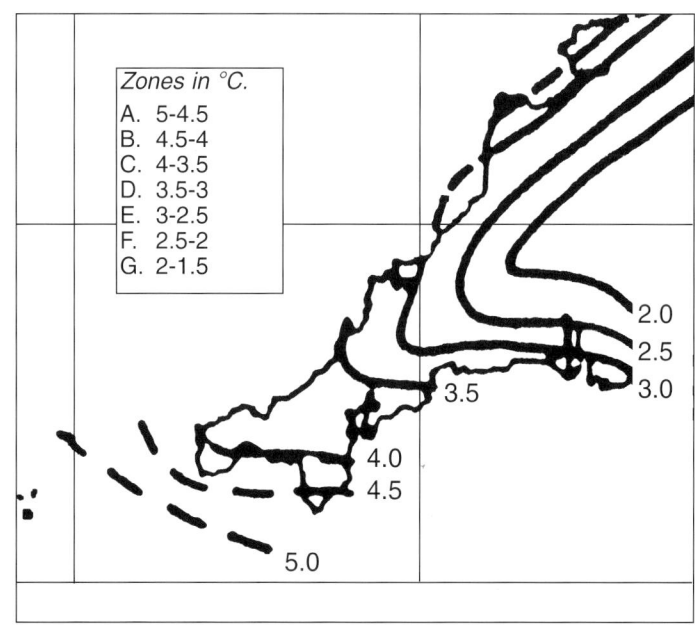

5. *Mean daily minimum temperature in February 1941-1970.*

with marginally hardy plants, such as *Citrus*, *Musa* or succulents, who is unwary enough to be caught by a September, or early October frost.

Wind

Norden, as long ago as the sixteenth century, described the 'fierce & furious wyndes' that 'sharply assayl the naked hills & dales', and nothing has changed.

In contrast to central and eastern England, which tends to be under the more stable influence of continental 'highs', Cornwall, especially in the west, is exposed in winter to the rapidly changing cyclonic conditions from the northwest which bring boisterous, squally weather. The north coasts, open to the Atlantic, and with a flat 'planed' surface compared with the south, receive the worst buffeting along a band which at the extreme west encompasses the whole of Penwith and the west coast of the Lizard.[8] As the wind speeds rise to gale intensity, this band spreads to cover the whole county, decreasing in force as it moves eastwards, slowed down by friction with the widening land, and impeded by the rising moorland. Naturally this simple pattern is considerably modified on the ground by the amount of shelter available, such as that in the valleys and estuaries of the south coast where, as we saw earlier, so many Cornish gardens are seated.

The discipline of recording the aspect for every garden in the ensuing list gradually brought to light how often sites for new houses were selected on south-east-facing slopes which were protected above from the north-west. Our survey of the climate quite clearly explains why this should be, and the review of the county's topography shows just where such places are found.

GARDEN HISTORY

The beginnings

It may appear fanciful to choose a starting point for garden history before the Norman Conquest, but the unique pattern of the prehistoric settlements in Cornwall has left its mark upon the landscape. The influence of the well-known Anglo-Saxon open field system here was not great, and is limited to the lines of incursion from Devon along the north and south of the county, and in the vicinity of the boroughs colonized by incomers. The critical period of 'enclosures' which changed the face of England during the eighteenth and nineteenth centuries, barely touched Cornwall, where records of enclosures often referred to winning land from the waste, rather than enclosing existing open fields.[9]

The typical early or 'Celtic' settlement was a solitary farmstead, or a small group of farms, with a 'close' attached to each dwelling, from which the surrounding waste was gradually brought into cultivation, by building walls and hedges out of stone laboriously dug up during clearance. Eventually these scattered homesteads joined up to create a patchwork of small square fields, such as are clearly seen along the road from St Ives, through Zennor to St Just.

The significance of this for garden history is that these settlements, many of which rose to the stature of manors by the Conquest or later, were agricultural in origin, where, as Tonkin remarked,

> the desire of our ancestors [was] to settle in our vallies, and to get, as they call it, in *the luthe* [dialect for 'in the shelter'].[10]

These were to become the 'gentlemen's seats' mapped by Norden, not a few of which, as our synopsis shows, ultimately grew into the mansions of the eighteenth and nineteenth centuries.

The records of these prehistoric settlements are inscribed on the countryside, but there survive written 'Lives' which recount tales of the invasion by Celtic 'saints', or missionaries, who established their solitary cells all over the county, leaving their names to posterity, to beatify Cornwall as 'the land of the Saints'. Some settled on existing sacred sites (the *lans* of place-names), or established new ones, but always separated from the *trevs*, or homesteads. Such is the origin of the many 'churchtowns', which may be sometimes sited at an inconvenient distance from the village. They were in time, however, joined by a parsonage, some of which, like *Lamorran* and *Ludgvan*, entered the ranks of the 'great' gardens of Cornwall.

The medieval period

One of the contributions of the Normans after the Conquest was, in the twelfth century, the impaling of nine deer parks, five of which were associated with their castles. Compared with the great English parks, they were small, and their distance from the Court, when communication with Cornwall, other than by sea, was difficult, soon led to their neglect, so that long before Henry VIII disparked them in 1542, they were already being grazed by cattle as well as deer, and in part were beginning to be cultivated. None of the Duchy parks has survived, but they were the forerunners of the later landscape parks, and created a taste among the great landowners. *Boconnoc*, a medieval park by royal licence, still flourishes and, despite the example of Henry VIII, new parks were impaled as soon as the reign of Elizabeth, and have continued to be created in each century since.

With one exception, there are no records, nor examples of early medieval gardens in Cornwall. We are fortunate, however, in possessing at *Tintagel Castle* a curious and possibly romantic survival, which has been the subject of a recent archaeological study linking it in design, if not in actuality, to the garden in the legend of Tristan and Iseult. As will be seen in the Norden sketch of about 1590 (see Fig. 74), it is rectangular with walls or fences high enough to create an *hortus conclusus* which, from other records, we know to have been characteristic of the period, and which was often associated with the Virgin Mary. The presence of such a garden, intended as a retreat within the confines of the Castle, suggests that there might have been similar gardens, as well as deer parks, connected with other castles throughout the county. Such a garden on the south face of St Michael's Mount is known to date at least from the eighteenth century, if not earlier, and a not inappropriately named '*Ladies*' (or perhaps originally 'Our Lady's') *Garden*' in the vicinity of the Elizabethan Star Castle on St Mary's, Isles of Scilly, even if later, follow in the same tradition.

A tentative date proposed for the *Tintagel* garden is about 1250. Earlier, in 1204, the men of Cornwall at great expense had purchased the 'disafforestation' of the whole county, which freed them from the burden of the 'forest law', which applied, not necessarily to a forest as we know it, but to tracts of land set aside, like deer parks and warrens, as royal game reserves, with severe penalties for trespass.[11] This new freedom provided an impetus to open up the waste further, so that many new farms came into existence and prospered. We may imagine that in some of the larger manors, and even the more considerable farms, gardens similar to that at *Tintagel* and other castles might have grown up, but in this period of great obscurity we can only speculate.

William of Worcester, in his *Itinerary* of 1478, listed thirty-four Cornish castles, most of which have now disappeared, some without trace. The men of Cornwall had petitioned Richard III in 1483, complaining of

> robberies, despoyleries of merchaunts, strangers, merthers, as well as by water as by land, entries by force and wrongful imprisonments[12]

which is evidence of the need that led the wealthier residents similarly to fortify their dwellings, by castellating their houses, building towers, and walling in their courtyards, perhaps with a gatehouse or barbican at the entrance. No complete house of this type survives, but

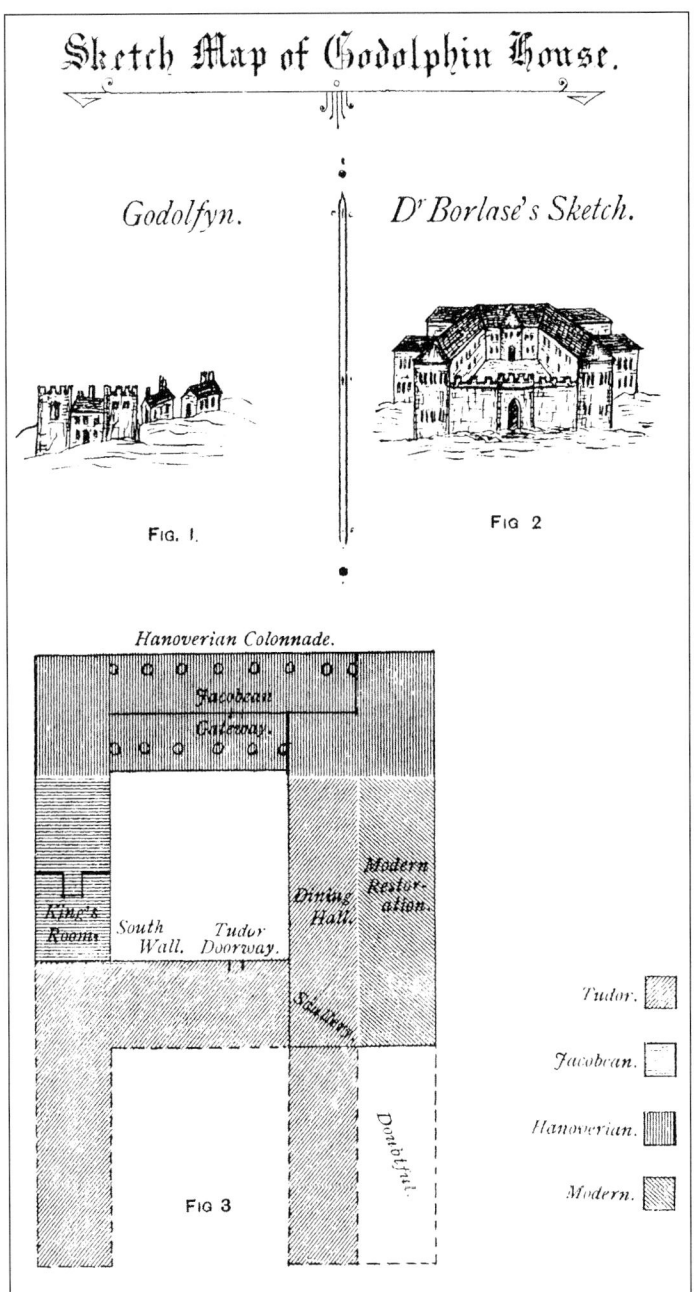

6. Godolphin, when a fortified house. Sketched by Borlase from the panel at Pengersick Castle.

enough relicts and illustrations remain to obtain a fair impression of how they might once have appeared. The tower at *Pengersick*, for instance, still exists, and its position, exposed to intruders from an easy landing on Praa Sands, evinces the need for protection in wilder times. *Pengersick*, though known as a 'castle', does not appear in Worcester, since it was built around 1510. The reconstruction by William Borlase offers an acceptable representation of this and other houses. Indeed, a sketch of about 1532 on the panelling in *Pengersick Castle*, shows the earlier house at *Godolphin* to be not dissimilar to this reconstruction (see Fig. 28). A map of Fowey in the time of Henry VIII shows *Place* as such a castellated building, with a tower, walls and gatehouse, and also *Boconnoc* in its deer park with a tower and castellation (see Fig. 112). There are similar sketches of *Arwenack* in Falmouth (see Fig. 44).[13] Nevertheless, all of the surviving houses from this period have been substantially altered, but among them perhaps *Tonacombe*, dating from *c.* 1480, presents us with the most realistic impression of a fortified house, with its walled Pleasance, massive oak front door, and the relicts of a possible portcullis.

By the turn of the sixteenth century, industrious farmers were increasing in prosperity, while mining had advanced sufficiently to make Cornwall the premier world supplier of tin and copper, so that it became possible from about 1550 to 1650 to improve farms and build manor houses. Norden, in 1590, reflected this movement in his long list of 'gentleman's seats' - some 180 of them. Nevertheless, only sixty-six of these, as our synopsis of seventeenth-century and earlier references shows, later became notable for their gardens. What, then, happened to the others? They did not all simply disappear, since many can be traced through later topographies, where they are revealed to have become farms as the original families died out or, perhaps passing on through an heiress, were leased off as the less desirable property. Some, of course, decayed, burnt down or were demolished. Whether they became mansions, or merely survived as yeomen's farms, they have all been rebuilt, remodelled, or at the least restored in a way that the study of their ancient gardens has become more a subject for the archaeologist than the historian.

The sixteenth and seventeenth centuries

It has been suggested that the period of the Commonwealth, in the mid-seventeenth century, acted as a watershed in garden design. The sparsity of records, however, makes it difficult to form a picture of Tudor and, except for Carew's description of *Hall Walk*, Elizabethan gardening in Cornwall before that time. Nevertheless, one fertile source of contemporary information may be found in the Glebe Terriers, written at the behest of the Bishops of Exeter in 1673 and 1735. Veronica Chesher in her review of them believed that

> the Cornish country parsonage house of the time, in the midst of its glebe lands and with its farm buildings, townplace [farmyard] and mowhay [rick-yard], had much in common with ... the larger farmhouses of the neighbourhood.[14]

But this does not necessarily make them irrelevant in a study of the gardens of 'great' houses and 'seats', since, if their service buildings and yards are discounted, there still remain many features which might be found at least in the smaller manor houses. We might expect the dwellings of the clergy, who were little more than small farmers, to have been conservative, when not old-fashioned, since they were not wealthy enough to 'improve' their livings. They may, then, be taken as examples of the type of design to be found some fifty years or more earlier, that is, before the Commonwealth.

All of the parsonages had 'courts', either enclosed by or joined to the building. Typically there was a walled forecourt with a gate or, among the most prosperous, a gatehouse. These courtyards might fulfil many functions, but the 'green court', for instance, was a grassed area where a visitor might graze his horse.[15] Every house - even the lowliest tenancy - possessed a walled 'garden' attached to the house. These were most commonly 'herb gardens', later termed 'kitchen gardens', where pot herbs, salads and green vegetables were grown; 'roots', in one case, being clearly distinguished as grown in 'plots'. Some of these gardens were planted with fruit trees - apples, pears or cherries, or perhaps a whole orchard of forty or more trees. There were 'bee gardens', presumably with blossoms, even 'dove' or 'pigeon gardens' with a culver house, and 'hop gardens'. Flowers are mentioned infrequently, but there were three 'arbour gardens', one 'by the parlour window', which is reminiscent of the medieval *hortus conclusus*. At least one garden, not unexpectedly at Tintagel, was planted 'for the defence of the dwelling house, from the North west windes', which could surely not have been the only one of its kind in the blustery Cornish climate. The grandest parsonages had 'walks' and 'bowling greens', that at Calstock possessing both.

Hals had described the decaying estate at *Park* as having 'gardens, walk and fish-ponds' beneath the 'tower-house'. Except for the ponds, which are nowhere mentioned in the Terriers, this description would fit the grandest of the parsonages. The phrase itself, indeed, may be regarded as a commonplace expression for these ancient gardens, for Gilbert also uses the same

7. Bake. A wide avenue leading to the front court through tall gate-piers with ball finials was a common practice in the late seventeenth and early eighteenth centuries. The end of the avenue often served as the bowling green. (Prideaux 1716-27)

phrase, 'ponds, walks, and gardens' for the destroyed old gardens at *Luney*, whereas more typically he uses the expression 'lawns, gardens and shrubberies' for contemporary gardens in 1820.[16]

The finest of the Tudor houses is undoubtedly *Cotehele*, which is castellated, with a tower, inner courtyards and a chapel. There is a bowling green and a pond, but the terraced gardens are late nineteenth century. *Trewarne* (or *Trewane*), another early house, although rebuilt in about 1645, has retained an earlier tower, which probably has been lowered. There are two front courts, one with a small gatehouse or barbican, with steps leading down to a pond. *Penheale* similarly has undergone many changes, but a sketch in the *Spoure Book* of *c.* 1690 shows the gatehouse of 1636, leading into the front court, with another court through a gate to one side (now the rose garden and parterre), and a formal walled garden on the other side. The present pond near the house, and the long lake were probably originally stew-ponds. So although there has been considerable remodelling of the house, and developments in the garden, the courtyards are in essence unaltered. The quite exceptional loggia to the gatehouse, facing in to the front court, indicates some Italian influence. Another loggia fronting a courtyard can be seen at *Godolphin*. Pevsner thought that it looked 'mid C17, and makes the accepted date of after 1712 ... seem highly unlikely'. There are also the 'remains of quite an elaborate garden' here. After the beginning of Elizabeth's reign, times became much more settled and peaceful, so there was no longer a pressing necessity to fortify houses. As early as 1547, for instance, Sir Richard Edgcumbe had his new house at *Mount Edgcumbe*, although castellated, built open and outward looking to the prospect. But the fashion for castles had taken root. Even a century later, *Ince Castle*, a square brick building more like Osterley Park and Syon House in London than anything in Cornwall, was erected, although it can claim to be no more than a pseudo-castle, perhaps aping *Trematon* on the neighbouring prominence. It was to be the first in a long line

8. Prideaux Place, the south front, with formal garden. The tiered branches of the central trees may have been trained in the medieval estrade *style. (Prideaux 1716-27)*

of mock castles and castellated houses. *Lanhydrock*, under construction at about the same time in 1635-42, had as an entrance to its forecourt a magnificent gatehouse, which is in effect an ornamental barbican, and already an anachronism. The long avenue had been planted before the gatehouse was completed, and wide avenues of trees leading to a front court were soon to be seen in other houses, such as *Bake*, illustrated on page 19, perhaps the finest being at *Mount Edgcumbe*.

A plan of *Lanhydrock*, dated 1694, showed a flower garden, bowling green, kitchen garden, 'Peare Garden', 'New Orchard' and 'Wilderness', that is a formal planting of trees or shrubs with winding paths, but much of this may have been planted after the Restoration, when the Robartes took up residence, at a time, wrote Polwhele, when 'most of the seats of gentlemen in Cornwall, were either newly built or materially repaired.'[17]

Without question the finest Restoration house in the county was that built for John Grenville at *Stowe* in 1679, which was modelled on a fashionable town house in Piccadilly. The approach ascended from the Coombe valley below, through trees and past the deer park to a gate into the forecourt where a broad stairway led up to the entrance door, thus integrating the house with the garden. Along the main front are three walled gardens, the farthest with a pavilion/gazebo, the nearest with a parterre.

Edmund Prideaux, who redesigned *Place* at Padstow early in the next century, left a collection of sketches made during two tours in 1716 and 1727, mostly to houses of his relatives, which represent designs which must have been created several years before. The illustration above of the south front of his own house, before it was altered, shows a formal geometric design with neat pointed trees which is related to a Dutch style of garden. Such designs may not have been uncommon, since his illustration of the garden at *Hexworthy* is very similar. However, his sketch of *Bake* (see Fig. 93), in East Cornwall, depicts a more intricate design of scroll-like parterres. These are reminiscent of the striking parterres in another walled garden, far away on the Roseland, at *Rosteague*, where four square divisions have been laid out, each with a different design following typical mid seventeenth- century patterns, in what has always been known there as 'The French Garden'.

The *Spoure Book*, which similarly contained sketches of family properties, includes two other remarkable gardens from the end of the seventeenth century. In the first, at *Bochym* on the Lizard, the terraces still survive, although unplanted when seen. In the Spoure sketch, the lower of the terraces has a design not unlike that at *Prideaux Place*, but here the surrounding trees are visible, characteristically radiating from the walled garden. The illustration of Spoure's own house at *Trebartha*, near Launceston, is even more intriguing. The layout is again not dissimilar, but two gateways which lead over a path separating one garden from the other have arches, surmounted with ball finials, to form an axis with a gazebo on the far wall, which bears a roof and ball designed to match the shape of the arches. This lower garden is divided into quadrants with narrow trees at each corner, and a statue at the centre. There is also a statue in the centre of the whole garden, holding a globe, aligned with those on the house, gateways and gazebo.[18] We see here indications of Italian influence, in gardens which might be termed in an 'Eclectic' style.[19]

In these examples of Restoration or late seventeenth-century Cornish gardens, there is evidence confirming that all the contemporary styles were to be found in the county during this period. But few have survived. The reason is not far to seek, for it is at least on record that in 1772 Sir Harry Trelawny at *Trelawne* ordered his Steward to destroy all of his old formal gardens. Similar gardens at *Heligan* were also destroyed. How many more of these civilized designs have gone the same way, we shall now never know.

The eighteenth century

The eighteenth century was a time of great social and cultural change. The ever expanding prosperity of mining spawned an industrial revolution which created great wealth for some, giving landowners the means and opportunity to 'improve' their grounds. Though remote, Cornwall was not cut off from the current of events and trends of fashion. Commerce attracted interests from outside the county, the universities afforded Cornish scholars the chance to associate with the great literary and scientific figures of the day and, perhaps above all, political links through Members of Parliament and the House of Lords, were even more influential. Addison, who expressed his views on gardening in the *Spectator*, focused attention on the political overtones. In his papers he declared his

> Whig patriotism, his confidence that the possession of land and its cultivation give the freeholder his political base and security ... To view your estates 'in a Prospect which is well laid out, and diversified with Fields and Meadows, Woods and Rivers ...' is to realise palpably the ideas of your citizenship and its place in traditions which go back to the Romans.[20]

The desire in this century for a 'Prospect' was to sound the death knell for many manor and other houses on typical Celtic sites, crouched snugly in

9. Antony House and its prospect in 1721. An early example of the growing fashion for siting mansions where they had a wide view of a varied countryside. (Country Life 1933)

valleys, sheltered and away from the coast. This, more than any other reason, accounts for their decline into the lower status of yeomen's farms. Warner drew the distinction between the old and the new very well:

> Beauty of situation does not appear to have been an object of regard with our forefathers; who rather courted the sullen gloom of sequestered hollows, than the cheerful variety of diversified prospects which the commanding eminence, or sloping declivity, affords.[21]

Charles Gilbert defines more particularly the qualities desired by the aspirants in his unfavourable comparison between *Catchfrench* - 'damp', 'under a hill', 'hidden' from view (notice the desire for outward show!) - and the nearby *Bake* which, by good fortune (for it was an ancient site),

> enjoys a most favourable and elevated situation, and few spots, perhaps, display a greater or more beautiful variety of home and distant scenery [the 'prospect']. Here indeed is a happy combination of all that is *sublime* [another eighteenth-century buzz word], and beautiful, soft, luxuriant, and *desolate* ... [a necessary ingredient in the 'sublime'].[22]

Another old house at *Kenegie*, in order to procure shelter from the prevailing south-westerly winds, in good seventeenth-century fashion, had sensibly turned its face away, and protected itself with trees obscuring a magnificent panoramic 'prospect' of Mount's Bay, which it had at that time preferred to view from its 'walks'. However, to keep up with the times, though unable to reorientate their house, the Harrises, as second best, built themselves a gazebo from which they could relish the scene.

Nicholas Morice, allied by marriage to the Herbert family who were landscaping Wilton and Highclere, by deciding after the turn of the century to improve his lands at *Werrington*, which had originally been purchased as a repayment for political services at the Restoration, was the first to introduce the new fashion for landscaping into at least the borders of Cornwall. There seems little doubt that he and his son were considerably influenced by William Kent, even if Kent had not taken a hand in the design (which he may well have done). Other influences were abroad. The poet Thomson's *Seasons* was opening the eyes of the cultured to natural scenery; Shenstone was at least as famous for his garden at the Leasowes as for his poetry, and greatest of all Alexander Pope, who knew and approved of Kent's principles, and sought a unification of the arts, was a correspondent of William Borlase at *Ludgvan*, and may have visited the Olivers at *Trevarno*. Charles Hamilton, the creator of Painshill in Surrey, was MP for Truro from 1741 to 1747, and it would be surprising if he had not discussed his ideas on landscaping with local landowners, such as William Lemon, John Enys, Thomas Hawkins of *Trewithen*, and others who were creating or improving their estates.

Lancelot Brown, who followed in Kent's footsteps, is not known to have ventured into Cornwall, although this does not mean that his principles were unknown, or that he did not have disciples. The appearance of the landscape at *Trelaske* is such that there is a legend that it may have been designed by the master himself. Francis Bassett, who began to restore the grounds at *Tehidy* in 1756, was evidently keeping up with the trends when he ordered his men to plant in 'clumps'. And at *Clowance* the St Aubyns, who had commenced an extensive programme of planting in 1723, when they introduced the plane tree into Cornwall, at the end of the century engaged John Nicholls, a local disciple of Brown, to relandscape their grounds.

But it was above all the career of Humphry Repton in Cornwall, which most clearly demonstrated the political influence upon the landscape.

The Prime Minister, William Pitt the Younger, had Cornish connections through his relationship to Lord Camelford at *Boconnoc*, who had, to quote Pevsner, 'laid out' his grounds 'with ... generosity ... and ... sensitivity to landscape effect'. In 1791 Repton had been consulted by Pitt about his own estate at Holwood Park, near Keston in Kent, and this resulted in an invitation to submit a Red Book to Lord Eliot, a relative by marriage, who had already begun to improve his grounds at *Port Eliot*. Although Repton was duly deferential, many of his suggestions, especially about the house, were not put into effect.

Pitt also recommended Repton to Reginald Pole Carew at *Antony*, another political supporter and MP, who became the channel for most of the other introductions into Cornwall. Repton considered his Red Book for *Antony*, which was the outcome of much fruitful discussion with Pole Carew, his *chef d'oeuvre*. In 1792, by Pole Carew's good offices, he was introduced to Francis Glanville, another MP, at *Catchfrench*. Glanville, in turn, was related both to Francis Gregor, MP for Tregony, at *Trewarthenick*, and to Lord Falmouth at *Tregothnan*. Repton produced Red Books for the former in 1793, and for the latter in 1809. Pole Carew had also written to Repton to inform him that his friend John Tillie Coryton, of *Crocadon*, had inherited

Pentillie, which he had the means and intention to restore and improve. This resulted in the sixth Red Book in 1810. The architect William Wilkins, an associate of Repton, at the same time added to *Pentillie Castle*. His son made further additions in 1815, and a year later remodelled the house at *Tregothnan*. It will come as no surprise to learn that Mrs Coryton was a cousin of Lord Falmouth.

Such, then, were the cross-currents and interrelationships in the eighteenth century, which brought to fruition so many fine gardens, which may still be seen today.

The nineteenth and twentieth centuries

Even though Repton continued to be active in the early years, it was John Claudius Loudon who was the more representative of the new century, by addressing a rising and prosperous middle class, both by the publication of his *Encyclopaedia* in 1822, and by the founding of the *Gardener's Magazine* in 1826. He personally visited four gardens in Cornwall - *Mount Edgcumbe, Pentillie Castle, Tor House* and *Trematon Castle* - although he had included ten in his earlier gazetteer,[23] among which *Carclew* perhaps reflected most clearly the new mood among garden owners. Sir Charles Lemon was himself a correspondent of the botanists William and his son Joseph Hooker, whom he later sponsored in his Himalayan expedition. It was on their recommendation that he appointed as his gardener at *Carclew*, William Beattie Booth, who was at that time working at the Horticultural Society's gardens at Chiswick. Booth was an expert on camellias, and had written the text to Chandler's *Illustrations and Descriptions of the Camelliae* (1831). He received the distinction of being made an honorary member of the Royal Horticultural Society of Cornwall, and later, in 1858, became assistant secretary to the Horticultural Society in London.

Worgan wrote in 1811 that

> most of the proprietors of lands in this county are directing their attention to planting, so that in thirty or forty years, Cornwall will present extensive wood-land scenery, both useful and ornamented.[24]

The thirst for new varieties was not confined to Cornwall. Sir Richard Acland, who had employed John Veitch, a Scotsman, to design his garden at Killerton in Devon, persuaded him to set up as a nurseryman in Exeter, where he engaged the brothers William and Thomas Lobb, whose father had worked at *Pencarrow* and later *Carclew*, to explore the American continents, and the Far East for new species.

Mid-century Joseph (later Sir Joseph) Hooker's Himalayan travels were introducing ever increasing numbers of rhododendrons, a species which had only appeared in this country during the first decade of the century. Their introduction inspired some of the more adventuresome of the gardeners to hybridize these new species, among whom Samuel Smith at

10. Larix Griffithii. The rare Himalayan Larch, grown at Coldrenick from seed sent from Sikkim by Sir Joseph Hooker in 1848. (G.Ch. 1907: i. 131)

Penjerrick and Richard Gill, gardener to D.H. Shilson at *Tremough* were the most notable.

Another early enthusiasm among gardeners was the 'acclimatisation of exotics'. In 1837 George Croker Fox of *Grove Hill*, Falmouth, who had a reputation for growing oranges, lemons and bananas in the open, won the Banksian

Medal of the Royal Horticultural Society of Cornwall for a list of newly introduced plants. His cousin Robert Were Fox at *Rosehill* and later *Penjerrick* continued the family tradition, while Augustus Smith at *Tresco* was encouraged by the unique climate on the Isles of Scilly to grow pelargoniums, mesembryanthemums and agaves in the open.

The Royal Horticultural Society of Cornwall, which had been founded in 1832, ran out of steam by 1861, despite the efforts of Canon Tom Phillpotts to revive it.[25] But the foundation of the Cornwall Daffodil and Spring Flower Society, by J.C. Williams of *Caerhays*, and his cousin P.D. Williams at *Lanarth in 1897*,[26] followed the lead of the flower growers of Scilly, who in 1886 had staged the first daffodil show to be held in the whole country. The interest in daffodil breeding, which had become of major commercial importance, on the mainland as well as on Scilly, was shared by the Williamses with George Johnstone of *Trewithen*.

By the end of the nineteenth century horticulture, and the collection of vast numbers of plants, had displaced the grand designs of the previous century. Algernon Dorrien Smith at *Tresco*, and John Davies Enys privately printed lists of more than 1,000 plants growing in their gardens, to be outstripped by Captain Pinwill, who in the 1880s listed over 4,500 mostly herbaceous plants growing at *Trehane*. J.C. Williams demonstrated his passion for new species by sponsoring, first the expeditions of Wilson and Farrer in China and the Far East, and then later those of Forrest. In this generosity he was joined by George Johnstone and Edward Bolitho of *Trengwainton*, in financing the journeys of Kingdon Ward

These new discoveries of camellias and magnolias, as well as rhododendrons, inspired a new breed of hybridist, no longer practising gardeners, but enthusiastic owners. E.J.P. Magor, a solicitor, at *Lamellen* was among the earliest, to be followed by E.G.W. Harrison, a retired General, at *Tremeer*, both of whom were at the forefront of rhododendron breeders. At *Tregrehan*, Gillian Carlyon, until her death in 1987, turned her hand to producing new camellia crosses, while David Trehane, at *Trehane*, became a leading authority on the subject, importing new varieties from New Zealand and Australia, to be followed later by his daughter, Jennifer. Of them all, J.C. Williams will perhaps be the longest remembered for his inter-generic cross *Camellia x williamsii*.

The complacent opening to the twentieth century during the Edwardian era was soon shattered by the onset of the First World War. Estates were never to recover from the depletion in the number of their staff by mobilisation and death, and later by the need for financial retrenchement. Nor did the remoteness of Cornwall let it escape the effects of destruction and neglect during another World War from 1939 to 1945, which was followed by even more far-reaching social and economic changes. Great houses were sold off as hotels, schools or hospitals, and their estates split up or neglected.[27]

The economic cutbacks of the post-war years, unfortunately, coincided with climatic changes, probably cyclic (since complaints of 'unseasonable' weather were common enough in the previous century), bringing high winds in December 1979 and January 1990, and freezing gales in January 1987, which ravaged the protective shelter in many gardens. In retrospect, it is now being realized that the forces of nature may have swept away much dead wood, which we had hesitated, or neglected, to touch earlier.

In the face of such adversities it is perhaps surprising that so many of the great gardens have been able to preserve at least some of their former beauty. The National Trust who, until recently, were concerned exclusively with the preservation of buildings, and the conservation of the countryside, have fortunately taken gardens under their wing, such as *Glendurgan*, *Trelissick* and *Trengwainton* in Cornwall. Another fifty historic gardens, or gardens on historic sites, appear in the current *Gardens of Cornwall Open Guide* for 1998. Numbered with them are twenty-one modern, that is post-war gardens, usually of more modest size. The National Gardens Scheme adds another twenty-two, many of which are new gardens of an acre or two, designed on a much smaller scale, which have been planted and are maintained singly by their owners, often in retirement, which are themselves evidence of changing social patterns and ambitions.

What then of the future? The profusion of gardening books and garden centres are proof, if any is needed, that gardening is not a dead art, while the growing interest in garden history and conservation augurs well for the future. As we move into the twenty-first century, times are certainly different, but they do not therefore look bleak.

NOTES

1. Fig. 1 is reproduced, with acknowledgement, to Prof. W.G. Balchin, from his *Cornwall, British Landscape Through Maps*, 9. 1967: 6. See also

R.M. Barton, *An Introduction to the Geology of Cornwall*, Truro, 1964.
2. All the sites printed in italics are described in the 'Topography' on the pages listed in the 'Index of Places' on page 332.
3. Fig. 2 is reproduced from the *County of Cornwall Development Plan*, 1952, vol. i, p. 21, with the permission of Cornwall County Council.
4. Fig. 3 is taken from *The Climate of Britain, The South-West Peninsula ... Climatological Memorandum* 139, 1986: 3, 5. [Crown copyright, reproduced with the permission of the Controller of HMSO.]
5. Fig. 4 idem.
6. *Maps of Mean and Extreme Temperature Over the UK, 1941-70*, Climatological Memorandum 73. Fig. 5. is based upon the map Figure 1.15. [Crown copyright.]
7. See *JRIC.* 1967: 267-90.
8. See *Maps of Hourly Mean Wind Temperature Over the UK, 1965-73*, Climatological Memorandum 79.
9. See Gilbert (1817: 363).
10. *Lake* (1870: iii.338). The Cheshers (1968) also write, 'Most of these farmsteads stand between the 200 ft. and 350 ft. contours, on platforms or in hollows on the hillside, sheltered by the slope of the hill and by clusters of trees planted for that purpose.' (pp.11-12).
11. The place-name *Catchfrench*, probably derived from the Norman French *chasse franche*, or 'free warren', may have originated during this liberation.
12. Quoted in G. Jackson-Stops and J. Pipkin, *The English Country House ...* 1985: 19, to explain the 'defensive inward-looking character of Cotehele'.
13. Hals, writing at the end of the seventeenth century, when describing ancient places such as *Park*, speaks of 'their tower-house' (*Lake* 1867: i. 310), and at Fentongollan (see *Tregothnan*), of 'a noble tower' (*Lake* 1870: iii. 344).
14. Potts (1974:xxxi).
15. See S. Landsberg, *The Medieval Garden*, 1995: 40.
16. In view of the paucity of evidence for these early days, William Bottrell's imaginative reconstruction of the ancient manor house and gardens at *Trewoofe* (1870: 245-87), may be commended as a true-to-life glimpse into the past, based, as it is, upon his own personal observations of the ruins 150 years ago, supplemented by the earlier memories and traditions of local inhabitants.
17. Polwhele (1806: 118).
18. The ubiquitous ball finials reflected the 'Copernican revolution', with its new perception of the world as a globe, represented here as borne on the shoulders of Atlas.
19. See Tom Turner, *English Garden Design*, 1986: 47.
20. J.D. Hunt, *Garden and Grove*, 1986: 184.
21. *Walk Through Some Western Counties ...*, Bath 1800: 74. Wordsworth, however, in his *Guide to the Lakes*, 'deplored the new residents "craving for prospects," which meant that their houses rose from the summits of naked hills, "in staring contrast to the snugness and privacy of the ancient houses"...' (M. Andrews, *The Search for the Picturesque*, Aldershot 1989: 7).
22. Gilbert (1820: 411-12), my italics.
23. On page 1247: they are Carclew, Clowance, Cotehele, Menabilly,* Pendarves, Port Eliot,* Pentillie Castle, Tehidy [he spelt it 'Tetredy'] Park, Trebartha Hall, and Trelawny [*sic*] House, the asterisks denoting 'show-places'. In the *Gardener's Magazine* (1837: 121-2), which Loudon edited, a supplement was published which added or revised entries for Tregothnan, Werrington, Boconnoc, Trelowarren, Clowance, Pendarves, Tehidy, and Trevethow [*sic*].
24. Quoted by Lysons (1814: clxxxiii. note d). They continue: 'Some of the principal planters of the present day, are Lord de Dunstanville, Sir John St. Aubyn, Sir William Lemon, Mr. Charles Rashleigh, Lord Grenville, Mr. Vyvyan, and Mr. Thomas of Chiverton.'
25. See A. Pearson, 'The Royal Horticultural Society of Cornwall', *JRIC.* 1974: 165-73.
26. See F.W. Shepherd, 'The Origins and History of the Cornwall Garden Society', *CG.* 1987: 10-30.
27. S.M. Turk and R.J. Murphy (R Poly SC. 1952: 35-9) report field studies at Pencalenick intended as a paradigm of the expected 'feral succession' in abandoned or neglected gardens, which would eventually lead to oak scrub, the typical 'climax' vegetation of these islands.

How to Use the Topography

The **topography** has been designed so that the location of gardens may easily be found. Those with known place-names can be traced through the *Index*, which contains much additional information. Explorations among unknown sites should begin by selecting under the appropriate *Chapter* (with its associated Ordnance Survey map), one of the *Localities* arranged around prominent towns. Each of these sections opens with a general *Introduction*, followed by a series of individual entries for the major parks and gardens, beginning with the grid reference, the OS codes for the larger scale and other maps, and an indication of those open to the public. Contemporary - post-Second World War gardens - are marked by an asterisk. Each section concludes with a *Supplementary List* of 'lesser known historic' and 'additional contemporary' gardens, which had received significantly less horticultural recognition than the main entries. The contents of the individual garden entries are described more fully in the following notes.

EXPLANATORY NOTES

Map references

The five chapters correspond with their respective Ordnance Survey maps. These are: The Isles of Scilly (*Explorer* 101); Land's End and The Lizard (*Landranger* 203); Truro and Falmouth (*Landranger* 204); Newquay and Bodmin (*Landranger* 200), and finally Plymouth and Launceston (*Landranger* 201) together with Bude and Clovelly (*Landranger* 190). Anomalies are noted at the end of the individual Introductions. A four-figure grid reference is given for each entry, followed by the number of the Ordnance Survey *Explorer* [**EX**] 1:25000 map; the *Geological Survey* [**GS**]; and the *Soil Survey* [**SS**] where this exists. In a few difficult cases a six-figure grid reference is given.

Historic references

(a) The *Chronological Bibliographies* at the end of the book, where more detailed references are to be found, are indicated under each entry by the generalized use of centuries, viz., **17th, 18th, 19th** and **20th C.** and **Illus.**, which represent respectively *early site*, *topographical*, *horticultural*, and *general gardening* references. The introductions to the bibliographies themselves should be consulted for a fuller explanation of this plan, which is felt to be more serviceable than the more conventional unselective form.

(b) In addition, specific references relating to individual gardens are noted under the entries themselves. Unless stated otherwise, the place of publication is London.

Preliminary notes

The *Preliminary Notes* to the garden entries contain much diverse information which needs to be explained in greater detail. They fall into five sections, as follows:

1. Place-names

The form of Cornish place-names is often thought to be strange, and their pronunciation puzzling. No more is intended here than to offer some general guidance.

(a) *Alternative names* are noted for three reasons: (i) where there has been a change of name, (ii) where older forms convey more clearly the original meaning or pronunciation, (iii) where early forms, such as in Domesday, have an intrinsic interest.

(b) *Derivations:* the meanings of Cornish elements in place-names, as found in such authorities as Padel (1985), are supplied, usually without comment. An explanation of certain recurring elements will save repetition in the entries:

An	literally 'and', is used to join two names, thus,'of, on, by, near the'.
Bos or **bod**	'dwelling' or 'home', commonly followed by a personal name.
Car	'enclosure', often with the sense of 'fort'.
Chy	'house', not usually followed by a personal name.
Lan	'sacred enclosure', thus a religious settlement or burial ground.
Nans	'valley' often corrupted to *lan* or *lam*, which can be confused with **lan** above.
Pen	'head', 'headland', 'top', or typically 'end'.
Pol	'pool' or 'pond', but can also mean 'creek' or 'cove'.
Porth	'cove', usually where a landing can be made.
Ros	normally 'heath', but with a secondary meaning of a 'promontory of land' (but not a 'headland' which is **pen**).
Tre	'farm', i.e., a prehistoric or 'Celtic' agricultural settlement (see Introduction).

The distinctions commonly made between two places of the same name are, in Cornish:

Veor = 'great'   **Vean** = 'little'
Wartha = 'higher'   **Wollas** = 'lower'.

The presence of the elements in current place-names may not always be obvious, through the operation of such processes as the mutation of consonants and shortening. These are subjects explained in more detail in the authorities. The books consulted are:

Padel, O.J., *Cornish Place-Name Elements*, 1985, Nottingham.

Pool, P.A.S., *The Place-Names of West Penwith*, 1973,

supplemented by

Dexter, T.F.G., *Cornish Names*, 1926, repr.1968, Truro.
Holmes, J., *1,000 Cornish Place-Names Explained*, 1983, Redruth.

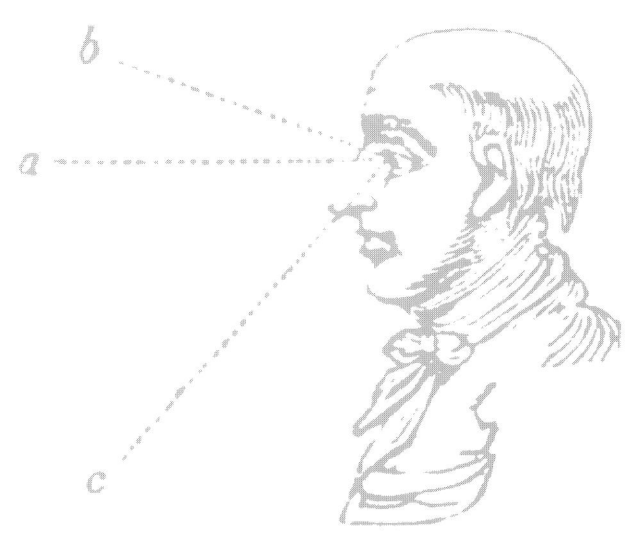

An ***** denotes an hypothetical form; **?** that the derivation is not known to the authorities; **[?]** that the place-name is not found in the authorities consulted.

(c) *Pronunciation:* A phonetic spelling with the accented syllable in capitals is given, with a rhyme where there may be a doubt. The general rule in Cornish is to accent the *last* syllable of a two-syllable word, and the *next but last* in words with more than two syllables. Exceptions in place-names are usually caused by the present spelling obscuring the original form of the words, or simply by Anglicizing, as in TREEba, instead of 'Trebba', and HELigan, instead of HeLIGan. Shortening is not uncommon, as in TREEVE for 'Trereife', TROUVE for 'Trewoofe', CRAZE for 'Caerhays' and TREGNY for 'Tregony'.

2. Topographical notes

(a) English Heritage has listed buildings since the 1970s, and parks and gardens since 1985. In each section there are three grades: I, II* and II. The criteria used are those of national (not local) importance, and in the case of gardens are primarily concerned with structure and design rather than with horticultural excellence.

(b) Aspect and altitude are taken from the OS maps, supplemented from other sources (usually indicated by the use of inverted commas). The geological notes are taken from the maps of the Geological Survey. Where specific information on soil is lacking, only a general indication, whether acid or alkaline, is attempted. The size of sites is given in acres, since this is still the measure usually found in the sources, although the metric equivalent is added in brackets, except in quotations. Estimated sizes are:

very small	an acre or less
small	up to 5 acres
medium	10 acres or more
large	20 acres or more
very large	50 acres or more
extensive	a few large parks.

Intermediate sizes are indicated by two words, for example, 'small to medium'.

3. Official designations

The conventional abbreviations for landscape, historical, and scientific value are used, viz.:

Landscape
*AONB	Area of Outstanding Natural Beauty
SAGLV	Special Area of Great Landscape Value
AGLV	Area of Great Landscape Value
*HC	Heritage Coast

Historical
*AM	Ancient Monument
AGHV	Area of Great Historical Value
HS	Historic Site

Scientific
*SSSI	Site of Special Scientific Interest
AGSV	Area of Great Scientific Value
CNCS	Cornwall Nature Conservation Site (Cornwall Trust for Nature).

An asterisk indicates National designations, the remainder are from the *Cornwall Countryside Local Plan*, 1985. Both categories have statutory significance, except for the **CNCS**.

4. Climate

This subject was covered in the Introduction, where the maps for rainfall (which is in inches), and the temperature zones are to be found.

5. Status

General information on the opening of gardens during the period 1983 to 1998 is supplied, but the annual official guides must be consulted for current details. *Of the contemporary gardens, only those which are no longer open have been described, as a matter of historical interest.*

The condition of parks or gardens open to the public, or otherwise accessible can be directly assessed, but for the rest, two broad categories are used:

(a) **Extinct**: Where the original has become non-recoverable, either by being built over or, in some cases, by being replaced by a 'residual' garden, i.e., one which bears no relation to the original.

(b) **Relict**: This includes gardens whose original design has been reduced, altered or neglected, but is still discernable, and perhaps recoverable. The great number of sites converted to other uses, such as hotels, schools and hospitals, fall into this category, but to varying degrees.

The comments under this head are based upon visiting, or at least viewing from the perimeter, the great majority of the places included in the Topography, with the intention and hope that they may assist in the selection of sites for more comprehensive surveys or further research.

1
The Isles of Scilly

The Isles of Scilly, although only some twenty-eight miles out from Land's End, for most of their history led an isolated existence, often with little more than a subsistence economy. The mild, equable climate, usually frost-free, and rarely dropping below the 5°C necessary for the continual growth of vegetation, barely compensated for a landscape, never exceeding 160 feet in altitude, barren of trees, quick draining, short of natural supplies of water and, except in a few places, not favoured with protection from unceasing sea breezes.

The earliest settlement in historic times was an outpost of the Abbey of Tavistock on Tresco, a site chosen, no doubt, because of the proximity of two fresh-water lakes. The Abbey seems to have succumbed to marauders from the sea, to be replaced by a garrison on the island of St Mary's, established from the time of Henry VIII to the early nineteenth century to protect the entry to the English Channel. The need to feed the military brought prosperity to the small population of inhabitants, by leading to a more extensive cultivation of potatoes which, with fish, became a staple diet. The peace following the end of the Napoleonic Wars, however, led to a total collapse of the fragile economy, followed closely by famine. The Duchy of Cornwall, to whom the islands belong, was forced by public opinion to resolve the chronic poverty aggravated by the neglect of the Godolphins who were the leasehold 'Proprietors'. The outcome of the surveys was a transfer of the lease to Augustus Smith, a young philanthropist from Ashlyns near Berkhamsted, who sought an opportunity to put his ideas into practice. His far-sighted, though despotic 'reign' was to earn him the title of 'Emperor of Scilly'. By the time of his arrival in 1834 it is probable that many exotic plants had already been introduced. The Hottentot Fig (*Carprobotus edulis*), and other mesembryanthemums, echiums, and at least *Aeonium cuneatum*, all of which are now naturalised, most likely owe their introduction to passing sailors from the Mediterranean and Canary Islands. The Steward's House, where Augustus Smith had at first lodged, had long been celebrated for its garden, with mulberry trees, fuchsias, geraniums and hebes. It was no doubt their attractiveness, and the potentiality of the unique climate that encouraged him to plant out his own garden with tender species, once he had decided to take up residence near the old Abbey on Tresco.

The evidence for the introduction from passing shipping is perhaps more secure in the case of the commercial species. It was a few potatoes given to Alexander Gibson of St Martin's from a Spanish vessel which initiated the lucrative trade in early potatoes mid-century. When this market began to fail, on the suggestion of Augustus Smith, followed up by William Trevellick at Rocky Hill on St Mary's, the early daffodils found growing wild over the islands were sent to market with spectacular success. Some of these tazetta narcissus had been growing around the ruins of the Abbey, perhaps since the time of the monks, but the presence of 'Soleil d'Or', 'Grand Monarque' and *Narcissus biflorus* around the Garrison lend some credence to the suggestion that they may have been introduced by the soldiers' wives. 'Scilly Whites' were prolific in certain orchards, especially at Newford, the farm of the former Lord Proprietor's agent. Certainly the narcissus 'Telemonius Plenus' is known to have been given to Mrs Gluyas, wife of the resident Dutch vice-Consul, and one of the 'Pioneers', by the captain of a French ship in the 1820s.

The narcissus trade was developed by Algernon Dorrien Smith, Augustus Smith's nephew and successor, who made a trial of over 350 varieties, some 240 of which he introduced from the Continent. From 1885 to the First World War the market in daffodils soared, exciting regular comment in the horticultural press,

11. Harvesting the crop: rival blooms. A favourite posed photograph by Gibson in the 1890s illustrates the kind of wicker basket used to gather blooms; here in a small orchard with protective hedges.

so that for a time every available piece of land was planted. To protect the fragile blooms from the elements, they were grown in small fields with high hedges, at first of elm, escallonia, tamarisk, and veronica (*Hebe*), but in the mid 1920s, deriving from the experience of A.A. Dorrien Smith during his expedition in the Antipodes, the use of pittosporum became virtually universal.

By the twentieth century the Isles of Scilly had become celebrated as 'Daffodil Land', receiving constant publicity. But after the boom years the bubble burst; the soil began to suffer exhaustion, pests and diseases spread, competition from home and abroad increased, and towards the end of the century the market itself receded. Growing was replaced by tourism as the major industry. 'Growers' came to depend as much on the cultivation of the visitors as of their fields, and the Abbey Gardens originally opened by Augustus Smith as a favour to his tenants, are now featured as one of the great tourist attractions.

Note: The Isles of Scilly, both in Topographies and administration, are independent of Cornwall. For this reason they have been treated as a separate section, with the more specific references printed under each entry.

THE ABBEY GARDENS, Tresco

SV89 14 : *EX 101* OPEN

Cornish tre + scawen = *elder tree; gardens of 17 acres (6.9 ha) with surrounding woodland listed grade I, sloping NNE to SSW from 20 metres to the Great Pool, on granite, soil 'acid over granite shale and shillet';*

rainfall 30-35", equable temperature with 9.2°C difference between the hottest (August 16.5°C) and the coldest (February 7.3°C), averaging 350 days with air temperatures above 5°, about the optimum for plant growth, humidity exceptionally high, frosts rare and usually not damaging, the major destruction being caused by high or chilling winds, especially if of long duration; the gardens are open daily, although launches to the island run regularly only during the summer season.

Augustus Smith took up his lease of the Isles of Scilly in 1834, lodging for a time on St Mary's until he had decided where he would eventually settle. The choice was to fall upon Tresco, where he set in hand the building of a house to his own design, perched on a rocky eminence above the Abbey ruins, with a prospect southwards over Oliver's Battery and the sea to Hugh Town and St Mary's. He was able to take up residence in 1838, and at once began work on his garden, which by his death in 1872 had already achieved the design in the accompanying plan, which is substantially that today. At first he developed the area around the house, described for the first time by a visitor in 1850:

> On entering ... you will be charmed with the gay profusion of flowers, some creeping on the ground, and others climbing the rock-work, which affords at once shelter from the winds, and inviting opportunities of display.

By this time Augustus was already 'hammering at the rocks beneath [his] study window to extend [his] mesembryanthemum plantations', to accommodate the new varieties he had received from Kew as a result of an appeal made to Sir William Hooker in 1849. Hooker, however, was less sympathetic when he wrote again four years later, although his son Joseph was 'astonished and delighted with the luxuriance and variety especially of the Cape and Australian vegetation ... displayed', when he visited the island in 1857. The Long Walk had by then been formed, 'where' Augustus wrote, 'most of my rarities are planted', and a year or two later he was informing his friend Lady Sophia Tower, that he was now

> at last finishing up the rocky slope beneath the Abbey at the east end, and have erected such a vast screen of rough masonry that it is fit to be part of Sebastopol, and has been christened the Malakoff, and it is to be crowned by a *chevaux-de-frises* of Aloes.

His collections of Aloes, or more properly Agaves, were to be the wonder of visitors for many years to come, and feature in all the earliest illustrations. The work progressed year by year. A garden below the rockery nearby the ruins, walled for protection, had been constructed early on, and below that the hop garden, or 'hop circle' as it came to be known, which had been 'enclosed with an outer circle of yews for a hedge' in 1851, when the deciduous trees were being replaced by evergreens for greater shelter. Below this again, 'the foundations of my green houses are rising', he wrote in 1856, and two years later he was

> very busy converting the veranda into stone ... The upper terrace is also intended to progress ... it is to be the chief feature of the gardens, and will, I fear, rather make the lower alleys, especially the long walk, not a little jealous ... I expect, however, when Neptune [actually a figure-head from a wreck] is raised on his throne at the head of the grand staircase that the eagle beneath will try to pick a quarrel. [The figure of a Mexican eagle was in a section of the garden known as Mexico.]

The design was reaching completion, and it was of the planting rather than of the construction that we next hear in 1859, when he announced that

> the new district called Australia, [which] though still in the rough, has some very brilliant productions, particularly of the Aralia tribe, Acacias and Cassias.

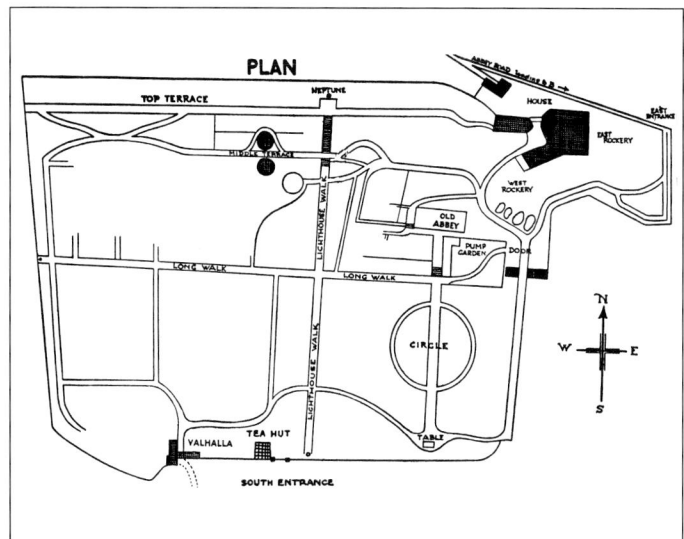

12. Plan of the Abbey Gardens, Tresco, in the 1940s.

The ornamental grounds had been extended by a 'new orchard and vegetable garden', and a year before his death, 'a grand croquet lawn [had] just been completed, large enough for a bowling green'. Two other features not mentioned in the letters are the Pebble Garden, where the beds were laid out in the form of the Union Jack, and the remarkable summer-house, adorned with carved figureheads from wrecks, which came to be known as Valhalla. Augustus, as North had remarked as early as 1850, was generous in allowing visitors, and there still survives his inscribed slate notice of welcome to all who 'abstain from picking flowers and fruit, scribbling nonsense and committing suchlike nuisances'. Alford, Dean of Canterbury, summarized the atmosphere of the garden in its early maturity, after a visit in August 1868:

> there are glades of Aloe and Dracoena [sic], varied with a multitude of outlandish trees, some beautiful, some strange rather than beautiful, but all contributing to give a curious foreign character to the place and to recall the villas of Cannes, or Nice, or Mentone, rather than those of England.

Augustus was not married, but arranged that he should be succeeded by his nephew, Thomas Algernon Dorrien, who adopted the name of Smith. Despite being at first inexperienced in horticulture, he applied himself to enhancing and extending the plantings in the garden, although he is perhaps better known for developing the narcissus trade on the islands. His son Arthur Algernon, however, had already acquired a reputation as a botanist before taking over from his father in 1918, and widening the range of plants from his contacts with Australia and New Zealand. He was also responsible in the 1920s for the pergola seat and pond on the middle terrace, which he named the 'Grecian rock terrace'. The latest advances in the design of the garden have been the addition of sculptures of the children and Gaia by David Wynne and, more recently, the creation of a new half-acre Mediterranean Garden to the award winning design of Carey Duncan-Haouach, which was featured in *Homes and Gardens* in 1993. As more and more visitors come to the islands, there has been a need to adapt to the requirements of tourism, but the essential character of the Abbey Gardens, which makes it unique in the British Isles, has not changed.

References: 19th C: *S.F. Tower,* Sketches in the Isles of Scilly, *1848: pl. 3; I.W. North*, A Week in the Isles of Scilly, *Penzance 1850: 18-19, the first description of the garden; S.F. Tower,* Scilly and its Emperor, *1873. [The Abbey copy contains many contemporary photographs.]; F. Le Marchant,* Flowers and Shrubs in Tresco Abbey Gardens, *1873-92, bound volume of 51 watercolours [in Tresco Abbey]; J.C. and R.W. Tonkin,* Guide to the Isles of Scilly, *Penzance 1882: 25-33, description by G. Vallance, gardener at the Abbey;* 20th C: *Official and other guides; C.F., G. and C. Dorrien Smith,* Mesembryanthemum, *vol. i. 1908, watercolour botanical drawings of 49 species;* Geranium, *vol. i, watercolour botanical drawings of 51 species and varieties of pelargoniums; G. Dorrien Smith,* Original Drawings, *2 vols., 53 watercolours of Scilly, Tresco and the Abbey Gardens [all three in Tresco Abbey];* Curtis's Botanical Magazine, *references listed in* JRHS, *1947: 190-91; J.W. Hunkin, 'The Gardens of Tresco', in* The Isles of Scilly, *E.A. Belcher, 1947: 33-59; P. Coats,* Great Gardens

13. The Neptune Steps. The size of the agaves in the Abbey Gardens frequently excited admiration. Here they border one of the principal features, in a sketch by T. von Erkenbrecher, a foreign visitor, which was circulated as a picture postcard about the turn of the century.

14. Armorel's Cottage. This abandoned dwelling on the depopulated island of Samson, with its solitary windswept elder obscuring an ancient tamarisk, was sentimentally identified with the fictional Armorel's Cottage. The walls beyond were built by Augustus Smith in his vain attempt to impale deer. (Photograph by Gibson)

of England, *1963: 194-207*; Architect. Digest, *1980: xxxvii 2-7*; R. King, Tresco: England's Island of Flowers, *1985*, quotes from many journal articles, reprinted watercolours of Francis Le Marchant, and the Dorrien Smiths, and the plant list of P. Clough and K. Spencer (1982); Scillonian, Winter 1996/7: 66. For the many journal and gardening book references, see 'Horticultural References' and '20th Century References' in the Bibliographies, pp. 277, 288. See also 'Plant Records', pp. 298-9.

SUPPLEMENTARY LIST

Armorel's Cottage, Samson
SV87 12 : *EX101*

The opening setting for the novel *Armorel of Lyonesse* (1890), by Sir Walter Besant, was the now deserted island of Samson, although the descriptions of the surroundings of the cottage better fit the luxuriant Holy Vale in the centre of St Mary's. One of the recurring features in the book is a tamarisk, which has led to the popular identification of a derelict house in the centre of Samson, with a solitary tree in its tiny garden, as the fictional Armorel's Cottage. John Savage, in his *Memoirs and Travels* of 1790, particularly remarked upon seeing a tamarisk on Scilly, which he regarded at that time as unusual and exotic. In about 1855, after he had depopulated Samson, Augustus Smith made a futile attempt to impale deer on South Hill, although he was rather more successful in the introduction of black rabbits, which are now occasionally seen on other islands.

References: Scillonian Autumn 1961: 230-33; Z.T. Cowan, The Story of Samson, *Cirencester 1991: 27-8*; E. Berry, The Samson Buildings, *Cornwall Archaeological Unit, 1994.*

15. *The Trevellick family. William Trevellick of Rocky Hill, one of the 'Pioneers' of the narcissus industry, is seen here with his wife, family and pickers, in a glasshouse used to bring the flowers into bloom before they were sent to market. They are of the variety 'Grand Monarque'. (Photograph by Gibson)*

The 'Ladies' Garden', Garrison, St Mary's
SV901 103 : *EX101*

A little south, along the path past the former coastguard cottages on the Garrison, is an overgrown walled area, with bedraggled Cordylines, which is occasionally referred to as The 'Ladies' Garden'. This most probably harks back to a time when Veronica Lodge, next to Hugh House, was used as officers' quarters. It may, however, be a relict of an earlier period, when enclosed private walled gardens were set up in the vicinity of castles, such as at Tintagel. Known in medieval times as an *hortus conclusus*, they were associated with the Virgin Mary, the 'enclosed' representing her intact virginity, which may be reflected in the name of this present garden, which originally may have been 'Our Lady's Garden'.

The Master Gunner's House, St Mary's
SV89 10 : *EX101*

The Master Gunner lived in a granite house (now known as the White House) which stands facing north-east below the Star Castle, overlooking Rat Island and the Quay at St Mary's. A report in the West Briton of 1 August 1818 reads:

> An Aloe [*Agave americanus*] growing in the garden of Mr. Tweson, [sic, ?Tovey] master-gunner of the Garrison of Scilly is well worth the attention of the curious for its extraordinary size. The flower stem is 22ft. high and 18ins in circumference, having 35 flower branches, exclusively of the top branch. The flower buds are now opening. It is the finest plant of the kind ever seen in the West of England.

The plant made such an impression that it was mentioned by John Forbes in 1821 and George Woodley in 1822. It provides evidence for the introduction of exotic plants to Scilly long before the arrival of Augustus Smith, since the Agave must have been planted in the eighteenth century, perhaps even by Abraham Tovey himself, the celebrated Master Gunner, who had rebuilt the Garrison Gateway in 1742. Col. George Vigoureux, who inspired a romantic novel by Sir Arthur Quiller Couch, was resident in the house at the time of the flowering, since the Star Castle had become uninhabitable.

References: J. Forbes, Observations on the Climate of Penzance, *Penzance 1821;*
G. Woodley, View ... of the Scilly Isles, *1822: 8;*
M. Tangye, Scilly 1801-1821, *Redruth 1970: 53.*

Rocky Hill, St Mary's
SV91 11 : *EX101*

Controversy has always surrounded the question of who should be credited with originating the narcissus trade. This may best be resolved by ascribing the suggestion to Augustus Smith, and the commencement of the trade to William Trevellick of Rocky Hill Farm, who was the leading member of that small band who came to be known as the 'Pioneers'. His fields, or 'gardens' as some termed them, always attracted the first attention of the early observers. The Cornish elm trees around the lower fields, although now growing freely, still show the line where they were pollarded to create a shelter hedge for the small bulb fields. The original farmhouse burnt down, to be replaced by a private residence, the new farmhouse being built higher up. The glass houses, where Trevellick is to be seen among his blooms and family, like so many others, have gone, or been reduced to mere packing sheds, the practice of sending daffodils to market in tight bud having sounded the death knell for hot houses. But Trevellick was also celebrated for creating above the old farmhouse a 'Little Tresco', planted with exotic trees and shrubs, many obtained from the Abbey Gardens themselves, which his successors, the Moyle family, later decorated with antiquities collected on the Islands. The garden was restored in 1960, and survives around holiday chalets.

References: J.C. Tonkin and B.P. Row, Lyonesse, *2nd edn. 1900: 64;* G.M. *1908: 27;* J.M. Stone, England's Riviere, *1912: 421;* Scillonian *1960: 163;* T. Moyle, 'I Remember', Scillonian, *Summer 1964: 101-4.*

The Steward's House, St Mary's
SV90 10 : *EX101*

The Steward's House, described as 'a replica in miniature of a Cornish manor house of the first part of the 18th Century', has had a chequered history; from 1750 the residence of the Godolphin stewards, then from about 1835 the chaplaincy where one of the chaplains in the 1860s 'hanged himself in a garret', a cheap lodging house for sailors, a 'ladies gown shop', and finally the Bishop and Wolf pub. It features here because Augustus Smith lodged with Johns the Steward when first visiting Scilly, where he saw a garden already celebrated by Woodley in 1822 as having

> good and extensive fruit and flower gardens behind, in which are some fine mulberry trees, and vines producing grapes of large size and excellent flavour.

Later memories recollected that it was

> full of rare plants and flowers brought to the islands by many visiting ships which entered the port of Scilly from worldwide journeys. There were mulberry trees, acacias, fuchsias, ironwood trees, palms, geraniums, and even bulbs flourishing in it.

This is good evidence for the source of the exotic plants on the islands, which may have provided the inspiration for Augustus Smith when he began to cultivate the Abbey Gardens. J.C. Owen, son of a Collector of Customs on Scilly, remembered many years later, how the ripe berries of the mulberry tree

> were too great a temptation to the youth of St Mary's, who attacked them each year with stones. Some stones were not accurately aimed and at length the late chaplain [T.S. Cunningham], tired of dodging the missiles as he walked in meditation up and down his garden paths, had the tree cut down, and its wood fashioned into a reading-desk and pulpit.

One suspects that Owen himself had been one of those youths!

References: G. Woodley, View ... of the Scilly Isles, *1822: 170;* J.C. Owen, Fair Lyonesse, *Bideford 1897: 29;* A.E. Richardson and C.L. Gill, Regional Architecture in the West of England, *1924: 156;* Scillonian, *1930 24: 413, 1949 100: 244-5, 1959 137: 47, 138: 70.*

2
Land's End and The Lizard

1. PENZANCE and ST IVES

The extreme west of Cornwall, and the old hundred of Penwith, present to view a landscape already denuded of trees before historic times, divided up into a patchwork of small prehistoric or 'Celtic' fields, and scarred by mining. In the farthest west, St Just became the focal point of the mining industry, although surrounded on all sides by small farmsteads, open to the ravages of the wind. Only in the valleys running down to the sea, such as at the ancient house of the Paynters at Boskenna, could the planting of trees be successfully attempted - an example followed by Dr Vernon Favell early this century at the neighbouring Penberth. In contrast, Arnold-Forster at the craggy Eagle's Nest perched high on a pinnacle above the north coast near Zennor cultivated his garden in hollows between rocks and hedges.

The principal fishing harbours grew up on the south coast at Mousehole and Newlyn, which later became an artists' colony, and on the north coast at St Ives, which, once the Great Western Railway acquired Tregenna Castle above the town as an hotel, began to be promoted among holiday makers as the 'Cornish Riviera'. Here in the narrow streets and alleys, where 'the abominable stench' of pilchards once 'assailed the nostrils', little gardens now glow over a long period with the vivid colours of mesembryanthemums, fuchsias and pelargoniums. It was, however, Penzance, on the site of the old Domesday manor of Alverton, that eventually emerged as the main port and market centre, receiving its charter as a borough in 1614, and becoming the coinage town for assaying tin and copper in 1663. By the turn of the nineteenth century, when the Napoleonic wars had made travel impossible, it took on a new life as 'the Montpellier of England', becoming prosperous enough for rich merchants and lawyers to begin erecting their mansions around the perimeter, facing the sea, and typically orientated towards the Mount. Among them the Bolitho family, who had gravitated from Penryn by way of Wendron, became dominant.

In about 1765, Thomas Bolitho (1742-1807) had settled at the Coombe, Chyandour - a house still to be seen nestling below the new flyover by-passing the borough - and there pursued his trade as a tanner. His sons entered into partnership with the adjacent tin works, long since gone, ultimately moving into banking. His four grandsons, burgeoning in wealth, built themselves what were described in *Lake's Parochial History* as 'modern palatial mansions'. Among their many benefactions was the laying out of the land between the Larrigan River and Newlyn Art Gallery as public gardens, to commemorate the 300th anniversary of the Borough's Charter, which were known as the Bedford Bolitho, and Richard Foster Bolitho Gardens.

The climate of Penzance is exceptional, enjoying during the last 150 years, except for brief lapses, winter temperatures comparable to those of the north coasts of the Mediterranean, and the mildest in England. Consequently even humble gardens in the town, until recent set-backs, flourished with exotic plants only surpassed on the Isles of Scilly. With the rising popularity of seaside travel, facilitated by the extension of the railway to Penzance in 1867, the Borough Council sought to enhance the reputation of the resort by creating in the grounds of the vacated Morrab House a unique sub-tropical garden. In this they were encouraged by the enthusiasm of those such as Thomas Bedford Bolitho, who at Trewidden had been experimenting with new and rare plants. However, the proximity to the sea which favours the land with an equable mildness, brings with it ferocious winds whose blasts required to be broken by belts of trees if these more tender species were to survive.

Today, of these old gardens only Trewidden lives on, the more celebrated Trengwainton owing its fame to the support given during the 1920s by Lt.-Col., later Sir Edward Bolitho to plant expeditions in Asia, which sent back seeds of rhododendrons for which this garden became famous. Other great gardens of the past, such as that of Canon Boscawen at Ludgvan Rectory, have fallen from glory, but even so, enough remains to reawaken a little of that fever of excitement once felt by those whose experiments in the 'acclimatisation of exotics' rivalled those along the coast at Falmouth.

BOSKENNA, St Buryan

SW42 23 : EX7, GS351/358

Boskene *1233 etc.; Cornish* bos + *kenow = puppy, pronounced bosKENna; house with date-stones 1678, 1858, and 1888, listed grade II*, cider house-stables, entrance gate-piers (early 19th C.), and sundial (early-mid 19th C.), each II; medium sized garden, south-west sloping 95-80m., on biotite granite, with acid soil, in an AONB and HC, an AGSV, and an AGHV with AM (cross); rainfall 35-40", temperature zone B; private.*

Tonkin, early in the eighteenth century, wrote of Boskenna long the residence of the Paynter family:

> Though this place lies near the sea, and very much exposed, yet has this gentleman, by means of furze ricks and other ingenious contrivances, raised several fair walks of trees about it, and made it a pleasant and profitable seat, which I mention here, that those who live under the same inconveniencies may imitate his industry.

Gilbert later described the house as

> encompassed with neat lawns, and sheltered with good plantations; from these declines a pretty sequestered vale, opening into the sea.

During the mid nineteenth century Boskenna was occupied by Charles Dacres Bevan (d.1872), a district court judge, who 'considerably improved and beautified it' (*Lake*), although Thurston, who included this among his select gardens, informs us that the grounds were developed in his time with 'a good rock garden' by Col. C.H. Paynter. It is now the residence of Helen McCabe, whose childhood home it was, and who has written about it. Part of the estate was purchased by Peter Paris, who established a successful flower business there. In retirement, from the middle 1970s, he turned his attention to the garden. His chief interest was that of a plantsman, rather than designer, and he has collected trees, shrubs and herbaceous plants, and more characteristically, in this context, alpines. F. Holland Hall in the *Cornish Garden* (1985: 22) published a good account of his plantings.

References: 17th, 18th, 19th (Gen.) and 20th C.

BOSKENWYN MANOR, Penzance

SW46 31 : EX7, GS351/358

Carne, *G. Ch. 1898, renamed Boskenwyn Manor after the Second World War; Cornish* carn = *rock, and* bos + keyn = *ridge +* gun = *white; grounds of about 14 acres (5.7ha), south sloping 85-60m., on metamorphosed Mylor slates, and phonolite and elvan intrusions, with acid soil, in an AGHV; rainfall 45-50", temperature zone C; private, divided between Boskenwyn Manor, Carne House, Boskenwyn Lodge, and Carne Vean (converted from former piggery), grounds relict, and separately maintained.*

The house at Carne was built in about 1880, when Charles Campbell Ross, MP, moved there from Morrab House in Penzance. The garden was described in the *Gardeners' Chronicle* of 1898 by Harry Roberts, a Redruth writer who expressed the hope that the new owner, F. St John Tupper (who was related to the Bolithos of Polwithen by marriage) would 'take advantage of its situation and make it one of Cornwall's most beautiful flower-gardens.' It is situated on the summit and side of a hill overlooking the town of Penzance, with views of Mount's Bay and St Michael's Mount, and had already been laid out in lawns, paths and shrubberies by Ross, with a 'fairly extensive' collection of plants, including a large number of rhododendrons and hollies. The property was used as a school during the Second World War, after which it was renamed Boskenwyn, the 'Manor' being added later. Today, the adjoining Trannack House, of a similar age, has a finer contemporary garden.

References: 19th (Hort.) and 20th C.

CASTLE HORNECK, Penzance

SW45 30 : EX7, GS351/358

Castelhornek, *1335; Cornish* hornek = *iron, i.e. 'strong'; house, late 18th, early 19th C. listed grade II*; medium grounds, east sloping 50-30m., on metamorphosed metabasic volcanic rocks, with acid soil, with an AM (Lesingey Round); rainfall 45-50", temperature zone C; now a Youth Hostel, with relict grounds, in plantations and agricultural use.*

The name 'Iron Castle' may refer to the prehistoric Lesingey Round on the hill behind, although *Lake* records that it was

> thought to be the site of a castle so denominated from its supposed strength, and built by the family of Tyes, who were lords of the district early

in the times of the Plantagenets, and whose title as baron Tyes became extinct in 1322.

If this be so, it is not mentioned by William of Worcester, the 'auntient ruyned castle' of Norden presumably referring to the Round. The present house was built, or remodelled, in 1720 by the Revd Dr Walter Borlase, brother of William Borlase of Ludgvan. He had issued a warrant in 1744 for the arrest of John Wesley, who, since the magistrate was not at home when he was brought to the house, was released. Gilbert thought that the

> gardens, shrubberies, walks, lawns, sheets of water, and plantations, which diversify the home grounds, ... render this one of the most agreeable residences in the neighbourhood.

The Borlase family continued in residence for many years, and are listed in the *Hort. Direct.* from 1889 to 1924. This is one of Thurston's selected gardens from which he cites only a *Pinus radiata* 'planted in 1850 to celebrate the coming of age of Mr Borlase, [which] now measures 90ft. by 19ft. 6in.' This Monterey Pine, which is still recognized as the largest in the county, has survived to the present day, but much of the grounds are now being farmed. The old house is now used as a Youth Hostel, and there are a number of holiday chalets in the garden below.

References: 17th, 18th, 19th (Hort. & Gen.) and 20th C.

CARNE, see Boskenwyn Manor

CHYMORVAH, Marazion

SW52 30 : EX7, GS351/358

Cornish chy + *morva = sea-marsh, or Morvah a saint's name, pronounced chyMORvah; pair of houses (c. 1860s) listed grade II; pair of gazebos with basement stores, and flemish bond garden walls, each II; small gardens south-west sloping 25-15m., on Head, with acid soil, in an AGLV; rainfall 40-45", temperature zone C; relict gardens, eastern house an hotel, western private.

These are an unusual, if not unique pair of attached large houses, which claimed to be the first in West Penwith with plumbed bathrooms. They were built on the cliff side opposite St Michael's Mount, presumably for two members of the same family, reputed to be wealthy mine owners who won the land at cards. It is recorded in the *Hort. Direct.* for 1908 that Col. T.W. Field was then resident, and that the garden continued to open until 1924, later under the name of T.F. Michell. The Fields, who are known to have been mine pursers, were later involved in smelting and banking, and may have been the family responsible for building the houses. There are two long, narrow walled gardens leading to the sea edge, ending with two gazebos and, in the case of the west house, a boat pen. The garden of this west house, which may have retained more of the original design, is described as divided into six sections. The Top Garden has a variety of shrubs sheltered by hedges planted 'in the Sissinghurst manner'; the Middle Garden has a large lawn with borders; the Herb Garden is laid formally with tiled paths and a slate sun terrace, where there had formerly been an orangery; the Kitchen Garden has a sunken greenhouse, and old cold frames; the Palm Garden is lawned and planted with *Cordyline australis*; and the Bottom Garden, which leads to the Gazebo, is grassed and planted with fruit trees.

References: 19th (Hort.) C.

EAGLE'S NEST, Zennor

SW43 37 : EX7, GS351/358

Small garden at 190m. altitude on biotite granite, with 'peaty acid soil', in an AONB and HC, a SSSI, and an AGHV; rainfall 45-50", temperature zone C; private.

The Eagle's Nest is perched on a high outcrop of rock a few hundred yards from the rugged north coast. The house was greatly enlarged in the 1870s by Professor Westlake, who laid out a tennis court, now a lawn, and planted a few sycamores, escallonia and hydrangeas. The creation of the garden as it is today dates from the 1920s, and is the work of William Arnold-Forster, a talented watercolour landscape painter, and a great worker for the League of Nations and the Labour Party. That there is a garden at all was the result of Arnold-Forster's painstaking experiments with plants, first described in *The New Flora and Silva* in 1938. 'These notes', he wrote,

> come from what must be one of the windiest gardens in the British Isles. So if in them you find a plant given good marks for wind-hardiness, you can feel sure that it will stand as much wind as your own garden is likely to offer. This place is ... in full view northwards, north-east and westward, so that nothing breaks the gales from Newfoundland and almost nothing tempers those from the south-west. Not a bush higher than Gorse survives at this level for miles around, outside this garden. Sycamore, Ash, Hawthorn struggle on, dwarfed and shaven slantwise, within garden walls, and a little gnarled Beech lives in the lee of a huge rock, so close-cropped

by wind that it has never managed to stray an inch beyond its shelter. So the plants I shall mention have been through a stiff ordeal.

How, then, was it all achieved? He was not very specific in this article, but the site is found to have been naturally provided with huge boulders out of which he created eighteen enclosures, separated from one another by granite walls topped by escallonia to act as wind-breaks. Within these enclosures the boulders are used to give added protection. It is not possible here to list all the plants recommended in the article, nor is there the need, for later, in 1948, Arnold-Forster published his book, *Shrubs for the Milder Counties*. Jane Taylor, who has written a sequel, refers to his 'helpfully subjective comments', which have served as a valued guide to more than a generation of Cornish gardeners. The house was purchased in 1955 by Patrick Heron, an internationally known abstract painter, who continues to maintain the garden.

References: 20th C.

FOXSTONES, see Penberth

GULVAL CHURCHYARD and VICARAGE

SW48 31 : *EX7, GS351/358*

St Welvela de Lanesky 1301, the Saint and Domesday manor names, pronounced GULval; now a one-acre (0.4ha) garden, and similar sized churchyard, south facing at 25m. altitude on Head; rainfall 40-45", temperature zone C; the top half of the vicarage garden was divided in the 1950s, and later developed, the garden and churchyard are relict.

William Wriothesley Wingfield, incumbent of the parish from 1839 to 1912, was described by the parochial historian as the 'gardener Vicar'. In the 1890s, together with the 'squires' William and Richard Foster Bolitho of Ponsandane, he newly laid out and planted the churchyard with exotic trees and shrubs. Among these, the most conspicuous was what became a thicket of *Embothrium coccineum* at the east end of the church, noticed by Thurston, but now sadly destroyed by the recent severe winters. The churchyard played a part in the parish winning the CPRE 'Tidiest Village Competition' for three successive years in 1962-4, which was believed to be a record. The vicarage grounds, originally of three acres (1.2ha), had also been planted by the Vicar, assisted in his old age by his niece Sybil Wingfield, who after his death retired to Pendrea House (q.v.) where she created a garden of distinction. W.W. Wingfield was involved during the year 1872 in an enquiry into the tithe for Gulval parish, which was pioneering the market gardening of early potatoes, fruit and other crops, the climate being comparable with that of the Isles of Scilly. The report of the enquiry was printed and provides a valuable insight into the contemporary horticultural scene.

References: 17th, 19th (Hort.) and 20th C; W.W. Wingfield, Parish of Gulval. Statement on behalf of the Vicar of Gulval, Penzance 1872.

HOGUS HOUSE, see Ludgvan Rectory

KENEGIE, Gulval

SW48 32 : *EX7, GS351/358*

Kenegy is the plural of keun *= reeds or rushes, pronounced KeNEGie; house late 16th, early 17th C., remodelled each century since, listed grade II, summer-house, mid 18th C. with reused features probably from old house, and gate-piers + walls with obelisks at former S, and main entrance, each II; medium grounds, west sloping 95-85m., on metamorphosed Mylor slates and phonolite intrusions, with acid soil, in an AONB and AGHV; rainfall 40-45", temperature zone C; now known as the Kenegie Manor Holiday Village, with relict grounds.*

Belonging in the sixteenth century to the Tripconeys, Kenegie passed to the Harris family from Hayne in Devon, so legend tells, as the consequence of the owner's dissipation, which eventually led him in 1598 to mortgage his estate to Arthur Harris, Governor of the Mount, who took possession. A charity named after 'Lady Tripconey' was funded, until the 1960s, from the rent of a small area at Trythogga, to which she retired. From the Harrises Kenegie came to the Arundells of Menadarva, who thereupon changed their name to Harris. In the nineteenth century there were a variety of occupants, including Sir Rose Price who lodged here from 1813 to 1817, while Trengwainton was being prepared for his occupation. Thomas Simon Bolitho of Penalverne similarly bought Kenegie in 1866 from William Coulson, a London surgeon from a Penzance family, a year before he too bought and moved to Trengwainton. Later the property became the home of Col. Otho Glynn Bolitho who transferred there from Poltair in the 1890s, 'and spent a considerable sum in rebuilding and modernising the mansion.' 'The grounds', wrote Gilbert in 1820,

> are clothed in some places with fine wood, and in others open, and diversified with agreeable walks, whence there is a delightful prospect of Mount's-Bay, the town of Penzance, and other interesting scenery.

16. Kenegie. Trees hid the splendid prospect from the house, which faced away into a formal garden, although the early eighteenth-century gazebo compensated with a better view. The open space in front was the bowling green. (Borlase 1758: 5)

All this is clear in Borlase's illustration of 1758, but the 'prospect' could not, as would have been desired in the eighteenth century, be seen from the house, which in medieval fashion nestled down, turning its face away from the prevailing south-west winds. The solution lay in the construction of a gazebo, with a small first-floor banqueting room reached by two external stairways, at the base of which may once have sat on plinths two pairs of 'Arundell Lions' (see p.180). The rear, not seen in the engraving, has a semi-circular bow window running from ground to roof level, which is so reminiscent of similar windows at Montacute, that it would not seem to be wholly coincidental. Bottrell described how the ladies used the upper floor for embroidery, taking tea, and watching the gentlemen bowl on the green between the gazebo and the house.

> This choice retreat was finished with decorative wood and plaster-work; over the fireplace may yet be seen the family coat-of-arms; a broad window, opposite the entrance, commanded a delightful view over miles of rich pasture, orchards, and gardens; the western hills, with several parish churches; St. Buryan tower, standing boldly out, like a lofty landmark, against the sky. [None of which, of course, would have been visible from the house.] In the ground apartment, which also contains a fireplace, gentlemen, after their exercise on the bowling-green, rested and partook of refreshments.

The estate was sold by the Bolithos in c. 1918. In 1954 it became an hotel and country club, which has gradually changed the nature of the grounds, so that, even though it is now all but obscured by the surrounding chalets, the gazebo, which is unique in Cornwall, is the principal remaining interest.

References: 17th, 18th, 19th (Hort. & Gen.) and 20th C; Illus.

LORAINE, St Ives*

SW521 394 : EX7, GS351/358

Garden of 2.5 acres (1ha), east sloping 80-70m., on metamorphosed biotite granite and Mylor slates, with acid and limed soil; rainfall 45-50", temperature zone C; private.

Loraine was built in the 1950s, on the site of a market garden adjacent to the Tregenna Castle Hotel, for J.F. Holman, an active member of the Garden Society, who was married to the film actress Linden Travers, sister of Bill Travers. There were mine workings in the vicinity (cf. Treloyhan), which would normally result in an acid soil, but where there had been prior cultivation the soil had been limed. As at other exposed gardens in St Ives, windbreaks are essential, and the climate is on the whole colder than Penzance. A drive sweeps up to the house, flanked by lawns and beds of trees and shrubs. Mr Gee, who had worked in the market garden, continued as the first gardener. He planned a rose garden with a seat sheltered by clipped yew hedges, and also a rock garden. The plantings at this time are recorded in an article by Phyllis Kimber in the *Gardeners' Chronicle*, 1965. In a recent sale notice, it is mentioned that the kitchen garden is 'discreetly hidden behind hedging and shrubs', and that a pathway through a pergola leads to a modern heated swimming pool. At the rear a 'wrought iron spiral staircase leads up to a paved sun terrace with iron balustrading and trellis work over which an established Wisteria is being encouraged', from which there are magnificent views. It would appear that these may be later developments.

References: 20th C.

LUDGVAN RECTORY, now Hogus House
SW50 32 : EX7, GS351/358

Lvdvha, Domesday 1086, the manor name, pronounced LUDjan; house, 18th C. extended early 19th and reduced 20th C., listed grade II*, gate-piers early 19th C. II; original garden small to medium, south-east sloping 75-65m., on metamorphosed Mylor slates, with acid soil; rainfall 40-45", temperature zone C; private house reduced with residual garden, the remainder is a housing development.

Canon Arthur Townshend Boscawen was the son of the Rector of Lamorran (q.v.), where he received a good schooling in the art and science of gardening. Although at first choosing the Army as a career, he followed his father into the Church. After serving his title in Bristol, he became incumbent at Buckland Monachorum in Devon (now 'The Garden House') ,and in 1893 was presented to Ludgvan, where the great Dr William Borlase, author of *The Natural History of Cornwall* had gardened. His father had already gained a reputation for cultivating plants from the Southern Hemisphere, in an area of his garden known as 'Australia'; his brother Arthur had joined the New Zealand Forestry Service, and Major Arthur Dorrien Smith, who was also introducing Antipodean plants into his garden at Tresco, was related by marriage. With such an ancestry, it might be anticipated that he would soon achieve a reputation as an expert on New Zealand plants. 'At Kew', it was written in his obituary in their *Bulletin*, 'we think of Arthur Boscawen's garden at Ludgvan as the place to which rare plants needing expert care and a favourable situation should be sent for trial.' The Rectory is set high on a plateau facing towards St Michael's Mount. It was planted out by Boscawen himself, with only a single assistant. Kingdon Ward's descriptive article is definitive:

> No attempt has been made to cut the garden up into departments. The lawn slopes down between belts of trees with outlying Palms striding on to the grass, and here and there a tall shrub marooned. Winding paths thread the massed vegetation, and suddenly the visitor comes on a bulge of rock work overflowing with wide waves of a precious creeper, or descends into a grotto whose angular slopes are plated with metallic foliage. For it is a remarkable feature of this garden, devoted to trees and shrubs, that the

17. Ludgvan Rectory, with 'palms striding on to the grass'. (JRIC. 1942: 5)

very rocks are covered with clinging carpets of woody plants.

Canon Boscawen was active in local horticultural circles, and conducted trials to show that anemones could usefully occupy a gap in the local crop rotation of broccoli and narcissus. He was Chairman from 1925 to 1937 of the Gulval Experimental Station, which was able to supplant the inferior yellow-curded type of broccoli with the white-curded, high quality variety now taken for granted. He won many awards, his greatest recognition coming when in 1922 he received the Victoria Medal of Honour, the highest award of the Royal Horticultural Society. This was one of Thurston's select gardens.

References: 17th and 20th C.

MORRAB GARDENS, Penzance

SW47 30 : EX7, GS351/358   OPEN

Cornish *morrep = seashore, or seaward portion of a parish, pronounced MORrab; 'stucco villa in the Georgian manner with columned porch', listed grade II, stone cross II; grounds of 3.5 acres (1.4ha), south facing on metamorphosed Mylor slates, with acid soil; rainfall 40-45", temperature zone C; public park since 1889, somewhat relict.

Morrab House, which was surrounded by a large walled garden, was built in 1865-6 by Samuel Pidwell, a wealthy brewer, on open land running down to the sea which, from Penzance to Ludgvan, was known as the 'Morrep', hence the name. It passed eventually to Charles Campbell Ross, senior partner of Batten, Carne and Carne, bankers, who was MP for St Ives and four times Mayor of Penzance. In the 1880s he moved up to Carne (q.v.), and in 1889 the property was purchased by the Corporation for a municipal park, the house becoming the home of the Penzance Library. A London landscape gardener, Reginald Upcher, was engaged to lay out the grounds, but his origins are somewhat obscure. Possibly he was related to the Upchers of Sherringham Hall, Norfolk (a Repton garden). Whatever the virtues of his design, his knowledge of exotic plants appears to have been limited, despite his receiving a silver medal for a paper he had delivered to the Falmouth Naturalist Society. The Royal Polytechnic Society judges expressed an opinion that, before publication, he should obtain a wider knowledge of planting in Cornwall. The *Gardeners' Chronicle*, in an editorial, was even more specific in its criticisms:

> Mr. Upcher has lately got together a list of the exotic plants flourishing in Western Cornwall, but he has weakened his case by including plants like Berberis Darwinii, Thuias,(sic) and Yuccas, which are hardy almost everywhere.

In planting, Mr Upcher seems to have depended on the advice and experience of local gardeners, so that the great reputation gained by the Morrab Gardens in subsequent years lay more in the hands of the gardeners and park superintendents, than with the original designer. When the Gardens opened in 1889, the announcement in the *Gardeners' Chronicle* read:

> The new Penzance public park promises to give a great impetus to acclimatization. One of its features is to be a Palm-grove, where tourists may fancy themselves in the tropics or on the Mediterranean shores.

A correspondent to the *Garden* described the Morrab Gardens six years later as containing

> a few groups of Elm and other trees, including Apples, Mulberries, and a quaint old Medlar with a twisted trunk, and evidently planted long before the gardens themselves were formed. A rock-edged pool is filled with aquatics and gold fish ... There are here some fine clumps of

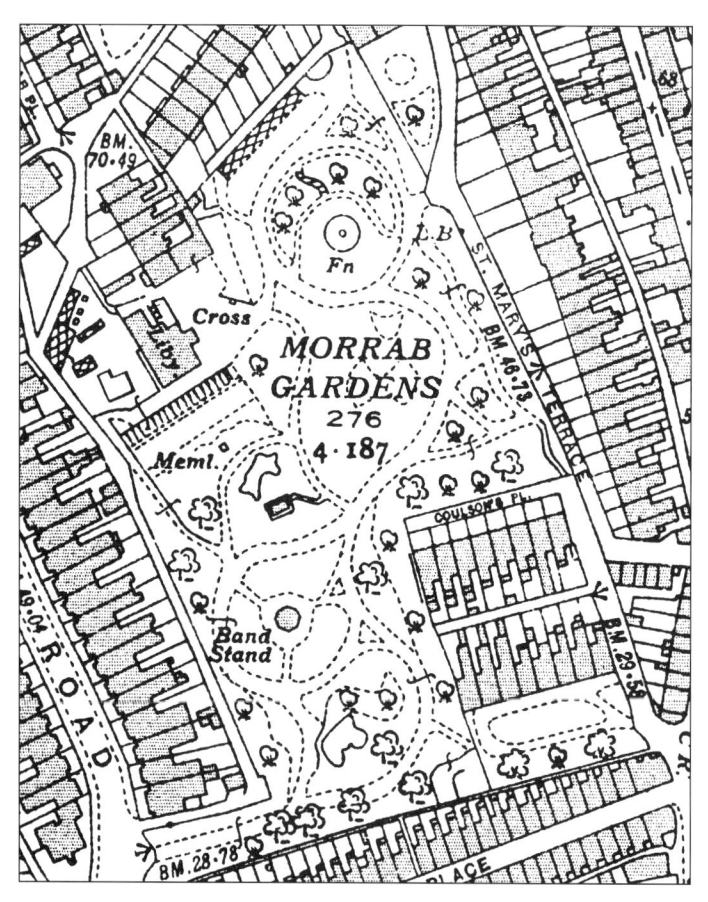

18. Morrab Gardens. This layout is somewhat more elaborate than that designed by Upcher, which his original plan and the early descriptions show to have been simpler. (Reproduced from the 1910 Ordnance Survey map C4/84/90)

Bambusa Metake [*Pseudosasa japonica*], and good plants of Cordyline australis, Agaves, &c., but isolated too much instead of being planted in bold groups.

Morrab had developed by 1930, when Thurston described it among his select gardens as laid out

with rows of *Cordyline*, tree-ferns, etc., and containing a fernery and palm house. The olive and *Musa ensete* fruit there.

The recent obligatory 'privatisation' of horticultural maintenance by local authorities, has destroyed the individuality, and much of the quality of these once famous gardens. There is a fuller description by F. Holland Hall in the *Cornish Garden* of 1986.

References: 19th (Hort.) and 20th C; C. Noall, The Penzance Library 1818-1968, Penzance 1968: 18-19.

THE OLD RECTORY, Marazion*

SW51 31 : *EX7, GS351/358*

A half-acre garden (0.2ha) at c. 15m. elevation on Mylor slates, with acid soil; rainfall 40-45", temperature zone C; opened 1993, 1995 NGS.

Although named the 'Old Rectory', neither the ancient parish of St Hilary, nor Marazion has had rectors. More recently it has been the residence of members of the medical profession, Dr Rob Senior arriving in the 1960s with an already large collection of cacti and succulents. The house has a balcony, creating below an open verandah on which grow several varieties of mature cacti, protected only against excess rainfall. Below the verandah two large beds are planted with a variety of agaves, aloes, aeoniums, cordylines, dracaenas, mesembryanthemums, puyas, other bromeliads and yuccas. In the lower garden, the other side of a lawn, in beds viewed from winding grass walks, are cultivated many rare and tender species of trees and shrubs. As in earlier days in Cornwall, some have originated in seeds brought home by travellers, such as members of the Cable and Wireless Company formerly at Porthcurno, or have been collected during personal expeditions. This garden was seriously damaged by the winter of 1987, which uncharacteristically was colder in west Cornwall than eastwards, but there have been recoveries and restorations. This is the only garden left in the county that can truly be said to be continuing the 'experimentation in the acclimatising of exotics', for which the Fox family and others in the nineteenth century were famous (but see also Lamorran House).

References: 20th C.

PENBERTH, St Buryan

SW39 23 : *EX7, GS351/358*   OPEN

Also known as Foxstones; *Cornish* pen + *perth = brake or thicket, pronounced* penBERTH; *gatehouse listed grade II; garden of 5 acres (2ha) on biotite granite, south-west sloping 45-20m. in a north-west, south-east valley, on acid soil, in an AONB and HC, an AGSV and CNCS, and an AGHV; rainfall 35-40", temperature zone B; open 1983-98 CGOG, two Sundays in April, and by appointment.*

The single-storey house with its stone terrace forms an arc with a view over the lawn down the valley to the sea. The entrance from the road crosses a stream through a bridge and gatehouse - designed by Drewitts of Penzance in 1912 - into a wide drive between thickly planted, sloping beds. The stream and valley run down the western side of the lawn, and beyond. This relatively sheltered area, littered with boulders, is planted with camellias, azaleas and other shrubs, some unusual and tender, with bog plants by the waterside. Along the eastern side of the house and lawn, the valley side rises steeply. Here the natural contours of the land, which is covered with rocks, have been augmented and heightened by the planting of windbreak hedges, to create sheltered nooks, where plants can be protected from the elements. This unusual garden was designed and laid out by Dr R. Vernon Favell after 1919, and has remained in the family, his granddaughter having been in residence since 1987. There is a wheelhead cross, without carving, probably pre-Conquest. This was one of Thurston's select gardens.

References: 20th C.

PENDREA, Penzance

SW47 31 : *EX7, GS351/358*

Pendre, *1238; Cornish* pen + an + tre = *'farm at the top of the village' i.e. the chief farm, pronounced* penDRAY; *originally small to medium grounds, east sloping 25-10m. on Head, with acid soil; rainfall 40-45", temperature zone C; house demolished, and grounds built over.*

Traces of earlier fabric suggested that Pendrea, considered by Courtney in 1845 the 'gem of the parish', was more ancient than the adjoining Ponsandane, which is perhaps confirmed in early prints where the house is seen enveloped in mature trees. In about 1834 John Sargeant Bedford had moved to Pendrea from the Bodmin branch of the East Cornwall Bank, on marrying the daughter of William Bolitho of Ponsandane. After his death, the succession of occupants is somewhat obscure before W.E.T. Bolitho, the son of William Bolitho of Polwithen, came to live here in the 1880s, until he removed to York House. The garden was listed in the *Hort. Direct.* during this time from 1889 to 1891, but it was not until Miss Sybil Wingfield, niece of the long-surviving vicar of Gulval became a tenant here in about 1919, after the death of her uncle, that its reputation began to grow. Thurston, who included Pendrea among his select gardens, described her as 'extensively' developing the grounds, as she had already done at the vicarage, so that they became one of the most notable gardens in the vicinity. Miss Wingfield was a contemporary of, and shared her enthusiasm with, Canon A.T. Boscawen, rector of the adjacent parish of Ludgvan, himself an horticulturist of distinction. She remained at Pendrea until the 1930s, which, after reverting for a time to the Bolitho family, was sold in 1954 to the Penzance Corporation. Subsequent developments and the demolition of the old house have, except for a few trees, led to the virtual extinction of the garden.

References: 19th (Hort. & Gen.) and 20th C.

PENLEE MEMORIAL PARK, Penzance

SW47 30 : *EX7, GS351/358* OPEN

Cornish pen + *legh (pl) = *flat stone or slab, pronounced penLEE; granite wheel-head cross, removed from the Green Market, II and AM; 15-acre (6ha) parkland on metamorphosed Mylor slates, with acid soil; rainfall 40-45", temperature zone C; public park.*

Land from 'Lower Morrab' was conveyed to the prosperous miller J.R. Branwell (of a Penzance family related to the mother of the Brontë sisters) between 1860 and 1865, after which he began to build his house, perhaps to the design of John Matthews, town surveyor at Penzance. It had along the east side a conservatory, and was surrounded by parkland of a quite different character from that at Morrab House. During this time, from 1889 to 1924, Penlee was listed in the *Hort. Direct.* After the Second World War, the property passed into the ownership of the Corporation as a Memorial. The entrance is through a shrubbery, leading to the house, now used as a museum and art gallery, alongside which is a formal, walled garden, with a small chapel. The parkland has been retained for the benefit of the public. The grounds were lovingly maintained and developed until his retirement, by the head gardener Ernie Cock, who became well known among local gardeners as an expert plantsman. A full description of the Park and its plants was given by F. Holland Hall in the *Cornish Garden* of 1984.

References: 19th (Hort.) and 20th C.

POLWITHEN, Penzance

SW46 30 : *EX7, GS351/358*

Polwithen was derived from the field name of the site (see Bottrell); Cornish pol + gwyth = *trees, pronounced* polWITHen; *originally medium sized parkland, south-east sloping 40-30m., on metamorphosed Mylor slates, with acid soil; rainfall 40-45", temperature zone C; grounds, except for small relict area near the house, extinct. Now the* Bolitho School.

The mansion and park at Polwithen date from *c.* 1870, when it became the seat of William, the third son of Thomas Bolitho II of the Coombe. He was succeeded in 1895 by his son W.E.T. Bolitho, who was living at that time at the adjoining York House, while his mother continued to occupy the family home at Polwithen. The garden was listed in the *Hort. Direct.* from 1889, but although by 1910 the house had become the Riviera Palace Hotel, the grounds continued to be listed under the name of W.E.T. Bolitho until 1916. Since he had no male descendants, the garden was eventually sold to the Clements Inn Safe Deposit and Contract Company, who began to develop the area as a residential estate - hence the present Clements and Kings Roads, at the juncture of which the former Lodge still survives. The hotel meanwhile had not prospered, so in 1918, after extensions, it became an Anglican girls' school - the School of St Clare, named after an ancient chapel. In 1995 this was succeeded by the co-educational Bolitho School, which takes its name from the Bolitho family. Even though Polwithen was a quite considerable park, it did not survive for many years, nor receive much notice. Little remains today save a sunken garden in front of the house, a few sad tree-ferns by the main door and some shrubberies to hint at past glories. The parkland to the rear has become playing fields which stretch to the former grounds of York House - at one time a Methodist girls' school, whose pupils mocked their sisters over the fence in their grey uniforms as 'grey donkeys'.

References: 19th (Hort. & Gen.) and 20th C.

PONSANDANE, Penzance

SW47 31 : *EX7, GS351/358*

Cornish pons = bridge + an + den = man, *hence 'foot-bridge', pronounced* PONzandane; *small to medium grounds, east facing at c. 5m. on alluvium, with acid soil; rainfall 40-45", temperature zone C; residential and nursing home with relict grounds.*

A vignette of 1843 shows Ponsandane as a thatched house with a verandah around it, which is how it was still described by *Murray* in

1859. It was here that William, son of the original Thomas Bolitho of the Coombe settled, probably on his marriage, to found the Gulval line of the family. The house was later enlarged or rebuilt by his son, Richard Foster, with a datestone that reads 1857. Thomas Simon Bolitho of Trengwainton, on taking possession of Kenegie, acquired the lordship of the manor of Lanisley from the Onslows, which he later, in 1893, decided to share between his son Thomas Robins and his cousin Richard Foster II. The latter was given the Gulval part, which he proceeded to develop as a model village, by providing a village hall, a smithy and an inn, and endowing the churchyard and various charities. The grounds of the house were laid out as parkland with vistas to the Mount, formal gardens in the area now occupied by a modern extension, and terraces along the front. Since the lane leading to St Ives and Gulval ran so close to the rear of the house, the kitchen gardens and greenhouses were set up in a walled garden across the road, which can still be seen (though now occupied by a bungalow) from the flyover at the beginning of the bypass, as can the lodge, where the original entrance has been diverted. Perhaps from this angle the garden today is not very impressive, but it was listed in the *Hort. Direct.* from at least 1870 to 1924. The house had been occupied by three generations of Bolithos, but after Richard Foster died in 1932 without heir, it was never again lived in by a Bolitho. After the Second World War it became a Methodist Fellowship Holiday Home, and then an hotel. It is now a nursing home.

References: 19th (Hort. & Gen.) and 20th C.

ST MICHAEL'S MOUNT, Marazion

SW51 29 : EX7, GS351/358   OPEN

St Michael is one of the patron saints of Cornwall; house listed grade I, other buildings etc. II; garden of 5 acres (2ha) listed grade II, at c. 18m.), on biotite granite, with acid soil, in an AONB with AMs (three crosses); rainfall 35-40", temperature zone B; National Trust since 1954, with Lord and Lady St Levan in residence, garden open 1983-98, daily April through May; Castle, Monday-Friday, April through October. There is an official booklet which has gone through several editions.

The Mount has had a long and interesting history, which is not strictly relevant to our purposes here. It has been the property for many years of the St Aubyn family, who also owned Clowance. (q.v.). Gilbert described the island as comprehending 'about seven acres of ground, whose herbage is sufficient to depasture about twenty sheep. Its surface is here and there diversified with plantations of firs'. The site of the earliest garden, which may date back to the time of the medieval nunnery, is

19. St Michael's Mount. The small garden on the south-east side. Pococke mentioned a 'hanging garden' here in 1750, which probably dated from much earlier. (G. Mag. 1833: 545)

on the south-east side, surrounded by eighteenth-century walls. It was seen by Pococke in 1750, illustrated in Lysons (1814), and described in 1833 by Thomas Rutger, who had been gardener both here and at Clowance for over twenty-five years. Rutger contrasted the *Pinus pinaster* planted *c.* 1783 (perhaps on the advice of Praed at Trevethoe), which after forty years had left 'scarcely a vestige', with the *Quercus ilex* planted in 1830, on the strength of his experience at Clowance, which he found to be thriving. He continued:

> On the south side, fully exposed to the wide expanse of the ocean, is a small garden ..., in three compartments, raised one above another ... In this garden several sorts of fruits have been matured, such as the peach, nectarine, plum, &c., with stawberries of the most delicious flavour; and there is now a myrtle tree in it of many years' standing. Other half-tender exotics might, no doubt, be introduced here with safety ... [he included a plan].

His words were prophetic, for Thurston, who included the Mount among his select gardens, reported in 1930 that a 'beautiful garden on the rocky southern slope has been extensively developed by the present Lord St Levan'. These are the nineteenth-century Terraces, with stone paths, steps and irregular beds, stretching to the west from the walled garden and enclosing a 'bower house' in a little wilderness out of view of the castle above. They also extended some way along to the east. On the northern slopes there were plantations when Dr Borlase visited and sketched the Mount in 1769, by which time the disused Civil War redoubts had already been planted out as gardens. Much earlier, and certainly before 1640, there had been a rabbit warren along by the sea to the east, which was later joined by other utilitarian features: a late eighteenth- or nineteenth-century ice-house cut in the rock higher up on the north, and nineteenth- and twentieth-century pigeon-holes built into the natural crevices. A map of 1843 also shows buildings which may have served as summer-houses. Certainly St Michael's Cave - a grotto to the west of the summit - was used as a retreat during the nineteenth and into the twentieth century. In 1895 the Mount was visited by the notable narcissus expert, F.W. Burbidge, who begged that specimens of the daffodils there should be collected by Dorrien Smith of Tresco. Burbidge wrote of the 'healthy luxuriance' of the tender Tazettas and other species he found there, concluding,

> the fact that the Narcissi luxuriated so well and flowered so early on this sunny islet has had a great economic result, for it was observations made here as to their growth and early blossoming that led to these beautiful flowers of the early year being introduced still further west, viz, to the Scilly Islands, where they now really form one of the most important articles of trade.

This applies even more directly to the spread of the industry along Mount's Bay.

References: 17th. 18th, 19th (Hort. & Gen.) and 20th C; Illus; A.H. Malan, More Famous Houses, *1902: 297; C. Hussey,* Guide to St Michael's Mount, *Marazion c.1930, partly from his* Country Life *article in 1924; J. Wake,* Guide to St Michael's Mount with a summary of its history from legendary times, *Northampton 1934; Anon,* St Michael's Mount a brief historical account and description, *Norwich 1969; P.Herring,* An Archaeological Evaluation of St Michael's Mount, *CCC Truro 1993: 41, 51 map.*

TREGENNA CASTLE, St Ives
SW51 39 : EX7, GS351/358

Tregene, Treghenen, 1301; Cornish tre + *personal name, or* + *kenow = puppy, pronounced* treGENna, *with a hard 'g'; house with 18th and 19th C. additions listed grade II; medium grounds, sloping north-east 90-60m., on metamorphosed biotite granite, with acid soil; rainfall 45-50", temperature zone C; hotel open to non-residents, with relict grounds and golf course.*

Tregenno appears on Norden's map of *c.* 1597, representing the seat of the Tregenna family. The ruins are believed to have survived until the early twentieth century. The 'Castle', however, was built on the heights above, overlooking St Ives Bay, in 1774 by Daniel Freeman, master builder of Penryn, probably to the designs of John Wood of Bath, for Samuel Stephens an 'opulent' merchant. It evoked from the 'elegant' Richard Warner of Bath no more than faint praise:

> Though this stile of architecture may in general be pronounced as little less than absurd when adopted in modern mansions, yet in the case of Tregenna, we allowed that it was justified by its situation. Its appearance from the Channel must be formidable; and it might possibly assist in deterring an enemy from attempting to land on an exposed coast, by holding out the semblance of defensive strength, which in fact it does not possess.

Neither have the grounds won any praise, except from John Betjeman who thought Tregenna

> a splendidly landscaped park with vistas of sea and headlands to the north and east in the

20. Tregenna Castle, probably by John Wood the younger, who also designed Acton Castle. At this time the prospect over St Ives and the sea took precedence over ornamental gardening. (Twycross 1846: 75)

Georgian manner which not even golf greens and tennis courts can destroy.

After a hundred years, even the Stephens family themselves tired of it (and St Ives), so that it was sold to the directors of the GWR in 1877, to become one of their three 5-star hotels.

> They then embarked on an extensive advertising campaign to publicise both hotel and railway; and it was this, more than anything else, which helped to transform St Ives into one of the great holiday playgrounds of the South West.

Pevsner reckoned the house had 'been ... extended out of recognition on the sides, and there is little left of the original interior work', described by Betjeman as 'all Edwardian-Adam style'. Since privatisation, the hotel has moved somewhat down-market from the days of its splendour, although the present owners are developing new ornamental gardens.

References: 17th, 18th, 19th (Gen.) and 20th C; Illus; J.H.Matthews, A History of the Parishes of St Ives ... etc, 1892: 319, 459-60, illus.43.

TRELOYHAN MANOR, St Ives

SW52 39 : *EX7, GS351/358*   OPEN

**Trelughion *1259; Cornish* tre + legh (pl) = *flat stone or slab; pronounced* TreLOYan; *the grounds originally of about 11 acres (4.5ha) are east sloping, 75-40m., on metamorphosed Mylor slates, with acid soil; rainfall 45-50", temperature zone C; now a* Methodist Guild Guest House, *opened 1996-7, NGS. Official leaflet.*

Treloyhan house was built in 1892 by Sir Edward Hain, a shipping magnate, on farmland, but the name is probably that of an ancient manor. The site, although having a spectacular view across St Ives Bay, was open and windswept. The grounds were laid out by F.W. Meyer, described in the *Gardener's Chronicle* as a 'well-known landscape gardener'. He was a German, trained at Proskau in Silesia, and brought to England in the late 1870s by Robert Veitch as his designer (see also Tredarvah and Boscawen Park). A.C. Bartlett, the renowned gardener at Pencarrow, wrote that he had utilized natural undulations to good effect, deepening some, and using laurels and *Rhododendron ponticum* to form screens and nurse plants.

21. Trengwainton, from the sale notice, 1866. Like all other Bolitho houses, it has a view of St Michael's Mount and the Bay.

These were then, in 1905, being removed, and the shrubs were 'already a feature'. Meyer specialized in rock work, creating from a mine burrow of the old Wheal Margery 'a rockery, which in the short space of seven years [had] become well furnished. A dripping-well suitably planted [was] one of the features ...'. Treloyhan was listed in the *Hort. Direct.* from 1908 to 1924. The rockery survives, but a seated lookout replaces the well which was removed after drainage problems. The garden is now only seven and a half acres (3 ha), but has been beautifully replanted since the Second World War by Dennis Hornby, the former head gardener.

References: 20th C.

TRENGWAINTON, Madron

SW44 31 : *EX7, GS351/358*   OPEN

Tregwaynton, 1317; *Cornish* tre + dy + guaintoin = *springtime,* pronounced trengWAINton; *house listed grade II, bothy, head gardener's cottage, kitchen garden walls, lodge, each II; original estate 773 acres (313ha), present garden 25 acres (10ha), listed grade II, with c. 100 acres (40ha) of woodland, south-east sloping 120-75m., on metamorphosed Mylor slates, soil 'lime free over clay', in an AONB, an AGSV, and an AGHV; rainfall 45-50", temperature zone C; garden National Trust since 1961, family in residence. There is an official leaflet with a guide to plants and plan by the late Simon Bolitho. Open 1983-98, March through October, Sunday to Thursday, and Good Friday.*

Trengwainton, according to *Lake,* 'was inhabited for a considerable period by the ancient and respectable family of Cowling', who sold the estate to Francis Arundell of Menadarva in 1668. The last Arundell almost rebuilt the house, which bears a date-stone of 1692, but after his death it was sold to the Praeds of Trevethoe who leased it as a farm. The landscaping of the grounds, however, is attributable to Sir Rose Price, of Penzance stock, who, after making a fortune in Jamaica planting sugar, returned intending to set himself up in a mansion. He first selected a site at Tredavoe, between Newlyn and Mousehole, where he raised up huge mounds on which to plant a shelter-belt, called by the locals 'The Chinese Wall', and now by the OS map, 'Price's Folly'. This being abandoned, he lodged from 1813 to 1817 at Kenegie, while acquiring and remodelling Trengwainton. Here he formed a terrace, and seventy-one acres (29ha) of plantations and shrubberies, 'laid out under the direction of Mr. George Brown', whose son was a land-agent for a London firm. He made 'ornamental' lodges, planted the main drives with laurels, and the barren hills with firs. In the valley to the west, three pools were made for fish and water-fowl, and an ice-house was constructed. Price was also responsible for the five walled gardens with west-sloping beds near the entrance, which are still a feature.

The Abolition of Slavery in 1833 ruined many plantation owners, and after Price's death in

1834, his heirs sold the estate to the mortgagees, whereupon it 'was soon taken possession by vulgar, greasy-looking men', until it was purchased by Henry Lewis Stephens (of Tregenna) in 1835. At that time there were

> 27 acres planted with pinasters; 34 with elm, oak, ash and birch, with a few beech and sycamore trees; and 10 with low firs &c ... The house ... was much too large for anyone to inhabit, and after some time one of the wings was taken down, leaving it still a considerable size.

After a period of use as a farm, the property, was purchased by Thomas Simon Bolitho, who moved there from Penalverne, like Rose Price, by way of Kenegie. His son, Thomas Robins Bolitho, who had a reputation as an agriculturalist, enlarged the house 'with little regard for architectural seemliness', and replaced Price's drive with the present carriageway. Being without issue, he left Trengwainton to his nephew, Lt.-Col. E.H.W. Bolitho (son of Edward Alverne Bolitho of Laregan), who was then living at York House.

At this juncture (1925), the garden, although listed in the *Hort. Direct.* from 1889 to 1924, had no great reputation; Thurston, for instance, included it in his select list, but had nothing to say about it, and cited only two plants. Col. Bolitho, however, with the help of J.C. Williams of Caerhays, P.D. Williams of Lanarth, who were his cousins, and Canon Boscawen of Ludgvan, began at once to develop the garden, so that when George Johnstone of Trewithen and Lawrence Johnstone of Hidcote in Gloucestershire offered him a share in Kingdon Ward's expedition to Assam and Burma in 1927-8, he readily accepted. He was fortunate in inheriting from his uncle his head gardener, A. Creek, who had been appointed in 1904, and proved expert in raising the seed sent from Ward, and in hybridizing rhododendrons. Several new features were formed. The stream along the drive, confined in a culvert, was opened up, and planted as the Stream Garden by G. Hulbert in the 1950s. The old drive became the Long Walk in which the new introductions were planted, and the walled gardens, although the ramped beds were still used for kitchen plantings, became a haven for tender plants. After Creek's retirement in 1934, the work of hybridizing was continued by G.W. Thomas. In 1961 Sir Edward Bolitho himself received the coveted Victoria Medal from the RHS, and in 1985 the present head gardener, Peter Horder, received the A.J. Waley Medal for his work with rhododendrons.

References: 17th, 18th, 19th (Hort. & Gen.) and 20th C; Manpower Services Commission, Trengwainton, *1982 (map only).*

TREREIFE, west of Penzance

SW45 29 : EX7, GS351/358

Treweruf, *1201; Cornish* tre + **yuf = lord, pronounced* TREEVE; *house 17th to 18th C. listed grade II*, stables and gate-piers (1780), kitchen garden walls 18th C., gate-piers and gate 18th C., each II; parkland of 13.5 acres (5.5ha), south-east sloping 50-30m., on metamorphosed Mylor slates, with acid soil; rainfall 45-50", temperature zone C; private, formerly open as theme park. There has been an official booklet.*

Trereife is a fine house of the Nicholls family, who were there possibly before the reign of Elizabeth I. They prospered, numbering among them a London barrister who made 'many improvements' to the seat, a Court Physician, and an MP. Early in the nineteenth century, the last male member of the family died at a young age, and his mother married the Revd Charles Valentine Le Grice, the boy's tutor and minister of St Mary's Penzance, whose son inherited the estate, since which time Trereife has been the home of the Le Grice family. The last Mrs Nicholls had come from the Usticke family (pronounced 'yewstick') of Botallack. In about 1780 yews were planted, which now cover the south wall of the house, which led her husband frequently to repeat the pun that there was '"yew" inside and outside the house'. There is a small park sloping away from the house to a lodge, but perhaps the estate has been better known in recent times for its daffodil fields, grown by the late Charles Le Grice, who was well known in the industry. Blight's description in 1861 is still recognizable today:

> The beautifully wooded grounds of Trereife, about a mile from the town, first attract attention; the roadway is here arched with a long avenue of noble elms; near its extremity it is crossed by another avenue, - the road turning from the left leads to Newlyn, - a few yards up on the right is Trereife House, almost buried in foliage; a yew tree is trained over the front of the building, giving it the appearance of a living wall of leaves ... The walks and peeps of woodland scenery around this place are very beautiful.

Lake added that 'there is an ancient rookery', and 'luxuriant shrubberies'. Trereife was listed in the *Hort. Direct.* from 1908 to 1924. In 1996 it was selected as the site for a proposed Cornish campus of the University of Exeter; however, plans for this were abandoned in 1998.

References: 18th, 19th (Gen.) and 20th C.

TREVAYLOR, Gulval

SW46 32 : *EX7, GS351/358*

Treveller, 1245; Cornish tre + ?, pronounced treVAYlor; house, 18th C. on site of an older house, extended and remodelled in 19th C., listed grade II, two sets of gate-piers, coach house, kitchen garden walls, lodge and walls, each II; small to medium grounds south-east sloping 90-80m., on metamorphosed Mylor slates, on edge of granite and diabase intrusions, with acid soil, in an AGHV; rainfall 45-50", temperature zone C. Until recently the Trevaylor Nursing Home, but came on the market in 1998; opened 1991-2 NGS.

Trevaylor had been 'for two or three centuries the property of the respectable family of Veale', the Revd Richard Veale, who died in 1625, being the first Protestant vicar of the parish. From 1788, however, the house was no longer occupied by them, but was let, among others, to Rose Price (later of Trengwainton, q.v.) who, it is said, laid out the grounds. In 1814, the Revd William Veale came to live in his family home, improving the house and rebuilding it in 1851. Blight gives a description of it at this time:

> At Trevaylor an avenue of trees forms a noble archway over the high road - the rooks have possession of the upper boughs. A very large ash, in an adjoining pathway field, is the finest tree of the kind in the west of Cornwall. [It has now gone.] The ash was formerly abundant in this part of the county ... One of the most extensive views of Mount's Bay is from the terrace-walk ... seven or eight of the surrounding parish churches are visible from this spot.

When Veale died in 1867 he had no male heirs, and the property was left to his nephew Sir Augustine Fitzgerald, who soon after leased it to John Borlase Bolitho who lived there until his death in 1876, being succeeded by his widow, and later by his sister, Mary. In 1914, when the property was inherited by Col. Cecil Richard Robyns Malone, who was successor to the Fitzgeralds, he wished to take up residence there himself, spending

> a considerable sum in rebuilding and enlarging the house, as well as laying out extensive gardens; he had a valuable collection of semi-tropical and hardy shrubs.

At the same time he built the lodge, opposite the front entrance, on such steeply sloping land that it had to be entered on the first floor. Meanwhile, Mary Bolitho, who had then been living at Trevaylor for nearly twenty years, transferred to Poltair (q.v.), a house which at one time had itself been a property of the Veales. Col. Malone's widow died in 1946, but his son continued the family presence in the parish at Rosemorran. This was one of Thurston's select gardens.

References: 17th, 18th, 19th (Gen.) and 20th C.

TREVERVEN, St Buryan

SW40 23 : *EX7, GS351/358*

Treverwen, 1312; Cornish tre + personal name, pronounced treVERvan; small to medium grounds at head of north-south valley from 85m., on biotite granite, with acid soil, in an AGLV and HC, and an AGHV; rainfall 30-40", temperature zone B; until recently a nursing home with relict grounds, but in 1997 came on the market..

Although Thurston included Treverven among his chosen gardens, it is not mentioned in any other of our sources. He wrote of it: 'The grounds were laid out by the Rev. J. Tonkin, uncle of the present owner, R.E. Tonkin Esq.' John Tonkin, the fourth son of Uriah, vicar of Lelant, had been curate of several local parishes, including St Buryan from 1856 to 1864, and was a local landowner. The garden around the house has now been adapted for the use of residents in the nursing home, but the valley garden, which would chiefly have caught Thurston's attention, is gradually returning to nature. In 1881, Tonkin married Mary Usticke Peters, heiress to the Penwarne estate (q.v.), to which he transferred.

References: 20th C.

TREVETHOE, Lelant

SW53 37 : *EX7, GS351/358*

Trevitho, 1150; Cornish tre + bedhow (pl) = graves, or bethow (pl) = birch trees, pronounced treVETHo; house mainly 19th C. stucco with additions listed grade II, north and south lodges, each II; originally a very large estate, south-east sloping 40-c. 10m., on metamorphosed Mylor slates, with acid soil; rainfall 35-40", temperature zone C; house is a residence and centre of a photographic laboratory complex, with garden and relict parkland, western plantations now the St Ives Holiday Village, with agricultural land in separate ownership.

In 1820 Gilbert described Trevethoe in its heyday:

> The house is rather modern [1761, remodelled from that in Borlase's sketch of 1748] ... There was formerly a deer-park at this place, now turned into grazing land, and a sheep walk. The pasturage ground in front of the house, is rendered agreeable by clumps of foliage, a fine carriage road, and an extensive serpentine canal. The more exposed part of this domain, is covered with plantations of Norway firs. On a bleak mountain, rising above the plantations at Trevethow, stands a hollow cenotaph, in the form

22. Trevethoe. A sketch by William Borlase of the old house in 1748. This was remodelled in 1761, which may account for an illustration not appearing in his Natural History *of 1758.*

of an Egyptian pyramid. It was erected some years ago, by John Knill esq. for the purpose (as it was said) of having his remains therein interred.

The 'firs' were one of the most celebrated features at Trevethoe, and their origin was described by Fraser in 1794:

> Mr. [Humphrey Mackworth] Praed has taken a great deal of trouble to raise his plantations, in a situation where they are exposed to both the south-west winds, and also the northern winds, being the highest ground between the Bristol Channel and St. George's, in that part of the country [i.e. at Trencrom]. After making a great number of unsuccessful experiments, at great expence [*sic*], in order to find out some hardy plant that would shelter the more slender trees, he was led to try the pine-aster fir, from observing that this tree grew well spontaneously, from some cones which happened to be accidentally scattered in one of his fields near the house.

Following upon this discovery, the *Pinus pinaster* was widely planted in Cornwall as a shelter tree. Gilbert's description still fits the view of Trevethoe on the estuary, when seen above from the right of the Hayle bypass. The 'canal', which has been filled in along the drive, has been widened into a lake with a small waterfall to the west of the house, with two bridges and ornamental plantations, including a long relict pergola, a grove of some twenty *Trachycarpus*, and the remains of a 'bamboo walk'. There is a more formal walled garden to the north of the house. The walled kitchen garden is of interest, having retained its greenhouses with an intact heating system, and there are dove holes in one of the outbuildings. Trevethoe had anciently belonged to the Bottreaux and the Godolphin families, coming into the possession of the Praeds in the seventeenth century. The estate having eventually passed down the female line, William Backwell-Tyringham chose to make Tyringham, rather than Trevethoe his home. It is now a large commercial complex, but the grounds are still maintained. They were listed in the *Hort. Direct.* from 1870 until 1924.

References: 17th, 18th, 19th (Hort. & Gen.) and 20th C; Illus.

TREWIDDEN, Penzance

SW44 29 : EX7, GS351/358   OPEN

Trewen, 1292; Cornish tre + guyn = white or fair, pronounced treWID'n; house listed grade II, kitchen garden walls with ramped beds, head gardener's cottage, and lodge, each II; garden and grounds of 37 acres (15ha), south sloping 90-70m., on metamorphosed Mylor slates, with acid soil, in an AGLV; rainfall 45-50", temperature zone C; private house, garden and nursery open 1983-98 CGOG, all year by appointment, and one Sunday each in March and April and two in May for charity. There is an official guide with a plan.

Trewidden appears as a place-name on the Ordnance Survey map of 1809, where there is known to have been a house at the time of Edward Bolitho's first marriage in 1830. It is probable that he moved there then; he was certainly responsible for the 1848 additions, which the English Heritage surveyors felt to have

> an overall architectural unity but the plan and elevations are deliberately irregular so as to resemble a house that has evolved over a period of time.

The impressive drive from the lodge entrance climbs some 150 feet (45.75m.), for most of the 500 yards (457m.) of its course between old stone Cornish 'hedges'. The garden began to be listed in the *Hort. Direct.* in 1889, under the name of Edward Bolitho, and continued after his death, in 1890, until 1924 under Thomas Bedford Bolitho, with George Maddern as gardener. The latter became well enough known to merit an obituary in the *Gardeners' Chronicle* upon his death in 1894, since he had been

> for a period of forty-five years gardener to the Bolitho family at Trewidden, and during that long time he carried out great alterations and improvements in the garden, one of the prettiest in the west of England.

It is reputed that Trewidden has the earliest tin workings in the county, and the pits of open-cast mining survive, two large cast-iron bowls used for purifying being preserved near the nursery. The Fern Pit has utilized part of these workings for what is claimed to be 'probably the best grouping of *Dicksonia antarctica* (Tree Ferns) in the Northern Hemisphere', obtained from early importations by the Treseders. The shallower pits have been named 'The Burrows'. 'Here,' wrote Charles Williams of Caerhays, who had married Thomas Bedford's daughter Mary,

> you have an ideal position for Rhododendrons of the large-leaf forms, and so different to some gardens, particularly the newer ones [i.e. in 1927], where the main idea seems to be to bed them out like Brussels Sprouts. The one disadvantage is that they are apt to get their roots into some form of mineral, which may have disastrous effects.

In a hollow near the Pit was created the Rock Garden, with a small pool fed by a waterfall, but which is perhaps most notable for its collection of *Erythroniums*. Thomas Bedford also gardened in Devon, at Greenway House on the Dart, which he purchased in 1882. It was from there that he introduced a plant of the Chilean Nut, *Gevuina avellana*, which became what the *Gardeners' Chronicle* thought to be 'probably equal to any other in the country'. There is still a specimen in the Mowhay Garden. The North Walk lies to the rear of the house, and it is here that probably some of the oldest plants are growing, including a *Magnolia obovata* planted in 1897 by Mary Williams herself, who continued to develop the garden after her mother's death in 1935. Her husband wrote:

> There has never been any attempt to make in this garden a collection of great numbers of various plants, but rather to grow some of the best shrubs, and to try and get these to grow into natural and beautiful plants.

Nevertheless, the range of plants listed in the various journal articles describing the garden (over 450 species and varieties in my calculations) are as numerous as in those describing the great gardens in Falmouth, so there is no doubt that, at the end of the nineteenth century, before Trengwainton began to acquire a reputation for its newly-introduced rhododendrons, Trewidden was acknowledged as the premier garden in Penzance, and was included in Thurston's select list.

References: 19th (Hort. & Gen.) and 20th C.

TREWOOFE HOUSE, Lamorna

SW43 25 : EX7, GS351/358   OPEN*

Trewoeff 1302; Cornish tre + goyf = *winter, pronounced* TROUVE, *as spelt in Paris (1824: 113), 'Troove'; garden of 2 acres (0.8ha) at c. 65m. altitude, on alluvium in biotite granite, with soil 'ph 6.5', in an AONB and HC, an AGSV, and an AGHV; rainfall 35-40", temperature zone B; open 1994-8 CGOG, Wednesdays May through September, and by appointment.*

Gilbert wrote that Trewoofe

> is a place of great antiquity, but the mansion is demolished, and the only remains of its venerable form is a door-way, which bears the arms of the Levelis family, viz. three calves' heads.

This came to be known as the 'Porch House', from which the doorway was removed after it became ruinous, although in 1987 it was re-erected. The Levelis family, according to a monument in St Buryan Church to Arthur, the last of them, who died in 1671, 'hath Flourished Here Since William's Conquest ful Six Hundred Years'. Moule noted that, 'On this estate is a [triple] entrenchment, in which is a subterranean passage [or fougou], where a party of royalists were concealed during the civil war'. Bottrell offers a fascinating reconstruction of the ancient house and garden, based upon authentic reminiscences, reasonable deductions, and generalizations drawn from similar cases. There was in his time an avenue, which had ended in a bowling green. The 'ladies' bower' in the house had opened onto a 'ladies garden', also accessed from the 'green court', with flowers and bee hives or boles. Beyond were vegetable, herb, hop and fruit gardens, surviving orchards, and perhaps a trellis walk. There were 'aquatic embellishments', a walled 'warren' and a 'pigeonry' or culver-house. He added the sometimes forgotten observation that the 'delight of old-fashioned pleasure-grounds ... were always designed for use as well as for recreation.'

By the beginning of the nineteenth century the estate had already been split up, the present Trewoofe House being modern, built in 1913, with a garden begun by Ella and Charles Naper of the Lamorna School of artists, several of whom painted here between the First and Second World Wars. The current owners, who are related, began a new garden in 1975. The leat to the former mill pool runs through the grounds (the pool was haunted according to Bottrell!), offering an opportunity for a bog garden, and there are beds containing several New Zealand shrubs, and some azaleas, rhododendrons and camellias. There are also collections of euphorbias, hostas, hellebores and iris, a conservatory, and a fruit garden with cordon and espalier trained trees. Wind and salt, however, remain problems endemic to the site.

References: 17th, 18th, 19th (Gen.) and 20th C; H. Bedford, Frank Gascoyne Heath ..., *Teddington, Middlesex 1995: 66-8, 78-9.*

TREWYN STUDIO, Barnoon Hill, St Ives

SW51 40 : *EX7, GS351/358* OPEN*

Very small town garden, now the Barbara Hepworth Museum; *open, Sundays, and Tuesday to Saturday.*

Barbara Hepworth came to St Ives with Ben Nicholson at the beginning of the Second World War, forming, together with Naum Gabo, the nucleus of an avant-garde school of artists. When she died in 1975, she asked the executors of her will to consider 'the practicality of establishing a permanent exhibition of some of [her] works in Trewyn Studio and its garden', which she had purchased in 1949. This they did, and the Museum, which from 1980 was administered from the London Tate Gallery, is now an integral part of the Tate Gallery St Ives, which opened in 1993. Statuary has always formed a prominent feature in garden design, and Barbara Hepworth was herself interested in the unity and relationship between sculpture and its context. In this tiny garden, we have the rare opportunity of seeing the works of a great artist in the setting in which she wished to place them.

References: 20th C.

YORK HOUSE, St Clare Street, Penzance

SW46 30 : *EX7, GS351/358*

House listed grade II; medium grounds, sloping south-west 60-45m., on metamorphosed biotite granite, with acid soil; rainfall 40-45", temperature zone C; Penzance Municipal Offices, *relict grounds.*

Lake *recounts the history of York House which*

> occupies a commanding position [above Penzance]; it was built by a Mr. Pope of Camelford. He conducted a business for some time at Bristol, from whence he emigrated to the United States, where he gained a large fortune, unknown and forgotten by his family. He afterwards returned to Penzance, recognised some of his relatives, and having purchased a few acres of ground, he built a good house thereon [in 1825] which became generally known as the Vatican ... Mr. Pope scarcely lived to inhabit his new mansion; and bequeathed it to his nephew [John Pope Vibert, who died in 1865].

The house had curious features, the windows showing 'the Gothick influence, and above the eaves ... a battlemented parapet with large stone obelisks after the Egyptian manner.' It was listed in the *Hort. Direct.* at least until 1870, after which there is no mention of the garden. W.E.T. Bolitho, son of William of Polwithen, moved to York House from Pendrea at the turn of the century, and seems to have remained there after his father's death in 1895, since his mother continued to live in the adjoining family home at Polwithen. He himself died in 1919, but his widow lived at York House until 1930. During this time, Col., later Sir Edward Bolitho, after retiring from the army lived here for a while, before inheriting Trengwainton in 1925. In 1931, the West Cornwall [Methodist] School for Girls moved to York House from Chapel Street, where it had been founded in 1884. The scholars from the neighbouring School of St Clare, at Polwithen (q.v.), seeing the new girls in brown uniforms, returned their uncomplimentary remarks about grey donkeys by calling them 'brown cows'. West Cornwall School closed in 1967. York House was subsequently acquired by Penzance Corporation for municipal offices.

References: 19th (Hort. & Gen.) and 20th C.

SUPPLEMENTARY LIST

LESSER-KNOWN HISTORIC GARDENS

Eden Valley, Vellanoweth, Ludgvan

SW50 33 : *EX7, GS351/358, SS.SW530*

Garden of 1 acre (0.4ha), sloping north-east on Mylor slates and alluvium, with acid soil; rainfall 40-45", temperature zone C; relict.

Eden Valley was built in 1888. Percy Waterer, who was distantly related to the Waterers of Knapp Hill, retired here from the City in 1907, laying out the garden 'to give the effect of a natural walk uphill'. The house, which had an extension at the back with a greenhouse on top, was without water, drainage or electricity. Miss Waterer, who had taught botany at the West Cornwall Girls' College,

Chapel Street, Penzance from 1920, took over the garden on her father's death in 1931. It was always a 'wild garden' with a wealth of wild flowers, but

> among this riot of foliage were specimen trees and shrubs, including immense clumps of bamboo. There were rhododendrons in full flower at Christmas and Camellias, Magnolias, Viburnum, Vaccinium, Cryptomeria, Azaleas, Myrtles and Tree Heathers grew enormously in sweet disorder.

Miss Waterer acquired a reputation as a plantswoman, especially for her collection of heathers, of which she once had 150 varieties. Her *Erica cinerea* 'Eden Valley' received the RHS Award of Merit in 1933, and of Garden Merit in 1984. The garden is being restored by the present owners.

References: 20th C.

Laregan House, Penzance

SW46 29 : EX7, GS351/358

Also Larrigan Cottage, *now* Higher Larrigan, *named after the Larrigan Brook, pronounced* laREGan *with a hard 'g'; now in apartments with a residual garden.*

This was originally the seat of Alexander Daniel (1599-1668) when Lord of the Manor of Alverton, there being no manor house. The present dwelling was built in 1814 by Thomas Pascoe, and was for a time the residence of Walter Borlase, who married Catherine Anne Bolitho. After his death, his nephew, Edward Alverne Bolitho, probably on his marriage *c.* 1881, came to Laregan, his aunt and nieces moving to the Coombe. After his death in 1908, the house was occupied by his sister-in-law Nora, daughter of William Bolitho of Polwithen. During this time, from 1889 to 1916, the garden was listed in the *Hort. Direct.* The grounds are now a school playing field, with perimeter trees, although the Lodge can still be seen to the south. The house has been reduced in size, with a residual garden in front, and the remains of the original plantations to the western side.

References: 18th, 19th (Hort. & Gen.) and 20th C.

Nancealverne, Penzance

SW46 30 : EX7, GS351/358

Cornish nans + *manor name, pronounced* nansALLvern; *house listed grade II*; small park, east facing at 50m. altitude, on metamorphosed biotite granite, with acid soil; rainfall 40-45", temperature zone C; private.*

Described in *Lake* as 'situated within beautiful wooded grounds', Nancealverne lies to the north-east of Rosehill. The house was built in the eighteenth century by a Mr Carveth who, through embarrassing circumstances, sold it to the Usticke family of Botallack. It later became the home of the Scobell Armstrongs. The Penzance bypass now cuts through the grounds, separating the Lodge, and opening up the house to view.

References: 18th, 19th (Gen.) and 20th C.

Newlyn West Churchyard and Vicarage, Newlyn

SW46 29 : EX7, GS351/358

Thurston wrote, 'An olive [*Olea europaea*], which grew outside St Peter's church was said by the Rev. W.S. Lach-Szyrma, formerly Vicar of Newlyn, to have been obtained from Genoa'. There was also an olive tree about 18 feet high in the vicarage, growing in a rockery. Mr Dorothy, the late head gardener of the Morrab Gardens, Penzance, had told him that it was transported to Morrab many years before. Although these trees have now died in severe winters, there are still exotic shrubs and trees to be seen around Newlyn church.

Reference: 20th C.

Penalverne, Penzance

SW46 30 : EX7, GS351/358

Cornish pen + *manor name, pronounced* penALLvern; *extinct, now* Penalverne Municipal Housing Estate.

Penalverne was the residence of the Grenfell family, before being occupied by Thomas Simon Bolitho, probably on his marriage in the late 1830s. His son, Thomas Robins, also took up residence there at about the time of his marriage in 1870, and inherited the property on his father's death in 1887. W. Roberts, a Madron man, and a local correspondent to gardening journals, wrote in 1881, 'we have Camellia trees in several gardens around here, notably at Penalvern [*sic*], where there is the finest specimen in Cornwall'. The garden was listed in the *Hort. Direct.* from 1891 until 1916, although early maps do not suggest that the design of the garden was very elaborate. In 1931 the house was demolished.

References: 19th (Hort.) and 20th C.

Poltair, Madron

SW45 31 : EX7, GS351/358

Cornish pol + ter = *clear, pronounced* polTAIR; *NHS geriatric hospital with residual grounds.*

Poltair was for many years the property of the Veales of Trevaylor (q.v.), but by his marriage to a coheiress, it came into the possession of Richard Hichens, a merchant from St Ives, who built a new house there. Otho Glynn Bolitho is recorded as residing here in 1873, and he continued to do so until after his retirement from the army, when he moved to Kenegie in the 1890s. Poltair was burnt down in 1905, and after it was rebuilt in 1912, Mary Bolitho, Glynn's sister, moved there from Trevaylor. Except for one notice in the *Hort. Direct.* in 1891, before Glynn had moved, there is no mention of the garden. At the death of Robins Bolitho of Trengwainton in 1925, who at that time owned Poltair, the property was bequeathed to Glynn's son, Bruce.

References: 18th and 19th (Hort. & Gen.) C.

Roscadghill, Penzance

SW46 30 : *EX7, GS351/358*

Roscaswall 1317; Cornish ros + personal name, pronounced roseCADGill; house listed grade II; very small garden at 70-60m. altitude, on metamorphosed biotite granite; rainfall 40-45", temperature zone C; private.*

The Cheshers (1968) believed that the house, built in the 1690s for John Borlase (1666-1755)

> demonstrates most of the features of a really modern house of the time, with its carefully symmetrical facade, elegant sash windows and equally elegant pedimented entrance, and its mansard roof, wide eaves and square-built appearance.

It later became the home of John Tremenheere (1758-1825), alderman and twice Mayor of Penzance, who belonged to an old and important Penzance family, related by marriage to the Borlases. Gilbert described it as 'situated on an elevated part of the country, and the prospects of the surrounding scenery, (which are multiplied in the distances,) have a fine effect'.

References: 18th , 19th (Gen.) and 20th C.

Rosehill, Penzance

SW45 30 : *EX7, GS351/358*

Cornish ros + hill (English), pronounced ROSEhill; house listed grade II; park of 8.5 acres (3.4ha), south sloping 70-55m., on metamorphosed biotite granite, with acid soil; rainfall 40-45", temperature zone C; private; there have been recent developments in the grounds.

Rosehill, described in Pool (1974) as 'one of the most elegant houses' of the early nineteenth century, was built in 1814 to designs of Robert Hitchens for Richard Oxnam, a merchant and banker. Gilbert felt that 'its bold situation [gave] it a fine view of sea and land. The drive through the grounds is also very fine, and the plantations have a thriving appearance.' John Vigurs, who resided there in the 1850s, according to Courtney, did more than 'either of his predecessors for the improvement of the place'. The property has a conservatory.

References: 18th, 19th (Gen.) and 20th C.

Rosemorran, Gulval, near Penzance

SW47 32 : *EX7, GS351/358*

Cornish ros + moren = bramble, pronounced roseMORan; house listed grade II, gate-piers, cross, each II; small to medium grounds at 93m. altitude, on metamorphosed Mylor slates, with acid soil, in a SAGLV with an AM (cross); rainfall 40-45", temperature zone C; private.*

Paris wrote in 1824 that he 'scarcely [knew] a situation where the skill of the landscape gardener could be exerted with greater advantage or effect' than Rosemorran, and *Lake* described it as a

> most interesting place, and one of the greatest ornaments to the neighbourhood. It was formed by the late George John, Esq ... He greatly improved and beautified the grounds by extensive plantations at Trye and Rosemorran Cairn.

The house is late eighteenth century, but it was afterwards remodelled as a *cottage ornée*, with Gothic-style features and a thatched roof said to be the longest in Cornwall. The listed wayside preaching cross has a wheel-head, with a carving of a cross on one side, and a crucifixion figure on the other. The early camellias were mentioned in the *Garden* of 1888, at a time when a correspondent well remembered 'the old-world garden, the picturesque porch, and the interesting native and other flowering plants which could be seen in and about the grounds.' The property has been occupied in this century by the Malone family, who were related both to the Johns of Rosemorran, and Col. Malone of Trevaylor.

References: 18th, 19th (Hort. & Gen.) and 20th C.

St Just-in-Penwith Vicarage, St Just-in-Penwith

SW37 31 : *EX7, GS351/358*

Stone cross listed grade II, AM; garden on biotite granite in an AONB and HC, and an AGHV; rainfall 40-45", temperature zone C.

Despite, or perhaps because of the rugged nature of the surrounding countryside, scarred by mine workings, St Just Vicarage and its garden attracted notice. It is described in *Lake* as

> pleasantly situated in a vale at a little distance to the east of the church. The house is commodious and well-built; a portico added by the late Mr. Buller has its gable inscribed "J.B. Vic. 1827". The gardens and shrubberies exhibit a considerable degree of luxuriance. In the grounds are preserved two ancient crosses, and a *men-an-tol* or holed stone.

References: 18th and 19th (Gen.) C.

Tredarvah, Alverton Road, Penzance

SW46 30 : *EX7, GS351/358*

Tredarvah, which adjoined Polwithen (q.v.), received only a passing mention in the *Gardeners' Chronicle* of 1889. It is included here since it had been listed in Veitch's Exeter Nursery catalogue of 1885 as one of the gardens planned by their German landscape designer, F.W. Meyer. This was one of those villa gardens, in Penzance as in other

Cornish towns which, probably for quite arbitrary reasons, received little or no notice in published records. Meyer also designed the grounds at Treloyhan, St Ives, and Boscawen Park, Truro. The original house was burnt down and the garden has been developed into separate holdings, erasing any sign of the earlier design.

References: 19th C. (Hort.)

Tregembo, St Hilary

SW57 31 : *EX7, GS351/358, SS.SW53*

Cornish tre + *kemer = *confluence, i.e. 'a farm where two streams meet', which describes the site exactly, pronounced treGEMbo *with a hard 'g'; house listed grade II*, coach house, cartshed etc, and bank barn, grouped around a rectangular farmyard II, gate-piers II; grounds 35m. altitude on metamorphosed Mylor slates and alluvium, with acid soil; rainfall 35-40", temperature zone C; farm.*

The fine house at Tregembo, built and remodelled in the seventeenth century, is distinguished by a Doric colonnade. The site is possibly pre-Conquest, since there is reference to an Edward Berner here before 1083. *Lake* confirmed that it

> is a place of considerable antiquity. It formerly belonged to the family of Grosse, from whom it passed by successive sales to King and Penneck; it was purchased by the latter in 1684. The house and grounds were considerably improved by Charles Penneck, Esq. [d.1801],

but were sold in 1802. Henry Penneck had been vicar of Paul parish from 1739 to 1771. The property subsequently passed to the Peters and Pascoe families. It was the home of the late Mr A.Tomlin who was prominent in the narcissus-growing industry along the shore of Mount's Bay.

References: 17th, 18th and 19th (Gen) C.

Treneere Manor, Penzance

SW46 31 : *EX7, GS351/358*

Cornish tre + an yar (pl) = *the hens, pronounced* treNEER; *house listed grade II*, garden walls, and kitchen garden walls each II; small garden at 50m. altitude, on metamorphosed biotite granite, with acid soil; rainfall 40-45", temperature zone C; private.*

In 1845, Courtney wrote that the grounds at Treneere 'till very lately ... had a most park-like appearance'. Gilbert described Treneere as 'situated on a pleasing elevation, about a mile north-west of Penzance, and the lands ... enlivened by a fine display of verdure'. But by 1974, according to Pool, they were 'becoming almost engulfed by housing development', although the mansion was 'set in a fine garden and still retaining a great deal of character ... It is an excellent granite ashlar building erected in [1758] by the Robyns family. The mansard roof and rounded dormer windows in the French manner are 19th century.' Members of the Oliver family had moved here from Trevarno (q.v.) earlier in the century, and to Ludgvan. There is a large, late eighteenth-century kitchen garden, with red brick walls and 'ramp coping'. Treneere housing estate was begun by the Corporation in 1938.

References: 17th, 18th, 19th (Gen.) and 20th C.

ADDITIONAL CONTEMPORARY GARDENS

See also: LORAINE, THE OLD RECTORY *and* TREWYN STUDIO *in the main section.*

Bodellan Farm, Porthcurno

SW38 23 : *EX7, GS351/358*   OPEN*

Cornish bos + ?*elen = *fawn. pronounced* boDELLan; *0.66 acre (0.27ha) garden, open 1997-8 NGS, one Sunday each in May, July and September, and by appointment.*

Bosavern Mill, St Just-in-Penwith

SW37 30 : *EX7, GS351/358*

Cornish bos + ?, *pronounced* bosAVERN; *1 acre (0.4ha) garden, open 1996 NGS.*

Described by the owner, Mrs J.A. Hilliard, Chairman of the Cornwall Garden Society, as a 'plantsman's garden, begun in 1989 on a near vertical, north facing slope, by the creation of granite terraces with a rockery, pool and stream.'

References: 20th C.

Tregilliowe Farm, near Crowlas, Ludgvan

SW53 31 : *EX7, GS351/358*   OPEN*

Cornish tre + kelli (pl) = *groves, pronounced* treGILLio; *2 acre (0.8ha) garden; open 1993-8 NGS, one Sunday each in June and July.*

Trelan, near the entrance to Trengwainton, Madron

SW45 31 : *EX7, GS351/358*

Treland, *Domesday 1086, Cornish* tre + lan, *pronounced* treLAN; *0.75 acre (0.3ha) garden in an AONB and AGHV; opened 1988-90 NGS.*

The garden of this country house won first prize in the 'Bloom in Britain' competition 1987-8. when there were lawns and colourful borders on several levels, from which there are views of Mount's Bay.

Trevegean, 9 Manor Way, Heamoor, Penzance

SW46 31 : *EX7, GS351/358*

Cornish tre + [?], *pronounced* TREVaGEEan; *0.33 acre (0.13ha) garden; open 1991-8 NGS, April through June by appointment.*

References: 20th C.

2. HAYLE and HELSTON

Hayle has, not unreasonably, been described as the 'cradle of the Industrial Revolution', and it is the only town in Cornwall that owes its existence entirely to industry. Hayle, which in Cornish means 'estuary', was originally in Phillack parish, on the north side of the river, and was part of the Domesday manor of Conarton, represented here by the ancient manor of Penpol. Tin had long been smelted in Cornwall, but copper ore, which required considerably more fuel, had been sent to Wales for processing. In the mid 1750s, however, a number of adventurers in the Camborne district decided to break the monopoly of the Welsh smelting interests, by setting up the Cornish Copper Company in Hayle. The company operated successfully until 1819, when it converted to an iron foundry. The need to import coal led to the development of a harbour, which was ingeniously kept free from silt by damming up a lake at high tide, which was then allowed to surge out at low tide to scour the channel.

With the prosperity of copper came merchants and engineers, among whom the Harveys of Hayle were foremost. They were associated with the celebrated Richard Trevithick. One of the offshoots of the copper smelting was the production of glassy slag blocks made from the *scoria*, or waste products. These blocks were used for workers' houses and other buildings, and are still to be seen there and in the hedges around Phillack. They were also used for the extension wing and stables at Riviere House, built for the managing partner of the Company.

What Hayle was like in those days is vividly described in *Hitchins*:

> The fumes arising from the furnaces of Copper-house, though less comprehensive in the extent of their influence than the sands, which have buried large districts of land in the neighbouring country, are scarcely less pernicious to vegetation in their effect and consequences. Some grounds in the vicinity have been nearly ruined, and the glass placed in the windows of the habitations, after a little while loses nearly all its transparency. No bees can live within the polluted atmosphere, and in the gardens many valuable vegetables will not thrive. Even at Riviere, the pleasant residence of Joseph Carne, Esq. though at a considerable distance, when the wind blows in an unfavourable direction, the smoke, impregnated with deleterious qualities, spreads desolation over the gardens, and blasts in a few hours, the promise of more auspicious breezes, and an inviting spring.

It is hardly surprising that the town attracted no wealthy residents, until the Downes and other large houses began to be built in the late nineteenth century.

In contrast, Helston, in the hinterland of The Lizard, was established by charter in 1201, by King John. At this time the River Cober was still navigable, but later in the thirteenth century it was cut off by the growth of Loe Bar. This was a temporary setback for the burgesses, who soon restored their fortunes by purchasing rights in the port of Gweek. As in the creation of other boroughs, the potential of Helston and its situation attracted, and was promoted by outside speculators, which is evidenced in the existence of Anglo-Saxon open fields around the town, and the addition of the Old English *ton* to the Cornish name of *Henlis*, meaning 'Old Court'. In these early days, Helston had no rival in the west nearer than Truro, since neither Penzance nor St Ives existed, and Marazion was insignificant. Similarly Gweek, until comparitively recent times, played an important part in the export of tin from the region.

It is no surprise to learn that soon after the Reformation, the extra-parochial Chapel of St Mary, in the centre of Helston, was converted into a Coinage Hall for the assaying of tin, during which process a corner (in French *coin*) of the ingot was cut off. The Hall was demolished in the nineteenth century, but the name of Coinage Hall Street (which soon surplanted the old name of 'Lady Street') remains. In the nineteenth century the wealthy families began to build their villas along the fashionable Cross Street, Lismore House and Penhellis having the finest gardens.

Despite the undoubted importance of Hayle and Helston, the great estates around them - including those of the Mohuns and Hawkins at Trewinnard, the Godolphins at Godolphin, the St Aubyns at Clowance and St Michael's Mount, and the Olivers at Trevarno in Sithney - were quite independent of them. So too were the estates on The Lizard - belonging to the Vyvyans at Trelowarren, the Bonithons of Bonython, and the Billets at Bochym. Penrose, however, with its associated manor of Nansloe, came more within the ambit of Helston. Bosahan, built on the Helford River in the early nineteenth century by Thomas Grylls, alone has any direct connection with a Helston family.

NB BOSAHAN, HALLOWARREN, LANARTH, MANACCAN GARDENS, POLDOWRIAN, TRELEAN, TRELOWARREN *in part, and* WYNLANDS, *all on The Lizard peninsula, are included in this section, although found on the OS Landranger 204 Truro and Falmouth map.*

ACTON CASTLE, Rosudgeon*

SW55 28 : EX7, GS351/358

Named after the Acton family, of Acton Scott in Shropshire; house listed grade II; small grounds, west facing at 50m., on Mylor Series slate, with acid soil, in an AONB; rainfall 35-40", temperature zone C; now in apartments, with contemporary garden.*

John Stackhouse, who was born at Trehane and in 1764 inherited Pendarves, decided in 1775, to build a house at Rosudgeon, named as a compliment to his wife Susanna's family. He had spent some time travelling and studying marine biology, and the house was 'admittedly ... for the express purpose of studying seaweed *in situ*'. He engaged John Wood the Younger, whom he had met in Bath while taking the cure for rheumatism, to design the house, which had subterranean tanks for his seaweeds. Stackhouse's various commitments in Bath and Pendarves led to periods away from the Castle, when it was looked after by John Carter, the smuggler known as 'King of Prussia', after Prussia Cove, their landing place. In 1788 Carter's brother Harry, having been embroiled with the Customs men at Marazion, fled with a price on his head. John, having entry, gave him refuge at Acton, by 'dragging himself along a dark passage' which Stackhouse had cut down to the shore, 'and suddenly into the splendour of the castle'.

It was undoubtedly John Stackhouse's eminence as a botanist, and the publication in 1795 of his *Nereis Britannica*, rather than any horticultural interest in the mansion, which rated a mention in the *Gardeners' Chronicle* of 1889. It was also in 1795, with his rheumatism worsening, that he cut the bathing pool in the rocks below the cliffs, in which direction the tunnel already led. In 1802 the Castle was sold to Buckley Praed, navigator for Nelson at the Battle of the Nile, who in 1837 was created Admiral to command the coastal defences from Fowey to Newquay. Acton Castle was already an hotel at the time of the 1889 article, but during its recent refurbishment into apartments, the seaweed tanks have been exposed, to form the centre-piece of a sunken circular garden, in the form of an amphitheatre.

References: 18th and 19th C. (Hort. & Gen.); H.Carter, The Autobiography of a Cornish Smuggler, *1894, reprinted Truro 1971: 19-20.*

BOCHYM MANOR, Cury, near Helston

SW69 20 : EX8, GS359, SS.SW61/71

Buchent, *or* Bocent, *Domesday 1086; Cornish, Dexter suggests* boch = he-goat + ?, *pronounced* botCHEEM; *house, late medieval, extended, remodelled and rebuilt by 1699, listed grade II*, gate-piers c. 1699 II*, clock tower, terrace walls, various buildings, gate-piers, and lodge with 1851 datestone, each II; medium grounds, east sloping 45-30m., on hornblende schist, with acid soil in an AONB and HC, and an AGSV; rainfall 35-40", temperature zone B; private, garden relict, grounds in agricultural use.*

Bochym has a long and chequered history. In 1549 John Winslade was executed for his part in Arundell's Cornish rebellion, after which the land was purchased by Reginald Mohun, who gave it with his daughter to Francis Billet The Billets died out in 1730, to be succeeded by the Robinsons, who later moved to Nansloe Manor. The house and the terraces, as sketched in the *Spoure Book* of *c.* 1690, which the listing describes as 'a rare survival of a late 17th century formal garden plan', must therefore be attributed to the Billets, but the present clock tower is much later and thought to have been erected to commemorate Queen Victoria's fiftieth anniversary in 1887. The Davey family were occupying Bochym during the second half of the nineteenth century, and it was remarked by *Lake* in 1867 that the 'grounds [had] recently been much improved'. This coincides with the time that, according to Bishop Hunkin, Veitch's Nursery had released William Lobb for three years to assist Stephen Davey with his garden. Lobb, who had previously worked at Scorrier, had been commended to Veitch by the Williams family, to whom the Daveys themselves were related by marriage, which would account for this curious arrangement. Bochym was listed in the *Hort. Direct.* from 1889 to 1916, during the residence of the Davey family, and was one of Thurston's select gardens, where he cited an 'unusually large', spreading mulberry (*Morus nigra*) which was still there when seen in 1991. The house was briefly an hotel, but except for old trees and shrubs along the drive, the garden is not planted. Fortunately, the seventeenth-century 'hard landscaping' remains intact. The garden to the lodge lost its former exotic appearance during recent severe winters.

References: 17th, 18th, 19th (Hort. & Gen.) and 20th C.

BONYTHON MANOR, Cury Cross Lanes, near Helston

SW69 21 : EX 8, GS359, SS.SW61/71

Cornish, Dexter suggests bos + an + eithin = furze, *pronounced* boNITHon, *with a long 'i'; house listed grade II*, 18th century gate-piers and walls II; a garden of 5 acres (2ha) with woodland sloping south, 75-60m., on* hornblende schist, with acid soil, in an AONB, and an AGSV; rainfall 35-40"; temperature zone B; the estate is run commercially producing especially asparagus and Cornish mineral water, and has recently added a wind-farm; opened 1987-93 CGOG, 1988, 1997-8 NGS, one Sunday in July. There is an official leaflet. Came on the market in 1998.

The original property, dating from c. 1277, was remodelled by Reskymer Bonithon in 1600, of which the north wing of the present house may have been part. The main front, built in the 1780s may have been designed by William Wood, a pupil of Thomas Edwards of Greenwich. For many years this was the seat of the Bonithon family, of which a junior branch resided at Carclew. In 1720, however, the estate was sold to Humphrey Carpenter, and thence passed in the nineteenth century to Capt. Joseph Lyle, the ancestor of the recent owner. At this time, according to *Lake*, it was 'surrounded by considerable thriving plantations'. These, consisting mainly of Beech and Monterey pine, had been planted in the late 1830s by Treseders' nursery, with paths surfaced with pebbles from Loe Bar, Helston. The main entrance drive has been edged more recently with lawns and blue hydrangeas, while a wide avenue of trees has lately been planted in the lawn of the garden front, creating a vista on to the landscape beyond. The main attraction, when open to the public, is the walled garden, which was landscaped by Treseders of Truro in 1961, to create a summer pleasure garden with a swimming pool, and a second section intended for vegetables, fruits and herbs. Latterly herbaceous borders have been added to extend the season of flowering. Lake Joy, which consists of three small areas of water, lies to the south of the walled garden, and here the Burncoose and Southdown Nurseries are creating around the natural water meadow and woodland glades new vistas for all times of the year.

References: 17th, 18th and 19th C. (Hort. & Gen.).

BOSAHAN, Manaccan

SW76 25 : LR204, EX8, GS359, SS.SW61/71   OPEN

Bosseghan, 1594, Bosahan, 1662; Cornish bos + *seghan = dry place, pronounced (and spelt in G. World 1904: 649), boSAIN; 19th C. cottage ornée lodge, listed grade II; grounds of about 15 acres (6 ha), and about 7 acres (2.8 ha) of woodland, in north-east facing slope and valley 75m. to sea, on Gramscatho Beds, with acid soil, in an AONB, and an AGSV; rainfall 40-45", temperature zone B; private, open 1983-98 CGOG, 1988, 1991 NGS, one Saturday in April, and one Sunday and Monday in May for charity, and by appointment.*

A house at Bosahan, described in *Hitchins* as 'an elegant modern built mansion' was erected by Thomas Grylls of Helston early in the nineteenth century, and, in the time of *Lake*, was 'surrounded with luxuriant plantations and meadows, and [had] an agreeable southern aspect.' The estate as it is now known began with the erection between 1884 and 1887 by Sir Arthur Pendarves Vivian of a new large mansion (with twenty-seven bedrooms) which, because of a tower and a small amount of castellation, was sometimes known as Bosahan Castle. Vivian also laid out the gardens and planted a large number of conifers. Although the area around the house was high and exposed, the two valleys running down to the sea afforded protection for tender plants, in what P.D. Williams of Lanarth regarded as 'one of the most happily chosen garden sites in Cornwall.' Sir Arthur Vivian lived to the ripe age of ninety-three. Bosahan was listed in the *Hort. Direct.* from 1908 until 1924, when the garden was gaining a high reputation for its collection of plants. Few gardens, thought one writer, 'possess greater charm or wealth of rare vegetation'. This was one of Thurston's select gardens from which he cited 103 plants. Among the more exotic, the tree ferns in the valley excited most comment, while Charles Curtis in the *Gardeners' Magazine*, thought that the

> bamboos grow with almost tropical luxuriance, ... you feel rather disappointed at not finding a well-tanned Britisher waiting with ready gun for tiger, crocodile, or other fearsome beast.

The stream which filled a small pool was surrounded with palms - *Chamaerops, Trachycarpus*, and a *Phoenix canariensis* which had survived 10° F. of frost. Contemporary writers were also enthusiastic in their admiration of the Lapageria Walk

> that extends 68 yards along the north side of a high wall, where red and white lapagerias are rampant - no other word suffices, and where on the rustic arches Clematis indivisa lobata is wonderfully fine.

In more recent times the 'new' mansion was found to be unmanageable, so in 1955 it was demolished and replaced with a smaller house, although the western walls were retained to create a courtyard garden to the rear. The main grounds, however, have remained as originally designed, excepting those parts around the house which have evolved with each reconstruction. There are a number of fine Victorian wrought iron gates separating the various gardens. The lawns are terraced, with balustraded steps, cannon, and a ha-ha where they meet the pasture. There is a pedestal sundial on the eastern lawn.

References: 18th, 19th (Hort. & Gen.) 20th C.

CLOWANCE, Crowan

SW63 34 : *EX8, GS352*

Clunewic, Domesday 1086; Dexter suggests Gaelic cluain = meadow, pronounced CLOWance, the 'ow' as in cow; house listed grade II, orangery, coach house, Pheasant Cottage, kitchen garden and walls, classical style Folly, boiler house, and three stone crosses, each II; very large estate, south facing slope 100-60m., on Mylor Series, metamorphosed slate and sandstone, and alluvium, with acid soil, with AMs (three crosses); rainfall 40-45", temperature zone C; house and park are timeshare, kitchen garden, and perimeter woods each in separate ownership. There is an official booklet.

Clowance was the farthest west of the ten Cornish gardens included by Loudon in his gazetteer of 1822, confirming that its importance was widely recognized even from these early days. Though much has been lost over the years, yet sufficient remains to leave some impression of what it once had been. The St Aubyns - a family, as Carew writes, 'whose very name (besides the conquest roll) deduceth his first ancestors out of France' - seem to have been long associated with the manor here, even though they also had connections with Devon. Their history at Clowance began in about 1380, with the marriage of Geoffrey St Aubyn to Elizabeth Kemyell (whose family had inherited the manor by marriage), after which they remained in possession until 1921. Several writers contrasted the grounds with their surroundings. Stockdale thought

> the plantations and grounds ... arranged with great taste and judgement, and tend greatly to enliven the dreariness of this part of the county,

caused no doubt by mining. Gilbert reveals that such activities may at one time have influenced the estate itself since:

> It would ... appear from Tonkin, that the woods which had grown in great abundance, were cut down by the second baronet, and when his son [Sir John St Aubyn] succeeded to the estate, he found it in a state of nakedness. In 1723, this gentleman began planting the grounds, upon an extensive plan, and among other improvements, introduced the plane tree, *[Platanus orientalis]* which is remarkable for its large leaf, and had not before been grown in Cornwall.

Four of these Planes, 'planted in the open grassland near the house, and known to date from 1723', were still there when visited by the Cornish Biological Record Unit in 1979. The high wall around the estate, some five miles in length, which at one time incorporated grand entrances, now mostly gone, dates from 1670, shortly after the Riding House, which may have been intended for the training of cavalry horses for the Parliamentary troops. The associated 'horse field', a large area to the east of the house surrounded by an ha-ha, not to keep the animals out but to keep the horses in, is probably the

23. Clowance in the 1750s, shortly before the rebuilding in the 1770s. (Borlase 1758: 22)

24. Clowance, risen 'phoenix-like from the flames' to the design of Piers St Aubyn, seen over the eighteenth-century lake and landscape. (Twycross 1846: 65)

'horse-close' mentioned in documents of 1667, which also refer to a deer park and a chapel.

Both the house and the grounds continued to evolve over the years. The print in Borlase shows the west face in 1758 with a rather formal garden layout, although Lord Pembroke (who was a distant relative of St Aubyn's wife) had already before this designed a new southern front. A few years later, between 1775 and 1776, when Robert Mylne was called in to advise on repairs, he suggested rebuilding. It was probably at this juncture that the orangery was constructed, and the parkland and pleasure gardens behind and to the west of the house developed. There had been a semi-circular box maze at the far end of what is now the putting green (which was itself originally a bowling green), and a parterre of which the surviving eight ancient Irish yews once formed an integral part. The grotto in the small walled garden nearby, which has been reconstructed from a fireplace once inside the old house, also probably dates from the eighteenth century. It bears a certain resemblance to the entrance to the grotto at Menabilly (q.v.).

The parkland stretches southwards from the house to the lake and cascade, with the ornamental King's Pond behind. There was a boat-house (one print, indeed, shows a sailing craft on the lake), and walks through the plantations which opened up vistas, such as the Temple Walk which led to a building, recently demolished (from which a roundel has been preserved in the foyer of the leisure centre), with a lily pond behind it. There was a Green Drive for riding, summer houses such as the Folly in the woods, and later, north of the stable block, a Victorian pets' cemetery. The kitchen garden, near the eastern entrance (now in separate ownership), is especially intriguing. Built into the wall is a classical-style gazebo for use as an office for the head gardener, where he has a view over the estate. On the outside of the boiler house are brick niches inhabited by dilapidated stone eagles, from the St Aubyn's family arms, contemplating pigeon cotes in the north wall. It is believed that much of the landscaping in the eighteenth century was the work of John Nicholls, a disciple of 'Capability' Brown, and father of Maria, Sir John St Aubyn's mistress. (It is not said which came first!) Later, in 1836 and 1843, the house suffered two fires, although on the latter occasion it rose 'phoenix-like from the flames' to a design of Piers St Aubyn. The garden was listed in the *Hort. Direct.* from at least 1870 to 1919, and was one of Thurston's select properties. The estate was sold in the early 1920s, after which the surviving descendants of the family transferred to their seat at Pencarrow.

References: 17th, 18th, 19th (Hort. & Gen.) and 20th C; Illus.

25. Downes. A perspective drawing by J. Dando Sedding, modelled on the Hortus Palatinus at Heidelberg, designed by Salomon de Caus (c. 1576-1626).
(*From* Garden Craft Old and New, *1891*)

THE DOWNES, Trelissick Road, Hayle

SW55 36 : *EX7, GS351/358, SS.SW53*

House, two terrace walls, and two summer-houses, each listed grade II*, statue (1934) II; small garden, listed grade II, north facing at 25m. altitude, on Mylor slates; rainfall 40-45", temperature zone C; The Convent of the Daughters of the Cross of Liège, garden relict but recoverable.

The Downes was designed in 1867-8 for William John Rawlings, an antiquarian, by Edmund Sedding, whose brother John Dando Sedding planned the garden, the accompanying perspective drawing of which he included some twenty years later in his influential book, *Garden Craft Old and New* (1891). The drawing does not, however, exactly represent the garden as it was more simply laid out, which suggests that it may have been a preliminary idealized sketch. For instance, the dividing yew hedge with its arch became a wall with steps down to a lower level; the arcaded hedges along the central path are now an avenue of pointed yews, and the rather indistinctly drawn domed temple at the end of the vista became a roofed summer-house with granite pillars, inspired by St Germoe's Chair in Germoe churchyard. The design today does, however, illustrate exactly the theories formulated by Sedding shortly before his death. An admirer of Repton, he believed that

> Art and Nature should be linked together ... To attain this result, it is essential that the ground immediately about the house should be devoted to symmetrical planning, and to distinctly ornamental treatment; and the symmetry should break away by easy stages from the dressed to the undressed part, and so on to the open country ... (135).

Sedding differed from Repton by creating a strong central axis, which draws the eye unerringly along the perspective from the formal, through the less formal, and so to the 'wilder effects upon the country boundaries of the place'. Such axial plans were to become a feature in the designs of several of the Edwardian architects who fell under his spell, among them Mawson and Lutyens. In order to break away from the more conventional Victorian bedding schemes, Sedding in his book, discussed the theories which the Egyptologist, Sir Gardner Wilkinson, expounded in his work *Colour and Taste* (1858), with which he had experimented at Downes, since all 'the patterns [of the parterres] were annually submitted to Mr. Sedding for approval, the colours being actually laid in pigments in the beds before planting', that is presumably, painted on the plan. Even though Harry Roberts in his article, probably echoing the policy of the *Gardeners' Chronicle*, believed 'the architect's influence in the garden ... to be essentially evil', he admitted that, 'The Downes is nearly perfect ... the place will appeal as a fine example of formal gardening, which has been pursued without altogether forgetting the beauty of hardy plants naturally grouped, and of unbroken greensward.' As the sole surviving,

26. Downes. The geometrical garden, as sketched by T. Raffles Davison, which leads by stages to a distant view of the estuary and Lelant Church beyond. (B. Arch. 1887: pl. 16)

even though relict example of a significant and influential High Victorian designer, it would not be frivolous to claim The Downes as one of the most historically important gardens in Cornwall.

References: 20th C; D.Ottewill, The Edwardian Garden, *1989: 27-37.*

ERISEY, near Penhale, on the A3083, The Lizard

SW71 17 : EX8, GS359, SS.SW61/71

Cornish, Dexter suggests eru = field + sech = dry, or chy, pronounced eRIZy; house listed grade II, gate-piers and walls, stables, farm buildings, and 18th C. deer-stile each listed grade II; medium to large grounds at c. 50m., on granite, surrounded by serpentine, in an AONB, an AGSV and an AGHV; rainfall 35-40", temperature zone B; private, relict front court, original grounds virtually extinct.

Erisey is situated upon one of the small islands of granite in an area of serpentine, on drier soil, fertile enough to grow wheat (there was a granary in which John Wesley preached) and to support 'extensive orchards'. The Erisey family can be traced back to the time of Edward I (1274-1307), achieving some eminence with James Erisey, Sheriff, in 1512-13, and a later James who commanded ships in Drake's expedition to the West Indies, and against the Armada. Richard and his wife Margaret built a new house here in 1620, as we know from the datestone over the door, with a chapel and inner court, but it was his son, also James, who planted 'handsome gardens and [made] many other improvements' in 1671, when the date was carved on the two tall gate-piers topped with ball finials at the entrance. A surviving deer-stile suggests that there was also a park at this time.

The present main front - the result of rebuilding in the eighteenth century, in a south-easterly direction - faces into a rectangular garden with central gates (now lost), which hung on piers matching those at the entrance. These are set into walls, surmounted by capstones which return to the end of the present house, as they must also have done to the earlier house. Originally, no doubt, this quite small front court would have been laid out as an ornamental parterre or knot garden, planted with flowers or herbs. Across the road, opposite the gate, once stood (as befits a descendant of one of Drake's commanders) a raised bowling green, reached by ascending a short flight of steps, enclosed on each side by two finely carved granite seats, with inward-facing canopies shaped like scallop shells, which might be taken as sentry boxes. By 1824 it was stated in *Hitchins* that the gardens retained 'only a small part of their former magnificence', which suggests that by this time the plantations at the rear of the house were also in decline. The Erisey family became extinct in the male line in 1722, their property passing by marriage into the possession of the Killigrews of Arwenack, who in turn sold it to the Boscawens as a farm, the hooded seats eventually being removed to Tregothnan.

References: 17th, 18th, 19th (Gen.) and 20th C.

27. Godolphin. The remains of the 'quite ambitious garden' are out of sight to the left of the engraving, while the deer park is on the slopes of the hill above. The garden with statues lay to the right of the foreground. (Borlase 1758: 12)

GODOLPHIN HOUSE, Godolphin Cross

SW60 31 : EX7, GS351/358   OPEN

Godolghan in Carew 1602, also known as Godolphin Hall; Cornish *go = slight or sub- + ?, pronounced g'DOLPHin; house listed grade I; once a very large estate, at 60m. altitude, on metamorphosed Mylor slates, with acid soil, in an AGLV; rainfall 40-45", temperature zone C; opened privately, on Thursdays May through August, and Tuesdays July through August. There is an official leaflet, with garden plan.

As early as 1535 Leland had reported that

> Thomas Godalcan, yonger sun to Sir Willyam buildith a praty House, and hath made an exceding fair blo House Mille in the Rokky Valley thereby. [There are] no greater Tynne Workes yn al Cornwal then be on Sir Wylliam Godalcan's Ground.

Carew confirmed that 'Godalghan Ball, or hill ...'

> hath, for divers descents supplied those gentlemen's bountiful minds with large means accruing from their tin-works, and is now possessed by Sir Francis Godolphin, Knight.

However, despite the illustrious career of certain members of the Godolphin famiy, we are sadly informed that, by the time of *Hitchins*, its ancient splendour [had] totally disappeared, and the principal parts exhibit a heap of ruins. The elegant portico which was built by Francis Earl of Godolphin, of white moorstone, brought from Tregoning Hill, had rooms over it that were never finished, and that now assist in swelling the triumphs of desolation.

It cannot, then, be surprising that enquiry of the present owner in 1985 was not encouraging. A recent visit confirmed that the original layout was virtually non-existent: the principal garden is now a field, and none of the earlier planting survives, except for a few trees, and a tall box hedge. This is not the place to plot the history of the house, nor the demise of the family, but the garden deserves a closer inspection. There still exist early sketches of Godolphin, showing it at that time to be a fortified and castellated house. Another sketch of *c.* 1535, on the panelling of Pengersick Castle, drawn from an aerial perspective, reveals an interior courtyard similar to Borlase's reconstruction of Pengersick itself. But these predate the present house.

The view in Borlase's *Natural History* of 1758, however, is much as it is today, but with a forecourt, enclosed by a fence, two pavilions at the outer corners, and an arrangement of trees designed for walks beyond the front court.

Borlase also informs us that there was a deer park, which is known to have existed to the rear of the house, on the hill, where several 'deer slades' (i.e deer-drives) have been identified. Pevsner, writing in 1951, believed that he had seen the 'remains of quite an ambitious garden ... in the solitude which surrounds present-day Godolphin'. This would have been what are known as the 'Side and Pond Gardens', which on an estate map of 1786 are shown as nine formal plots with hedges, a grand central walk running east to west, with ponds to the north. In the surrounding groves and avenues there had been statues, which were known to have existed in 1890, but are now gone. A courtyard behind the stables to the right of Borlase's print, accessed from the house, is known as the 'King's Garden'. Long before Pevsner, Lawrence Weaver (in *Country Life*, 1915) had lamented the departed glory:

> Still more tragic than the dishonour which time has brought to the old building is the laying waste of the gardens. The old generous plan is still visible, with a "mount" [perhaps no more than the debris from the ponds?] beyond a noble box hedge, some dilapidated steps at changes of level and two fine pools which have lost their shape.

It is comforting to be able to report that the rising interest in garden history has led to a professional survey of the grounds being undertaken at Godolphin, which may shed even more light on the garden and its design.

References: 17th, 18th, 19th (Hort. & Gen.) and 20th C; Illus.; P Herring, et al., Godolphin, Breage, *Cornwall Archaeological Unit, Truro 1997.*

LANARTH, St Keverne

SW76 21 : LR204, EX8, GS359, SS.SW61/71

Cornish lanherch = *a clearing, pronounced* laNARTH; *house listed grade II, gate-piers II; grounds of 11 acres (4.4 ha), north-west sloping 100-80m., on gabbro troctolite, with acid soil, in an AONB, and an AGSV; rainfall 35-40", temperature zone B; private.*

Lanarth became the seat of the Sandys family after Anthony Sandys purchased the estate in 1617. Lt.-Col. William Sandys, on his return from India in the early nineteenth century, built 'an elegant house' there, a 'house, gardens, and grounds,' so *Hitchins* informs us, that 'have been raised to their present state of perfection at a vast expence; and [which] include every convenience which a retired situation can be expected to secure.' George Williams of Scorrier purchased the estate in the 1860s, which he used as a shooting box, but when it passed to his son Percival Dacres in 1891, he then proceeded, as Thurston - who included this among his select number - tells us, to create a garden

> out of a three-acre meadow and an eight acre wood on the crest of a hill and very exposed, and by the conversion of the old walled garden into a herbaceous garden. The newly acquired ground is stocked with rare trees, and hybrid shrubs, largely raised from seed.

P.D. Williams was to earn an equally wide reputation for his work in raising narcissus, as for his collection of trees and shrubs. During his time the garden was listed in the *Hort. Direct.* from 1908 to 1924. After his death in 1935, the estate passed to his only son, Michael, and despite 'brambles and other war-time nuisances' it still held its place as 'one of the two or three outstanding gardens in the county', in the opinion of Bishop Hunkin, who wrote a most valuable account of it in the *JRHS*. Michael Williams died in 1963, leaving the estate to his godson, Paul Tylor. Some of P.D.'s 'most interesting specimen plants', quoted by Hunkin from the list P.D. Williams had made in 1931, as well as many other trees he planted, still remain. Sadly, others, including the original tree of the 'Lanarth' form of *Magnolia cambellii*, have been victims of the recent gales, but Mr and Mrs Tylor are endeavouring to restore the woodland garden. Another well-known plant raised at this garden is the *Hydrangea* 'Lanarth White', which received the Award of Merit in 1949, and of Garden Merit in 1984. It is widely available in nurseries.

References: 17th, 18th, 19th (Gen.) and 20th C.

LISMORE HOUSE, Cross Street, Helston

SW65 27 : EX8, GS359

Named from the Michaels family connection with Lismore in Ireland; house listed grade II, garden walls by house, water pump, and kitchen garden buildings dated 1839, II; 2.5 acre (1 ha) garden listed grade II, sloping south, on Mylor Beds; rainfall 40-45", temperature zone C; private, but traditionally open for the Furry.

Lismore House, built in 1835 for Glynn Grylls, third son of Thomas Grylls of Bosahan, a solicitor in Helston, has for its setting a fine example of an early nineteenth-century town garden. The house itself is well seated on a platform with a lawn sloping gently away. Adjoining the house to the west is a walled garden with evidence of glass-houses on the walls, and believed at one time to have been a rose garden. At the foot of the slope on this same side is a small serpentine pond, with trees on the rising ground behind, now enveloping a summer or 'bark' house. Alongside, and immediately opposite the house, is a second large walled garden, evidently intended for vegetables, rising to a coach house and bothy, accessible from a back alley, but embellished on the garden front with a cornice and parapet, to serve as an 'eye-catcher' from the house. There is a terrace in front, slightly bowed, with railings, and with partial urns fixed to the walls. On the exterior of the walled garden at the north-west corner is a rustic stone grotto-like arch, and in the wall itself a cast iron pump dated 1844. The lawn has on its eastern side a large bed with mature ornamental trees and shrubs. The gardens were maintained and developed from 1937 by Mrs and the late Dr Michael. The property recently changed hands.

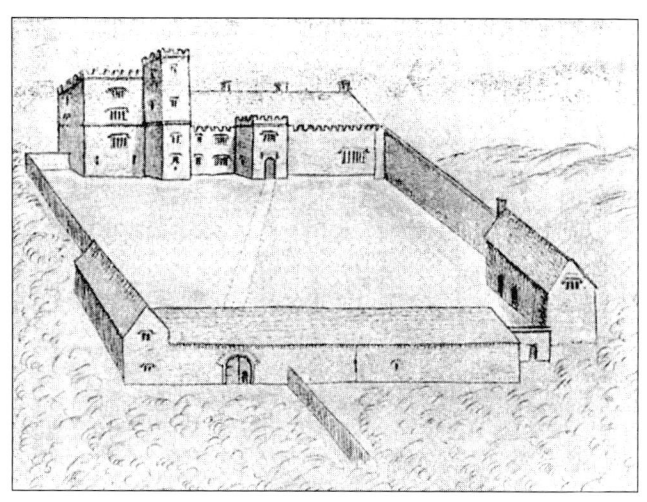

28. Pengersick Castle (above) and Godolphin. The representations by William Borlase in 1734 of the paintings of Pengersick and Godolphin, the homes of William Militon (d. 1565) and his wife Honor Godolphin, on the walls of the 'Castle' show their similarity as fortified houses. (After sketches in the Morrab Library, Penzance)

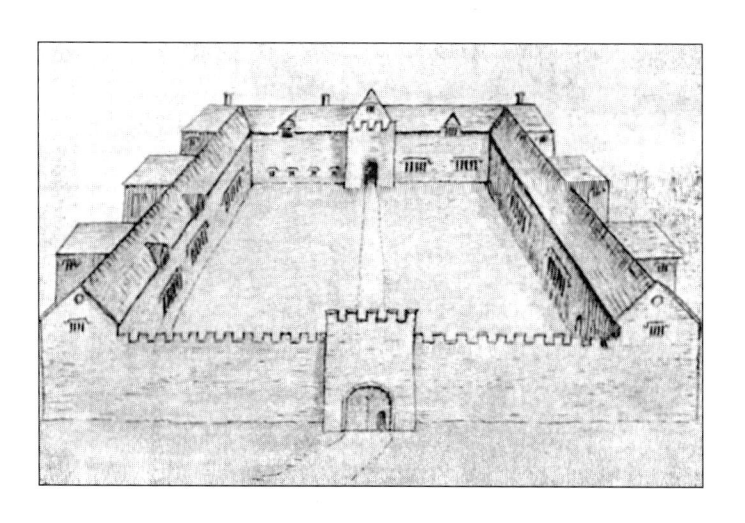

NANSLOE MANOR, Helston

SW65 26 : EX8, GS359, SS.SW61/71

Cornish nans + *loch = pool, usually near the sea, pronounced nansLOW; house 18th C. possibly earlier origins, with 19th C. added wing listed grade II; small to medium grounds, south-west sloping from 45m., on Mylor Beds; rainfall 35-40", temperature zone C; hotel, open to non-residents.*

Lake describes Nansloe as

> the seat of the Robinsons, after their removal from Bochym in Cury, ... pleasantly situated on the eastern bank of the little river *Cober* or *Loo*, near the head of the Loo Pool; the house was built by that family *circa* 1734. Latterly it was purchased by A.W. Young, Esq., M.P. for Helston, the present owner.

Nansloe, a former manor, was incorporated into the Penrose estate in the eighteenth century, so when it was turned over to the National Trust, they came into possession of land on both sides of the Pool. It was then decided that the house at Nansloe, with its grounds, drive and walled garden should be sold off. Although the surrounding trees have matured, the Pool can be seen across the neat lawn and the fields beyond. The tiled floor of a former conservatory survives on the south side of the house, and the lodge has an intriguing cobbled area with initials, apparently those of a former chauffeur.

References: 17th, 18th and 19th C. (Gen.).

PENGERSICK CASTLE, Praa Sands

SW58 28 : EX7, GS351/358

Cornish pen + *cors (adj) = reedy, pronounced penGERsick with a hard 'g'; house listed grade I, annex added 1927-8, and altered 1968; at 40m., on metamorphosed Mylor slates, in an AONB with an AM (Castle); extinct.*

The description by Maton at the end of the eighteenth century, when Pengersick was a ruin, paints a more realistic picture of its condition down the centuries than is gained from its present shape.

> About four miles from Marazion, and a half an one from the high road, towards the coast, stands Pengerswick Castle [*sic*], of which a square stone tower, of three stories, with a smaller one annexed, and some fragments of walls are the only remains. The door, on the north, is machicolated. The different apartments are now used as granaries and hay-lofts, but the wainscoat, which is of oak, remains perfect. This wainscot is very curiously carved and painted, and there are several quaint pieces of poetry

inscribed on the panels. A winding stone stair-case leads to the top of the principal tower, which commands a good view of the surrounding country.

Pengersick should properly be described as a fortified manor house, rather than a castle. It was built around 1510, and according to Leland, 'one Henry Force was Lord of it'. No doubt the proximity to a long stretch of sand which afforded an easy landing made it necessary to seek some security from marauders in wilder times. The actual plan of the original is a matter of conjecture, but Borlase's reconstruction may suffice to give a general impression of a typical fortified house, of which very few survive that have not been substantially altered, as indeed has Pengersick itself. The present and former owners have been endeavouring to recreate a Tudor garden here.

References: 17th, 18th, 19th (Gen.) and 20th C; Illus; B.Tuck, Pengersick Castle, Redruth 1984.; P Herring, Pengersick, Breage, Cornwall Archaeological Unit, Truro 1998.

PENPOL HOUSE, Penpol Avenue, Hayle

SW56 37 : EX7, GS351/358, SS.SW53   OPEN*

Cornish pen + pol, that is 'creek's head', pronounced penPOL; the house with its garden walls, well and gates are listed grade II; a 2 to 3 acre (1.2 ha) garden on the Gramscatho Beds, with river deposits causing an alkaline soil; rainfall 40-45", temperature zone C; open 1983-98 CGOG, 1987, 1991, 1994 NGS, June through July by appointment. There is an official leaflet.

Penpol, originally in the parish of Phillack on the other side of the river, came within the Domesday manor of Conarton, which included much of the land that later became the town of Hayle. Although a family named Penpoll is known to have resided in the parish, the property belonged to the Godolphins from the fourteenth century. The house, which has had a varied history, is sixteenth-century in origin, but has been extended and remodelled in each century since. It was leased in 1731 by John 'Merchant' Curnow, who was one of the pioneers of Hayle as a port and industrial town. The lease passed from him to Richard Oke Millet, who had married a Curnow daughter, until eventually he purchased it in 1788. A bizarre event is recounted of his successor, Dr Richard Millet, who was resident at Penpol up to 1863, in which he was accused by his brother-in-law, Dr Edmonds, of poisoning his half-brother, Jacob Millet, by the extraordinary expedient of mixing aconite in the horse-radish sauce served with his beef, although he was acquitted on trial. The family of Ellis, who are the present owners, had formerly been partners in one of the early smelting companies, but later, in 1815, founded the Hayle Brewery, taking a lease on Penpol in 1890, which was ultimately purchased by Col. John Ellis in 1921.

The garden as it now is seen, however, has been created since 1945, to become one of the most notable among contemporary Cornish gardens, not least because, unusually for the county, it lies on alkaline soil. This has enabled a long alley of delphiniums with box edging to be planted along one wall of the former kitchen garden, and this has become one of its more celebrated features. Adjoining this alley there is a formal pond garden enclosed by hedges, and edged with herbaceous and shrub borders. This garden extends westwards from the walled entrance courtyard.

To the north of the kitchen garden, and adjoining the west side of the house, the area is divided into two by a path. By the house itself is the 'Grey Garden', so called by the late Ellis sisters who created it, although it is now planted in a more colourful cottage-garden style. Across the pathway is a greenhouse with a vine. The earth outside, intended for the roots of the vine, was found on cultivation to be full of bones of various shapes and sizes. Evidence on similar sites suggests this was a not uncommon practice in Cornwall: presumably the bones acted as a fertilizer. Proceeding farther northwards, now beyond the rear of the house, the grounds open into the 'Cider Press Garden', which has been laid out formally with hybrid and floribunda roses, and beyond this a circular planting of old-fashioned roses. To the west of these gardens is a grassed area planted with ornamental and fruit trees, with a wild garden adjacent to the old-fashioned rose garden. Yet farther beyond, and to the north of these gardens, is a large lawned area on two levels, surrounded with a double line of perimeter trees for protection. This satisfying design, in compartments, has created a garden of continually varying interest, with plantings which are unusual if not unique in this part of the world. The front entrance gates were until recently approached by an avenue of trees, but, despite protests from many sources, these were removed by the local authority in March 1980.

References: 18th, 19th (Gen.) and 20th C; V. Bliss, The History of Hayle, Penwith District Council 1978: 47.

29. Penrose and Loe Pool, 'as if it were a serpentine lake especially made as a vista for the house', with the bath-house on the right. (Twycross 1846: 64)

PENROSE, near Helston

SW64 25 : *EX8, GS359, SS.SW61/71*

Cornish pen + ros*, pronounced* penROSE*, often anglicised to* PENrose*; house listed grade II, stables and 'garden building', each II; a 1,600 acre (648 ha) estate, on north-east facing side of south-east sloping valley 60m. to the sea, on Mylor Beds, with acid soil, in an AONB and HC, a SSSI, AGSV and CNCS; rainfall 30-35", temperature zone B; donated to the National Trust in 1974, house private.*

There is mention of a John de Penrose in the records as early as 1281, but the family becoming extinct, the estate then passed to a niece, who in 1770 sold it to Hugh Rogers, of Treassowe in Ludgvan parish. He was succeeded by his brother John who began to extend his lands, establishing a deer park in 1785. The old house, which had been built for the Penroses in the seventeenth century, was also improved by the new owners, who added elegant stables with a clock turret. At the same time the grounds were relandscaped to take fuller advantage of the prospect over the Loe Pool, which included a Temple Plantation although no temple seems to have survived. They then extended the estate further by incorporating Degibna Woods, as well as the nearby Nansloe Manor, from the other side of the Pool. During the nineteenth century there were further developments, including the bath house erected in about 1837 which has been restored by the National Trust. This was followed about ten years later by a bridge over the river, clearly intended to act as a feature in the view which, as Pevsner remarked, overlooks 'Loe Pool as if it were an artificial serpentine lake especially made as a vista for the house'.

It was at about this time that the Helston Lodge was constructed in a Victorian Tudor style, but the Bar Lodge, built later in 1895-8 by the estate workmen to designs of G.H. Fellowes Prynne, was rather more elaborate, being adorned with a wooden balustraded balcony, where the Rogers family sometimes took tea. It was intended to open into an impressive new drive to the house, which was never completed. John Jope Rogers, who resided at Penrose during the second half of the nineteenth century, had a lively interest in horticulture, which led him to contribute several valuable articles to journals. In 1860-61 there was a particularly severe winter, after which Rogers wrote two articles describing its effect - the first to the *JRIC*, listing the damage to trees at Penrose, and the second to the *Gardeners' Chronicle*, with a longer list, which may have included examples from other gardens in Cornwall. His interest in climate continued, resulting in a second article to the *JRIC* in which the effects of the bad winter of 1878-9 were compared with those of nearly twenty years earlier. There were many fine trees at Penrose, especially among the new introductions of conifers, which were the subject of further articles. One of these, *Abies religiosa*, was believed to have first fruited in this country at Penrose. This is a species which is still uncommon in Cornwall today. The garden was listed in the *Hort. Direct.* from 1908 to 1924, and was one of Thurston's select gardens.

References: 17th, 18th, 19th (Hort. & Gen.) and 20th; Illus; S.H. Toy, The History of Helston, *1936: 598-601; B. le Mesurier and L. Luck,* Coast of Cornwall 12, Loe Pool and Gunwalloe, *National Trust 1987.*

RIVIERE HOUSE, Phillack

SW56 38 : EX7, GS351/358, SS.SW53

House listed grade II; small garden, south-east sloping 20-10m., on Gramscatho Beds; rainfall 40-45", temperature zone C; now in apartments.

Riviere House was built in 1791 for John Edwards, manager of the Cornish Copper Company. It later became the home of the geologist Joseph Carne, FRS. The mansion stands out prominently on the north side of Hayle Pool, to the west of Phillack church, above the King George V Memorial Walk. It is surrounded by a square enclosed garden with lawn, old trees and shrubs. Kilvert in 1870 described how he

> climbed over a gate at the foot of a hill close by the creek shore and climbed a steep path through a pretty wood, part of the grounds of La Rivière, to the mansion, a white square formal house. In the plantation was a path leading down to a celebrated well in a dark cool square chamber cut in the rock. We went through a door in the wall into the fine granite-walled garden of La Rivière.

The well-known author Compton Mackenzie moved here from Cury vicarage, and was resident from 1908 to 1910. He later described his gardening experiences in the pages of the *New Flora and Silva.* 'The name of Riviere,' as is remarked in *Hitchins,*

> will be long remembered, as being, with a trifling variation in orthography, the appellation of that castle in which Theoderick resided; when the Irish saints, who were subsequently murdered by him, landed on his territories. This venerable castle, or palace, has probably long since been buried in the sands which have greatly encroached on this estate, and which would, in all probability, have proved entirely destructive to it, had not their progress been arrested, as in other parishes, suffering from similar accumulations, by introducing thick plantations of the sea rush [*Juncus maritimus*]. The most interesting circumstance relative to this sand is, that on this estate (and much more so on the coast of Gwithian parish) it is passing into a state of hard stone or rock. Dr. Paris has read a paper on this subject to the Royal Cornwall Geological Society, in Penzance.

Riviere Castle was also mentioned by William of Worcester (1478), and it was undoubtedly these Riviere Towans, with their romantic associations here, as well as the more familiar Cornische in the Mediterranean Riviera, which prompted the GWR, in its promotion of St Ives as a holiday resort, to coin the punning expression 'The Cornish Riviera'.

References: 17th, 18th, 19th (Gen.) and 20th C; Compton Mackenzie, My Life and Times, Octave 4, 1907-1915, *1965: 40-1.*

TOLROY, St Erth

SW56 35 : EX7, GS351/358, SS.SW53

Talary Veas, Lanhydrock Map c. 1693; Cornish tal *= brow of hill + [?], pronounced tolROY; grounds of 30 acres (12 ha), at c. 60m., on phonolite to north, Mylor slates to south; rainfall 40-45", temperature zone C; grounds extinct, now the* Tolroy Manor Holiday Village.

Talary Veas was depicted as an uncultivated area in Trenhayle on the Lanhydrock map of the Robartes land, prepared by Joel Gascoyne in 1696. It was situated at the narrowest point in Cornwall, a mere three miles across, where, from a height on Trenhayle could be seen both St Michael's Mount and St Ives Bay. The land was poor, but in 1842/3 when owned by the Praed family of Trevethoe, it was shown on the tithe map as hedged and divided into fields. By 1871, it had come into the possession of John Harvey Trevithick, a partner in Harveys & Co. of Hayle, who died there in 1877. He was succeeded by Henry Harvey Trevithick, his son, who was listed by the *Hort. Direct.* as opening the garden from 1908 to 1916. Charles Henderson, in 1923, wrote on his copy of the Tolroy map that it was 'at that time the residence of Henry Trevithick esquire who had laid out extensive wooded grounds in the 30 acres which had been furze in the 1690s'. An impression of woodland can be seen high to the left of the Hayle bypass, when driving toward the Lelant roundabout, but on closer inspection the vast leisure centre and 'holiday village' will be found to have erased all traces of the fine house and pleasant surroundings that linger in the minds of the older local residents.

References: 20th C.; V. Chesher and J. Palmer, Three Hundred Years on Penwith Farms, *Penwith Local History Group 1994: 58-62.*

TRELEAN, St Martin in Meneague

SW74 25 : LR204, EX8, GS359, SS.SW61/71 OPEN*

Cornish tre + [?], pronounced treLEAN; 20 acre (8 ha) south-north valley garden from 61m. to the sea, on Gramscatho Beds, with acid soil, in an AONB, an AGSV and CNCS; rainfall 35-40", temperature zone B; open 1983-98 CGOG, 1991, 1993-5 NGS, by appointment April through October.

The history of the Trelean garden became a legend in the lifetime of its creator, Sqn.Ldr. George Witherwick, a dentist in the RAF who, for thirty years had cultivated a four-acre (1.6 ha) garden in Surrey. In 1979 he and his wife decided to retire to Cornwall, arriving with 'four lorry and seven estate-car loads of trees, shrubs and plants of all kinds.' Trelean was at that time an untouched valley, beginning six to seven hundred yards away from the farmhouse, along an old path known as Doodes Lane. A stream runs the length of the valley down to the sea, which is overhung by indigenous trees. 'In fact', he writes,

> the whole valley is wooded, with a two-acre area in its upper third of mostly bracken. It is this area which now largely constitutes the garden, which is different from most, having no pretence at formality, no lawns, spacious or otherwise, no cement or tidy, edged beds, no rockeries or concrete pools.

Indeed, the progress down the valley itself is distictly hazardous, where will be found 'semi-concealed notices to the effect that "no compensation is payable to the under 65s."' This is a garden of character, not to say eccentricity. It out-Cornwalls the Cornish valley gardens by not even attempting to introduce any plan or design, other than that of simply growing plants, of which there are a huge variety. After establishing the immigrants in their new home, and beginning to introduce trees and shrubs which could not be grown in Surrey, George Witherwick turned his attention to the hybridizing of rhododendrons, having received some instruction in the art by the celebrated nurseryman, Mr Gill of Penryn. He produced, among others, 'Trelean Pink Blush'.

It would clearly be impossible in a brief note such as this to do justice to the plants recorded at Trelean, which by 1988 had already exceeded 1,200. The interested reader is referred to published articles that concentrate upon the plants, and to George Witherwick's forthcoming book. One records with regret that as this note was being penned, news sadly came of his death, but the future of this remarkable garden at present seems to be assured.

References: 20th C; G.T. Witherwick, In a Cornish Valley., A Nature Diary, *Wadebridge, 1988.*

TRELOWARREN, Mawgan-in-Meneage

SW72 23 : LR203 and 204,
EX8, GS359, SS.SW61/71 OPEN

Trellewaret, Domesday 1086; Cornish, Dexter suggests tre + lowern = fox, pronounced treloWARRen; house listed grade I; garden around the house of c. 32 acres (13 ha) listed grade II, with extensive grounds and woodland, sloping north-south, highest point 100m., house at 76m., to creek level; in Meneague Crush Zone, with acid soil, in an AONB, an AGSV and CNCS; rainfall 35-40", temperature zone B; private house, garden and estate. House partly leased to a religious charitable trust. Opened 1987-9 CGOG, but since independently. There is an official booklet.

The size of the estate at Trelowarren, and the long history of the Vyvyan family who, so legend tells, escaped from the sinking land of Lyonesse on horseback, make it impossible to do more here than present an outline of some of the salient features. The manor was mentioned in Domesday as being owned by Earl Harold who was killed at Hastings, but the Vyvyan family, with whom it is usually associated, inherited the estate by marriage in 1427, when it was no more than a small manor house with a chapel opposite, set low in the landscape for shelter from the bleak and uninterupted moorland of The Lizard peninsula. This medieval house was first extended by John Vyvyan in the sixteenth century, then further enlarged by Sir Richard Vyvyan (1611-65), the first baronet, who rebuilt the chapel to form part of a new courtyard. The stables followed in 1697, the William and Mary dovecote a year later, and a clock was added in the eighteenth century. Sir Richard (1732-81), the fifth baronet, who had been a student of William Borlase at Ludgvan, between 1753 and 1760 engaged the architect Thomas Edwards of Greenwich to remodel the house in the new Georgian fashion, while the chapel was decorated with fine 'Strawberry Hill Gothic' plasterwork.

A plan from this period by Dionysius Williams (in the Record Office) shows a 'Rococo' type garden, but the history of the grounds as we now know them may be said to have begun with Sir Vyell Vyvyan (1767-1820), the seventh Baronet, in the late eighteenth and early nineteenth centuries. He carried out much of the original road building and estate planting, which included shelter belts around the house to afford greater protection from the elements. He also created within the existing woodland, Pleasure Gardens

30. Trelowarren in 1806, before the alterations by Sir Vyell Vyvyan. (Polwhele, 1806: iv. 116)

to the south of the house, where in 1820 was planted the celebrated 'Sir Vyell's Oak'. The estate was then separated from the unenclosed moorland and rough pasture of the Goonhilly Downs by the digging of an ha-ha on the southern boundary of the woodland.

Sir Vyell's successor, Sir Richard Rawlinson Vyvyan (1800-79, eighth Bt.), continued to carry out extensive work on the house, and developed the garden and estate. Until this time, the entrances had been either from St Mawgan, or via the 'Double Lodges' on the St Keverne Road. In 1833 a new drive was laid, planted for some 550 yards (500m.) as an 'Ilex Avenue', with a lodge built on the Garras road. Later, in 1846, it was expected that Queen Victoria would visit the estate, and it was decided that she should come up the scenic Helford River, landing at a newly built quay at Tremayne, and over the new Ton Bridge, built for this same purpose.

Sir Richard was also responsible for three walled gardens. One, which later came to be known as 'Lady Vyvyan's Garden', was built immediately west of the north wing, utilizing stone salvaged from the fire at Nanswhyden (q.v.), in which were placed glazed Gothick 'folly' windows, incorporating on one corner the Turret Folly. The second, an acre in extent, built east of the stables, was intended as a Botanic Garden, where plants were to be arranged both according to the systems of Linnaeus and Decandolle. In the centre there was to be a 'temple' to act as a botanical library, and it was proposed that the 'entrance will be formed by two folding iron gates, the pillars of which will terminate in busts of the founders of the two systems'. It is not known how far this project ever advanced. Yet another small walled 'Melon Garden' was constructed, in the vicinity of the stables, which is now used as a nursery.

One of Sir Richard Vyvyan's most lasting garden features has been the formal lawns around the house, with wide granite steps adorned on each side with urns, leading up to the raised walk and Pleasure Gardens. In the woodland there is to be found a 'Mount', over 50 feet (15.25m.) in height, making it the highest point on The Lizard peninsula, which was known as 'Three Seas Point' since from it the Channel could be seen on both sides of the Lizard, as well as the Atlantic. Today, because of the growth of trees, only the latter is visible.

More recently, during the post-war years, and after the death of her husband, Sir Courtney Vyvyan (1858-1941), Trelowarren became well-known in the writings of Lady Clara Vyvyan (a daughter of Mrs Powys Rogers, née Williams, of Tregye), who restored the Pleasure Grounds, as well as creating her own garden. She herself died in 1976. The estate has now been opened up to the public with a restaurant, craft centre, pottery, small nursery and woodland walks, as well as housing an evangelical religious centre. The garden, which is being restored, was listed in the *Hort. Direct.* from at least 1870 to 1924, and was one of Thurston's select gardens.

References: 17th, 18th, 19th (Hort. & Gen.) and 20th C; Illus; Lady C. Vyvyan, The Old Place, 1952, Letters from a Cornish Garden, 1972, etc.

TREVARNO, Sithney

SW64 30 : EX8, GS352   OPEN

Cornish tre + [?], pronounced treVARNo; estate of c. 750 acres (304 ha), including garden about 30 acres (12 ha), in north-west, south-east valley, 75- c. 50m., on Mylor Series metamorphosed slates and sandstone, and alluvium, with acid soil; rainfall 40-45", temperature zone C; private, open 1983-94 and 1996 CGOG, and from 1997 open daily all year. There was an official leaflet.

With good reason, Trevarno can claim to be the finest of the maintained historic gardens in this section. The manor was first mentioned in 1296 as the house of Randulphus de Trevarno. It has subsequently been owned by the Killigrews, Carminows and Courtneys. It eventually came to the Oliver family, one of whom was believed by Gilbert to have married the heiress of Trevarno. According to Betjeman, the poet 'Pope stayed here in the eighteenth century as a guest of the father of Dr Oliver the biscuit inventor', with whom he was certainly in correspondence. William Oliver, MD, FRS, practised in Bath and wrote a treatise on the waters there. He died in 1764.

After the Olivers had moved to Ludgvan and Treneere in Penzance, Trevarno was purchased by Christopher Wallis, a wealthy attorney of Helston, 'by whom [in the 1830s] vast improvements were made to the house and grounds'. His grandson, Christopher Wallis Popham, the child of his daughter, after inheriting, remodelled the house in 1839 to the design of George Wightwick, and built the walled garden, with two conservatory-greenhouses. One of these, overlooking the lakeside terraces, is of particular interest. It is in the form of a two-storey cottage-folly, joined gable-end on to the outer side of the wall, while on the inner side it becomes an ornate conservatory, with a high central aisle and two lower apses on either side. It seems probable that the most unusual serpentine yew tunnel walk, 13ft.(4m.) high and 165ft.(50m.) long, parallel to the north wall of this walled garden, was constructed at the same time.

The estate came up for auction in 1874, and was bought by William Bickford Smith, eldest son of George Smith, 'the eminent writer on historical and religious subjects', and whose grandfather had been the inventor of the safety fuse. Trevarno remained in the same family until 1994, when it was sold. Betjeman described William Bickford Smith as a 'learned artist', and it is certainly to his initiative that we owe the principal elements of the present garden. He extended the lake, adding the boat house in a neo-Gothic style, with a tiled bellcote spire at the open gable end, and created the formal lakeside terraces, ornamented with bedding schemes, rose gardens and herbaceous borders, interspersed with gravel walks, which have now been grassed over. A rockery with its grotto, pool and stepped mount, was constructed on a spot where Wesley is reputed to have preached, and above it, along the drive, a pinetum was planted, containing around 120 specimens, which seem to have escaped Thurston's notice when compiling his list of conifers. William Bickford Smith also made considerable additions to the house, to the designs of James Hicks, increasing it in size to forty-six rooms. Among the principal features were a 'portico, with granite pillars of the Ionic order', a billiard room, and a library of such magnificence that it prompted Kelly's *Directory* (1883) to include a detailed description. It was, they wrote,

> a spacious apartment, 42 by 32 feet, the floor is of parquet oak inlaid with ebony and Italian walnut, and the cornice is decorated with the emblazoned coats appertaining to the family; the collection of books comprises over 7,000 volumes [the number increased in subsequent editions]: the oil paintings are, with few exceptions, from the brush of Mr. Bickford-Smith himself.

Trevarno passed in 1919 to John Clifford Bickford-Smith, who added to the plantings, as did Michael Bickford-Smith after the Second World War. He was also responsible for the bog garden, and for commencing a dogs' graveyard. Peter Bickford-Smith, until recently Chairman of the Cornwall Garden Society, took over the estate in 1975, engaging Drewitts of Penzance in 1980 to reduce the house to its original size.

One of the most impressive features added during his time was the greatly enlarged cascade into the lake. Other interesting items in the garden are a sundial on the lawn to the south of the house; an Edwardian wooden summer-house on a bank above the east lawn, beyond which is an Italian garden, now redesigned, with a cast iron fountain; the steps leading to the yew tunnel, guarded at the top by two red stone lions; and a paved aromatic garden adjoining the north side of the house. The future of Trevarno is at present unknown, but the new owner has expressed his intention to maintain and continue opening this most worthwhile garden.

References: 17th, 18th, 19th C (Hort. & Gen).

TREWINNARD MANOR, St Erth

SW54 34 : *EX7, GS351/358, SS.SW53*

Cornish tre + guyn = *white, fair* + arth = *height, pronounced* TreWINnard; *house including garden walls and gate-piers to the north listed grade II*, coach house, including courtyard walls and gate-piers II*, farm buildings II; small garden, at c. 25m. altitude, on Mylor Series slate, with acid soil; rainfall 35-40", temperature zone C; private.*

According to Lysons, the 'barton of Trewinnard

> belonged to an ancient family of that name, two of whom were successively members for the county in the reign of Edward III. The last who appears to have possessed this barton was William Trewinnard, one of the members for Helston, in the reign of Henry VIII. From the Trewinnards it passed to the Mohuns, who some time resided at Trewinnard.

Their 'some time' residence was occasioned by their widespread interests throughout the county. Leland mentioned their 'fair Lordship' at Trewinnard in 1534, but in 1650 the estate was purchased by John Hawkins from a family who were later to settle at Pennans and, in 1715, at Trewithen (q.v.). They became the possessors of an early eighteenth-century coach, reputed to have been purchased from a Spanish ambassador, which they used until 1777, after which it was stored in the coach house until 1919, when, after restoration, it was given to the Truro Museum. The possession of such a coach speaks greatly for the social position of the Hawkins in the vicinity, although it raises questions about its utility on many of the Cornish lanes at that time. The eventual plight of this once important estate is sketched for us in *Lake*:

> Trewinnard house has been so much altered latterly as scarcely to leave a trace of what it had been in former times. The gardens shewed pleasing specimens of cut yew, trim box, and trained thorn hedges. There was also a building, detached from the house, supposed to have been an ancient chapel ... the old mansion and grounds had the advantage of a stream of water, brought with great art over very uneven ground from a distance of two or three miles, conducted into almost every field, and supplying the house. Trewinnard is now divided between the families of St. Aubyn, of Clowance, Hawkins, and the representatives of the Praeds: one third to each.

This fine house is at present the residence of Sir John Nott, former MP for St Ives and Minister of Defence.

References: 17th, 18th, 19th (Hort. & Gen.) and 20th C; 'Cornubia', Historical Notes on the Parish of St Erth, *1936, chap.11.*

SUPPLEMENTARY LISTS

LESSER-KNOWN HISTORIC GARDENS

Gwithian Churchyard

SW58 41 : *EX7, GS351/358*

St Gocianus, *patron saint; pronounced* GWITHian.

The Lysons noted that:

> In the parish of Gwythian the fig-tree [*Ficus carica*] appears to be naturalised to a greater degree than perhaps anywhere in the kingdom. We observed a considerable group in the church-yard, and were assured that there were many in the neighbouring hedge-rows.

Kilvert, in August 1870, also recorded in his *Diary*, that he had found in

> the churchyard, overhanging the road ... a magnificent fruit-bearing fig tree, covering a vast space of ground. The figs on the top of the tree only, ripen and become fit to eat.

Thurston discovered one tree still flourishing in the 1920s, but when visited in 1992 only a seedling about 10 feet high, growing out of the foundation of the south wall of the chancel, was surviving. See also Manaccan, and Newlyn East.

References: 19th (Gen.) and 20th C.

Manaccan Churchyard

SW76 25 : *EX8, GS359, SS.SW61/71*

Cornish ?manach + ?*an = *monk's dwelling, place of, pronounced* maNACKan; *in an AONB and HC, an AGSV, and CNCS.*

Lake noted that:

> A large and flourishing fig-tree [*Ficus carica*], the

trunk of which is about ten inches in diameter, grows out of the western part of the south wall of the church. It is known to have occupied its present position for at least a century.

Thus it was there around 1770. Even though this was deleterious to the fabric of the church, the tree still existed, and had reached the top of the tower when recorded by Thurston in the 1920s. It is less high today. See also Gwithian and Newlyn East.

References: 19th (Gen) C.

Penhellis, Cross Street, Helston

SW65 27 : EX8, GS359, SS.SW61/71

Cornish pen + ?, pronounced penELLis; house listed grade II; garden small to medium, on Mylor Beds, with acid soil; rainfall 35-40", temperature zone C; Residential Home with relict garden.

Penhellis is a 'stucco Italianate villa', designed c. 1838 by George Wightwick, which has one of the few gardens described in Kelly's *Directory* (1893):

> Penhellis, the residence of F.V. Hill esq. is beautifully situated on the slope of a hill at the north-west end of the town; it has very well laid out grounds, which contain many beautiful specimens of flowering shrubs and a splendid ornithological museum, all the specimens in which were shot in the county, and include a water rail caught by the beak by an oyster at Helford river near Helston.

Hill was Town Clerk of Helston, clerk to various other bodies, and an alderman. The property is not mentioned in any other of our sources.

References: 19th (Gen.) C.

Penmare, Hayle

SW57 38 : EX7, GS351/358

Cornish pen + [?], pronounced penMAIR; hotel, grounds now extinct.

Listed in the *Hort. Direct.* of 1890 and 1891 as the residence of W. Hosken, one of a family of millers. It is now an hotel on the road east out of Hayle, with nothing left of the grounds save a large car-park, surrounded by houses.

References: 19th (Hort.) C.

Weath Garden, Helston

SW65 27 : EX8, GS359, SS.SW61/71

Cornish gwyth = trees, pronounced WEETH; small garden at river level, on Mylor Beds, with acid soil; rainfall 35-40", temperature zone C; relict.

Weath Garden was listed in the *Hort. Direct.* in 1908 under the name of A.H. Michell, who does not appear in the Kelly's *Directory* of that time. Weath is part of the Penrose estate, and in recent years has been used for allotments. It occurs only on this single occasion in our sources, and little or nothing is known of its history locally.

References: 19th C. (Hort.).

ADDITIONAL CONTEMPORARY GARDENS

See also: ACTON CASTLE, PENPOL HOUSE and TRELEAN under the main entries.

Carnowall, Black Rock, Praze

SW665 341 : EX8, GS352   OPEN*

Cornish carn = tor + ughel = high, pronounced carNOWell; 1.5 acre (0.6 ha) garden, at 500 feet (152m.) altitude; open NGS 1997-8 mid May to mid July by appointment.

Flambards Victorian Village Garden, Culdrose Manor, Helston

SW67 26 : EX8, GS359   OPEN*

Garden in 20 acre (8 ha) theme-park; open 1997-8 NGS, Easter through October.

Hallowarren, Carne, near Manaccan

SW77 24 : LR204, EX8, GS359, SS.SW61/71   OPEN*

Cornish [?], pronounced HALowarren; 1 acre (0.4 ha) garden in an AONB, and an AGSV; open 1987 CGOG, 1997-8 NGS one Sunday each in May and June in association with Wynlands, q.v.

Reference: Pring (1996: 98).

Paradise Park, bird sanctuary, Hayle

SW55 36 : EX7, GS351/358, SS.SW534   OPEN*

Open 1994-6 CGOG, 1997-8 NGS, all year.

Poldowrian, near Coverack, The Lizard

SW74 17 LR204, EX8. GS359, SS.SW61/71   OPEN*

*Cornish pol + *douran = watering place, pronounced polDOWrian; in an AONB and HC, an AGSV and CNCS, and an AGHV; open 1983 ,1985-98 CGOG, April through June by appointment only. There is an official leaflet.*

Reference: 20th C.

Woodland Nursery, Garras, The Lizard*

SW70 23 EX8, GS359, SS.SW61/71

Garden in an AONB, and an AGSV; opened 1989-97 CGOG, 1991, 1993-7 NGS .There has been an official leaflet.

Reference: Pring (1996: 123-4).

Wynlands, Choon, near Manaccan

SW753 246 LR204, EX8, GS359, SS.SW61/71   Open*

0.5 acre (0.2 ha) garden, in an AONB, and an AGSV; open 1997-8 NGS, one Sunday each in May and June in association with Hallowarren, q.v.

3. CAMBORNE and REDRUTH

Camborne and Redruth, in the eastern section of the ancient hundred of Penwith on the granite of the Carnmenellis extrusion, lies open on the north coast to the Atlantic Ocean. This area, one of the richest in mineral resources, became the most extensively mined in Cornwall, with the result that all of the great houses in the district may be expected ultimately to have derived their wealth from the mining industry.

The oldest among the local families were the Bassets, reputed to have come over with the Conqueror, and whose estate at Tehidy had been mentioned in the Domesday Book. Leland in 1535 described their deer park at Carn Brea as, even at that early date, 'now defacid', no doubt by industry, although Tonkin, in the early eighteenth century, found the 'castle and park wall ... still standing'. Nevertheless, he had

> been informed by several old men ... that all the rocky grounds under Carnbray Castle, and from thence to Porth-Treth, were covered with stout trees in their remembrance; so that squirrels, of which there are many, could leap from one tree to the other all the way. These were mostly destroyed in the Civil Wars, and the rest were cut down by the old Lady Basset, ... so that now there is not the least sign of any trees ever having grown there. (*Lake* 1868 :ii.220)

This was to result in major problems from exposure when reafforestation was later attempted.

Inland, in the more protected areas upon richer soil, the Beauchamp family as early as the sixteenth century had established themselves at Trevince and later at Pengreep, while in the seventeenth century Rosewarne and Pendarves were settled by families of the same name. But the destruction of native woodlands meant that the mining industry would need to look elsewhere for its fuel. This, they found, could be imported most conveniently from Wales, just as they came to see that it would also prove more economic to export the prepared Cornish ores for smelting. Thus a two-way traffic developed with the Welsh: importing coal for fuel, and exporting ore for smelting, which passed through the newly constructed harbour of Portreath, built at the former Basset's Cove, where an ingenious sloping twin railway carried the coal up and the ore down without engines, by the force of gravity.

It was this Welsh connection which brought into Cornwall among others the family of Williams. James Williams is known to have emigrated to Cornwall some time before 1654, where his grandson John settled at Burncoose.

His grandson, another John, was to become one of the most successful mine speculators the county had known, and it was he who 'built and planted' Scorrier. As the family grew, so they expanded into the adjoining Tregullow and overflowed into the houses even of the Beauchamps themselves. The gardens at each of these houses have received a measure of notice in the principal gardening journals of the day, but the greatest horticultural reputation of the Williams family was to come rather from the estates outside the district which they acquired as their mining interests broadened.

John Williams retired to Sandhill Manor in Gunnislake, for family reasons, but also to pursue his speculations in the silver mining of the area. It was as a consequence of the family's interest here that his grandson later acquired the nearby Werrington Park in 1882. Their partnership with the Fox family in their Iron Foundry at Perran-ar-worthal resulted, on the Foxes' withdrawal, in the occupancy of Goonvrea and Tredrea, just as the departure of the Vivians from Pencalenick provided an opportunity for another branch of the family to settle near Truro. Lanarth, on The Lizard, had been purchased in the 1860s by George Williams of Scorrier to satisfy his passion for shooting, but in the hands of his youngest son, P.D. Williams, it was to gain a reputation at the turn of the century not only for its plantings, but also for the breeding of narcissus. But it was Caerhays, where the Trevanions had bankrupted themselves carrying out Nash's extravagant designs for the castle, which under J.C. Williams became elevated to the stature of what has been described as 'the greatest garden in Cornwall'.

A concentration upon these great estates should not, however, lead us to neglect the many large houses built by others who profited from the mining industry: attorneys, engineers, mine captains, and bankers. It is probably largely fortuitous that only two, Tolvean at Redruth and Basset Villa at Camborne, appear in the sources upon which we rely, but as in other towns, a glance around the once fashionable areas will reveal that there must have been many other residences adorned in the days of their prosperity with large gardens of equal worth.

NB BURNCOOSE, PENGREEP, SCORRIER, TREGULLOW, TREVINCE, and TRESKEWES, although in the vicinity of Redruth, are to be found on the OS Landranger 204 Truro and Falmouth map.

BURNCOOSE, Gwennap

SW74 39 : LR204, EX104, GS359   OPEN

Broncoys 1277; Cornish bron = breast of hill + cos = wood, pronounced burnCOOZe; house listed grade II, 18th C. lodge and gate-piers II; grounds of 30 acres (12.2 ha), south sloping 100-80m., on Mylor Series metamorphosed greenstone, with acid soil; rainfall 50-60", temperature zone C; private residence, and the Burncoose and Southdown Nursery. There is an official leaflet, with a guide to plants and a plan. Open 1983-98 CGOG, daily all year, and 1987, 1997 NGS.

Burncoose was the first of the houses to be built by the Williams family, after James Williams had emigrated from Wales to Stithians, sometime before 1654. It was John, grandson of James, who first settled here in 1715, although the present house dates from the early nineteenth century, with extensions and remodelling in mid-century. A curious feature is described by C.C. James (n.d.):

> In the grounds there is a tunnel approximately 75 yards long which permits the passage of cattle and horses to the surrounding fields. The ground above the tunnel is levelled off and forms a portion of the garden.

The property was 'improved' by John Williams III in the early eighteenth century, and by his nephew in the nineteenth century, but Thurston, who included Burncoose among his select gardens, suggests that 'the garden was in great measure created by Mrs Powys Rogers (a daughter of J.M. Williams of Caerhays), who lived at Burncoose from about 1890 till 1916', after which she and her husband moved to Tregye (q.v.), Hamilton Davey says of her that she was:

> A genuine lover of gardening … [and] a determined opponent of that self-assertive style of horticulture which obtains in connection with suburban villadom under the refined name of "bedding out." For correctness in the massing of plants, Burncoose can be cited as an object-lesson, every plant introduced into the garden being placed in position with some definite object in view.

He also made reference to her collections of 'rare Alpine flora' and bamboos. Subsequently the garden suffered some neglect, particularly during the war years, and sustained damage from a freak storm in December 1979. In 1984, however, the Southdown Nursery, who are now producing a vast range of ornamental and exotic plants, moved here from Redruth to take a central place on the estate, occupying, with the walled garden, 7 acres (2.8 ha) of the grounds. The private entrance to the property is now separated, rising from the lodge along a drive lined with choice exotic trees and shrubs. Further south, from this point edged with fine stone kerbs, it becomes one of the paths through the main plant collection to the west of the house, in front of which a lawn with a sundial in its centre slopes gently to a stone ha-ha, beyond which there is a pond, added in the time of Mrs Rogers or shortly before. Along the perimeter are mature trees some 150 years old, including Holm and Lucombe oak, and a large Monkey Puzzle tree, believed to be one of the tallest in England. Burncoose has remained in the possession of the Williams family, Charles, the present resident, belonging to the Caerhays line.

References: 18th, 19th (Hort. & Gen.) and 20th C; Illus.

GLADYS HOLMAN HOUSE, see Rosewarne

PENDARVES, Camborne

SW64 37 : EX104, GS352

Cornish pen + ?dar derivative = oak, pronounced penDARvis; Georgian house demolished 1955, Boteto Lodge, gate-piers, coach-house, and Ramsgate Lodge, each listed grade II; large park, west sloping 105-80m., on Mylor Beds metamorphosed slate and sandstone, with greenstone, granite and alluvium, and acid soil, in an AGLV with AMs (two crosses and an altar slab); rainfall 40-45", temperature zone C; farm and relict parkland.

The origin and development of the Pendarves estate are not well recorded. Certainly the family itself is ancient, and well connected by marriage, both to the Prideauxes and the Godolphins. They numbered among them a sheriff, in 1685, and a knight, in 1714. But like so many other families, the Pendarveses failed in the male line, and became extinct, the estate passing to the Revd Dr Stackhouse of Trehane, whose son Edward (who previously had adopted the name of Wynne with an inheritance) also took the name of Pendarves when he came into possession of the estate. The grounds, which are near Clowance, like that park, are enclosed by an encircling wall. The house, according to *Hitchins* was

> erected on a pleasing eminence, which commands an extensive view over the western part of the county. The southern front overlooks a large piece of artificial water, which considerably adds to the elegance of the whole.

To the east of the house, Gilbert wrote, there

> is a neat shrubbery, through which is carried a walk, opening into a once beautiful grotto, or fossilary, the roof of which, even in its present

31. Pendarves. The earliest representation of an ha-ha in Cornwall, with figures arranged as in an exedra. (Borlase, 1758: 14)

delapidated state, appears to represent a firmament of twinkling stars. These brilliant gems, which lined the whole interior, were collected by Mrs. Percival [née Pendarves], from the neighbouring mines [*c*.1747]; and when we consider that this grotto is still the grandest ornament belonging to Pendarves, it is truly surprising that it should be also the most ruinous. The building has been robbed of many of its most valuable ornaments, the door-way broken down, and the interior filled with lumber.

This sad state of affairs represents the condition during the period that the original Pendarves family was becoming extinct. A print in Borlase's *Natural History* (1758), however, indicates what at least they had been planning at this time, even if, as seems likely, it never wholly materialized. The scene is significant as recording, in structural detail, the earliest known ha-ha in Cornwall. The central third of the front exhibits an unusual and original feature which, if it had been backed by a wall or hedges, would qualify as an *exedra*. In this instance the magnificent view, which may be sampled near Four Lanes, on the B3297, was intended as a natural backcloth to the statuary. Here, then, we can see the full accomplishment of the eighteenth-century gentleman's dream of a 'prospect'. Alas, the scheme probably was never completed, else surely Gilbert would have mentioned the statues. Nevertheless, the estate was for a time to enjoy a reprieve. It had been included by Loudon among the ten Cornish gardens in his gazetteer of 1822, but this was updated in his *Gardener's Magazine* in 1837. 'Edward Wynne Pendarves', it was announced, has

> greatly improved this place, by extending the grounds, and giving them a park-like appearance; also by altering the approach on the south-west, and adding another at the north-east; which, with many acres of new plantations, adds considerably to the beauty of the place.

He also commenced an estate village at the adjoining Treslothan, with its own church and vicarage, where he is interred in a grand mausoleum overlooking the park. The garden was still being listed in the *Hort. Direct.* from 1889 to 1924, now under the name of W. Cole Pendarves (formerly Wood), his great-nephew who succeeded to the property. But by 1930 it rated no more than a passing mention by Thurston. Thus a few years later, after the Second World War, the estate went into a decline, the house was demolished, the timber sold off, and it is now desolate and forgotten.

References: 17th, 18th, 19th (Hort & Gen.) and 20th C; Illus.

PENGREEP, Gwennap

SW74 38 : LR204, EX104, GS352

Pengrypp, 1500; Cornish pen + krib = *ridge, pronounced* penGREEP; *house listed grade I, sundial, laundry and cottages, two separate late 18th C. stables, early-mid 19th C. coach house, 18th C. gate-piers and walling, each II; large grounds, on south-east side of a south-west, north-east valley, sloping 75-40m., on Mylor Series metamorphosed slate and sandstone, and alluvium, with acid soil, in a CNCS; rainfall 50-60", temperature zone C; private.*

Pengreep was originally a farm, to which the Beauchamp family transferred from Trevince in the early eighteenth century, to establish a new seat. They enlarged the house shortly afterwards. During the nineteenth century it was occupied by John Michael Williams (whose great-grandmother had been a Beauchamp), from some time before the 1850s, until in 1890 it became the residence of members of the Ford family who were related by marriage to the Beauchamps. In 1865 J.M. Williams extended the dwelling but, nevertheless, even though the present house derives from three periods, it was thought worthy of being given a grade I status by the English Heritage surveyors, since they considered it to be 'predominantly [a] mid C18 house and as such ... a fine and complete example.' Gilbert, with his usual keen eye, pin-pointed the most striking attractions in the grounds:

> The gardens, shrubberies, and plantations, are ... very fine, but its most interesting features are the lawn walks, ponds and waterfalls.

These similarly had impressed William Beckford of Fonthill, who visited Gwennap in 1787 while waiting for the weather to change before boarding ship at Falmouth. He wrote:

> in a sheltered valley, lies ... [Pengreep] wrapped up in shrubberies of laurel and laurestine. Copses of hazel and holly terminate the prospect on almost every side, and in the middle of the glen a broad, clear stream reflects the impending vegetation. This transparent water, after performing the part of a mirror before the house, forms a succession of waterfalls which glitter between slopes of the smoothest turf, sprinkled with daffodils; numerous flights of widgeon and Muscovy ducks were sprucing themselves in the edge of the stream, and two grave swans seemed highly to approve of its woody retired banks for the education of their progeny.

The lakes, with their cataracts, which appear to have been created from the stream at a later date than this note, lie along the south of the drive, the first near enough the road for it to have been used to water the horses of passing coaches. In the lawn on the northern side is a curious mound of uncertain origin, surmounted by an ancient surviving oak, which appears in a painting from the early 1800s. In the centre of the carriage ring in front of the house is a sundial with the Beauchamp arms, and to the north-east of the house are the foundations of a once-large conservatory, which looked out over a garden with regular formal paths, now a plantation of camellias and rhododendrons. The estate of Pengreep is adjacent to that of Burncoose. Even though Thurston included this among his select gardens he only cited one plant, and the garden was never listed in the *Hort. Direct*, nor has it been open in the more recent guides.

References: 18th, 19th (Hort. & Gen.), 20th C.

ROSEWARNE, Tehidy Road, Camborne, now Gladys Holman House

SW64 40 : EX104, GS352

Cornish ros + gwern = *alder-trees, pronounced* roseWARN; *house listed grade II*; small reduced grounds in centre of the town;* Gladys Holman House Residential Home.

Rosewarne is a Greek Revival-style house, built about 1815 for the Harris family, and restored in 1911 by James Miners Holman. The ancient manor house of Rosewarne is farther along Tehidy Road, and is now known as Rosewarne Wollas. William Harris, who was sheriff in 1773, had made his fortune mining. The property passed to his daughter but, so *Lake* informs us, 'unfortunately both her and her son [were] hopeless lunatics.' The description in *Hitchins* of the house in its early days is couched in a balanced and almost philosophic style:

> The situation of the house is not elevated, and consequently the prospects from it are not extensive; but its local beauties amply compensate for these deficiencies. The garden and walks with which the house is surrounded, exhibit fertility in her neatest attire. The house is rather conveniently large, than magnificently spacious; but its accommodations, that are adapted to every necessary purpose, render it a delightful habitation for such as prefer retirement and the charms of nature, to the artificial grandeur of tumultuous life.

Kilvert, the day before ending his Cornish visit in August 1870,

> walked round the pretty flower garden and fine kitchen garden [at Rosewarne] and visited the ferns and fruit houses.

Despite the apparent madness of the owners (which today might have been diagnosed less severely), in Capt. Frederick Townley Parker, who was deputed to look after their affairs, they had a good steward, for in 1920, when the estate was sold, he had increased it in size, by good management, to 4,000 acres (1,619 ha).

References: 17th, 18th, 19th (Gen.) and 20th C.

ROSEWARNE EXPERIMENTAL HORTICULTURE STATION, near Camborne

SW64 41 : *EX104, GS352*

Large grounds of 109 acres (44 ha), south-west facing, sloping 75-50m., on Mylor Series metamorphosed slates and sandstone, with acid soil; rainfall 40-45", temperature zone C; formerly Ministry of Agriculture, now the Duchy College, *opened 1983-5, 1987-8 CGOG.*

The Experimental Station was opened for the Ministry of Agriculture in December 1951, by the late Mr Fred Shepherd who was its first Director. It was established by the National Agricultural Advisory Service, formed in 1946, as one of around a dozen such places

> sited to cover the main climatic and soil conditions of England and Wales and all the main agricultural and horticultural enterprises. One was to be in the milder south west and it [was] ... Rosewarne, which became the centre for all the commercial horticultural crops of the region.

The site selected was a ridge of barren land, which had once formed part of the Rosewarne estate. The history and development of the advisory services, and in particular the work of the station, are too long to be described here, but they were admirably covered by Mr Shepherd himself in an article he contributed to the *Cornish Garden* of 1991, after the closure. The Government's financial restrictions were begun in 1977, leading eventually to the complete cessation of advisory work in 1989. The future of the site, by now fully equipped for trials and scientific work, was in doubt. In many counties over this period, parallel educational facilities in horticulture had been set up, but in this Cornwall had come late in the field, only recently commencing horticultural courses at the Duchy College. Providentially, this was to be in time to take over some of the facilities at Rosewarne, which for the present has, therefore, given the premises a reprieve.

References: 20th C.

SCORRIER HOUSE, near Redruth

SW72 43 : *LR204, EX104, GS352*

Scoria, 1321, Scorrier 1794; the derivation is uncertain, but probably not the Latin scoria, *a word which means dross or mine waste, pronounced SCORia; house 1910 listed grade II, 18th C. ha-ha II; garden of 5 acres (2 ha), parkland 20 acres (8.1 ha), and extensive woodland, at c. 115m. altitude, on Mylor Series slates and sandstone, and elvan intrusions, with acid soil, and AMs (two crosses); rainfall 45-50", temperature zone C; private, opened 1990-93 CGOG.*

John Williams II, grandson of John of Burncoose, who was described in *Lake* as 'one of the most extensive and most successful managers of mines, as well as adventurers, the county ever produced', built and planted Scorrier in 1778. The house was sited near to the areas of mining from which the Williamses were obtaining their wealth, and several observers point to the contrasts in the landscape, as, for instance, Warner:

> We ... flattered ourselves with a morning of much information and amusement at Scorrier House, the residence of John Williams, esq; which retires from the road to the right, about two miles from Redruth; and though placed in a country naked of picturesque beauty, enjoys, by the judicious management of the grounds around it, and the taste of their plantations, a very agreeable home view.

The 'information and amusement' came from 'viewing the extensive mineralogical collection', for which John Williams was well known. The gardens were to become even more celebrated as a consequence of their gardener, William Lobb (1809-63), who both worked here and, after being recommended by the Williams to Veitch's nursery, sent back plants and seed from his expeditions, including *Fitzroya plicata* (1849), *Sequoiadendron giganteum* (1853) - of which there was once an avenue at Scorrier - and *Thuja plicata* (1853).

The Pinetum, in a two-and-a-half acre (1 ha) walled garden where the collection is planted, therefore forms one of the more important features of the garden. The trees are set informally, in groups or singly, in a meadow with mown paths. There is also what was described in 1881 as 'one of the finest and best managed Camellia walls in England ... Its length is 380 ft., and it is 20 ft. high.'

Michael II, son of John Williams, inherited Scorrier, but lived at Trevince where he purchased Caerhays in 1854 (q.v.). His son, George, rebuilt Scorrier in its present form in about 1862, after a fire, greatly improving the grounds, but retaining the lawned terrace with a ha-ha, 100m. long and one metre high, built of uncoursed granite rubble. The front lawn was adorned by several handsome classical urns. George married Charlotte Mary Davey of Bochym (q.v.), and was probably responsible for persuading Veitch's nursery to release Lobb to assist Stephen Davey to restore the garden there. He also, in the early 1860s, purchased Lanarth from the Sandys (q.v.). Among the features at Scorrier are a fine conservatory, recently restored, a Folly Dairy, and a Quartz Grotto garden, with formal rose arches. A circular quatrefoil knot garden with a sundial in the centre, surrounded by beech hedging was planted in 1989. The garden was listed in the *Hort. Direct.* from at least 1870 to 1916, and was one of Thurston's select gardens. It remains in the possession of the Williams family.

References: 18th, 19th (Hort. & Gen.), 20th C.

TEHIDY PARK, near Camborne

SW64 43 : EX104, GS352

Tedintone, Domesday 1086, Tyhidy, 1236; Cornish, Dexter suggests from hedhy = to stretch out, i.e. extensive, pronounced TIDDY; the house, with pavilions designed by Thomas Edwards of Greenwich for John Pendarves Basset 1734-9, and conservatory of 1863, sold in 1917 as a hospital, but burnt down 1919 and rebuilt by 1922, listed grade II, south and east lodges c. 1790 II; over 1,000 acres (405 ha) in 19th C., north-west and south-east sloping, c. 85-60m., on Falmouth Series metamorphosed sandstone and slate to the north, and Mylor Series metamorphosed slate and sandstone to the south, with acid soil, in an AONB and HC, an AGSV and CNCS; rainfall 40-45", temperature zone C; the relict grounds, a Cornwall County Council Country Park and golf course; and the former NHS hospital buildings vacated in 1988 with 42 acres (17 ha) of the estate now developed as residences.

Although it has become sadly decayed in this century, Tehidy was important enough to be included among the ten Cornish gardens in Loudon's gazetteer of 1822. The Bassets, who may have come over with the Conqueror, are known to have obtained the manor by marriage in about the middle of the twelfth century, but the mansion, to designs by Edwards, was not begun until 1734, as a result of the family's increasing wealth from their mining interests. With the house came the laying out of the surrounding grounds, first under the direction of John Pendarves Basset (from *c.*1734 to 1739), followed by his nephew, Francis, who succeeded him. However, 'The Park', as it came to be known, was principally the work of Lord de Dunstanville (1757-1835). Gilbert's long description, together with several prints, is today the only means we have of knowing what it was like in the days of its glory.

> The southern side of the house opens into a lawn, which, after a gentle descent, falls into a flat, filled with a sheet of fresh water, the sides lined by deep foliage. From the grounds which rise on the opposite side of this lake, there is a fine view of the house, and a great portion of the park, with its beautiful plantations, and winding walks. The north side of the building is backed by a large mass of foliage, opening to a noble terrace, skirted by a rich variety of plants and evergreens. These are protected on either side, during a rapid ascent, by several rows of trees, whose interwoven branches, form a body capable of resisting the strongest winds. This terrace, with its delightful embellishments, formerly terminated at a Grecian temple, "Dedicated to Bacchus and social mirth." Over the pediment stood a figure of the jolly god, and at the entrance were the figures of two lions, carved in stone. Since the removal of this building, the vista opens suddenly upon a range of high lands, which once included a large portion of the deer park. It borders on the North Sea, and affords most extensive and diversified prospects. The whole extent of the park and ornamental grounds, is upwards of seven hundred acres. The entrance is at a neat lodge on the southern side, which is built in the rustic style [a thatched *cottage ornée*], and over-run with vegetation. The plantations exceed one hundred and thirty acres, ninety of which have been planted by the present nobleman, and are in a very flourishing state.

The Tehidy plantations were raised on a once barren and exposed site. Lord de Dunstanville described his method in the *Annals of Agriculture* of 1794:

> I have been planting for 15 years ... I find the pinaster is the tree that answers best, both because it penetrates through the bed of spar stone more easily than any other tree, and also that it stands our north-west winds which the Scotch will not. I use the pinaster as Lord Fife does the Scotch Fir, as a nurse for other trees. Under its shelter I plant silver spruce and Weymouth firs, larches, Spanish Chestnut, oaks, planes, beech, lime, birch, sycamore etc. The spruce, larch and Weymouth are hardly to be raised except in sheltered situations. Of the forest trees the plane, ash and sycamore answers best. I plant my pinasters at two years old, and two or three years after I put in the other trees. When I make a plantation I carefully preserve the furze, fir, etc., as of great use in sheltering the trees. Never destroy the weeds, as they keep the roots of the trees moist, which is a great object in our dry soil. [*Quoted from Tangye, 1984*].

32. Tehidy in 1781, before being redesigned by Lord De Dunstanville; here with the deer park in front and the temple on the extreme right. (Watts 1781)

This advice was widely circulated and followed by other estates. But while the gardens and Lord de Dunstanville's skill were admired, the design was not without its critics. Edward Luckhurst, writing in 1878, though not unaware of his achievements, informed his readers that he was 'going to indulge in a little faultfinding ...':

> One would like to see more clumps, more grouping, more individuality in the features of the grounds themselves, and instead of a series of long interminable stretches of wide walks with parallel bands of turf on which are the specimens, an occasional cosy nook formed by a semicircular belt of trees and shrubs, with shrub clumps out on the turf; winding walks leading to circular enclosures formed in a similar way, but not having a heterogeneous collection of shrubs upon the lawn, but with one or more specimens of a distinct species or several species of the same genus to impart a distinct character to that particular lawn ... Another feature which might be introduced here with the happiest effect is an avenue. From the principal entrance a drive runs in a straight line through the park for a considerable distance without overlooking any agreeable prospect or feature of interest, and which moreover in stormy weather must be still more bleak and dreary here.

These criticisms are significant, not so much for Luckhurst's opinions, as for the light they throw upon the nature of Dunstanville's design. But we have reached a point where we must echo his concluding remark that, 'Here I [too] must leave Tehidy, not that the subject is exhausted ...'. Those whose interest has been aroused will find their curiosity satisfied by Michael Tangye's two excellent books, although there is, perhaps, space to mention one or two other features, such as the statue of the Antonine (Farnese) Flora in Coade stone which used to stand over the entrance to the house; the extensive kennels and dogs' cemetery; an ice-house near the lake dug in 1781; the designs by Nesfield for a parterre perhaps never executed; the extremely handsome courtyard gates which once led into the

33. Tregullow. Many of the trees in the parkland at this time, only twenty years after the house was built, had not yet reached maturity. (Twycross, 1846: 84)

park, and 'Lady Bassett's Retreat' restored as the Gazebo. There also survive two pretty thatched *cottage ornée* lodges at the south and east entrances. The garden was listed in the *Hort. Direct.* from at least 1870 to 1924, but by 1930 had declined too far to figure among Thurston's select number.

References: 17th, 18th, 19th (Hort. & Gen.) and 20th C; Illus; M.Tangye, Carne Brea, Redruth, *1981;* Tehidy and the Bassets, Redruth, *1984.*

TREGULLOW, near Scorrier

SW72 43 : LR201, EX104, GS352   OPEN

Cornish, James suggests tre + kellyow = *groves, pronounced* treGULLo; *house listed grade II, lodge and gate posts II; grounds of 15 acres (6 ha), east facing slope 105-85m., on Mylor Series metamorphosed slate and sandstone, with acid soil; rainfall 45-50", temperature zone C; private house with relict grounds, open 1985-8, 1992-8 CGOG, one Sunday in May for charity.*

The classical style house at Tregullow was built in 1826 for William (after 1866 Sir William) Williams, the fourth son of John Williams II of Scorrier, on his marriage, but has since been somewhat altered and reduced in size. It has attached on the south-east corner a fine Victorian conservatory of five bays with a three-bay canted end, ornamented with coloured glass, and 'an elegant internal iron frame'. To the rear there is an unusual ice-house, in the form of a tunnel. The park, which is edged by railings, on the north is separated from the house by a low granite balustrade. The principal entrance lies to the south, where there is a small lodge with gate-piers 'linked by unusual stone railings with narrow round-headed openings and rounded copings.' The story goes that on one occasion a note was found affixed to this front gate, which read:

> Pray, Sir Billy, do not weep.
> We've stolen one of your fat sheep.
> For you are rich and we are poor,
> And when that's gone we'll come for more.

There are two walled gardens to the south-east, cut into the valley side, one of which is of an unusual oval shape, although both are now unused; the other can be seen from the public

34. Tregullow. Part of the Yew Walk. (G. 1891: 237)

road which passes north from the Lodge. The grounds consist principally of a wooded valley with sheltered slopes, planted with many fine trees, of which the *Saxegotha conspicua*, Prince Albert's Yew, introduced by William Lobb in 1847, is perhaps the most notable. The extensive shrubberies, as is common in Cornwall, are mainly planted with rhododendrons and camellias, with some acers and magnolias. But one of the more striking features of Tregullow had been the Yew walks, which were extolled by C.A.V. Conybeare, MP, then resident there, writing in the *Garden* of 1891:

> In the garden here is an avenue 60 paces long, bordered on the left with a thick hedge of English Yews at least 20 feet high, and on the right with some Irish Yews, many of which attain a height of nearly 30 feet. There is also a second avenue some 90 paces in length, sheltered by a line of thirty-eight splendid Yews standing so closely together as to form practically a continuous wall or belt. Almost every one of these is from 25 feet to 30 feet high, and many of them have a circumference of something like 24 feet at about 5 feet from the ground. It will thus be seen that their proportions are very fine.

Only one of these avenues is now intact, the other having lost one side. The local Gwennap Horticultural Society, established in 1858, at one time held its annual August Show at Tregullow, whose gardens were listed in the *Hort. Direct.* from at least 1870 until 1891, and figured among Thurston's selected estates. The property has remained in the Williams family, although Sir William's son Frederick lived for a time near their Foundry at Perran-ar-worthal, at Goonvrea (q.v.), while his youngest son, Richard, married Georgiana Sophia, daughter of the Revd Thomas Phillpotts of Porthgwidden (q.v), and his grandson, Robert, the daughter of E.B. Beauchamp of Trevince (q.v.), thus following a fashion among gardening families for forming alliances. Tregullow, like other Cornish gardens, suffered neglect during and after the Second World War, but since the 1970s there has been an active programme of restoration and replanting.

References: 19th (Hort. & Gen.) and 20th C; Illus.

TREVINCE, Gwennap

SW73 40 : LR204, EX104, GS352

Trefensa 1277, Trevince 1768; Cornish, James suggests tre + hins = path, pronounced treVINCE; house remodelled c. 1870 with parts from 17th and 18th C. listed grade II; medium to large estate, on a south-east facing slope 85-60m., on Mylor Series slate and sandstone, elvan, and alluvium to the south, with acid soil; rainfall 45-50", temperature zone C; private.

Trevince, although originally one of the largest and most important holdings in the parish, was not itself a manor, but formed part of the Pensignance or Trevarth manors. The earliest reference is to a Robert de Trefyns in 1281, the Beauchamps coming into possession through marriage to a daughter of the Trefyns in the fifteenth or sixteenth centuries. In the early eighteenth century, however, they chose to transfer their seat to Pengreep, leasing off Trevince, which eventually was taken up by Michael II, second son of John Williams II of Scorrier whose great-great-grandmother had been a Beauchamp. According to Gilbert, he 'considerably improved' the property, but upon his death in 1858, Trevince was again occupied by a member of the Beauchamp family. This was E. Beauchamp Tucker, a descendant in the female line, who changed his surname to Beauchamp. He continued the process of improvement, so that ten years later, *Lake* was able to describe Trevince as 'pleasantly situated near the church,' with a house that 'has latterly [i.e. in 1866] been almost reconstructed, and is now [a] handsome and commodious residence ...' where one of the farm buildings had been surmounted by a clock. In *Murray*, whose interest was so often more in industry and antiquities than in horticulture, the reader was advised that, 'The gardens [were] well worthy of a visit. Here camellias of all shades flourish in the open air throughout the year,' which was evidently written at a time when camellias were still believed to be tender plants. Since Trevince was listed in the *Hort. Direct.*, probably from before 1870 until 1924, such visits would have been welcomed, and its continuing reputation won it a place among Thurston's select gardens. Howard Longueville Dillon Beauchamp, who inherited the estate from his father Howard Charles in 1964, extended the collection by the addition of large-leaved rhododendrons, but maintained an interest in camellias until his death in 1988. He was succeeded by his daughter, Vanessa, and she and her husband, besides replacing the old trees, are introducing new plants, to give the garden a more year-round interest.

References: 17th, 18th, 19th (Hort. & Gen.) and 20th C.

SUPPLEMENTARY LISTS

LESSER KNOWN HISTORIC GARDENS

Basset Villa, Basset Road, Camborne

SW64 39 : EX104, GS352

Named after the Bassets of Tehidy; house listed grade II; small garden at 85m. altitude on metamorphosed greenstone, with acid soil; rainfall 40-45", temperature zone C; now the St Claire Residential Home, with relict garden.

This house, in a once fashionable Camborne street, was listed open in the *Hort. Direct.* for 1908 as the residence of Mrs Bickford. There were several houses in this road recorded in Kelly's *Directory* as 'Basset Villas', but this was generally known at the time as the 'White House'. Its interest is principally as a representative town-house garden, of which there were several in Camborne, many larger, and some more elaborate.

References: 20th C.

Penventon, West End, Redruth

SW69 41 : EX104, GS352

Cornish pen + fenten = spring, pronounced penVENTon; small grounds at 115m. altitude, on Mylor Series metamorphosed slate and sandstone, with greenstone; rainfall 40-45", temperature zone C; large hotel complex, with residual garden.

Among our sources Penventon is only mentioned in Twycross, with an illustration, as having 'well planted' lands. This substantial house was that of the Steward to the Tehidy estate, and it was from here that, in the 1850s, John Penberthy Magor moved to Lamellen (q.v.), which his wife had inherited.

References: 19th C (Gen.); Illus.

Polstrong, near Camborne

SW62 39 : EX104, GS352

Cornish pol + *strongk = dung, pronounced polSTRONG; house listed grade II; small to medium grounds, south sloping 60-50m., on Mylor Beds, metamorphosed slate, with acid soil; rainfall 40-45", temperature zone C; relict garden, private.

The entrance to Polstrong is situated about a mile and a half from Camborne along the old A30. Although the gate-posts leading down to the house through a tree lined drive survive, the two plain lodges have been demolished, to be replaced by two matching private dwellings. The immediate grounds are not large, but the land drops away steeply to a watery valley which has been used as a trout farm. There is an impressive 'two-storey aisled conservatory' attached to the house, large enough to accommodate tall exotic trees, and the walled garden has a summerhouse with stained glass windows at the entrance, as well as an attractive small glasshouse on the far wall. Polstrong was recorded open in the *Hort. Direct.* of 1908 as the residence of J.R. Daniell, and in 1916 of Capt. R.A. Thomas, in whose family it remained until 1997.

References: 20th C.

Tolvean House, West End, Redruth

SW69 41 : EX104, GS352

Cornish toll = hole + vean, pronounced tolVEAN; small garden, at 115m. altitude, on Mylor Series metamorphosed slates and sandstones, with acid soil; rainfall 40-45", temperature zone C; NHS hospital, with residual garden.

Tolvean House is adjacent to, and may have been built on grounds originally belonging to Penventon to designs by James Hicks. It was recorded as open in the *Hort. Direct.* from 1889 until 1924 as the residence of Alfred Lanyon, a JP, and member of a prominent family in the town. William Dallimore, from Kew Gardens, judged it in 1904, to be

> one of the tidiest and best kept places I saw in Cornwall. Throughout the whole place there was scarcely a weed to be seen, while the collection of plants indoor and out was good and remarkable for good cultivation. Mr. Bowden, the head gardener, is between seventy and eighty years of age, but is full of projects for the improvement of the place as any young man would be.

Nothing but a lawn with perimeter trees remains.

References: 19th C. (Hort.).

ADDITIONAL CONTEMPORARY GARDEN

Treskewes, Trewithen Moor, near Stithians*

SW72 37 : LR204, EX104, GS

Cornish tre + scawen = elder + *ys = place of, pronounced treSKEWS; 1 acre (0.4 ha) garden; rainfall 50-60", temperature zone C; opened 1989 CGOG and NGS; currently on the market.

A very damp garden begun in 1976 on the site of an old slaughter house, hence with rich soil, sloping down to the Trethellen river. Primulas and Himalayan plants became a speciality and were grown in great variety. Penny Black also has a reputation for dried flower arrangements, about which she has written and appeared on television.

References: Penny Black, A Passion for Flowers, a Celebration of a Cottage Garden, with inspirational ideas using fresh, dried, and pressed flowers, 1992; and five other books on pressed flowers and pot-pourri.

3
Truro and Falmouth

1. TRURO

Truro owes its origin to its position at the confluence of four rivers, the Calenick, Kenwyn, Allen and Tresillian, and to the convergence of important roads from the west (along Kenwyn Street), the north (along Pydar Street), and the east (along St Clement's Street). Although, until very recently, never the county town, which, because of the difficulty of communication with England, was sited first at Launceston, and then Bodmin, it has gradually through the centuries increased in importance. It was not a Domesday town site, but seems to have come into existence during the twelfth century under the care and protection of Richard de Lucy, the feudal Lord of Kenwyn. The present city has spread into two adjoining manors, that of Newham, once a rival, and the Duchy manor of Moresk. The wealth of the town was based upon the coinage of tin, the weekly market, an annual fair, and overseas trade. Now that Lemon Quay has been filled in as a car-park, and the town extended inland, it is perhaps difficult to imagine Truro as an important harbour, although the river remains tidal up to this point. By the later eighteenth century the town had grown to become the social centre of Cornwall, with its own theatre, philharmonic society, assembly rooms and, in Lemon Street, town houses modelled on those in Bath. Like that city, it began to attract many residents during the 'season', who also possessed country estates. By the Quay there are still several fine Georgian houses, which were built for wealthy and prominent Truro families: The Mansion House, Prince's House, The Great House and the Old Mansion House, some of which once had quite elaborately designed gardens.

As in Helston and other boroughs, the Anglo-Saxon influence at first was quite strong, so that around the town there were open fields divided into strips. On two of these 'stitches', during the mid-nineteenth century, were built Alverton, the house of a banker, and Tremorvah, the house of a vice-Warden of the Stannaries. Across from them, the estate of Tregolls had come by marriage into the possession of Admiral Spry of Place Manor on the Roseland, who was then able to retire there in the winter, more to enjoy the social life than for business. Later in the nineteenth century, as the town expanded outwards, Lemon Street was extended into the Falmouth Road, where new large Victorian villas were erected, of which Glanmor is but one example.

As Truro increasingly became a centre during Georgian and Victorian times, so links were forged with the surrounding estates. The Enys family, whose estates were nearer Falmouth than Truro, were nonetheless prominent in the business and shipping at Truro, whereas William, son of the wealthy Lewis Charles Daubuz, who had leased the Enys Mansion House and was Mayor of Truro, bought an already established estate at Killiow. Whatever influence Lord Falmouth might wield in Truro from his estate at Tregothnan, he derived from his long ancestry and widespread interests, whereas Trelissick, at a greater distance, was being built up by 'guinea-a-minute' Daniell, one of Truro's *nouveau riche*.

These factors have perforce influenced the selection of properties for inclusion in this section. For instance, Carclew might seem more appropriately grouped with other houses in the Perran-ar-worthal district, which clearly look towards Falmouth, except that in the days of its greatest horticultural reputation, it was the home of the Lemon family. Their name, given to a Street and Quay in Truro however, proclaims otherwise, that their business interests lay in a different direction.

ALVERTON HOUSE, Truro

SW83 45 : *EX105, GS352*

Alwaretone, *Domesday 1086, manor name of Penzance; Old English* Alward, *a Saxon landowner* + tun = *town, pronounced* ALLverton; *Convent, with clock-tower entrance 1898, designed by Ninian Comper, and the Chapel 1910, by E.H .Sedding, listed grade II*; small grounds, south-east sloping from c. 25m., on Falmouth Series sandstone and slate, with acid soil; rainfall 40-45", temperature zone C; now the* Alverton Manor Hotel, *with relict garden.*

Alverton was built in the 1830s by the banker William Tweedy, on the site of one of the medieval-type strip fields owned by notable Truro families. He named it Alverton, the manor name of Penzance, because of his relationship with the Boase family there. He was treasurer of the Royal Horticultural Society of Cornwall until his death in 1859, after which the *Hort. Direct.* recorded the garden as still being opened by his widow in 1870. It is at present somewhat reduced in size, first by the sale of the site for St Paul's Church School in 1895 (now the Tregolls Manor Residential Home), and then by the widening of Tregolls Road in 1967. There was formerly a lodge to the north of the drive, and a small lake to the south fed by a stream that at one time ran down the hill. Behind the house there is a walled garden with a greenhouse, both of which are now unused. An early map shows paths and a structure along the northern boundary, which may have been a summerhouse. Several mature trees survive, among them a much admired 'cut-leaved' beech (*Fagus sylvatica var. heterophylla*), and large arboreal rhododendrons. In 1883 the property became the Convent of the Epiphany, after which the building was much enlarged, but in 1988, when the Convent moved to Copeland House (formerly Lis Escop), after the Cathedral School closed, it was opened as an hotel.

References: 19th (Hort. & Gen.) and 20th C.

BOSCAWEN PARK, Truro

SW83 43 : *EX105, GS352*   OPEN

Cornish bos + scawen = *elder tree, pronounced* bosCAWN; *originally intended to be about 23 acres (9.3 ha) at river level, on Falmouth Series sandstone and slates, with acid soil; rainfall 40-45", temperature zone C; open at all times.*

The need for an area in Truro for recreation was realized as early as 1864, when a memorial was presented to the City Council:

> The undersigned believe the health and comfort of the people of Truro would be greatly promoted by the establishment of a pleasure ground, ... your memorialists believe the mud lands between Waterloo Quay and Sunny Corner offer an attainable site for such a pleasure ground, where from 20-30 acres of waste land might be reclaimed and converted from a nuisance to a means of health and recreation.

Little was done until the late 1880s, when Lord Falmouth donated the foreshore between Waterloo Quay and the Mill Stream, and the Duchy sold that between there and Sunny Corner for a nominal sum. The park was designed by F.W. Meyer, the landscape gardener at Veitch's Exeter Nurseries. The *Gardeners' Chronicle* in 1894 wrote:

> The plan shows extensive areas of turf devoted to sports, and breadth and openness are not lost in a too great amount of tree-planting.

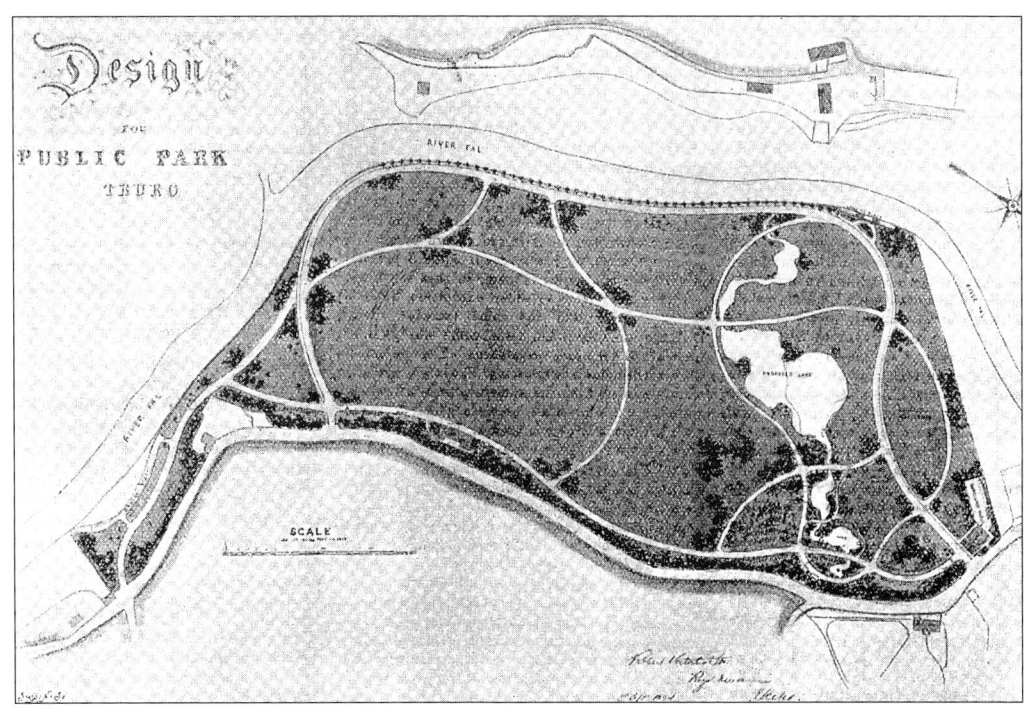

35. Boscawen Park. The original design by F.W. Meyer of Veitch's Exeter Nursery, as printed in the Gardeners' Chronicle. *(1894: ii. 730)*

The completion of the scheme depended on reclaiming land from the river, which by 1910 had not advanced beyond five acres (2 ha). As late as 1934, the *Gardening Illustrated*, even though including a list of trees obtained from Mr Ernest Allen the gardener, described the park as 'still in the making, only a portion at present being complete'. The slow progress, and subsequent developments, have somewhat modified Meyer's original plan, although there are ornamental bedding schemes and a lake near the road.

References: 19th (Hort.) and 20th C.

BOSVIGO HOUSE, Bosvigo Lane, Truro

SW81 45 : *EX104-5, GS352*   OPEN*

Cornish, Dexter suggests bos + Wiga = *proper name, pronounced* bosVIGo, 'I' *as 'eye'; house listed grade II; garden 3 acres (1.2 ha) on Falmouth Series sandstone and slate, with acid soil; rainfall 40-45", temperature zone C; garden and small nursery, open 1987-98 CGOG, 1987, 1991, 1994-5, 1998 NGS, Wednesday to Saturday, March through September.*

Bosvigo at the commencement of the eighteenth century was the property of the family of Sholl (who were also at Condurra, q.v.), from whom it was purchased in 1741 by the grandfather of Sir William Lemon of Carclew. 'The house,' so *Lake* informs us,

> which is situated in an agreeable little valley about half-a-mile from Truro, was built by Francis Benallack, Esq., who afterwards sold it to Henry Rosewarne, Esq., M.P. for Truro ... who enlarged the buildings ... [it] is now [1868] occupied by John R. Paull, Esq., solicitor.

Paull's family remained there for the best part of a century. The present house has been reduced in size, isolating a handsome Victorian conservatory which, with its plants, has become a feature of the garden. Around the house are enclosed walled areas, each with a different plan, planted particularly with herbaceous beds for colour and foliage effect. On the southern side of the house the sloping woodlands have walks among many unusual plants. Bosvigo is exceptional in Cornwall for its range of herbaceous plants, and for their associations.

References: 19th (Gen) and 20th C.

CARCLEW, Perran-ar-worthal

SW78 38 : *EX104-5, GS352*   OPEN

Cornish ?cruc = *barrow, hillock* + lyw = *colour, pronounced* carCLEW; *house ruins listed grade II*, chapel, coach house, barn, each II*, lodge 1871, garden walls and terraces, each II; garden listed grade II; very large estate, with garden of 5 acres (2 ha) east sloping 85-25m, on Mylor Series slate and sandstone, with 'acid loam, limey near house in kitchen garden', in an AONB, and an AGHV with an AM (barrow); rainfall 40-45", temperature zone C; grounds and garden part relict, and in divided ownership; open 1983-98 CGOG, 1987, 1991-8 NGS, last Sunday in April, and all in May for charity, or by appointment.*

Carclew was, until the reign of Henry IV, the property of the Daunger family, who brought it by marriage to the Bonithons, who continued there until in 1677, the male line having died out, it came to Samuel Kempe. 'The said Mr. Kempe', so Tonkin informs us,

> built a noble house here, which he did not live to finish, and had laid such a plan for avenues, gardens, &c, as when brought to perfection would have made it one of the pleasantest seats in the county.

The plan may have been preserved on a map of Trefusis by Crow and Marsh, dated 1764. The property, after at first reverting to the Bonithons on his wife's death, was eventually sold to the 'great' William Lemon in 1749. Although of humble birth, he had become wealthy by industry and skill in mining, engaging Thomas Edwards of Greenwich (who was active in designing West Country houses) to enlarge Kempe's house 'by the addition of colonnades, offices, &c. [rendering] it one of the most uniform and elegant buildings belonging to the county of Cornwall,' as is seen in Borlase's print of 1758. Gilbert continued:

> The ground on the north and west sides of the buildings, is occupied by a fine shrubbery and by beautiful gardens, which, with the ponds and walks, are remarkable for a combination of natural and artificial beauties, and wear a soft luxuriant tint, even in the most dreary seasons of the year. The park and plantations occupy a circumference of several miles, and afford an excellent range for deer, of which there are a great abundance. A considerable portion of the lands is also laid out in a sheep walk, and pasturage for cattle. The principal entrance is at a handsome lodge, near the road leading from Truro to Penryn. The drive from hence to the house, is through an avenue, nearly a mile in length, shaded with lofty foliage, (chiefly evergreens) and lined on each side with a hedge of laurel, that seems to indicate an everlasting spring.

Robson, in 1874, described the drive in not dissimilar terms in the *Journal of Horticulture*, but entry is now more usually made along the short-

36. Carclew. The house in the 1750s, as designed by Thomas Edwards of Greenwich. (Borlase, 1758: 11)

er route higher up. In Gilbert's time, the property was in the possession of Sir William Lemon (the grandson of the original owner), who was responsible for laying out the garden and grounds as described in the article. He was followed on his death by his son, Sir Charles Lemon, who became chairman and a founder member of the Royal Horticultural Society of Cornwall. He was fortunate in his appointment of William Beattie Booth as his gardener, for Booth had been working at the London Horticultural Society's new garden at Chiswick under Lindley, where he became an expert on camellias, supplying the text for Alfred Chandler's *Illustrations and Descriptions of the Camelliae*, 1831. While at Carclew, he also wrote plant notes in the *Botanical Register*, and articles in the *Gardeners' Chronicle*. He was appointed assistant secretary to the London Horticultural Society in 1858, after leaving Carclew, but had to retire through ill health.

Sir Charles was himself a keen plant collector, and in 1837 had proposed offering a silver medal to the Packet commander who introduced the largest number of new plants. Although no winner was announced, he entered a list of his own collections from seamen in the succeeding *Report*. He also corresponded with the Hookers, and was one of the sponsors of Joseph Hooker's Himalayan expedition. He had engaged as his gamekeeper Joseph Lobb, the father of William and Thomas Lobb, who thus were able to gain early experience at Carclew which was to stand them in good stead when later they became plant collectors for Veitch's nursery at Exeter. *Murray* is alone in suggesting that Lucombe had also been gardener here, but in this he is almost certainly mistaken, even though Elwes may have written that one of the Lucombe oaks at Carclew was 'the largest he had ever seen'. Booth, indeed, had described one of these oaks in 1851 as 'about 76 years old', which Sir Charles believed to be one of the originals.

Carclew was among the ten gardens in Loudon's gazetteer of 1822, and it was regularly named among accounts of new and exotic plants from that time onwards. The main gardens were arranged in a dell surrounding the 'Higher Pond' which stood above the 'Wheel Pond' from which water was raised to the house. On the western slopes of this valley were two terraces. An illustration of the formal garden and greenhouse on one of these terraces as it was in 1874 has been included here, since this is a type of bedding not usually associated with Carclew today, although Robson described other formal areas in his article. The estate had by then passed to John Hearle Tremayne (see Heligan), who had married Lemon's sister, and it was listed in the *Hort. Direct.* from at least 1870 until 1924 in their family name. Tragically the magnificent house at Carclew, to which additional colonnades had been added at each side, was gutted by fire in 1934, and since then the estate has gradually

37. Carclew. One of the terraces above the Higher Pond, in the late nineteenth century. (J. Hort., 1874: 405)

been colonized by smaller dwellings. The parkland in front of the ruins is now in the grounds of Trevorick (q.v.). A new Carclew House was built by Jack Siley in 1963 at the top of the old terraces, which are now divided into six compartments, in one of which is an interesting pillar sundial. They lead down to the old Pond Garden, to which he added a rotunda, where many notable trees have survived. The greater part of the main garden area, as distinct from the estate, is therefore still owned and maintained as an intact whole.

References: 17th, 18th, 19th (Hort. & Gen.) and 20th C; Illus; W.B. Booth, Cottager's Manual ..., *Truro 1834;* History around the Fal, *part V, The Fal Local History Group, 1990: 20-51.*

COPELAND COURT, see Lis Escop

KILLIGANOON, Carnon Downs

SW 80 40 : EX104-5, GS352

Kellygnohan, *Assize Plea Rolls 1296; Cornish* kelli = *a little grove* + *cnow = nut-trees, pronounced* KILLYgaNOON; *house and adjoining garden walls listed grade II; medium size grounds (originally about 140 acres (56.66 ha)) in north-west, south-east sloping valley, 100-40m., on Falmouth Series sandstone and slates, and the Portscatho Series below the garden, with acid soil; rainfall 40-45", temperature zone C; house private, but with a leisure centre. The garden is not open, but a public footpath runs above the western edge.*

Killiganoon was built in about 1750 for Richard Hussey, a barrister who became Attorney-General. His elder sister married the father of the Revd Robert Walker of St Winnow (q.v.), and his third sister married the grandfather of Sir Richard Hussey-Vivian, first Baron Vivian of Glynn (q.v.). After his decease in 1770 the estate passed to a Mr Dagge, an attorney, from a notable Truro family, and afterwards to Admiral Spry of Place, Antony, 'who considerably enlarged the house and improved the plantations.' In 1874-5 the house was slightly remodelled by James Hicks after a fire the year before. Gilbert wrote that:

It stands nearly at the head of a singular valley, which opens with peculiar remoteness, between two rising hills, and faces a paddock, the sides of which are lined with charming foliage. The whole is hidden from the eye, unless at a near approach, and when seen, it presents a most striking contrast to the more elevated bleak lands which compose the adjoining plains.

The fronting rectangular 'paddock' was walled in the eighteenth century, to form the principal garden, which now leads down by steps to a second level. Beyond this the 'singular valley' encloses a sequence of seven small lakes. The gardens were renovated between 1960 and 1984, and are being replanted by the present owner, who is also clearing and opening the lakes. Thurston, who included this among his select gardens in 1930, cited a Lucombe oak in his lists.

References: 18th, 19th (Gen.) and 20th C.

KILLIOW, Playing Place
SW80 42 : EX104-5, GS352

Cornish kelli (pl) = groves, pronounced KILLio; house and coach-house each listed grade II*, seven other buildings II, terrace walling, and kitchen garden walls each II, well head II; very large estate, south-east facing slope 85-40m., on Portscatho Series sandstone and slate, with acid soil; rainfall 40-45", temperature zone C; house private, coach-house etc. converted to residential apartments, grounds - golfing range, and agricultural. Has been on the market since 1996.

Killiow is an estate of some antiquity, being known before the time of Norden (1597) as successively the seat of the Killiows, Vivians, Tredenhams (in Norden's time), Haweises and Gwatkins. Robert Lovell Gwatkin, who was married to the niece and co-heiress of Sir Joshua Reynolds, 'almost rebuilt the mansion, increased and improved the extensive gardens and plantations, and made the whole into a handsome and tasteful modern residence.' It was he who was responsible for the serpentine (or crinkle-crankle) eastern wall of the kitchen garden, which is a rare and probably unique example in the county, and for the later terrace walling, which 'follows the contour and continues beyond' the house 'to the north and east looping round the kitchen garden from the parkland/farmland below, like a ha-ha' (EH listing). The house was again remodelled, around 1850, possibly to designs of Paxton. There is an early description of the garden by Thomas Pettigrew, of Cardiff Castle, who in 1879 was accompanied by the gardener, Mr. Braund,

> through the plant houses and over the grounds and gardens, which were well cultivated. We noticed some fine specimens of Rhododendrons and Coniferae in the pleasure grounds, and a large raised bed of the hybrid tuberous-rooted Begonias in full bloom and in luxuriant health in the flower garden ... My friends were surprised and much pleased to see the decided improvements that had been made on this estate and its surroundings since their first acquaintance with it some thirty years ago. Much of the land which was then barren waste is now crowned with thriving plantations and fertile fields. Agricultural improvements here have not been forgotten; the land has been thoroughly drained and well cultivated, and is now bearing fine crops. On the lawn opposite the mansion a party of workers were busy making a second crop of hay, not by female labour [!], however, but by machinery.

This description calls for some comment. In the first place, it would seem that Gwatkin's 'improvements' might not have been as 'extensive' as Gilbert had suggested, or that there had been substantial later development after the estate passed to the Daubuz family. The large plant-houses, however, have now gone, their beds being occupied by tender outdoor plants, but Thurston (in 1930) was still able to cite several conifers, which were also listed among notable trees at the RHS Conifer Conference in 1931.

The references to agriculture are of particular interest, since it has been suggested that Killiow may be regarded as a Cornish example of a *ferme ornée*, or ornamented farm, in which parkland and farming are integrated. The Revd John Daubuz, Rector of Creed, who had purchased the estate in 1860 from William Daubuz, was clearly as interested in produce as in ornamentals, for it was reported in 1894 that he had organized an inspection of fruits at Killiow, from Bunyard's Nursery, and from his own stock, among them named varieties of eight apples, two cherries, fourteen pears, and ten plums, with between ten and twenty trees of each variety. The garden was listed, at least from 1870 in the *Hort. Direct.*, during his time, and after the turn of the century by his son, John Claude Daubuz, who was a prominent figure in the county, and owner of the Carvedras Tin Smelting Works in Truro. After his death in 1915, Killiow disappeared from the *Directory*. More recently the estate passed to the Penrose family, and is partly used as a golfing range.

References: 17th, 18th, 19th (Hort. & Gen.) and 20th C.

LAMORRAN RECTORY
SW87 41 : EX105, GS352

Lannmoren *969*; *Cornish* lan + St Morenna, *pronounced* laMORRan; *extinct garden on steep south-west facing slope, from c. 55m., on Portscatho Series sandstone and slate, with acid soil, in an AONB, and in part an AGSV; rainfall 35-40", temperature zone C; the remodelled parsonage was transferred to Tresillian in the 1890s, and the garden abandoned.*

The rectory garden at Lamorran, once one of the most celebrated of Cornish gardens, was a bare field in 1850, a 'wilderness' in 1930, and today has virtually disappeared without trace. So passes the glory of this world. The Hon. and Revd John Townshend Boscawen was the younger brother of Evelyn, Sixth Viscount Falmouth, who was named after the famous diarist and landscape designer John Evelyn (1620-1702). He was brought up in the rectory at Wooton, near Dorking, where Evelyn had helped to redesign his brother George's garden in 1652. Roy Strong saw Evelyn as opening a new chapter in English gardening: 'the garden [became] ...a living instance of man's understanding of the processes of nature ... Horticulture and the myriad phenomena of nature are studied for themselves.'

Lamorran had been described similarly as 'one of those gardens teeming with plants of great horticultural interest and the attraction of which was not the decorative style of gardening but the intrinsic value of the lessons that might be learned there.' Evelyn had been one of the first to be elected to the Royal Society: Boscawen was elected a Fellow of the Linnaean Society in 1886. Edward Luckhurst, writing in 1877, was impressed at the way Boscawen, by his 'great and pioneer work' had solved 'many a horticultural problem, evolving lessons of ... value'. 'Expediency might suggest' a barrier of sturdy fast-growing trees as a shelter-belt, he continued,

> but correct taste never would agree to it, for the work would clash with every line and curve of nature. The difficulty was overcome skilfully and well by making tree-clothed banks from the natural slope at an irregular acute angle up the valley, so as to offer the least amount of resistance to the wind while it turned it away past the garden completely.

Evelyn had built for himself at Wooton 'a little study over a Cascade, to passe my Melencholy houres shaded there with Trees, & silent Enough ...'. Boscawen too valued the quiet seclusion of his remote garden. His great friend Capt. Pinwill, at that time creating a remarkable garden at Trehane, told how Boscawen, hearing his approach, hid in the broom cupboard, whereupon his wife rapped on the door, saying, 'You can come out now Boscawen, it's only Pinwill'. Lamorran has returned to a wilder nature than was ever intended, but many of the valuable plants were rescued, and are growing at Tregothnan, the family seat. This was one of Thurston's select gardens.

38. Lamorran Rectory. The garden with its 'tree clothed banks [on] the natural slope at an irregular acute angle up the valley'. (G. Ch. 1881: i. 751)

References: 17th, 19th (Hort. & Gen.) and 20th C; R. Strong, The Renaissance Garden, *1979: 216, 221.*

LIS ESCOP, now Copeland Court, Kenwyn, Truro

SW82 45 : *EX104-5, GS352*

Cornish lis = mansion + escop = bishop, *pronounced* LIS EScop; *small garden, on south-east facing slope, 70-45m., on Portscatho Series sandstone and slate, with acid soil; rainfall 40-45", temperature zone C; now the* Convent of the Epiphany, *with extinct/relict grounds.*

The creation of a Cornish diocese in 1877 necessitated the provision of a suitable house for the new bishop. Kenwyn Vicarage, described by Wesley, who had lodged there, as 'a house fit for a nobleman; and the most beautifully situated of any I have seen in the county', had been remodelled in Queen Anne style. The Vicar, 'finding his expenses increasing and his receipts diminishing, desired to occupy a smaller house', and so was prepared to vacate the parsonage, a new vicarage, now known as Frere House, being provided for him. A.C. Benson, the first bishop's son, described the Victorian garden at that time:

> there was a sunny circle of turf with rose-beds, and a big old-fashioned summer-house with alcoves, its open front flush with the wall, and built out behind the shrubbery. Then the winding path led down through trees and shrubs to the house, to another lawn with flower-beds, where a great lime-tree, feathered down to the ground, and gave good shelter in summer heat. Beyond the shrubbery was a large vegetable-garden, and beyond that again an orchard with bee-hives and white cob-walls.

He concluded, rather patronizingly:

> the whole place, though fairly trim, was not in any sense smart.

Little was done by Benson, or his successor Wilkinson, while Bishop Gott chose to reside at Trenython (q.v.). It was left for Bishop Stubbs to rectify the deficiencies of the property, for which he enlisted the help of E.H. Sedding, who became a close friend, and his eventual biographer. He arrived with some knowledge of and interest in horticulture, having, as a vicar, divided his glebe into allotments for the benefit of his parishioners, and written about his Deanery garden while at Ely. He laid out 'the garden at Lis Escop on a larger scale than the original, with the same excellent taste as he displayed in furnishing his house'. He greatly admired his architect's uncle, John Dando Sedding, and a photograph in his biography shows a layout which, in embryo, is similar to designs in his *Garden-Craft Old and New* (1891). He constructed an equatorial sundial from the pinnacle cross of St Mary's, Truro, and wrote a verse inscribed around it.

Bishops come and bishops go. When John Wellington Hunkin arrived three bishops later, his gardener described the grounds as 'in a mess'. Hunkin, a Truro man, born at the Parade, seems to have had no gardening experience before returning to Cornwall, but in a short time, not only was his interest aroused, but he became one of the county's foremost horticultural writers. He was aided from the beginning by experts such as Canon Boscawen at Ludgvan, a memorial article on his death being Hunkin's first contribution to horticultural literature. Soon after, in 1942, he began a series of gardening articles in the *Guardian*, a 'quality' Church paper, now defunct, sending forty in all, the last not being published because of his death. He also wrote important, and always scholarly articles in the *JRHS* on Tresco, Lanarth, Pencarrow, Caerhays, and Trehane, as well as a masterly survey, with the title 'A Hundred Years of Cornish Gardens'. In the summer of 1945 he drew up a plan of Lis Escop, at a scale of a quarter-inch to a pace, with a list of 225 trees and shrubs with their positions numbered.

Although he wrote that, since Bishop Stubbs' time, 'no Bishop of Truro has wanted to change his residence or ever will', this has not proved the case. The next bishop did move, and Lis Escop was purchased by the Copeland family of Trelissick for the the Cathedral School. It was renamed Copeland Court. At the demise of the school in 1982, the more recent school buildings were converted into Diocesan Offices, and since the closure of the Convent of the Epiphany (now Alverton Manor Hotel), the house has been occupied by a small number of nuns.

References: 20th C; A.B. Donaldson, The Bishopric of Truro 1877-1902, *1902: 58; E.H. Sedding,* Charles William Stubbs, *Plymouth 1914: illus. p.38; A.C.Benson,* The Trefoil, *1923:178-87; M.Moore,* Winfred Burrows, *1932:134; A. Dunstan and J.S. Peart-Binns,* Cornish Bishop, *1977; Bishop Hunkin's JRHS articles are cited under their subjects: the* Guardian *articles, though seen, are not listed.*

PENCALENICK, St Clement, Truro

SW85 45 : *EX105, GS352*

Cornish pen + kelin (adj) = holly, *pronounced* pencaLENick; *house dated 'M.H.W. 1881' listed grade II, thatched* cottage ornée *lodge II; medium to large estate, sloping south and east from house, at 30m. altitude, on Portscatho Series sandstone and slate, with acid soil, in an AONB, an AGSV, and in part a CNCS; rainfall 35-40", temperature zone C; relict grounds, now the* Pencalenick Residential Day School.

39. Pencalenick in 1888, soon after the new mansion had been built, and the terraces and Italian garden laid out. The prospect looks across the Tresillian River to the wooded slopes of the Tregothnan estate. (Photograph in RIC)

Pencalenick, then known as Lower Penair (see Penair), was a tenement of the Duchy manor of Moresk, and it was not until the beginning of the eighteenth century, when the property came into the possession of the Foote family of Lambesso, that the history of Pencalenick proper began. The Footes not prospering, in 1743 the estate was mortgaged to William Lemon, after whose death it was sold to the Vivian family. The Vivians were descendants of Johnson Vivian, who had moved from Camborne to Truro in the first half of the eighteenth century, becoming wealthy enough to purchase Pencalenick in 1758. From him the property passed to his younger nephew, the Revd John Vivian, who was responsible for laying out the grounds, which were described in *Hitchins* as of 'late years ... considerably ornamented and improved'. A later descendant, John Vivian Tippett, who changed his name to Vivian, was in 1832 the initiator of the Horticultural (later the Royal Horticultural) Society of Cornwall, and its first President. Gilbert described the house as

> a handsome brick building, situated on a knoll, rising almost perpendicularly from the end of a navigable lake [the Kiggon pond, then a creek of the river], and backed by a mass of foliage. The buildings, gardens, walks, and plantations, have a very beautiful effect when viewed from the adjoining road, leading from Truro to St. Austell. [That is, of course, the earlier road past Penair, arriving in Truro down St Clement's Hill, (see Tregolls).] On a pleasing elevation which faces the house, stands a handsome freestone obelisk.

The obelisk, since it bears no inscription, has aroused much speculation. This may be no more than a 'folly', but one of several explanations is that it was placed there by one of the Vivians to commemorate his escape when the floor in front of the fire-place collapsed, possibly as a result of mining. He 'grabbed the mantlepiece thereby saving himself from an early demise'. This was a suggestion from the grandson of Michael Henry Williams, of Trevince and Tredrea (q.v. where he was already acquiring a reputation for horticulture), who purchased Pencalenick in 1880. Three years later he had the old house demolished and a new and far grander mansion built in 'arid Victorian French Gothic' (Betjeman) to the designs of J.P. St Aubyn.

Thurston, when naming Pencalenick among his selected gardens, wrote that, as well as the house, 'the grounds [also] owed their development to Michael Williams'. Among his additional features was an Italian garden elaborate enough to evoke comparison with Pencarrow, though now relict. His son, Henry Harcourt, continued his enthusiasm for gardening, being especially interested in the growing of fruit, which caused him to be selected as a judge at the RHS in London on several occasions. On his father's death in 1902, he took up many civic and county responsibilities, among them becoming a member of various agricultural committees during the First World War. In the 1920s, he began large plantations of Japanese larch, Douglas Fir, ash, sycamore and chestnuts. During his time, Pencalenick was listed in the *Hort. Direct.* from 1908 to 1924, but in 1916, after he had moved to Penair, his wife's mother, Lady Harriet Salusbury-Trelawny, occupied part of Pencalenick until 1932, followed until 1935 by his widow, who had married Lord Rendlesham.

During the Second World War, however, the house was requisitioned by the military, first for British and American troops, then later for Italian prisoners of war, who were used to fell trees on the north slopes, prior to the commercial planting of conifers. In 1970 the garden formed the subject of a survey by the Adult Education Department of the University of Exeter, who, although they listed many species of plants, found that of the twenty-five exotic shrubs cited in Hamilton Davey's 'Acclimatisation ...' article of 1897, only eight had survived. They described Pencalenick as 'A Cornish Garden in Decay '...

> where once flourished rose-garden and neat lawns, shy creatures like the squirrel and nuthatch are busy in great trees high above a sheet of Rhododendron blossoms and flowering shrubs - a happy meeting of East and West - making a part of a tributary of the Fal seem like some head-stream of the Mekong and adding to the charms of the County a piece of the Assam-Tibetan border.

References: 17th, 18th, 19th (Hort. & Gen.) and 20th C; R. Foss, ed. Pencalenick: a history in words and pictures, *Falmouth, 1998.*

PENMOUNT, Truro

SW82 47 : EX104-5, GS352   OPEN*

Originally Penhellick; Penmount *is a composite Cornish and English house name pronounced* penMOUNT; *house listed grade II; medium to large grounds, south-east sloping 95-65m., on Portscatho Series sandstone and slates, with acid soil, in an AGLV; rainfall 40-45", temperature zone C; now the* Crematorium, *grounds open to the public.*

Gilbert wrote:

> Penhellick, formerly the seat of the Collinses [related to the Collins of Treworgan and Truthan (q.v.)], was purchased from that family by the late general Macarmick, who erected here a very noble mansion, and gave it the name of Penmount ... The house is situated on a high bleak spot, about a mile from Truro, without a shrub to shelter it; but there is a deep valley on its western side, which is more fertilized and picturesque.

According to *Lake*, General William Macarmick, who succeeded his father James as a wine-merchant in Truro, 'pulled down almost every hedge on the place; opened his doors to all, [and] attracted the high and the low by politeness, gaiety and festivity.' But the new house seemed doomed, for he was almost immediately appointed Governor of Cape Breton in America, and the dwelling remained unoccupied, its next purchaser dying before taking up residence. As *Hitchins* relates, the eventual owner, 'finding the house in a ruinous condition ... proceeded to demolish the superfluous parts, and to repair the remainder ...'. Later, in the second half of the nineteenth century, Penmount became the home of the Carus-Wilson family, Dorothea, the second daughter of E.S. Carus-Wilson, marrying Michael Williams III, and Frances Jane, his third daughter, marrying Thomas Bedford Bolitho of Trewidden (q.v.).

In 1956 the property was converted into a crematorium. The grounds are now well kept, with attractively planted rose borders, in a garden named after the Henderson family, Major J.S. Henderson, who last resided there, having married Margaret, the youngest daughter of E.S. Carus-Wilson. His son, the noted Cornish scholar Charles Henderson, wrote the first history of Cornish gardens in 1928, and in 1930 contributed a chapter on Cornish woodlands to Thurston's *Trees and Shrubs of Cornwall*.

References: 17th, 18th, 19th (Gen.) and 20th C.

POLGWYNNE, Feock

SW82 38 : EX104-5, GS356   OPEN*

A former name of Porthgwidden; Cornish pol + guyn = *white or fair, pronounced* polGWIN; *3.5 acre (1.4 ha) garden, south-east sloping 30m. to the sea, on Portscatho and Falmouth Series sandstone and slate, with acid soil, in an AONB; rainfall 40-45", temperature zone C; open 1983-98 CGOG, 1987, 1991-8 NGS, all year by appointment, and one Sunday each in April, May and June for charity.*

Polgwynne was built to the east of Porthgwidden, in one of the walled gardens, between 1923 and 1930, when Mr and Mrs H.K. Neale were owners. At that time it covered about six acres (2.4 ha). The present grounds, which have been developed since 1966, are smaller, but they also include part of the plantation from Porthgwidden down to the sea, which was added as a protection against further development. The garden falls away in three terraces. The first, of stone, is in front of the house, from which there are views across the lawns to the estuary beyond. The second is a large rectangular lawn. On the west is a bed of shrubs, beyond which, through a doorway, is entered a small formal walled garden with a rectangular pond. Beyond this is a much larger walled garden, now grassed over, in which are the greenhouses described by Canon Phillpotts in 1852. Across the lawn of the third terrace, a rill runs into the foliage below, where, in the south-east corner there is a summer house. The whole garden is beautifully designed and richly planted, including what is believed to be the largest female *Gingko biloba* in Britain.

References: 20th C.

PORTHGWIDDEN, Feock

SW82 37 : EX104-5, GS352

Aqua de Porthgwn *1284 (Assize Plea Rolls);* Cornish porth + guyn = *white, hence fair, thus 'fairhaven',* *pronounced porthGWIDDen; clockhouse, courtyard and kitchen garden walls (c .1855), listed grade II; grounds of 8 acres (3.25 ha), south-east sloping, 40m. to the sea, on Portscatho and Falmouth Series sandstone and slate, with acid soil, in an AONB, and along river an AGSV; rainfall 40-45", temperature zone C; original grounds divided, house since 1961 in apartments, garden relict.*

Porthgwidden was built in 1829 for Edmund Turner, MP for Truro, and sold in 1842 to John Phillpotts, MP for Gloucester and a barrister, who was brother to the Bishop of Exeter. His son, 'Tom' Phillpotts, even as a curate at St Austell had evidenced his interest in horticulture by being chosen as a judge in the Tywardreath Gardening Society Flower Show, the oldest in Cornwall. He became an active member of the Royal Horticultural Society of Cornwall almost from its foundation in 1832. It is not, then, surprising that he carried these interests with him to Feock, where he became Vicar in 1844, by gift of his uncle the Bishop, and took up residence at Porthgwidden, rather than at the vicarage, by gift of his father.

Porthgwidden already had an established garden and a fashionable terrace (see illustration) which would have won the approval of a garden designer writing in 1842, who rejoiced that the

40. Porthgwidden. The terrace with its view across the Carrick Roads marked a return to the earlier practice of dressing the grounds in the vicinity of the dwelling. (Twycross 1846: 87)

'old system of having nothing but shaven grass, and bare gravel around the house' was 'fast giving way to the introduction of walled or balustraded terraces, and all the rich decorations of the old gardens'. Perhaps because the grounds were already laid out, Phillpotts became better known for scientific horticulture than landscaping, so that Porthgwidden was described as 'the Mecca of West country horticulturists and scientists'.

Phillpotts was for many years Steward of the Horticultural Section of the Bath and West Show and, with others along the Fal estuary, experimented with the 'acclimatization of exotics'. In 1850 he built himself extensive greenhouses in which he grew not only melons and cucumbers, but ornamental orchids and stove plants, publishing his method for retaining the humidity when heating the air, in the *JRHS* of 1852. He saw the social benefits of garden cultivation, and had heard 'of many cases where drunkards had been reclaimed from the error of their ways'. He was quick to see the benefit to small farmers of the new markets opened up by the Penzance to London railway. There was a Swiss-style boat house on the shore, now converted to a dwelling, and a rotunda-type open gazebo, now in an adjoining garden. The first bishop of Truro, later Archbishop of Canterbury, lodged at Porthgwidden for a while until a suitable episcopal residence was completed. His son, A.C. Benson, wrote a pen sketch of Tom Phillpotts at this time:

> [he] was a type of clergyman now almost extinct ... He had no pomposity, but one felt him at once to be a personage ... He did not treat my father with any marked deference, as most of the clergy did, but as a county magnate like himself.

Porthgwidden was listed in the *Hort. Direct.* from at least 1870 until 1891, and was one of Thurston's select gardens.

References: 19th (Hort. & Gen.) and 20th C; Illus; A.C. Benson, The Trefoil, *1923:175-6; 'Porthgwidden and Tom Phillpots', Feock ... some aspects of local history, III, Extra-mural Department, University of Exeter 1975: 38-53.*

TREGOLLS HOUSE, Truro

SW83 44 : *EX105, GS352*

Cornish tre + *collas = hazlett, pronounced treGOLLS; originally medium to large grounds, north-west and south-west sloping, at 25-15m., on Falmouth Series sandstone and slate, with acid soil; rainfall 40-45", temperature zone C; house demolished, grounds reduced and relict.*

The tenement of Tregolls, consisting of two Cornish acres, was held in 1337 by Thomas Tregolls. In the eighteenth century it was in the possession of the Thomas family, and from 1770 to 1775 it was a school for young ladies. It came to the Sprys of Place Manor when Admiral Thomas Davy Spry married Anna Maria Thomas, heiress to the estate. Thereafter they spent much of their winters there.

The main highway to St Austell then passed south of the grounds of the house, via St Clement's Hill, arriving at Tresillian by a still existing steep and tortuous route along the borders of Penair and Pencalenick. In 1827 discussions took place to route a new road, either through Penair from Kiggon Bridge, or on Lord Falmouth's suggestion, west of Pencalenick, which would involve cutting through the grounds of Tregolls. After difficult negotiations with the Sprys, who used this land as a nursery, the Tregolls Road was formed inside the western boundary of their estate. Subsequently the house became the residence of Robert Tweedy, younger brother of William Tweedy, who had built Alverton across the road. It was listed in the *Hort. Direct.* from at least 1870 until 1891 under his name or that of G. Evans.

During part of this period, the mansion was occupied from 1879 by the Truro Grammar School, of which Lewis Evans was headmaster, which transferred to Newham House about 1891. The mansion has also served as a house of residence for the girls of Truro High School, but proved unsound in the mid 1980s, and was demolished. The coach-house and the former lodge remained occupied, and are set, with a pond, in wooded grounds extending to some twenty acres (8 ha), which are currently destined for development. The central reservation of the Tregolls Road, widened in the mid 1960s, is attractively cultivated with bedding schemes, which contributed to the city winning the 'Britain in Bloom' award in several years.

References: 17th, 18th, 19th (Hort. & Gen.) and 20th C; Illus; R.E. Davidson, The History of Truro Grammar School *, Mevagissey, 1970: 76-8.*

TREGOTHNAN, St Michael Penkevil, Truro

SW85 41 : *EX105, GS352*   OPEN

Cornish tre + ?goth = water-course + nan, *pronounced* treGOTHnan; *house listed grade I, clock-tower and stable yard II*, walls, railings and gate-piers, ha-ha, lodge, and gate-piers, each II; garden listed grade II*; grounds of about 50 acres (20 ha), south-west sloping, 75m. to river, on Portscatho Series sandstone and slate, with acid soil, in an AONB, and an AGSV; rainfall 35-40", temperature*

41. Tregothnan. From the 'noble terrace with a parapet, conducting to a spacious lawn', is seen the prospect of the river opened up on the advice of Repton. (Twycross 1846: 10)

zone C; private, open 1983-98 CGOG, one Sunday each in April and May. There has been an official leaflet.

Tonkin described Tregothnan as the seat of a family of that name

> till Johanna, the daughter and heir of John Tregothnan, by her marriage in ... 1334, with John Boscawen, of Boscawen Rose, in the parish of S. Burian, brought Tregothnan to this family, whose principal seat it hath been ever since, now just four hundred years; who have greatly enriched themselves, as well as enobled their blood, since that time, by marriages with the heiresses of Albalanda, Trenoweth, &c., and by matching themselves into the most eminent families of the county ... [such as St Aubyn, Carminow, Courtenay, Trevanion, and Godolphin].

It was not, however, until the time of Hugh Boscawen in the seventeenth century, that the family began to come into prominence. His second son and successor built the first mansion at Tregothnan (illustrated in *Country Life 119*, 1956: 1054), of which two rooms survive. Before this time it was the neighbouring manor of Fentongollan which had been in the ascendance, coming to the Carminows of Respryn by marriage, whose son, so *Hitchins* (quoting Hals) informs us, kept open house with sumptuous entertainment at Christmas. His son, however, squandered his inheritance and the estates were sold, being bought by Hugh Boscawen in 1676.

> When this last purchase was made, a venerable mansion, that had been erected by the Carminows with lofty towers and a fine chapel, graced the premises; but these were all demolished by Mr. Boscawen. A farm house now occupies the site, and not a vestige remains to indicate its departed grandeur.

Hals declared that, 'the chief stones thereof [were] carried to build the gates and houses of Tregothnan.' Celia Fiennes, Hugh Boscawen's first cousin, visited and described the new house standing

> on a high hill in the middle of a park with several rows of trees, with woods beyond it ... There is a court walled round with open iron gates and bars ... the drawing-room ... goes into the garden which has gravel walks round and across, but the squares are full of gooseberry and shrub trees and looks more like a kitchen garden ... out of which is another garden and orchard, which is something like a grove - green walks with rows of fruit trees. It is capable of being a fine place with some charge

Hugh Boscawen's nephew, another Hugh (c. 1666-1734), who succeeded him in the estate, was created Viscount in 1720 for personal services to George I. His son, Edward (1711-61), the Admiral, who had built for himself a house in London, left designs for the 'palladianising' of Tregothnan, but it was his grandson, Edward, the first Earl (1787-1841), who was to improve both the house and the grounds. Reginald Pole Carew of Antony, in a letter to Repton dated 25 July 1809, wrote:

> Lord Falmouth ... has just succeeded to His Family Seat ..., a fine Place, with a very bad House, ... where good advice will probably, ere long be thought very desirable.

He suggested a visit in September, the date that Repton wrote in his Red Book that he was 'on the spot' at Tregothnan. 'It is clear,' wrote a later Lord Falmouth, in 1968,

> that many of his recommendations were carried out, noticeably the shelter belt to the south-west of the house, which provides an attractive walk to the kitchen garden flanked by a double line of very old *Camellia japonica*.

Repton was followed by William Wilkins, junior, the son of his former associate, who enlarged and refaced the old Cromwellian house in Regency style, based upon the Tudor manor of East Barsham, and the Rectory of Great Snoring, near Walshingham in his native Norfolk. It was also at about this time, according to *Hitchins* (ii.358), that the tower of the abandoned old church at Kea was purchased 'as presenting a conspicuous and pleasing object from the grounds of Tregothnan,' that is, as an eye-catcher. The distinctive entrance gates and railings, however, are usually attributed to Lewis Vulliamy, who in 1845-8 also enlarged the house, and designed the arched gate-house at Tresillian Bridge, leading into the four-mile scenic drive along the Tresillian river.

Nevertheless, the designs did not pass without criticism. Edward Luckhurst, in a two-part article in the *Journal of Horticulture* of 1877, was rather more blunt in his criticism and advice than usual, and than perhaps would be suffered by garden-owners today. He did not like the double row of camellias mentioned above; 'duty compels me to say that the arrangement is a mistake; the formal aspect of such long lines robs the scene of that grace which it ought to possess ... '. He did not like the terraces: 'One turns from this pleasant scene [of the Fal] with regret, for, most unfortunately, the terrace is not in harmony with it, ... [it] is now occupied with circles of Box embroidery and spar of various colours'. The description of this 'broderie' parterre is similar to that by Nesfield at Tregrehan, and designs exist which suggest that he may have worked here as well. Luckhurst believed that they 'might be dispensed with advantageously', and so they have been, but for other reasons, and without regard to his advice.

At about this time, the Hon. and Revd John Townshend Boscawen was Rector of Lamorran (q.v.), and he, and his brother Evelyn the Sixth Viscount (1819-89), were engaged in the development and planting of the grounds, in a manner approved by Luckhurst. They were both the sons of Canon the Hon. John Evelyn Boscawen, at one time Rector of Wooton, near Dorking, the home of John Evelyn the famous diarist and horticulturist, to whom they were related. J.T. Boscawen of Lamorran was the greater gardener, and probably took the lead. A catalogue preserved from 1862 shows that of 330 lots of rhododendrons on sale at his garden, 110 were bought for Tregothnan.

The view from across the terraces and deer park to the River Fal, often with large ships anchored, is both striking and perhaps the most familiar, but earlier writers concentrate more upon the vista across the lawn from the summer-house, and the variety of the plantings in this area. Adjoining the house is a quite magnificent stable yard, designed by Wilkins, where the great north-west camellia wall runs the full length of the stable, some 70 yards (64m.) long and 25 feet (7.6m.) tall, planted with camellias trained up to the roof guttering. Tregothnan, one of Thurston's select gardens, was listed in the *Hort. Direct.* from at least 1870 to 1924. Although it is now only open on special occasions, it will be realized that (Luckhurst notwithstanding!), such an opportunity ought not to be missed.

References: 17th, 18th, 19th (Hort. & Gen.) and 20th C; Illus; C. Hussey, English Country Houses: Late Georgian, *1958: 140 et seq.*

TREGYE, Feock

SW80 40 : EX104-5, GS352

Tregy, 1327; Cornish tre + ky = *dog, pronounced and sometimes spelt* treGUY; *house listed grade II; estate of about 30 acres (12 ha), valley garden about 5 acres (2 ha), sloping north-south 65-20m., on Portscatho Series sandstone and slate, with acid soil; rainfall 40-45", temperature zone C; now the Duchy Grammar School with relict grounds, and a separate private valley garden.*

Tregye had been a farm since at least the fourteenth century, and had come into the possession of the Boscawen family. During the early nineteenth century, however, this was the residence of the Penrose family, William having built a new house, with a date-stone 'W.P. 1809'. They continued there until 1889, when John Richard de Clare Boscawen, youngest son of Lord Falmouth, made extensive alterations, adding his own date-stone 'J.R. de C.B. and M.F.L.B. 1891-2'. During the intervening period until the work was completed, he lived with his wife at Porthgwidden. His father was at that time developing the garden at Tregothnan, and he too began to lay out the grounds around his new house and drive with 'semi-formal planting of conifers, camellias, and rhododendrons'. A valley garden was also created a little distance from the house at about the turn of the century, which was given the name 'Happy Valley'. The two pools, one with a grotto, were later dug out of the little stream that flows through. Here, Thurston recorded:

> There is a beautiful Weeping Willow (*Salix babylonica* Linn.) ... [which] is a descendant of the tree over Napoleon's grave, and was brought from St Helena by Colonel Byng (now Lord Byng of Vimy) about 1902.

In 1916 the property became the home of Edward Powys Rogers, who had married Charlotte, sister of J.C. Williams of Caerhays Castle. Since 1890 she had been creating a fine garden at Burncoose (q.v.), and now began to develop the garden at Tregye, particularly in the valley. This was one of Thurston's select gardens, from which he cited forty-eight plants.

At the beginning of the Second World War the house was taken over by the military, and subsequently has been an hotel, and is now a school. Twenty-five years ago the Happy Valley was separated, and has since been restored and rejuvenated in a most remarkable way by Edward Needham. A very large number of introductions of species rhododendrons, and other rare and unusual plants have been made from the wild, giving the garden that freshness and special atmosphere with which the famous valley gardens of the nineteenth century, like Penjerrick, must once have been endowed.

References: 17th, 18th, and 20th C; 'Tregye', Feock ... some aspects of local history, III, Extramural Dept., University of Exeter, 1975: 17-25, with map.

TREHANE, Probus

SW86 48 : EX105, GS352 and 346   OPEN

Cornish, Dexter suggests tre + han = *summer, or* Hanna *a personal name, pronounced* treHAIN; *house ruins listed grade II, coach-house II; garden of 5 acres (2 ha), east facing slope 90-75m., on Grampound Grit or Ladock Beds sandstone and slate, with acid soil, in part in a CNCS; rainfall 40-45", temperature zone C; private, open 1983-1998 CGOG and for charities, alternate Sundays late March through August. Official guide.*

The Trehane family was already described as 'ancient' in 1288, and remained in possession of the barton until the mid-seventeenth century, when the estate passed by marriage to John Scawen of Molenick, near St Germans. His grandson sold out to John Williams of Carvean, who was related to the Williams family then at Trewithen. It is believed that the bricks from which in 1700 he began to build his new house had come from clay below the lake there. Despite Gilbert's rather dismissive remarks that it had 'a large white front, in conformity with the style of building which prevailed about a hundred years ago ... and does not appear to have undergone much improvement,' it had been described, before it was tragically gutted by fire in 1943, as one of the most beautiful houses in Cornwall.

After John William's death, the Revd William Stackhouse, vicar of St Erme, came into the property by marriage to the heiress, whose son John achieved a reputation as an eminent botanist, building Acton Castle (q.v.) for the study of seaweeds. The succession at Trehane, which so often seems to have passed along the line through heiresses, came eventually in 1861 to Capt. William Stackhouse Church Pinwill, who returned from India upon resigning his commission in 1868 to take up residence at Trehane, where he became a notable horticulturist, placed by Bishop Hunkin as second in the hierarchy of Cornish gardeners. He was a contemporary of the Hon. and Revd J.T. Boscawen at Lamorran, and a great friend of P.D. Williams of Lanarth, who together shared their experiences, and benefited from the new plants being introduced by Wilson and Forrest, which were being distributed by Veitch of Exeter.

Capt. Pinwill's sister had married the headmaster of Probus School, who became Archdeacon of Bombay. After his retirement he travelled a great deal in Europe, enlarging the range of the garden by sending home to his brother-in-law interesting plants from Greece, Italy, Switzerland and the Pyrenees. Pinwill became well known for 'his great generosity and the help which he [gave] to many people in starting their gardens', for his knowledge of plants and their cultivation, and the magnificent specimens in his garden, such as the massive dark pink form of *Magnolia campbellii*, and the *Davidia involucrata* which became one of the largest in the country. He was awarded the Victoria Medal, the highest accolade of the RHS, in 1915, and in an obituary it was said of him that, 'His type of gardening, his skill, and his great generosity, were only equalled by the late Canon Ellacombe of Bitton', who had become a legend in his own day. His reputation has recently been amply confirmed by the re-appearance of his 'Plant Index' from 1888 to about 1900, with entries for some 4,500 plants growing in the garden, the great majority, unusually for Cornwall, being herbaceous.

After Pinwill's death in 1926, the succession again reverted to daughters, so that, especially after the gutting of the house, which post-war restrictions prevented re-building, the garden went into a steep decline, until David Trehane, a descendant of a branch of the family originating in Linkinhorne, bought the estate in 1963. In subsequent years much restoration has been undertaken, and new developments made, especially in the trials of camellias, a species on which David Trehane is one of the leading authorities in the country. The dwelling is now in the converted stables, which bears a rainwater head with the arms of the Williams and Courtenay families. The intriguing 'little temple or pleasure house', which stands outside the grounds overlooking the railway, erected in memory of William Stackhouse in 1861, with windows displaying the family arms in stained glass, has unfortunately been vandalized, but the relics of the old house contain one of the largest colonies of the Greater Horse-shoe bats in the county. This is a plantman's garden, in compartments, so rich in species and varieties, that, unlike so many Cornish gardens, visitors are surprised always to find so much of interest throughout its long open season.

References: 17th, 18th, 19th (Hort. & Gen.) and 20th C.

TRELISSICK, Feock

SW83 39 : EX105, GS35　　　　　　　　　OPEN

Trelesyk, Assize Rolls 1280; Cornish tre + *gwlesyk = leader, pronounced treLISsick; house listed grade II*, water-tower, lodge, kitchen garden walls and 8 various buildings, each II; 25 acre (10 ha) garden listed grade II, with 376 acres (152 ha) of parkland; garden east sloping, 50m. to river, park south sloping, on Portscatho and Falmouth Series sandstone and slate, soil 'shillet over clay, lime free', in an AONB, and an AGSV with an AM

42. Trelissick. An unusual parkland for Cornwall, dotted with trees, and with wooded walks designed to provide vistas of the river. (Gilbert 1820: ii. 808)

(cross); rainfall 40-45", temperature zone C; house and estate, with an endowment, donated to the National Trust in 1955; house private, garden open through March to end of October. Official leaflets and guides with plans.

Descriptions of Trelissick have focussed more upon the parkland, which is of a type unusual in Cornwall, than the gardens which are mostly post-Second World War. Although there had almost certainly been a dwelling here since before 1280, little is known of the early history of the site. The first modern house was built about 1750 for Capt. John Lawrence of the Cornwall Militia, to designs by Edmund Davy, grandfather of the celebrated Humphry Davy. After Lawrence's death in 1790, the estate was bought ten years later by Ralph Allen Daniell, son of Thomas Daniell of Truro, chief clerk and successor to Sir William Lemon, who was probably the richest man in Cornwall, known from the profits of the Seal Hole mine at St Agnes as 'Guinea-a-Minute' Daniell.

He added substantially to the estate, so that he could ride all the way to Truro on his own lands, but it was his son, Thomas, who in 1825 engaged Peter Frederick Robinson to rebuild the house, adding to the south front a six-columned Ionic portico to the proportions of the temple of Erectheus at Athens, and a window copied from the temple of Minerva Polias to create what Pevsner described as 'the severest neo-Greek mansion in Cornwall'. He laid out miles of rides and carriage roads through the beautiful hanging woods along the west side of the estuary, and planted, particularly beech and deciduous oaks, in the park. He was also responsible for the neo-Greek Old Lodge at the entrance. His life of splendour in the end ran through his capital, so that he was eventually obliged to sell his estate to Lord Falmouth, who sold it on to John Davies Gilbert, son of the compiler of the *History of Cornwall* (1838), and a keen agriculturalist, who introduced a considerable flock of sheep to the parkland. However, dying in 1854, he did not enjoy the estate for many years, bequeathing it to his son, Carew, who survived until 1913.

Considerable additions were made during this time. A second storey was raised on the wings of the house, and 'a fair sprinkling of foreign trees and shrubs' were introduced 'from his wanderings into remote regions of the globe', such as the Far East and Australia. In his replantings in the park he favoured the sweet chestnut, and began laying out the Carcaddon area as a garden, in 1866 connecting it to the main grounds by one of the first reinforced concrete bridges.

Trelissick was listed in the *Hort. Direct.* from at least 1870 until 1924, but its attraction would still have been as much for the walks and spectacular views as for the ornamental plantings. Indeed, when Thurston visited Trelissick, which was one of his select gardens, in the late 1920s, even though he was able to find many fine trees to cite in his lists, it was still largely a shrubbery of *Rhododendron ponticum*, laurel, aucuba and other shade-bearing shrubs beneath a canopy of oak and beech, with some fine conifers. After the death of Carew Davies Gilbert the house was let in 1913 to Leonard Daneman Cunliffe, Governor of the Bank of England, who bought part of the estate in 1928, which, on his death in 1937 he bequeathed to his daughter, Mrs Ida Copeland.

With her, and her husband Ronald Copeland, Managing Director of Spode, the history of the garden proper began, many of the flowers painted on their porcelain being grown at Trelissick. Together they planted the main garden and the Dell area with trees and shrubs, including hybrid rhododendrons obtained from Bodnant. In 1955 Mrs Copeland donated the house, garden and surrounding park and woodland to the National Trust, who have continued the replanting, particularly on the Carcaddon side. They have also opened up vistas, such as that to Tregothnan, and created woodland walks. Among the many features, the log summer-house, and the water-tower with its squirrel weather-vane, from the crest of the Gilbert family, may be selected for mention. Trelissick is principally a modern plantsman's garden, but contained within parkland continuously managed and beautified since the mid-eighteenth century, where, amid smooth lawns, are well placed groups of oak and beech framing the views south to the Carrick Roads.

References: 18th, 19th (Hort. & Gen.), 20th C; Illus; Feock ... in the nineteenth century, II, Feock Local History Group, Exeter 1973: 34-43; Manpower Services Commission, Trelissick, 1982.

TREMORVAH, Truro

SW83 45 : *EX105, GS352*

Formerly Conium; *Cornish* tre + *morva = sea-marsh, pronounced* treMORvah; *house with small residual garden; occupied by* Cornish Mutual Assurance Co. Ltd.

In the early nineteenth century, Gweal Conium was the name of a field to the north-east of Truro, owned, medieval-style, in strips, by several local families. A 'new Gothic Mansion', named 'Conium', was advertised in 1826 with the description:

> In the pleasure grounds (which are tastefully laid out) is a grotto, the entrance to which is through

a subterranean passage; near it is a hermitage and fish pond ... this place is well-known to be the greatest subject of curiosity and admiration to strangers visiting Truro.

In 1841, Philip Prothero Smith, vice-Warden of the Stanneries, built a new house here, which thereafter was to be known as 'Tremorvah'. Upon his death, and that of his widow, the estate, which included five meadows, in all forty-five acres (18 ha), was acquired by Richard B. Chellew, a shipowner. The gardens during this period, from at least 1870 to 1916, were listed in the *Hort. Direct*. On Chellew's death in 1929, the estate was sold, and became a residential development. Nothing now remains of the garden save the *cottage ornée* lodge, and a belt of mature trees, shielding the recently-built Penhaligon Court from Tregolls Road.

References: 20th C.

TREVORICK, Carclew

SW78 38 : *EX104-5, GS352*

Cornish, Holmes suggests tre + *personal name,* Uuoroc *or* Moroc, *pronounced* TreVORick; *other details as for Carclew; private.*

The Carclew estate was divided up *c*.1960, when much of the garden, including the ruins of the old house, became the property of Mr Jack Neale, whose dwelling is known as Trevorick. The new Carclew House, until his death in 1988, was the residence of Judge R.C. Chope, and is now that of his widow.

VICTORIA PARK and WATERFALL GARDENS, Truro

SW82 45 : *EX104-5, GS352* OPEN

The Waterfall Gardens *are 0.75 acre (0. 3ha), and* Victoria Park *some 4 acres (1.6 ha), steeply sloping on Falmouth Series sandstone and slate, with acid soil; rainfall 40-45", temperature zone C; open to the public.*

During the development of Truro towards the end of the nineteenth century, the remaining freeholds of Lord Falmouth in the City were auctioned off in 1891, which afforded an opportunity for the purchase of a plot of land leading to the Tregear waterfall, near the St George's Methodist Church, which was 'presented to the City in 1893 by ... alderman E.G. Heard.' This was 'prettily laid out [by John Mitchinson, the Truro nurseryman] with flower beds, shrubs &c., and skirted by the Kenwyn stream, which [created] an ornamental waterfall', giving the garden its name. Subsequently new legislation made it possible for the Council itself to provide pleasure gardens at public expense, which resulted in the laying out of the Victoria Park on the steep slope between the Waterfall Gardens and the Castle Hill, now the site of the Crown Court, which was opened in 1898 in commemoration of the sixtieth year of the reign of Queen Victoria. Kelly's *Directory* (1910) recorded that

> there are sub-tropical plants, an ornamental fountain and a band-stand; a drinking fountain was presented by Alderman T.L. Dorrington J.P. in commemoration of the 81st birthday of Her ... Majesty ... and an aquarium of fresh water fish by R.B. Chellew esq.; a caretaker's lodge has also been erected by Alderman Dorrington, in commemoration of the coronation ... of the King and Queen.

The gardens continue to be well maintained. The railway viaduct towers over both gardens, from which the view of the Park provides a charming introduction to the City as the traveller enters the station from the east.

References: 20th C.

SUPPLEMENTARY LISTS

LESSER-KNOWN HISTORIC GARDENS

Bodrean, near Truro

W84 47 : *EX105, GS352*

Also on the OS Explorer Map 105, 1997 as the 'Rookery'; Cornish bod + dreyn = *thorns, pronounced* boDRAIN; *early 19th C. house, 18th C. to rear, listed grade II; grounds at 95m. altitude, on Grampound Grit, sandstone, and slate slightly calcareous, in an AGLV; rainfall 40-45", temperature zone C; private.*

Originally the property of the Prynne family, Bodrean was in 1939 used by the Society of St Francis for homeless men. After being occupied by troops during the Second World War, it became an hotel, but is now private, with the surrounding land in agricultural use. It is included here as typical of estates around Truro described in Barratt (1988).

References: 17th, 18th, 19th (Gen.) and 20th C.

Comprigney, Truro

SW81 45 : *EX104-5, GS352*

Cornish cloghprennyer = *gallows, pronounced* comPRIGney; *garden of about 4 acres (1.6 ha) at 55m. altitude, on Portscatho Series sandstone and slate, with acid soil; rainfall 40-45", temperature zone C; private.*

Although the name is derived from a word meaning 'gallows', *Lake* describes Comprigney as 'a genteel residence'. The property of the Vivians of Glynn, this was the birthplace in 1718 of a descendant, the Revd Thomas Vivian, who was famous in his day for various works of theology. 'His son, John [who became vice-Warden of the Stanneries] ... may be called, according to Tregellas, the founder of the copper trade in Cornwall'. It was, however, a later resident, William Nicholas Gill, a draper in Truro, who is listed as resident in the *Hort. Direct.* from 1890 to 1919, being followed in 1922 by George Coulter Hancock, who 'considerably enlarged and improved the house' to the designs of Cowell, Drewitt and Wheatley. He was succeeded by Brig. 'Tony' Mulock, secretary of the Cornwall Spring Flower Society, which preceded the present Cornwall Garden Society. There are established gardens; a walled rose garden to the south-east, a formal garden on the south-western side with a *Cedrus atlantica glauca*, Wellingtonia, cherry trees and other shrubs, while a lawned area at the rear, screened by a yew hedge contains a *Gingko biloba*.

References: 18th, 19th (Hort. & Gen.) and 20th C.

Condurra, St Clement's

SW85 43 : EX105, GS352

Cornish *kendowrow = joint-waters, pronounced conDURRa; small garden at river level on Portscatho Series sandstone and slate, with acid soil, in an AONB, and an AGSV; rainfall 40-45", temperature zone C; private, reduced grounds.

Condurra was advertised in the *Sherborne Mercury* of 1798, as a new brick house with thirty-eight acres of meadow, and 'fine gardens', described by Gilbert as the residence of the Sholl family. It later had passed through many hands, including that of the Vicar of St Clements, eventually arriving by purchase with the Vivians of Pencalenick. It was under their ownership that the house burnt down in 1853, never to be rebuilt. Gilbert had reported the tradition that

> this place was once the dwelling of Condurra, earl of Cornwall, who submitted to the authority of William the Conqueror, at his arrival in England.

Perhaps encouraged by this romantic past, a more recent owner of the cottage adorned the gate and walls with bizarre ornaments of a Celtic type, and kept a peacock on the terrace. He also possessed an authentic gondola, moored in the river, in which he would transport himself, at the right state of tide, in the garb of a gondolier, to drink at the historic Wheel Inn at Tresillian.

References: 18th C.

Glanmor, Falmouth Road, Truro

SW82 44 : EX104-5, GS352

Small urban garden on Portscatho Series sandstone and slate, with acid soil; rainfall 40-45", temperature zone C; private, reduced grounds.

Glanmor was originally the property of R.F. Michell, a prominent and prosperous timber importer and merchant. Pettigrew, in the *Journal of Horticulture* described Glanmor as

> a pretty little place on the outskirts of Truro, ... whose gardens were laid out by Mr. Mitchinson [a Truro nurseryman] about seven years ago [i.e. 1872]. They are neatly laid out and tastefully planted with trees and shrubs, which have grown remarkably well.

The grounds have now been reduced and divided, but still flourish.

References: 19th (Hort.) and 20th C.

Killagorden, Idless, near Truro

SW82 46 : EX104-5, GS352

Cornish kelli = grove + [?], pronounced killaGORDen; house, coach-house. and lodge each listed grade II; grounds in valley sloping north-east to south-west from 60m., on Portscatho Series sandstone and slate; rainfall 40-45", temperature zone C; private.

Killagorden is an ancient tenement recorded in the *Parliamentary Survey* of 1649, although in the nineteenth century it acquired for a time the name of 'Rosedale'. The house, with parts from about 1510, is mainly seventeenth century, with eighteenth-century bays. The early nineteenth-century lodge was built in the Gothick style. It lies in the valley of the River Allen, secluded among plantations of trees, with some parkland. During its occupancy by an American, it was visited by, among others, the film star Katherine Hepburn. Bishop Hunkin, in his review of Cornish gardens, mentions a later resident and gardener, Ivens Knowles, whose wife, Lilian, was an economic historian, and Professor at the London School of Economics.

References: 17th, and 20th C.

Lambesso, near Truro

SW84 44 : EX105, GS352

Cornish lan + bedewen (pl) = birch trees, pronounced lamBESSo; house, and gate-piers each listed grade II; grounds at 45m. altitude, on Portscatho Series sandstone and slate, with acid soil, in an AONB; rainfall 40-45", temperature zone C; private.

Once the seat of a family of this name, Lambesso formerly belonged to the manor of Moresk, and was the site of the Duchy prison. The seventeenth-century house, built by John Foote, Mayor of Truro and great-grandfather of the dramatist Samuel

Foote, known as the English Aristophanes, is now the residence of Charles Thomas, former Professor of Cornish Studies at the University of Exeter. The estate once extending to seventy-two acres (29 ha) included the Lambesso Woods. The gate-piers now stand on each side of the public road, which runs over part of the original entrance drive.

References: 17th, 18th 19th (Gen.) and 20th C.

Moresk, Truro

SW82 45 : *EX104-5, GS352*

Moireis, Domesday 1086, pronounced morESK; *grounds south-west sloping c. 30-15m., on Falmouth Series sandstone, slate and alluvium, with acid soil; rainfall 40-45", temperature zone C; extinct.*

Early in the nineteenth century, Lewis Charles Daubuz, a Huguenot, having acquired mining interests in Cornwall, leased the Mansion House in the City, and the farm, gardens and plantations at Moresk, on the outskirts of Truro, both belonging to the Enys family. His son, William, resided at Killiow (q.v.). In 1840 Stephen Treseder leased the

> farm and gardens, walled gardens, gardeners house and other buildings, plantations and shrubberies, five acres well sheltered and watered on a slope, aspect SW ... and five closes of rich land adjoining the ... gardens.

Here the Treseder family began their nursery. John, at first seeking gold, had

> travelled widely in Australia, New Zealand and Tasmania discovering many new shrubs and plants to cultivate in gardens and parks.

Since their closure early in the 1980s, the nursery grounds have been developed into detached houses, with well cultivated gardens, but the 'Daubuz Moors' were presented to Truro by the Enys family for the public benefit.

References: 17th, 18th, and 19th (Gen.) C; From Moresk Road to Malpas, *Truro Building Research Group 1988: 50-51, with full account of the Daubuz and Treseder families; see also C.G. 1987: 62, and 1989: 87 for Treseder plant introductions.*

Newham House, Truro

SW82 44 : *EX104-5, GS352*

English derivation; house listed grade II; small garden at 20m. altitude, on Portscatho Series sandstone and slate; rainfall 40-45", temperature zone C; private, residual gardens.

The house, originally the manor of Newham, was built by the wealthy Truro merchant, R.A. Daniell. It was, according to *Lake*, 'pleasantly situated on the western bank of the river Fal [i.e. the Truro river, tributary of the Fal] ... and stands within a well-wooded lawn.' A few trees are still left surrounding the house, on the left-hand side of the Truro bypass, towards Falmouth, forlornly looking down on the Newham industrial estate, and across the dual carriageways of Morlaix Road, carved out of its grounds, to the Newham housing estate on the other side. It was, from about 1891 to 1909, the Truro Grammar School, until this became the Cathedral School, and was transferred to the Cathedral precincts.

References: 18th, 19th (Gen.) and 20th C; R.E. Davidson, The History of Truro Grammar and Cathedral School, *Mevagissey 1970: 78-81.*

Penair, St Clement, Truro

SW84 45 : *EX105, GS352*

Pengarth, Caption 1337, also Higher Penair; Cornish *pen-arth = promontory, pronounced penAIR; *estate originally 133 acres (54 ha), south-east facing slope, 90-40m., on Portscatho Series sandstone and slate, in an AGLV; rainfall 40-45", temperature zone C; formerly a Nursing Home, with relict grounds, but on the market since 1996 as apartments.*

Penair House was formerly the seat of the Launce family, passing, after successive sales, to the Vivians. Admiral Reynolds came into the property by marriage and his son, Sir Barrington, built a new house from which there was a good view of the surrounding country. 'The home grounds,' Gilbert tells us, 'are well laid out, and sheltered by extensive plantations.' Lady Reynolds was recorded as living there, in the *Hort. Direct.* of 1870, but the house continued to be listed, occupied by other residents, until between 1911 and 1916 Harcourt Williams from Pencalenick (q.v.) began to take up residence here, where he remained until his death in 1927.

References: 17th, 18th, 19th (Gen.) and 20th C; Illus.

Polwhele, Truro

SW83 47 : *EX105, GS352*

Cornish pol + hwilen (pl) *= beetles, pronounced* polWHEEL; *late 19th C. Tudor Gothic house with 16th C. core, listed grade II; originally medium to large estate, sloping north-east to stream, 95-50m., on Portscatho Series sandstone and slate, with acid soil, in an AGLV; rainfall 40-45", temperature zone C; school with relict grounds.*

Both the place and family of Polwhele have a long and distinguished history. William of Worcester recorded a castle here, and Norden was the first to mention a member of the family. Richard Polwhele is well known as the author of the *History of Cornwall*, commenced in 1803, and the *Hort. Direct.* was still listing another member of the family, T.R. Polwhele, as resident there from at least 1870 to 1908. During this time the building was extended, the southern part and the whole eastern front to the design of Gilbert Scott. The house and grounds are now occupied by a private school, which also acts as choir school to the Cathedral. An ice-house was discovered here in 1997.

References: 17th, 18th, 19th (Gen.) and 20th C.

Ruanlanihorne Old Rectory

SW89 42 : *EX105, GS352*

Cornish St Ruan + lan + horn/corn = *corner, pronounced* ruanLANihorn; *in an AONB, and an AGSV; relict.*

The reputation of this place was sufficient for *Lake* to consider it worth recording that adjoining the churchyard of Ruanlanihorne, 'are the old rectory house and gardens; the latter border the creek, and have always been remarkable for early produce, and for abundant crops of grapes.' The 'new' rectory has itself been sold off, and is presently known as the 'Old Rectory'.

References: 18th, 19th (Hort. & Gen.) C.

Saveock House, near Chacewater

SW77 44 : *EX104-5, GS352*

Cornish sevi (adj) = *strawberries, pronounced in Cornish* saVAYoc, *but anglicised to* SAVeock; *grounds at c. 75m. altitude, on Falmouth Series sandstone and slate; rainfall 40-45", temperature zone C; private.*

Gilbert writes:

> Seveock House [sic], the seat of Michael Allen, esq. is situated on the western side of this parish [of Kea], about four miles west of Truro. It is a neat uniform building, with suitable offices for a genteel establishment. It stands at the head of a handsome lawn, lined with several rows of trees, which after an easy descent, terminates at a sheet of water, surrounded by foliage, and gravel walks.

Lake, however, in 1868, wrote in the past tense that it 'was a genteel and commodious residence', since it had been sold off to become a farm. The 'sheet of water' has gone.

References: 18th, 19th (Gen.) C.

Southleigh, Lemon Street, Truro

SW82 44 : *EX104-5, GS352*

House listed grade II; small grounds on Portscatho Series sandstone and slate, with acid soil; rainfall 40-45", temperature zone C; house in apartments, grounds built over, garden extinct.

The development, early in the nineteenth century, of new houses along Lemon Street, led to a demand for plants in their gardens, which were supplied by J. Chappel, 'late Gardener to the Right Hon. Lord Bridport'. 'Mr Chappel first advertised in the Sherbourne Mercury in 1798 and was in business at the top of Lemon Street, where Southleigh now stands, until 1822'. The house was built on his nursery in 1831, originally as the vicarage for St John's Church across the street, but passed into private ownership, when the parsonage was relocated in the Falmouth Road. William Paul, a solicitor, lived here until his death in 1841, and the garden was listed in the *Hort. Direct.* for 1870 by Joseph Roberts, his son-in-law and partner in the practice.

References: 19th (Hort.) and 20th C; Lemon Street and its Neighbourhood, *University of Exeter Extra Mural Department, n.d. pp. 18, 24 with map.*

Treliske, Truro

SW80 45 : *EX104-5, GS352*

Trelesyk, *Assize Plea Rolls 1260; Cornish, Dexter suggests* tre + losc = *burnt, pronounced* treLISK; *originally medium to large grounds, at 90m. altitude, on Portscatho Series sandstone and slate, with acid soil; rainfall 40-45", temperature zone C; the original house is now a school with residual grounds, the remainder of the estate being occupied by the* Treliske Hospital *and a golf course.*

William Teague, a working miner who had made a fortune at Tincroft and Carn Brea mines, at first rented Pencalenick from the Vivians, but when in about 1873 Mrs Vivian was not prepared to sell, he erected for himself a mansion to the designs of James Hicks, on land forming part of a farm known as 'Liskes'. The garden was listed in the *Hort. Direct.* from 1908 to 1924, as then the residence of Sir George Smith, a county magistrate, or his widow.

References: 19th (Gen.) and 20th C.

Truthan, near St Erme

SW83 51 : *EX105, GS346*

Cornish tre + [?], *pronounced* TRUTHan, *the 'u' as in truck; house, well-house, and gate-piers, each listed grade II; grounds at 82m., on Ladock Beds, or Grampound Grit; rainfall 40-45", temperature zone C; private.*

The site of Truthan was originally part of the manor of Cargoll, owned by the Bishop of Exeter, but long in the possession of the Borlases. An earlier building on the site was the seat of John Jago, Sheriff of Cornwall in the mid-seventeenth century, and Courts were held here in 1684. The present house is early eighteenth century, probably including parts of the earlier building. The manor had been acquired by Sir Christopher Hawkins, of Trewithen, early in the nineteenth century, who disposed of it to Edward Collins. Gilbert wrote that 'Truthan House is of modern date, and, with the grounds, has been greatly improved by the present proprietor' [i.e. Collins], who died in 1855, but his son, who inherited the property, resided at Newton Ferrers, since which time it has passed through

43. Truthan. 'The grounds are laid out with great taste, and were greatly improved' by Edward Collins. (Twycross 1846: 45)

several hands. There survives a small park, and a walled garden adjacent to the house with ornamental trees.

References: 17th, 18th, 19th (Gen.) and 20th C; Illus.

ADDITIONAL CONTEMPORARY GARDENS

See also BOSVIGO, PENMOUNT and POLGWYNNE in the main section.

Bosbigal, Old Carnon Hill, Carnon Downs

SW79 39 : *EX104-5, GS352*

Cornish bos + [personal name?], pronounced bosBEEgal; 0.5 acre (0.2 ha) garden; opened in 1983 CGOG.

The garden of the late Fred Shepherd, VMH, former President of the Cornwall Garden Society, who had been the first Director of the Rosewarne Experimental Horticulture Station. As would be expected his own garden was exemplary and varied, and included a National Collection of Schizostylis and 300 cultivars of narcissus.

Calenick House, near Truro

SW82 43 : *EX104-5, GS352*

Cornish *clunyek = marshy place, pronounced C'LENick; house, and clock-tower each listed grade II*, early 19th C. weigh-house II; very small garden; opened in 1989 CGOG.

Calenick was notable for its smelting works, an extensive chandlery, and a crucible manufactory. The early eighteenth-century building, formerly a count house for the smelting works, has survived, along with the clock tower (dated 1752), and some of the original buildings put to a new use. The small garden has shrubs, herbaceous borders and old roses.

References: 19th (Gen.) and 20th C.

Carclew Mill, Perran-ar-worthal

SW77 38 : *EX104-5, GS352*

For the derivation see Carclew; small garden in an AONB, and an AGHV; opened in 1988-9 CGOG and NGS.

Adjacent to the Carclew estate, this is predominantly a woodland garden, with azaleas, rhododendrons, camellias and magnolias. There was a sunken water garden.

Garvinack Farm Woodland, Tregavethan, Truro

SW77 48 : *EX104-5, GS352* OPEN*

Cornish *cor = hedge, or boundary + [?], pronounced garVINack; open 1989-98 CGOG, mid March through April, by appointment, and one Sunday in March for charity.

Reference: Pring (1996: 69).

High Noon, Ladock

SW89 50O : *EX105, GS346* OPEN*

Part of Nansawsan House; open 1994-8 NGS, in combination with Ladock House, one Sunday in early May.

Ladock House, Ladock

SW89 50 : *EX105, GS346* OPEN*

Ladock is the saint's name, pronounced LADock; house, formerly the Rectory, listed grade II; open, in combination with High Noon, 1994-8 NGS, one Sunday in early May.

References: 20th C.

Nansawsan House, Ladock

SW89 50 : *EX105, GS346* OPEN*

Cornish nan + sawsan = Englishman, pronounced nanSAWsan; open 1994-8 NGS, one Sunday in mid May, and by appointment.

Piper's Barn, Penpol, Feock

SW81 39 : *EX104-5, GS352*

2 acre (0.8 ha) garden in an AONB, at river level; opened in 1983, 1985 CGOG.

A neat garden, described as 'beautiful for its imaginative use of water, richly planted'. The designer has now moved away.

Roseland House, Chacewater

SW75 44 : *EX104-5, GS352* OPEN*

Garden with a small nursery, open 1992-8 CGOG and NGS, Tuesdays April through July, and one Sunday each in the months of May to August for charity.

Reference: Pring (1996: 102).

Springfield Farm, Allet, near Truro

SW79 48 : *EX104-5, GS352* OPEN*

Open 1992-8 CGOG, two Sundays each in June and July, and by appointment.

Reference: Pring (1996: 104-5).

Towan Camellias, Trevilla Hill, Feock

SW82 39 : *EX104-5, GS352* OPEN*

Cornish towan = sand-dune; 3 acre (1.2 ha) nursery in an AONB; open 1997-8 CGOG, daily except Saturdays February through April. Came on to the market mid 1998.

Treworder Mill, Kenwyn, Truro

SW79 46 : *EX104-5, GS352*

Cornish tre + *gor-dre = over-farmstead, pronounced TreWARDer; grounds of 2.75 acres (1.1 ha) in a CNCS; opened 1994-6 NGS.

In the sixteenth and seventeenth centuries Treworder had been a substantial house of eight rooms, and two for servants, occupied by the Coryn family, though later divided. The present gardens of the Mill, in a tranquil setting bordering on the Kenwyn river with views of mature woodland, is planted with a wide range of moisture-loving plants, including candelabra primulas and hostas. Above the well-planted natural pond is an orchard of young trees. There are terraces, a summer-house and a greenhouse. The property came on to the market in mid 1997.

References: 19th (Gen.) and 20th C.

2. FALMOUTH

A town such as Falmouth, with a parish church dedicated to King Charles the Martyr who was executed in 1649, clearly cannot be of any great antiquity. In the previous section, Truro was shown once to have possessed an important harbour, although lower down the River Fal the Bishop of Exeter had founded Penryn, which received its charter as early as 1265, on ground belonging to Glasney College, quite explicitly as a rival to Truro. Both towns, however, were enraged when in the sixteenth century the Killigrews of Arwenack had both the temerity and the foresight to realize that Smithick on their estate, nearer the sea, had the potential for an even better harbour.

Falmouth now has the distinction of being the finest natural deep-sea harbour in Europe. It received its charter late, by Cornish standards, in 1661. In its first phase it was little more than a fishing port, but from 1688 until 1852, when the trade passed to Southampton, it was the headquarters of the Royal Mail packets. During this period of prosperity many fine houses were built, especially by the more successful Packet captains. Perhaps the best, and certainly the finest Regency building in Cornwall, is Marlborough House, built for Captain John Bull, and named after his ship. Penmere was another house, later known for its garden, which was built by a Captain Bullock. The packets brought with them overseas trade and travel, which made Falmouth one of the principal ports of the county, attracting a variety of merchants and speculators. Among them were the Foxes, a west country Quaker family from Wiltshire, who had married into, and were partners with the Were family at Wellington in Somerset, and into the Croker family in Devon. They progressed to Cornwall, from Catchfrench to Par, from whence the first George Croker Fox eventually came to settle in Falmouth. Here he built Bank House (until recently the YMCA), near Arwenack, in 1759, and opened his shipping offices along the road, overlooking the harbour, where they are today. If not the most important family in Falmouth, they built, developed or resided in at least fifteen of the properties whose gardens received notice during the last century, alongside which the reputation of others pales into insignificance.

The first George Croker Fox had two sons, the elder of whom built Grove Hill House in 1788, sited above Bank House in a 'grove' of the woods of the Arwenack estate, at the corner of a road which is still known as Wood Lane. No doubt he laid out the grounds at the same time, but it was his son, the third George Croker, who began the tradition of horticulture for which the family became famous, by submitting to the Royal Horticultural Society of Cornwall in 1837 a detailed list of 223 tender plants which he was cultivating in the open in his garden, and for which he received a Banksian Silver Medal. Many of these plants were recent, but some orange and lemon trees had been planted early in the century. He also later built Goonvrea, above the Foundry at Perran-ar-worthal, in which the family had an interest, but he died in 1850 without descendants.

His younger brother, the first Robert Were Fox, however, had four sons, three of whom were to continue the tradition begun by their uncle; Joshua, the second son, who farmed Tregedna at the lower end of Penjerrick, having fallen from grace by marrying outside the circle of Friends. Robert Were the second was the most distinguished among them, being elected a Fellow of the Royal Society for his scientific work, which was further promoted by his daughters, Anna Maria and Caroline, who together founded the Royal Polytechnic Society of Falmouth.

Robert Were, although renting part of his father's property at Penjerrick, first built himself a house at Rosehill along the Lane from Grove Hill. Little is known of his gardening activities there, since this was overshadowed by the later, greater reputation of Penjerrick, which came into his possession in 1839, after which he began to develop it in association with his son, Barclay, who tragically never lived to enjoy the fruits of his labours. Rosehill was to gain its reputation later in the century, after it had been sold to Howard Fox, Robert Were's nephew, in 1872. Howard was the son of a younger brother, Alfred, who had built his house, Wodehouse Place, alongside Rosehill. He too began to develop his estate at Glendurgan at about the same time as his brother at Penjerrick, but little was heard of the garden there until after his death. The youngest of the four brothers, Charles, also came to Trebah, the neighbouring garden to Glendurgan, during the mid-1820s, although Bishop Hunkin, in his article on Cornish gardens, credits the planting there chiefly to Charles Hext, who purchased it in 1906. Such then are the principal Fox gardens, but some account must be taken of others, who benefited from the mild climate of the area.

Tremough, during the time of William and Daniel Shilson, was renowned for its rhododendrons, grown from seed sent by the Hookers from the Himalayas, and for the activities of

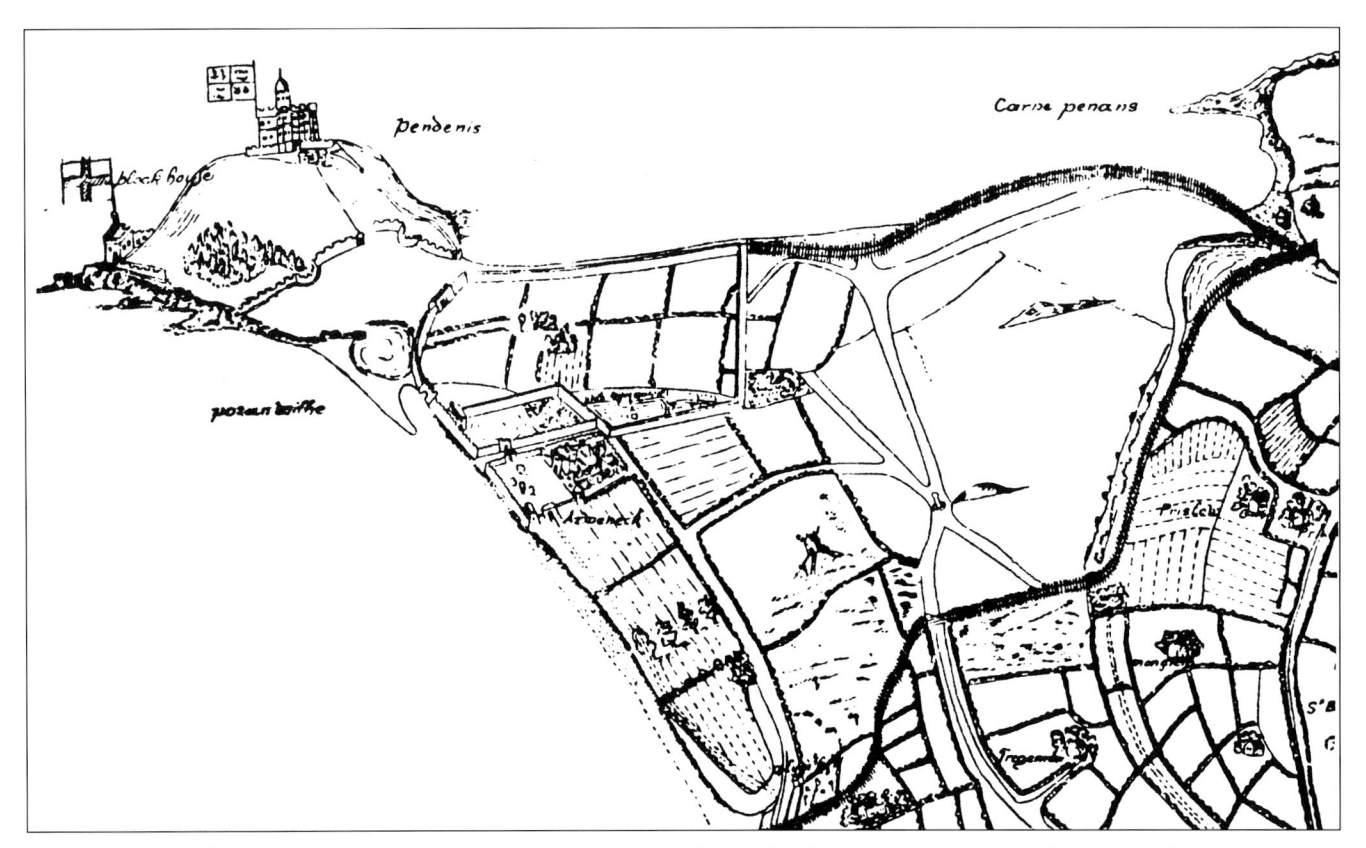

44. Arwenack. The Arwenack estate from Lord Burghley's map of c. 1580. The house is shown fortified, with a barbican leading into a front court. Towards the castle a large walled area encloses fields and a stewpond, and at the bottom left corner an ornamental garden. There are pallisades along Gyllyngvase to Swan Pool, returning to the shores of the estuary via Prislow, evidently intended to impale deer. The line of the present Arwenack Avenue, parallel to the shore, had already been laid out, but as yet without trees. (JRIC. 1887: 160)

their gardener, Richard Gill, in hybridizing. Boslowick, first developed by a member of the Tilly family, who had preceeded the Shilsons at Tremough, was known for its fine collection of acacias, and the attractive gardens at Penwarne began to be planted in the 1900s. Finally, the ancient estate at Enys must not be passed over, since with Arwenack it was the earliest of all Cornish gardens to receive any recognition, and this in a Cornish manuscript play on the Creation, dating from around 1450.

ARWENACK, Falmouth

SW81 32 : EX8 & 105, GS352

Cornish war *ar = on the + winnic = marshy place, pronounced arWENack; house listed grade II*, 18th C. gate-piers, well, Killigrew monument, each II; very small residual grounds, north-east facing, near sea level, on Mylor Series slate and sandstone, in an HS; ruined house with extinct grounds, and a small contemporary garden.

The history of Arwenack and the birth of Falmouth are synonymous, so can but lightly be touched on here. The manor was inherited by the Killigrew family, of Killigrew in St Erme parish (near Truro), in the reign of Richard II, by marriage with an heiress, where, according to Lysons, 'John Killigrew Esq., who died in 1567, built ... what was then esteemed the finest and most costly house in the county.' When Walter Raleigh landed here upon returning from the coast of Guinea, there were no more than a few fishermen's houses in an insignificant village named Smithick, but in 1663 Sir John Killigrew began to build several new houses, against much opposition from Penryn, Truro and Helston, who rightly foresaw this as a rival to their position as the principal ports.

Arwenack House was burnt down at the time of the Civil War, some say by Sir John himself, a zealous Royalist, who had been governor of Pendennis, to prevent it falling into Parliamentary hands, or as others believe by the then envious governor of the Castle. Whichever, it was never rebuilt, but was, as *Lake* describes, 'partially fitted up for the occasional residence of the family'. The local authority has done a service to the garden historian by erecting a useful sign at Arwenack which records from ancient maps four successive plans of the house and its surrounding gardens. The description of the ruined house by Beckford (of Fonthill) in 1787 may be quoted as of particular interest.

> Just out of the town, in a sheltered recess of the bay, lies a grove of tall elms [see Grove Hill House], forming several avenues, carpeted with turf. In the central part rises a stone pyramid, about thirty feet high, well designed and constructed, but quite plain, without any inscription. Between the trees one discovers a low white house, built in and out in a very capricious manner, with oriel windows and porches, shaded by bushes and prosperous bay. Several rose-coloured cabbages, with leaves as crisped and curled as those of the acanthus, decorate a little grass plot, neatly swept, before the door. Over the roof of this snug habitation, I espied the skeleton of a gothic mansion, so completely robed with thick ivy, as to appear like one of those castles of clipped box I have so often seen in a Dutch garden.

The pyramid had been erected by Martin Killigrew in 1737, and was later moved up the hill, only to come to rest finally on the shoreline, in the present car-park. A *History* in 1872 recollected that there had once been

> a deer park, gardens, a grove and a long avenue of trees, then called the walk. (now the Ropewalk.) [Gilbert remarked that 'contemplation had long been excluded from this spot by the noisy wheels of the ropemakers.'] The walk or rather walks, which are about 200 fathoms long, consist of three parallel and contiguous ways, with rows of elms between and on each side of them. Two of the ways are used as ropewalks, and the other is a cart road. About twenty years ago, the old trees, which were much decayed from age, were cut down, and young trees planted.

Susan Gay reported in 1903 that 'none of the original trees in the old avenue are now standing', having succumbed to great storms in 1703, 1758, 1764 and 1790. Of those that remained, it was noted, many 'from Age and the Shallowness of the Soil [were] now actually Dead on their Leggs'. The Avenue with gate-piers, Grove Hill, and the Rope Walk, still survive as street- and place-names in Falmouth, and, as McCabe writes, 'Every effort has been made to recreate the appearance of old Arwenack, including a courtyard with little parterres surrounded by neatly clipped box hedges', which can be viewed from the road.

References: 17th, 18th, 19th (Hort. & Gen.) and 20th C; Beckford (1787, quoted in Redding 1842: 133); Tregelles (1884:ii.115-195).

BOSLOE, Mawnan Smith

SW77 27 : EX8 & 105, GS359, SS SW61/71

Cornish *prys = thicket + *loch = pool (see Boslowick), pronounced bozLOW; house listed grade II, lodge, entrance gateway, terrace wall and settle, each II; medium garden south-east sloping, 40-25m., on Gramscatho Beds, with acid soil, in an AONB and HC, and an AGSV; rainfall 40-45", temperature zone C; purchased by the National Trust in 1980, as holiday cottages, garden opened 1983-90 CGOG, 1991, 1993-5 NGS.

Bosloe was built in 1880 for the Fox family, who owned the adjacent Glendurgan (q.v.), on the site of a cottage named after William Pitt, Earl of Chatham, to which later additions were made, as is indicated by the date 1903 on a rainwater head. Over the turn of the century the resident is recorded as having been William Welsford Ward, JP. The house stands on a stone terrace, with a terraced lawn below, in the corner of which is a granite settle, with a curious stone feature of uncertain nature. The lawn ends with a neat ha-ha. There is an impressive vista of the Helford River, framed by plantations of trees on each side of the lawns. The drive has been densely planted with evergreen azaleas, and the garden to the east of the lawns is dotted with camellias and rhododendrons, all of which make a colourful spectacle at the time the garden was previously open. The gardener's bothy, which is let as a holiday cottage, has dove holes in the gables.

References: Coast of Cornwall No 16, Helford River, *National Trust, 1989: 4.*

BOSLOWICK, Falmouth

SW79 31 : EX8 & 105, GS352

Presloweth 1503; Cornish *prys = thicket + *loch = pool + yk = diminutive, pronounced bozLOWick; extinct, formerly medium to large sized garden; now a public house, and housing estate.

Boslowick was included in a 1783 list of estates belonging to the Manor of Penryn-Foreign, and by 1841 there was a mansion there, owned by James Bull, a Falmouth solicitor, 'with yard, garden, orchard. lawns, plantations, and 39 acres.' James was the descendant of a family of packet captains, which included the famous John Bull of Marlborough House (q.v.). Tobias Tilly, who similarly was a descendant of another packet captain, by his marriage to John Bull's niece in about 1834, became related to this family. Thus it was that Harry Tilly, the third child of Tobias and Henrietta (née Bull), born in 1839, was eventually to take up residence at the Bull residence of Boslowick. The senior line of the Tilly family were by this time well established at Tremough (q.v.), where they had built the Barton and created an Italian garden. The early maps, however, do not suggest that the garden at Boslowick had any such elaborate designs, although it was reputedly 'a fine garden at the beginning of the century [which] specialised in growing peaches (though not for sale).' It was also numbered among Thurston's select gardens in 1930, as containing 'a good collection of acacias', of which he cites *A. juniperina* (an especially tender species), *longifolia*, *melanoxylon*, *riceana*, and *verticillata*.

References: 20th C.

CARWINION, Mawnan Smith

SW78 28 : EX8 & 105, GS359   OPEN

Cornish car + gwyn = white, fair, pronounced carWINion; garden of 9.5 acres (3.8 ha), in south facing valley, 65m. to the sea, on Gramscatho Beds, with acid soil, in an AONB, and an AGSV; rainfall 40-45", temperature zone C; donated by Cecil Rogers to the National Trust in 1969, who also own 20 acres (8.1 ha) of woodland. The garden, managed by Anthony Rogers, is open, 1983-98 CGOG, 1988, 1991-8 NGS, all year round.

Carwinion was bequeathed to a younger son of the owner of Penrose (q.v.), possibly to the Revd John Rogers, who was rector of Mawnan from 1806 to 1838. It became the residence of his son Reginald (born 1819), who built the house, with a long drive ending in a late eighteenth-century carriage ring. His grandson, another Reginald (born 1854), was probably responsible for the planting and design of the garden in the late nineteenth century, in association with the Fox family at Glendurgan and Trebah (q.v.), who were his cousins. It is possible that the family helped to finance various plant expeditions, from which they and neighbouring gardens profited.

The Carwinion valley, indeed, has similarities with those of the Fox gardens, although it is longer and narrower. From the end of the eighteenth century it was dominated by a wooden structure known as 'The Rogers' Tower', described in *Lake* as 'an observatory'. This collapsed in the 1930s, and its site is now marked by a mound. There are few changes from the appearance of the grounds as seen in the first edition of the Ordnance Survey, although a former orchard to the south of the house has been replaced by two additional ponds, and the walled garden grassed over. To the south and east of the house, lawns slope down towards the walled garden. Of the former herbaceous borders in this area, only a stone sundial now survives. The present owner has planted camellias, eucryphias and species rhododendrons, and in 1986 began a reference collection of some eighty to ninety species of bamboos, which has been featured in the national press, more than half of which are cultivated in the walled garden. This was one of Thurston's select gardens in 1930, from which he cited sixteen plants, including a *Leucodendron argenteum* grown from seed brought back by Commander Arthur Rogers from South Africa.

References: 19th (Gen.) and 20th C; K. Bradley-Hole, 'Glorious Jungle', Daily Telegraph, 31 March 1990; C. Haddon, 'Gardens of Paradise', Sunday Times, 8 April 1990.

ENYS, Mylor Bridge

SW79 36 : EX104-5, GS352

Cornish enys = island, tongue of land, pronounced ENis; house including 18th C. service wing, clock tower, walls and gate-piers together listed grade II; barn, coach-house and stable c. 1840, together II; 210 acre (85 ha) parkland and relict garden listed grade II, east and north-east sloping 70-c. 25m., house at 40m., on Mylor Series slate and sandstone, and alluvium, with acid soil in an AGLV with an AM (cross); rainfall 45-50", temperature zone C; has opened on special occasions in the spring for charity.

Enys was the first garden ever to have received public notice in Cornwall, and can claim to have been among its greatest. 'It is generally understood', *Hitchins* records, that

> Enys ... has been in this family ever since the days of Edward I, for so high this family can be traced. In the Cornish play, brought into Oxford in 1450, and of which the manuscript is still preserved in the Bodleian Library, Enys and some other lands [such as Arwenack (q.v.)] are given as a reward to the builder of the universe.

The garden was also celebrated for its beauty in the 1709 edition of Camden's *Magna Britannia*, which is the first notice of a Cornish garden in a published volume. In 1824, *Hitchins* considered that the gardens 'still preserve their beauty'. The illustration from Borlase (1758) shows them as they were in the first half of the eighteenth century. There will be noticed a long walled garden to the east of the house, with two pavilions with cupolas, and a turret on the far end wall. Along the south wall is a long narrow kitchen garden. The interior of the main walled garden is laid out in paths and appears to have had a central structure. The mature trees on the far left of the view are elsewhere shown to have led to a former entrance from the south-east. The house itself is seated on a level area edged with walls, at the western corner of which is a small building, which is described as a 'dairy' on a

45. Enys. Even though this engraving dates from the mid eighteenth century, the layout of the garden is at least seventeenth-century, and in part considerably older. (Borlase 1758: 7)

later estate map of *c.* 1779, which also confirms the existence of the other features. In addition it includes a fish pond in the position of one of the surviving ponds (not visible in the print), with parkland and orchards. What is here seen and mapped is a garden which had been in existence for some considerable time. The walled garden with its gazebos and walks is almost certainly seventeenth century, and the fish ponds even older. As it appears today it is much shortened, although the pavilions survive, now with slate roofs, the northern having been converted into a gardener's cottage, and the southern into an apple store. Gilbert, in 1820, described the grounds as

> still remarkably beautiful. There is also a very delightful shrubbery, with a fresh water lake, a handsome temple [now disappeared, unless he was referring to the 'dairy'], and most delicious walks, shaded with a rich variety of foliage.

The 1839 Tithe map, however, introduces a new phase, when the garden was substantially altered. As early as 1748, a John King, whose identity is so far unknown, is mentioned as having planned alterations. Much later, in 1833, John Samuel Enys engaged Henry Harrison, a London architect who had worked on several Cornish houses, to produce designs for the garden as well as the house. Among these later features are the 'Ladies Garden', illustrated in the *Gardeners' Chronicle* in 1889, replacing part of the kitchen garden, which leads on through an arch to an enclosure known as the 'Colonel's Garden' (Col. John Enys, 1757-1818).

To the south of the house is a formal lawn with a rosary and a pool which probably predated the new house. A sundial placed there in memory of Jane Enys in 1865, now removed from its pedestal, has a topograph around its rim. The lakes in the lower valley, joined by a small cascade, retain the atmosphere which captivated the photographers in the early horticultural journals. A waterwheel there, which lifted water to the house, can still be operated. Enys has always been noted for its bluebell woods which, with the destruction of many trees by storm damage, have become an open sheet of blue, and are now a spectacle when seen in association with an immense copper beech in early foliage. The courtyard and its buildings are of interest, especially for the fine stone Italianate clock tower, and the horse mill which is in a workable condition. Some of the shaped pieces of granite in these buildings are believed to have originated in the demolished medieval Glasney College at Penryn. Later in the nineteenth century the horticultural reputation of this garden was much enhanced by the plant collections of J.D. Enys. 'During his sojourn in foreign lands', wrote Hamilton Davey,

> Mr. Enys greatly enriched Enys and other grounds by the seeds and plants he was

constantly sending home [especially from New Zealand and Patagonia]. Perhaps the most prized of his introductions is the Chatham Island Forget-me-not *(Myosotidium nobile.)*

In 1907 he privately published a booklet of *Trees and Shrubs and Plants growing at Enys*, which listed in excess of 1,000 varieties. Many, through age and storms, have now disappeared, but the former gardener, Richard Dee, endeavoured to locate those which have survived. Enys was listed in the *Hort. Direct.* from at least 1870 until 1924, and was one of Thurston's select gardens. Since occupation by the Netherlands Navy during the Second World War, the house has not been used as a residence, and the savage gales of 1979 wreaked much havoc, but there are signs that the importance of this garden is beginning again to be recognized, although its future remains in doubt.

References: 17th, 18th, 19th (Hort. & Gen.) and 20th C; Illus.

FOX ROSEHILL GARDENS, see Rosehill

GLENDURGAN, Mawnan

SW77 27 : EX8 & 105, GS359; SS.SW61/7　　　　OPEN

Cornish, Dexter suggests glyn = narrow river valley + dur = water + gan, goon = by a down, *pronounced* glenDERgan; *grounds of 40 acres (16 ha), garden of 25 acres (10 ha) listed grade II, sloping 70-10m. to estuary, on Gramscatho Beds, soil 'acid over shillet with some clay', in an AONB, and an AGSV, in part a CNCS; rainfall 40-45", temperature zone C; donated by Cuthbert Fox and family in 1962 to the* National Trust, *open daily through March to end of October, with an official guide.*

Glendurgan, considered by some to be the best planted and designed valley garden in Cornwall, seems to have escaped notice in horticultural literature until after it appeared among Thurston's select gardens in 1930. He there described the estate as purchased by Alfred, the third son of Robert Were Fox I, between 1821 and 1829, although it seems more probable that, as in the case of his brothers at Penjerrick and Trebah, he did not come into full possession until the 1830s. His son, Wilson Lloyd Fox, informed Thurston that:

> When Alfred Fox first planted it, he favoured *Pinus Pinaster* for standing the wild winds, and their cones at present furnish the squirrels with food. From time to time he added a great variety of trees and shrubs, and made several orchards. There is a very puzzling labyrinth made of laurel, presumably 70-80 years old [i.e. 1850-60, during his childhood, although now usually dated much earlier in 1833], and camellia trees of like age. It is remarkable that the place has been under the management of only two head gardeners since 1825.

These were John Peters, gardener for fifty years, and Willian Eddy for fifty-five years, who were followed by George Sanderson for thirty years. Glendurgan is a larger garden than the adjoining Trebah, but does not have the same direct view of the river from the house, although the valley ends at the picturesque little fishing village of Durgan. Barclay Fox in 1833 described a visit when he 'assisted Uncle A. in cutting down his trees & drinking his tea.' This felling, perhaps, may have been the prelude to the laying out of the garden, since the planting of the maze, reputedly modelled on that at Sydney Gardens, Bath, is usually dated (perhaps wrongly) in the same year. (The date 1883 in Trinick [1981] seems to be a misprint.) Barclay also vividly described the occasion on 8 April 1837 when the thatched cottage burnt down:

> The crowd of villagers there assembled were eager in their condolences with his Honour [Alfred], who showed himself the hero throughout & caused, I imagine, admiration & wonder. He was the merriest of the party, looked on the bright side of it & gave all the operatives some porter, which was the finest trait of all.

Well, of course, he still had his fine mansion in Falmouth, and perhaps was glad of the excuse to build a new house on his country estate. It would have been at this same time that the south-east wall was constructed behind the new house, originally intended for fruit, but now with the addition of a western wall, planted out as a formal garden. Alfred was also responsible for the front entrance and the curving drive. While the admirable overall design and foundation planting may be attributed to Alfred Fox, there is a certain indefiniteness about his son's account of the later developments, which may explain why the garden did not arouse any horticultural interest before it was inherited, on the death of his widow in 1890, by her fifth son, George Henry Fox, who was a keen botanist. It was to him that many of the conifers are due, as well as the fragrant and tender rhododendrons, for which Penjerrick, under the care of his cousin Robert, was becoming famous. He died in 1931, to be succeeded by his eldest son, Cuthbert Lloyd, who, assisted by his wife, increased the range of species and varieties. 'Many of the plants now at their best', wrote Michael Trinick,

> date from this period, Asiatic rhododendrons and magnolias, cornuses, camellias, hydrangeas and

eucryphias ... also some unusual plants - aloe, persimmon and evergreen oleasters.

He added:

> Perhaps their particular contribution ... was their sense of restraint. Instead of planting up every corner, so tempting in Cornwall where plants grow quickly, they left glades and sweeps of grass and encouraged wild flowers to grow beneath the trees.

In 1962, on the bicentenary of the arrival of the Fox family in Falmouth, the house and garden at Glendurgan were donated to the National Trust, although Cuthbert Fox continued to live in the house and manage the garden, being followed by his son, Philip. At present restoration work is in hand, seen most notably in the cutting down of the laurel hedges of the maze to encourage their regeneration. Glendurgan differs from Penjerrick and Trebah, not so much from the exigencies of the terrain, as by a different concept of design.

References: 19th (Gen.) and 20th C; Barclay Fox's Journal, *ed. R.L. Brett, 1979: 57, 104;* Coast of Cornwall No 16, Helford River, *National Trust 1989: 5.*

GOONVREA, Perran-ar-worthal

SW77 38 : EX104-5, GS352

Cornish goon = *upland pasture* + *bre = hill, pronounced goonVRAY; originally an estate of about 20 acres (8 ha), east, south-east sloping 45-10m., on Mylor Series slates and sandstones, with acid soil, in an AGLV; rainfall 45-50", temperature zone C; house demolished after fire in 1980s, now a residential development with relict gardens.*

It is difficult to imagine today that Perran-ar-worthal was, during the nineteenth century, a hive of industrial and commercial activity. Beside their Foundry, which they shared with the Williamses, the Fox family were also importers of wood from Norway (hence the Norway Inn) at the now abandoned wharves. Several of the family had residences here, among which was Goonvrea, erected in the first half of the nineteenth century for George Croker Fox III of Grove Hill. He died in 1850 without issue, just at a time when there was a serious slump in the copper trade, which seems to have affected the family fortunes enough to cause them eventually to relinquish their partnership in the Foundry to the Williamses, who took over not only the business, but also two of the larger Fox houses at Tredrea (q.v.) and Goonvrea. The latter was then occupied by F.M. (later Sir Frederick Martin) Williams, a director of the Foundry. The upper storeys of the house, at that time an hotel, were destroyed by fire in about 1980, and the remainder was demolished in 1989. There had been a gazebo, bowling alley, walled garden - in which have now been built separate dwellings - and wooded walks, some of which have survived. Little, however, is known of the garden in earlier times, although it was listed in the *Hort. Direct.* at least from 1870 during the time of F.M. Williams, and in 1916 under J.P. Paull.

References: 19th (Hort. & Gen.) and 20th C.

GREATWOOD, Mylor

SW81 36 : EX104-5, GS352

Formerly Wood Cottage, *Gilbert 1820; medium size gardens, east sloping 25m. to shore, on Mylor Series slate and sandstone, with acid soil, in an AONB; rainfall 40-45", temperature zone C; private, in apartments.*

Joseph Fox was the second son of George Fox of Par, by his second marriage, who became the head of the medical line of the family in Falmouth. He remained at Bank House when his brother, George Croker, left to build Grove Hill House in 1788. His son, Joseph, also studied medicine, at Edinburgh, St Andrews and the London Hospital, but becoming of independent means on the death of his father, he practised medicine for only seventeen years, retiring to Wood Cottage in 1800, which at that time was probably part of Carclew, 'the bottom of [whose] interesting grounds', wrote Gilbert,

> is washed by the deep slow-moving waters of Restronguet Lake, whose gentle murmurs produce a pleasing effect, particularly at the flowing in of the tides.

By this time the cottage had been enlarged sufficiently to be described as the 'seat of Joseph Fox, M.D.'.

> The situation and embellishments of this charming retreat render it a place of uncommon interest. The moss-house, walks, and resting seats, are constructed with that superior taste, and philosophic arrangement, which give a varied beauty to the multiplicity of objects which nature and art have here assembled together. The avenues, which open through the woods, let in a diversity of pleasing objects, romantically situated on the juts of Falmouth Harbour; and the variety of trading vessels which are constantly coasting up and down the river, and give it an air of gaiety and general cheerfulness.

Gilbert, as a vendor of medicines, would have been well acquainted with Joseph Fox, who himself described his 'seat' modestly in an adver-

116 Truro and Falmouth

tisement in 1805 for a manservant, as 'Garden Grounds and a small Farm (together about fourteen acres).' In the latter years of the century, however, the house, after some remodelling, was rather grandly renamed Greatwood. Michael Trinick located here the second of a pair of the 'Arundell Lions', which had once sat on the steps at Bank House, one of which had previously been removed to Glendurgan. After the death of Joseph Fox in 1832, the house passed through several hands, many vicissitudes and a period of near dereliction, but has now been restored 'in an exemplary fashion'. The terraced gardens are still charming when viewed from the river.

References: 18th, 20th C.

GROVE HILL HOUSE, Wood Lane, Falmouth

SW81 32 : EX8 & 105, GS352

House listed grade II; very small residual garden, south-east sloping from c. 35m., on Mylor and Falmouth Series slate and sandstone, with acid soil; rainfall 40-45", temperature zone C; original garden extinct, house developed for holiday letting.

George Croker Fox I had moved from Par to Falmouth in 1759, where he built Bank House along the shore from Arwenack. His eldest son, George Croker II, in 1788 moved up higher into the woods of Grove Hill on the other side of the Arwenack Avenue to build himself a new house. The 'elegant' Warner of Bath, in 1809 considered that Arwenack

> and Mr. Fox's beautiful seat, ... which lies in its neighbourhood, and possesses every circumstance of beauty, and advantage of situation, are the only private residences that claim any attention in the vicinity of Falmouth.

His son, George Croker Fox III, was the first of the family on record to engage in those experiments in the acclimatization of exotics for which they later became famous. Grove Hill was the first of the houses along Wood Lane to be built, with a garden much more extensive than at present, running down to the Dell, where there was a lodge known later, because of its design, as the Swiss Cottage. But rather than its design, it was the range of plants grown which aroused the greatest interest, as it still does today. When in 1837 the recently formed Royal Horticultual Society of Cornwall offered their Banksian Medal 'for an account of the largest number of new and hitherto undescribed plants, which shall have

46. Grove Hill. The house stands high above a lawn sloping down to the former walled garden, greenhouses and fish ponds, in an area now known as the Dell. (Twycross: 1846: 68)

flowered in the possession of the Competitor', Croker Fox submitted a carefully compiled list of 223 plants which received the award. The list opens with a description of the garden, of which the climate at that time is perhaps the most intriguing. It was generally mild, with little ice or snow, but

> cold winds prevail in the spring - in summer, the thermometer stands nearly as follows.- At the highest 74 [Farenheit]; at the lowest, 48; average temperature, 61.- In winter, at the highest, 51; at the lowest, 23; average temperature, 37.

Although certainly equable, this is a colder climate than one is usually led to expect, and suggests that much attention must have been given to the protection of, for instance, the two varieties of orange which had survived, one for ten, the other for twenty-three years, and a lemon for seventeen years. Among the longer-surviving trees were an *Acacia armata,* for 16 years (which had only been introduced to the country in 1803), a *Metrosideros floribunda* (*Angophora intermedia*) for twenty years, and a *Leptospermum ambiguum* [?], for seventeen years. The dates of planting out extended from 1807 for a *Myrtus communis* to a mere year or two, showing that the introductions had been a continuous, on-going process.

The Foxes, with their shipping offices facing the harbour, were in a peculiarly fortunate position to acquire exotic species from the many seamen who used the port. The coming of the railway in the mid 1860s, however, by cutting into the lower end of the grounds, was an augur of the garden's demise. Croker Fox III had no issue, so that after his widow's death the estate passed to his nephew, Barclay Fox, and after his untimely death to his son, Robert, under whose name it was listed in the *Hort. Direct.* from 1908 until 1916. But already, by that time, the steady expansion of the town was eating into the grounds, so that today little remains of this once famous and most innovative garden but a lawn and a few trees.

References: 19th (Hort. G Gen.) and 20th C; Illus.

GYLLYNGDUNE GARDENS, Falmouth

SW81 31 : *EX8 & 105, GS352*   OPEN

Cornish, Holmes suggests an gylen dhown = *deep nook or bay, pronounced* gillingDOON; *medium estate, south sloping to the sea, on Falmouth Series sandstone and slate, with acid soil; rainfall 40-45", temperature zone C; house now the* Gyllyngdune Hotel, *the remaining grounds the* Princess Pavilion *and Gyllyngdune Gardens public park, open all year.*

In 1838 General William Jesser Coope engaged George Wightwick to design a house for him on Gyllyngvase, to be named 'Summerlands'. At the same time he purchased the advowson of the rectory of Falmouth from Lord Wodehouse, into which his son, William John, was inducted. Unfortunately, the General was killed in an accident shortly after the house was completed and his son had become rector, who then himself took up residence in his father's place, after which the house became known as Gyllyngdune. There had been an isolated house along the shore at Gyllyngvase as early as 1806, as a date-stone in the garden of the hotel shows, but the new dwelling was much grander, and the first edition of the Ordnance Survey shows that a quite elaborate garden, with some parkland, had been created at the same time.

The house itself is now an hotel, which has retained the coach house and front lawns, although the lodge with fine iron gates is now separated from the grounds by Emslie Road. Alongside, to the west of the hotel and stables, has been built the Princess Pavilion, the original walled garden to its south being laid out as a lawn, ornamented by bedding schemes, and with a central bandstand. From this area two sets of steps flanked by vases run down to a terrace, on which stood the stove houses, once used for tender plants, but recently demolished. From this terrace a path then leads along one side of a hollow from which the building stone for the house had probably been quarried, which has been planted as a rock garden, with a central circular bed. Along this path there is excavated in the rock face a seat in the form of a shell grotto, semi-circular in plan, with a central division containing a peep-hole. On a prominence to the right stands a primitive arch, consisting of two slender square columns, supporting a similar slab of granite. A tunnel leads out from the floor of the quarry across Cliff Road (which was a later development) down steps to the beach.

The paddocks and parkland on each side of the quarry, once part of the estate, are now occupied by other buildings; but on the present promenade, although originally within the grounds of the property, there is, raised on a mound, a summer-house or gazebo which, because of crosses in the gables, has wrongly been termed a 'chapel', although it may well have been used as an oratory. When viewed from the sea, the whole Gyllyngdune estate still stands out conspicuously from the later developments, by reason of its mature trees and plantations. This complex (other than the hotels) is preserved by the local authority as a leisure area, but although still used as a public park, its interesting survival as a relict Victorian private garden is commonly forgotten. The Revd W.J. Coope sold the Gyllyngdune estate in 1863 for the then not inconsiderable sum of £10,000, to Sampson Waters (d.1866), who had mined in South America. His successors sold it in 1903 to the town for pleasure and winter gardens, which they opened in 1907, the Pavilion being added in 1910. (See also the Queen Mary Gardens.)

References: 19th (Gen.) and 20th C.

KIMBERLEY PARK, Falmouth

SW80 32 : *EX8 & 150, GS352*   OPEN

Urban public park of about 7 acres (2.8 ha), on Mylor Series slate and sandstone, with acid soil; rainfall 40-45", temperature zone C; open all year.

Kelly's *Directory* (1893) records that:

> The public garden, called "Kimberley Park", at Berkeley Vale ... was laid out and presented to the inhabitants in 1877 by the Earl of Kimberley K.G. as an ornamental recreation ground.

The garden still handsomely serves that same purpose today. The park was laid out by John Simpson Tyerman, formerly of the Liverpool Botanic Gardens, then living at Penlee House, Tregony (q.v.). The opening was announced in *The Times* of 26 May, and Thurston included the park among his select gardens, citing fifteen trees. The Dracaenas (i.e. Cordylines) also received a mention in the *Garden* of 1880, and the *Gardeners' Chronicle* referred to plants submitted to the Falmouth Naturalists' Association exhibition in 1889. The Earl of Kimberley (which is in Norfolk) had inherited the Killigrew estates in Falmouth, through the marriage of an ancestor to a member of the Berkeley family, hence the names of the Park and the Vale. (See further under Arwenack for the Killigrew family.)

References: 19th (Hort.) C.

LANTERNS, Restronguet Creek, Mylor

SW81 37 : *EX105, GS352*   OPEN*

0.5 acre (0.2 ha) garden, on Mylor Series slates and sandstone, in an AONB; rainfall 40-45", temperature zone C; open 1990-98 CGOG, and NGS, daily, all year.

Lanterns, through which a stream runs to the Restronguet Creek, lies above the Pandora Inn. This is a plantsman's garden, begun in 1966, with a wide-ranging collection of species and varieties, both for the waterside and dry areas. By reason of its position it is possible to grow tender plants such as *Parochetus communis*, and the *Salvias elegans* 'Scarlett Pineapple' and *guarantica* in the open all year round. Alpines, always unreliable in the damp Cornish climate, are rarely attempted, but here *Soldanella villosa*, which is notoriously difficult to flower, flourishes. More intensive cultivation is made possible by the use of the two heated greenhouses, and a conservatory. Douglas Chapman, who was chiefly responsible for the hard landscaping, died in 1994, and his wife Irene until recently struggled, with some help, to keep the garden open.

References: 20th C.

MARLBOROUGH HOUSE, Silverdale Road, Falmouth

SW79 31 : *EX8 & 105, GS352*

House listed grade II*, early 19th C. gates, railings and flanking walls II*, stables II; relict garden, sloping south-west from c. 10m., on Mylor Series slate and sandstone, and alluvium, with acid soil; rainfall 40-45", temperature zone C; grounds reduced in size, house private.

'Falmouth owed a great deal of its former prosperity to its being the packet station, first established about the year 1688.' The packets sailed, according to *Lake*, for the 'Garonne, West Indies, Lisbon, New York, Corunna, Gibraltar and other places,' and by 1782 eighteen packets were sailing to the West Indies and America alone. Many of the packet captains were able to amass a sufficient capital to build themselves fine houses for retirement, such as Penmere (q.v.). Among them was John Bull who, in his ship the *Marlborough*, had achieved a great reputation for the daring and bravery necessary in the protection of the mail against the piracy of the French. In 1805 he inherited a cottage, built about 1713, which he named after his ship and began to enlarge into what A.L. Rowse described as 'one of the most beautiful houses in England', a view endorsed by the London Georgian Group after a visit in 1990.

The graceful illustration in Twycross shows this splendid Regency house in its original form in 1846, before the two wings had been raised to the first-floor level by his son. Unusually, Twycross included a jolly garden scene, which perhaps justifies the presence of Marlborough in the present context. Bull began to improve his estate, in 1824 ordering 500 elm trees and 150 additional apple trees. Among his subsequent orders were 300 more elms, 2,000 thorns, 1,000, followed by another 1,000 beech, and 200 Scotch firs. In 1825 he ordered another 1,000 thorns, and in 1828 another sixty apples.

47. Marlborough House, described as one of the most beautiful Regency houses in the country. (Twycross 1846: 89)

In the large-scale OS map of 1880 the formal layout of the garden can clearly be distinguished, with its orchards, plantations and hedge trees leading down to 'The Captain's Walk' by the Swan Pool (so named for its former use by the Arwenack estate). Bull personally assisted in the planting of what Thurston described as the 'beautiful Marlborough or Bull's avenue ... of tall Cornish elms'. The Bull family continued at Marlborough until 1947, after which the house was purchased by Prof. H.G. Hanbury QC, who with his wife took an interest in cultivating the garden, though now on a scale reduced by urban expansion. John Bull himself could claim to have been a 'celebrity', but among others who have lived here were, in the 1930s, the aviator, Amy Johnson, and in the 1970s the fictional characters of the long-running television series, *The Onedin Line*, which harboured at Charlestown (see Duporth).

References: 19th (Hort. & Gen.) and 20th C; Illus; M.E. Philbrick, 'Some Falmouth Packet Captains 1729-1832', History around the Fal, part II, 1983: 65-77.

MELLINGEY, Perranwell

SW77 39 : EX104-5, GS352

Velingie Mill 1590; Cornish *melyn-jy = mill-house, pronounced meLINgee; lodge with walling etc. listed grade II; originally a 14 acre (5.6 ha), now a 7 acre (2.8 ha) garden, south sloping 20-10m., on Mylor Series slate and sandstone, with acid soil; rainfall 40-45", temperature zone C; original house burnt down and grounds partially built over, modern house and garden opened 1983-4 CGOG.

A farm at Mellingey is shown on a map of 1691, and in 1872 *Lake* recorded it as the property of John Jose, but Barratt dates the house 'in or about 1883', extended to designs by James Hicks. Jose was a successful miner who had made a fortune in South America which enabled him to own much property in the parish. The gardens, which were listed in the *Hort. Direct.* from 1908 until 1924 under his widow's name, were at that time 'one of the main features of this property'. The house, however, was burnt down in 1940, and stood in ruins for the next dozen years before being taken down. A new and smaller house has since been erected on the site, with the same name, although much of the original grounds have been built over. However, the attractive ornamental lodge, with its handsome gate-piers and walling, now known as Bay Tree Lodge, survives on the main road to indicate the general direction of the former drive.

The present garden is still substantial. There is a lawn in front of the property, and to the side, with formal gardens and a fish pond. Steps lead down to further terraces also laid out with trees and borders, beyond which are mature woodlands with meandering pathways running below to the Creek at the bottom of the valley.

References: 19th (Gen.) and 20th C.

MENEHAY, Falmouth

SW78 32 : EX8 &105, GS352

Menehy, Lay Subsidy Rolls *1327; Cornish *meneghy = sanctuary, pronounced* MENehay*; 18th C. remodelled house listed grade II; small to medium south facing grounds at 75m. on Mylor Series slate and sandstone, with acid soil; rainfall 40-45", temperature zone C; private.*

Menehay, which means in Cornish 'sanctuary' - that is, land belonging to a monastery (Latin *monarchia*, cf. **meneghy*) - was part of the manor of Penryn-Foreign, belonging to the Bishop of Exeter. In 1841 the house was described as with 'mowhay [i.e. rick yard], yard, road, watering, plantations and 16 fields totalling 75 acres.' Although owned as lessee to the Bishop by Richard Mitchell Hodge, it was at that time occupied by Elizabeth Weymouth. The 'old garden' was described by Thurston, who included this in his select list, 'as being developed by Mr Charles Phillips', who had added a small Pinetum. It had already been listed in the *Hort. Direct.* under his name in 1919 and 1924. In 1904 he had introduced small plants of the New Zealand tree-fern, *Dicksonia antarctica*, one of which Thurston (who cited some seventy other species, including magnolias, from here) described as having attained a girth of 6 feet 4 inches in 1928. Two from this planting still survive. Since 1939 Menehay has changed hands several times, but the present owners are endeavouring to restore and develop the gardens there.

References: 20th C.

MEUDON, Mawnan Smith

SW78 28 : EX8, GS359

Cornish *merthyn = sea fort, pronounced MEWdun*; house listed grade II; grounds of 18 acres (7.3 ha), in an east facing valley 60m. to the sea, on Gramscatho Beds and raised beach, with 'acid shale, sand and clay soil', in an AONB, and an AGSV; rainfall 40-45", temperature zone C; the* Meudon Hotel, *open to non-residents.*

The background to Meudon is recounted in *Hitchins*:

> The barton ... was for some time a seat of the Carveths ... Of this barton Mr. Kempe purchased the lease ... [and] built on it a house for his own residence; which, with the estate, was carried by his widow to her second husband, the late Francis Gregor, Esq. of Trewarthenick [q.v.]; under whose representative, it is now held on lease by Mr. Fox.

This refers to the seventeenth-century farm, still existing alongside the hotel, which was itself remodelled and enlarged in the 1970s from another house built at the beginning of the twentieth century on the site of two 300-year-old coastguard cottages. It was at this time that much of the grounds were laid out.

> The hanging gardens were brought back to their full glory during the years 1945 to 1963 when the property belonged to a Lady Worley. The then head gardener Joseph Hojek, started work in the gardens, just after the war and was so very much the "instrument" of their success ... The setting for Meudon is unusually beautiful, the garden abounds with rare flowering shrubs, giant rhododendrons and azaleas, eucalyptus, magnolia, camellia, banana and chilean flame trees sweep down to the private beach, just north of Rosemullion Head.

References: 18th, 19th (Gen.) and 20th C.

NANSIDWELL, Mawnan Smith

SW78 28 : EX8, GS359

Lansidwell, Hitchins *1824; Cornish nans + ?, pronounced* nanSIDwell*; house listed grade II; garden of 5 acres (2 ha), with additional 4 acres (1.6 ha) of woodland, at 60m., on Gramscatho Beds, with acid soil, in an AONB, and an AGSV; rainfall 40-45", temperature zone C; the* Nansidwell Country House Hotel, *open to non-residents.*

Hitchins wrote in 1824:

> Lansidwell, commonly called Nansugell, which is now a farmhouse, was for many years a seat of the Newcourts. This is now the property of Mr. Richard Fox [from the medical line of the family].

There is still a farm, but the house (now an hotel) was built in 1905, to the designs of the architect, Leonard Stokes, for Sir Sidney Rowlatt, a judge. The garden which was created during this period was listed in the *Hort. Direct.* from 1919 until 1924. Within the last ten years, it has been laid out in terraces, and is well planted with a variety of azaleas, rhododendrons and other shrubs, with striking views and vistas across Falmouth Bay to Pendennis. There is a round pond on the lower terrace, with a statue of Mercury in the centre. The walled garden has beds neatly edged with golden box, now grassed over, but with espalier fruit trees. It includes the relict of a greenhouse, or conservatory, with two wall niches. To the rear is a quarry rock garden and fernery, with a banana plant close to the house itself.

References: 18th, 19th (Gen.) and 20th C.

PENJERRICK, Budock

SW77 30 : *EX8 & 105, GS352*   OPEN

Penhegerik, 1327; Cornish pen + nans + ?, pronounced penJERRick; *Higher Penjerrick house, cottage ornée listed grade II; garden of 15 acres (6 ha), listed grade II, south-east sloping 80-10m., on Mylor Series metamorphosed slate and sandstone, with acid soil, in an AONB; rainfall 40-45", temperature zone C; private, open 1983-98 CGOG, 1993-4, 1996-8 NGS, Wednesday, Friday and Sunday, March through September, or by appointment.*

Penjerrick was originally part of the Penwarne estate, which was split into several parts, of which in the late eighteenth century George Croker Fox II occupied one part, and his brother Robert Were Fox I another. Their sons succeeded them, although an entry in Barclay Fox's

48. Penjerrick. 'I doubt if there is one [garden] which can compare with Penjerrick in a certain indescribable effect – the effect of landscape gardening carried out with the most exquisitely cultivated taste.' (G. Ch. 1874: i. 309)

Journal on 24 June 1839, to the effect that 'Uncle G.C. & my father' were 'the new owners', suggests that while they may have been managing their sections for several years, they were not in full possession. In March 1837, Robert Were Fox II of Rosehill had introduced his son, Barclay, to farming at Penjerrick. Barclay had already been keeping his colt there, but two years later, their new status as owners offered the freedom to develop the garden in their own way. They began with

> a day of grand havoc ... slashing the big trees right & left. [They] had 7 men with hatchets, ropes & saws, & by evening the lawn looked like a battle field - heaped with prostrate corpses of trees.

Work continued through July and into September, when, on the 28th Barclay wrote:

> Fresh changes & improvements have opened a beautiful vista of the meadows below. With their fringe of fine trees they are a vast additional beauty.

He had written on the 19th that, after his repairs and improvements to the house, he felt it a 'real unfeigned pleasure to be at last settled in at Penjerrick as a home.' Early the next year, in March, we find him 'making a beautiful entrance', the drive of which, on a second visit, he 'laid out ... before breakfast'! Towards the end of the year they began digging the pond. On Christmas Eve, he wrote:

> Met my father at Penjerrick, where the pond-scenery lit by a bright sun looked surpassingly lovely. Where the old muddy lane was, is now a beautiful glade (the hedges being thrown down) sloping to the pond, from whence 3 or 4 elms, a towering poplar, and a noble ash start up in the foreground in fine bold drawings, beyond the pond which mirrors back the tall trees bending over it.

On 22 January he was, 'Busied with my father ... about the rockery', by which he probably meant the rock work by the pool, where by 4 February he had 'accomplished some very effective grouping & building with the large rocks carried yesterday.' By this time the house had been extended 'to provide a second home for Barclay's parents and sisters as well as himself.' Penjerrick is the earliest and archetypal Cornish valley garden, a genre which is often dismissed as without conscious (or evident) design. These extracts should dispel that myth. Barclay Fox knew exactly the potential of the site and how to achieve it, before it became what the listing terms 'a plantsman's garden', for when his father first gave him the management of the farm on 19 March 1837, he wrote:

> This is an object which will suit me best of any I could name. The loveliness and interest attached to the spot from old associations, invest it with a charm to my mind far beyond any pecuniary advantages.

Tragically, Barclay died in 1855, and his father out-lived him by twenty-two years. He had already, perhaps inspired by his uncle at Grove Hill (q.v.), begun experiments with exotic plants at Rosehill (q.v.), an enthusiasm he was to carry with him to Penjerrick, where he retired in 1872. An article by H.M. (undoubtedly Henry Mills, head gardener at Enys), in the *Gardeners' Chronicle* (1871) described the garden at this time. R.W. Fox had created

> a cave-like passage, which leads into what may be termed an underground grotto, with a sky-light. It is here that the filmy Ferns are seen enjoying their situations, as if they were in a state of Nature.

This grotto led on to a fern house. 'Mr.Fox,' he wrote, 'receives seeds from all quarters, and buys anything he thinks will grow at Pengerrick [sic].' He was 'an ardent lover of Conifers', of which he possessed 180 kinds. Another article in the same journal of 1874 emphasizes that the beauty of Penjerrick depended on more than nature.

> The spot is naturally lovely, but not exceptionally so ... but I doubt if there is [anywhere] which can compete with Penjerrick in a certain indescribable effect - the effect of landscape gardening carried out with the most exquisitely cultivated taste.

R.W. Fox died in 1877, after which his only surviving daughter, Anna Maria, continued to live and develop the garden here until her death in 1897. Hamilton Davey believed that until one had a journal comparable to that of her sister, Caroline, 'one half of the history of Penjerrick, and that perhaps its most important, will be comparatively unknown.' The head gardener, Samuel Smith, who had been appointed in 1889, was responsible for most of the plantings of rhododendrons and proved an expert hybridizer. Henry McLaren of Bodnant, in the *Rhododendron Society Notes* (1928), wrote a comprehensive survey of the Penjerrick hybrids. He believed that:

> The success of the recent planting is perhaps due in part to the fact that the Rhododendrons, which are the main under planting, are kept in the nursery, not only until they are big enough to flower regularly but, above all, until they are big

enough to be in scale with the large trees beside and beneath which they are to grow.

The garden was listed in the *Hort. Direct.* from 1889 to 1924, and is ranked high among Thurston's select gardens. The old house, 'too small to be designated a mansion and far too romantic to be called a villa', was replaced by the present dwelling in 1935. Penjerrick has suffered in post-war years from the rising cost of labour, and the dire effects of storms, but Hamilton Davey's words still ring true: 'how much Cornwall owes to Penjerrick is a question she may never learn to answer quite justly.'

References: 19th (Hort. & Gen.) and 20th C; Barclay Fox's Journal, ed. R.L. Brett, 1979.

PENMERE, Mongleath Road, Falmouth

SW79 32 : *EX105, GS252*

Cornish pen + [?], pronounced penMEER; grounds of around 5 acres (2 ha), east sloping from c. 55m., on Mylor Series slate and sandstone, with acid soil; rainfall 40-45", temperature zone C; now the Penmere Manor Hotel.

Lake described Penmere in 1867 as 'the handsome and pleasantly situated residence of Alfred Lloyd Fox, Esq', who was the eldest son of Alfred Fox of Wodehouse Place and Glendurgan. He had come to reside there in about 1863, although the house was originally built for Capt. Bullock of the Packet Service who, according to Thurston, had laid out the grounds. They were developed over the turn of the century by Horton Bolitho, eldest son of John Borlase Bolitho of Trevaylor, near Penzance. Of *Eucalyptus globulus*, Wilson Lloyd Fox (Alfred Lloyd's youngest brother) wrote to Thurston that

> there were three trees in a row at Penmere, ... which I have always considered to be the highest, and probably among the earliest planted in England, and between 80 years and 100 years old. The tallest was blown down on 17th of January 1926. Mr Horton Bolitho furnished me with the following measurements. Five years ago the tree measured 120ft. in height, and 11 ft. in girth. Some of the top branches appear to have broken off. It now measures on the ground 102 ft.; girth at 5 ft. from the ground 12 ft. 2 in. and at the base 15 ft.

Thurston added that the 'girth of the two surviving trees at Penmere were 11 ft. 10 in. and 10 ft. 8 in. in 1928.' Although the hotel which occupies the site maintains the surrounding grounds, the garden is not now mentioned in its brochure as a feature.

References: 19th (Hort. & Gen.) and 20th C.

PENMORVAH, Mawnan Smith

SW78 30 : *EX8 & 105, GS352*

Cornish pen + morvah = sea marsh, pronounced penMORvah; small to medium garden, south sloping from c.70m., on Mylor Series metamorphosed slate and sandstone, with acid soil, in an AONB; rainfall 40-45", temperature zone C; now the Penmorvah Manor Hotel, *open to non-residents.*

The entrance to Penmorvah lies immediately opposite that of Penjerrick. It was thus by chance that Charles Curtis visited the house of the Revd Ed. Hensley, rector of Parkham in Devon, when surveying gardens in Cornwall for the *Gardeners' Magazine* in 1908. 'Let me say,' he wrote, that

> Penmorvah with its six acres of garden and orchard, is one of the best kept places I saw in the Falmouth district. Larger gardens contained rarer tress and shrubs, and finer scenery, but for smart up-keep Penmorvah is more after the style of the better gardens in the home counties and northwards.

Part of the garden is still maintained around the hotel.

References: 20th C.

PENWARNE, Mawnan

SW77 30 : *EX8 & 105, GS352*   OPEN

Cornish pen + guern = alder swamp, pronounced penWARN; late 18th C. house listed grade II*, two stables, trap house, two sets of gate-piers etc, each II; garden of 12 acres (4.9 ha), south-east sloping 85-55m., on Mylor Series metamorphosed slates and sandstone, with acid soil, in an AONB; rainfall 40-45", temperature zone C; private, opened 1983-98 CGOG, 1988, 1991, 1993-8 NGS, by appointment, and one Sunday each in March and April for charity.

The manor and barton of Penwarne were anciently in the hands of a family of the same name. In 1820 the house was described by Gilbert as 'modern, and commands fine views over a diversified district, and the distant sea.' John Penwarne, an attorney in Penryn, moved to London where he died in 1836 at the age of eighty, the property being sold to Michael Nowell, a merchant of Falmouth, passing in the 1870s to the Revd Michael Nowell Peters, vicar of Madron. Over the turn of the century it was the residence of the Revd John Tonkin (see Treverven), and it was probably during this time that the grounds, as they are now seen, were laid out. Nevertheless, in the succeeding years Penwarne is recorded in Kelly's *Directory* merely as the residence of a farmer. Thurston, who included this among his selected gardens, said no more than that it had 'well-kept grounds.' They are so still.

There is a lake by the side of the house, edged with tree ferns. The lawn to the garden front is surrounded by fine trees, with a walled garden to the west, in which a swimming pool has recently been constructed, but otherwise, except for small beds, grassed over. Below the lawn is a lower terrace, with grass and fruit trees. On the eastern side a stream runs down a valley into a small pond, along the sides of which have been planted a variety of trees and shrubs, which have now reached their maturity. There had once been a chapel at Penwarne, which was removed in the 1860s, stones from which were used to build the tower by the pond. The previous owner now lives at Estray Park (q.v.).

References: 17th, 18th, 19th (Gen.) and 20th C.

QUEEN MARY GARDENS, Falmouth

SW80 31 : *EX8 & 105, GS352*　　　　　　OPEN

Named after the wife of George V; small garden on the foreshore of Gyllyngvase beach; public pleasure garden, open at all times.

The entry in Kelly's *Directory* (1926) reads:

> Queen Mary Gardens, opposite the bathing beach, were opened to the public in 1913, and were the gift of the Earl of Kimberley, the cost of laying them out being borne by the Hon. Mrs. C.S. Goldman [wife of the MP]; in front is a new promenade.

The Earl had already, in 1877, presented the town with the Kimberley Park (q.v.), which was named after him. In 1903 the Council purchased the Gyllyngdune estate (q.v.), which until then occupied the land right down to the beach. This provided the opportunity to extend the cliff road, thus creating a promenade the whole length of the cliff up to and beyond the Falmouth Hotel. The laying out of the Queen Mary Gardens, therefore, formed a part of the development of Gyllyngvase into the principal 'bathing' beach of the resort. (See also Raffles, below.)

References: 20th C.

RAFFLES, Fenwick Road, Falmouth

SW80 32 : *EX8 & 105, GS352*

Originally The Cottage, *renamed* Raffles Hotel *after its more famous namesake in Singapore; garden of 1.5 acres (0.6 ha), at 35m. altitude, on Mylor and Falmouth Series slate and sandstone, with acid soil; rainfall 40-45", temperature zone C; now known simply as* Raffles, *the property is at present on the market.*

Raffles is an old house, built in about 1770, and formerly known as The Cottage, Melvill Road, since Fenwick Road had not then been created. The occupant during the late nineteenth, and into the twentieth century, was William Mitchell Grylls, a banker, and partner with the Williamses of Tredrea and Scorrier, but for our purposes the reputation of the garden dates from 1947, when the novelist Howard Spring, with his wife Marion, moved there from Hoopers Hill, Mylor. In her autobiography, *Memories and Gardens*, Marion Howard Spring wrote at length of her reminiscences of Falmouth.

> The Falmouth house had always been known as The Cottage. We called it the White Cottage, after our Pinner house; though it was hardly my idea of a cottage it was certainly white ... The garden was once bigger than it is today. Indeed, it ran right down to the sea. Then [in 1866] came the branch railway line which linked Falmouth with Truro. It cut the garden in two.

This means that the lower garden would have once run down to near where the Queen Mary Gardens are today (q.v.). Her book continues with several chapters in which she described her own garden, and those of others she had visited. One chapter opened: 'Cornish gardens on the whole used not to pay much attention to herbaceous plants ... But I dreamed of having a good long bed ...' She made her dream come true, and believed that her 'border was a success, and looked very well against the lawn ...' She described how on 'the right of the White Cottage, as you face it, there [was] a fine conservatory 45 feet long and 25 feet wide'. It was dilapidated, and she wrote that after it was restored she grew tender plants and cacti there. 'The dining-room ... [looked] upon a little enclosed garden', which the Springs felt 'called for very formal treatment', and which they achieved by the construction of a pond, with a water garden and a summer-house.

For the first eight or nine years they annually held a sale for the Royal Cornwall Polytechnic Society, which was based in Falmouth. When, as time went on, this proved too much for them both to organize, the garden itself was opened for charity four or five Sunday afternoons each year. After the departure of the Howard Springs, the property became an hotel, adopting a more romantic name, but the garden which they had created continued to be, and still is, one of its principal attractions.

References: Marion Howard Spring, Memories and Gardens, *1964: chaps 22-32, with illustrations.*

ROSEHILL, Wood Lane and Melvill Road, Falmouth

SW80 32 : EX8 & 105, GS352   OPEN

Now Fox Rosehill Gardens; house listed grade II; grounds of 2 acres (0.8 ha), sloping south-east from c. 35m., on Mylor and Falmouth Series slate and sandstone, with acid soil; rainfall 40-45", temperature zone C; Falmouth School of Art, and public park, relict of original garden, open all year.

Rosehill was leased in 1821-2 by Lord Wodehouse to Robert Were Fox, FRS, who, in about 1839 began with his son Robert Barclay to develop Penjerrick (q.v.), to which he retired in 1872. Rosehill was then purchased by his nephew Howard, son of Alfred Fox, his neighbour at Wodehouse Place. The fame of Penjerrick during this time, however, rather overshadowed that of Rosehill, although a visitor noted orange, date and lemon trees, as well as aloes in the open, among 300 naturalized exotic species. R.W. Fox was a scientist, who saw the acclimatization of tender foreign plants as an experimental discipline, whereas Howard Fox, his successor, was inspired by his experience of sub-tropical plants on his travels, to design a Mediterranean type garden. As early as 1880, in the very first notice of Rosehill in an horticultural journal, the author remarked that:

> In this lovely spot [Dracaenas] are made use of in a novel and picturesque manner. Through the lawn there is a charming vista, through which an extensive view of the sea can be obtained from the house, and on each side of this opening is a row of these plants, backed by choice Conifers, the whole forming an avenue worthy of imitation.

It was, indeed, imitated along the road into Falmouth, which was planted and named 'Dracaena Avenue', ending a few hundred yards short of Rosehill itself. The popularity of this Mediterranean style of planting spread through the seaside resorts of Cornwall, and into South Devon. The Morrab Gardens, Penzance, opened in 1889, is an instance, and the invention of a 'Cornish Riviera' by the Great Western Railway exploited the idea to promote tourism. By 1908, Charles Curtis, editor of the *Gardeners' Magazine*, was to write: 'I cannot call to mind one [garden] in England, that is so altogether un-English as that of Rosehill.' The whole made up 'a picture of the character one associates in idle moments with a "Chateau d'Espagne"'. It was the intention of the family that Rosehill as a whole should be given to the people of Falmouth, and to this end the greater part of the garden was donated as a public park. Later a gift of the house and its surrounds followed, which was intended as a museum, but the local authority felt themselves unable to accept. Thus the two have become separated - the house and grounds, after being for a time an hotel, becoming the School of Art, and the remainder the Fox Rosehill Gardens.

References: 19th (Hort.) and 20th C.

49. Rosehill. Howard Fox admiring the Musa ensete *in his Mediterranean-style garden. (G. Ch. 8 Dec. 1894)*

ROSKROW, near Mabe Burnthouse

SW76 35 : EX104-5, GS352

*Cornish *ros + krow = hut, properly pronounced rosKROW to rhyme with 'cow', but often Anglicized to rhyme with 'crow'; original garden extinct, now a modern house and other developments.*

Charles Henderson's commentary in 1922 on his sketch of Roskrow, which is the only representation of the mansion to survive, cannot be bettered. It was at that time the residence of John

Pendarves, whose grandfather had bought it in 1614 from Harry Roscrow.

> The picture ... shows the house as Mrs Delaney must have known it in 1717. It shows moreover, that what she described as a gloomy medieval fortress was nothing but the typical Tudor Cornish house. The massive walls - that still appear beside the present entrance gate - are shown to have been part of a terraced & ornamental garden. These & the garden walls in the lower right hand corner alone survive. When Roskrow passed to the Bassets it became a secondary residence, first a dower House, then a leasehold house - finally a farm. Becoming ruinous, it was pulled down at the beginning of the present century, & then an entirely modern mansion erected a little in front.

Mrs Delany, the young wife of the decrepit Alexander Pendarves, later became celebrated for her *Autobiography*, published in 1861, and was a friend and correspondent of Dean Swift. During the early nineteenth century Roskrow was leased from Lord de Dunstanville by Robert Were Fox I, and was later the residence of his widow, and of his grandson, Robert Barclay Fox and his wife, during the years of his failing health.

References: 17th, 18th, 19th (Gen.) and 20th C; J. Palmer, The People of Penryn, *Truro, 1986: 8, 10-11.*

50. Roskrow. Sketch by Charles Henderson from an original map preserved in the Royal Institution of Cornwall. Notice the ramped beds in the bottom left corner.

TREBAH, Mawnan

SW76 27 : EX8, GS359, SS.SW61/71   OPEN

Trevraybo *1327,* Treba *1679; Cornish* tre + ?, *pronounced* TREBBA, *although usually Anglicised to* TREEbaa; *mid - late 19th C. game-larder listed grade II; garden of 25 acres (10 ha) listed grade II, south sloping valley 65m. to the estuary, on Gramscatho Beds, with acid soil, in an AONB, an AGSV and in part a CNCS; rainfall 40-45", temperature zone C; now The Trebah Garden Trust, open 1983-98 CGOG, 1991, 1993-8 NGS, daily. Official guide, plan etc.*

The house at Trebah was built for the Nicholls family *c.* 1750, but later became the property of Robert Were Fox I. His son, Charles, occupied the estate in 1826, but did not become the owner until it was given to him by his father in 1842, at which time he began to extend the house. This stands at the head of a valley, with a clear view all the way to the river and the country beyond.

We may speculate, since there is little hard evidence, that he would have begun to lay out the general framework of the garden, which in outline is fairly staightforward, bringing up gravel for the paths from the shore and digging the upper pools. The shelter-belts were already there, so that planting could begin, although the complete absence of any reference to Trebah in the horticultural literature of the time suggests that, as in the case of his brother Alfred at Glendurgan, it may not yet have been distinctive enough to have aroused comment. Although Charles died in 1878, and left the estate to his daughter, Juliet, and her husband, Edmund Backhouse, the garden continued to be listed in the *Hort. Direct* in his name from 1870 until 1891. The first notice in an horticultural journal, however, did not come before 1904, when S.W. Fitzherbert, a regular correspondent on West Country matters, wrote:

> For the natural beauty of its grounds, ... none can excel Trebah, the residence of Mr. E. Backhouse ... The sloping sides of the valley are steep and irregular in outline and, being well covered by trees, the lower levels are amply protected from both east and west winds. This spot offers a happy home for sub-tropical plants and shrubs, of which full advantage has been taken, with the result that many fine examples of rare plants are to be met with growing with unaccustomed vigour in this sheltered sanctuary.

The house was covered with flowering climbers, and in an isolated position on the lawn was 'the finest specimen of *Exochorda grandiflora* that [he] had ever seen.' The collection of rhododendrons was also very fine, especially the fragrant varieties for which the other Fox gardens were becoming noted. 'Numbers of Cordylines [were] dispersed about the grounds', but there was, as yet, no mention of the Trachycarpus which have now become so much a feature of this garden. These were planted in the time of Charles Hawkins Hext, who bought Trebah from Edmund Backhouse's son, Sir Jonathan, in 1906. Although he had died eleven years later, in 1943 Bishop Hunkin still found it natural when describing the garden to associate it with both him and his wife, who survived until 1939, 'under whom [he considered] it certainly reached its height'. Fortunately we are able to form some picture of Trebah during this time, from a description in the *Garden* of 1913, where the anonymous author remarked on the design.

> The rather steep, sloping banks on either side of the valley are intersected with pathways, but so cleverly has the work been carried out that it is seldom one gets a glimpse of the paths, except in the immediate vicinity. Indeed, natural effect is aimed at throughout and successfully secured, harmony of colour and contour being a striking feature.

Fitzherbert had singled out the bamboos for special comment, but now there were noticed in addition tree ferns and palms: *Phoenix canariensis* as well as the Trachycarpus. The 'water garden' extending 'practically the whole length of the gardens,' in the form of a rivulet leading to the lower pools, had also become a feature. Harry Thomas, the head gardener, who was responsible for much of the planting, emulated his fellows at Penjerrick and Glendurgan in the hybridizing of rhododendrons, by crossing *R. arboreum* with *griffithianum* to produce 'Trebah Glory' and 'Trebah Gem', which won pride of place as the frontispiece of the second of Millais' classic books on the species.

Bishop Hunkin, however, stated quite bluntly in the end that now the Hexts 'have both gone ... the garden is no longer being kept up as it used to be.' And so it remained until in the 1980s the property was purchased by Major 'Tony' and Mrs Hibbert, who instigated an energetic programme of restoration and development. By 1987, when the magnitude of the task became overwhelming, the garden was offered to the National Trust, who, without an endowment, felt they must turn it down. In desperation, a solution was sought by opening the garden on a commercial basis, out of which grew the successful foundation of The Trebah Garden Trust, which it is hoped and expected will maintain the grounds for the foreseeable future.

References: 19th (Hort.) and 20th C.

TREDREA, Perran-ar-worthal

SW77 38 : EX104-5, GS352

Cornish tre + tre, *pronounced* treDRAY; *residual garden, south-east sloping 35-5m., on Mylor Series slate and sandstone, with acid soil; rainfall 40-45", temperature zone C; grounds now divided into separate residences, some with good gardens.*

George Fox of Par had married twice. His eldest son, Edward, from his first marriage, half-brother to George Croker Fox of Falmouth, had settled in Wadebridge, where the family became prominent merchants (see Gonvena). George II, Edward's eldest son, however, became associated with his cousins in their copper mines at Gwennap. On his marriage, he built a house at Tredrea, Perran-ar-worthal, on land belonging to the Bassets of Tehidy, where in 1791 the Fox family had established a Foundry making pumping machinery, of which his son, George III, eventually became manager.

It would appear, however (the case is somewhat obscure), that in about 1825 he, and others of the family, suffered financially from speculations in Chilean copper, which resulted in his having to resign from the Foundry, in favour of his cousin Charles of Trebah (q.v.). This led to his removal, first to Exeter, and then to the Lake District, where he passes out of our picture. Charles then took over Tredrea until, in 1848, all the Fox family pulled out of the company, leaving it to the Williamses who had become their partners. Michael Henry Williams, second son of Michael II of Scorrier, and MP for Truro, now became Director of the Foundry, and lived at what Lake described as 'the agreeable seat of Tredrea', which passed on to his son, Godfrey Trevelyan. Little is known of the garden in these early years, other than through family letters, although *Hitchins*, evidently referring to Tredrea, had commented:

> The plantations raised round the abode of Mr. Fox, thrive with peculiar luxuriance, and give variety to the diversified scenery, which arises from the effects of labour and machinery [i.e. at the Foundry], and the commanding hills which fringe the borders of Carclew.

Michael Henry Williams, who later created the garden at Pencalenick (q.v.), was the first to receive horticultural recognition, being listed in the *Hort. Direct.* from at least 1870 until 1890. The garden was visited by J. Robson, correspondent to the *Journal of Horticulture*, in 1874. 'My expectation,' he wrote, was that

> most likely many half-exotic plants would be there luxuriating out of doors, together with

healthy Camellias, Rhododendrons, and the like, and this anticipation was fully realised, whilst under glass many interesting Orchids and other stove plants are cultivated, some specimens of the latter far exceeding those often met with in the most celebrated plant-growing establishments near London.

Orchids became a speciality at Tredrea, and of its gardener, J. Murton, who sent a list to the *Gardeners' Chronicle* two years later. Robson observed that

> [of the] many fine Orchids cultivated [there]; and in regard to their being all so large, it may be said that there is not the motive to multiply them as is so often done in a nursery, and sometimes also in private gardens. Here it would seem that a really good specimen is more valued than several small ones: hence almost everything was large and fine.

In the twentieth century the house was to become an hotel. It still survives, divided into apartments, but the grounds are now separated into spacious housing plots, some of which have been well cultivated, incorporating mature trees and features from the original estate.

References: 19th (Hort. & Gen.), 20th C; H.A.F. Crewdson, George Fox of Tredrea, *privately printed, Chichester 1976: 1-9 and pedigree.*

TREFUSIS HOUSE, Mylor

SW81 34 : EX8 & 104-5, GS352

Cornish tre *+ ?*fos *= dyke, pronounced* treFEWsis; *house rebuilt to a design by Hicks in Scottish Baronial style in 1891, listed grade II, kitchen garden walls II; medium to large grounds, south sloping valley 65-5m., on Mylor Series slate, sandstone and head, in an AONB, and an AGLV; rainfall 40-45", temperature zone C; private.*

Leland's 1534 statement that 'There dwelleth an auncient Gentilman [ancient in ancestry, not in age!] caullid Trefusis at this point of Penfusis', is echoed by other writers down the centuries. The family are still there today. Tonkin wrote:

> The house is extremely pleasant by its situation, and would be much more so were it built a little higher up. To the south of the house is a fine grove, and a walk, at the end of which is a pleasure house, built by this gentleman's father, from whence there is a very beautiful prospect.

In 1787 Trefusis was visited by William Beckford, author of *Vathek*, while waiting for his sea-passage. (Beckford was later to develop Fonthill on a grand scale.) But a few years later, Stockdale found the property was 'going rapidly to decay'. In Gilbert's opinion:

> The situation [was] remarkably grand, and it might be converted into one of the finest seats in the kingdom.

However, even though it was for a time the home of George Croker Fox III, one of the gardening family of Falmouth, its potential as the site for an exceptional garden seems never to have been fulfilled. Fox was resident in January 1814, and lent his assistance when the transport ship carrying invalids with their families from Wellington's army, tragically sank in a gale while anchored off Trefusis Point, with much loss of life. Trefusis is not alone in not being developed as an ornamental garden, and is a useful reminder that the 'great' gardens of Cornwall, and many of the less than great, were the fruit of an enthusiasm for plants and landscape design which was by no means shared by all the gentry and landowners.

References: 17th, 18th, 19th (Gen.) and 20th C; U.M. Redwood, Trefusis Territory, *Falmouth 1987.*

TREMOUGH, Falmouth

SW76 34 : EX8 & 104-5, GS352

Cornish tre *+* mogh *= swine, pronounced* treMOW; *early-mid 18th C. extended and remodelled house listed grade II, late 19th C. lodge, garden walls and steps, and gate-piers, each II; small to medium relict grounds, sloping 110-85m., on Granite, with acid soil 'full of granite gravel'; rainfall 40-45", temperature zone C; until 1998* Tremough Convent *and school.*

S.W. Fitzherbert wrote in 1900, brooking no argument:

> In the gardens of D.H. Shilson, Esq., at Tremough, Cornwall, is to be seen the most representative collection of Himalayan Rhododendrons, and hybrids of the same section in the British Isles.

The barton had been for many years in a family of that name, before eventually being sold to John Worth who, so Tonkin informs us,

> had for some time before a considerable mortgage on it. Mr. Worth had built on Tremogh [sic] a very large house of moorstone, and hath enclosed a small park for deer.

But fortune did not smile on him, for, as *Lake* records:

> the house fell to ruins, the grounds were neglected, and the whole estate became the subject of litigation. It was afterwards purchased by Mr. Tilly of Falmouth [see also Boslowick], whose son sold it to ... B. Sampson, Esq. [see Tullimaar], from whom it passed to William

Shilson, Esq., the present proprietor and occupier. To the last two or three proprietors Tremough is indebted for its substantial and commodious house, its beautiful grounds, and its elegant lodge entrance.

It is with the Shilsons that we shall principally be concerned. Tremough had come to William Shilson as a bequest from Benjamin Sampson in 1864. Twelve years later Henry Mills, gardener at Enys, was to write an unusually detailed account of the garden for the *Gardeners' Chronicle*, which is worth quoting at some length. 'This garden,' he wrote,

> is noted for the splendid collection of Rhododendrons which the late Mr. Shilson raised from seed, the greater part of which he received from the late Sir William Hooker. Some of these Sikkim varieties attain to an unusual size, and flower in the open borders at this place. There are many hybrids here, crossed by the late Mr. Shilson from the varieties above mentioned, which are of great beauty and great variety. Another feature of Tremough is good plant growing, both in greenhouse and stove. For some years past the plants from this place have taken a leading position in all the horticultural shows in this county ... [exciting] the admiration of all visitors, and [bringing] forth high commendations from the professionals present. Tremough ... cannot be said to be little - nearly twenty acres being set apart for gardening purposes and pleasure grounds, lawns, &c. The soil rests on granite, and is full of granite gravel, which the Rhododendrons and the so-called American plants delight in.

He continued with a survey of the plants, chiefly rhododendrons, which were to be seen, some in vast numbers - 137 *R. ciliatum*, 145 hybrids, over 800 in borders, and so forth. But it was no one species garden, for

> An avenue of Limes opposite the entrance [to the house] runs down to the bottom of the lawn. On the south front is an Italian garden, a plan of which I enclose [but which was not printed], with the style of bedding-out, &c. Attached to the house is a conservatory, 32 feet by 18 feet ... In the wall garden are eight glass-houses - Azalea-house, Orchid-house, stove, early vinery, Erica-house, Fig-house, and Peach-house. There are also three ranges of brick pits for growing Melons and Cucumbers outside.

The contents of this lavish range of houses are then detailed.

> The kitchen garden is some little distance from the wall garden, and was well furnished with seasonable vegetables. Terrace walls are covered with Camellias, so also is every bit of wall near the gardens ... In the wall garden is some rockwork, with Ferns and plants suited to the place, a fountain, in the centre of a pond containing gold and silver fish, giving it a pretty finish. The place, and especially the plant growing, is a credit to the young gardener, Mr. Gill.

This article, written by a practical gardener from one of the principal estates in the county, is of considerable interest for its comprehensive coverage of all the various aspects of a large and flourishing Victorian garden. But it was for their specialized growing of rhododendrons that the Shilsons and their gardener were to achieve their greatest reputation. Nearly a quarter of a century later, Fitzherbert reported in the *Gardeners' Chronicle* (1900) that:

> Hybridising has been consistently carried on ever since the time that the late Mr. Shilson started his collection of Himalayan Rhododendrons; and the head-gardener, Mr. R. Gill, is able to point with pride to numerous lovely hybrids of his own raising.

Gill was allowed to run his famous 'Penryn Nursery' from Tremough gardens itself, and was later to join his son at his Kernick nursery, from which the 'Gill Hybrids' were circulated to gardens up and down the county. Indeed, as Fitzherbert went on to announce, Kew itself had

> been enriched in its turn by a fine assortment of Rhododendrons from Tremough gardens, six truckloads of large bushes having been lifted under the superintendence of Mr. Watson, of the Royal Gardens, and safely transported to the Temperate-house.

Astonishing photographs were published to illustrate this herculean exercise. But however successful, interest was not to be confined to rhododendrons: 'About ten years ago [i.e. *c.* 1890]', Fitzherbert went on,

> an extensive alteration in the grounds was carried out, and numerous Coniferae were planted. These have made fine growth, and bid fair to become one of the features of the garden.

Tremough later became a Catholic girls' school, until its closure in 1998. Sue Bradbury has recently traced its history from the earliest days, through to its later development as a Convent and a school.

References: 18th, 19th (Hort. & Gen.) and 20th C; S. Bradbury, The Story of Tremough, *Trewirgie 1994.*

51. Tullimaar, the terraced gardens. The tidal estuary, with its wharves, is now entirely silted up. (Twycross 1846: 85)

TULLIMAAR, Perran-ar-worthal

SW78 38 : EX104-5, GS352

House listed grade II, early 19th C. kitchen garden walls, and the east 'Truro' and west 'Falmouth' lodges both of c. 1834 are each II; medium sized garden, steeply south sloping, 30m. to the river, on Mylor Series slates and sandstones, and alluvium, with acid soil; rainfall 45-50", temperature zone C; private.*

'Tullemaar [sic] was erected in 1829,' writes Rex Barratt, 'by Benjamin Sampson the owner and manager of a powder factory at Cowsawes [sic] who died in 1840.' He was succeeded by his nephew of the same name, who had changed his surname from Cloak. After a case in the Chancery Court, the estate passed to William Hockin, his sister's son, and then to Francis Hearle Cock, 'a solicitor whose offices were in Pydar Street.' It was during the latter's time that the gardens were listed in the *Hort. Direct.*, and subsequently by his widow and other residents from 1889 until 1924. The illustration of the terracing along the steep valley side in Twycross, however, dates from a much earlier period in the 1840s. Even though the trees have now grown considerably, the impressive lines of the terracing can still be discerned when viewed from the other side of the valley.

Kilvert spent a holiday here with the Hockins from 19 July to the 6 August 1870, which he recorded in his Diary. 'From the bedroom window,' he wrote,

> I look out upon the front of the house and the rich mingling of the purple beech tints with the bright green of the other trees about the lawns and shrubberies. From the other window nothing is to be seen but the trees and side lawn and terraced grey gravelled walks of Tullimaar, the brown sands, mud and shrunk stream of Restronguet, the rich sloping oak woods dark and impervious, rising from the river bed opposite. Down the river beyond the woods may be seen the back of a rounded hill, and up the river the glint of white buildings on the river side, through the trees, the white walls and chimneys of an iron foundry.

In the twentieth century, Gen. Eisenhower briefly lodged here in 1944, while reviewing troops before D-Day, and is reputed to have survived an assasination attempt by an American soldier. More recently, Tullimaar has been the home of Princess Marthe Bibescu - a descendant of Napoleon, and former literary hostess in Paris, who died in 1973 - and the Cornish Nobel prize-winning author, Sir William Golding.

References: 19th (Hort. & Gen.), 20th C; Illus.

WODEHOUSE PLACE, Wood Lane, Falmouth

SW80 32 : *EX8 & 105, GS352*

Named after Lord Wodehouse; small garden, south-east sloping from c. 35m., on Mylor Series slate and sandstone, with acid soil; rainfall 40–45", temperature zone C; now holiday apartments.

This, the 'home of the Fox family since Mr Alfred Fox built the house about 1821,' was one of Thurston's select gardens, probably only because it belonged to a member of the Fox family, since he cited no more than a *Chamaerops fortunei* from there, even though it was, nevertheless, probably the highest in the county. Wilson Lloyd Fox had written to him:

> When Alfred Fox settled there, no tree or house interfered with the view of the shore line of the Bay stretching from Pendennis Castle to the Manacles. Now the sea is barely visible. The finest trees and shrubs have disappeared. Formerly there was a beautiful *Ailanthus glandulosus* (tree of heaven), and also a large Cedar of Lebanon. There is a fine Dracaena, one of the oldest in the neighbourhood.

Wodehouse Place adjoins the garden of Rosehill. Wilson Lloyd Fox was in a good position to describe it, since he was the youngest son of Alfred Fox, and had lived there as a boy. At the time he was writing, the property was owned by Cuthbert Lloyd Fox, his nephew, and the son of his brother George who had inherited the property in 1891, after his mother's death. The name given to the house emphasizes once again that so many of these places were part of the Arwenack estate, which had been inherited by the Wodehouse family, later Earls of Kimberley.

References: 20th C.

SUPPLEMENTARY LISTS

LESSER-KNOWN HISTORIC GARDENS

Budock Vean, Budock

SW76 27 : *EX8, GS359, SS.SW61/71*

Cornish St Budocus + vean pronounced BEWdock; medium to large grounds, south-west sloping, 45m. to creek-side, on Gramscatho Beds, with acid soil, in an AONB and HC, and an AGSV; rainfall 35–40", temperature zone C; the Budock Vean Hotel, with golf course and relict grounds. There is an official leaflet.

Gilbert wrote:

> Budockvean, the seat of Benjamin Pender, esq. is pleasantly situated on the banks of the Heyl [i.e. Helford River], and on the lower part of the grounds, is a landing-place for boats, and other small vessels. The house has an ancient appearance, and opens into a lawn, lined with foliage. It had formerly an attached chapel, and a burial place. The latter is converted into a mowhay. [i.e. rick-yard].

The chapel is a link with the small Celtic religious house originally at this place, which passed into the possession of the Bishop of Exeter, because of the valuable Ferry rights at Helford Passage. The Penders sold the estate after the First World War. The new owners then disposed of some of the land for building, the mansion and outbuildings being either demolished or radically altered for use as a Country Club. After a period of dereliction, it has become a hotel and golf course, with a wooded valley leading to the jetty.

References: 18th, 19th (Gen.) and 20th C.

Carmino, Fenwick Road, Falmouth

SW80 31 : *EX8 & 105, GS352*

Named after the place and family name of Carminow; Cornish, Dexter suggests car + menou = very small, pronounced carMINo; small urban garden; private.

Carmino was the house of Wilson Lloyd Fox, the youngest son of Alfred Fox of Glendurgan, who corresponded with Edgar Thurston during the preparations for his book on Cornish trees and shrubs, providing him with information on the Fox family and other matters. Even though the garden of Carmino is modest in size, Thurston in his survey cited seven plants from there. W.L. Fox received a brief recognition in the *Gardeners' Chronicle* of 1889 for plants he had sent to the Falmouth Naturalists' Association exhibition, to illustrate winter flowering in Cornwall.

References: 19th (Hort.) and 20th C.

Trevissome House, Flushing

SW79 34 : *EX8 & 104-5, GS352*

Pronounced treVIZum; house listed grade II; reduced grounds of 4 acres (1.6 ha), south sloping, 30m. to the sea, on Mylor Series metamorphosed slates and sandstone, in an AONB; rainfall 40–45", temperature zone C; holiday residence and marina, garden partly built over and relict.

Trevissome, on the riverside opposite the marina at Falmouth, was formerly the property of the Bishop of Exeter. The present house is of early nineteenth-century origins, possibly incorporating an earlier dwelling, but with considerable later extensions. The grounds were listed as open in the *Hort. Direct.* from 1916 to 1924, first as the residence of Dunbar Buller, and later of W.H. Dowman.

In January 1922, Captain Dowman, having first seen the *Cutty Sark* in Falmouth Harbour when she took refuge from a channel storm, followed her to Lisbon where he purchased her from the Portuguese later that year. He then, upon returning to Falmouth, restored the ship to its former glory. He also over the years imported statuary to ornament his quite substantial gardens, but these were taken away some twenty-five years ago, and the grounds gradually built over. The house is now divided into holiday flats for those who use the sixty-five moorings on the private waterfront with its two slipways.

References: 19th (Gen.) and 20th C.

Treworgan, Mawnan Smith

SW78 28 : *EX8, GS359*

Cornish tre + personal name (Gurcant?), pronounced treWORgan; grounds of 8 acres, eastern facing valley, sloping 60m. to the sea, on Gramscatho Beds, with 'acid shale, some clay and sand', in an AONB, and an AGSV; rainfall 40-45", temperature zone C; private.

Treworgan was built in the latter part of the nineteenth century, with mullioned windows and a castellated entrance tower, as the residence of John Cole, JP. It occupies the south side of an east-facing valley, with Meudon along the north. The lodge leads to an entrance drive through lawned areas, flanked by trees and shrubs. A formal rose garden has recently been created by the front door. To the east, steps lead to a formal lawned area with cherries, camellias, shrub borders, hydrangeas, tree heathers and other shrubs. There is a kitchen garden adjoining the coach-house with greenhouses, fruit and herb gardens. The larger part of the grounds are typical of Cornish wooded valley gardens leading down to the sea, in which are found camellias, rhododendrons, gunnera, tree ferns, azaleas and spring bulbs. The *Hort. Direct.* has Treworgan opened by Mrs Hodgkin in 1916. It is now the residence of TV presenter Hugh Scully.

References: 20th C.

ADDITIONAL CONTEMPORARY GARDENS

See also LANTERNS and RAFFLES in the main section.

Calamansac House, Port Navas

SW75 26 : *EX8, PF1370, SS.SW61/71*

*Cornish *kyl = nook + ?, pronounced, according to Henderson (1934), C'MANjack; in an AONB, and an AGSV; opened 1990, 1992 CGOG.*

Calamansac House, built in 1930, is sited in a large area cut out of the surrounding woodland, opening up spectacular views of the Helford River. Several holiday cottages have since been built, around which have been created informal plantings. Oliver Rackham writes that the Calamansac Woods of 31.7 acres (12.8 ha) are 'well documented back to the thirteenth century [and have] a long history of coppicing'. Though not the most important, it 'is one of the woods that make the special character of the Helford River, with their continuous oak canopy going down to the water's edge ... [and] is very conspicuous for its size.'

References: 20th C; O. Rackham, Calamansac Wood ... a report on its conservation for Kerrier District Council, *Cambridge 1987.*

Elim Cottage, Broads Lane, near Mylor Bridge

SW79 36 : *EX104-5, GS352*

Opened 1983-8 CGOG, 1987-8 NGS.

This garden was commenced by a Mrs Stevens in the early 1920s on an old orchard, of which some trees are still standing. The chief plantings are of rhododendrons, azaleas and magnolias, which have now grown to a size where they densely cover the ground, leaving only narrow walks. The garden is of particular significance since it has preserved many of the old Gill hybrids, which are (or were) clearly labelled. The garden, after a change of ownership, is no longer open to the public.

Estray Parc, between Penwarne and Penjerrick

SW77 30 : *EX8 & 105, GS352*   OPEN*

Estray anciently signified a field for stray animals; 3 acre (1.2 ha) garden in an AONB; open 1997-8 CGOG, 1993-8 NGS, one Sunday each in April and May.

References: 20th C; St Budock, vol.ii, The Budock Parish History Group *1993: 49.; Pring (1996: 66-7).*

Glensilva, Trefusis Road, Flushing

SW81 33 : *EX8 & 105, GS352*

A composite name: glen = valley + silva = wood; the house was originally built by a Dr Crossman as a nursing home; opened 1983-4 CGOG.

A garden on three levels, reached from the house terrace by twin curved stone stairways. There are 'trees, rhododendrons, camellias, roses, perennials' and a 'rock garden'. The lawns are irregular, and run down to the shore. There is a summer-house and a lily pond.

Missenden, Church Road, Mylor

SW80 35 : *EX104-5, GS352*

In an AONB; opened 1987-8 CGOG.

Small mature garden laid out in 1913; extensively redeveloped since 1971. Slopes gently to Mylor Creek. The emphasis was on spring-flowering shrubs. Two orchid houses and a water garden.

Oak Tree House, Perran-ar-worthal

SW77 38 : *EX104-5, GS352*

Opened 1988-91 GCOG, 1989, 1991 NGS.

A spring garden of camellias and rhododendrons planted since the early 1960s on several levels. The house is off the A39, opposite Perran Wharf.

The Old Vicarage, Church Road, Perran-ar-worthal

SW77 38 : *EX104-5, GS352*

House listed grade II; opened 1988-91 CGOG, 1989 NGS.

The house was built as Perran vicarage in the early 1840s, but was sold in 1982. Since then the garden has been remodelled and terraced. It is laid out with lawns, rockeries, and well-stocked borders. There is a putting green, and a circular slate terrace with a fish pond. The shaft of an incised granite cross, said to have been moved from the Glebe field, has been listed grade II.

Rosemary Cottage, Passage Hill, Mylor Bridge

SW80 36 : *EX104-5, GS352*

Opened 1983-5, 1989 CGOG.

A recent garden with a 'fairly wide selection of shrubs and herbaceous plants', begun in 1979.

Torwalla, Tresahar Road, Falmouth

SW80 32 : *EX8 & 105, GS352*

Cornish tor = *belly or swelling +* wollas, *pronounced* torWOLLa; *opened 1987, 1989 CGOG.*

A secluded town site with a south-sloping 'triangular shaped garden laid out most originally.' A shelter-belt of deciduous and coniferous trees has been planted since the late 1970s, to allow the development of perennial beds and tender shrubs. The 'aim is all round colour and winter foliage'.

Trenarth, Constantine

SW75 28 : *EX8, GS359, SS.SW61/71*   OPEN*

Cornish tre + *arth or *garth = *height, pronounced* treNARTH *2 acre (0.8 ha) garden, in an AONB, and an AGSV; open 1996-8 NGS, one Sunday in August.*

Treviades Gardens, Constantine

SW74 28 : *EX8, GS359, SS.SW61/71*   OPEN*

Cornish tre + fyades =*'one who flees', pronounced locally according to Henderson (1937)* 'Vizzis'; *Barton and garden walls c. late 16th C., remodelled 18th C. listed grade II*; Treviades Barton and Wollas open as two linked gardens, both in an AONB, and an AGSV; opened 1996, 1998 NGS one Sunday in July.*

The manor of Treviades was in the possession of the Trefusis family from 1320 until it was sold in 1920. By 1649 it consisted of two adjoining farms, one being three times the size of the other. The larger Barton is described by Henderson as a typical small Cornish manor house of the period 1580-1650, forming three sides of a rectangular courtyard, the fourth side being a high wall with a gateway. 'The front of the house, however,' he wrote, 'faces, not into the court, but into a small enclosed garden on the south side.' A doorway to one side gave access to the road, the other to an orchard. 'Below the garden the ground drops 7 or 8 feet to a farm lane, so the garden has the effect of having been raised up on a terrace.' The present owners have developed and opened both farms in association; on the lower one, a small water garden fed by two springs was discovered and restored.

References: 20th C.

Zoar, Mylor

SW807 367 : *EX104-5, GS352*

A 1 acre (0.4 ha) garden in an AONB; opened 1996-7 NGS.

A long, narrow garden begun in 1986, planted in sections with trees and shrubs. There is an interesting collection of dwarf conifers around a small pond.

Phormium tenax variegata

3. GRAMPOUND, ST MAWES, and MEVAGISSEY

This final section covers the area around and within a triangle formed by the three towns of Grampound, St Mawes and Mevagissey, which has at its centre the town of Tregony. Although today each is small and, except for tourism, unimportant, they all have a long ancestry. Grampound owed its initial success to its bridge, known to have been there at least from 1296. In 1302 it was named Grauntpount, from the Norman French *grand-pont*, and in Cornish *Ponsmur*, both meaning the great bridge, so-called because it was the main medieval highway to cross the River Fal. It was granted its charter by the Earl of Cornwall in 1332, with, notoriously, two members in Parliament, but by the mid-fifteenth century it had declined in importance. Of three tanneries which were there in the nineteenth century, only one now survives, belonging to the Croggon family, whose house, The Hollies, has a fine contemporary garden. Grampound is in the parish of Creed, to the south, where part of the former rectory garden has been opened. Garlenick, in the same parish, with the ancient woodlands of Trenowth, is away to the north. Along the main road, which gave Grampound its reason for existing, there are to the east the now decayed estate of the Hawkins at Pennans, and to the west their estate at Trewithen, beautifully improved by the Johnstone family.

Tregony, once with the Norman castle of the Pomeroys, like Grampound sent two members to Parliament from 1294 to 1832, for, unlikely as this must seem now, it was once a flourishing medieval port, until by 1600 it had become silted up. Penlee House, at the top of the hill, is a nineteenth-century house, in which lived a former Curator of the Liverpool Botanic Gardens. Closely aligned with the town is the estate of the Gregors at Trewarthenick, for which Repton produced a Red Book. Francis Gregor was a friend and associate of Jeremiah Trist, the vicar of Veryan to the south, who was wealthy enough to build himself a mansion at Behan Park, while his son expensively landscaped the vicarage.

St Mawes is today best known as a yachting haven, but this too had been esteemed as a town in the thirteenth century, and had sent its quota of two members to Parliament. Later, probably as a consequence of the Castle built in 1540, it was classed as a borough. At Lamorran House, near the Castle, an ambitious contemporary garden is under construction, which is taking full advantage of the favoured position to hazard exotic plantings. Although some distance away, St Mawes is in the parish of St Just in Roseland, famed for its churchyard, which was probably first 'improved' in the early nineteenth century by the Revd Dr Rodd, who emanated from the well-cultivated Trebartha Hall in Northill. It was much enhanced by the importations of the Treseders, who once had a nursery alongside. But some of the most interesting older gardens are to be found on a tongue of land the other side of the Percuil River: the ancient Place Manor, built on the site of a former Priory; Trewince, with a park and its own quay, and most intriguing of all, Rosteague, with a walled 'French Garden' enclosing four elaborate parterres.

Mevagissey has been a fishing port since 1400. It never became a borough, nor was represented in Parliament, but its quaintness has always appealed to the tourist, who will now additionally be attracted to the no-longer 'lost' gardens of Heligan, cultivated by the Tremayne family for some three centuries. Finally, Caerhays Castle stands alone on the coast, to the west of Mevagissey. Part of the great Domesday manor of Branel, Caerhays has a long and colourful history. It is difficult to resist quoting the conclusion to Charles Henderson's scholarly article charting the demise of the Trevanions.

> The huge expense of building the castle is said to have ruined the family, and the incubus of the great unfinished pile demoralised those who dwelt within it. It is said that at the last, shooting the eyes out of valuable family portraits with pistols after dinner became a pastime of the lord of Carhays. Another story goes that Mr. Trevanion, having invited his wealthy relative, Lady Burdett-Coutts, to visit him in the hope of mending his broken fortune, wrecked all his schemes by giving way to unreasonable mirth when his dog bit her footman on her arrival. The baroness drove home again in high dudgeon, and the last Trevanion of Carhays, with a last whimsical jibe at Nemesis, had the dog's portrait painted and headed for bankruptcy ... The portrait of the dog that bit the footman hangs in the servant's hall, and is the sole relic of a once great family of Trevanion that remains at Carhays.

Nonetheless, as our following entry will tell, the garden remains one of the most highly acclaimed in the county.

NB St Austell appears both on the OS Landranger 204 Truro and Falmouth *map, and the OS* Landranger 200 Newquay and Bodmin *map, but the gardens there will be discussed in the next chapter, as will* TRENARREN, *which, although it clearly belongs with St Austell, is found only on the Truro map.*

BEHAN PARK, Veryan

SW91 39 : EX105, GS353/354

Formerly known as the 'bowling green'; Cornish vean + parc = field, pronounced BE'AN Park; house listed grade II; small to medium parkland, south sloping, 60-50m.; on Veryan Series slate, limestone and radiolarian chert, in an AONB and HC; rainfall 35-40", temperature zone C; National Trust offices and residential apartments.

Jeremiah Trist succeeded his father as vicar of Veryan in 1781, and having married an heiress became a local landowner. In about 1807, with the bishop's permission, he built a house more suitable to his status on grounds he owned to the north of the church, commonly known as the 'bowling green', but called in Cornish *parc behan* - 'little field'. Not knowing the meaning, he incongruously named his new mansion Behan Park, 'so', his scholarly neighbour Whitaker, the historian and rector of Ruanlanihorne, acidly remarked, 'a bowling green of Cornwall was expanded by force of folly into a park of England.' The property, however, clearly impressed Samuel Drew, who wrote of it in *Hitchins*:

> Behan-Park ... is delightfully situated on a rising ground, that affords a prospect which is rather pleasing and diversified than extensive. A beautiful lawn stretches before the house, which is encircled by shrubs of various kinds, separated by an effectual barrier, which art has concealed from the eye, except to those who inspect it more nearly [i.e. an ha-ha]. The gardens, walks, and appendages, are all appropriate, and characterize the same taste that is conspicuous in the decency which the church exhibits. A small piece of water lying at some distance, enlivens the variegated scenery.

Trist was on familiar terms with neighbouring landowners, but especially with the Gregors of Trewarthenick, who in 1792 had engaged Repton's services, and he may have been influenced by his suggestions there. He was skilled in horticulture, and with the Revd Robert Walker of St Winnow, and Admiral Penrose of Ethy was asked to revise Worgan's *General View of Agriculture in Cornwall*, of 1811, contributing a section on the management of woods, plantations and willows (pp. 99-103, see also pp. 171-7). He was responsible for planting many trees in Veryan, and for building the famous round houses, to mark the limits of his land, which have become a distinguishing feature of the parish, and the subject of various legends. They were in fact constructed to a design of Admiral Penrose for improved workmen's cottages. The house and grounds are much as described, although an avenue of May trees, which until recently led from the Park gate, has now gone.

References: 18th, 19th (Gen.) and 20th C.

CAERHAYS CASTLE, St Michael Caerhays

SW97 41 : EX105, GS353/354　　　　　　　OPEN

Caryhays, 1366-1540 see Henderson (1935: 185); Cornish car + hay = enclosure, pronounced C'RAZE; house listed grade I, service buildings, garden walls, gateway and folly tower, higher lodge, lower lodge, each I, ornamental tower, cowhouse, bridge (dated 1910), each II; grounds of 60 acres (24 ha) listed grade II, north-east, north, and east sloping 70m. to the sea, house at 25m., on Grampound Grit, with basalt and dolomite intrusions south-west to north-west below house, with acid soil, in an AONB and HC, and an AGSV and CNCS; rainfall 35-40", temperature zone C; private, open 1983-98 CGOG, Monday - Friday mid-March to first week of May, and also various Sundays and holidays for charity. There is an official guide.

'The manor and barton of Caerhays,' according to *Hitchins*,

> belonged at a very early period to the Arundell family, from whom it passed [c. 1379] with an heiress to Trevanion of Trevanion, in which name it continued until the year 1767, when the male branch became extinct by the death of William Trevanion.

The estate then passed to John Bettesworth, his sister's son, whose son took the name of Trevanion in 1801. It is perhaps of passing interest to know that Lord Byron's grandmother had been a Trevanion. The early history of the house is critically reviewed by Tonkin. John Trevanion, who inherited in 1703, he wrote,

> has bestowed a good deal of money in buildings, gardens, &c., on this place but as there is nothing of regularity observed it may be more properly called a pleasant romantic seat than a complete habitation; and although it faces the south, yet it lies too much under a hill, and is therefore cold and damp in winter. The house anciently stood to the north of the present, towards the brow of the hill, according to my opinion in a far better situation. The place where it was built is still called haller, that is the hall; but the old desire of our ancestors to settle in our vallies, and to get, as they call it, in the luthe [dialect 'shelter' or 'protection'], inclined one of the Arundells to remove the house to where it now stands, and that was done so long since that nothing remains but the name to point out this ancient building.

Between 1805 and 1807, John Bettesworth Trevanion engaged the celebrated John Nash to

52. Caerhays Castle, designed by John Nash in 1808. (Gilbert 1820: ii. 845)

build the present Castle, although the tradition that his former associate, Humphry Repton, had visited here has, upon investigation, received no confirmation.

The Castle is entered through an impressive castellated gate-house on the shore. Jones, in her book *Follies and Grottoes* (1974), however, inclines to Tonkin's opinion of the earlier dwelling by classing the whole project as a 'folly', which certainly bankrupted the Trevanions, although Pevsner considered it 'picturesque'. The estate was eventually purchased in 1854 by Michael Williams II of Scorrier (although at the time he was resident at Trevince), who during a period of unemployment occupied a large number of Cornish miners in removing the top of a hill which, despite Nash, obscured the view from the Castle to the sea. He was succeeded by his son, John Michael, who was married to Elizabeth Maria, daughter of Stephen Davey of Bochym (q.v.), who continued to live at Caerhays after her husband's death, which probably was one reason why her son, John Charles, purchased Werrington for himself.

'J.C.,' as he came to be known, may be regarded as the founder of the great reputation of Caerhays as a plantsman's garden of national, if not international reputation. He was the sponsor, or contributed to the cost of, several plant-hunting expeditions, notably those of Forrest, Wilson, Farrer and Kingdon Ward, and the gardens reflect their discoveries of rhododendron, azalea, magnolia and camellia. Other collections were made of hydrangea, *Lithocarpus* and *Nothofagus*. Seeds from these various expeditions were sent back to the contributors, and were propagated and planted in the grounds above the Castle, which included the complete collection of Wilson's Kurume azaleas.

Many of these introduced specimens and varieties flowered for the first time at Caerhays. Fortunately, J.C. Williams scrupulously recorded the progress of his garden in a Garden-Book which, beginning on 1 January 1897, continued with entries for 1,650 days until 1934. He was also a regular contributor to the *Rhododendron Society Notes*, for whom he prepared a list of 264 species and natural varieties growing in the garden in 1917. Bishop Hunkin has done a service by summarizing the contents of the Garden-Book in two articles in the *JRHS* of 1943.

For many years J.C. interested himself in hybridization, making perhaps twenty or thirty crosses a year, which were then ruthlessly selected on flowering some four years later. Twelve appear in the *Register*: 'Blue Tit', 'Humming Bird', and 'Yellow Hammer', being the best known, and 'Royal Flush' being considered by the late Lionel Rothschild as the finest hybrid ever produced. Of equal, or perhaps greater fame were the camellia crosses made between *Camellia japonica* and *saluenensis*, which have become known as *williamsii* camellias. Among these are 'J.C. Williams' and 'Mary Christian', named after J.C. and his wife, and 'Charles Michael', named after his gardener. The most famous of all, 'Donation', however, was not bred at Caerhays, but by Col. Stephenson Clarke at Borde Hill in Sussex (but see Trewithen).

Julian Williams, the grandson of J.C., in an article on Caerhays camellias regretted that the notes on hybridizing were often lost or cryptic, and that many of the plant labels in the garden had disappeared or become illegible, which has made identification difficult. Such is an ubiquitous problem in gardens! Finally, J.C. shared with his cousin P.D. Williams at Lanarth an interest in raising daffodils, which he began in 1893. Many were never named, but not a few are to be found in the *Register*, several of which have received a F.C.C. or Award of Merit.

Caerhays was listed in the *Hort. Direct.* from 1908 until 1924, and was one of Thurston's select gardens. In a recent list of Champion Trees, compiled by the late Alan Mitchell, thirteen were recorded, to which Walter Magor (of Lamellan) in his review added another nine. Continuity of ownership, coupled with long-serving head gardeners since 1885, has ensured the maintenance and survival of this, probably the most important plantsman's garden in Cornwall.

References: 17th, 18th, 19th (Hort. & Gen.) and 20th C; Illus; J.C. Williams, List of Rhododendron Species Growing at Caerhays Castle in July 1917, RHS.; J.G. Millais, Magnolias, 1927: 105, 118, 122, 156, 194, 205, 234); H.Montgomery-Massingberd, The Field Book of Country Houses, 1988: 108-11.

GARLENICK, near Grampound

SW94 50 : *EX105, GS347*

Also Garlinnic; Cornish *cor = hedge or boundary + ?, pronounced garLENick; house listed grade II*, garden walls and gazebo II; medium sized estate, north sloping 75-45m., on Grampound Grit, in an AGLV; rainfall 40-45", temperature zone D; private.

From 1554 Garlenick was the seat of the Wooldridge family from Shropshire, who continued there until early in the nineteenth century, when the property was bought by the Revd George Moore, who substantially rebuilt the seventeenth-century house, incorporating his date-stone, 'G M 1812'. The eighteenth-century walls and gazebo are constructed in Flemish bond red brick, on a rubble plinth, but only Stockdale among our sources makes any mention of the 'beautiful gardens and fish ponds', of which the latter may have been of medieval origin. There remain the old garden walls, with a gazebo, which is well maintained, but little more of the former gardens remain. Thurston cited from here only an *Amelanchier canadensis* and a *Quercus suber*, the 'cork oak', with a girth of 14 feet 8 inches, which the owners believe to be the largest in the West Country. The garden has suffered from Dutch Elm disease, and, since it was exposed to the freezing winds in 1979, several of the old large Arboreum rhododendrons succumbed to the frosts.

References: 17th, 18th, 19th (Gen.) and 20th C.

HELIGAN, St Ewe

SW99 46 : *EX105, GS353/354*   OPEN

Cornish heligan = willow tree, or possibly the name of a stream, pronounced heLIGan (although often Anglicized to HELigan); house listed grade II, steward's house, lodge and walls, stables, stable walls, Palm Cottage, and shippon (cow-house), each II, also kitchen garden walls, walls attached to the house, and pre-Conquest Cross, each II; grounds of 57 acres (23 ha) listed grade II, sloping south and south-east 95-25m., with house at 80m., on Grampound Grit and basal conglomerate, with acid soil, in an AONB with an AM (cross); rainfall 40-45", temperature zone D; house in apartments with surrounding garden private, remainder now The Lost Gardens of Heligan, open 1992-8 CGOG, 1996-8 NGS, daily all year. Official guide and plan.

The manor of Tremayne is situated in St Martin in Meneage on the banks of the Helford River. John Tremayne of this family, who was Sheriff in 1486-7, had a brother, Richard, who resided at Tregonan, not far from Heligan. The manor of Heligan itself is recorded in *Hitchins* to have been,

> at an early period the property of the Heligans, from whom it passed by female heirs to the Tregarthians, and Whitleighs, and from the latter by co-heiresses to the families of Grenville and Hals. Towards the conclusion of Elizabeth's reign [in 1569], Heligan was purchased by Sampson Tremayne [d. 1626/7].

His son, William, then built a Jacobean house in 1603, to which a William and Mary style front block was added by Sir John Tremayne (d. 1693/4) almost a hundred years later, in 1692. When the fashion changed, the Revd Henry Hawkins, son of John Tremayne, effected a Georgian transformation in 1810, which was then improved by his son, John Hearle Tremayne. Nevertheless, despite all this remodelling, one cannot quarrel with W. Robert's judgement in the *Gardeners' Chronicle* of 1896, that the

> house, from an architectural point of view, has very little that is either striking or beautiful about it - it is severely plain, but large and substantial.

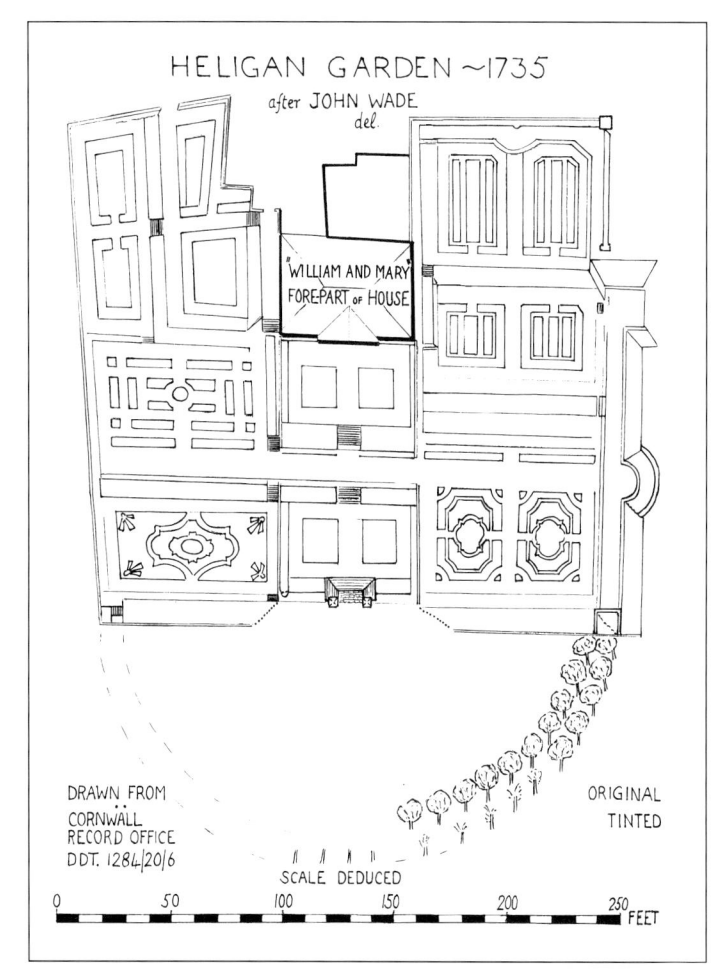

53. Heligan. The elaborate, but at that time rather old-fashioned formal garden, had been swept away by 1774 in favour of more natural landscaping. (C.G. 1987: 73)

As the house developed, so too did the garden, in design following fashion just as closely. In 1692 a walled garden court 60 feet (18m.) wide and twice as long was laid out in front of the house, but in 1735 John Tremayne expanded this by 'creating a parterre style garden at various levels flanking the garden court and both sides of the house'. About forty years later Thomas Gray was commissioned to draw up a plan of the garden which showed that tree planting had already begun along the west drive, and that the structure of the garden had reached that stage where it was to provide the framework for the plant collections of the nineteenth century.

The Revd Henry Hawkins Tremayne, curate of Lostwithiel, had unexpectedly inherited not only Heligan, but also the other family estates at Croan (q.v.) and Sydenham in Devon, but it was his son, John Hearle Tremayne, who was the first to attract attention for his plant collecting. In 1825 he received the seed of *Benthamidia fragifera* (now *Cornus capitata*), brought back by Sir Antony Buller from Nepal, which in 1832 he planted out as an avenue in the Lower Drive leading down to Heligan Mill. In 1896 William Roberts wrote that 'Heligan may be almost described as the birthplace of Cornus capitata', for which it had received notices in the *Gardeners' Chronicle* in 1841 and 1843. Only one or two of the original trees still survive, but plans are afoot to restore the avenue.

The main Himalayan plantings, however, have been attributed to John, the son of J.H. Tremayne. Sir Joseph Hooker, who had travelled in the Himalayas between 1847 and 1850, had been sponsored by Sir Charles Lemon at Carclew, who was John Tremayne's uncle. It was only natural, therefore, that when seed and seedlings were sent out from Kew, some were sent to Heligan, where they seem to have survived better than at Tremough, Penjerrick or Carclew. Indeed, their plants had the reputation of being finer than their parent specimens seen by Hooker himself. Many have now grown into large, if rather gaunt plants.

John and his son, John Claude (b. 1869), were also enthusiastic collectors of bamboos, of which they grew a large enough number of varieties to challenge comparison with Menabilly (q.v.). The lower garden, in which three pools were created, became known as the 'Japanese Garden' (now the 'Jungle'), where various conifers and other trees were planted, some of which have grown into magnificent specimens, among them the tallest *Cedrela sinensis* in Britain, and probably the biggest *Abies nordmanniana*, *Pinus thunbergii* and *Podocarpus totara*. Among the more exotic specimens noticed by writers was a *Chamaerops excelsus* planted in 1850, which by 1896 had grown to 20 feet (6m.), and the tree ferns brought over from Sydney, Australia by the Treseders.

Heligan was listed in the *Hort. Direct.* from at least 1870 until 1924, and was one of Thurston's select gardens, but already by this time the management of such extensive grounds was becoming increasingly difficult, so that for many years the estate became quiescent, and the properties let out. In 1990 a process of resuscitation was begun, which has brought into the public eye features which, although there for the pleasure of the owners, had not impressed the more plant-conscious horticultural writers. These include the rock garden and grotto, and the ravine garden and wishing well. An Italian garden, enclosed and with a small rectangular pond and a summer-house, was so unlike other gardens of this type that its name was questioned, until an Italian visitor remarked on its similarity to the gardens of ruined houses in Pompeii. In the recent restoration, great emphasis has been placed upon the Victorian produce gardens - the vegetable garden, the walled melon yard, the fine wall of bee-boles, and the flower garden with dipping pool. 'Mrs Tremayne's Garden', now the 'Sundial Garden', has recently been restored. Roberts felt that this

> very charming enclosure, of about a quarter of an acre, filled with all kinds of old-fashioned flowers, which produce a gay succession from January to December ... more nearly approaches my own idea of what an old English flower garden ought to be like than anything I have ever seen.

In recent years, Heligan has been the most highly publicized, and therefore the best known Cornish garden - principally for its commendable restoration project. In our context it must be evaluated as essentially a nineteenth-century plantsman's garden, alongside many others in the county as great or greater, most of which have never been 'lost'.

References: 17th, 18th, 19th (Hort. & Gen.) and 20th C.

THE HOLLIES, Grampound

SW93 48 : EX105, GS353/354　　　　　　OPEN*

House listed grade II; a garden of 1-2 acres (0.4-0.8 ha), south-west sloping, at 50m. altitude, on Grampound Grit, with acid soil, in an AGLV and HS; rainfall 40-45", temperature zone D; open 1983-98 CGOG, 1987, 1991-3, 1995-8 NGS, by appointment, April through September, and one Sunday each in May and June, for charity.

The Hollies dates possibly from the early eighteenth century, with mid- to late-nineteenth-century alterations. It is a town house fronting immediately on to the single road of the ancient town of Grampound. Behind the house is a courtyard garden with outbuildings and a greenhouse, leading into another enclosed area of lawn with perimeter borders, which again leads on into a smaller paved enclosure, appropriately planted with alpines and other similar plants. These enclosures represent the town garden, but beyond there would originally have been a medieval 'stitch', and it is in these fields that the larger part of the garden has been created, in the form of island beds variously planted. The sequence and design add to the charm, but it is the wide range and expert plantings by Mrs Croggon which raise this garden well above the average. Across the road the leather tannery (which was the last in the country to use traditional methods with oak bark) has long been in the Croggon family.

References: 20th C.

LAMORRAN HOUSE, Upper Castle Road, St Mawes

SW84 33 : EX105, GS352　　　　　　OPEN*

For derivation see Lamorran Rectory, after which parish this is named; garden of 3 acres (1.2 ha), south-east sloping from 60-15m., the upper garden on Portscatho Series, the lower on Falmouth Series sandstones and slates, with acid soil, in an AONB and HC; rainfall 35-40", temperature zone C; open 1989-98 CGOG, Wednesday and Friday, April through September, or by appointment, and one Sunday each in April and May for charity.

The garden at Lamorran House was re-created by Mr Robert Dudley-Cooke, who moved from his house in Surrey in 1982, bringing with him many rhododendrons, and particularly evergreen azaleas, of which there are 500 specimens, some of which had begun their life in Cornwall. In an article in the Cornish Garden, he outlined his aims in developing this garden: (1) 'That the garden should be landscaped, i.e. levels constantly varying. That it should be an intimate garden, i.e. winding paths leading to new vistas and with plenty of running water', (2) evergreens to predominate for year-round cover, (3) to have a sub-tropical look in its coastal setting, (4) some woodland for the larger rhododendrons, and (5) the wide variety of plants chosen for visual effect rather than botanical significance.

The Japanese Garden with a waterfall and grotto was the first to be formed, followed by work on the lower garden, which at that time was overgrown with blackthorn and brambles. Here a Mediterranean-type garden was created, surmounted by a small temple, and an Italianate pond. It has been necessary to provide shelter from the south-west wind from Falmouth, and scorching easterlies in the early year. Where protected, such plants as acacias, of which there are twelve species, callistemons, grevilleas, cassias, metrosideros and *Albizia lophantha* are flourishing. On a succulent bank there is a selection of agaves and lampranthus, with bougainvillaea on the wall beneath the temple.

Travels in the Mediterranean region inspired an enthusiasm for palms, varieties of which have been planted throughout the garden, the more common, such as *Cordyline australis*, but also *Phoenix canariensis*, *Butia capitata*, and other rarer species. Other plants such as the various forms of *Yucca, Dasylirion, Beschorneria,* and succulents such as the *Aeonium* enhance the sub-tropical effect. The garden is continually evolving, and more recently has enveloped part of the former Riviera garden below. This fascinating and unique garden continues the tradition in the acclimatization of exotics of the Falmouth gardens at Grove and Rosehill, among others. Although on an altogether grander scale, Lamorran may be compared with the Old Rectory at Marazion, although there the interest in rare and subtropical plants is more explicitly botanical.

References: 20th C.

MEVAGISSEY VICARAGE

SX01 45 : *EX105, GS353/354*

SS Meve et Ide in Poudre *1427*, i.e. *SS Meve and Issey, pronounced* mevaGIZy; *on Grampound Grit and conglomerate, in an AONB; rainfall 40-45", temperature zone D; now* Mevagissey House *holiday accommodation.*

Mevagissey has one of the few parsonages which inspired Gilbert to write a description of any length, but probably chiefly because of the view:

> The vicarage-house ... is a most charming rural retirement. It is situated about half way up a narrow valley, full of meadows, smiling with verdure, interspersed with masses of lively foliage, and the eye, having glanced over this delightful sweep, rests on the glittering waters of Mevagissey Bay. The building being in the cottage style, very happily corresponds with the surrounding scenery, and the gardens produce flowers and fruits in great variety and perfection.

However, when the Revd Edward Carlyon became vicar in 1840, he found this 'cottage', now the site of the Sunday School, dilapidated and too small for his requirements. So in 1846 he built what is now Mevagissey House, on his glebe land. It was in the garden of this house that Thurston had heard in 1930 that a *Kalmia latifolia* flowered about every second year. He also wrote of a

fine tree [of *Laurus nobilis*] and many shrubs in the vicarage garden ... The leaves were formerly requisitioned in connection with the preparation of tinned "sardines" at the now extinct factory at Mevagissey.

References: 18th, and 20th C.

PENLEE HOUSE, Tregony

SW92 45 : *EX105, GS353/354*

Cornish pen + *legh = *flat stone, pronounced* penLEE; *house listed grade II; grounds of 2 acres (0.8 ha), at 50m. altitude, on Portscatho Series slate and grit, with acid soil, in an AGLV and an HS; rainfall 35-40", temperature zone C; opened 1983-4 CGOG, now the* Penlee Nursing and Residential Home.

Penlee House was built by Richard Gurney, the rector of St Cuby, Tregony, in the 1820s. However, the garden did not come to the notice of horticulturists until 1871, when the house became occupied by John Simpson Tyerman, who retired there from Liverpool. From 1861, Tyerman had been Curator of the Botanic Gardens in Liverpool, where, with the borough architect, a Mr Robson, he had designed the Palm House, in which he had successfully germinated the double coconut of the Seychelles (*Gdnrs' Ch.* i.1874: 113-14). Later, in 1877, Tyerman was engaged to design Kimberley Park in Falmouth (q.v.).

There had once been a Victorian conservatory along the whole east side of Penlee House, which may have dated from the time of Tyerman's residence. In his early life he had spent some time working in nurseries, before being accepted into the service of Kew in 1858. Evidently he was still propagating plants at Tregony in his retirement, for Charles Williams of Caerhays had told Bishop Hunkin that

> as a boy he used frequently to ride over to see about getting plants from Tyerman's at Tregoney [sic] ... One of the plants from his garden at Penlee ... was figured in the *Botanical Magazine* (1872), t. 5959 - *Senecio pulcher*, a handsome grounsel, introduced from Uruguay by Mr. Tyerman himself. [He was] commemorated by a rare Rhododendron *R. Tyermanii*, a specimen of which [in 1943 was] at Penjerrick.

Tyerman, who died in 1889, had also a reputation as a naturalist, specializing, if such a word is appropriate for a man of such varied achievements, in ferns and mosses, a hare's-foot fern *Duvalia tyermanni* being named after him, and in conchology, where he made a notable collection of shells, and had a seashell *Marginella tyermanii* named after him. A later occupant of the house who took a great interest in the gar-

54. Pennans. The celebrated avenue had by this time been cut across by the turnpike. The left wing of the house is now gutted, but there is some evidence that it may never have been completed. (Twycross 1846: 47)

den, which he opened to the public, was the late Dr K.O. Parsons, a physician, who was also a celebrated horologist. This Penlee House should be distinguished from Penlee House in Penzance, which became a Memorial Park.

References: 19th and 20th C; Nora McMillan, 'Lever and his Shell Collection', Journal of the History of Collections, 4 no. 2 (1992) pp. 297-9.

PENNANS, between Grampound and Hewas Water

SW95 48 : EX105, GS347

Cornish pen + nans, pronounced penNANS; house listed grade II*, early-mid 18th C. stables, and garden walls each II, the walls, which are incomplete, are of interest, 'Early-mid 18 C. Red brick, laid in Flemish bond ... about 4 metres high, enclosing a large rectangular area with one cross wall running east/west. The walls were probably formerly enclosing an orchard and kitchen garden' (EH); garden extinct, now a farmhouse.

The tenement of Pennans was mentioned in the Parliamentary Survey of 1649. The house, which was formerly the seat of the Huddy family, was built in about 1680, but was remodelled and extended to its present form *c.*1700-20 by Philip Hawkins, an attorney of a Devon family. Although the house is illustrated in Twycross entire, with its avenue, the front left as seen today is gutted. Curiously there is no sign of there ever having been any communication between this wing and the main house, which led the English Heritage surveyor to surmise 'that it may never have been completed'. Philip Hawkins leaving no male issue, the estate passed with his second daughter to the Carlyons of Tregrehan. In 1824, *Hitchins* recorded that:

> It is now occupied as a farm house, around which appear the fading memorials of departed grandeur. The lofty brick walls which formerly enclosed an extensive garden, still remain; but in some places they are verging to decay, and in others the creeping ivy mounts above their summits. The ancient pillars on which the gates were formerly suspended, have been demolished within the memory of the present generation; and the statues of lead which once decorated the appendages of the house, have also of late years been removed. When the turnpike road was made, that branch which leads from St. Austell to

Truro, was carried across some fine rows of trees, that grew with the utmost regularity, and formed a shady walk leading from the house to a piece of water in an adjoining vale. To prevent the connexion from being cut off by the intersection of the turnpike road, a tumulus was raised on each side among the trees, from which was turned a lofty arch formed of brick, beneath which travellers pursued their way, and over which carriages belonging to the house could pass without inconvenience. But when Pennance [sic] ceased to be the residence of grandeur, the arch was suffered to fall into decay, and its sounding echo was heard no more. About forty years since [i.e. in the 1780s] it was taken down, to prevent accidents; and the tumulus on one side still remains.

Evidently the problem of motorways is no new thing! The remains of the 'tumulus' is still apparent at the entrance to Pennans, and the 'piece of water', surrounded by trees, can be seen in the lower part of the field opposite.

References: 17th, 18th and 19th (Gen.) C; Illus; Borlase:Original Letters V 88, 1753, in Morrab Library, reprinted O. Corn. 1979-85: 389.

PLACE MANOR, St Anthony in Roseland

SW85 32 : *EX105, GS352*

Cornish plas = *palace or mansion, from the English; house and lodge each listed grade II; grounds in north facing valley, 35m. to the sea, on Portscatho Series sandstone and slate, with acid soil, in an AONB, and an AGSV and CNCS; rainfall 35-40", temperature zone C; has been an hotel, but is now private.*

The house, which may be seen across the Percuil River from St Mawes, occupies the site of the Augustine priory of St Anthony founded in 1124, and adjoins the parish church, but the present building, although it includes part of a sixteenth-century wing, was mostly remodelled and extended in *c.*1840, in what *Lake* described as a 'palatial style'. The estate came into the family of Spry when George Spry purchased it from Sir Richard Vyvyan of Trelowarren in 1635. A seventeenth-century lease mentions, as well as 'wharfs, quays and fields', a 'bee garden, dove house, garden and nurseries', but, apart from the private walled garden, the house now stands with only woodland behind, and a plain lawn in front leading down to the shore. The Spry family also owned and sometimes resided at Killiganoon and Tregolls (q.v.). Place Manor, Anthony should be distinguished from Place House, Fowey, Prideaux Place, Padstow, and Rame Place.

References: 17th, 18th, 19th (Gen.) and 20th C; Illus.

PROBUS GARDENS, Probus

SW90 47 : *EX105, GS352* OPEN*

Cornish = saint's name; 7.5 acre garden (3 ha), south sloping 90-85m., on Grampound Grit, sandstone and slate, with acid soil; rainfall 40-45", temperature zone C; open all year round, but best season from May through September. There is a guide with a plan.

The original 'County Demonstration Garden' was laid out in the two-acre grounds of Methleigh House (the Technical Institute), St Austell in the 1960s by Mr Eric Trevan, under the direction of Peter Blake, County Horticultural Advisor. The expansion of the College, however, soon led to the search for a new and larger site, which was resolved in 1971 when Mrs Johnston offered a place on the Trewithen estate, now known as the Probus Gardens. The project was to a great extent Peter Blake's own inspiration and design, which at that time was unique in the country. The 1988 guide clearly outlined the purpose and intention of the garden:

> The Centre has been established to illustrate in the form of permanent demonstrations and planting displays, a comprehensive range of garden practices, plant utilisation and the results of modern garden techniques and research.

Among the various objects, two were particularly designed to help and interest general visitors:

> To improve their gardens thus assisting them to utilise their soil and surrounds to their best possible potential

and:

> To draw attention to the close association which exists between plants and medicine (e.g. herbs), history and geography, (e.g. exploration of new countries, plant collecting) and the problems associated with the study and understanding of the Countryside.

Some sixty-five different sections were planted

> ranging from ideas on design to lawn treatments, from collections of roses and heathers to fuchsias and lilies. [There is an] historical garden and nature trail, observation bee-hives, geological collection and much more

However, in line with the Government's policies on privatisation and financing, the County Department of Horticulture and its staff were gradually dissolved during the 1990s, so that the fate of the Centre hung in the balance. Nevertheless, for the time being, a way has been found for it to survive, with certain modifications aimed at preserving as many of its educational functions as can be supported by admission charges, and other means of private funding.

References: 20th C.

ROSTEAGUE, Gerrans

SW87 33 : EX105, GS352

Cornish ros + ?*daek = *perhaps 'full of riches' or a personal name, pronounced* rosTEAGUE; *house listed grade II*, summer-house and garden walls, and culver-house each II; small to medium grounds, south-east facing at c. 30m. altitude, on Portscatho Series sandstone and slate, with acid soil, in an AONB and HC, and an AGSV; rainfall 35-40", temperature zone C; private, occasionally open.*

Rosteague is a house dating from the fifteenth and sixteenth centuries. It was purchased in 1619 by a family who, the previous century, had removed to Lavethan in Blisland from Kent, where Richard Kempe had been sheriff in 1528. They married into the local families of Spry at Place, Hobbs at Trewince, and Cregoe at Tregeare - once a rich manor.

Nicholas Kempe mid-century reversed the house to face the sea. It was remodelled by John Kempe around 1700, at a time when he may have improved the grounds, building the large walled garden, which has been quartered and entirely taken up with four parterres of elaborate and differing figurations, and has traditionally been known as 'The French Garden', in the belief that the designs may have had some affinity with Versailles. Certainly they are compatible with patterns known to date from the 1660s. They constitute a unique survival in Cornwall, and may never have had an equal, since, with the Kempe family connections 'up-country', the inspiration may have come from seeing similar gardens in London or the Home Counties.

There is an interesting nineteenth-century summer-house in the north-east corner of the walled garden, with a beehive-shaped roof thatched with Somerset reeds, supported on rustic tree trunks, where you would need to stoop to enter. This, too, is intriguing, since such beehive summer-houses can still be seen in Somerset, where the reeds originated. It may date from the time that Henry Harris - who was related to the Harrises of Rosewarne (q.v.), - extended the house in 1820. There is a culver house at some distance from the dwelling, thought to be medieval, and there was a small deer park in the nineteenth century, and possibly earlier.

References: 17th, 18th, 19th (Gen.) and 20th C.

ST-JUST-IN-ROSELAND CHURCHYARD, St-Just-in-Roseland

SW84 35 : EX105, GS352   OPEN

Small to medium sized churchyard and memorial garden, steeply north sloping, 30m. to the sea, on Portscatho Series sandstone and slate, with acid soil, in an AONB and HC, and in part an AGSV; rainfall 35-40", temperature zone C; open at all times. There is an official guide book to the church and churchyard, and a leaflet on the 'Granite Stones'.

St Just Churchyard, in a 'sequestered nook', produced, thought Gilbert, 'a valuable subject for the pencil of the artist, and admirers of landscape scenery.' *Murray's Guide* in 1859 advised that it was 'worth visiting', and many thousands have visited it ever since. *Hitchins* observed that the 'stones of the building appear from their grit to have been brought hither from some distance and probably by water', some perhaps from a quarry, mentioned by Leland, between Pentewan and Black Head. He quotes Whitaker as affirming that:

> This circumstance ... accounts for what nothing else can account for, the strange position of St. Just Church, with its parsonage at the bottom of the bank, shelving down to an arm of Falmouth Harbour, even on the very brink of the water.

There are, nevertheless, other accounting factors, such as that the anchorage was probably of much greater importance in the past. *Hitchins* adds:

> By the present minister, the Rev. Dr. Rodd, this house has been much improved, and both the buildings and gardens have assumed a degree of elegance to which they were strangers in former years.

Edward Rodd (rector 1803-36), by bringing with him the horticultural expertise of his

55. Rosteague. A plan of the parterres in the walled garden.

family at Trebartha in Northill (q.v.), which he was to inherit in 1836, may have originated the plantings in the churchyard. They were considerably enhanced later in the century, when John Garland Treseder returned from Australia and founded a nursery alongside. Among the embellishments was a series of granite stones inscribed with verses and epigrams, lining the path down to the church, placed there by the Revd Humphrey Davis, rector from 1901 to 1930. In 1984 the Manpower Services Commission set up a project to enlarge the churchyard to designs by Neil, the grandson of J.G. Treseder, to include a pool fed by a rill. As a result of a legacy from Mrs Anne Groves, it became possible at the same time to lay out the opposite side of the road to the churchyard as Memorial Gardens, which have opened up new and higher vistas to the Creek. Thurston cited lime trees (*Tilia vulgaris*) at St Just, but the official guide lists many other species, probably of greater interest.

References: 19th (Gen.) and 20th C.

TREWARTHENICK, Tregony

SW90 44 : *EX105, GS352*

Cornish, Holmes suggests tre + Uyethenoc *or* Guethenoc *a personal name, pronounced* trewarTHENick; *house listed grade II; large grounds listed grade II, east sloping 70-20m., with house at 60m., on Portscatho Series, sandstone and slate, with acid soil, in an AONB, and an AGSV; rainfall 40-45", temperature zone C; private, in apartments, opened 1985, 1992-3 CGOG.*

'The manor and barton of Trewarthenick' wrote Gilbert,

> was anciently the property of Richard Peynell, who it is probable, obtained it in marriage with Mary, daughter and coheiress of John Penham, of the city of Exeter. It was transferred by this lady, during her widowhood, to Thomas Seely, and sold by one of that family, in the year 1640, to John Gregor, esq. ancestor of the late proprietor.

In the sixteenth and seventeenth centuries the Gregors were successful merchants in Truro, who had further improved their condition by good marriages, such as that of Francis Gregor with Joan Prideaux, and John with Elizabeth, daughter of Walter Moyle of Bake, who in 1686 as the date-stone reads, had built 'a fine new house'. In her *Memoirs* (c.1850), Sarah Gregor (née Glanville, of Catchfrench), however, believed Trewarthenick in 1791 to be

> very destitute of beauty, with few plantations, and the surrounding ground cut up into fields and regularly tilled, and a public cart road (since turned) ran close to the house which had its least agreeable offices [including a piggery] in near connection with it ...

that is, an estate which might be termed a *ferme ornée*. A year later, in 1792, Francis Gregor, her uncle, invited a visit from Humphry Repton, who then prepared a Red Book. These Red Books in Cornwall are all confined within a close family and political circle. Gregor was himself related to the Glanvilles at Catchfrench for whom Repton was to prepare a Red Book in 1793, and

56. Trewarthenick. Sketch by Edmund Prideaux, 1727.

57. Trewarthenick. This 1831 engraving is from the same viewpoint as that of Prideaux, after the grounds had been improved and the house enlarged following the visit of Repton in 1792. (Allom 1831: 64)

like Glanville he was an MP and supporter of Pitt, who had introduced Repton to his brother-in-law at Port Eliot.

In December 1792 Pitt issued a proclamation calling out the local militia, as a defence against possible invasion by the French. This triggered Francis Gregor into action, which his neighbour, Whitaker, rector of Ruanlanihorne, regarded as 'near-panic'. He continued to be occupied in these matters for many years, being, as his niece thought, 'in his element' organizing and taking part in exercises.

Once over, the Napoleonic wars were followed by a time of shortage and hardship, which factors militated against Gregor having the leisure to occupy himself too greatly in the improvement of his estate, although it is believed that the house was remodelled to Repton's designs. Stone for the house was obtained from a quarry in the grounds, which received ornamental planting about 1820.

In 1825, however, the property was inherited by Gregor's niece, Sarah Glanville (whose husband had changed his name from Booker to Gregor). She began at once to refurbish the estate which had lain unoccupied for several years. She first engaged the London architect, Henry Harrison, who had assisted Soane at Port Eliot, to enlarge the house with two wings (now removed), and then began to improve the grounds, perhaps in consultation with her uncle's Red Book, which can now be seen in the County Record Office. A comparison between the 1727 sketch by Edmund Prideaux, and Allom's print of 1832 is instructive. The fields can be seen to have been opened up to leave a more natural landscape, and plantations now define the boundaries and obscure the service buildings to the left of the house. The avenue through which, in Prideaux's sketch, curved the main approach, has been dispersed, and the entrance resited. There is pool in the park land below. These all follow the advice in the Red Book, and from the maturity of the trees must date from the time of Francis Gregor himself.

The 'Spring Garden' to the south, beyond the walled garden, and extended as suggested by Repton, is sheltered by huge laurels planted in 1828, enclosing an area with impressively large rhododendrons, and rather less mature magnolias. It seems probable that the small 'picturesque' garden with a pond to the north of the house may also date from this period. The subsequent history during Victorian and later times is evident enough in what has survived. Along what appears to have been the ha-ha in front of the house, twelve yews have been placed, now grown to a size virtually to block out completely the prospect over the park, which below is separated off by a wire fence planted with spotted aucuba.

The area to the west of Repton's new approach, now known as the 'Summer Garden', has been brought into cultivation 'out of bracken and brambles' during the last twenty-five years. Here, at the southern end, are beds of camellias, while to the north are large islands with a variety of flowering trees and shrubs. The historic landscape at Trewarthenick is now past its maturity, but there has been some commendable planting since 1945, and recent efforts have begun towards restoration. The garden here is not often open, and was neither listed in the *Hort. Direct.*, nor visited by Thurston.

References: 17th, 18th, 19th (Hort. & Gen.) and 20th C; Illus.

TREWINCE, Gerrans

SW86 33 : EX105, GS352

Cornish tre + guyns = wind, pronounced treWINCE; extended house listed grade II*, gate-piers, two cottages, and quay, each II; medium to large grounds, sloping south-east, 60m. to the sea, on Portscatho Series sandstone and slate, in an AONB and HC; rainfall 35-40", temperature zone C; now Trewince Manor self-catering accommodation, with relict gardens.

This fine house was built in the early 1750s, with extensions to the south in about 1930. Gilbert writes:

> Trewince, formerly a seat of the Courtenays, and successively of the Hobbses, and Johnses, is now the residence of the widow of the late Richard Johns, esq. Trewince House is a handsome free-stone building, and the grounds around it are well laid out, and afford delightful prospects.

The Johns family were influential in the parish during the eighteenth and nineteenth centuries since the rectorial tithes, acquired by Edward Hobbs in 1661, had eventually passed to them by 1729, after which they continued at Trewince until 1876, obtaining their income both from their leases as major landowners, and from their involvement in the pilchard industry, operated from a 'cellar' [i.e. a warehouse] at their quay. They were succeeded in 1897 by the Thomas family, John Collette Thomas, who had made a fortune in London, extended the house and lived here in style. The grounds, which are entered through impressive gate-piers surmounted by eagles from the Hobbs' coat of arms, despite adaptations to the holiday trade, still retain a park-like quality.

References: 17th, 18th, 19th (Gen.) and 20th C.

TREWITHEN, Probus

SW91 47 : EX105, GS353/354   OPEN

Cornish tre + gwyth = trees, pronounced treWITHen; house listed grade I, two pavilions (c. 1740) each I, barn with two engine houses, with an engine dated 1811 by Trevithick II*, pavilions and walls adjoining farmhouse, each II; garden of 25 acres (10 ha) listed grade II*, south facing 85-80m., on Grampound Grit, and basal conglomerate, with acid soil; rainfall 40-45", temperature zone C; private, garden and nursery open 1983-98 CGOG, 1991, 1993-98 NGS, Monday to Saturday through March to the end of September, and Sundays in April and May. Official history, guide, and plant list with plans.

Tonkin described Trevorva which had come into the possession of the Dorset family of Williams as having a road which was 'one of the deepest and worst in the whole country'. In his time they lived 'at a place adjoining called Trewithan, where,' he believed, 'the family removed, probably disliking the dirty situation at Trevorva'.

> After the Williamses had flourished for some time at Trewithan, Courtenay Williams, when he had foolishly squandered away a pretty estate and a good fortune too, which he had with his wife ... sold this barton ... to Philip Hawkins, esq. brother to the Rev. Dr. Hawkins of Pennance [i.e.Pennans (q.v.)].

Hawkins 'much improved this seat ... made good gardens [and] new built [a] great part of the house' in 1723. Around 1730 James Gibbs drew up new designs, but he did not live to see these brought to fruition and, since he had no issue, the estate reverted to his nephew Thomas, son of his sister Mary, who had married Christopher Hawkins of Trewinnard (q.v.).

In 1738 Thomas Hawkins engaged Thomas Edwards of Greenwich, who was active in Cornwall at the time, to enlarge the house. In 1763-4 alterations were made to designs by Sir Robert Taylor. Although Tonkin had written that Philip had 'made good gardens, &c,' it was Thomas who was responsible for the major planting. There survives in the County Record Office a notebook written by him in 1745 with the title, 'The Care and Cultivation of Trees', and a 'Diary' written in 1757 by his father-in-law, James Heywood, which together with the 'Plan of the Barton House, Plantations and Gardens of Trewithen' supplements the print in Borlase's *Natural History* of 1758. There were woods to the south and south-west which protected the house from the prevailing winds, avenues radiating to the east and north, and in the centre of a 'pleasing labyrinth' stood a 'Statue of Pomona'. Thomas died in 1766 to be succeeded by his son, later Sir Christopher Hawkins, who was more

58. Trewithen. The straight-sided rows of beech were planted in the mid eighteenth century by Thomas Hawkins, but were remodelled with winding edges and vistas by George Johnstone in the early twentieth century. (Borlase 1758: 23)

interested in enlarging his estate than improving his grounds. A contemporary rhyme about him ran:

> A park with no deer;
> A cellar with no beer;
> A house with no cheer;
> Christopher Hawkins lives here.

He too was without issue, the property passing to his nephew, Christopher Henry Thomas Hawkins. He being a minor, the property was managed by his father, John, who was responsible for planting the holm oaks to the north of the house from acorns collected from his own house at Bignor Park in Sussex. Gilbert had little to say about the garden at Trewithen. Unusually it is *Hitchins* which contains the fuller description:

> Its views are commanding, and it is a conspicuous object from many places at a considerable distance; but its aspect is unfavourable being directed towards the north, and exposed to the violence of storms which blow from that quarter. The grounds in its vicinity however, render it pleasant, and the trees, which in several directions surround this mansion, impart to it a degree of correspondent dignity.

On the death of C.H.T. Hawkins, who never lived at Trewithen, the property passed again to a nephew, whose son succeeded him upon his death a year later. The designs by Nesfield during this period for a parterre seem never to have been implemented, but with the succession of George Horace Johnstone began what has been called 'Trewithen's Golden Age of gardening'. First Johnstone believed 'it was necessary to take an axe and claim air and light from amongst the trees, first for the house and those that live in it, and then for the plants that must share the fortunes of the owner.'

One hundred hybrids of *Rhododendron arboreum* were then planted, two of their own hybrids from which were named 'Alison Johnstone' after his wife, who came to live with him on their marriage in 1910, and 'Jack Skilton' after his gardener, who received the RHS Long Service Medal in 1959. The creation of the garden as it is today was ironically a consequence of a war-time Government order for tree-felling. This provided an opportunity to reshape the lawn with its straight avenue of trees stretching from the house, into a glade over 200 yards (183m.) long, flanked with winding edges, planted up with trees and shrubs arranged to provide vistas and perspectives from several viewpoints.

Trewithen is renowned for its outstanding collection of tender and rare plants, many from Asia, which are unique to this garden. There is available a select list of the plant collection drawn up by Nigel Holman (of Chyverton). Among other species there is an outstanding collection of camellias, some of their own raising, such as 'Elizabeth Johnstone', which was named after their daughter, and 'Glenn's Orbit' which first flowered as the astronaut completed his orbit of the earth. Their plant of 'Donation' was struck from a cutting from the original at Borde Hill in Sussex which later died, and is reputed to be the source of many of the subsequent specimens. George Johnstone achieved also a high reputation for his raising of daffodils. Other features of the garden include the Water Gardens, indicated on the plan of c.1745, laid out in the shape of an eagle, the Hawkins family emblem, which is being restored after the storm of 1990; the old walled kitchen garden planted with herbaceous borders, rare and tender climbers, and with a lily pond and summer-house; and the Cock Pit, a former quarry, imaginatively planted with tree ferns in the early twentieth century, now a rock garden. Trewithen was listed in the *Hort. Direct.* in 1919 and 1924, and was one of Thurston's select gardens.

References: 17th, 18th, 19th (Hort. & Gen.) and 20th C; Illus.

TRIST HOUSE, formerly Veryan Vicarage, Veryan

SW91 39 : *EX105, GS353/354*

The present house is named after three former vicars; the parsonage and terraces listed grade II, lodge II; grounds of 4 acres (1.6 ha), north-west sloping 80-65m., on Grampound Grit to south-east and Veryan Series slate, limestone and radiolarian chert to north-west, with acid soil, in an AONB and HC; rainfall 35-40", temperature zone C; private, relict garden.

After the death of his father, Samuel Trist exchanged his Devon living with his successor, to become the third in the family to be installed as Vicar of Veryan. Since his mother continued in residence at Behan Park, with his sister Charlotte, who had inherited most of the family estate, he therefore took over the vicarage from his brother Thomas, and in 1831 began to rebuild it, with a lodge incorporating ornamental masonry from St Nun's Chapel in Grampound, to the designs of Harrison, a London architect also used by Sarah Gregor in renovating Trewarthenick. She is believed, in her improvements to the grounds there, to have incorporated some of the suggestions of Repton not followed out by her uncle. Trist may, therefore, have been influenced by her in laying out his own garden, at a cost of £1,000, which, in comparison with the £3,000 spent on the house, is a vast sum, indicating extensive landscaping.

Although overgrown and somewhat dilapidated when last seen, the grounds still survive. There are terraces at three levels at the garden front of the house, ornamented with vases, and with a central pillar on which stands what appears to be a medieval stoup, leading to a lawn. To the west, beyond some fruit trees, by the walled garden, is a large-scale rockery in the Victorian 'heaped style', and possibly the remains of a grotto. Also to the west is a pool, perhaps an old mill-pond, fed by a stream. The plantations of trees merge into more natural woodland. The use of masonry from a chapel in a neighbouring parish (much to the chagrin of the incumbent!), and a medieval stoup as a garden ornament, reflects the widespread and quite cavalier attitude of the clergy towards antiquities at this time. The vicarage was sold in 1980, and the present owner is restoring the garden.

References: 20th C.

SUPPLEMENTARY LISTS

LESSER-KNOWN HISTORIC GARDENS

Lanhadron, near Pentewan

SW99 47 : *EX105, GS353/354*

Lanlaron Domesday 1086, Nansladron on OS maps; Cornish nan + lader = thieves, pronounced lanHADron; original estate, with an AM (a cross-base), extinct.

Norden described Lanhadron in about 1597 as

> a auntient howse of the Arondells, where was the most statelieste parke within the Shire, now vtterly decayde, and the woodes rooted vp, and the land sowed with corne. There is an oke within the circuit of this decayde parke, called Arondells oke, which is sayd to bear Leaues as whyte as whyte paper: some suche Leaues are ordinarye on manie okes, but to be so generall is more straunge.

Carew mentions one called the Painter's Oak in the hundred of East;

> but whether the [white leaves] partake any supernatural property, to foretoken the owner's soon ensuing death, when his leaves are all of one colour (as I have heard some report), let those affirm, who better know it: certain it is, that divers ancient families in England are admonished by such predictions.

About a century later, Tonkin in his manuscript writes of the Arundell oak:

> I had myself a very fine plant (which was a seedling found in a hedge on Lanhadron, not far from the place where the old one grew, and dropt there I suppose by some bird), lately growing in my garden at Treleven, which being forced to remove it in a wrong season, ... I lost, to my great regret, though I took all imaginable care of it, and perhaps too much.

References: 17th, 18th, 19th (Gen.) and 20th C.

Luney, Grampound

SW96 48 : *EX105, GS347*

Cornish leven = *smooth* + *-i* = *name suffix in river names, pronounced* LOONy; *estate extinct.*

Gilbert writes:

> Luney was a seat of the Mohuns, who removed here from Creed ... The house, and the attached offices, were built by the Mohuns, in a style of great strength and durability, and are yet standing; but the ponds, walks, and gardens are all destroyed.

The expression 'ponds, walks, and gardens', distinguishes ancient from contemporary gardens, which Gilbert described as with 'lawns, gardens and shrubberies'. The Mohun family were also at Boconnoc, Hall, Rosteague and Trewinnard, each of which once had elaborate gardens.

References: 18th and 19th (Gen.) C.

Tredinnick, Veryan

SW92 42 : *EX105, GS353/354*

Cornish tre + reden = *bracken, pronounced* treDINick; *house, garden and courtyard walls etc, and gate-piers, together listed grade II, grounds at 75m., on Portscatho Series sandstone and slate; rainfall 35-40", temperature zone C; farm with contemporary garden.*

The present farmhouse is seventeenth century, remodelled in the seventeenth and eighteenth centuries. It was, wrote Gilbert,

> formerly a leasehold seat of the Trevanions who purchased it in the latter part of the seventeenth century, of the Bullers. Richard Trevanion, governor of Pendennis Castle built a good mansion at this place, which has been burnt. He also planted several portions of the ground with young trees, which have since given a new feature to its surface. The lease expired about 1804, when it became the property of James Buller, esq.

There are dove-holes in the south wall of the house.

References: 17th, 18th and 19th (Gen.) C.

Trenowth, Grampound

SW93 50 : *EX105, GS347*

Trenwit Domesday 1086, Cornish tre + noweth = *new, pronounced* treNOWTH; *the Barton House, and a pair of cottages, each listed grade II; originally a large estate, Trenowth House garden 18 acres (5.5 ha), sloping north-east to the River Fal, 100-45m., on Grampound Grit, with acid soil, in an AGLV, a SSSI and CNCS; rainfall 40-45", temperature zone D; the* Barton *is a farm,* Trenowth House *is a private residence.*

The family bearing the name of this Domesday manor are of great antiquity, Michael de Trenowith serving in Parliament in 1338. They became extinct on the male line in 1497. Only the site of the old manor house now remains, but the Barton House, of seventeenth to eighteenth century vintage, survives as a farmhouse. The residence is a neo-Georgian house, designed by a Truro architect, possibly Cornelius, in 1928. The formal garden, designed by the same architect, reflects the taste of the time.

The terrace garden is rectangular, originally with a slate terrace in front of the house, and a flat lawn leading to a low wall. The adjoining water garden is similar, but with unusual angular L-shaped ponds, set in flat lawns, with shrubs and specimen trees. The gardens formerly extended into the surrounding woodland, where there are magnolias, camellias, azaleas and rhododendrons, and the remains of kitchen gardens and orchards. Much of the estate is covered with ancient woodland, which has descended from that mentioned in the Domesday survey.

References: 17th, 18th, 19th (Gen.) and 20th C.

ADDITIONAL CONTEMPORARY GARDENS

See also THE HOLLIES, LAMORRAN HOUSE *and* PROBUS GARDENS *in the main section.*

Creed House, Creed, near Grampound

SW93 47 O : *EX105, G353/354*   OPEN*

St Creda the patron saint; part of the garden of the former rectory, open 1993-8 CGOG, NGS, mid April through September, by appointment, and one Sunday each in May and June for charity.

Reference: 20th C.

Riviera Gardens, St Mawes

SW84 33 : *EX105, GS352*

Open 1987, CGOG.

Described when last open as 'semi-natural gardens with New Zealand and Australian trees and shrubs,' the greater part has now been incorporated within the Lamorran House gardens above (q.v.).

Trewollack and Ker Vean, near St-Just-in-Roseland

SW85 34 : *EX105, GS352*

Cornish tre + [?wollas], *pronounced* treWOLLack, *and* ker = *fort* + vean, *pronounced* KER vean; *in an AONB and HC, and in part an AGSV; opened 1985, CGOG.*

There is a small shrub garden associated with a nursery. Ker Vean has grounds of two acres (0.8 ha) around the cottage, with 'old oaks, apple orchard and daffodils, pine and birch trees dating from 1930'. Since 1978 there have been additional plantings of trees, shrubs and tender plants. There are three acres (1.2 ha) of adjoining woodland.

4
Newquay and Bodmin

1. ST AUSTELL, LOSTWITHIEL and FOWEY

Of the three towns which are most prominent in this section, St Austell is both the largest and the most recent. It owes its origin and increasing prosperity entirely to mining, but in two forms. Much of the early growth of the town was based, as in other Cornish mining towns, on tin - in particular the rich mine at Carclaze, two miles to the north, which operated continuously from the sixteenth century until 1851 - but though relatively ancient, the town seems never to have received a charter.

St Austell's greatest prosperity came in the late eighteenth century, as a consequence of the experiments carried out by the Wedgwoods in their endeavour to increase the strength and quality of their ceramics. From this time St Austell became the centre of the china-clay industry, which, with tourism, forms a major part of the Cornish economy, although there are rumblings that this product can be administered more easily outside Cornwall, and obtained more cheaply outside the British Isles.

As in other business centres, such as Truro or Penzance, men of various professions began to build their town villas and country estates. The Coode family of bankers and solicitors were at Trevarthian (now the Mid-Cornwall College), Moor Cottage next to Trewhiddle, and Polcarne, the only one of their estates to have remained intact. The Rashleighs, who originated in Fowey, were also influential locally. Charles Rashleigh built the harbour (named after him) at Charlestown, to export clay, and landscaped Menacuddle, Prideaux House and Duporth. Other landowners won a reputation for their planting, including the Lakes at Trevarrick Hall (now built over, but from a distance still conspicuous for its trees), and the Polkinghornes at Trewhiddle (now almost submerged under a holiday park). In this century, Medland Stocker, prominent in the industry, built Trelawney in the town, and de Cressy Treffry, a merchant, planted his garden around Penarwyn at St Blazey Gate.

Some of the estates in the vicinity are of greater antiquity. The Sawle family reputedly came over at the Conquest, and their park at Penrice, though near, had an existence independent of St Austell. Similarly, Tregrehan, once the seat of the Bodrugans, and now of the Carlyons, predates the town. Trenython, nearby in Tywardreath parish, however, was a nineteenth-century mansion built for Colonel Peard who had fought with Garibaldi in the Italian wars of independence. Opposite Tregrehan is one of the finest of the contemporary gardens, at Pine Lodge. Along the coast from the Rashleighs' former estate at Duporth, the post-World War II camellia garden at Porthpean looks out over the sea. Lower towards Black Head is Trenarren.

Lostwithiel is a town of much greater antiquity, and once of great importance, first as a ford at the high-water mark of the Fowey estuary, then under the protection of the Manor of Bodardell and the royal dukes who resided at Restormel Castle, and lastly as the principal Stannary town, with the Court, and the so-called 'Duchy Palace'. In its latter days it lost its place as a port, as did so many other towns on up-river sites, to Fowey, which was nearer the sea. Restormel House, below the Castle, has a fine natural view down river, but could scarcely be described as a 'designed' landscape. Among the most prominent families, from at least the sixteenth century, were the Kendalls, whose estate at Pelyn has only recently passed out of the family. Here, too, the extensive woodlands show little sign of design, except where a long carriage-ride winds through them. Castle, nearby, which some believe to have a better claim to be the Arthurian headquarters than Tintagel, alone has a reputation for its plantings.

Fowey has a long history, much of which is connected with Place and the heroic deeds of the

Treffry family, among which the incident in the time of Henry VI described by Leland, when 'the wife of Thomas Treffry, with her men, repelled the French out of her house, in her husband's absence', is not the least courageous. Its natural harbour made Fowey in the fourteenth century the most important port on the south coast, but it suffered from one serious defect: the valley sides were too steep for the town to expand. The Rashleigh family grew into prominence here, residing at Kilmarth, and Menabilly, which was for a time one of the premier gardens in Cornwall. William Rashleigh in the mid-nineteenth century preferred a more 'marine residence', and built himself Point Neptune poised over the sea. On the east side of the estuary Hall, set a little inland, created its famous Walk above Bodinnick in the sixteenth century, and in more recent years at Polruan, a garden has grown up on an equally spectacular site at Headland. Farther up river at Golant, Torfrey received a notice for its garden, but of rather more significance are the estates of Ethy and the manor and vicarage of St Winnow, where Admiral Penrose, and the Revd Robert Walker, with Jeremiah Trist, the vicar of Veryan at the beginning of the nineteenth century, were active in the development of agriculture in the county. The beauty of the woods along the creeks of the Fowey river is nowhere more enchanting than at St Cadix on the site of the Priory, where, as so often, the founders of religious houses have chosen with an uncanny knack idyllic spots conducive to contemplation.

NB In this section TRENARREN, *although in the vicinity of St Austell, appears on the* OS Landranger 204 *map for Truro and Falmouth, and* TREDUDWELL, *near Fowey, on the* OS Landranger 201 *map. They are both indicated in the appropriate map references.*

BOCONNOC, near Lostwithiel

SX14 60 : EX107, GS347   OPEN

Bochenod, *Domesday 1086*, Turris Blekennock, *Worcester 1478; Cornish* bos + Cynoc *personal name, pronounced* boCONock; *house listed grade II*, stables and carriage house, dovecote early 18th C., bathing pool and bath house early 19th C., obelisk, two classical shrines, four lodges 19th C., each II; garden, deer park and extensive grounds listed grade II*, sloping 140-40m., house at 60m., on Staddon Grit to north and Meadfoot Beds, calcareous slate, grit, and thin limestone to south, with acid soil, in a SAGLV, and in part a SSSI and CNCS, with an AM (cross in Deer Park); rainfall 40-45", temperature zone E; private, open 1983-98 CGOG, 1987, 1991, 1993-8 NGS, one Sunday in April and three in May, for charity.*

The manor of Boconnoc was owned in the fourteenth century by the Carminows, passing to the Courtenays in the fifteenth, but Henry Courtenay, Marquis of Exeter, being executed for treason in 1538, it came eventually into the possession of the Mohuns in 1579, the house being rebuilt by Sir William Mohun, the last Earl of Devon. In 1717 the estate was sold to Thomas Pitt, Governor of Madras, from the proceeds of his sale of the Pitt Diamond. Three years later, he was able to greatly extend the house. His grandson, Thomas, first Baron Camelford, who inherited the estate in 1761, in association with Charles Rawlinson, a carpenter from Lostwithiel, made further additions to the house in 1771, and is reputed to have engaged Sir John Soane in its repair. He also made extensive improvements to the park, which included several miles of carriage drives, and the erection of an obelisk (1771) in memory of his wife's uncle Richard Lyttleton, framed by two classical shrines. In these activities he may have been influenced by his brother, William, later first Earl of Chatham, who was a patron of Capability Brown and himself an amateur landscaper of considerable ability. In 1793, he was succeeded by his son, Thomas, the second Baron, who, as an exponent of the 'Picturesqe' style, was also able to make his contribution to the development of the estate. Gilbert's description offers a useful insight into their combined intentions:

> The mansion is situated in a delightful lawn, of nearly one hundred acres, which is neatly varied by new plantations, and straggling trees. The surrounding dells and ravines are watered by the river Lerran, over which the wooded hills rise in beautiful succession, and thicken into such stupendous shade, that every other object soon becomes lost in the impenetrable gloom. Amongst this variety of hill and dale, fertility and barrenness, the first Lord Camelford had a ride carried on, for at least six miles in circuit, which has given an easy access to every part of the grounds, and from which, the pleasing scenery of nature is viewed in all its different attitudes, whilst the decorations of art are lost to the eye, and almost to the imagination.

It is reported that William Mason, who from student days had a long association with the vicar, visited Boconnoc some time around the 1780s. Polwhele wrote of the occasion:

> The rural simplicity of the quiet vallies ..., and the manner in which the unadorned paths through them and the adjoining woods were carried by the taste and judgment of their owner, pleased his fancy and met his approbation. Some particularly favorite spots he frequently revisited

59. Boconnoc, where 'the intrusions of art were not only concealed, but they were so contrived as to give additional charms to the simple scenery of nature, without betraying any symptoms of design'. (Hitchins; print from Gilbert 1820: ii. 910)

... The principal brook in these grounds (the Lerryn ...) he was so fond of, that he lamented to his host his not having seen it before he printed his third book of the English Garden. [1772-81] The Cornish Lerina (he observed) was a much handsomer nymph than his Nottinghamshire Ligea, and had he been earlier acquainted with her charms, should certainly have occupied her place in his poem.

When in 1804 Thomas was killed in a duel, the estate passed to William Wyndham, Lord Grenville, and Prime Minister, who was married to his sister, Anne. It was during their time, in 1840, that the planting of the Pinetum began, when the beech trees below the house were often admired as the finest in the county. On the death of Lady Grenville in 1865, the estate passed to a nephew, George Matthew Fortescue, and has remained in this family ever since. He also made significant additions to the collection of conifers, around 1898.

During the Second World War the mansion was occupied by American troops, and it now suffers from subsidence, so that the family has taken up residence at the Stewardry, which was formerly the parsonage. The deer park, which was first impaled by the Carminows in the fifteenth century, has survived the many changes, although it is now on a different site.

During the Civil War Boconnoc had been the scene of two notable battles, in January 1643, and in 1644, when Charles I made his headquarters here, and attended service in the church. In 1890 Miss Courtney recorded a legend from those times:

> not long ago stood the stump of an old oak, in which, in 1644 when Charles I made this seat his head-quarters, the royal standard was fixed. It bore variegated leaves. According to tradition, they changed colour when an attempt was made to assassinate the King whilst he was receiving the sacrament under its branches. The ball passed through the tree, and a hole in the trunk was formerly pointed out in confirmation of the story.

Gilbert, quoting an earlier writer, reported that the upper part of this oak, about nine feet above the ground, was broken off by the wind in March 1783. As for the ball which was said to have passed through the trunk, the writer cynically added, 'a hole made by woodpeckers was shown to confirm the tale ...'

References: 17th, 18th, 19th (Hort. & Gen.) and 20th C; Illus; M.A. Courtney, Cornish Feasts and Folk-Lore, 1890: 104; J. Harris, The Artist and the Country House, 1979: 254; Polwhele, Biographical Sketches, 1831:ii.26n; J. Wallis, The Cornish Register, 1847: 38.

CASTLE, near Lostwithiel

SX09 58 : *EX107, GS347*

(Castle by) Lantien, Domesday 1086; house listed grade II, 19th C. watermill, granary, and cowhouse each II; grounds of 14 acres (5.7 ha), including gardens of 4 acres (1.6 ha), south sloping 30-20m., on Head and Valley Gravel, in a SAGLV; rainfall 45-50", temperature zone D; private.

The site of Castle is within the Domesday manor of Lantien Parva, near the stronghold of Mark, the Arthurian king of Cornwall at Castle Dore. There is evidence of an eighteenth-century dwelling here, but the present house was built by Richard Foster around the time of his marriage in 1835, with further additions made in the 1880s. The Foster family of Lostwithiel were tanners, and partners in the East Cornwall Bank, but Castle was 'later leased to others. In the 1870s and 1880s, after the demise of Richard Foster, it was occupied by Colman (later Sir Colman) Battie Rashleigh, before he inherited the family seat at Prideaux House (q.v.). During the First World War Castle was leased to the Austrian Count Fabrice (reputedly a descendant of the Hapsburgs), who was granted asylum in England. It is rumoured that Rudolf Hess was interrogated here during the Second World War.

This was one of Thurston's select gardens, which in 1930 had 'some very fine conifers in the grounds', of which he cited seven, including a *Sequoia sempervirens*, which Bruce Jackson (co-author of Dallimore's *Handbook to the Coniferae*) told him 'must be one of the largest redwoods in the country'. This was confirmed in 1979 by its inclusion in Alan Mitchell's *Champion Trees*.

There is a carriage ring before the house, with a central pond and fountain, and an extensive walled garden to the rear, also with a central pond. An area of two acres on the other side of the lane, with a garden house, was devoted to sporting activities, such as tennis and putting. The garden has admittedly been neglected for many years, so that its present horticultural interest lies chiefly in its mature trees.

References: 17th, 19th (Gen.) and 20th C.

DUPORTH, near St Austell

SX03 51 : *EX107, GS347*

Cornish du = two + porth, pronounced duPORTH; house with many later additions listed grade II; very large relict or extinct grounds, in a south-east valley sloping 50m. to the sea, on Meadfoot Beds, calcareous slates, grit and thin limestone; rainfall 40-45", temperature zone D; now the Duporth Holiday Resort.

Charles Rashleigh, who was a younger son of Jonathan Rashleigh III of Menabilly (q.v.), and married to Grace, daughter of the Revd Henry Hawkins Tremayne of Heligan (q.v.), settled in St Austell, where he prospered at first from the mining of tin, and built himself a house (now the White Hart Hotel) in the growing town. He was also responsible for the creation of a suburb at Mount Charles, and in 1791 began the construction of a harbour at West Polmear (or Porthmear), which flourished and came to be known as Charlestown. (In recent years, the port was used for many scenes in the popular television series, *The Onedin Line*.)

With the development of copper mining and china-clay, the prosperity of the town and harbour grew, and Charles Rashleigh built himself a 'handsome marine residence' at Duporth which was described in *Hitchins* as

> delightfully situated. It is about half a mile from Charlestown, lying in an easy vale, that in a south-east direction opens its bosom to the sea. The house has been considerably enlarged by its present possessor, and the gardens are cultivated with much care.

Charles had three daughters, but no sons to succeed him, so that it was George Freeth (*c.* 1800-82), a Duchy officer and his wife who were recorded in the *Hort. Direct.* as resident from 1870 until 1891, and Henry Hodge, RN, or his widow, from 1908 to 1924. The whole area is now taken up by a vast caravan park and leisure centre, which makes it difficult to envisage what the garden once may have been, although there remains a wooded valley along the western side, with some recent plantings of ornamental trees and conifers.

References: 17th, 18th, and 19th (Gen.) C.

ETHY, Lerryn

SX13 57 : *EX107, GS347*

Teuthy, Leland 1534, also Tethy; Cornish [?], pronounced EEthy; house listed grade II*, pair of gates, and garden walls, each II; 17.5 acres (7 ha), south-east and south-west sloping 95-5m., on Meadfoot Beds, calcareous slate, grit and thin limestone, in an AONB; rainfall 40-45", temperature zone D; private, the woodland, originally *part of the estate, is separately owned by the National Trust. The property was given to the Trust by Lord St Levan as an endowment for St Michael's Mount, but the house has been sold.*

The manor of Ethy was successively in the families of Stonard and Cayle before the sixteenth century, when it became the seat of the Courtenays. In 1790 it was sold by the Earl of Mount Edgcumbe to David Howell, who was followed in 1845 by his son, Francis. The present house, of a classical design, is no earlier than the mid-eighteenth century, with mid-nineteenth century extensions. What Gilbert believed 'may be justly thought classed among the most agreeable residences in the county' was leased to Admiral Sir Charles Vinicombe Penrose in 1798, where, so Lake reported,

> he entered with his characteristic alacrity of character into agricultural pursuits and improvements, by which he was always greatly attracted.

In 1811, while resident here, Penrose, in conjunction with the Revds Robert Walker of St Winnow and Jeremiah Trist of Veryan, revised and contributed to Worgan's *General View of the Agriculture of the County of Cornwall*. One of his novel ideas, which was published in the book (see pp. 27-30), was a plan for round cottages as workmen's dwellings, a specimen of which (now gone) he had built at Ethy barton. This became the model for Trist's more famous round houses at Veryan.

One of the greater attractions of Ethy is undoubtedly its position on the Lerryn river. 'Ethy House', wrote Samuel Drew in *Hitchins*,

> is situated on the margin of Lerrin creek, on some elevated ground, from which the command is extensive, and the prospects are diversified. The house is well adapted for a genteel and retired residence, being surrounded by gardens, trees, a woody scenery, and a fertile soil, which adds charms to this pleasing retreat. From some walks contiguous to the house, the river ... opens its bosom to the view, skirted on each side with trees and shrubs, which give a pleasing solemnity to the scene, while they enliven the senses with their picturesque diversity.

The garden itself, although among Thurston's select number, is relatively plain. He refers to a *Ficus carica*, trained over a pergola, which extended for 41 feet (12.5m.), and was once one of the features, although it is now departed. However, Thurston does not mention the parterre with circular and curved box hedges, which has survived. The fine walled enclosures, which are of eighteenth-century origin, with moulded granite steps, incorporate remains of stonework from the earlier manor house. The mansion in its woodland setting may be viewed from the opposite side of the creek.

References: 17th, 18th, 19th (Gen.) and 20th C.

HALL, Bodinnick

SX13 53 : EX107, GS347   OPEN

Cornish hall = *moor; garden extinct, Walk at 45m. altitude, in an AONB and HC; donated to the National Trust in 1945.*

The quite considerable mansion of the Mohuns at Hall is believed to have been three storeys high. But like so many of the Cornish, the Mohuns were on the wrong side in the Civil War and suffered their great house to be destroyed, so that nothing remains except, perhaps, a chimney, and a ruined chapel. Their cliff walk, however, survives, known from early days as 'View Hall', which in dialect would appropriately have been pronounced 'View 'all'. No description can match that of Carew, who, around 1600, had undoubtedly trodden the ground himself,

> cut out in the side of a steep hill, whose foot the salt water washeth, evenly levelled, to serve for bowling, floored with sand, for soaking up the rain, closed with two shorn hedges, and banked with sweet scenting flowers: it wideneth to a sufficient breadth for the march of five or six in front, and extendeth to not much less than half a London mile: neither doth it lead wearisomely forthright, but yieldeth varied and yet not overbusy turnings, as the ground's opportunity affordeth; which advantage increaseth the prospect, and is converted on the foreside into platforms, for the planting of ordnance, and the walker's sitting; and on the back part, into summer-houses, for their more private retreat and recreation.

This passage is significant as the first detailed account of Elizabethan horticulture in Cornwall: the manner of levelling, drainage and planting. Little but the actual path remains, although there survives a shelter, mentioned by Gilbert (1820: 901), which is old even if not one of the original 'summer-houses'. It was here, in August 1644, that some unknown person shot at King Charles from the harbour, as he paraded along the Walk, only to wound a seaman in his company. There are some colourful accounts on record, but the more sober report of one of his lieutenants puts the incident into a truer perspective. The shot, even assuming that guns at that time, and at that distance, possessed sufficient precision, was a long way off putting the King's life at risk.

A monument at the start of the Walk commemorates those who fell in the Second World War, and the donor, Col. Shakerley. Sir Arthur Quiller-Couch, a native of Fowey, who cultivated a garden near the beginning of the Walk, is also commemorated on a monument at the end, by the summer-house.

References: 17th, 18th and 19th (Gen.) C; Coast of Cornwall 21, Fowey, National Trust, 1990: 10-13.

HEADLAND, Battery Lane, Polruan by Fowey

SX12 50 : *EX107, GS347*   OPEN*

Garden of 1.25 acres (0.5 ha), sloping from 30m. to the sea, on Meadfoot Beds, calcareous slates, grit and thin limestone, in an AONB and HC; rainfall 35-40", temperature zone D; open 1983-98 CGOG, 1987, 1991-8 NGS, Thursdays, mid May to mid August. There is an official leaflet.

The Headland is on the eastern side of the estuary of the Fowey River, where it meets the sea, with views along the coast to the Dodman, and as far as The Lizard on a clear day. A flight of 100 steps leads down to a sandy beach. Although open to salt-laden winds, there is always shelter to be found somewhere, and the south-facing path is generally frost free. The owners write:

> Monterey pines tower over the "North Col" and many lampranthus blaze on the "South Face". In crevices are aloes, sedum, erigeron, sempervivum, and in "Wattle Alley" are gums and wattles. On the rock garden are junipers and cupressus, and red-hot pokers between them. Everywhere are foxgloves, valerian and wallflowers, ... scabious, aquilegia growing wild. Torquay palms rustle in the breeze.

This unique garden, begun in 1974, has often been televised, and was used as a setting in the film *Stolen Hours*.

References: 20th C.

KILMARTH, Polkerris

SX09 52 : *EX107, GS347*

Cornish *kyl = nook or back + mergh = horse, pronounced kilMARTH; house listed grade II; grounds of 12 acres (4.9 ha), at 80m. altitude, on Meadfoot Beds, calcareous slate, grit and thin limestone, in an AONB and HC; rainfall 40-45", temperature zone D; private.

Kilmarth, described in *Lake* as 'a beautiful marine residence', was anciently the seat of the family of Baker, but the present mansion was built after the Rashleigh family had acquired the estate. Jane Rashleigh, the unmarried daughter of Jonathan Rashleigh I of Menabilly (q.v.), had lived here during the first half of the eighteenth century until her death. Later, her great-nephew, William, lived here, until in 1810 he inherited from his uncle the family home at Menabilly, which lay across the valley.

During his time at Kilmarth, William began to acquire a reputation for the collection of exotic plants, which he carried with him into his new demesne. After his departure, the property was variously occupied, Evelyn William Rashleigh being recorded here in the latter years of the nineteenth century. He was from another branch of the family, which eventually inherited Menabilly, although he himself later moved to Stoketon (q.v.). When, in this century, after a period of absence, the Rashleighs returned to occupy their family seat, it was to Kilmarth that Dame Daphne du Maurier (Lady Browning) retired, after leaving Menabilly, until her death in 1988. The house provided her with the setting for her novel *The House by the Strand* (1969). The reply to an enquiry by Major Magor from Lady Browning did not encourage any expectation that Kilmarth would today have much to show for itself. There is a small enclosed garden to the front of the house, with wooden railings and steps leading down to the lawn and parkland, but in a recent sale notice, 'All the grounds' were described as 'capable of being kept on a low cost basis,' which suggests that they are not elaborate.

References: 18th, and 19th (Gen.) C.

MENABILLY, near Fowey

SX10 51 : *EX107, GS347*

Cornish men = stone or meneth = hill + *byly plural of obel = pebbles, pronounced MENably; house listed grade II*, west lodge probably 18th rebuilt 19th C., stone cross, grotto, each II; garden listed grade II; estate of 280 acres (113 ha), with north - south river valley, sloping 60m. to the sea, on Meadfoot Beds, calcareous slates, grit and thin limestone, with acid soil, in an AONB and HC, and a CNCS in part, with AMs (two crosses); rainfall 40-45". temperature zone D; private.

Menabilly is the principal seat of the Rashleigh family, of whom a selective pedigree is included in the Index of Persons below. The Rashleighs were of Devon origin - in 1529 Philip Rashleigh from Barnstaple began trading in Fowey, 'Where,' wrote Carew, 'I may not pass in silence, the commendable deserts of Master Rashleigh the elder [Philip's son, John], ... for his industrious judgement and adventuring, in trade and merchandise, first opened a light and way to the townsmen's new thriving'. John, who married

Alice Lanyon, thereby acquiring for the family valuable properties in Madron, built a fine house in Fowey, which is now the Ship Inn, but in 1596 his son, John II, bought land at Menabilly outside the town, and began to build his house there. This was completed by his son, Jonathan, but being on the wrong side in the Civil War, his new house was looted. It was probably as a consequence of this that his grandson (his son pre-deceased him), Jonathan II, who married Jane Carew of Antony, and their son, altered and restored Menabilly in 1710-15.

60. Menabilly. The Grotto, from a painting by G. Boney in 1805, of which the present whereabouts are not known.

The history of the garden proper began with Philip II, who in 1702 succeeded his father (even though he was not to die until 1762). Borlase wrote of him:

> Every thing that belongs to the flower-garden, and grows in any part of England, will thrive and flourish here, as the late accomplished and courteous Philip Rashleigh Esq; of Menabilly did formerly manifest [he died unmarried in 1736], and his present sister, Mrs. [Rachel] Hawkins, (widow of the late Reverend Dr. Hawkins of Pennans [q.v.]) now at Pencoit, can satisfy the most curious.

This tradition was followed by Philip III (the son of Jonathan III), who is perhaps better known for his collection of minerals, part of which is now housed in the new Rashleigh Gallery in Truro Museum, and for his Grotto at Polridmouth. Owing to dilapidation and defacement this was unfortunately closed in 1940, and we must rely on contemporary descriptions, of which the most comprehensive is that of Paris (1824: 206). The passages in square brackets are from *Hitchins*:

> it stands at the extremity of a long grove, and is constructed with the finest species of marble and serpentine, brilliant crystals, pebbles and shells, in the form of an octagon, two of the sides [internally] are appropriated to the door and the window, which front each other, the six remaining sides form receptacles [niches], four of these contain specimens of ores found in the county, [of tin, lead, iron, and copper, each kind being classed separately], and two are filled with organic fossils, polished agates, jaspers, &c. The intermediate spaces are occupied by shells, coraloides [specimens of quartz, fluors], and various other substances; the roof is composed of *Stalactytes* of singular beauty, and which produce a very striking effect as seen through the rough formed arch which composes the entrance; in this grotto are preserved two links of the chain, which formerly were found in Fowey harbour by some fishermen in the year 1776, they are of a triangular form incrusted with shells and corals, supposed to be part of the chain which extended from tower to tower for the ancient defence of the harbour [the diameter of the link is about sixteen inches; the iron is nearly decomposed]; among the mineralogical specimens in this grotto one of *Calcedony* deserves particular notice for its beauty and magnitude; in the middle of the grotto is a table inlaid with 32 polished specimens of granite all found in the county of Cornwall.

The fame of Menabilly grew during the tenure of William, Philip III's nephew, who had already begun to acquire a reputation for his collection of exotic plants while residing at Kilmarth (q.v.), so that in 1822, when Loudon included Menabilly among the ten Cornish gardens in his gazetteer, it was starred (along with Port Eliot) as a 'show-place'. By this time the old formal gardens around the house had been swept away by Gray, a disciple of Brown, much to the dismay of Sir Colman Rashleigh of Prideaux [see Pring 1996: 20]. Of three *Quercus cerris* over 100 feet (30.5m.) high in 1930, Miss Alice Rashleigh wrote to Thurston:

> The oaks were believed by William Rashleigh to be American oaks. He planted them in 1810 when he inherited the estate from Philip Rashleigh. When he came into possession, he found a small closet on the spot, the only convenient retiring house on the establishment. He made more suitable arrangements in the house, and set up a granite pedestal with the date when he took the house, and picked up three acorns, which he planted round it, to make a picturesqe object.

William's eldest son, William II, was disenchanted with Menabilly, and chose to build himself a 'marine residence' named Point Neptune, in

Readymoney Cove, which was virtually without a garden. His brother Jonathan V, and his son Jonathan VI were left to continue and enrich the family tradition. It was during this time, in the mid-nineteenth and early twentieth centuries, that the serious plant collections were formed. Hamilton Davey, in his notable article of 1897 on 'Acclimatisation of Exotics ...', begins by extolling the virtues of the garden:

> Far and near Menabilly is the subject of admiration among lovers of gardening, and if there are circumstances under which envy becomes a venial offence, it may well be elevated to the rank of a virtue when it concerns the place now under notice.

From his list of plants, one group may be selected, which became a speciality - namely the collection of bamboos: *Arundinaria*, fourteen varieties, *Bambusa*, seventeen varieties, and *Phyllostachys*, sixteen varieties - in all a collection of forty-seven varieties, reckoned by S.W. Fitzherbert in 1903 as 'probably as comprehensive as any in the country, and to which Mr Rashleigh [i.e. Jonathan VI] has for many years devoted much attention.' Unfortunately a recent census in 1990 could find only eight surviving, although this is probably the largest of the original collections to have survived to the present day. Fitzherbert also mentioned another speciality:

> Of Eucalypti there is a fine assortment ... Mr Rashleigh is trying about thirty species raised from imported seed in various positions in the gardens in order to test their hardiness.

They feature prominently in Elwes and Henry's *Trees of Great Britain* (1906-13), and later in Thurston (1930). H.C. Watson had earlier, in the *Kew Bulletin* of 1893, referred to another collection:

> On one side of the garden there is a valley, one side of the slopes of which is planted with many rare Coniferae, and other trees and shrubs, obtained chiefly from Kew, Mr. Rashleigh having always maintained an active correspondence with the Royal Gardens. This slope has been named the "Hooker Grove," in compliment to Sir Joseph Hooker.

A full collection of papers relating to the plantings at Menabilly from 1790 to 1880, during the time of William II and Jonathan V and VI, is

61. Menabilly. The lawn, with trees and shrubs planted out as specimens. (G. Ch. 1886: i. 817)

lodged in the County Record Office, but has never been seriously studied. In more recent times the family have been absent from Menabilly, and for many years the house was tenanted by Daphne Maurier. It was the setting for several of her novels, notably *The King's General*, and *Rebecca* (Manderley being Menabilly). She moved to Kilmarth (q.v.), another Rashleigh house, when the family returned to their original seat. No apology is necessary for the length of this note, since, especially in the nineteenth century, Menabilly, listed in the *Hort. Direct.* from at least 1870 to 1924, must be classed among the greatest of the Cornish gardens.

References: 17th, 18th, 19th (Hort.& Gen.), 20th C; Illus.

MENACUDDLE, St Austell

SX01 53 : EX106 and 107, GS347　　　　　　OPEN

Cornish meneth = *hill* + gwythel = *thicket, pronounced MENacuddle; chapel listed grade II*, and an AM; in an east facing steep river valley from c. 120m. altitude, on granite, with acid soil; rainfall 45-50", temperature zone D; public gardens.*

62. Menacuddle. A view of the waterfall and chapel in 1820. (Gilbert 1820: ii. 866)

The background history of Menacuddle is usefully summarized in *Hitchins*:

> The lands of [Menacuddle] ... are said to have been originally granted by Edward VI to Sir Thomas Pomeroy of Hugh Pomeroy, from whom in process of time, they passed to the Edyveans. By one of this family this estate was sold to Charles Rashleigh, Esq. of Duporth by whom it has been lately sold to Joseph Sawle Sawle, Esq.

Menacuddle was celebrated for an artificial waterfall emanating from a well in the floor of the ruined chapel, the waters of which 'roll through a narrow dell, darkened with leafage, and strewed with enormous rocks' to flow away under Menacuddle bridge. This picturesque description is illustrated in the print in Gilbert's *Survey*. He wrote:

> The trees are of various sorts, in general grown to a good size, and intermixed with evergreens. There is a variety of intricate walks carried through the inclosure; also ponds, stored with fish of gold and silver hues. The upper walks stretch over the steep acclivities, in zig-zag directions, accompanied by rustic seats, formed of rough blocks of wood, covered with moss, and entwined with ivy. Opposite a rustic building called the Hermitage, stands a pedestal, capped with an urn, bearing a profile likeness of the late earl of Mount Edgcumbe.

Menacuddle well and walk were restored by Sir Charles Sawle in memory of his son, who fell in the First World War, and the grounds presented to the local authorities as public gardens.

References: 18th, 19th (Gen.) and 20th C; Illus.

PELYN, near Lostwithiel

SX09 58 : *EX107, GS347*

Cornish pen + lyn = *pool, pronounced PLIN; house listed grade II*; originally very large estate, now 140 acres (57 ha), in a north-west, south-east valley, sloping 110-90m., on metamorphosed Meadfoot Beds, calcareous slate, grit and thin limestone, with acid soil, in a SAGLV and a CNCS; rainfall 40-45", temperature zone D; private, but recently vacated by the Kendalls.*

For more than three centuries the seat of the Kendall family, Pelyn was described by Gilbert as:

> situated in a solitary retirement, on the western side of the river Fowey, where it is so concealed in woods, as to be seldom seen but by those who visit the family.

The house was built about 1600, and remodelled in the eighteenth century. Carew praised 'Mr. Will. Kendall's hospitality ... [which] exceeded all others of his sort.' This hospitality evidently con-

63. Penrice. The deer have now gone, but the house still sits comfortably among the trees of various hues. (Twycross 1846: 32)

tinued down the centuries, for a ballroom was attached to the eighteenth-century house, which was restored after a fire in 1860. The wide terrace in front of the house, entered by drives from both east and west, is well adapted to accommodate several vehicles, and conjures up a picture of torch-lit carriages driving through from town to deliver the occupants to the festivities. The grounds, which are extensive, save for a small garden behind the house, and some parkland to the east, are almost all given over to woodland, but there was in the 1850s a long scenic carriage ride, circling widely around Trethevy, through the Carmear Woods, via Puddle to Pelyn, passing over three bridges *en route*. 'Pelyn', wrote Gilbert,

> is supposed to have been at an early period, the site of a religious house [dedicated to St Chad]; and indeed the gloomy silence which prevails in this retired seclusion, must have been admirably adapted for those austere habits which characterized the devotionals of former ages.

He continues, however, that St Chad's

> festival was formerly observed ... in a very convivial manner ... To the right of the mansion ... there is a small summer-house, standing on four stone pillars ... In this summer-house, about a century since, four friends, a Mr Kendall, of Pelyn, Mr. Glynn, Mr.Young, and Mr.Trelawny, met annually on the 2nd of March, to celebrate the saint's day

- no doubt with great merriment! Only the site of the summer-house remains, from which there would have been a view of the garden and parkland, and perhaps, before the trees grew tall, of the sea in the distance. There is an intriguing tunnel nearby, which may, upon further investigation, prove to be the relict of an ice-house.

References: 17th, 18th, 19th (Gen.) and 20th C.

PENRICE, between St Austell and Charlestown

SX02 49 : *EX107, GS347*

Cornish pen + *red = *water-course, pronounced* penRICE; *house listed grade II, north-east gateway II; medium to large estate, west sloping, 80-40m., on Meadfoot Beds, calcareous slate, grit and thin limestone, with acid soil, in an AONB, with a CNCS; rainfall 45-50", temperature zone D; now a residential home.*

The manor was, for many generations, in the family of Sawle, reputed to have 'come from

Normandy with William the Conqueror.' John Sawle died in 1789, the estate passing by way of a female cousin to Admiral John Graves, brother of Thomas Graves of Thanckes (q.v.). His son, Joseph Sawle Graves, after his father's death in 1811, assumed the name of J. Sawle Sawle. The present house is a late Georgian building. 'It lies,' wrote Samuel Drew (himself a St Austell man) in *Hitchins*,

> about a mile and a half from St Austell; but [the house] having a northern aspect, it is less influenced by the genial warmth of a summer's sun. During Mr.Sawle's minority the gardens were only partially rescued from that disorder into which they had been suffered to run, before the estate came into the possession of this family. Much therefore remains for the present possessor to accomplish.

A deer park had been impaled in about 1785, which continued into this century. The venerable rhododendrons and plantations have suffered from age and recent storms, although there have been new plantings within view of the house. The gardens had been listed in the *Hort. Direct.* from 1908 to 1924, and became one of Thurston's select estates, where, among the half dozen citations are an *Eriobotrya japonica*, grown from seed collected abroad by Lady Graves-Sawle, a *Quercus robur* planted on the coming of age of Richard Graves-Sawle, and a *Cupressus macrocarpa* on the front lawn, planted by Sir Joseph Graves-Sawle (d. 1885). 'Many trees in the densely wooded grounds', Thurston wrote in 1930, 'were planted by the grandfather of the present owner Sir Charles Graves-Sawle'. Mrs Rosemary Cobbold-Sawle, who, when she died in 1973, was the last surviving member of the family, directed in her will, that Penrice should become an old people's home, which it did in 1978.

References: 17th, 18th 19th (Gen.) and 20th C; Illus.

PINE LODGE, Cuddra, St Austell

SX04 52 : *EX107, GS347*   OPEN*

Garden of 5 acres (2 ha) in 30 acres (12 ha) of park, lake and woodland, 25-15m. altitude, on alluvial acid soil; rainfall 45-50", temperature zone D; open 1985-98 CGOG, 1991, 1993-8 NGS, Wednesday to Sunday, and holiday Mondays, April through September.

Pine Lodge is situated in the former Cuddra plantation, which was part of the Tregrehan estate. It adjoins Cuddra House, and is in the vicinity of the Cuddra and Crinnis mines. The garden, begun in 1948, has been evolving over the last seventeen years. The bungalow is approached off the A390 along a drive, which passes through an existing plantation. The original garden began with a terrace and formal garden in front of the house, which led on into an informal area of lawns, with winding grass paths through island beds planted with a wide range of rare and unusual plants. The area beyond was next developed into an arboretum, large enough for the specimen trees not to be cramped. The accessibility of water made it possible to create a quite sizeable lake in a field above the house, which was planted with water lilies, and surrounded with wide beds of plants which would flourish in such a situation.

At a later stage, the entrance itself was improved: a pathway was paved through the plantation to arrive at the front of the house between two waterfalls cascading down huge rocks, feeding into a large pond, over which the house was reached by a bridge. The arboretum was next extended on one side into a Pinetum, where the trees are graded in size eventually to form a semi-circular amphitheatre. The lower side of the arboretum is to be retained as parkland, and a new lake formed from mine workings. The most recent creation has been the 'Slave Garden', so named from a central feature, around which is a circle of beds filled with perennial plants graded to shade the colours in the sequence of the rainbow. In the surrounding lawn, well spaced out, is a collection of fourteen magnolias. At present a Japanese Garden is under construction to designs seen on a visit to that country. The plants are all labelled by Mrs Shirley Clemo, who is an expert plantswoman, while her husband Raymond is responsible for the management and landscaping. This is an ambitious garden, which as it matures has become one of the finest contemporary examples in the county.

References: 20th C.

PLACE HOUSE, Fowey

SX12 51 : *EX107, GS347*

Cornish plas = *mansion (from the English); house early 16th C. with mid to late 15th C. origins, front dates from 1791, mainly 1817-45, listed grade I, walls and gateways II, tower described by Leland fell in 18th C; medium grounds, at c. 50m. altitude, on Meadfoot Beds, calcareous slate, grit and thin limestone by the house, Dartmouth Beds, silts and slates north of the house, in an AONB and HC, and on an HS; rainfall 40-45", temperature zone D; private.*

Place House, which has a long and interesting history, was much modified during the early nineteenth century, in what Pevsner described as 'an overwhelming display of early C19 to Early Victorian Gothic', which, upon completion, as seen in a contemporary painting, left the immediate surrounding grounds much as they are today. The nearer access above the house, curving down from opposite Place Road, as well as the long scenic drive northwards, both probably date from this same time.

It was the prospective development of the area bounded by these drives which, no doubt, prompted a consultation with Thomas Mawson, the first garden designer to dub himself a 'landscape architect', and the first President of their Institute, although it would appear that it did not issue in a full commission. Nevertheless, there remain a few features which seem to owe something either to his influence, or a common taste in design. Across the drive to the north of the house is a circular, perhaps once a rose garden, divided into sectors, with a semi-circular flight of steps leading up higher. Passing along at this level, one arrives at a substantial summerhouse, with a view across the river, and below it a terrace where once there had been a pergola. These are all characteristic of Mawson's style, to be seen in paintings of certain gardens he had designed. A long scenic walk from this garden runs along, and down to river level, through a tunnel to a castellated gateway. The slopes above the walk are well clothed with trees. Place was listed in the *Hort. Direct.* from 1908 to 1916.

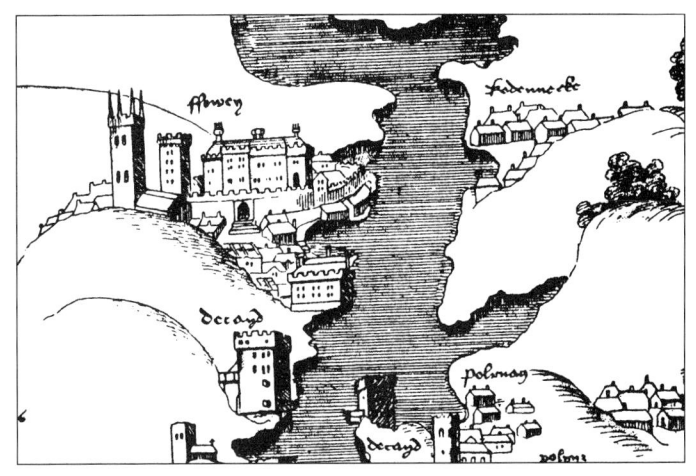

64. Place, Fowey. A fortified house, with tower, gatehouse and castellated walls. Detail from the Henry VIII map of Fowey harbour. (Lyssons 1814: 108)

References: *17th, 18th, 19th (Gen.) and 20th C; Illus; S.C. Hall,* Baronial Halls, *i.1848; G. Beard,* Thomas H. Mawson, *1976: 60.*

65. Place House, Fowey, exhibiting an 'overwhelming display of early nineteenth-century to Early Victorian Gothic'. (Pevsner: Twycross 1846: 57)

PORTHPEAN HOUSE, St Austell

SX03 50 : *EX107, GS347* OPEN*

Cornish porth + vean, *pronounced* porthPEAN; *mid 19th C. stucco house listed grade II; garden of 3 acres (1.2 ha), east sloping, from 45m., on Head, with 'shaly' acid soil; rainfall 40-45", temperature zone D; open 1984-96 CGOG, 1988 ,1991, 1993-4 NGS, two Sundays in March, and one each in April and May, and by appointment.*

The garden at Porthpean, once an inn, was laid out on a low cliff directly above the beach, by Maurice Petherick, in the mid 1950s. There is a panoramic view of the sea, particularly from the top of the garden. At first there was little more than a ragged line of tamarisks to ward off the salt-laden gales. These were replaced by a variety of shrubs and trees - bay, elder, ash and pittosporum. In other parts of the garden there are large, well-established beeches, chestnuts and Monterey pine, to act as windbreaks. Even so the garden is quite grey with salt after bad gales, and artificial shelter has sometimes to be used. The garden was designed for a collection of camellias, of which some 200 were planted during the first five years. Detailed records were kept in a card index of the varieties planted. An especial charm of this garden is the natural carpet of primroses which are generally in flower at the same time as the camellias.

References: 20th C.

PRIDEAUX HOUSE, near St Blazey

SX05 56 : *EX107, GS347*

Cornish pry = mud, china-clay + ?, *or possibly* près d'eaux, = near the waters, *pronounced* PRIDoh; *house, screen wall and gazebo together listed grade II, gateway with railings and piers II; large estate, sloping south-east to river valley, c. 130m. each side, house at 105m. sloping to 35m., on coarse granite, with acid soil, in an AGLV with an AM (Prideaux Camp); rainfall 45-50", temperature zone D; private.*

The old manor at Prideaux was already the property of the Rashleighs, but John (later Sir John) Colman Rashleigh built his new house not far from the manor in about 1808, 'at the head of a narrow but very picturesque valley, and [commanding] an extensive prospect of sea and land' (*Lake*). He was created a baronet in 1831, but by the fifth baronet, Sir Harry, the succession had passed to a nephew of the Stoketon branch of the family, the sixth baronet Sir Richard (born 1958) by then having inherited Menabilly. Stockdale had singled out for attention the 'very fine bold promontory, nearly opposite the house, and the lands about it ... ornamented with young plantations,' which are now the Warren Wood, and the Pengall Plantation. An interesting account of the problems met when these woodlands were raised is given in *Hitchins* by Samuel Drew, who knew the area well:

> The hill on which Mr. Rashleigh laid out his plantation, has an aspect fronting the north-west; and its declivity is on the margin of a deep and narrow vale that is enclosed between this hill and another, which has since been partially planted. Through this vale a strong current of wind from the north and north-west often passes, the piercing qualities of which rendered every precaution necessary that prudence and foresight could suggest. Many efforts were accordingly made, before he succeeded. Trees of various kinds and in various stages of progression, were introduced; but his early exertions were abortive. Experiment succeeded to experiment; some part of the hill was sowed with acorns; another part with beech-mast, and others with the seeds of ash and sycamore. But none of these seeds could easily be matured to perfection. In springing up they afforded a flattering prospect; but the spiry grass soon overpowered them, and the expence of constantly weeding them was too great to justify an unremitting perseverance. (1824: i.562)

The solution lay in the planting of the pinaster fir, introduced by Praed of Trevethoe (q.v.). The advice of Lord de Dunstanville (see Tehidy) might also be read in this connection. The garden here was listed in the *Hort. Direct.* from 1890 until 1916. Both the garden itself and the plantations and woods on the surrounding heights present an impressive picture. An exercise track for horse-riding has been laid out, which runs along the eastern side of the valley. Prideaux House should be distinguished from Prideaux Place in Padstow, the seat of the Prideaux-Brune family.

References: 17th, 18th, 19th (Hort. & Gen.) and 20th C; Illus.

RESTORMEL CASTLE, near Lostwithiel

SX10 61 : *EX107, GS347* OPEN

Cornish ros + tor = hill + *moyl = bald, *pronounced* resTORmel; *castle at an altitude of 65m., on metamorphosed Meadfoot Beds; AM managed by* English Heritage.

Restormel is more a subject for history than for horticulture. 'It stoode' wrote Norden in 1590,

> sometimes in a parke of fallowe deare, but amongste others it was disparked in the time of King Hen. the 8. If the proportion of necessarie offices [i.e. privies] in auntient decayde buyldinges may argue equall hospitalitie, here was noe want; ... and it is to be thowght that in

those dayes they buylded for vse, and not as men now doe their great and glorious howses for ostentation, great halls and litle meat, large chymnies and litle smoak.

The views of a more romantic age are well expressed by Stockdale, where his ideal of 'the picturesque' in nature was reflected in contemporary landscaping:

The ruins are richly overgrown with ivy, and being almost embosomed in wood, are very pleasing objects to the lovers of the picturesque, as well as to impress the mind with the most sublime ideas of the instability of human grandeur.

References: 17th, 18th, 19th (Gen.) and 20th C; Illus.

ST WINNOW

SX11 57 : *EX107, GS347*

Sanwinvec, Domesday 1086; Cornish = saint's name, pronounced WINno; house listed grade II; grounds of 4 acres (1.6 ha), at 20m., on Dartmouth Beds, silts and slates; rainfall 40-45", temperature zone E; former vicarage, now private.

The manor is mentioned in Leland as belonging before 1470 to Margaret, Lady Huntingdon. It was eventually purchased by John Rashleigh of Penquite, son of Jonathan III of Menabilly, whose son Colman Rashleigh (later of Prideaux House) sold it to the Revd Robert Walker. In October 1800, Staniforth

rode to St Winnow ... where we saw some very pretty flowers & several fine plants & a beautiful arbutus & some medlars loaded with fruit & a very nice greenhouse & good kitchen garden - the situation of the house is beautifully retir'd under the high ground to the N.E., with the church in front about 100 y'ds distant & the River Foy close to it, of wch the beautiful seat of Mr. John Rashleigh on the opposite side of the river at Penquite there is a fine view.

Gilbert wrote that 'the handsome mansion and grounds of the Rev. Robert Walker', were seated a little farther up the hill than the aged manor house, to the south of the church, the 'buildings are modern, and the grounds altogether rich in verdure. The landscape scenery round St. Winnow,' he believed, was 'perhaps as fine as in any part of England.' Walker shared agricultural interests with his neighbour, Admiral Penrose at Ethy, and with the Revd Jeremiah Trist of Veryan. He had experimented with the breeding of pigs and cattle, and with his associates joined in the revision of Worgan's *General View of the Agriculture of ... Cornwall* (1811). The garden today, except for an old orchard and a few trees and shrubs, is chiefly under grass.

References:17th,18th, 19th (Gen.) and 20th C.

TREGREHAN, St Blazey Gate

SX05 53 : *EX107, GS347*   OPEN

Cornish tre + ?*crygh *= wrinkled, pronounced* treGRAIN; *house 18th-19th C., lodge mid 19th C., each listed grade II; grounds of 20 acres (8 ha) listed grade II*, on south facing slope, 65-15m., with house at 55m., on Meadfoot Beds, calcareous slate, grit and thin limestone, alluvial on margins, with acid soil; rainfall 45-50", temperature zone D; open 1987-98 CGOG, 1991, 1993-8 NGS, daily mid March to mid June. There is an official booklet.*

The estate at Tregrehan, formerly in the possession of the Brodrugans and Mount Edgcumbes, has since 1565 been occupied by the Carlyon family, who extensively planted the parkland during the eighteenth century. In 1840 the earlier house began to be modified to designs by the celebrated local architect, George Wightwick, for Edward Carlyon, who had grandiose ideas for

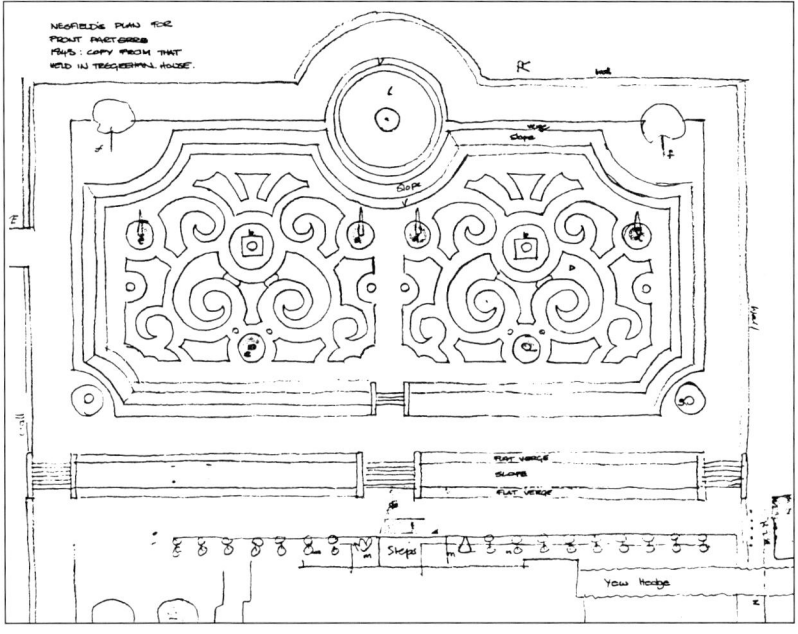

66. Tregrehan. The terrace and parterres from Nesfield's plan of 1843.

the improvement of his grounds, which led him also to invite the up-and-coming Nesfield to design a parterre to the south of the enlarged house, and a new entrance court, or carriage ring for the West Front.

Nesfield's plan, dated 1843, is still held at Tregrehan. He wrote that 'the Parterre should be separated from the Entrance Court by Yew hedges, kept clipped and grown in such a man-

67. Tregrehan. The terrace in front of the house, three years after Nesfield had produced his design, is still immature, and made visible only by the erect pointed yews. (Twycross: 1846: 47)

ner as to cause arches over communicating walks'. As will be seen from the plan, there is a terrace in front of the house, with stone balustrading, urns, a sundial and steps, which lead down through the parterre to a round pool with central fountain. The parterres themselves, in the style known as 'broderie', composed of coloured gravel and grass, were embellished with statues of the Four Seasons.

A small kitchen garden had been shown on the tithe map of 1839, but in 1845 Edward Carlyon had the present large walled garden built, to the north-west of the house, having at its centre a circular pool with a 'charming dolphin fountain', said also to be by Nesfield.

'The fine Pinetum', as Thurston observed, 'is a special feature of the grounds, which contain one of the choicest collections of rare trees and shrubs in the County'. W.J. Bean, who visited Tregrehan in 1916, wrote that it had 'a full complement of rhododendrons' and stood out 'above all the Cornish gardens for the richness and health of its conifers'. The *Hort. Direct.* listed Tregrehan from at least 1870 to 1924, and it was one of Thurston's select gardens. Today, there are also many trees from the Southern Hemisphere, reflecting the family's interest in New Zealand, and the garden is famous for the camellias raised by the late Miss Gillian Carlyon. The outsize conifers, many of them the largest of their species in Cornwall or the whole of Britain, are no longer young, so that a programme of replanting has been begun by Mr Tom Hudson, Miss Carlyon's successor.

References: 17th, 18th, 19th (Hort. & Gen.) and 20th C; Illus.

TRENYTHON, near Tywardreath

SX10 54 : *EX107, GS347*

Cornish, Dexter suggests tre + eithin = gorse, *pronounced* treNITHon *with a long 'i'; grounds originally of 131 acres (53 ha), in south-west sloping valley, 100-25m., on Meadfoot Beds, calcareous slate, grit and thin limestone, and Dartmouth Beds and Head at south-west end, with acid soil, and an AM (cross); rainfall 40-45", temperature zone D; Trenython Manor Country Club, open to non-residents, garden opened 1990-93 CGOG, 1996 NGS, came on the market in 1997.*

Trenython was built for John Whitehead Peard on the estate of Little Penneck in 1869-70, it is said, on the recommendation of Garibaldi, who visited him when he had retired to Penquite. Col. Peard, a youth of 'great stature and extraordinary muscular strength', was the son of the courageous Vice-Admiral Peard. This colourful character was once famous as 'Garibaldi's Englishman', joining his forces in 1859, and receiving from Victor Emmanuel the Cross of the Order of Valour.

The mansion, with a *porte-cochère*, is, not surprisingly, handsomely decorated in the Italian style, with marble pillars from the Temple of Diana at Ephesus, intended for a local Chapel, installed in the vestibule, since they had been refused by a Christian place of worship because of their pagan origin. The prospect from the house, which stands at the head of the valley, through which runs a stream, branching off into Pinnock Woods below, looks over the clay works and harbour of Par, to St Austell Bay and Black Head. The house, ornamental gardens and woodland may be viewed in the distance to the left of the road from Par to Fowey. Peard had landscaped the grounds near the house into steep terraces leading down to where the stream filled a pool set in a glade, thence to drain away over a waterfall, surrounded by a rockery.

The former plantings of bananas (*Musa basjoo*), and the *Trachycarpus fortunei* and bamboo varieties which still survive in luxuriant clumps, were the essentials of all exotic valley gardens. Perhaps the crowning glory today is the grove of seventy-two ornamental maples, a feature unique in Cornwall, planted by Mr Pearce, a former gardener, following a short stay at Westonbirt after 1945. Trenython was purchased by Bishop Gott as his residence in 1891, because he was not able to house a large and valuable family library in Lis Escop, and was listed from 1908 to 1924 in the *Hort. Direct*. It was subsequently the Railway Convalescent Home, and is now a holiday centre.

References: 19th (Gen.) and 20th C.

TREVARRICK HALL, St Austell

SX00 52 : *EX107, GS347*

Cornish tre + ?*arth = adjective of height, pronounced treVARick, with a short 'a'; house listed grade II; very small residual garden on an east facing slope, at 80m., on metamorphosed Meadfoot Beds, calcareous slates, grit and thin limestone, with acid soil; rainfall 45-50", temperature zone D; private.

Trevarrick, which was built in the early nineteenth century by Henry Lakes, is still standing, but with only a tiny lawn and two huge monkey puzzle trees to reflect its former glory, although there is a hint of the past when the hillside is viewed from the town, where the dwellings are seen to be interspersed with fine trees, some perhaps planted as replacements when the area was developed. It was described in *Hitchins*, in its greater days in 1824, as

> a modern built house, and pleasantly situated. Behind it, on a winding hill, the trees which have been planted by its present possessor, thrive with much luxuriance; and the scenery around, though not extensive, is diversified with pleasing varieties.

Thurston, who included this among his select gardens, tells us that the conifers, which once had been a speciality of the garden, were planted by Robert Gould Lakes, the second son of Henry. In 1885, W. Napper wrote:

> There are very few places that can vie with Trevarrick for remarkable specimens of exotic trees and plants. The two trees of Benthamia fragifera [*Cornus capitata*] there are said to be the largest specimens in Britain.

He was clearly astonished at the size of these and other trees, of which he gives the measurements, but he also found the rock garden

> well furnished with rarities, and it almost took [his] breath away when [he] saw here the Mitraria coccinea quite 14 feet across and covering a small hillock. This plant is usually found in the greenhouse.

R.G. Lakes was in the custom of sending flowers or notes to the various journals, which he did from 1880 to 1897, but when Charles Curtis visited and described the garden in 1908, it was the Hitchins family who were in residence there, although his memory (or notes) was at fault when he stated that this was the old home of the Shilsons, for they had lived not at Trevarrick, but at Tremough and Trewhiddle, which follows. In view of the status, convenience of access to the garden, and the enthusiasm of the owners, it is perhaps surprising that Trevarrick was never listed in the *Hort. Direct*.

References: 17th, 18th, 19th (Hort. & Gen.) and 20th C.

TREWHIDDLE, near St Austell

SX00 51 : *EX107, GS347*

Trewidell 1650; Cornish, Dexter suggests tre + gwidhal = Irishman's, pronounced treWIDDle; medium to large relict grounds, south sloping from 50m., on Meadfoot Beds, calcareous slates, grit and thin limestone, with acid soil; rainfall 45-50", temperature zone D; now the Trewhiddle Holiday Estate.

Trewhiddle was recorded in the Parliamentary Survey of 1649 as in the possession of one Nicholas Trewidell. By the 1820s the estate was the home of the Polkinghorne family. 'The house', wrote Gilbert, 'is a modern stone building, sheltered by flourishing plantations,' *Hitchins* adding ... 'its adjoining grounds, have been raised to their present state of commanding respect, by their present possessor [Francis Polkinghorne], at a vast expence.' Mid-century it had been for a time the property of Thomas Graves Sawle, but Thurston, who included this among his select gardens, informs us that the 'grounds were well laid out by the late owner Mr Henry Shilson', son of William Shilson of Tremough (q.v.), who was listed in the *Hort. Direct.* from 1919 to 1924. The present holiday park has considerably cut into the estate, although the house itself retains its character, looking down over a steeply sloping lawn to a stream planted with trees and conifers. There are still many old rhododendrons and shrubs in this area, preserving some of the original atmosphere. The long drive is at first wooded, but soon becomes overwhelmed with chalets and caravans.

References: 17th, 18th, 19th (Gen.) and 20th C.

SUPPLEMENTARY LISTS

LESSER-KNOWN HISTORIC GARDENS

Fowey Hall, Fowey

SX12 51 : *EX107 GS347*

Small grounds, at 65m. altitude, on Meadfoot Beds, calcareous slate, in an AONB and HC; rainfall 40-45", temperature zone D; holiday accommodation.

Fowey Hall was built in the grand manner, with a terrace and curving stairways, in the early years of this century on the site of a former hospital dedicated to St Blaize, by Charles, later Sir Charles Hanson. The small garden was announced as open in the *Hort. Direct.* from 1919 to 1924, probably for its bedding schemes. Hanson, who 'came of local stock, had emigrated to Canada, where he made a fortune and returned to London, of which city he became Alderman in 1909 and Senior Sheriff two years later. In 1917 he was chosen Lord Mayor and created a baronet.' The Hall was taken over by the American army during the Second World War, and is now a centre of the Countrywide Holiday Association.

References: 20th C.

Lanwithan, Lostwithiel

SX11 59 : *EX107, GS347*

Cornish lan + gwyth = trees; house dated 1827 on rainwater head with some additions, listed grade II; small grounds on valley side, west sloping 25-10m., on Head and Valley gravel, in an AGLV; rainfall 45-50", temperature zone E; private.

Lanwithan is described by Twycross as a 'handsome house, in the modern style, pleasantly situated and commanding agreeable prospects'. It was built for William Foster (1775-1849), from a Lostwithiel family of bankers, to take advantage of the sunnier side of Lostwithiel, and still continues in the family. The grounds in the print in Twycross are not extensive, and much as today. The sloping meadow which is now separated by a wire fence from the surrounding plain garden, is known as 'The Lawn', which may have preserved an earlier meaning, signifying 'well-maintained fields used not (as in a 'park') for grazing cattle, but as a setting for ornamental trees and shrubs'. Lake announced that the house (unusually for the time) was in 'telegraphic communication' with the railway.

References: 19th (Gen.) and 20th C; Illus.

Lostwithiel, 1 Queen Street, Lostwithiel

SW10 59 : *EX107 GS347*

Thurston wrote in 1930, 'The garden of the house now occupied by Dr Rudge was made by Miss Frances M. Hext, who died about 1896, and contains some good trees.' Dorothy de L. Nicholls, in a letter to Major Magor (of Lamellen) in 1984 wrote: 'Until about 1965, Dr Rudge's house was occupied by various people who cared for the garden. But a few years ago, being about 200 yds long, half the land was sold for building. Yesterday I peered over the new dividing wall to see the whole levelled and laid out as a well-used fowl run. So no shrub nor tree remains except the magnificent Tulip tree, the bole measuring over 7 ft.' This immense and handsome tree still flourishes in a walled enclosure.

References: 20th C.

Moor Cottage, St Austell

SX01 51 : *EX105 and 107, GS347*

Medium grounds, at 30m., with south-east facing slope above, on Meadfoot Beds, calcareous slate, grit and thin limestone, and alluvium; rainfall 45-50", temperature zone D; private.

Moor Cottage is 'delightfully situated in a valley surrounded by rich plantations', immediately adjoining Trewhiddle, and can be seen from the road not to have developed significantly from its appearance in the print accompanying Twycross's description. It was the house of Edward Coode,

68. Moor Cottage, built for Edward Coode in the early nineteenth century, although not without attraction, received little notice. (Twycross 1846: 84)

from the St Austell family of bankers, in 1867 occupied by the Revd George Lambe, incumbent of Charlestown, although still remaining in the possession of the Coode family. It has no particular history as a garden, but is included here since it was considered in 1846 worthy of an illustration among the *Mansions of ... Cornwall*.

References: 19th (Gen.) C; Illus.

Penarwyn, St Blazey Gate

SX06 53 : *EX107, GS347*

Cornish *pen-arth = promontory + guyn = fair, pronounced penARwyn; small to medium grounds, south sloping, 25-15m., on Meadfoot Beds, calcareous slates, grit and thin limestone; rainfall 45-50", temperature zone D; grounds extinct, house with residual/relict garden.

Penarwyn was built in the late nineteenth or early twentieth century for John de Cressy Treffry, of Treffry, Clunes and Co., general merchants in Par. The garden was recorded as open from 1908 to 1916 in the *Hort. Direct*. The northern part of the grounds are now occupied by the Doubletrees School and Hospital, and the southern section, with the name Penarwyn Woods, is a residential development, but interspersed with many fine trees from the original garden. The gate-piers and a wall with an arch survive at the southern entrance. The house itself has been divided, the residential side with a circular lawn in front and the remains of a sunken garden, both perhaps part of the original garden.

References: 20th C.

Point Neptune, Fowey

SX119 511 : *EX107, GS347*

In an AONB and HC; extinct, the house in apartments.

Lake observes:

> Point Neptune is the beautiful and pleasantly situated marine residence of William Rashleigh, Esq. The position it occupies commands a fine view of the harbour and adjacent scenery; and the carriage road leading to it winds its way by the side of the well-wooded and romantic valley. By the side of the carriage road is a foot path, the use of which Mr. Rashleigh and his lady have generously and opportunely presented to the respectable inhabitants of Fowey, of all classes.

The Italianate house was built by William Rashleigh II, eldest son of William I of Menabilly, at Readymoney Cove (Cornish *redeman* possibly = stony ford), in preference to residing at Menabilly. Two years before his death in 1867 he built the Rashleigh Mausoleum on St Catherine's Point opposite, where he, his wife and his daughter are buried, with his family pets buried nearby. He was succeeded at Point Neptune by his daughter, Edith Frances, who was married to Sackville George Stopford-Sackville.

References: 19th (Gen.) C.

Polcarne, St Austell

SX01 52 : EX106 and 107, GS347

Cornish pol + carn = tor, pronounced polCARN; urban garden of about 2 acres (0.8 ha), at c. 65m. altitude, on metamorphosed Meadfoot Beds, calcareous slate, grit and thin limestone, with acid soil; rainfall 45-50", temperature zone D; private.

Polcarne was built in 1864 on a prominent site in St Austell for a member of the Coode family, who were bankers and solicitors in the town. Of several other substantial family properties, this is the only one to have survived intact, and is of especial interest since the garden, created at the time the house was built, has remained virtually unaltered. It has recently been given protected status by the local authority. Members of the Coode family also built and occupied Moor Cottage, Trevarthian and Pond Dhu (not described here) all in St Austell, and Polapit Tamar (q.v.).

References: 19th (Gen.) C.

Restormel House, Lostwithiel

SX10 61 : EX107, GS347

Now Restormel Manor, Cornish ros = high hill + tor = hill + moyl = bald, pronounced resTORmel; late 18th C. house incorporating 16th and 17th C. material, listed grade II; garden of c. 2 acres (0.8 ha), south facing, at 25m. altitude, on Head, in an AGLV; rainfall 45-50", temperature zone E; Duchy property, private residence.

Restormel House, classed by Betjeman as 'Strawberry Hill Gothic', had earlier been described by Stockdale as a

> low embattled structure, said to have been erected on the site of an antient chapel ... [as a consequence of which it was frequently referred to as 'Trinity House']. The valley in which this house is built, with the castle on the eminence near it, forms for the artist a very pleasing picture, and have often been admired.

It commands, wrote Gilbert,

> a perspective view of a delightfully wooded valley, lined on each side with an elevated ridge of oak; the river, after having fallen over different cascades, is seen passing through the Gothic arches of Lostwithiel Bridge.

The owners and tenants of this property form a list of some of the principal families of the county: Gregor of Trewarthenick, the Earl of Mount Edgcumbe, John Hext, and Sir C.B. Graves Sawle. The main plantings of trees, camellias, rhododendrons, hydrangeas and other shrubs are along the drive from the south-east.

References: 18th, 19th (Gen.) and 20th C; Illus.

St Cadix House, St Veep

SX13 54 : EX107, GS347

House, extended c. 1710, listed grade II; the grounds are in a north-south steep valley leading to the River Fowey, on Dartmouth Beds, silts and slates; rainfall 40-45", temperature zone D; private.

Leland mentions the little priory on the northern side of the creek dedicated to St Juliott and St Cyric, founded by William, Earl of Moreton, about the time of the Norman Conquest. It was considered to be a cell of the priory at Montacute in Somerset. *Hitchins* recorded that: 'The abbey house ... and the chapel are quite dilapidated. The cemetery is turned into a garden, and many of the stones are incorporated in some adjoining buildings.' It was at that time the property of the widow of Richard Wymond. St Cadix House was described by Gilbert as standing

> in a secluded situation, at the foot of a hill, adorned with charming foliage. The principal front commands a pleasing view over the solitary lake, and the ebb and flow of the tides, which run beneath its shrubberies and shady walks, are happily adapted to dispel that sameness which would otherwise prevail.

Dressed stone, tracery, column bases, and mullions in the garden are possible remains from the Cluniac Priory, dissolved in 1536, and probably sited to the north of the present house.

References: 17th, 18th, 19th (Gen.) C.

Torfrey, Golant

SX11 54 : EX107, GS347

*Cornish tor = belly + *bre = hill, i.e. round-topped hill, pronounced TORfrey; 1.33 acre (0.5 ha) garden, east facing at 80m. altitude, on Dartmouth Beds, silts and slates, in an AONB; rainfall 40-45", temperature zone D; private.*

Torfrey was part of the manor of Lantyan, settled by the Couch family in the 1700s, John Couch having a half-acre nursery there in 1744, which was still in existence under his name in 1840, although by 1804 Oliver Slyman had already purchased the property. The present house was designed and built as his residence by William Grundy, an architect, with two date-stones for 1886 and 1888. It has two gables, with Doric colonnades of granite in front of each bay, possibly added later, and a small bell tower to the side. In the wall by the entrance there is a niche, perhaps intended for a vase or figure. Over the lawn, framed by trees, there is a fine view across the Fowey valley to the country beyond. To the south of the lawn are the remains of a greenhouse and pergola, beyond which is a substantial rockery which once carried water down to the pond. There had been a 'Banana House', now a loggia. When seen, the house was being refurbished and the garden was long neglected; however, it had been listed in the *Hort. Direct.* in 1916 under the name of Mrs A.E. Mills, a descendant of the Grundys, and in 1930 Thurston cited an *Hydrangea petiolaris*, which was said to have come from Menabilly. The barton to Torfrey, across the road, is now a vinery.

References: 18th, 19th (Gen.) and 20th C.

Tredudwell Manor, near Lanteglos by Fowey

SX15 52 : *LR201, EX107, GS347*

Cornish tre + *personal name, pronounced* treDUDwell; *17th C. house, remodelled 18th C. listed grade II; grounds at 80m. altitude, on Dartmouth Beds, silts and slates; rainfall 40-45", temperature zone D; agricultural land.*

Gilbert writes:

> Tredudwell, formerly a seat of the Trevanions [see also Tredinnick], afterwards of the Eveleighs, and since of Canon Howell, is a commodious mansion, with suitable offices. It opens into a neat lawn, and the estate contains one hundred and twenty-three acres of fine cultivated land.

Lake, over half a century later, also remarked on the 'well-cultivated land'. There is no sign that there has been any ornamental garden here. Lt.-Col. Shakerly of Tredudwell, donated Hall Walk to the National Trust after the Second World War.

References: 18th and 19th (Gen.) C.

Trelawney, Tremena Road, St Austell

SX01 52 : *EX106 and 107, GS347*

Named after the Trelawny family, pronounced treLAWNey; *small to medium size urban garden, at 100m. altitude, on metamorphosed Meadfoot Beds; rainfall 45-50", temperature zone D; extinct, now a housing estate.*

T. Medland Stocker, one of the original directors of English china-clay, built his house at St Austell in the early twentieth century. It was reported in the *Hort. Direct.* as open from 1919 to 1924. The whole area has recently been built over, the estate being known as Trelawney Park. Coleraine, a more recent garden, is in the same road. This house must be distinguished both from Trelawny in Altarnun parish - the original home of the Trelawny family, - and Trelawne in Pelynt parish: note the difference in pronunciation and spelling.

References: 20th C.

Trenarren, near St Austell

SX03 48 : *LR204, EX105 & 107, GS347*

Cornish *dyn = *sea-fort* + garan = *crane, pronounced* treNARRen; *18th to 19th C. house listed grade II; small to medium grounds, south facing valley from 55m. to the sea, on Meadfoot Beds, with acid soil, in an AONB; rainfall 40-45", temperature zone C/D; private.*

It was recorded in the Parliamentary Survey of 1649 that Samuel Hext held the tenure of Trenarren, and it has remained in the family until the present day. Thomas Hext rebuilt the house in the early years of the nineteenth century. 'It stands,' so *Hitchins* recorded, 'on elevated ground near a promontory called the Blackhead. The prospect from the house is very extensive, but its situation is much exposed to the tempests'. The property was, until his death in 1997, leased to A.L. Rowse, the distinguished historian, who wrote about it in the *Cornish Garden* of 1981.

References: 17th, 18th, 19th (Gen.) and 20th C.

Trevarthian, Palace Road, St Austell

SX01 52 : *EX106 and 107, GS346*

Cornish tre + ?margh = *horse, pronounced* treVARTHian; *grounds on metamorphosed Meadfoot Beds; rainfall 45-50", temperature zone D; extinct, now the* Mid-Cornwall College.

Trevarthian, the residence of Arthur Coode, one of the St Austell family of bankers and solicitors, was built in the second half of the nineteenth century. The garden was listed as open in the *Hort. Direct.* from 1908 until 1916, but although the house has survived, the grounds have been swallowed up in the campus of the Mid-Cornwall College.

References: 20th C.

ADDITIONAL CONTEMPORARY GARDENS

See also HEADLAND, PINE LODGE, *and* PORTHPEAN *in the main section.*

Benbole, Edgcumbe Road, Lostwithiel

SX10 59 : *EX107, GS347*   OPEN*

Garden of 1 acre (0.4 ha); open 1997-8 CGOG, three Saturdays in May.

Churchtown Farm Field Studies Centre, Lanlivery

SX07 58 : *EX107, GS347*

When established by the Spastics Society in 1974, as an outdoor centre for handicapped people, Peter Macfadyen introduced an horticultural training course. Training greenhouses were built, a botanic collection created, and a garden developed with rockeries and pergolas. The centre has now moved in other directions, under different leadership, but some of the features of the original plan remain.

References: 20th C.

Coleraine, Tremena Road, St Austell

SX01 52 : *EX106 and 107, GS347*

Opened 1987-8 CGOG.

This two-acre garden was planted some forty years ago, and has a fine collection of camellias, rhododendrons and magnolias, and a good sized eucalyptus and embothrium. The display of shrubs is especially colourful, enhanced by daffodils and bluebells.

Furzeball Cottage, Pont near Bodinnick

SW145 527 : *EX107, GS347* OPEN*

In an AONB and HC; open in 1989-92, 1997-8 CGOG, 1989, 1991-2, 1997-8 NGS, mid-May to mid-June, Wednesday to Sunday, or by appointment.

Reference: 20th C.

Jarn Syvy, Bodinnick

SX13 52 : *EX107, GS347*

Opened in 1983-4 CGOG.

Described as an interesting garden of about one and a half acres (0.6 ha), and designed for shelter in an exposed position. Possesses some rare plants.

Water Meadow, Luxulyan

SX05 58 : *EX107, GS347* OPEN*

1.5 acre (0.6 ha) garden, part of the grounds of the former Luxulyan Vicarage, now known as King's Acre; open 1995-8 NGS, one Sunday in June or by appointment.

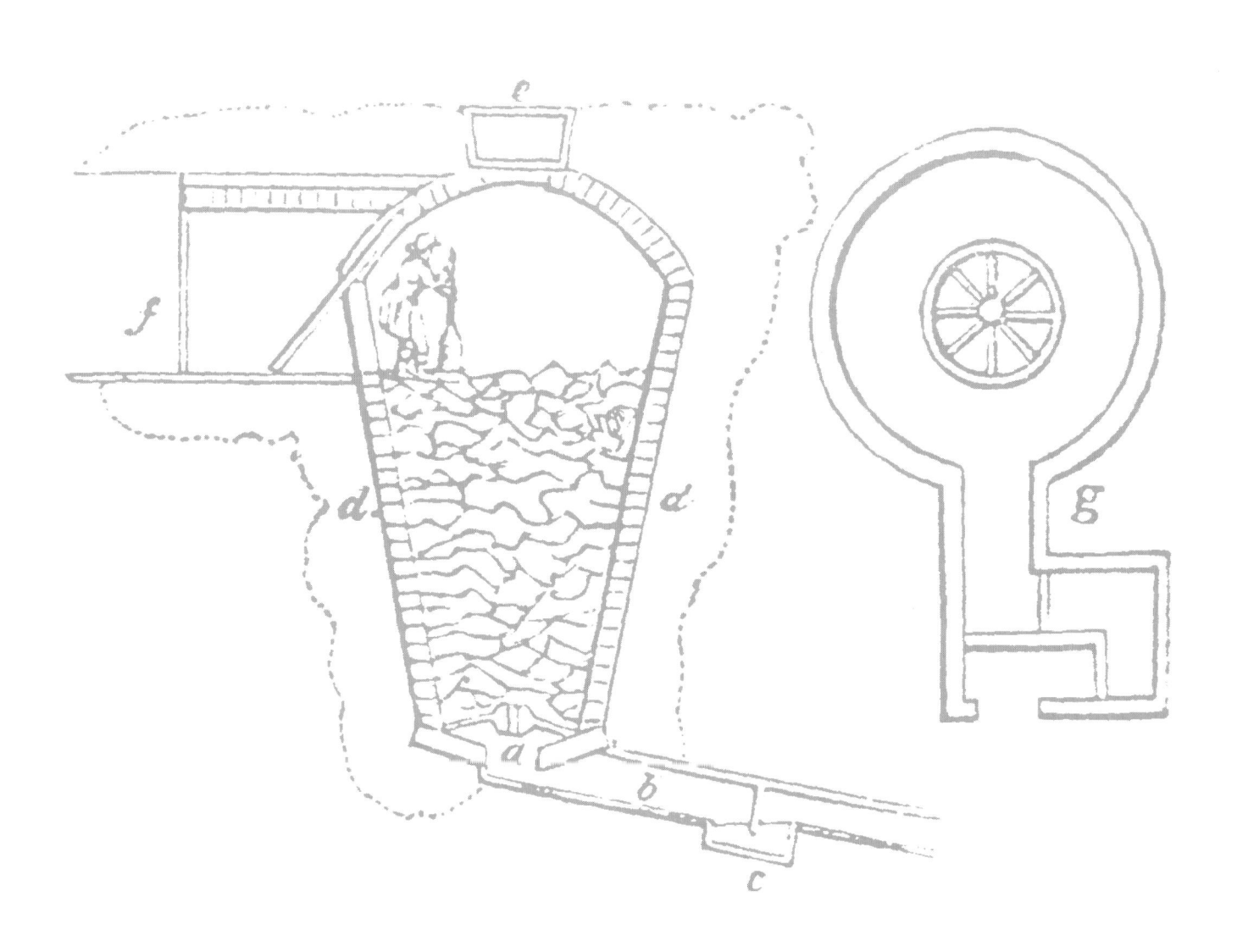

2. NEWQUAY, PADSTOW and WADEBRIDGE

The three towns which serve as the focal points in this section, although they have arisen from different origins, shared a common history as fishing ports. This was from the outset the function of Newquay until, with the coming of Treffry's railway in 1875, increasing hordes of tourists began to flood in. Originally with the manor name of Towan Blustry, the little fishing village became literally a Newquay when protective stonework was built around the harbour, as in many other small ports, during the fifteenth century.

Padstow had always been a centre of population, for the same reason as Bodmin, because a monastery of St Petroc had been established there, which is reflected in its former name of Petrockstow. Its wide sandy estuary proved ideal for fishing pilchards with a seine net, which was to provide secular employment and prosperity. It never, however, rose to the level of having members of Parliament, and was only incorporated for a short time from 1582 until 1590.

The origin and history of Wadebridge is also encapsulated in its name, which originally was Wade, derived from the Old English *waed* - a ford - which marks an early medieval low-tide crossing of the River Camel which, at high tide, until it began to silt up, could serve as a port. A weekly market and two annual fairs, established in 1312, increased its prosperity, and the bridge built in about 1468 - which still stands in a modified form - ensured its continuing importance. It should not escape notice that all three towns (with the exception of Towan Blustry), have English names, which emphasizes once again that towns in Cornwall are rarely Celtic in origin, but were either founded, or developed, by incomers.

Newquay could boast no great houses until the Regency craving to sniff the sea air led a few wealthy landowners - of whom G.W.T. Gregor who built the Tower in 1835 was the first - to set up their marine residences, much to the annoyance of the locals. Among these, only Treveddo received any notice for its garden. Once the railway arrived, however, the town increased in size and popularity and began to move steadily down-market, although the Trenance Gardens still deserve to be counted along with the parks at Morrab in Penzance, and Kimberley in Falmouth. There are, however, ancient and great houses in the vicinity of Newquay, chief among them Trerice, now restored by the National Trust, and also Tresillian House to the south, while farther off to the south-west is Chyverton, the unique eighteenth-century landscape park designed by John Thomas, a Truro attorney. Farther west along the coast, Rosemundy was one of the principal houses at St Agnes. Newquay had been in St Columb Minor parish, and around St Columb Major there is a group of once important estates: Carnanton to the west has been cut into by the St Mawgan airfield, while below, Nanswhyden, a once beautiful house, though burnt, lingered on in the memory. Trewan, an extraordinary Gothic house built by the Vyvyans, looks down on the parish and over the handsome old rectory, built for a bishop and enclasped in a moat.

Central to Padstow is the fine Prideaux Place which dominates the town, although a rich merchant in about 1803 sought to rival this ancient site by building a grand house on Sanders Hill, which was forthwith demolished by the Prideaux-Brunes, when he was discovered to be heavily in debt after his death.

The principal house in Wadebridge is Gonvena, which was built in 1780 by Edward Fox, who stemmed from the same family as the Falmouth line of Foxes. A little farther along the estuary is the old estate, and modern garden at Dinham, while to the south, along the Polmorla valley, near St Breock the mother parish, the Crag had a reputation for its garden in the early twentieth century. Away north, near Port Isaac, an old Victorian garden has been uncovered at Long Cross, which is being restored in association with an hotel.

NB ROSEMUNDY in St Agnes, which is on the OS Landranger 204 Truro and Falmouth map, fits more appropriately into this section.

CARNANTON, St Mawgan

SW87 64 : *EX106, GS346*   OPEN

Carneton 1303; Cornish, Dexter suggests carn + e an = of the + ton = meadow, pronounced carNANton; house listed grade II*, stables, kennels, school-house, gate-piers, railings and gates, and gate-piers, each II; estate c. 2,000 acres (809 ha), large parkland partly reduced, in north facing valley, sloping 110-60m., on Dartmouth Beds, purple and green slates, in an AGLV; rainfall 40-45", temperature zone D; private, part of the grounds taken into St Mawgan airfield, open CGOG 1997-8, one Sunday in May.

Even though identification with the Domesday 'Carnetone' is no longer accepted, Carnanton is an ancient site, having once a castle named Castle-Fust mentioned by Worcester (1478), and a chapel licensed in 1331. The manor had been the property of the Earls of Warwick, but was conveyed to the Crown in the reign of Henry VII by their heiress, Ann Neville. It became the

69. Carnanton, after the re-orientation of the main entrance porch, and the extension. All but one of the trees that darkened the house were removed, but this splendid example has survived. The steps in the distance lead up to a raised walk, where the new 'eye-catcher' end to the school-house lies just off the print to the left. (Morris 1866-80: iv. 25)

house of the notorious Attorney General Noy who, although setting out with liberal sympathies, later incurred much popular odium in the reign of Charles I by his revival of the forest laws, the soap monopoly, and the writ of ship money, so that at his death it was said his heart was found shrivelled up like a leather purse.

The estate came into the family of Willyams of Roseworthy in Gwinear (originally from Stowford in Devon), by marriage, at the end of the seventeenth century. The house dates from around 1710, but was remodelled and re-oriented by the Willyams in the 1830s. It was described in the listing as a fine example of an early eighteenth-century house, with a well proportioned entrance to the east. A school house built for the children of estate workers, incorporates earlier features including a doorway from the Tudor house. Its right gable end, dated 1845, which faces the garden to the south, in front of the house, is treated in Gothic style as an eyecatcher. The well-preserved stables, described as a rare survival in a complete state, combine the use for carriages, riding and driving horses, with that of working farm horses to the rear, together with an estate workshop and forge. There are also kennels. Gilbert thought that, although gloomy, it had

> good gardens, but there is a stiffness prevailing throughout the whole; and the trees [presumably yews] have been cut into such grotesque shapes, that every vestige of their natural beauties is destroyed. On the western side of the house is a beautiful sheet of water, with a walk carried round its borders: also a neat summer-house, overhung with willows, and other drooping leafage.

The house has now been opened out, by the loss or removal of the oaks which once surrounded it, but the lake has disappeared as a consequence of the airfield and new water courses. The woodlands which were felled during the First World War, have mostly regenerated, although there has also been considerable replanting. The view from the house, over lawns and ornamental planting to the woodlands and hills beyond, is now most impressive. Beyond the sloping lawn, formal gardens are being developed incorporating a wall from the Tudor house, with a yew walk, the adjacent woodland being underplanted with rhododendrons and other suitable shrubs. Although the Willyams have been active in local affairs, the grounds have never, except for being listed in the *Hort. Direct.* from 1890 to 1924, received much horticultural notice. The recent opening has revealed the measure of that loss.

References: 17th, 18th, 19th (Hort. & Gen.) and 20th C; Illus; C.Lee, Vale of Lanherne, *Redruth 1984: 37-41.*

CHYVERTON, Zelah

SW79 51 : EX105, GS346   OPEN

Cornish chy + war = on + ton = grass, *pronounced* CHIVerton; *house listed grade II*, bridge (c. 1780) II*, stables and lodge, each II; grounds of 140 acres (57ha) listed grade II, sloping north-east 70-30m., on Grampound Grit, with soil of 'loam and shale, very acid'; rainfall 35-40", temperature zone C; private, open 1983-98 CGOG, 1991-8 NGS, Monday to Friday, March to June, by appointment only.*

Chyverton, as so many places in Cornwall, was once in the possession of the Arundells, but the land was sold to John Rosogan, whose ancestors held the estate on lease, in the reign of Queen Elizabeth. In 1724 it was purchased from them by John Andrew of Trevallance, the maternal great-grandfather of John Thomas, whose family had emigrated from Glamorganshire in the mid-seventeenth century. He was described as an 'eminent attorney' of Truro, who became, for thirty-four years, vice-Warden of the Stannaries. As his wealth grew he moved from his offices in Truro to Chyverton, where in the 1770s he improved his estate by creating a park and planting ninety-four acres (38 ha) of woodland, having remodelled the house some ten years earlier. *Hitchins* was mild in his praises: 'The site is pleasing, the gardens are commodious, and the ancient grounds are embellished with extensive plantations.' Gilbert is somewhat more sympathetic:

> It is situated in a part of the country, where Nature appears in her most forlorn attire; yet by industry and expense, Chiverton displays many beauties, consisting of neat sheets of water, fine gardens, and thriving plantations.

It is only in recent years that the importance of this eighteenth-century landscape has become appreciated. It is not, however, immediately apparent whence Thomas had received his inspiration, other than that his first wife was the widow of John Beauchamp of Pengreep which, like many other estates of the time, had been 'improved'. Nevertheless, he was able to create at Chyverton a small park which displays the classic principles of landscape style rarely, if ever, to be found in such a pure state in Cornwall.

From the house, there is a prospect down over sloping lawns to a bridge crossing a serpentine lake, with plantations on each side of the valley leading up to Tinker's Castle (originally 'Hunter's Tower') - a folly intended as an eye-catcher on the horizon, though now extended into a house, and obscured by the growth of trees. The significance of this design, although still intact, was over-shadowed by the horticultural interests of the more recent owners.

In the early nineteenth century the estate passed by marriage to the Peter family of Harlyn, John Thomas Henry Peter (1810-73) marrying the daughter of John Penberthy Magor of Penventon, who inherited Lamellen (q.v.). His grandson, E.J.P. Magor, who later became celebrated for his collection and hybridizing of rhododendrons, was often at Chyverton in his boyhood, which he loved, and had hoped to inherit from his aunt. She, however, felt she must leave it in the Peter family, who in 1924 sold it to Treve Holman. He then began to plant the estate with rhododendrons and magnolias, with advice from Harold Hillier, but finding after his return from the war, that the magnolias had the better survived neglect, decided to concentrate upon this latter species.

Treve Holman was succeeded by his son, Nigel, who, with his wife, continued to develop the garden after 1959, independently designing a wooden bridge over the stream which has been likened to that in Monet's garden. Until interest became aroused quite recently in the design of the garden, it was the magnificent collection of plants, especially the magnolias, which was the glory of Chyverton. The present owner claims that it is only here that trials of new introductions, for which Cornwall was once famous, are still continuing, and there is much justice in his claim.

References: 18th,19th (Gen.) and 20th C.

GONVENA HOUSE, Wadebridge

SW99 72 : EX106, GS335/336

Cornish guyn = white + meneth = hill, *pronounced* gunVENna; *house listed grade II, ha-ha II; relict, part extinct estate, sloping south-west to river from 30m., on Middle Devonian grey slates; rainfall 35-40", temperature zone D; house now in apartments, grounds a residential development.*

The Wadebridge line of the Fox family, who became wealthy merchants in the town, was founded by Edward Fox, the eldest son of George Fox of Par by his first wife, and half-brother to

George Croker Fox of Falmouth. His eldest son, George, moved away to build Tredrea in Perran-ar-worthal (q.v.), but his younger son, Edward II, continued in the family business. He purchased the barton of Gonvena from John Hoblyn in 1790, after which he

> erected thereon the present mansion house, laid out the gardens, and planted the ornamental plantations, shrubberies &c.

The house, high above the estuary, was particularly conspicuous, with its two brick elevations visible from the centre of the town. *Hitchins* recorded that:

> When this house was first erected it was exposed to storms, and some serious injuries were sustained in the buildings ... But of late years, since the trees planted round this mansion have acquired a degree of maturity, it has been sufficiently sheltered, to suppress all apprehensions of such a returning calamity. The plantations and gardens are laid out with much taste and judgement; and the latter are kept remarkably clean and neat.

The ha-ha dates from the time of the building of the house, and is constructed of horizontally coursed slate stone piers with vertically coursed slatestone retaining walls. The house, which was sold by the Fox family in 1829, has survived, and even though the grounds have been divided between smaller residences, they are still surrounded by, and interspersed with, many fine mature trees.

References: 18th, 19th (Gen.) and 20th C; H.A.F. Crewdson, George Fox of Tredrea ... privately printed, 1976: 1.

LONG CROSS VICTORIAN GARDEN, Trelights

SW98 79 : *EX106, GS335/336* OPEN

Garden of 3 acres (1.2 ha), at 100m. altitude, on Pillow Lava (spilite), in an AONB and HC; rainfall 35-40", temperature zone D; Hotel, open to non-residents, and open 1983-98 CGOG, 1987, 1991-2, 1994-8 NGS, daily. Official leaflet with plan.

The discovery at Long Cross of the structure of an old Victorian garden, designed by a Capt. Allerdyce at the turn of the nineteenth century, with maze-like hedged pathways, a pond, a folly, and a mount from which are panoramic sea views, led, around 1980, to its revival and replanting. There has been added a modern reproduction of a traditional dovecote.

References: 20th C.

NANSWHYDEN, St Columb Major

SW87 62 : *EX106, GS346*

Cornish nans + gwyth = trees, wood, pronounced nansWEEDdn; mansion burnt down 1803, farm house, front gate walls, coach house, granary, kitchen garden walls, all listed grade II; original garden extinct.

70. Nanswhyden. This engraving of the house before it burnt down in 1803 shows that it possessed a quite substantial garden in the mid eighteenth century. (Borlase 1758: 8)

The passing of Nanswhyden has always lingered in the minds of Cornishmen, as did the demolition of the earlier mansion at Stowe, and perhaps that at Sanders Hill. From 1581 this was the chief residence of the Hoblyn family. An account is given in *Hitchins* of the origin of the building:

> Nanswhydden House, as it lately stood, was begun in the year 1740, at which time the eastern wing was added to the old house that then occupied the site, and was left standing by Robert Hoblyn, Esq. then member of parliament for Bristol. But a proposition having been made by some Cornish gentlemen to nominate Admiral Boscawen and himself to represent the county of Cornwall at the ensuing general election, Mr. Hoblyn was induced to pull down all the old parts of his house that had been left standing, and to add a new body and another wing, to correspond with the wing already built, that the whole might appear with elegant uniformity. The building was thus undertaken, and accomplished accordingly; but before the time of the anticipated election arrived, Mr. Hoblyn and Admiral Boscawen were no more.

Gilbert describes the house:

> The basement story was built of granite, the upper part with a light coloured slate, or killas, and the whole lined with brick: the door cases, windows, pediment, and balustrades were of the Ionic order. The shell of this structure, was erected by that able architect Potter ... The chimney pieces, which were finished in Italy, were remarkably elegant, in respect of the richness of marble, the delicacy of design, and the excellence of the sculpture.

Although Gilbert, and others, attribute the design of the house to Potter, it is now thought more probable that he was no more than the contractor to Thomas Edwards of Greenwich, who designed several other Cornish houses of the time (see *Country Life 132* 1962: 775). The general layout of the grounds can be seen in the print from Borlase. Two lines of trees running along each side of the grounds are shown in the Ordnance Survey first edition of 1809, not long after Nanswhyden was burnt in 1803. The estate remained in the Hoblyn family for some years, but it eventually passed to William Shilson of Tremough, and is now a farm. The platform where the house stood, and the fast decaying dovecote, are all that remains.

References: 17th, 18th, 19th (Gen.), 20th C; Illus.

PRIDEAUX PLACE, Padstow

SW91 75 : EX106, GS335/336　　　　　　　　OPEN

Cornish plas = palace, mansion (from English) + family name, pronounced PRIDoh; house listed grade I, entrance gate I, footbridge, The Rink (stables), south entrance, stables, footbridge with fortifications, dairy and grotto, temple and grotto niche, garden seat on terrace and two artifacts, each II*, horse trough and grotto niche, shell house (remains), garden walls, sunken garden, each II; garden c. 5 acres (2 ha) and deer park c. 5 acres (2 ha) listed grade II, sloping east 55-45m., on Middle Devonian grey slates, in an AONB, and HS with an AM (cross); rainfall 30-35", temperature zone D; private, open 1993-8 CGOG and NGS, daily (except Friday and Saturday), Easter to mid October.

Carew wrote in 1602:

> Mr. Nicholas Prideaux, from his new and stately house, thereby taketh a full and large prospect of the town, haven, and country adjoining, to all which his wisdom is a stay, his authority a direction.

Nicholas Prideaux the elder, a lawyer and steward of the Prior, bought the fee-simple of Padstow after the dissolution of Bodmin Priory, where his

71. Prideaux Place. Sketch by Edmund Prideaux in the 1730s, showing an elaborate seventeenth-century garden. The 'Wilderness' (see page 313) was to the left.

72. Prideaux Place. The redesigned east front. (Borlase 1758: 4)

descendant, Sir Nicholas, rebuilt the dwelling into a 'stately house' in 1592. This was considerably remodelled by Edmund Prideaux, who inherited it in 1728. He also redesigned the garden after a visit to Italy in 1739-40. His keen interest in architecture and garden design is evident in a series of sketches made on two tours in 1716 and 1727, chiefly to the houses of his relatives.

His depiction of the south front of Prideaux Place, before its alteration (see Fig. 8), shows the formal garden divided into four quadrants, with central trees, it would appear, trained in an *estrade* form, with clipped conical bushes, probably yew, along their edges. Such a design has parallels not only among his own sketches, but also in the *Spoure Book* of *c.* 1690, and may be taken as typical of a late-seventeenth century Cornish garden of a Dutch type.

His drawing of the east front is considerably more elaborate. Along the front of the house is a long terrace with central steps between pillars surmounted by what appear to be vase-shaped finials. To the extreme left can be seen a square building, perhaps that used to house his 'Roman antiquities'. The obelisk, later moved and now gone, and the temple are also clearly in view. It is somewhat more difficult to decipher the foreground, except that it would appear that the Wilderness (made in 1734), of which he gave a separate plan (see Fig. 118), and the bowling green are away to the left.

By 1758, however, when his son Humphrey had succeeded him, fashions were changing. The print in Borlase, which is very similar to that signed by J. Dayman among the Prideaux collection, shows a much altered scene. The whole house with its terrace has been castellated, the central steps have become a gate-house or barbican, with the continuation of the terrace armed with cannon. The whole foreground has now been opened up as a deer park, with a walled garden to the left. This park is one of only three to have survived to the present day. It bears a legend that if the deer were to die out, so too would the family. The obelisk has disappeared, but not the temple.

Changes were still to come when the Revd Charles Prideaux-Brune (the 'Brune' was added in response to the will of his maternal uncle) became the owner in 1793. From then until his death in 1833, he carried out further extensions and alterations. The dairy, for instance, was now adapted as a grotto, and a grotto niche in the form of a round arch with large scattered rocks was incorporated into the terrace. He was also responsible for the rock work at the stable yard water trough. The shell house, and the Victorian sunken garden, formerly with a handsome conservatory on the end platform, date from 1878 and were designed by Charles Glynn Prideaux-Brune (b. 1821). This fine formal garden was restored in 1992, though planted with a simpler labour-saving bedding scheme. The conservatory was not replaced. Prideaux Place is a house and garden richer in features than can all be mentioned here, but the illustrations, better than words, plot the course of its earlier history. It was listed in the *Hort. Direct.* from 1889 to 1924, and was included among Thurston's select gardens, but not visited by him.

References: 17th, 18th, 19th (Hort. & Gen.) and 20th C; Illus.

ROSEMUNDY, St Agnes

SW72 50 : LR204, EX104, GS346

Goen Enis *alias* Rosemundy, Parl. Survey *1650*; Cornish ros + mon-dy = *mineral-house, pronounced* roseMUNdy; *remodelled and extended 18th C. house listed grade II; medium grounds at c. 90m. altitude, on Ladock Beds or Grampound Grit, with acid soil, in an HC; rainfall 35-40", temperature zone C; now the* Rosemundy House Hotel.

Maurice Bizley writes:

> Rosemundy is a large 18th century house with perhaps some older portions. A gracious dwelling with a wide frontage and canopied doorway [which] was for more than a century the residence of a succession of landowners, mine pursers and country gentlemen. It formed part of the Donnithorne estate in the 18th century. Then John James purchased it with much other land in Breannick, Pennick and Mingoose. After his death, Thomas Humphries lived there and then for seventy or eighty years it was the Carne family seat. Many beautiful trees and shrubs were planted in the grounds, especially by the members of the last named family.

'William Naylor Carne,' wrote Susan Gay in 1903,

> is one of the Cornish "gardeners", and his green-houses hold rare ferns and plants, while in his garden are to be seen fine shrubs and flowers, well sheltered by large trees.

Luckhurst had described the plants in Carne's garden, in the *Journal of Horticulture*, 1877, to which he more than once applied the epithet 'snug', or 'snug and cosy'. It was listed in the *Hort. Direct.* from 1916 to 1919. For a time after the First World War, this was a Social and Moral Welfare Home, before becoming an hotel. The extent of the grounds has contracted, but on 8 July 1954 a grassy 'theatre' or 'playing-place' was opened by Bishop Morgan, and the Revd Clifford Lever, superintendent minister of the Truro circuit, which is still used for festivities.

References: 17th, 18th, 19th (Hort. & Gen.) and 20th C.

ST COLUMB MAJOR RECTORY, St Columb Major

SW91 63 : EX106, GS347

House, flanking walls, gateway and gate over the moat, each listed grade II*, entrance gate-piers II; very small garden, at 45m., on alluvial soil; extinct, former garden now a car-park or built over.

Cornwall was without its own bishop from 1050, when Edward the Confessor joined Devon and Cornwall as the Western See with its seat at Exeter, where it remained for centuries. The ecclesiastical ferment of the nineteenth century aroused great hopes that Cornwall might again have its own bishop. Dr Samuel Edward Walker, Rector of St Columb, the most richly endowed parish in the county, expressed a willingness to forego some of his benefits to this end, and in the 1850s engaged the celebrated Truro ecclesiastical architect, William White, a pupil of Sir Gilbert Scott, to build for him a rectory capable of being used as a bishop's residence. Although this project was not thought to have been a 'very wise or practical one,' it was conceded that the 'rectory and its grounds would have made a charming episcopal residence'. The design incorporated remnants of an earlier building erected in the fifteenth century by John Arundell, Dean of Exeter. It was, wrote Moule,

> situated in a steep but fertile valley ..., surrounded by a spacious lawn, and the acclivities of the hill, which rises towards the town, have been judiciously planted. A stream runs through the valley, which contributes to the freshness and beauty as well as to the calm and undisturbed retirement of the scene. The building is quadrangular, with a gatehouse and moat, and it is necessary to cross a bridge to reach the porch, thus in its plan emulating the castellated style of building adopted by the neighbouring gentry [such as at Trewan, q.v.].

The new rectory, 'more like a small medieval college than a parsonage,' has been judged 'a deeply picturesque composition.' The grounds, once adequate and well planted, are now so reduced that they would scarcely merit a mention in a survey of historic gardens, were it not that the moat, a feature unique in Cornwall, was retained by White in his design.

References: 19th (Gen.) and 20th C; A.B. Donaldson, The Bishopric of Truro 1877-1902, *1902: 31.*

SANDERS HILL, Padstow

SW91 75 : EX106, GS335/336

Sanders *in Polwhele (1806) and others, but in some subsequent writers also* Saunders Hill, *both with or without an apostrophe; house demolished, garden extinct.*

Like the departed houses at Nanswhyden and Stowe, Sanders Hill, now the recreation ground, Lawn, and car-park in the centre of Padstow, made a great impression during its erection, being depicted in no less than three contemporary collections of prints. Moule, for example, who was not given to writing detailed descriptions of houses, is unusually expansive:

73. Sanders Hill. This 'striking ornament to the town' of Padstow, erected in about 1803, was demolished in the 1820s. (Gilbert 1820: ii. 652)

On the southern side of the town is Saunders' Hill, a mansion erected by Thomas Rawlings, Esq., about 1803, from designs by *Richards*; on the front is an Ionic portico, opening upon a vestibule and tribune. The library contains a collection of mineralogical specimens, and some family portraits by *Opie*. The plantations around Saunders' Hill are beautifully diversified by the natural inequalities of the ground. The spot is enclosed by a bold and irregular contour of hills, whence the arm of the sea, which forms the harbour of Padstow, appears as a spacious lake, and the water, from the bright colour of its sandy bed, preserves its cerulean hue. In an opposite direction, is a richly cultivated valley, in which the town is situated. Mr. Rawlings, of Saunders' Hill, died in 1820; his brother is the present vicar of Padstow.

Gilbert in 1820 considered

> the plantations and walks ... laid out with considerable propriety and taste. The gardens and shrubberies are also very fine, and the whole, although in its infant state, is a striking ornament to the town and its environs.

'Some idea of its beauties and the grandeur of the situation may be formed,' he wrote, from the print reproduced here from his book. By 1824 the sad fate of the house, which in 1806 Polwhele had hoped would 'promise durability to the town which it adorns', is succinctly told by Stockdale. It had

> been lately taken down, owing to the death of that gentleman, and its materials sold by auction, as the property could not be more advantageously disposed of.

A slump in the property market might appear to have been no new thing, but the reality was rather more grim. The Rawlings had become the paramount merchants in Padstow, but Thomas, on his death, was found to be heavily in debt. 'After the crash ... the Prideaux-Brune family', wrote Rawe and Ingrey,

> acquired Saunder's Hill among other Rawlings property: viewing a second mansion in Padstow with disfavour, they sold off the building, and its contents, stone by stone, floor by floor.

References: 18th, 19th (Gen.) and 20th C; Illus; C. Berry, Padstow 1895-1925, *Padstow 1976: 30-37.*

TINTAGEL CASTLE, Tintagel

SX04 89 : *EX 109, GS322*

The walled garden at Tintagel Castle has been a well-known feature for many years. Leland, in the mid-sixteenth century, recorded 'a ground quadrant wall as yt were a garden plot', and Sir Richard Grenville's plan of 1583 describes the enclosure as 'a garden walled.' The illustration from Norden (*c.* 1590) quite clearly shows this garden, then enclosed with higher walls, or perhaps fences, than now exist. The interior plan is simple. There is a single entrance on the southeast side, leading on to a perimeter path, which also bisects the area. Between the edge of the path and the wall is a space of about twenty inches, which may have served as a sheltered flower border. The two sections surrounded by the paths may simply have been lawns, or could have been medieval 'flowery meads', planted with such flowers as violets, primroses, periwinkles or daisies. Turf seats were common in such gardens, but there is no evidence left to show that there had been one here. As it stands, however, this is a not untypical small medieval *hortus conclusus*. Peter Rose, in an informative article in *Cornish Archaeology*, has reviewed the various ways in which such a plot may have been cultivated at that time.

The date and age of this garden is not known, other than that the Castle itself is thirteenth-century. In certain versions of the Arthurian Legends, King Mark's Castle is located in Cornwall, and more especially at Tintagel. More particularly, part of the romance of Tristan and Iseult takes place in a garden at King Mark's Castle. Oliver Padel has made the interesting suggestion that Richard, Earl of Cornwall, indeed might have acquired Tintagel and established a castle there precisely because it was focal in the internationally renowned romances of Tristan and Iseult as well as having significant associations in local folklore. The romantic castle which Richard created would naturally have had a garden as one of its components.

References: 17th C; P. Rose, 'The medieval garden at Tintagel Castle', Cornish Archaeology, 33, 1994: 170-82.

TRENANCE GARDENS, Newquay

SX81 61 : *EX104 & 106, GS346*   OPEN

Cornish tre + nans, pronounced treNANCE; medium size grounds in north-east, south-west valley, at river level, on alluvium in Meadfoot Beds, with 'acid and alkaline soils'; rainfall 30-35", temperature zone C; public park.

With the growth of the holiday industry in Newquay, the upper part of the Trenance Valley was laid out as a public garden in 1906, and the narrow track widened for vehicles. The sunny, sheltered nature of this valley was seen as a pleasant contrast for visitors to the more bracing air of the sands and cliffs. The gardens had the advantage, especially in an area which is predominantly alkaline, of having on the slopes a thin acid soil in which camellias, rhododendrons and heathers could be grown. The lower, flatter section is slightly alkaline and used more for brilliantly coloured formal bedding schemes. A wide variety of shrubs and trees are grown, among which is a dawn redwood (*Metasequoia glyptostroboides*), raised from the original batch of seeds sent to this country.

In 1933 the gardens were extended by damming up the stream flowing into the Gannel, to provide a large boating lake, a quarter of a mile long (402m.), and 70 yards (64m.) wide, around which have been planted flower gardens.

References: 20th C; M. Haigh, and D. Woolgrove, Explore Newquay, *Newquay 1974: 37-44, including plan.*

74. Tintagel Castle. The garden with high walls, it would appear of pallisading, is clearly seen on the island to the right. (Norden 1597)

TRERICE, Newlyn East

SW84 58 : EX106, GS346   OPEN

Trevret Domesday 1086; Cornish tre + res = *ford, pronounced T'RICE; house listed grade I, garden walls and gate-piers, lions, and outbuildings, each II; grounds of 6 acres (2.4 ha), sloping west towards river from 30m., on Meadfoot Beds, black calcareous slate, with Felsite intrusions, 'limey'; rainfall 35-40", temperature zone D; the* National Trust *were donated the estate by Sir Richard Acland in 1943, and came into possession of Trerice itself in 1953, open 1983-98 CGOG, 1987, 1991, 1993-8 NGS, daily August, but otherwise from the end of March through October with the exception of Tuesdays and Saturdays.*

Trerice has been more celebrated for its delightful Elizabethan house than for its garden. That there was once a family named Trerice is known, but it is lost in the mists of time, the male branch becoming extinct in the reign of Edward III, when the estate came by marriage to the Arundells in about 1330. Thereafter this branch of the family became distinguished as the Arundells of Trerice. The Elizabethan house was built for Sir John Arundell about 1570. Michael Trinick wrote that it is half-hidden

> by elms, its curving grey gables command no distant view, for this is a close country, and Elizabethan builders cared more for sheltered places, and the presence of pure spring water, than for a wide prospect.

By default of male issue, the estate passed from the Arundells to the Aclands, but Gilbert found there 'little appearance of its once fruitful gardens, raised terrace, and expansive lakes.'

The gardens as they are now have been laid out with due regard for the style and antiquity of the site, since 1953, when the National Trust came into possession of the house, which had been in various ownership.

The forecourt, once probably cobbled, was turfed and planted with borders in 1969, but the present garden walls probably date from no earlier than the beginning of the nineteenth century. From this forecourt, steps lead up north to the bowling green, also a nineteenth-century feature, with level terraces above, all of a type described by Graham Stuart Thomas as 'nearly unique in Cornwall'. To the south, illustrations had shown a 'Dutch Garden', but all signs of design had vanished, so that in 1972 this area was planted with herbaceous borders, and beyond as an orchard, with a collection of old apples, arranged in a *quincunx* pattern, where the trees are in line from whichever angle they are viewed (compare Bake). F. Holland Hall has written a comprehensive article on the planting at Trerice in the *Cornwall Garden* (1986: 26-9).

The presence of two listed 'Arundell Lions' offers an opportunity to enlarge upon their ancestry. These particular lions are known to have originated from Kenegie, near Penzance (q.v.), the seat of the Arundell Harrises from Menadarva. They were taken from Kenegie when the Harrises removed to their other seat at Lifton, in Devon, but were brought back to Trerice by the National Trust when they were threatened by road widening. The late Michael Trinick, who hunted out these beasts, found four others, two with 'severe', two with 'benign' expressions. The 'severe' pair, now at the entrance to Bosvathick in Constantine (SW75 30), since they are associated with unusual gate-piers matched at Kenegie, he believed almost certainly must have come from there, where they may have sat with the Trerice pair, all four (surely too many?) at the foot of the stairway up to the gazebo. But Bottrell had earlier recorded in 1880 (p. 23) that a pair of lions had actually been seen at the *gates* of Kenegie. Were *these* then perhaps the Bosvathick pair? If so, this would have left only the Trerice lions to guard the gazebo. The puzzle remains.

The two smaller 'benign' lions however, are certainly known once to have guarded the entrance to Bank House in Falmouth, the single survivor later being removed to the Foxes' other house at Glendurgan. Its mate was found in 1979 in the undergrowth at Greatwood, a former seat of Joseph Fox, who was born at Bank House. These two smaller lions - undoubtedly relations of the four great Arundell Lions - now share a home with the Foxes at Glendurgan.

References: 17th, 18th, 19th (Gen.) and 20th C; Illus; H.A. Tipping, English Homes, Early Renaissance, *1912: 129.*

TRESILLIAN HOUSE, Newlyn East

SW85 58 : EX106, GS346   OPEN

Cornish, tre + Sulgen = *personal name, pronounced* treSILLian; *house listed grade II; grounds of 20 acres (8 ha), west sloping 70-55m., on Meadfoot Beds and calcareous slates; rainfall 35-40", temperature zone D; private, open 1998 CGOG, April through September by appointment.*

'Tresillian,' wrote Twycross,

> was originally held by a family who bore that name; and Sir [Robert Tresilian], Lord Chief Justice of England, who was executed at Tyburn in 1388, was Lord of the Manor. With his daughter and heiress it passed to John Hawley, and subsequently, by purchase, became the property of the family of Davies, who sold it, in

1694, to Samuel Gully, Esq., of Leigh in the County of Devon, ancestor of the present inheritor.

The core of the present house was built during the occupancy of the Gully family, but on the death of Richard Gully in 1792, there was no-one to succeed him, and the estate was left to his nephew, the Revd John Bennet. His son, Richard Gully Bennet, married Loveday, of the Tehidy family of Bassets, in 1820, and for sixty years resided at Tresillian. In 1846 it was announced in Twycross that

> [the] old house will shortly give place to a new structure in the modern style, a view of which we have been enabled to give through the kind assistance of the architect.

However, after the death of Richard Gully Bennet, the family did not reside in the house for some years. When Capt. Leonard Bennet inherited his uncle's estate in 1928, he found the house neglected and the grounds overgrown. He rectified this situation by cutting down trees to open up a view of the pond, building a greenhouse, erecting a pergola, and planting flowering shrubs.

After the Second World War, in 1947, the estate was sold, and in the 1970s became the residence of the owner of the home farm, now a 'theme park' known as 'Dairyland', who has further developed the grounds. The walled garden, in particular, which dates from the eighteenth century, has been laid out in Victorian style over the past ten years, by the knowledgeable head gardener, John Harris, with old varieties, and plants formerly used as organic remedies against pests and diseases. In 1993 he also began a reference collection of sixty varieties of Cornish apples, interspersed with medlars and quinces, as part of a plan to create at Tresillian an authentic representation of historic gardening practices in the county.

References: 17th, 18th, 19th (Gen.) C; Illus; R.G. Kerswell, The Bennets of Tresillian, *Durham, 1994.*

TREVILLET, Bossiney, near Tintagel

SX08 88 : *EX109, GS322*   OPEN

St Nectan's *(or* Knighton's*)* Kieve; kieve = *stone trough; a rift in a complex area of the Upper Devonian rocks, in an AONB and HC, and an AGSV; private, access on request, after payment.*

Although not strictly a garden, the cascade at St Nectan's Kieve, in the grounds of the abandoned mansion of Trevillet, deserves a place in our survey as a Cornish specimen of the 'Picturesque'.

The Wood family, according to Gilbert, had built a 'small temple, or summer-house' (by then a ruin) at the top of a spectacular waterfall (like Sir Michael le Fleming at Rydal in the Lakes, and the Duke of Atholl at Dunkeld) where

> the beauty and solemnity of this charming cascade, is greatly heightened by the solitude of the situation, [and] the grandeur of the rocks, [and where] the waters are heard falling with a most tremendous crash, the noise of which, reverberated by the adjoining cliffs, strikes the spectator with admiration and delight.

This description calls to mind the 'agreeable horror' of Bishop Berkeley before the manifestations of nature, and Burke's analysis of the 'sublime' in his *Enquiry* (1759). Here, in place of the lays of Bards in Wales, or the cult of Ossian in Scotland, are 'Legends of a Celtic hermit, lonely sisters and Knights of the Holy Grail' (Betjeman). Although remote, and off the beaten track of the fashionable searchers after the Picturesque, the temple at St Nectan's Kieve was, nonetheless, a private expression of the same sentiment.

75. St Nectan's Kieve. This sombre illustration, with two travellers in admiration before a cascade pouring through an arch, over-topped by a ruined temple, is an epitome of the Picturesque 'sublime'. (Gilbert 1820: ii. 586)

182   Newquay and Bodmin

References: 18th and 19th C (Gen.); C.M. Andrews, The Search for the Picturesque, Aldershot, 1989: 171-2, 213-4 and illustrations.

TREWAN HALL, St Columb Major

SW91 64 : *EX106, GS347*

Cornish tre + [?guan = weak], pronounced TRUAN as spelt in Gascoyne (1699); house and attached garden walls listed grade II*, early 19th C. farm buildings, house, gate-piers each II; medium to large estate, sloping south, 115-100m., on Meadfoot beds, calcareous slate, grit and thin limestone; rainfall 40-45", temperature zone D; now a camping and caravan park. There is an official history.

76. Trewan Hall. The Gothic house erected by John Vivian in 1633, is seen here as it was in 1820. It was remodelled by William White in 1870. (Gilbert 1820: ii. 668)

The mansion of the Vivian family at Trewan is of fifteenth-century origin, and the most important seat in St Columb. When in 1633 John Vivian moved from his old family home at Trenoweth, he considerably altered this old house, building a grand hall, with a plasterwork 'Genesis' ceiling similar to that at Lanhydrock, and recording the date of completion in 1635 on a fireplace. After the death of his son in 1691, the estate passed to his son's granddaughter, Mary, who had married Sir Richard Vyvyan of Trelowarren, in whose family it remained until 1920, although for a number of years it was not occupied.

The house was again extensively rebuilt in the 1860s to the designs of William White, who was probably selected on the evidence of his recent work on St Columb Rectory (q.v.), during the course of which some of the old features, such as the plaster ceiling, were lost. New farm and service buildings were added in a matching Gothic style, which, though artistically apt, might appear pretentious for their humble use.

Lake described the position of Trewan as

> pleasantly seated on the brow of a hill, facing the south, and sheltered by plantations. Its elevated position above S. Columb town, commands an uninterrupted view of a fine picturesque scenery of hill and valley.

The kitchen garden, whose walls are attached to the rear of the house, is entered through an arch. At the end of a path running from this point through the plantation of trees is a small temple-like building, clearly intended to be the focal point of a vista, with a pitched roof over an empty niche with a half-domed ceiling, such as might once have contained a statue, other ornamental object, or perhaps less probably a seat. The illustration in Stockdale depicted deer in front of the Hall in 1824. However, this is the only evidence for a park or paddock at Trewan. The present owners have confined their caravan and camping activities to the adjacent fields, thereby to a great extent preserving the ambience of the house and its immediate grounds.

References: 17th, 18th, 19th (Gen.), 20th C; Illus.

SUPPLEMENTARY LISTS

LESSER-KNOWN HISTORIC GARDENS

The Crag, Polmorla

SW98 71 : *EX106, GS335/336*

A garden of 5 acres (2 ha), on Middle Devonian grey slates; rainfall 35-40", temperature zone D; opened 1983-6 CGOG.

The origin of this garden is described in a recent local history:

> A mile up the valley, just beyond Polmorla, was another iron works, The Factory, (it was first a fuse factory and hence the name). It was started by Mr. G.H. Harris, 'Millwright, Machinist, Brass Founder, Mill Furnisher, Carriage Builder, Agricultural Machinery'. The Crag, a large house on the north

side above the Factory, was built by Mr. Harris for his third wife who survived him.

The garden was laid out on the side of this steep valley at about the turn of the nineteenth century, but had fallen into a decline since its pre-Second World War heyday. It still has great potential, and was being restored and replanted with spring bulbs, rhododendrons and flowering shrubs, but the advancing age of the owner made the preparations necessary for opening no longer possible. This 'Crag' should be distinguished from another, probably better known 'Crag', now a holiday complex at Maen Porth, Falmouth.

References: J.West, St Breock and Wadebridge, Redruth 1991:43.

Dinham, near Wadebridge

SW97 74 : EX106, GS335/336

Cornish dynan = *fort, a diminutive of* dyn, *pronounced* DINam; *house listed grade II, and late 18th, early 19th C. buildings now holiday accommodation also II; small garden, sloping south-west 25-20m., towards the Camel estuary, on Middle Devonian grey slates, in an AONB, and an AGSV; rainfall 35-40", temperature zone D; opened 1983, 1989 CGOG.*

The house at Dinham is of seventeenth-century origins, though it was probably rebuilt in the late eighteenth and early nineteenth centuries, using older material. The garden is modern, with herbaceous and shrub borders, including some unusual plants. A small parterre with box hedging is at present being developed. There are views over the Camel estuary from the woodland walks. Thurston (1930) records an interesting recollection of the Revd I.N. Smith-Pearse:

> In my youth I knew a mighty elm in a sheltered dell sloping to the Camel estuary, popularly said to cover an acre of land. A considerable part is still standing, but split into three parts, possibly from a stroke of lightning. It was the subject of a lawsuit some forty years ago between Miss Yeo of Dinham and Preb. Sanford of St Minver House. The Court gave Mr Sanford possession of the tree with the proviso that he paid Miss Yeo compensation for damage done to the boundary hedge. (p.220)

References: 19th (Gen.) and 20th C.

Harlyn House, Harlyn near St Merryn

SW87 75 : EX106, GS335/336

Cornish *ar = *facing* + lyn = *pond, perhaps here referring to the bay, pronounced* HARlyn; *house listed grade II*, dovecote II*, gate-piers II; the garden at 35m. altitude, in an AONB, an AGSV, and an AGHV, is not significant; private.*

The 'pleasant residence' of Harlyn was formerly the seat of the Tregewe family, passing through the female line, first to the family of Michel, and in 1632 to the Peter family who were originally from Devon. The house, which no doubt incorporates earlier fabric, remodelled and extended, has a date-stone for 1798.

There is a curious dovecote, probably originating in the eighteenth century, which more resembles the modern version on a pole or upright, than the medieval form. There is a substantial central pillar, built of slates, supporting a head with sixty nest holes. 'It belongs to a period when dovecotes were ornamental features and not a necessary source of fresh meat.' (Penhallurick, 1978). The barton became widely known as the site of a rock known as Catacleuse, which was used for the pillars of churches, and fonts, notably at St Merryn and Padstow.

References: 17th, 18th, 19th (Gen.) and 20th C.

Lanteglos by Camelford Rectory, Camelford

SX08 82 : EX109, GS335/336

Cornish nans + eglos = *church, pronounced* lanTEGlos; *in an AGLV; now the* Lanteglos Country House Hotel.

The description in *Lake*, although not specifically mentioning the nature of the garden, is suggestive of ornamental design:

> The handsome rectorial mansion, certainly one of the largest and best in the county, was built by the late rector the Rev. Roger Bird. It is an Elizabethan structure; in one of the gables is a shield of granite bearing the initials and date R.B. 1847. In the lawn is preserved an ancient Norman font with cable mouldings; near by, on a rockery in the centre of an ornamental sheet of water, is placed for preservation the head of an ancient granite cross.

These antiquities were not particularly evident on visiting this pleasant garden, but there is an interesting headstone commemorating a pet dog.

References: 19th (Gen.) C.

Nansough, Ladock

SW87 50 : EX105, GS346

Nanscugh, in Gilbert (1820), perhaps a misprint; Cornish nans + hoch = *pig, pronounced* nanSOW (*to rhyme with* 'cow'); *house listed grade II; grounds south-west sloping 50-30m., on Grampound Grit; rainfall 40-45", temperature zone D; private.*

The house is early nineteenth-century. Gilbert wrote of it: 'The barton of Nanscugh, is the seat of Charles Andrews, esq. who has rebuilt the house, and surrounded it with thriving plantations,' which lie at the bottom of the valley along a stream. The present owners have built steps down from the front lawn, and are developing the ornamental plantings.

References: 18th and 19th (Gen.) C.

Newlyn East Churchyard, Newlyn East

SW82 56 : *EX106, GS346*

Thurston notes that, 'At Newlyn East a fig-tree [*Ficus carica*] is growing out of the south wall of the church, and is propped up by a wooden pole in the ground'. There is an illustration. The tree is still there, and its continued existence is perhaps ensured by a legend that anyone who touches it will die! See also fig-trees at Gwithian and Manaccan.

References: 20th C.

Tolcarne House, Newquay

SW81 61 or 62 : *EX106, GS346*

Cornish tal = *brow, front* + carn = *rock, pronounced* tolCARN; *extinct.*

Gilbert writes: 'Tolcarne, the property of Thomas Tinney, gent. is a modern building, with good gardens and lands, in a high state of cultivation.' Thurston describes and illustrates an unusual elm at this place:

> A few trees close to Newquay, including the well-known arched trees at the gate of Tolcarne House have been referred by Dr C.E. Moss to U[lmus] campestris. The arch of the Tolcarne tree (Pl.xxxi) measures 7 ft. 6in. from the ground to the top. It has been suggested, in connection with the origin of the arch, (a) that the tree fell, and rooted itself again; (b) that a bough was trained downwards, and induced to strike root. The present owner of the house says that, according to tradition, the tree was blown down in a northerly gale, and took root.

Tolcarne, and the tree, have disappeared under expanding Newquay.

References: 18th, 20th C.

Treveddo, Tower Road, Newquay

SW80 61 : *EX104, GS346*

Cornish tre + bedewen = *birch trees, pronounced* treVEDDo; *now the Bredon Court Hotel.*

Newquay grew in popularity as a resort during the nineteenth century. The Tower, built in 1835 for G.W.T. Gregor, a wealthy landowner, being one of the first seaside residences. The outsiders, or 'foreigners' as the locals called them, bought land and built villas which, when it was proposed to build the Atlantic Hotel, led to riots. In 1891, nine years before the hotel was opened, some wealthy residents established golf links on the Warren above Fistral Bay. Treveddo was built alongside The Tower at about this time, perhaps to benefit from the links which it overlooked. At first an A. McCarthy was recorded in Kelly's *Directory* as residing there, but after the First World War it was P.B. Wallace, according to the *Hort. Direct.*, who opened the gardens from 1919 to 1924. The house eventually became the Knowle Links Hotel, and is now the Bredon Court Hotel.

References: 20th C.

ADDITIONAL CONTEMPORARY GARDENS

Ferny Park, Bossiney, Tintagel

SX07 89 : *EX109, GS322*

In an AONB and HC, and an AGSV; opened 1995, NGS.

A half-acre garden, with a stream creating a natural feature.

Grignan, Bolingey near Perranporth

SW763 530 : *EX104, GS346*   OPEN*

Cornish *gruk = *heather* + nans, *pronounced* GRIGnan; *opened 1989-98 CGOG, 1989-97 NGS, three Sundays in May and one in June.*

Reference: Pring (1996: 72-3).

The Japanese Garden, St Mawgan

SW87 66 : *EX106, GS346*   OPEN*

Open daily all year, 1997-8 CGOG.

Reference: C.G. 1997: 36.

Lower Treneague, south of Wadebridge

SW98 71 : *EX106, GS335/336*

In an AGLV and a CNCS; opened 1989-90 NGS.

Described when open as: 'A tree lined valley garden of several acres, partly wild, newly landscaped, still being developed', which can be seen from the road.

Maen Anneth, Roche

SW986 605 : *EX106, GS347*

Cornish maen = *stone* + anneth = *dwelling, pronounced* MAIN ANneth; *opened 1988-91, CGOG.*

Sited at an altitude of 185m., this one and a half acre (0.6 ha) informal garden was begun in 1974. It has been designed to afford protection from exposure to winds, by creating small areas, planted with island beds. Although intended for year-round interest, it is at its peak in the spring.

3. BODMIN

Bodmin is the only town in Cornwall to be mentioned in Domesday, where it was recorded that the Canons of St Petroc owned sixty-eight houses and a market. There seems, then, little doubt that Bodmin was at that time the most populous place in the county and, after receiving its charter in the thirteenth century, remained so until the sixteenth century. Although without a Norman castle, the strong religious life around the original monastery would appear to have been enough to sustain the markets and fairs which brought great wealth with them. An early nineteenth-century house, until recently used as the municipal offices, now stands on the site of the Priory, with its grounds a public park.

After a relative decline in the seventeenth and eighteenth centuries, Bodmin re-emerged in the nineteenth century as a route centre. Polgwin, the house of Charles Hext, for instance, where the garden was once open, was one of several villas built along the old coaching road dropping down into the town from the north. The eventual loss of the town's status has been said to have been in part the consequence of a refusal to allow the railway - the most significant means of communication in the nineteenth century - into the town. The transfer in 1988 of the Law Courts to Truro - which already held the County Hall and Cathedral - spelt the end for Bodmin as the County Town. Over the centuries, with the advancing ease of transport, Cornwall's centre of gravity moved from Launceston, to Bodmin, and finally to a site which is truly central.

A number of important historic gardens are grouped around Bodmin, which, although a convenience for the traveller, does not imply that they were therefore dependent upon the town for their creation. The Robartes family at Lanhydrock, like many others in Cornwall, benefited from the Restoration, and enlarged and improved their house and lands out of the great profits of their mining interests. Glynn, to the east, is another ancient estate, belonging to a family of that name, which in the nineteenth century was purchased as the seat of Sir Richard Hussey Vivian of Truro, who had distinguished himself in the Napoleonic Wars. North of Bodmin there is a cluster of gardens, the greatest among them being Pencarrow, where the creation of a great estate occupied the time and attention of Sir William Molesworth, once he had been relieved of the affairs of state. There had been other estates nearby: Park, once the domain of the Earl of Huntingdon, was long since defunct, while the adjacent Croan Manor with a seventeenth-century house had passed through many hands. Within the Domesday manor of Colquite, a former estate of Lord Marney, to the north-east, are preserved ancient woodlands, which clothe the valley of the Camel river. Tredethy, the seat of the Hexts, a family already mentioned as residing in Bodmin, is sited where these woodlands form the centre-piece of a panoramic view from the house. Another Domesday manor at Lancarffe, where the Hexts had lived before moving to Tredethy, has been developed since the 1930s in a most interesting and varied manner.

Not all of the gardens in this section are centred upon Bodmin. The parish of St Tudy is particularly rich in gardens, both ancient and modern. The oldest is Wetherham, donated to the church as a residence for the Rector in the sixteenth century. During the nineteenth century Lamellen became noted for its rhododendrons under the Magor family, who encouraged Major-General Harrison in his retirement after the Second World War, to their cultivation and hybridization at Tremeer - another old house and garden. At Tremayne Cottage, in the lane up to Wetherham, is a modern garden which belies the name of the house, since the wide range of plants and features is anything but typical of a cottage.

In conclusion, two ancient gardens deserve to be mentioned, even though they are inaccessible to the public. Lavethan, in Blisland parish, is a manor which still possesses the atmosphere of great antiquity, while Trewarne (Trewane), in St Kew parish, although much changed down the centuries, has preserved the remains of medieval features which have yet to yield up their full significance.

CROAN MANOR, Egloshayle

SX02 71 : *EX109, GS335/336*

Cornish crowan = *little hut (Dexter suggests St Crewenna or Crouwenna 1269), pronounced CROWan; house listed grade II, barn, three sets of gate-piers, garden walls and dovecote (remains), kitchen garden walls + two pavilions + gate-piers and iron gates, each II; medium grounds, south facing at 70m. altitude, on Upper Devonian grey slates, with diabase and epidiorite intrusions; rainfall 40-45", temperature zone E; private, opened 1983 CGOG, ownership now changed.*

Croan was anciently a seat of the Roscarrack family, and was sold, after being occupied by others, to Edward Hoblyn of Bodmin. From the Hoblyns it was, through an heiress, eventually bequeathed to the Revd Henry Hawkins Tremayne of Heligan, in whose family the estate remained until recently. The house, which was

77. Glynn. Sketch by Edmund Prideaux, 1727. Notice the railings to the front court, and the two pavilions to the side court. The service buildings were behind, with a detached dovecote higher up.

probably rebuilt for Edward Hoblyn, has a date-stone of 1696, although with earlier origins. The front court has railings and upon the kitchen garden walls there are two early eighteenth-century pavilions, and the remains of a dovecote of the same period. Members of the Tremayne family moved here from Heligan after the Second World War, bringing with them artifacts from their larger and, in post-war circumstances, less manageable estate. They described Croan in 1983, on the single occasion that it has recently been open, as 'an old Cornish garden with rare trees and shrubs'. It is a place of great interest which deserves deeper research.

References: 17th, 18th and 19th (Gen.) C.

GLYNN, Bodmin

SX11 64 : EX107, GS347

Glin Domesday 1086; Cornish glynn = a narrow river valley, pronounced GLIN; house listed II*, mid 18th C. service buildings, coach house, SW lodge with railings, terrace walls and steps (c. 1830), each II; large grounds, south sloping to river 90-25m., on Staddon Grit, head and alluvium, Middle Devonian slate to the north-east, with acid soil, in a SAGLV with an AM (ornamented cross-shaft), and in part a CNCS; rainfall 45-50", temperature zone E; private, until recently the Glynn Research Institute.

Although the manor of Glynn belonged for many generations to an ancient family of that name, the elder branch became extinct in the early fourteenth century, and the estate passed to the Carminows, who carried it by an heiress to the Courtenays. Early in the seventeenth century, however, it was returned by purchase to a younger branch of the Glynn family, who were resident there when Hals, with unaccustomed accuracy of etymology, described the name as

> taken and given from the ancient natural circumstances of the place, where lakes, pools, and rivers of water abound, and groves of trees or copps, flourish and grow.

Two sketches by Edmund Prideaux show Glynn in 1727. The direction from which the main front is drawn is not signified, but it is probably facing south-west. There are courts on two sides enclosed by railings, from which two pavilions with pointed roofs at each end of the right-hand side look down to the river valley below. The second sketch, an oblique view, which is not reproduced here, reveals the service buildings behind the house, and above, a round structure which could be a large dovecote. Below, in our illustration, and to the right, is a large, regularly planted area, presumably an orchard.

The plantations of trees which are such a feature of the whole Glynn valley were already present, some in a mature state. The regular alternation of tall trees with intermediate shrubs, perhaps thorns, in the hedges should be noticed, as well as single specimens all with long naked trunks, which have an artificial appearance as if cut for visual effect. It is now known that it was the practice of the time to prune young trees in this way, both to accelerate growth, and to improve their appearance. (See Banks [1991: 192]).

In 1805 a new house was built by Edmund John Glynn, who, communicating only by writing, was declared lunatic by his uncle, who then had the house remodelled in 1819. Betjeman discerned in the design of the library window the possible influence of Wyatt, but thought it more probable that the architect had been William Richards, to whom a similar house at Sanders Hill in Padstow is more certainly attributed. This remodelled house, however, was destroyed by fire, even before the interior was completed, after which the Glynns disappeared from the district. The shell was bought by Sir Richard Hussey Vivian of Truro, of the St Columb Major family of Vivians, who had distinguished himself in the Napoleonic Wars. He was probably responsible for the portico on the entrance front, the tall pillars supporting broad eaves on the garden front, and the attached orangery and dairy.

The steps down from the house once led to an Italian garden, but the conservatory and dairy are now without roof or glass, and the Italian garden is a lawn. Nevertheless, the huge arboreal rhododendrons and azaleas in the American Garden above the formal bedding are still conspicuous from the road and the railway to the south, where there are two lodges leading in from the east and west. Glynn was listed in the *Hort. Direct.* from at least 1870 to 1908 in the name of Lord Vivian, and became one of Thurston's select gardens. The Vivian family remained here until 1947, after which it was neglected for over twenty years, and feared doomed for demolition, until it was reprieved in 1962 by the arrival of the late Dr Peter Mitchell, a Nobel Prize winner, who eventually restored it to become the Glynn Research Institute. This has recently closed, and the future is uncertain.

References: 17th, 18th, 19th (Hort. & Gen.) and 20th C; Illus.

HENGAR, St Tudy

SX07 76 : EX109, GS335/336

Cornish hen = ancient + car, *pronounced* HENgar; *house with date-stone 1905, and gate-piers listed grade II; medium grounds at 130m. altitude, on Middle/Upper Devonian grey slates; rainfall 45-50", temperature zone E; Hengar Manor Country Club, open to non residents.*

Hengar was the manor house of Penrose-Burden, which extended into the parish of St Breward. It was successively the seat of the Billings, Lowers, Trelawnys and Michells. Rowlandson used to stay here with Matthew Mitchell, a banker, to 'make his charming watercolour sketches of North Cornwall' (Betjeman), although he visited and made drawings of many other places in the county. The estate later came into the Onslow family, and the present house was re-orientated from east to west, for Sir William Wallace Rhoderick Onslow, in 1905 - the year after the former house had burnt down.

The park-like grounds, with two lakes, entered along a drive lined with trees, have now in part been developed as a chalet park, with a nine-hole golf course. An earlier walled garden joined to the north-west side of the rebuilt house is of some interest. It is entered through a central doorway in the far wall to a central path flanked on each side by two large and ancient yew trees. The whole garden is on two levels, parallel to the side of the house, with steps in the centre and both extremities, and with a raised walk around the perimeter on three sides. In the north-east corner there is a deep sunken garden, with steps to a small terrace, having stone seats at each end. From this, further steps lead down to a lower paved level adjoining the house, at one time with formal beds, but now paved over.

References: 17th, 18th, 19th (Gen.) and 20th C; Illus.

LAMELLEN, St Tudy

SX05 77 : EX109, GS335/336

Landmanvel *Domesday 1086; Cornish* nans + *personal name, pronounced* laMELLen; *house listed grade II*, kitchen garden walls, lodge, gate-piers, bridge over River Allen, all mid 19th C., each listed II; grounds of 37 acres (15 ha), listed grade II, in valley sloping west 100-50m., on Upper Devonian grey slates, with acid soil, in an AGLV; rainfall 40-45", temperature zone E; private, opened 1987 CGOG.*

The late Major E.W.M. (Walter) Magor returned from Kenya to Lamellen in 1961, to begin a rescue operation after twenty years of neglect, following the death of his father, E.J.P. Magor. In the ensuing years he himself became an authority on rhododendrons, and for many years was editor of the Rhododendron Society's year book. In 1985 he wrote a definitive history of Lamellen in the *Cornish Garden*.

Lamellen had been mentioned in Domesday, but the name Nansmayl-wyn - or Maylwyn's valley - found in a document of 1280 is probably more nearly the original meaning. A house was built there in 1698, as a date-stone records, by Samuel Furnis. The Magor family originated in Mousehole, and were bankers at Kenwyn, Truro, becoming involved in the founding of the

Redruth Brewery. In 1825 John Penberthy Magor of Penventon (q.v.) had married Elizabeth Ann Moyle, who became the heiress to the Lamellen estate. On moving there in 1849, as *Lake* recorded, he

> built the present tasteful Elizabethan mansion, and made other considerable and judicious improvements, only a few years before his death.

His interest in horticulture while still at Penventon is seen in an article on *Salvia patens* in the *Botanical Register* of 1838, from a specimen exhibited by him at a meeting of the Royal Horticultural Society of Cornwall. There are no records of his 'judicious improvements', which probably referred to the basic tree-planting, but the great reputation of Lamellen dated from the time of his grandson, E.J.P. Magor. He had often visited and loved Chyverton (q.v.), which he hoped to inherit from his aunt, but since she believed that the estate should remain in her husband's family, from 1901 he applied himself seriously to gardening at Lamellen. He

> visited Glasnevin, Edinburgh and Kew (several times), and the 'Truro Daffodil Show' every year, and kept careful records of plants which took his fancy. From the beginning, he was buying plants and planting rhododendrons, which he got from Gill, James Veitch, Reuthe, T. Smith of Daisy Hill Nursery, Newry, Gauntlett, Penjerrick and Menabilly, and even in 1903 Messrs. Regel & Kesselring of St Petersburg.

He obtained seed from E.H. Wilson's expeditions of 1899-1902 and 1903-5, eventually providing material for illustrations in the *Botanical Magazine*. In 1909 he joined Reginald Farrer collecting alpines in Switzerland, but on his marriage had to decline an invitation to the Chinese expedition. From 1911 onwards he began making hybrids, notably between Himalayan species, of which over a hundred were registered, 'Damaris' and 'Lamellen' perhaps being the best.

> As his hybrids and new species came to flowering, he contributed an annual article to the 'Rhododendron Society's Notes' describing them. Under the pseudonym 'Peter the Hermit' he also contributed a regular article to 'Gardening Illustrated' entitled 'Notes from a Cornish Garden'.

Lamellen was listed in the *Hort. Direct.* from 1919 to 1924, after which date Magor used to issue a 'List of Surplus Plants for Sale' to members of the Rhododendron Society, from which he sent plants as far afield as to Joseph Gable in Pennsylvania, Wada in Japan, and Hobbie in Germany. He also later supplied Sir Eric Savill with many of the foundation plants in what is now the Savill Gardens, and the Valley Garden in Windsor Great Park. Towards the end of his life Col. (later General) Eric Harrison came to live at the neighbouring Tremeer (q.v.), where the former owners, the Hexts, were cousins of the Magors. E.J.P. was able to arouse in Harrison an enthusiasm for rhododendrons, of which the General himself became a leading hybridizer.

When Walter Magor took over Lamellen, it had become a jungle, and he was advised by Dr Harold Fletcher of the Edinburgh Botanic Garden, to 'Cut the whole lot down'! However, he struggled to restore the garden, and 'made considerable progress in clearing and re-planting, and found most of his father's foundation plants, and some of his earlier hybrids.' A sale was held of seedlings and young plants, which, although not financially rewarding, gave 'the satisfaction of knowing that all [his] father's young hybrids and the Chinese species were passing into good hands.' E.J.P. Magor had regarded camellias as stove plants, too tender for North Cornwall, and planted hardly any. In latter years, Walter Magor wrote, this had been remedied, and 'we have started small collections of Eucryphias, Hollies, Nothofagus and Podocarpus'. Major Magor died in 1995, but his daughter, Mrs J.D. Peter-Hoblyn, and her husband continue to live at Lamellen.

References: 17th, 19th (Gen.) and 20th C.

LANCARFFE, near Bodmin

SX08 68 : *PF1347, GS335/336*   OPEN

Lancharet, Domesday 1086; Cornish lan + gof = *smith, pronounced* lanCARF; *house, re-orientated 1680, with later alterations, listed grade II*, stables II*, cross II; 4.5 acre (1.8 ha) garden, south facing at 142m., on Middle Devonian grey slate, with acid soil, in a SAGLV, with an AM (inscribed stone); rainfall 50-60", temperature zone E; open 1983-98 CGOG, by appointment.*

The history of Lancarffe is summarized in *Lake*:

> The manor of Lancarffe ... held of the honor of Bodmin, or of S. Petrock, belonged, temp. Richard II., and for several years afterwards, to the family of Whalesborough, who then held it under the Bevilles ... [it was eventually in 1787] sold to Francis John Hext, Esq., father of Admiral William Hext of Tredethy [q.v.], the present proprietor. The mansion has latterly [i.e. in the 1860s] been occupied as a farm house.

In the twentieth century the property was owned by the Rawlings family who, in the 1930s, designed the terraces and planted a maple avenue. The present owner, Richard Gilbert, has developed the grounds by planting many trees and shrubs. He inherited Lancarffe from his father, who bought it from Admiral Sir Bernard Rawlings in 1956. The terraces are edged with two long lonicera hedges, leading above the house to a small garden with steps up to a round pond with a fountain. Beyond this and above the drive is a formal walled garden, with a rectangular pond, well planted with wall shrubs. Further along is a woodland garden with azaleas, rhododendrons, camellias and magnolias. A small hedged area adjoining the stables encloses the ancient cross. This is a most worthwhile garden to visit on the rare occasions it is open.

References: 17th, 18th, 19th (Gen.), 20th C; Illus.

LANHYDROCK, near Bodmin

SX08 63 : *EX107, GS347*   OPEN

Cornish lan *+ saint's name, pronounced* lanHIGHdrock; *house listed grade I, Church, gatehouse, gateway and walls at east entrance, also I, coach house, service buildings, walls etc. to garden east and north of house, and a pair of lodges, each II*, 8 urns, urn in higher garden, Treffry cross, Joseph's cottage, holy well, barn, garage, kitchen garden and gardener's house, stables, east lodge, each II; parkland with gardens of 25 acres (10 ha) listed grade II, sloping east '130-100m.', on Meadfoot Beds, calcareous slate, grit and thin limestone, in part metamorphosed, soil 'ph 4.5 good medium loam', in a SAGLV, and in part a CNCS; rainfall 50-60", temperature zone E; house and park donated to the* National Trust *by Lord Clifden in 1953, open 1983-98 CGOG, 1987, 1991-3, 1997-8 NGS, daily (except Mondays unless Bank Holidays) March (house from April) through October. Official guides.*

Lanhydrock originally belonged to the Priory of St Petroc at Bodmin, but was obtained by the Glynn family of the nearby Glynn at the Dissolution, passing to the Lytteltons. In 1620 the estate was purchased from Lyttelton Trenance (to whom the property had come by marriage) by Sir Richard Robartes (1580-1634), who was then residing in Truro. Although he never lived there himself, he began to build the house at Lanhydrock, which was completed by his son, John (1604-85), between 1635 and 1642. John Robartes was also responsible for the gatehouse and a long avenue of sycamores leading up from Respryn Bridge. The house, at this time with four sides, enclosed an inner court. 'A plan of 1694' described in the official guide, shows a deer park of 259 acres to the south of the avenue ... [much] now occupied by the Great Wood. To the south-east of the house is shown the Flower Garden, now occupied by formal beds [etc], and before the east wing, lies the Bowling Green. Close by is shown the Pheasantry, the Kitchin Garden, the Peare Garden, the New Orchard and the Wilderness, the whole together with the house, the outer court and the stables occupying 22 acres.

This describes a not untypical late-seventeenth century house and grounds, repeated on a greater, or more usually lesser scale at many other sites. In 1740 the Lanhydrock estate passed to Mary Vere Robartes, widow of Thomas Hunt of Cheshire, and on her death in 1758 to her son, George (d.1798).

Following the current fashion for bringing the lawn right up to the house, he demolished the east wing of the house, opening up the inner court and leaving the gatehouse isolated and disconnected - the entrance path, as shown in the Akermann aquatint of 1827 (reproduced on the cover of the official guide), even winding around to avoid it altogether. He also added a double row of beech trees on each side of the sycamore avenue and extended the woodland. On his death the estate passed to a niece, who was married to Charles Agar, Viscount Clifden (1769-1811).

When their son, Thomas James Agar (1808-82), inherited the property in the middle of the nineteenth century, he assumed the name and arms of the Robartes family, using his great wealth, derived from the family's mining interests, for the general improvement of his estate and tenants. Thus he stood among the many prosperous landowners and industrialists who turned to the fashionable architects of the day to enlarge their houses. George Gilbert Scott (he was not knighted until 1872), a renowned Gothicist, would seem a natural choice in 1857 to extend the ancient house, and to re-incorporate the gatehouse in formal gardens beside and in front of the house.

The illustration on page 190, which dates from 1903, shows the parterre to have been quite elaborate, with edged bedding and gravel paths, which may be compared with Nesfield's *broderie* parterre at Tregrehan (q.v.). The paths are now of grass, and the beds contained within box hedging. The Higher Garden behind the house was first laid out as a shrubbery at about this time. The remodelling of the house was put in the hands of Richard Coad, of Liskeard, from Scott's office, who was also turned to after the disastrous fire of 1881 for the rebuilding, by

*78. Lanhydrock. The 'Upper Garden East' in 1903, still with the broderie parterres designed by Gilbert Scott. (*Country Life*)*

which time he had his own practice. In 1870 *Lake* recorded that the 'rows of aged trees [in the Avenue] have latterly been sheltered and protected by parallel rows of thirty young beech trees', and this replacement continued through the nineteenth and into the twentieth century.

The seventh Lord Clifden (1885-1966), who inherited the estate in 1930, began the process of replanting the slopes behind the house (which he described as then being nothing but clumps of Portugal Laurel) with ornamental trees and shrubs more in line with the current trends than the old Victorian shrubberies. The thatched gardener's cottage, last occupied in 1885, was made a feature, and is now used as a shelter. He also purchased the splendid bronze urns, once part of Lord Hertford's collection at the Chateau de Bagatelle in the Bois de Boulogne, which had been modelled for Marie Antoinette by Louis Ballin, goldsmith to Louis XIV.

In 1953 Lord Clifden donated Lanhydrock to the National Trust, although he continued living in the house with his sisters until his death in 1966, the family's occupation ending with the death of his surviving sister in 1969. Since this time the Trust has built on the existing foundations. A semi-circular herbaceous border, with two quadrants, for instance, which had been planted by Lady Clifden in 1914, was in 1972 completed by the addition of two further quadrants, replacing a derelict greenhouse and potting shed. From the top walk of the Higher Garden there is a panoramic view eastwards over the house to the Fowey valley, Caradon Hill and Bodmin Moor beyond. Landhydrock was listed from at least 1870 until 1924 in the *Hort. Direct.*, and was one of Thurston's select gardens.

References: 17th, 18th, 19th (Hort. & Gen.) and 20th C; Illus; J. Nash, Mansions of England, *1841: iii. pl. 6; Manpower Services Commission,* Lanhydrock, *1982.*

LAVETHAN, Blisland

SX09 73 : *EX109, GS335/336*

Cornish, Dexter suggests Ian + Adwen = *saint's name?, pronounced* laVETHan*; house listed grade II*, steps to terrace, gateway to gatehouse, ha-ha, two barns, Holy*

Well House, well house, and medieval cross, each grade II; grounds of 5 acres (2 ha) around the house, south sloping 100-70m., on Middle Devonian grey slates and alluvium, in an AONB, and in part a CNCS; rainfall 40-45", temperature zone E; private, with holiday lettings.

Lavethan is a manor of great antiquity, the house dating from the early to mid sixteenth century, probably with earlier origins. It was partly remodelled with a date-stone of 1653, and again in later centuries. In Norden's day it was the house of Humphry Kempe, whose family had originated in Kent, but who married into old Cornish families, such as the Boscawens, St Aubyns, and Courtenays of Boconnoc. In 1619 they had also purchased Rosteague from the Mohuns.

The estate was at one time much larger, and included a small deer park. The Lavethan Wood is now owned by the Woodland Trust, but some parkland remains, separated from the house by an ha-ha, running down to the Waterloo river. There are three ancient crosses, one believed to be of medieval origin. The approach to the house, by an oak-lined drive, arrives at a flight of steps up to a terrace at the north-west, incorporating earlier stonework. A castellated seventeenth-century gateway 'of particularly fine quality' was re-erected here to form an archway to the gatehouse on the north-west, which had originally been at the Mansion-house on Blisland Green. To the south-east there is a small courtyard garden. Gilbert observed that the

> planted hills and vales belonging to this charming villa, are so connected with those of the vicarage, that they must appear to the stranger, as one and the same place ... The house is old, and has lately undergone considerable improvement, and near it are fine gardens, lawns, and groves. The lower parts of these diversified grounds, are washed by the waters of the Camel, and together with the church tower, form the most beautiful assemblage of rural scenery, which is to be found on the banks of the river.

References: 17th, 18th and 19th (Gen.) C; Illus.

MAIDENWELL, Cardinham*

SX14 70 : EX109, GS335/336

Maiden refers to the Virgin Mary; 25 acre (10 ha) garden, south-east sloping, at 238m. altitude, on coarse grained granite, with acid soil, in an AONB, and an AGSV; rainfall 50-60", temperature zone F; opened 1984-90 CGOG, 1988 NGS. There was an official leaflet.

The garden is centred on a fourteenth-century farmhouse, reroofed in a Spanish style in the 1950s. It was created by the late Marika Hanbury Tenison, a well-known cookery writer, from about 1960. This could only be accomplished on this elevated and exposed site by the establishment of windbreaks on all sides except the east, where the valley drops away. The garden boundaries include ornamental areas, woodland and water meadows. The more recent plantings were chosen

> both for rarity value and their affinity with the surrounding landscape. This [was] an important aspect at Maidenwell and every effort [continued] to be made to complement distant views and the 'feel' of the surrounding moor rather than excluding it.

One recent development was a new heather garden, interplanted with hebes, brooms and dwarf rhododendrons. This merged into a broad planting of evergreen azaleas. *Betula jacquemontii* were chosen to augment the common birches planted in this new garden, guaranteeing white stems from an early age. An attempt was made to achieve autumn and winter interest by special attention to coloured stems and good leaf-colour. There are several *Fothergilla monticola*, a *Cercidiphyllum japonicum*, and the unusual *Daphnephyllum macropodum*. A fountain stands at the top of the garden as a memorial to Marika, Robin Hanbury Tenison's first wife, but the property passed into other hands in 1990, and is no longer open. The description given here refers, therefore, to the garden before that date, which, in view of the unusual nature of the site, and the measures taken to cultivate it, seems worth preserving.

References: 20th C.

MICHAELSTOW HOUSE, see Tregenna House

PENCARROW, Washaway, near Bodmin

SX03 71 : EX109, GS335/336

Pengvare Domesday 1086; Cornish pen + car in the plural, pronounced penCARRo, as in arrow; house late 17th or early 18th C. origins on an earlier site, partly rebuilt 1760-75, probably by Robert Allanson of York, remodelled c. 1844, listed grade II, pair of lodges, lower lodge, cottages, fountain, grotto and rock garden, garden house, walled kitchen garden, ice-house, each II; garden of 50 acres (20 ha) listed grade II, house south facing, rising 75-150m., on Middle Devonian grey slates, with acid soil, with an AM (Pencarrow Round); rainfall 40-45", temperature zone E; private, open 1983-98 CGOG, 1995-8 NGS, daily (except Friday and Saturday) Easter to mid-October. Official guide.*

79. Pencarrow. 'On [the] eastern side is a rockery, in imitation of one of the neighbouring tors, and composed of rocks of time-worn granite, with shrubs interspersed; dense masses of American plants, with lofty trees in the background, crown the rockery, bound the garden on the west as well as on the east, and present a gay appearance when in full flower.' (Twycross 1846: 27)

The origins of Pencarrow are succinctly summarized in *Hitchins*:

> The barton of Pencarrow was inhabited by the Pencarrows until the days of Henry VII. in which reign it was forfeited by attainder, its possessor siding with Richard III. against Henry. After this event it was successively in the families of Walker and Molesworth. John Molesworth, a younger son of a Northamptonshire family, settled at Pencarrow in the reign of Elizabeth.

The subsequent history of the Molesworth family, and their alliance with the St Aubyns is clearly outlined in the genealogical table in their official guide, and need not detain us here.

The present house was remodelled in about 1844 by George Wightwick, and the grounds, which are our primary concern, laid out by Sir William Moleswoth, the eighth Baronet, who inherited the estate in 1831, when aged twenty-one, shortly after becoming an active politician. He rose to some merit, and as the Chief Commissioner of Works arranged for the opening of Kew Gardens to the public. The grounds at Pencarrow were planned and executed between his political activities, and with the assistance of his local constituents, with whom he was popular for his help through the bad times before the repeal of the Corn Laws.

The condition of Pencarrow in 1820 had been described by Gilbert:

> The gardens and shrubberies are large and flourishing. The deer park is dotted over with firs, and other straggling trees, and skirted with umbrageous woods, which form in the distance, a diversity of pleasing swells.

Molesworth began with the lawn in front of the house, creating an elaborate semi-elliptical Italian Garden, with a central fountain copied from that in the Piazza Navonna in Rome, with vases and an ornate balustrade. The gardens were described in 1842 as 'beautifully laid out, in beds of various forms and devices,' planted with 'the newest sorts of Dahlias, and of the choicest Pansies, Verbenas, Petunias, and Alstromerias', which is in contrast to the stark simplicity of the present design. Between 1831 and 1834 a rockery, with a grotto and cave, were formed by the gardener, Mr Corbett, along the western side. A writer in the *Gardeners' Chronicle* of 1842 described this as

> one of the best specimens of rockwork we have seen ... the stone is brought from the adjoining hills ... The stones were not dug out of a quarry, but were lying on the surface of the soil, with the lichen, moss &c., growing about them; consequently they have a more natural effect than if they were taken out of the earth.

These rocks, some of immense weight, were carted by his tenants, and numbered in his garden book. Brent Elliott has qualified his description of Corbett 'as a pioneer of naturalism' by adding, 'although later rock gardens placed greater emphasis on laying stones on their natural bed.' But any comparison of igneous granite with the bedding of sedimentary rocks is clearly inappropriate. Corbett was actually attempting to reproduce the haphazard distribution of granite blocks on a 'clitter slope', as seen on Bodmin Moor, which Twycross explicitly confirms, hence his retention of their surface plant growth, and the notes on position in the garden book. The journal-writer continued:

> In this rockery are planted most of the best varieties of rock plants ... In one part an artificial bog is formed [bogs are frequent on the Bodmin Moors], which has every appearance of being natural ... In this bog we found, to our astonishment, that singular little plant the Dionaea muscipula or Venus's fly-trap ... Here also we found Pinguicula grandiflora, and Parnassia Caroliniana, in most vigorous growth.

The present state of the rockery does not exactly leave the impression here suggested. It seems probable that the camellias, Himalayan rhododendrons, pieris, yuccas etc., illustrated in Luckhurst's article of 1878, were later plantings, and that the maturity of supposedly 'dwarf' conifers, which can still overtake the unwary, may have altered the original conception.

In about 1842, William Molesworth followed these innovations by planting the main, mile-long drive with a collection of trees raised from seed obtained from the mid-century plant hunters, such as William Lobb, Sir Joseph Hooker and David Douglas, and from Veitch's nursery in Exeter. His last task was to plant up the Green Drive leading to the Camelford Gate, and an American Garden of conifers, rhododen-

80. Pencarrow. Here the rockery in the late 1870s is reaching maturity. (J. Hort. 1878: ii. 70)

drons and some camellias under a canopy of beech and elm. Before his death in 1855 he was able to boast that he had planted a specimen of every conifer, save ten, capable of growing in the Cornish climate. The planting was continued by his sister, Mrs Ford, and the succeeding members of his family. Corbett, his gardener (who is on record as having invented 'Corbett's hygrothermanic apparatus' for heating greenhouses!), was succeeded by another notable gardener and horticultural writer, A.C. Bartlett.

As early as 1842, a fine and healthy specimen of *Araucaria imbricata* (now *A. araucaria*), about five feet (1.7m.) in height had been recorded as growing at the base of the rockery. It is claimed that it was at Pencarrow that a guest, Charles Austin, was the first to remark on seeing his first *Araucaria*, that: 'It would be a puzzle for a monkey'. A fine avenue of Monkey Puzzles was later planted, leading from the Double Lodges at the far end of the garden, which, though somewhat bedraggled with age, are still surviving.

Among other features of the garden should be mentioned the lake, with the nearby wishing well, the ice-house, and palm house, the 'Rounds' ancient encampment after which Pencarrow may have been named, the cockpit by the drive, the Celtic cross, and the ample kitchen gardens, now commercially producing deliciously superior strawberries. The garden was listed in the *Hort. Direct.* from at least 1870 until 1916, and was one of Thurston's select gardens. Much of the grounds became derelict during the Second World War, and from then until his untimely death in 1998, Lt.-Col. Sir Arscott Molesworth-St Aubyn cleared and replanted. 'By 1991 he had planted out more than 160 different species of specimen conifers ... many introduced since Sir William's day, more than 570 different species and hybrids of the genus Rhododendron, and more than sixty different Camellias.'

References: 17th, 18th, 19th (Hort. & Gen.) and 20th C; Illus.

SKISDON LODGE, St Kew

SX023 770 : *EX109, GS335/336*

House, and two sets of gate-piers, each listed grade II; small grounds, south facing at 40m. altitude, on Upper Devonian slates; rainfall 35-40", temperature zone E; house in holiday flats, with the coach-house in separate ownership.

Skisdon Lodge is possibly eighteenth-century or earlier in origin, but it was heavily remodelled in the mid nineteenth century, by which time it was considered to be the chief residence in the parish of St Kew. Gilbert had described it, with an illustration, as 'a very neat mansion, situated in a verdant paddock, and surrounded with fine shrubberies, walks, and gardens' - words which remain applicable today.

References: 18th, 19th (Gen.) and 20th C; Illus.

TREDETHY, Helland, near Bodmin

SX06 71 : *EX109, GS335/336*

Cornish tre + ?, *pronounced* treDETHy; *house listed grade II; medium to large estate, south facing slope, from 100m., on Middle Devonian grey slate, with acid soil, in a SAGLV; rainfall 40-45", temperature zone E; now the* Tredethy Country House Hotel, *open to non-residents.*

Tredethy, sometime a seat of the families of May and Lang, 'became the property of the Hext family through the marriage of Francis John Hext, Esq., grandfather of the present proprietor with Margaret, daughter of Elias Lang, Esq., and heir of her brother who died without issue' (*Lake*). Gilbert described the house as

> a neat modern mansion, delightfully situated on the brow of a steep woody hill, on the western side of the river Camel. The lawns, and outgrounds, are richly clothed with timber, and the whole barton is in a high state of cultivation.

Except that the house, of early seventeenth-century origin, was 'improved' and extended, as a date-stone announces, in 1868, Gilbert's description is still applicable.

Additional and more specialized trees have been planted on the higher levels, within sight of the house, to create a magnificent panorama from the front terrace. Among the trees by the path there is a small dogs' cemetery, and in the lower garden a lake. This is one of Thurston's select gardens, which was listed in the *Hort. Direct.* from 1908 to 1924, under the name of various members of the Hext family. In 1930 it became the home of Prince Chula of Thailand, whose brother, Prince Bira, achieved celebrity as a racing driver. It was a hostel during the Second World War and is now an hotel.

References: 17th, 18th, 19th (Gen.) and 20th C; Illus.

TREGENNA HOUSE, Michaelstow, near Blisland

SX07 78 : *EX109, GS335/336*

From the early 1900s renamed Michaelstow House; *Cornish, see Tregenna Castle; lodge, with date-stone 1876,* and entrance gate-piers etc. each listed grade II; gate-piers east of house II; medium grounds, house north-east facing at 110m. altitude, on Middle/Upper Devonian grey slate, with acid soil; rainfall 45-50", temperature zone E; now the Michaelstowe Holiday Village.

Tregenna was completed in 1869 by William Hocken, a native of the parish, on his return after accumulating 'considerable additional wealth as a Manchester merchant.' It was built, so Maclean tells us,

> upon lands which have been in the possession of his family for several generations. The principal front is constructed of fine granite ashlar, and the other portion of local stone of considerable beauty of colouring. The whole is completed in the most costly manner, whilst the stables and other auxiliaries are very perfect of their kind, the gardens being well stocked and prolific.

Lake also describes the property in unusually glowing terms, continuing:

> On the lawn before the southern front is a large circular pond or basin, the circumscribing wall of which is of wrought granite. On the eastern side are excellent walled gardens, with green houses, and conservatories of the most perfect description, and arranged in the best possible manner. The chief entrance to the grounds is now being constructed in a style suitable to the elegant place to which it leads.

The completed entrance remains impressive, leading along a curved drive, planted with ornamental trees, beside a round pond, to a view of the house across the front lawn. To the rear of the house the 'granite basin' has been removed from its 'circumscribing walls' on the lower terrace, to lie in the grass above the steps on the upper terrace, while the fountain lies in a far corner. The walled gardens, at a great depth below the eastern side of the house, now serve as a car-park. There has been considerable modification in creating the holiday village, but there are still interesting relicts of an opulent Victorian estate, built and walled in granite ashlar.

References: 19th (Gen.).

TREMEER, St Tudy

SX06 76 : EX9, GS335/336   OPEN*

Cornish tre + meur = *big or great, pronounced* treMEER; *house listed grade II; about 13.5 acre (5.5 ha) garden south-east sloping, 110-90 m., on Middle/Upper Devonian grey slates, with acid soil; rainfall 40-45", temperature zone E; private, open 1983-98 CGOG, 1987, 1991-8 NGS, daily April through September. In 1998 became a residence of the present Govenor of the Bank of England.*

It is recorded in *Hitchins* that:

> Tremeer ... which was the ancient seat of the Lowers, was the birth-place of Sir William Lower, who distinguished himself as a dramatic writer, and of Dr. Richard Lower an eminent physician in the reign of Charles II. This gentleman coming into Cornwall when George Fox, the celebrated Quaker, was a prisoner in Launceston gaol, paid him a visit; and was so convinced of the truth of his doctrines that he embraced the principles for which he was imprisoned, and joined that community. Dr. Lower distinguished himself as an author in "a treatise on the heart".

A Dr Reed bought the property in 1790, and built the core of the house in 1798. Gilbert added that he also 'adorned it with shrubberies and gardens'. It passed to Admiral Hext through marriage to Dr Reed's daughter, and was enlarged by his family in 1899 (date-stone), in an 'Arts and Crafts' style. The English Heritage report suggests that the terraces on the south-east may have been of seventeenth-century origin: there were lawns and formal beds in front of the house, and paths, with a brook flowing at the lower end of the garden, which had been tapped to feed a leat, probably for a mill.

It was here that Maj.-Gen. E.G.W. Harrison came in 1939 in retirement to hunt, and, following Churchill's example, to take up painting. Within a fortnight of his arrival, however, he was recalled to the army, and was not able to settle at Tremeer until 1946. The inspiration for his interest in the breeding of rhododendrons and camellias came from E.P.J. Magor, who at Lamellen (q.v.), a few miles away, had one of the finest collections in Cornwall. He began hybridizing with the help of the Magors, and George Johnstone of Trewithen, and benefited from the new varieties which had been introduced from the expeditions of Farrer, Forrest, Wilson and Kingdon Ward.

The garden at Tremeer was remodelled. The formal beds were grassed over to form a wide lawn, and beyond this Gen. Harrison fashioned large beds in which to plant his rhododendrons, with grass paths winding between. The leat was extended to form a wide lake on the lower levels. With military precision, manuscript books were kept from the start of his hybridizing experiments, which remain with the house. At this stage, except for plants received from Lamellen or Trewithen, the garden was still immature.

In 1961, however, Gen. Harrison married Mrs Roza Stevenson of Tower Court, Ascot, widow of J.B. Stevenson, chairman of the RHS Rhododendron Committee, and editor of *The Species of Rhododendron* (1930). She brought

81. Tremeer. The terracing is thought to be seventeenth-century. In 1899 another storey was added to the 1798 house in a not inappropriate 'Arts and Crafts' style. (Twycross 1846: 79)

with her many mature plants to add to his collection. At this time Gen. Harrison himself possessed 1,000 rhododendrons and 300 camellias, to which were now added 200 rhododendrons, and about as many azaleas from Tower Court. In 1978 he eventually felt that it was time for him to give up, and leave the garden to others, who have preserved if not developed it. Gen. Harrison's great reputation for rhododendrons must not, however, obscure the fact that he planted a great variety of other species to extend the flowering season, and created a bank of heathers, cistus and dwarf azaleas on a slope at the rear of the house. Now that it has reached maturity a casual visitor might be forgiven for imagining that this is one of the great historic gardens, rather than an entirely post-Second World War creation.

References: 17th, 18th, 19th (Gen.), 20th C; Illus.

TREWARDALE, Blisland

SX10 71 : *EX109, GS335/336*

Cornish tre + [?], uncharacteristically pronounced TREWerdale; house listed grade II*, carriage house and stable, ha-ha, and gate-piers each II; medium estate, south-west sloping 150-130m., on Middle Devonian grey slate, and alluvium by stream, with acid soil, in a SAGLV, with AMs (crosses); rainfall 45-50", temperature zone E; private, occasionally open.

Trewardale is described in *Lake* as

> pleasantly situated in a finely wooded lawn, with its principal front to the south ... The grounds, which are tastefully and judiciously laid out, are well watered by a tributary to the Camel.

This was formerly the seat of the Robyns family, who became bankers, and were related by marriage to Col. Robyns Malone of Trevaylor (q.v.). From them it was purchased by William Browne, who married Honour Spry and settled here in about 1680. Their date-stone, WB - HB 1680, is found on the reconstructed gateway near the walled garden adjacent to the west of the house. The house itself originated in 1773, and was extended in 1839, after the estate had passed by marriage to the Revd John Basset Collins, whose mother was an aunt of Lord de Dunstanville of Tehidy (q.v.). It has remained with the Collins family ever since.

There are two drives: the northern, or rear drive from the east is of beech; the southern enters through unusual castellated gate-piers with railings, along a drive amply edged with lawns, planted with various ornamental trees and shrubs. To the south of this drive, sloping steeply to the stream, is a now derelict walled garden, which, as that near the house, is without walls on the southern side. The carriage house has a wall sundial, and the lawn in front of the main house runs down to a finely constructed early ha-ha. This is a well-preserved eighteenth- and early nineteenth-century estate, whose chief ornamental plantings are along the drive. The gardens were listed in the *Hort. Direct.* in 1890 and 1891, in the name of Mrs Collins.

References: 18th, and 19th (Gen.) C; Illus.

TREWARNE, St Kew

SX04 78 : *EX109, GS335/336*

Originally (and on OS map) Trewane; Cornish tre + gwern = alder trees, pronounced treWARN; house listed grade II*, gatehouse (possibly 19th C. 'folly' using older materials) II, well house II, gate-piers II; small grounds, south sloping 110-90m., on Middle Devonian grey slates, with elvan intrusions, in an AGLV; rainfall 40-45", temperature zone E; private.

Trewarne, or Trewane as until recently it was usually known, is described by Pevsner as one 'of the most perfect Cornish mid C17 manor houses (c.1645), with garden, garden wall, and contemporary entrance.' The estate came into the possession of the Nicholl family, who were related to the Nicholls of Penvose, in 1525. They lived there 'in great respectability' for four generations, before the present house was rebuilt. It is reputed that about this time Charles II sheltered here as Prince of Wales and, after the Restoration, presented the family with two silver warming pans 'for the comfort of the ladies of the Manor' - perhaps because he had not been too cosy there himself! At the rebuilding, the old tower was retained. It may once have had a flat roof with a castellated parapet, for the house seems to have lost a top floor, which might have been gabled, since a number of coping stones, finials, and scrolled gable-ends were found in the garden, and the steps from the gatehouse are constructed from mullions.

The steps lead down from a walled garden, or court in front of the house to a large pond, which, since Gilbert had written of the 'remains of good gardens, and fish-ponds', may have been formed by joining up smaller ponds. In the garden to the east of the house is a well in an arched recess, which is reputed to be an holy well, over which once stood a chapel, believed to have been licensed in 1150. A fifteenth-century lantern cross of Catacleuse stone once stood in the grounds, which made the rounds of the houses of subsequent owners of Trewarne, ending up in St Neot churchyard.

References: 17th, 18th, 19th (Gen.) and 20th C; J. Harris, The Artist and the Country House, Sotheby 1995: 178.

WATERGATE, Trelill*

SX04 78 : *EX109, GS335/336*

Garden of 3 acres (1.2 ha), sloping south-west from 90m., on Middle Devonian grey slates, with acid soil, in an AGLV; rainfall 40-45", temperature zone E; opened 1984-97 CGOG, 1989, 1994, 1997 NGS.

Walter Magor of Lamellen, a near neighbour, wrote in his obituary of Capt. J.N. Hicks, RN, that at Watergate

> he created almost entirely by his own efforts a delightful shrub garden, in which he planted some of the most attractive camellias, magnolias, rhododendrons and other flowering shrubs available. Nor were herbaceous and bulbous plants overlooked. At the Truro Show, he was successful particularly with his daffodils, and also with camellias. (C.G.1974: 33)

The grounds lie in a sheltered valley, where the stream which runs through it has been used to create a water garden with a variety of primulas and other moisture-loving plants. This garden has been maintained and developed since 1975 by Lt.-Col. G.B. Browne, the size and quality of planting being compared by David Hunt to those included by Thurston in his survey of the premier Cornish gardens in the 1930s.

Reference: Pring (1996: 122).

SUPPLEMENTARY LISTS

LESSER-KNOWN HISTORIC GARDENS

Colquite, St Mabyn

SX05 70 : *EX109, GS335/336*

Chilcoit, Domesday 1086, Cornish, Dexter suggests kyl = nook + cos = wood, pronounced colQUITE; very large estate, in all 388 acres (157 ha), south sloping to river from 110-20m., on Middle Devonian grey slates, with acid soil, in a SAGLV, and CNCS in part; rainfall 40-45", temperature zone E; private.

In the sixteenth century Colquite was the manor of the Marney family, of Layer Marney Hall in Essex, although the

> old mansion ... [of which there are remains], together with a detached chapel, was taken down some years ago, and a plain modern house erected as a future family residence [for the Deeble Peters].

Gilbert continues:

> The manor of Colquite, has some of the most beautiful wood and rock scenery which accompany the windings of the Camel. The views at, and a little to the north of Dunmeer Bridge, are particularly bold and picturesque.

Colquite Woods are now maintained by the Forestry Commission. The immediate surroundings are in lawns, but there are interesting modern geometrically-designed formal herb beds in the walled garden. The house and ancilliary buildings have recently been refurbished to create a shooting estate. There is also a farm.

References: 17th, 18th, 19th (Gen.), 20th C; Illus.

Park, Egloshayle

SX03 71 : *EX109, GS335/336*

Extinct.

Mentioned by Leland (1535) as the 'Manor Place' of 'Hastinges Erle of Huntendune', Park was anciently the seat of the Peverells. Hals, in the 1730s, stated that:

> On this lordship ... those gentlemen had their deer-park, some of the walls and fences being yet standing; their tower-house, and other buildings answerable, their gardens, walk and fish-ponds beneath the same, the ruins whereof are yet extant.

By the end of the eighteenth century, the estate had decayed, the remains of the mansion surviving only in the stables to a farmhouse, now in a neat garden.

References: 17th, 18th and 19th (Gen.) C.

Penvose, St Tudy

SX05 77 : *EX109, GS335/336*

Cornish pen + fos = dyke, pronounced penVOSE; grounds, north-west sloping, 100-50m., on Upper and Middle Devonian grey slates, in an AGLV, and in part a CNCS; rainfall 40-45", temperature zone E; farm.

In the time of Norden (*c.* 1590) Penvose was the seat of Humphry Nicholl, whose ancestor Otho was MP for Lostwithiel in 1436. In Gilbert's time the house, built in 1640 by Anthony Nicholl, MP (d. 1658) had

> long been stripped of that splendour and dignity, which once graced its apartments ... The greater part of the old buildings are yet standing, and some of the windows are beautified with stained glass, displaying the arms of Nichol, impaling those of Specott, Mohun, Prideaux, Giffard, Rous, and some others. The grounds are very beautifully wooded.

Maclean, writing in 1879 confirmed that the

> Mansion House at Penvose is still standing and is now a farmhouse. It is approached through a garden, entered by an arched gateway in front, having a square hoodmoulding, on the drop-ends of which are the initials A.N. and within the spandrils the figure 1646, shewing that it was erected by Anthony Nicholl in that year. The house consists of two portions at right angles to each other, which, with a partly ruined portion, enclose a small quadrangle, which is bounded by a long building, now used as a store. This extends to the main road and adjoins the entrance.

There were more recent farm buildings dated '1817' and 'S.T. K[ekewich]. 1847'. The woodlands are along the River Allen, and especially around the site of the old manor to the north.

References: 17th, 18th and 19th (Gen.) C.

Polgwin, Castle Street, Bodmin

SX07 67 : *EX107, GS347*

Also Polgwyn, Cornish pol + guyn = white, fair, pronounced polGWIN; town garden sloping south from c. 90m., on Middle Devonian grey slate, with acid soil; rainfall 50-60", temperature zone E; house in apartments, with relict garden.

The old coaching road from the north entered Bodmin down Castle Road and Castle Street. Among the large villas on the east side of the road is Polgwin, opened in 1908, as reported in the *Hort. Direct.*, by Charles Hawkins Hext, manager of the Liskeard District Bank, who in 1910 moved to Trebah (q.v.), and continuing thereafter under H.D. Foster, another banker, until 1924. The house is approached by a curved drive, with thick plantations to the right, revealing the house with steps down from a terrace on to a lawn.

References: 20th C.

The Priory, Bodmin

SX07 66 : *EX107, GS347*

On the site of St Petroc's Priory, the present early 19th C. house, listed grade II; medium sized park, at 90m. altitude, on Middle Devonian slate, on an HS; rainfall 50-60", temperature zone E; house, Bodmin Municipal Offices until May 1992, with residual garden, grounds a public park.

Gilbert wrote:

> The site of the priory is now occupied by a neat modern mansion, the seat of Walter Raleigh Gilbert, esq. It has some excellent gardens and shrubberies, and the lawn is enlivened by a beautiful fresh water lake.

William Pennington, Mayor of Bodmin, from a family of bell-founders, became a tenant of the remains of the Priory in 1765, on condition that he erected a mansion on the site. He bought the freehold in

82. The Priory, Bodmin. The house built by William Pennington in the last years of the eighteenth century, and its lake, have both survived. (Gilbert 1820: ii. 629)

1788, having fulfilled the conditions some twenty years earlier, the house passing to Gilbert by marriage to his niece. The lake and its surrounds survive; the remainder of the grounds are a public park.

References: 18th, and 19th (Gen.) C; Illus.

St Benet's, Lanivet

SX03 63 : *EX107, GS347*

Tower listed grade II*, 18th C. pinnacle II; very small grounds, east facing at 90m. altitude, on metamorphosed Meadfoot Beds; rainfall 45-50", temperature zone E; now an hotel.

St Benet's is an early fifteenth-century Benedictine religious house, which passed to the Courtenay family following the Dissolution. After 1720 much of the building was demolished, but in 1817, the Revd F.V.J. Arundell, who had much improved Landulph Parsonage (q.v.), 'fitted it up with much taste' as a residence. 'The remains are in a narrow valley, almost surrounded by wood, with a rapid stream in the front which,' thought Stockdale, who always had an eye for the picturesque, 'adds greatly to the beauty of this romantic spot ...' of which he himself made a drawing. *Murray* also believed that it would 'have a charm for a sketcher'. As it stands Pevsner felt it looked 'essentially C19 Gothic, with C15 windows built into a regular 1859 façade.' Today, McCabe thought it 'beautifully kept, with an attractive garden in front.'

References: 17th, 18th, 19th (Gen.), 20th C; Illus.

ADDITIONAL CONTEMPORARY GARDENS

See also MAIDENWELL, TREMEER *and* WATERGATE *in the main section.*

Bodwannick Manor Farm, near Lanivet

SW03 65 : *EX107, GS347*   OPEN*

Open 1997-8 NGS, one Sunday each in April, May and June.

Butt's Parc, Churchtown, St Tudy

SX06 76 : *EX109, GS335/336*

Cornish parc = *field; opened in 1985-6 CGOG.*

A garden of flower beds and herbaceous border, with an additional four acres (1.6 ha) of meadow.

Kingberry, Bodmin

SX07 67 : *EX107, GS347*   Open*

1 acre (0.4 ha) garden; open 1997-8 NGS, one Sunday each in June and August.

Lower Hamatethy, St Breward

SX09 78 : *EX109, GS335/336*

Hamotedi, *Domesday 1086; Cornish* *havos = *shieling, i.e. marginal land + ?, pronounced* HAMatethy; *in a SAGLV, an AGSV, and an AGHV; opened 1983-90 CGOG and NGS.*

This new and remarkable garden is situated on a site sloping from 160 to 150m., on the high moor, in a wooded valley with a boulder-strewn stream running through. It was planted with shrubs, bulbs and perennials among the natural rocks, with a bog garden, and extensive use of ground cover. Since a change of ownership the garden has not been opened, so that its present condition is not known.

References: 17th, 18th and 19th (Gen.) C.

Newton House, Lanhydrock

SX09 630 : *EX107, GS347*   OPEN*

Part of the Lanhydrock estate, 3 acre garden (1.2 ha) in a SAGLV; open 1996-8 NGS, two Sundays in June. Came on the market mid 1998.

References: 20th C.

Oak Lodge, Nanstallon, near Bodmin

SX019 676 : *EX107, GS347*

In a SAGLV; opened 1995-7 NGS.

A developing seven-acre woodland garden.

Old Mill Herbary, Hellandbridge

SX065 715 : *EX109, GS335/336*   OPEN*

In a SAGLV; open 1987-98 CGOG, 1988, 1991-4 NGS, daily (except Wednesday) April to mid October.

Reference Pring (1996: 87-8).

Tremayne Cottage, St Tudy

SX065 760 : *EX109, GS335/336*

Cornish tre + men = *stone, pronounced* treMAIN; *opened 1985 CGOG, 1991 NGS.*

A fine established garden of two and a half acres (1 ha) including woodland. Many of the trees and flowering shrubs have matured, presenting a pleasing show of colour and foliage in their season. There is a rose garden, a well-designed large water garde; a pool stocked with carp, and a small aviary.

Wetherham, St Tudy

SX06 75 : *EX109, GS335/336*

Opening in 1998 CGOG, subject to planning permission.

References: 19th (Gen.) C.

5
Bude and Launceston

1. BUDE and NORTH-EAST CORNWALL

The gardens in this present district are widely scattered and, in contrast to the previous sections, they are distributed between two Ordnance Survey maps (Landranger 190 and 201). Their division here into three groups has been made simply for the sake of convenience, an arrangement which in itself illustrates most clearly a point made in the Introduction, that the towns in Cornwall do not naturally form the nucleus of more than a relatively small area. They serve more as useful location points for the gardens than as any indication of the influence they may have exerted in their creation, indeed some of the estates came into existence quite independently of, and sometimes prior to the town's existence.

The first of our groups, to the extreme north of the county, on the OS Landranger 190 map, in a quite striking manner also confirms another of the observations made in the Introduction - namely that gardens along the north coast, open to the sea and ravages of the north and north-west winds, are thin on the ground. For instance, along this strip, west of the A39 from Port Isaac to the county border at Morwenstowe, no more than six places received a mention in our sources as possessing any sort of garden. Indeed, even among this small number, only two were of any significance, while four of them are now extinct. Moreover, except for Bude, which is not of any great antiquity, and perhaps Camelford, there is no town of substance in the whole of this region north of Wadebridge. This is not to say, of course, that there were no settlements or old manor houses in this area, where they are probably just as frequent as in other localities, but they were not in situations that encouraged their development into mansions with parks, or were such as would lead to the creation of new estates during the years of prosperity.

It might be thought fortuitous, or merely a consequence of the sources used, that all of these six gardens lie in, or north of Bude. But it is not without significance that of these only Stowe, the great house of John Grenville, Earl of Bath, ever made any mark in the county, and then chiefly by reason of the extraordinary eventuality that it seemed no sooner built, than it was pulled down again, as being inconvenient. To the garden historian, Tonacombe alone retains any interest - not so much that it was ever very important in itself, but since, probably because it was isolated, it has survived as a relatively intact example of a Tudor manor house.

Ogbeare Hall, some way to the south, and sited well inland on a tributary of the River Tamar, only a mile or two from the Devon border, has so far been left out of account. Nevertheless, even though more favourably placed than those previously mentioned, this estate also fell into a long decline from Elizabethan times until it was revived late in the nineteenth century. Its position, at a distance from Launceston, would not justify its being held over to the next section, although in character it might more reasonably be identified with other properties along the mid-reaches of the Tamar, such as Polapit and Werrington Park, than with the other six gardens, away north of Bude.

These two latter parks, however, as well as Penheale Manor and the neighbouring Treludick, clearly do fall within the ambit of Launceston, even though ranged along the lower southern-most edges of the Landranger 190 map. They have therefore been grouped with other mid-eastern Cornish gardens, to follow in the next section.

MERKJASTEINN, Flexbury, Bude

SX21 07 : *EX111, GS307/308*

The name is Flemish, now changed to Foster Melliars; a small garden, at c. 15m. altitude, on Bude Formation sandstone and blown sand; rainfall 35-40", temperature zone E; house in apartments with residual garden.

Merkjasteinn is situated with its entrance opening into East Fairholme Road, Flexbury. The house was built by Robert Aubrey Foster-Melliar in the early years of the twentieth century, with a name, no doubt, derived from some undiscovered connection with Belgium. After his death it became for a time a school, and is now in apartments. Robert himself was the son of the Revd Andrew Foster-Melliar, Rector of Sproughton in Suffolk, a regular correspondent to the *Journal of Horticulture*, who was an expert on roses and author of *The Book of the Rose* (1894), which went through four editions. His son had written a small volume of poems and two novels, so it was probably his horticultural ancestry and literary reputation which led him to be invited by Theo Stephens, in 1934, to open the first issue of his well-loved magazine *My Garden*, which ran until 1951.

Foster-Melliar's lively and droll articles, describing his experiences in creating his garden at Flexbury, in the teeth of gales and blown sand, were immediately published in book form in 1936, with the title *My Garden by the Sea*. The illustration of the garden in the book might, perhaps, suggest that it was rather ordinary and unimportant in comparison with the 'great' gardens of Cornwall, but its inclusion here may be justified on literary, if not on horticultural grounds. The author is still remembered in Bude for his connection with a nursery, as owner of a shop in the town, and as a town councillor. Little other than the house, however, has survived the urban expansion to preserve his name.

References: 20th C.

83. Merkjasteinn. In the early twentieth century the tennis court took the place of the bowling greens of earlier times, to be superseded today by a swimming pool. (From R.A. Foster Melliar, My Garden by the Sea, 1936)

OGBEARE HALL, North Tamerton

SX30 96 : *EX111, GS323*

Cornish googoo = cave + ?, pronounced OGbeer; 19th C. house with 15th C. hall listed grade II; medium grounds, south sloping 130-95m., on Crackington Formation shale, with acid soil; rainfall 35-40", temperature zone F; residential home, not open to the public.*

Ogbeare Hall is one of the undiscovered gardens of Cornwall, although here is a house where once lived the famed Leonard Loves (or Lovice), who in 1576 was 'Generall receaver to ye Queenes Maiestie of all hur revenewes in the Cou'tyes of Devon and Cornwall', as a brass in North Tamerton Church informs us - a house, moreover, whose gardens had been announced in the *Hort. Direct.* as open to the public from 1889 until 1916. Gilbert wrote of it:

> Ogbeer [*sic*] House is certainly a building of great antiquity, and its large mullioned windows, loaded with iron bars, give it an air of gloomy dignity. It is now inhabited [as were so many of these deserted old places in Cornwall] by a farmer. The lands are well tilled, and abound with cultivated hills, and valleys filled with woods and pasturage.

Perhaps the 'iron bars', and the mile-long drive off the Boyton-N. Tamerton road, with its inauspicious entrance, may explain its obscurity. Little of the sixteenth-century house survives now, except the magnificent Great Hall, which bears comparison with Cotehele, and the tower-like entrance porch.

For our purposes the history of Ogbeare begins in the 1880s, when it came into the hands of a Major Holt of Farnborough Grange in Devon. He it was who is recorded in the Kelly's *Directory* of 1883 as having 'recently ... restored and enlarged' the house. It would appear (although writers so often seem to omit such information) that he also laid out the grounds at the same time. A local writer found the appearance of them 'incongruous, as if a Victorian villa from a prosperous suburb had been placed in this remote Cornish district', criticism which stems, I imagine, from the rather artificial looking coloured foliage and conifers, and the pristine condition of the 'building of great antiquity'.

Gardens, however, are meant primarily to be enjoyed from within, where they should - so some late nineteenth-century designers argued - be distinguished from the landscape beyond, though leading into it (e.g. see The Downes). The ground in front of the Hall falls away steeply, and has been terraced. On the level, just below the platform on which the house sits, there is a formal rectangular lily pond. The view from this point is seen over the trees planted at lower levels, and framed on each side by deciduous and evergreen trees of various hues. Its neatly maintained, peaceful isolation is its own justification. At the valley bottom there is a lake fed by a stream from the adjoining woodland, two acres (0.8 ha) in extent, with islands.

References: 17th, 18th, 19th (Hort. & Gen.) and 20th C.

STOWE, near Kilkhampton

SX21 11 : EX126, GS307

Carriage wash, cottage wall 'part of kitchen-block?', real tennis court partly used as a shippon (cow-shed), each 17th C. and listed grade II; in an AONB and HC, and an AGSV; house demolished, garden and stew ponds extinct.

If one were uncharitable, the great house at Stowe, built in 1679, might be dubbed a folly, perpetrated by John Grenville, created Earl of Bath in 1661 for his services in the restoration of the monarchy. Stowe was probably designed and built by John Fitch, who earlier had been responsible, under Grenville, for constructing the Citadel at Plymouth. The mansion was clearly modelled, as were so many of the new houses after the Restoration, on Clarendon House in Piccadilly, which had been designed by Roger Pratt in 1664. In this decision lay the folly, to build here in Cornwall a town house, as Borlase observed, in 'a situation so distant from London & so bleak & naked in it self (expos'd as it is to the North Sea without the shelter or beauty of one tree)'. Grenville's fortunes were declining when he died in 1701, and by 1739 his successors had begun to demolish the house of his pride. On this event Baring-Gould, paraphrasing Polwhele, commented:

> Within the memory of one man, grass grew and was mown in the meadow where sprung up Stowe House, and grew and was mown in the meadow where Stowe had been.

The investigations of the Ancient Monuments Commission have been able to discover on the ground the old and new houses with their gardens, but this would not have been possible without the assistance of a plan of the estate by the celebrated cartographer Joel Gascoyne, a water-colour copy of an oil painting and two sketches by Edmund Prideaux, drawn in about 1716.

In the first of these sketches, the main entrance to the house can be seen between two pillars, leading up to a grand stairway, necessitated by the slope of the land. The second sketch, made lower down in the woods of Coombe valley, shows this same elevation high above, dominating the steep carriage drive, eventually arriving, as seen in the water-colour, through a deer park, described in Gascoyne's plan as the King's Park. The first sketch also shows along the south side of the house a sequence of three walled gardens, in which the archaeologists detected signs of terracing and steps to accommodate a slope not clear in the drawing. The planting in these compartments, in the water-colour and in the plan, is more

84. Stowe. The finest Caroline house in Cornwall, but 'bleak and naked in it self (expos'd as it is to the North Sea without the shelter or beauty of one tree).' (Sketched by Prideaux in 1716)

elaborate than in Prideaux's sketch, which suggests that there had been a process of simplification over the years. On the wall of the third compartment, towards the service quarters, there is a gazebo, from which the grounds and the coast could be surveyed. Borlase described Stowe as 'far the noblest house in the West of England', by which he would have intended to include the whole estate. Certainly it was one of the grandest houses ever to have been built in Cornwall, and a unique example here of the Caroline style.

References: 17th, 18th, 19th (Gen.) and 20th C; Illus; R. Drew, History of the Parish and Church of Kilkhampton, *1926: 64-79.*

TONACOMBE, Morwenstow

SX20 14 : EX126, GS307

An English name; pronounced TUNacombe; house, in which it is 'possible that materials from Stowe were used', listed grade I, Red Cross Stone in Pleasaunce c. late 12th century II*, two barns, two pairs of gate-piers (which may have originated at Stowe) and walls, each grade II; small garden at 125m., on Bude Formation sandstone, in an AONB and HC, an AGSV, with an AM (cross); rainfall 30-40", temperature zone D; private, but a public footpath passes through the grounds.

The old manor house of Tonacombe was mentioned as early as 1272, but the existing buildings are probably of *c*.1480. It has remained to this day in the family of the Waddons, who acquired the place by marriage in 1646. In her *Historic Gardens of England* (1938), Lady Rockley (the former Hon. Alicia Amherst) included only two Cornish gardens, viz. Lanhydrock, and Tonacombe,

> [the] low-crouching stone buildings [which] are still surrounded by a stone wall for defence, now enclosing the garden, which is laid out in a formal style with straight lines and cut trees, quite in keeping with the old house. Near by,

among gnarled stunted Oaks, lies a singular group of fish ponds, much as they were in the fifteenth century.

The precincts of the house are entered though gate-piers surmounted by eagles, along a walled drive, more strictly a front courtyard, known as the 'Street'. The heavy oak doors of the house, which has three small inner courts, show evidence of a possible former portcullis. The entirely enclosed 'Pleasaunce' to the east of the house, is a good example of a medieval *hortus conclusus*. Charles Kingsley, in *Westward Ho!*, modelled the dwelling of the Leighs, 'that great rambling dark house on the Atlantic cliffs in Morwenstowe parish,' on Tonacombe, which he named 'Chapel'. There was in his day a Chapel House in the parish, and there is still a Chapel farm at the nearby village of Shop.

References: 17th, 18th, 19th (Gen.) and 20th C.

SUPPLEMENTARY LIST

LESSER-KNOWN HISTORIC GARDENS

Cleave House, Morwenstow

SX20 12 : *EX126, GS307/308*

Extinct; in an AONB and HC, and an AGSV.

Cleave House was described in 1820 as a 'neat mansion surrounded by beautiful open grounds, quickset hedges, and fine walks.' It formed part of the Duchy of Cornwall, and was held on lease by the Waddon family from the neighbouring Tonacombe, passing in marriage to the Revd Oliver Rouse, and thence, on his decease in 1781, to James Martyn who bequeathed it to the Revd John Rouse. The whole property was obliterated by the construction of the Cleave Camp airfield.

References: 17th, 18th and 19th (Gen.) C.

Eastaway Manor, Morwenstow

SX21 13 : *EX126, GS307/308*

House listed grade II; small to medium grounds, at 125m., on Bude Formation sandstone, in an AONB and HC, and an AGSV; rainfall 35-40", temperature zone D; now Eastaway Manor Hotel, *with relict grounds.*

Eastaway House originally belonged to the Priory of Launceston, but was afterwards annexed to the Duchy in 1540, since which time there have been a number of different occupants, some associated with the nearby Cleave House, and Tonacombe. The present house is early nineteenth century, incorporating part of a late seventeenth-century building at the rear. Gilbert wrote in 1820 that it 'is charmingly situated at the head of a small valley filled with lawn, gardens, and plantations, which form together, a truly rural and pleasing residence.' The lawns still look out over the woodland in the valley below.

References: 17th, 18th and 19th (Gen.) C.

Flexbury Hall, Bude

SX21 07 : *EX111, GS307/308*

Sited at 40m. altitude, on Bude formation sandstone and blown sand; rainfall 35-40", temperature zone E; the house is in apartments, with a small residual garden.

'Long the seat of the Daymans,' according to Gilbert, 'and of late years greatly improved'. Charles Dayman was for a time curate at Poundstock, but in the *Hort. Direct.* for 1924 Flexbury was listed as the dwelling of F.L. Winter. The main entrance to the Hall, with heavy red brick pillars and retaining walls, opens into Poughill Road, opposite Ocean View Road, and the house faces east into a small residual garden, and on to a housing development, part of which is within the still-standing garden walls.

References: 18th, 19th (Gen.) and 20th C.

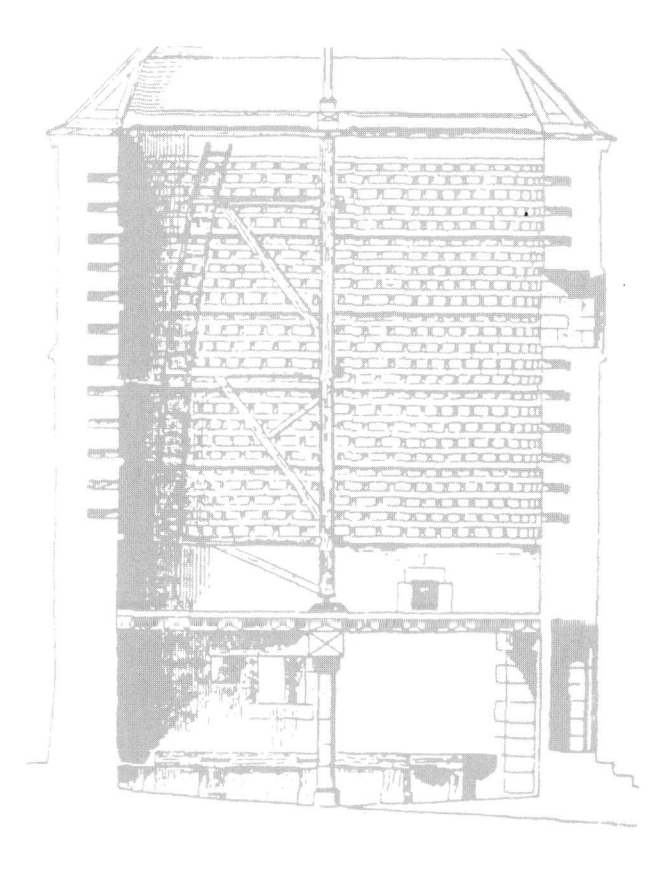

2. LAUNCESTON

The dearth of gardens in the previous section, along the exposed western side of Bodmin Moor, was due to the isolation of the region from the main stream of traffic, and the harsher geographical factors. Here on the eastern side of the Moor, the gardens have been more influenced by the configuration of the rivers which span the area, than by their proximity to Launceston, ancient and important though that town was.

Even though this eastern section of Cornwall has been divided for our purposes laterally into three segments, the pervasive dominance of the River Tamar throughout its length must never be forgotten. Its influence is exerted not only along the north-south course of the river itself, but also transversely through its tributaries, some of which, like the Ottery, the Inney, and especially the Lynher, are substantial rivers in their own right. These influences will become more apparent as we look more closely at the distribution of gardens in the area.

Polapit Tamar, in the north, takes its name from the river, although not within sight of it, while a little lower down the Ottery flows through Werrington to form a distinctive feature and feed a lake, until eventually joining the Tamar close to the borders of the Park. Penheale Manor, with two lakes, and Treludick, with a pond, also benefit from streams which run into the Ottery. Launceston stands a little west of the river on another smaller tributary, the Kensey, along which, if its course is traced through, also will be seen to lie Trebursye, Tredidon - still with a fishing lake - and Tregeare, each watered by small streams which run down to the Kensey River. The tree-clad Lawhitton churchyard and rectory, as well as the nearby grounds of Hexworthy, are all safely raised above the flood plain of the Tamar where it is especially wide below Launceston. Farther south, Sir John Call took advantage of un-named streams to create a lake in his new property at Whiteford.

An imaginary line to mark the southern-most limit of this present section has been drawn at Gunnislake. However, this is not entirely arbitrary, since from ancient times, until as recently as the construction in 1961 of the road-bridge at Saltash, this was the first crossing of the Tamar. It was here, to Sandhill Manor, that John Williams of Scorrier retired with his young wife in 1832. Only Trelaske, among our parks, is found near the Inney, up-river at Lewannick, but when this tributary has run out its course, it joins the Tamar where it twists among the woodlands opposite the Duke of Bedford's famous garden at Endsleigh in Devon.

The Lynher, the greatest of the tributaries, which by the time it meets the Tamar at its mouth will have swollen sufficiently to have become its rival, here, in mid-Cornwall, begins as a trickle flowing down from the Moors. But this small stream which modestly enters the grounds of Trebartha Hall to feed the swan pond, sweeps out again at the other end under Castick Bridge as a fully-fledged river. This transformation has been effected by the waters collected on the high moor by the Withey Brook, which roars in a torrent down over the rocks in Castick Wood to augment the emerging outfall of the lake. More peaceably, a few miles south at Berriow Bridge, a contemporary garden has been created along the banks, around an old cottage, which has inspired others in this, and the neighbouring village of Middlewood to arrange a biennial garden opening.

We shall meet the Tamar and Lynher again in the next section, where they are joined by other tributaries, but they will then form only one aspect of a wider perspective. Here, in mid-eastern Cornwall, where the water-courses form a network, it is easier to appreciate how these rivers and streams are not simply the necessary providers of water, but the very forces which have etched out and sculpted the landscape.

NB Since the gardens in this section are evenly divided between the OS Landranger 190 *and* 201 *maps, the appropriate number will be entered in each map reference.*

HEXWORTHY, Lawhitton

SX36 80 : *LR190, EX112, GS337*

Derivation probably English; house remodelled c. 1700 with additions listed grade II; garden of about 6 acres (2.4 ha), east sloping 85-60m., on Culm Measure shales, with acid soil; rainfall 40-45", temperature zone F/G; private.

'The Bennet family,' so *Hitchins* informs us,

> had formerly a seat in this parish called Hexworthy, with a considerable freehold estate. This is now the residence and property of Edmund Prideaux, Esq. who is related to the Bennet family by a previous marriage between their ancestors.

The grandfather of this owner was the artist of the accompanying sketch, which shows a house not dissimilar in style to that of today, but with a typical seventeenth-century garden, terraced, and with cut trees, bounded on each side by walls, and with railings and a gate to the front. All this has given way to lawn, except that there still remain a few traces of former topiary.

85. Hexworthy. Sketch, dated 1716, by Edmund Prideaux of a seventeenth-century Dutch-style terraced garden.

Gilbert believed that 'the planted hills form some of the most beautiful scenery which overhangs the Tamar.' The grounds at present, however, are said to be overgrown, although in 1930 this was one of Thurston's select gardens, which had been listed in the *Hort. Direct.* from 1889 to 1916. There are still relicts of ornamental planting which may include some of those he cited. 'There are two trees [of *Juglans regia*] in a field at Hexworthy,' he wrote,

> where a row of walnut trees formerly stood by the side of the main road. According to tradition, a former owner of the place used to take his wife there to beat her. This probably had its origin in the old rhyme:
>
> > A spannel, a wife, and a walnut tree,
> > The more you beat 'em, the better they be.

Hexworthy has been much used for hospitality, and among the guests is reputed to have been Oliver Cromwell in 1646, who slept here before taking Launceston Castle from the Royalists. There is within the house a small private chapel, with a Gothic doorway.

References: 17th, 18th, 19th (Hort. & Gen.) and 20th C; Illus.

LANDUE, Lezant

SX35 79 : LR201, EX112, GS337

Landew *1308*; Cornish *lann + *du = *black*, pronounced lanDEW; *country house listed grade II, house rebuilt early 19th C., barn early 19th C., cart-shelter, lodge dated 1812 in Picturesque Gothic style, gate-piers to lodge, late 18th C. gate-piers and quadrant walls, each II; extensive estate of 700 acres (283 ha), in east-west valley 94-75m., on Culm Measures shale and chert; rainfall 40-45", temperature zone F/G; private.*

Landue was originally in a family of that name, until it was sold to Thomas Trefusis in 1582, passing in the female line to Edward Herle, who was responsible for the present façade to the fifteenth-century building. The estate was sold again in 1820 to Thomas John Phillipps, and then in 1867 to the Tregoning family, who continued here until the 1990s, and were listed in the *Hort. Direct.* from 1908 until 1924. This was included among Thurston's select gardens, but chiefly for 'an avenue of good oak trees [*Quercus robur*] in the old drive, planted between 1820 and 1827.' To the north and west of the house are shrub gardens, and to the east a woodland garden with a summer-house. There is also a wooden Victorian conservatory adjoining the dwelling. The surviving members of the Tregoning family wrote in 1989 that the garden contained 'an old well, rhododendrons, azaleas,

eas, and magnolias typical of a Cornish garden, a weeping beech and a 'Tulip' and Medlar tree. This large estate is chiefly given over to parkland and agriculture.

References: 17th, 18th, 19th (Gen.) and 20th C.

LAUNCESTON CASTLE

SX33 84 : LR201, EX112, GS337   OPEN

Dunhevet Domesday 1086; Cornish Dunhevet, Dexter suggests is dun = hill + heafod = chief, Holmes suggests for Launceston, lan + Stephen (the parish) + ton = town (English), pronounced variously, but properly, as sometimes anciently spelt, LANson with A as in 'lance'; castle on prominence at c. 150m., pillow lava and shalstein in shale, in an HS; AM managed by English Heritage.

The many published references are usually to the former deer park, and the picturesque ruins, but *Lake* has recorded that the third Duke of Northumberland and the fourth, who died in 1865,

> are said to have expended £3000 in making walls, walks, and plantations, around and throughout the ruins, thereby rendering the castle and grounds more accessible to the public; and staying or hiding the progress of decay. The park was held on lease by Edward Coode, Esq., of S. Austell.

There is an illustration. The Dukes at that time owned Werrington Park (q.v.).

References: 17th, 18th, 19th (Gen.) and 20th C; Illus.

PENHEALE MANOR, Egloskerry

SX26 88 : LR190, EX9, GS323   OPEN

Pennehel Domesday 1086; Cornish pen + hel = hall, pronounced penHEEL; house listed grade I, stables, and gatehouse each I, gate with gate-piers and flanking walls, gate-piers, walled garden with pavilions, row of three cottages (Lutyens), each II*, dovecote, lodge and gate-piers, and various outbuildings each II; medium-sized garden in very large estate listed grade II, east sloping 130-100m., mainly on Meldon Shale, with acid soil; rainfall 40-45", temperature zone F; private, open 1983-98 CGOG, 1989 NGS, one Sunday each in May and June.

The manor of Penheale was, until the reign of Henry VI, in the family of the Bottrells, passing by marriage to the Hungerfords, who in 1572 sold it to George Grenville, whose family had been tenants for two generations, and were probably the first to have resided there. The second George Grenville, having no sons, sold the estate to Sir John Specott, from Somerset, whose family were related by marriage. He built the magnificent stables which bore a date-stone on their completion in 1620, although there were additions in 1676, the dovecote to the rear dating probably from the early eighteenth century. Specott was succeeded by his second son, Paul, whose initials, with those of his wife, Grace, and the date 1636 are over the front door of the house. However, his most substantial monument is the fine gatehouse opposite, with its loggia facing into the front court. The subsequent history is summarized by Ralph Edwards in *Country Life* (1925):

> Towards the end of the eighteenth century Penheale fell upon evil days. Divided into three separate dwellings in George III's reign, it suffered still harsher usage in Victorian times and was almost ruinous when the present owner [Capt. Norman R. Colville] acquired it.

Nevertheless, in 1867 *Lake* was able to pronounce it to be

> one of the finest and best preserved specimens of ancient manorial residences in the county ... The adjoining gardens and fish ponds are in good keeping with the mansion; and the main entrance is through an avenue of fine lime trees, whose growth is only excelled by the magnificent chestnuts and oaks of the surrounding groves.

This assessment is confirmed in the print in Twycross (1846), reproduced on page 208, and the rather thin sketch in the *Spoure Book* of *c.* 1690 shows that the basic plan was already in existence much earlier. Indeed, through the lower gate a layout can faintly be traced, which might correspond to Gilbert's 'noble terrace, with a bowling green, and a fine fish pond.'

Norman Colville moved to Penheale from Scotland for health reasons in 1920, and along the way had been impressed by Castle Drogo in Devon, which inspired him to engage Sir Edwin Lutyens to restore the house. Lutyens' additions lie to the right hand of our illustration, and were described by Pevsner as

> like a London block of flats. Yet it stands up perfectly to the old work, by virtue of its obstinate originality.

Lutyens also designed the parterre below, to replace some ramshackle buildings, Gertrude Jekyll's advice being requested on the planting. The long wall which encloses the garden in the foreground of the print has a pavilion at each end, and outside is planted up as a camellia wall facing on to a lake, with an island which was, no doubt, one of the fish ponds referred to earlier. Today the line from the rose garden through the upper gate-piers and steps, and on through the lower, forms the main axis of a large, level

86. Penheale. In the 1920s Edwin Lutyens restored and enlarged the old house, also creating a parterre to the right of the picture. The gate at the far side of the front court now leads out on to the plat, with its four 'rooms' enclosed by high yew hedges. (Twycross 1846: 56)

square plat below the house, enclosed and revetted by walls, which gives the impression of being four times the area of the square enclosing the house and it courts. Along the whole of the house side is a long raised terrace with beds edging the wall.

From this terrace the plat is seen to be quartered like a parterre (indeed it was so called by Mrs Colville), except that the enclosing hedges are of yew, some eight feet high, forming four compartments, or rooms. These hedges are reminiscent of, and clearly inspired by those at Castle Drogo. Between the terrace and the first two hedges is a long grass walk, with herbaceous borders on each side, both below the terrace and against the hedges. A similar border has been planted along the hedges on the far side of the plat, looking out over the parkland.

Gertrude Jekyll had left some designs for beds, which may have inspired some of the planting for which Mrs Colville and the gardener, Mr J.R. Moffat, are chiefly responsible. The apparently square 'rooms', however, are deceptive, since inside they are subdivided into smaller compartments. In particular, on the far left side (as seen from the direction of our illustration) a swimming pool has been constructed, 'designed to Greek proportions', within a compartment which overlaps two of the rooms. If now one were to stand on the far side of this pool, enclosed in an area fringed with nothing but grass and dark yew hedges, there opens up a long vista, at right angles to the main axis, all the way to the right-hand edge of the plat, where there are gate-piers with ball finials, leading down a semi-circular flight of granite steps, both admittedly modelled on those at Newton Ferrers (q.v.).

From these steps there is a view of a rectangular lake, long enough to be termed a 'canal', bounded by trees, leading the eye to the woodland garden beyond, which is planted with rhododendrons, camellias and magnolias. This canal has been formed out of one (or perhaps more) of the old fish ponds. There is an intricate inter-relationship of squares and rectangles in this garden: around the house, for instance, there are the square courts and gardens, with their angular rose-beds, parterres, square pavilions and the cubic outline of Lutyen's extension. The axial line from the house joins this square house enclosure to the much larger square plat with its four square rooms. A cross-axis at right angles from within and between these rooms ties in the swimming pool with the rectangular canal beyond, leading to the woodland garden.

Such an insistent geometrical formality is most unusual in Cornwall, which makes Penheale, in addition to its wonderful planting, so fascinating. It has no parallel, except perhaps on a much smaller scale at The Downes, Hayle.

References: 17th, 18th, 19th (Gen.) and 20th C; Illus; J. Brown, Gardens of a Golden Afternoon, *1982: 173 (where the reference to Jekyll's plan, preserved in the University of California, is given).*

PENHEALE BARTON, Penheale Manor

SX26 88 : *LR190, EX109, GS323* OPEN*

For details see Penheale Manor; open 1994-8 CGOG, one Sunday each in May and June.

The Barton, the residence of Mrs Norman Colville, with a date-stone for 1835, now serves the function of a dower house to the Manor. It has a narrow forecourt, and a large square walled garden to the rear. Mrs Colville, who was responsible for much of the planting in the Manor, in 1989 carried her interest in flowering herbaceous plants to her new garden, where they are planted in island beds, and in borders along the walls, interspersed with shrubs of various heights. The terrace has some climbers.

Reference: Pring (1996: 90).

POLAPIT TAMAR, Boyton, near Launceston

SX33 89 : *LR190, EX112, GS323*

Cornish pol + pit = *pit (English), i.e. 'pool in a pit' hence mine working, pronounced* POLapit; *house listed grade II, stables and carriage house with the date 1866 on rain-water hoppers, dairy and cold store mid-19th C., garden terraces, north lodge, south lodge, gate-piers and railings, each II; large estate in east-west valley 126-70m. with house at 90m., on mainly Namurian shale, with acid soil; rainfall 40-45", temperature zone G; divided into apartments.*

Polapit, 'a handsome and costly mansion', was built for Edward Coode in 1866, and was further extended for R.C. Coode in 1901-3 to designs by Robert P. Whellock, which included a ballroom with chambers above. The house stands in a depression adjoining, but without a view of the Tamar, and is surrounded on the higher ground by plantations. To the south of the house is a terrace with retaining walls of dressed granite, with a flight of steps leading down to two lower terraces. Along the east side of the drive down from the north lodge are the sheltering walls of the former kitchen garden, in a small valley. This is an impressively large estate and house, with many good trees. However, there is little sign today of what must once have been fine ornamental gardens, when Polapit was listed in the *Hort. Direct.* from 1908 to 1924.

References: 19th (Gen.) and 20th C.

TREBARTHA HALL, Northill

SX26 77 : *LR190, EX109, GS337* OPEN

Tribertha *Domesday 1086; Cornish* tre + [?], *pronounced* treBARTHa; *Barton listed grade II*, threshing barn II*, two lodges with gate-piers, granary, and two bridges, each II; very large estate, east sloping 250-130m., on granite, and Upper Devonian metamorphosed slate and alluvium, with acid soil, in an AONB, an AGSV and CNCS, with AMs (three crosses); rainfall 50-60", temperature zone F; private, open 1983-98 CGOG, 1987, 1991, 1993-8 NGS, one Sunday each in May, June and September. Official guide and plan.*

'The manor of Trebartha,' according to *Hitchins*,

> is said to have belonged to Walter Reynell, a knight of Gascony, so early as the reign of Richard I. at which time he was Castellan of Launceston. About one hundred years afterwards, it was the property of a family called Trebartha, who ... became extinct in the male line during the reign of Henry VII. at which time the property was carried by an heiress to the Spoures, with whom it continued until the year 1729.

Trebartha was then bequeathed to the family of Rodd. The dwelling figures in the *Spoure Book* of *c.* 1690, where it appears as an old Cornish house with courtyards, arched gateways, and a quite elaborate garden, quartered, each quadrant with a statue in the centre and pointed trees at each corner, and with a pavilion on one wall, which together suggest an Italian influence.

All this was taken down in the eighteenth century by Col. Rodd, who erected on its site what Gilbert considered 'a large tasteless building, which appears to be deplorably destitute of architectural ornaments', but near the house

> are good gardens and a shrubbery, with hot houses, and several neat gravel walks. The whole is surrounded by extensive plantations, the extremities of which are sheltered by an amphitheatre of bold hills, which bear on their bleak brows, tors of a most sublime and frowning appearance. From a stupendous elevation on the northern side, a considerable stream descends, and the roar of its waters in their falls over the different precipices, is heard at a great distance. The beautiful also, is here associated with the sublime; for the foliage of forest trees is seen delightfully clothing the sides of the heights, and forming a pleasing contrast to the bare and bleak elevation by which they are protected.

87. Trebartha Hall. A remarkable Italianate garden in which the sphere motif is repeated on the gate-piers and arches, the roof ridges and dormer windows. The figure in the lower garden probably represented Atlas. (From a sketch by Henderson, based upon the Spoure Book, c. 1690)

becoming available from plant collectors. The Swan Pool, landscaped with other interesting specimens, dates from the turn of the century. There had been a boat shed here, and alongside, a grotto-like boat pen within a mound of earth, with a path to the top which serves as a Mount affording a view over the lake. In the level parkland is a well, which has been surrounded by a collection of ancient crosses and mile-stones. The history of the site has been related by Bryan Latham in his book Trebartha - the House by the Stream (1971), and Christopher Latham has written an excellent guide to The Trees of Trebartha (c. 1983). The word 'magical' has become a cliché when applied to Cornish gardens, but the stillness of the Swan Pool broken only by the distant roar of the torrent and the sighing of the great trees which tower up the slopes above, induces an atmosphere to which this over-used word is not inapplicable.

The house, maligned by Gilbert, became dilapidated during wartime occupation by the military and as a prisoner of war camp, and was demolished in 1948, the family now living in unobtrusive modern houses.

References: 17th, 18th, 19th (Hort. & Gen.) and 20th C. Illus.

TREBURSYE, near Launceston

SX30 83 : LR201, EX109, GS337

Trebursii 1199; Cornish tre + Bursige = Old English personal name, pronounced treBURSEy; lodge and gate-piers listed grade II; medium grounds, south sloping to brook, 155-140m., on Culm Measures shale, with acid soil; rainfall 35-40", temperature zone G; now Trebursye Manor Residential and Nursing Home.

Trebursye was originally in the possession of a family named Gedys, but the 'heiress ... carried it in marriage to Sir John Eliot, who died in the tower of London, in the time of Charles I', although the estate continued in the Eliot family. The Tudor Gothic house, reputed to have been to the designs of Sir Jeffrey Wyattville, was built in about 1810 for William Eliot on a new site which, although 'large and noble', Gilbert thought exhibited 'a singular association of modern taste, with ancient gloomy magnificence.' When he unexpectedly inherited the Earldom of St Germans in 1823, the estate was sold to David Howell of Ethy, from whom it passed mid-century to Charles Gurney (1805 - c. 1890), who was listed in the Hort. Direct. from at least 1870. He was succeeded in 1908 by Miss Gurney.

Thurston referred to 'a plantation of conifers and other trees,' noting that Trebursye was then

Two years later Loudon was to include Trebartha among the ten Cornish gardens in his gazetteer of 1822, and fifty years on, Lake believed it 'to be reckoned among the best and most stately seats of the county.' It was listed in the Hort. Direct. from at least 1870 until 1924, in the name of Francis Rashleigh Rodd, and was one of Thurston's select gardens. The property was purchased by Bryan Latham in 1941, at a time of import shortage, to take commercial advantage of the timber in the woods and Castick Plantation, both probably planted by Edward Hearle Rodd in the early nineteenth century.

The American Gardens and Upper Terraces were later developments, probably from mid-century, when many new varieties were 'in the possession of Mr Gwillin Vowler'. Except for these notices, little has been said about the garden, other than by Betjeman who, in 1964, thought 'the landscape park looked as though it had been laid out by Repton', perhaps recalling that he had worked at Port Eliot. In the late 1990s, however, such a connection is hard to imagine since, although the sloping parkland down to the tree-lined brook undoubtedly has its attractions, the house has been much extended, and surrounded with recently-planted mixed flower beds. The drive has suffered from being cut through by the A30 Launceston bypass, thus detaching it from the attractive thatched lodge, with its most unusual gate-piers surmounted by pyramids supported on four balls.

References: 17th, 18th, 19th (Hort. & Gen.) and 20th C; Illus.

TREGEARE, Egloskerry

SX24 86 : LR190, EX109 and 111, GS323

Cornish tre + car, pronounced treGEAR; house listed grade II, lodge with date-stone JCBL 1868, gate-piers and walls, stables, gazebo, gateway and walls, each II; park and plantations of 433 acres (175 ha), south sloping from 172m., on Crackington Formation shale and grit, with acid soil, in an AGLV; rainfall 40-45", temperature zone G; private, at present on the market.

Tregeare is a large estate, which seems in the passage of time to have excited little attention. It was but vaguely reported in *Hitchins* that it had for 'many years, perhaps many generations, belonged to the family of Baron', words echoed in *Lake* some fifty years later. Twycross alone has the information. Jasper Baron had demolished the old manor house, which was in Egloskerry parish, and in 1790, as a stained glass window records, built a grander house quite nearby (now in Laneast parish), which was completed around 1820 in the Georgian Palladian style. It was approached by a drive from an entrance which later, in the nineteenth century, was made more impressive by the addition of a lodge, cottages and gate-piers set back from the road behind a grassed area, making it evident that this was the approach to an estate of substance.

The drive itself is flanked on each side by ornamental plantations, which include magnolias and rhododendrons of early introduction. The site of the old house was to the right, but on the left (or south) there is, within the woodland, a walled garden, with two greenhouses, between which an archway - dated 1582 and from the earlier dwelling - has been erected. The drive eventually arrives at the porticoed entrance to the house from the east, but the main front looks southward to plantations of trees along the east side of the parkland and on the horizon, with arboreal rhododendrons along the west side, to a small lake. This park is now divided into three by hedges, which, although not recent, evidently are not original, since the presence of an ha-ha (and the print in Twycross of 1846) would seem to imply that it had formerly been open and grazed, if not by deer, then by bullocks. Immediately to the west of the house is an area of well-maintained woodland with an orchard, and an impressive thatched stone gazebo, believed to have been converted into a game-larder and apple loft from an earlier dovecote. Jasper Baron's son, William, had been sheriff in 1825, but the estate was inherited by his sister, Elizabeth, wife of John King Lethbridge of Launceston, whose son, John Christopher Baron, was responsible for building the lodge in 1868 and developing the estate.

References: 18th, 19th (Gen.) and 20th C; Illus.

TRELASKE, Lewannick

SX28 80 : LR201, EX109 & 112, GS337

Cornish tre + losc = burnt, pronounced treLASK; keeper's cottage, probably mid 16th C. with earlier origins, listed grade II, gate-piers reputed to have been moved from Lydcott in Morval parish, II; originally very large estate, garden sloping south-east, 170-150m. from house, on Pillow lava and shalstein, with acid soil, and an AM (cross); rainfall 45-50", temperature zone F/G; private.

The family succession at this barton has been summarized in *Lake*:

> In 1242 Trelaske was held by Sir Roger Treloske, who was succeeded by Sir Andrew Treloske, and has ever since been held by descendants of the family, the present proprietor, Edward Archer, Esq., being descended by marriage from the Uptons.

The Uptons had themselves descended on the female line. Gilbert wrote:

> The buildings are seated on the northern side of a park, which gently slopes to a sheet of water overhung with a variety of stately foliage. At an agreeable distance from the house, are some neat modern stables, over which is a handsome clock; and nearly adjoining, are good kitchen and flower gardens. The whole at this time [c. 1820] presents a melancholy appearance, from the house being uninhabited, and from the uncultivated and neglected state of the grounds. There is however an air of dignity diffused in every part of this domain, from the appearance of its extensive woods, rising and falling in beautiful

88. Trelaske. The quality of the planting by the Archer family gave rise to the legend that the landscape had been designed by 'Capability' Brown himself. (Twycross 1846: 77)

succession over hill and dale. The trees are principally oak, which have grown to an immense size, are very aged, and still very flourishing: their wide spreading branches and luxuriant leafage, are beautifully contrasted by the slender firs, which rise in stately clumps over the principal eminences.

It was undoubtedly this scene, so well described in this passage, and illustrated in Twycross (1846), which fostered the rumour that 'Capability' Brown may have landscaped the parkland and lake, although there is no evidence that he ever worked in Cornwall. Nevertheless, when this estate was reviewed in the *Gardeners' Chronicle* in 1848, it was placed under their 'Farm Memoranda', rather than in the horticultural section. When Thurston included Trelaske among his select gardens in 1930, it was still occupied by Philip, a member of the Archer family. The house, with an orangery and early camellia house, has passed through several hands, the recently converted stables being currently on the market. *Hitchins* has recorded that there was formerly a manganese mine on the estate, 'from which small quantities of this semi-metal were raised'. It had a regular lode about ten fathoms from the surface.

References: 17th, 18th, 19th (Hort. & Gen.) and 20th C; Illus.

WERRINGTON PARK, near Launceston

SX33 87 : *LR190, EX112, GS323*

Vluredintona, Domesday 1086; house listed grade I, south lodge, gate-piers and walls, north lodge and walls, gate-piers and walls, ha-ha, estate office, carriage house, tunnel possibly an ash-house or larder, ice-house 'a good example of its type', kitchen garden walls 18th or early 19th C, each II, White Bridge, 'the parapets ... rebuilt in the 19th century replacing a white painted balustrade' (see Gilbert 1820 ii.: 522) II, Terrace House possibly Pococke's Hermitage ('at the time of the inspection (1987) the Terrace House was considerably overgrown and some of the upper sections had fallen away') II, the Sugar Loaves II, 'The park also contains two cockpits, their terraces remaining', Church of St Martin I, entrance, vicarage etc. each II; parkland c. 400 acres (162 ha) listed grade II, sloping 100-60m. south and west from the house, mainly Meldon chert, Namurian shale, and river deposits, with acid soil, in an AGLV, and with an AM (round); rainfall 40-45", temperature zone G; private, opened 1997 NGS.

Werrington, with its parkland of considerable historical importance and interest, was formerly one of the residences of the Abbot of Tavistock, which, although at one time half in the county of Devon, belonged always in the Archdeaconry of Cornwall. It was purchased in 1650 from the nephew of Sir Francis Drake, by William Morice, of a family believed to have originated in Caernarvon, who had been knighted and appointed Secretary of State and Privy Councillor as a reward for his services in restoring the monarchy. The grounds as they were during his time may be seen in a sketch made by Edmund Prideaux in 1716 from a point near the present Yeolmbridge - St Stephen's road.

The house was later modified and the estate extensively landscaped for his son, Nicholas Morice, so Pevsner believed, with the help of William Kent. However, until further evidence or documents are forthcoming, this supposition must remain largely circumstantial. However, the suggestion is not without some substance, since Morice, by his marriage to Catherine, daughter of the Earl of Pembroke, had become allied to the Herbert family. The Herberts were all active members of that circle where the aesthetic theories of the Palladian movement were under discussion, and were themselves actively engaged in the landscaping of Wilton in Wiltshire, and another branch at Highclere in Hampshire. In the absence of actual plans, we are fortunate in possessing a concise though detailed contemporary description of 1750 by Richard Pococke, an indefatigable traveller of wide knowledge and experience, of his perambulation around Werrington, making it possible to identify the sites of the various features, which are mostly now gone.

> It is a very fine rising ground on each side of the river Atre [Ottery], and beautifully improved in wood and lawn; to the left [of the later White Bridge, facing toward the house], on a heigth [*sic*], is a building to represent a ruinous castle [now Castle Hill], and lower in the park Sr William [son of Nicholas Morice] began a temple of the sun, which appears in a wood: to the right there is a very fine terrace [now the Terrace Gardens], winding round the hill, and above it opposite to the house, a triumphal arch, on the model of that on Sidon Hill, at Highcleer. Descending we come

89. Werrington. Sketch by Edmund Prideaux, 1716. The line of trees, centre left, is in the position of the present 'Lime Walk'. Notice that the church at this time adjoined the house.

90. Werrington. View c. 1820 taken from the same position as the Prideaux sketch, showing the lake, and clumping of trees characteristic of the Palladian School of William Kent. Notice that the church has been moved away from the house. (Gilbert 1820: ii. frontispiece)

to a hermitage, like that at Richmond [which had been designed by Kent], and beyond it is a model of what is called the Tomb of Horatii, near Albano [still extant]. Returning down towards the river there is a large alcove trellis seat [near the ford by the later Duchess's Bridge], and above the river forms a beautiful serpentine river ... To the west [of the house] is a small building in a wood [named on Borlase's sketch of 1557 the 'Warren House']; and farther on the hill is the church built by Sr William Morris [in 1742], with a Gothick tower and turret on each side of it :.. This park is to be looked on as one of the most beautiful in England.

The various features will repay individual consideration. Pococke immediately detected a close resemblance between the Hermitage at Werrington and that built by Kent in 1730 for Queen Caroline. This was an example of a 'rusticated' structure. The description of the trellis seat at Werrington exactly fits two surviving examples at Rousham, known to have been designed by Kent. In the same way a 'temple of the sun', was characteristic of Kent's work at Stowe. Pococke, from his travels, also remarked on the similarity of the triumphal arch at Werrington to that of Morice's wife's relatives at Highclere, which can still be compared in illustrations. The original of the 'Tomb of the Horatii', which has puzzled some commentators, has now been located, and was probably seen at Albano on one of those Italian tours so common at the time, being introduced to inspire a fashionable meditation on the transience of human life, typified by Gray's immensely popular 'Elegy'. It is surely no coincidence that Kent modelled the central arch of his Hermitage at Rousham on one he had seen at Albano. The 'White Bridge', illustrated and described by Gilbert as ornamented with palisadoes and surmounted with capitals, may have been inspired by the much grander Palladian bridge at Wilton, the estate of another relative. Gilbert wrote more generally that

> [the park] which is of great extent, appears before the beholder, in some places clumped with firs, or strewed with finely spreading trees; in others enlivened by winding walks.

Indeed, these are exactly in the 'Natural Style' advocated by Kent and the Palladian school. The changes made to the landscape may be observed in a comparison of the Prideaux sketch and the Gilbert print, which were both drawn from roughly the same position. Even the church itself had been moved. Otho Peter described it as an evil hour when the last baronet determined to move the place of worship and churchyard in order to build the still extant bowling green:

> Day by day the parishioners watched with outraged feelings the carts removing their dead [none too carefully it seems] ... and many a curse is said to have been hurled at the author of the sacrilege ... A malediction rested on the family of Morice from the date of this changing of the site of a house of God. Sir William died childless [in 1750], and within 30 years the estate had passed to strangers.

The first stranger was the Duke of Northumberland, who purchased the estate for the political influence he obtained by owning a 'pocket borough'. He became a patron of Charles Gilbert, the historian, and took some interest in the estate, building the Duchess's Bridge at the other end of the lake, and a 'Temple' to compete with that built by the Duke of Bedford at Endsleigh, which the Williams later demolished.

His successors, however, lost interest after the electoral reforms of the 1830s, so that by 1882, when the estate was bought by J.C. Williams, ostensibly for the shooting, it had been neglected for several years. It was, however, to prove invaluable as an overflow from his principal residence at Caerhays, to accommodate the increasing number of seeds and specimens received from plant expeditions sponsored by his family. These were planted in the seven-acre (2.8 ha) Terrace Gardens facing the house across the lake. Among them were rhododendrons grown from seed sent from Forrest's expeditions. They had been carefully labelled, but many of the labels have become detached or illegible. Some of these plants have achieved a great size, and become interlaced. In addition to the rhododendrons, there is an interesting variety of other trees and shrubs around the estate.

References: 17th, 18th, 19th (Hort. & Gen.) and 20th C; Illus; Otho Peter, The Manor and Park of Werrington, *1906; M. Jourdain,* The Work of William Kent, *1948: fig. 112.*

WHITEFORD HOUSE, Stoke Climsland

SX35 73 : *LR201, EX108, GS337*

The name is of English origin; former service range now a house listed grade II, garden walls, temple, each II; relict and part extinct large garden, at c .100m. elevation, on Upper Devonian slate, and alluvium; rainfall 45-50", temperature zone F; Duchy property.

When John Call from Launcells returned after twenty years in India, he was persuaded to settle in Stoke Climsland, in proximity to Callington, hoping to prove that it had some ancient link with his name. He then purchased Whiteford which, in the early part of the seventeenth century, had been the property of the Clarkes, from whom it had passed to the family of Addis (the house being illustrated in the *Spoure Book, c.* 1690). Here, in about 1775, he built Whiteford House, which Gilbert considered to be 'one of the most elegant modern mansions in this neighbourhood,' to be visited later, in 1842, by Loudon and his wife. 'From each front of the mansion,' Gilbert wrote,

> there is a fine sweep of lawn, and on the southern side a handsome shrubbery, ornamented with an Italian fountain. The northern side is backed by a large plantation of evergreens, and in front of this stands a neat temple, from which the waving foliage sweeps round in a circuitous form, and encloses at the bottom a very extensive canal, crossed by a neat bridge, under which is a cascade. In the middle of the canal, are several small islands, planted with firs and laurel, and rendered interesting by the number of swans, and other water birds, continually gliding over the surface of the waters. The gardens at Whiteford, are large and valuable: the hot houses produce pineapples, grapes, American aloes, and many rare plants, - the gleanings of different countries. The whole of these are well attended to, as are also the various walks that are carried through the shrubberies and open grounds.

In 1784, John Call was elected MP for Callington, and two years later was appointed one of the Commissioners of Crown Lands. He was created first Baronet in 1791, and died in 1801. 'Unhappily the idyllic squirearchy he established at Whiteford,' writes Sheila Lightbody,

> did not long survive; his great-grandson, the 4th Baronet, ran a racing stud at Newmarket [for the proverbial Gordon Bennet] and gambled for high stakes, and a hundred years after its erection Whiteford House was empty and desolate, and the estate suffered from an absentee landlord. In 1901 the house was boarded up and fast falling into decay, and a few years later [in 1912] it was demolished, when the property was purchased by the Duchy of Cornwall.

The service wing of the house was divided into cottages, but later converted to a house. The garden walls still survive as does the temple, dating from about 1799, with a figure relief in *Coade* stone, which when it was seen by Pevsner in

SUPPLEMENTARY LISTS

ADDITIONAL HISTORIC GARDENS

Darley, Upton

SX27 79 : LR201, EX109, GS337

In an AGLV.

Under his entry for *Quercus robur* Thurston wrote:

> Perhaps the most notable existing oak in the County is a tree at Darley, the former home of the Darleys of Darley, in Linkinhorne parish, which is known as the Darley Oak. It is recorded in the History of the Parish of Linkinhorne from the MS. of W. Harvey written in 1727 (Bodmin, 1876) that "in the plaisance of the village stands the great natural curiosity known as the Darley Oak. At the height of 3 feet from the ground (where there are many excrescences), it measures 36 feet in circumference. Being hollow, and having convenient openings for ingress and egress, it is capable of housing small pleasure parties, which it often does in the season. Although reasonably supposed to be upwards of 500 years old, it is still healthful and vigorous, and producing acorns".

There is an illustration of this ancient oak as it was in the 1920s. Even though one side of the trunk has been lost, it still exists, and appears in good health in the garden of Darley Farm.

References: 17th, 19th (Gen.) and 20th C.

Lawhitton Rectory

SX35 82 : LR190, EX112, GS337

Landsithan c. 830, now known as The White House; Cornish, Dexter suggests lan + gwedhen = tree, pronounced laWHITTon *house listed grade II; private.*

Thurston cited two trees - one from Lawhitton Rectory, the other from the churchyard. The grounds are still well covered by trees and, as viewed from the road, compare favourably with the more celebrated Hexworthy close by. The Rectory was built in 1801 by Charles Marshall, who died in 1826, and the garden was probably laid out by him or his successors, James Duke Coleridge, LL D (1826-39), and Francis Du Boulay, son-in-law and chaplain to the Bishop of Exeter.

References: 19th (Gen.) and 20th C.

Manaton, South Hill

SX33 72 : LR201, EX108, GS337

On the OS map as 'Lower Manaton'; house, well house and gate-piers, each listed grade II; grounds sloping south to north 150-125m., on Culm Measures and Upper Devonian slate; rainfall 45-50", temperature zone F; farm, and residences.

The mansion was rebuilt by Francis Manaton, and has a date-stone F M 1687. The well house is seventeenth century, and may also have been built by him. Gilbert wrote:

> Below the house, are to be seen some old fish ponds, and in the middle of each, a spot of ground, which has a fir tree, grown to an immense size, although rooted in a watery soil. The plantations have been greatly thinned, but enough remains to shew the ancient state of this once respectable residence.

The lakes are still there, with an area of shrubs and ornamental trees, entered through a gateway with piers surmounted by hounds. There is a recent plantation of trees to the left of the driveway from the higher gateway down to the lakes, beyond which is a cluster of buildings.

References: 17th, 18th, and 19th (Gen.) C.

Sandhill House, Gunnislake

SX42 71 : LR201, EX108, GS337

House listed grade II, stables, gate-piers, kitchen garden walls, each II; grounds originally of 20 acres (8 ha), at 110m. altitude, on granite; rainfall 45-50", temperature zone F; now an hotel.

Sandhill, probably of seventeenth-century origins, was enlarged in 1790 by the Revd John Russell, in Regency style, although there have been later additions. At the same time he also built the stables and kitchen garden walls, which have a 'row of square brick pigeon holes with slate perches, and a granite date-stone of 1637, probably resited.' John Russell's son is reputed to be the Jack Russell who bred the terrier named after him. One of the principal interests of this place is its connection with the Williams family. John Williams of Scorrier, with Robert Were Fox I and Charles Carpenter of Moditonham, purchased the mineral rights of Duchy manors, and obtained

> a lease which [secured] to them the right of searching for silver in the whole manor of Calstock. This was procured in consequence of some silver lodes having been discovered in this manor early in the same year, 1811. (*Hitchins* 1824:ii. 305.)

John Williams had already (in 1809) purchased the manor of Calstock, and established himself in the vicinity. One reason for his move from Scorrier appears to have been that, after the death of his wife, Catherine, in 1826, he was again married, to

---

1951 was a cattle byre. In about 1982 this was restored by the Landmark Trust, and is now used as holiday accommodation.

References: 17th, 18th, 19th (Hort. & Gen.) and 20th C; Illus.

a younger local woman, which is said to have caused his sons and daughters to fear for their inheritance. As a consequence, he made settlements upon them, and retired to Sandhill in 1832, where he died in 1841. The rights in the manor passed to John Michael Williams of Caerhays Castle, and it was his presence in Calstock which was one factor in the eventual purchase of Werrington Park by his son John Charles in 1882.

References: 19th (Gen).

Tredidon Barton, Tregadillett

SX27 84 : LR201, EX109, GS337

Cornish tre + [?], pronounced treDIDon; house, granary and monument, each listed grade II; grounds sloping south-east, 150-130m., on Culm Measures shale, in an AGLV; rainfall 40-45", temperature zone G; farm, grounds have recently become Tredidon Trails *leisure park.*

The deeds of Tredidon are said to go back to 1417, but the present farmhouse is of late sixteenth century origins, with extensions and remodelling in each century since. This was anciently the property and residence of the Tredidon family, which passed by descent and sale to Henry Spry. 'It is situated,' wrote Gilbert, 'on an eminence facing a lawn, and has a shrubbery and good gardens. The barton contains about two hundred and forty acres of land, clothed with fine timber.' The house still has a number of mature trees around it, and a small conifer plantation north of the drive entrance. There is a stream, and a small lake used for coarse fishing. Perhaps of greatest interest and curiosity is a mausoleum erected in about 1865 for James Bucknell on his favourite spot. 'It is said that he intended the rest of his family to be buried here but a dispute with the local vicar meant that no-one else was allowed to be buried here on unconsecrated ground.' [But contrast the Rashleighs at Fowey, see Point Neptune.]

References: 17th, 18th, and 19th (Gen.) C.

Treludick, Egloskerry

SX25 88 : LR190, EX109, GS323

Cornish tre + ?, pronounced treLUDick; late 16th C. house listed grade II, gate, gate-piers, walls and railings II*, stables, and farm buildings II; grounds east-sloping, 130-110m., mainly Meldon Shale; rainfall 40-45", temperature zone F; farm.*

Gilbert wrote that Treludick, 'which is a very ancient dwelling, has been of late much improved [by Peter Hurdon, whose family had resided there for about sixty years], and is surrounded with several acres of thriving plantations.' The house is late sixteenth century, possibly remodelled for the Baron family [see Tregeare], with a date-stone of 1641 reset in the stables. Among the farm buildings is a butterwell, still [in 1988] used for its original purpose. Along the eastern front of the house, enclosing a front court, are handsome railings, with ornamented gates and gateposts, dating probably from the early eighteenth century. The grounds slope down from the front to a stream and pond. There are small plantations of trees to the north around the settlement as a protection. There is no 'garden' in the ornamental sense, but the house and grounds form a charming unity.

References: 17th, 18th, and 19th (Gen.) C.

Tremeal Farm, Launceston

SX31 83 : LR201, EX112, GS337

Pronounced treMEAL; *extinct, now* Tremeal Manor Farm, *holiday cottages, with residual garden.*

It is recorded in *Hitchins* that:

> Tremeal which was formerly a seat belonging to the Vyvyan family, was sold by the late Sir Vyel Vyvyan of Trelowarren. This is now a farm house, and is the property of Samuel Archer, Esq.

Gilbert adds:

> the mansion-house of Tremeal, though of modern erection, has been in great part demolished, Mr. Archer having for some years taken up his abode in Devonshire. The grounds are very fine, and stored with a quantity of excellent timber: the trees are chiefly oak, elm, beech, and sycamore.

All this has now gone.

References: 18th and 19th (Gen.) C.

ADDITIONAL CONTEMPORARY GARDENS

See also PENHEALE BARTON, *in the main section.*

Berriow Bridge and Middlewood Gardens, North Hill

SX27 75 : LR210, EX109, GS337　　　　　　　　OPEN*

Cornish, Dexter suggests berrow = possibly pl. of bar = hill-top; *a group of village gardens in an AGSV, open 1989, 1991, 1993, 1995, 1997 NGS, alternate years, one Saturday and Sunday May/June.*

Higher Truscott, near Launceston

SX30 85 : LR201, EX109, GS337　　　　　　　　OPEN*

1 acre (0.4 ha) garden open 1990-91, 1993-4, 1996, 1998 CGOG and NGS, one Sunday each April, May and August.

Reference: Pring (1996: 76-7).

Trenance, Launceston

SX33 84 : LR201, EX112, GS337　　　　　　　　OPEN*

Cornish tre + nans, *pronounced* treNANCE; *a 1.75 acre (0.7 ha) garden open 1995-8 NGS, one Sunday each in May and July.*

3. SOUTH-EAST CORNWALL

This final section covers a broad area of interior, coastal and riverside landscape, dissected by river valleys which make communications roundabout and difficult. Such towns as there are tend to serve areas confined within natural boundaries, each with its own characteristics and local justification. They will need to be taken one by one.

To the west, Liskeard lies at the head of the long valley of the East Looe River, which opens into the sea almost due south. The town grew up on the site of a former castle, to which, unusually, had been annexed two deer parks - the Old and Lady Park, so-named after a former chapel dedicated to the Virgin Mary. The place-names still survive, if not the parks, which are also commemorated in the Norman-French place-name of Doublebois, which signifies the two 'forests' or game reserves. There are several estates around Liskeard, such as the ancient Treworgey to the north, with the nearby Domesday manor of Rosecraddock resettled in the nineteenth century by a relative of the Treworgey Connocks. Doublebois House, another late nineteenth-century property, lies along the road to the west. In Liskeard itself, Westbourne and Luxstowe are but two among several fine houses which date from the time of the town's growth in prosperity as a business centre. Lewis Foster, one of a banking family, built his house (now a hospital) on the road out of town to the south, naming it Trevillis after a Domesday manor a few miles away. Carved out of this estate, which is now partly built over, is Moyclare, the celebrated garden of the late Mrs Moira Reid, a great plantswoman. A little to the west, at Coombe, is Trelidden, a natural garden created by Marjorie Blamey, who has gained a wide reputation for her accurate and beautiful botanical drawings of wild flowers.

An unusually large group of contemporary gardens around St Neot's have been opened as a result of the enthusiasm of the late Mrs Bridget Okely, who was organizer of the National Garden scheme in Cornwall.

The town of Looe, due south down the valley from Liskeard, had its origin as a fishing village, which became elevated to the rank of a proprietory borough with two members of Parliament. Its growth in more recent times, however, has been due to its popularity as a seaside resort. Among the earliest of those gentry who acquired a taste for sea air in the late eighteenth century was John Lemon, MP for Saltash, and later of Truro, who built himself a cottage at Polvellan, opposite the headland of Trenant Park, the property of his brother-in-law, but neatly tucked away from exposure to any onslaught from the open sea. Waterloo Villa, on the contrary, named to commemorate the victory, was built on the west-facing slopes of the estuary in a more exposed position. As the days of the great battle receded into the past, the house acquired the apparently bizarre title of Klymiarvan, which is, nevertheless, no more outlandish than the Cornish for 'culver-field'. The nearby parks at Trelawne, in Pelynt parish, and at Morval House and Bray, both in Morval parish, all pre-date the rise in popularity of Looe as a watering-place.

To the east of Looe is St German's, where the River Lynher opens out into the Tamar to form the twin estuary of the Hamoaze. This ancient place was once the seat of one of the Cornish bishoprics, until in the eleventh century the ecclesiastical centre was transferred to Exeter, although the Priory itself continued for several centuries up to the Dissolution. The Quay took its name from the Priory, as 'Porth Prior', but was soon changed to Port Eliot when John Eliot purchased it from John Champernowne who, as legend has it, almost by accident, acquired the estate from Henry VIII. Port Eliot is now one of the two gardens in mainland Cornwall with an English Heritage Grade I for national significance.

East of St German's, towards Saltash and Torpoint, the great natural beauty of the landscape has given birth to many parks and gardens, chief among them Mount Edgcumbe, the other Grade I garden.

The importance of a 'prospect' for the eighteenth-century and later landscapers has been remarked upon several times already. Where, then, could there be a finer opportunity for such a view than over the extensive waters of the estuary, and the lower reaches of the Rivers Tamar and Lyner? The various inlets, or bays along the mouth of the Tamar have been called 'lakes', and as such present a broad perspective to the designer seeking a prospect. Wolsdon House, for instance, built above St John's village, has taken just such advantage of the first of these lakes after leaving the promontory of Mount Edgcumbe. In 1819 Loudon visited Tor House, which was then as celebrated for its view over the river to Devon, as for its garden, but, alas! this was to become hidden as Torpoint grew in size. A little farther along, however, Admiral Graves could satisfy his gaze with the sight of Devonport Dock over the Thanckes Lake, from a house that was later transferred to Portwrinkle. Antony had long been established to the north of Torpoint, at the mouth of the

Lynher, across the river from Trematon and Ince Castles on the other bank. Farther up the Lynher at Sheviock, Trethill House had been sited high enough, even though inland, to look along the estuary to the horizon. Sconner House, perhaps designed by the great Repton himself, and later to become the Dower House to Port Eliot, was placed where it could look across the river to St German's Quay opposite.

One of the simple pleasures of the populace of Plymouth in the nineteenth century, and still so today, was to take a boat by river to Cotehele Quay and beyond. Such a trip presents a more authentic impression of the estates along the river than can be gained from any enumeration of the towns - Saltash, Calstock, Callington and Gunnislake. Passing by the humble Mary Newman's Cottage at Saltash, but recently restored, is to be seen beyond the mouth of the Lynher the now reduced grounds of Moditonham House at the head of the Kingsmill Lake. Here Parson Arundell drained the mudflats at Landulph, so that he no longer needed to take a boat from his vicarage to church at high tide. Around a turn of the river, in the woods above the Quay, is Pentillie Castle, with its Folly Tower in which, if legend is to be believed, old John Tillie is still sitting, crumbling away after his death, with his pipe and bottle before him on the table. Alongside at Halton, but now long gone, there had once been a deer park. Past Cotehele Quay, if the voyage can be extended that far, under the great railway viaduct at Calstock, the river winds almost full circle around the former seat of Salusbury Trelawny at Harewood, until the weir puts an end to any further travel.

The rich variety of properties over this south-eastern corner of Cornwall more than compensates for the scattered distribution of estates in the central section, and the meagre offerings of the north.

ANTONY HOUSE and WOODLAND GARDEN, Torpoint

SX41 56 : EX108, GS348   OPEN

Antone, Domesday 1086; house listed grade I, forecourt and sundial (removed 1988) I, dovecote II*, stables, entrance lodge, walls + piers and gates to NE, screen wall and piers, kitchen garden walls, claire-voie, bath house, dovecote (remains), each II; garden and woodland each of 25 acres (10 ha) listed grade II, sloping from 60m. north-west to sea, with house at 25m., on Upper Devonian slates, with acid soil, 'medium loam on shale', in a SAGLV, and an AGSV; rainfall 35-40", temperature zone D; house and garden donated to the National Trust by Sir John Carew Pole in 1961, open Tuesdays, Wednesdays, Thursdays and Holiday Mondays, April through October, and Sundays June through August; woodland given to Carew Pole Garden Trust 1975, open 1990-98 CGOG, 1994-8 NGS, daily, March through October. There are official guides.

91. Antony. Sketch of the elaborate garden front by Edmund Prideaux, 1727.

92. Antony. The entrance front. (Twycross 1846: 36)

Antony had a long history before the arrival there of the Carews in the late fifteenth century. It had always been of importance for the much-frequented ferry at Antony Passage, and as agricultural land, held by the families of Haccombe, Archdeknes, Dawnay and Courtenay. It was through the marriage of Sir Nicholas Carew of Mohun's Ottery in Devon with Joan Courtenay, that Antony came to her fourth son, Alexander (d. 1492), great-great-grandfather of Richard Carew the historian, who described 'our cold harbour' as 'the poor home of mine ancestors'.

This may not have been entirely modesty, for Norden found it merely 'profitablye and pleasantly seated', and dwelt more, as did Carew himself, on his 'verie artefically contryued ... ponde of Salte water ... stored with muche and greate varietye of good Sea-fishe'. The 'banqueting house' on a small island to a design of his friend Sir Arthur Champernowne of Dartington, however, was never erected. A new house was built at Antony between 1711 and 1721 for Sir William Carew (1689-1743) on a new site, the medieval house probably being in the region of Tomboy Hill near the old dovecote. According to Lysons it was to designs of James Gibbs, which was doubted by Christopher Hussey, although Pevsner considered 'the composition and proportions [to be] worthy of a better name than that of the unknown designer of Puslinch, suggested' as the alternative.

In 1713 Humphry Bowen of Lambeth made a garden, approximately 575 ft (175m.) long by 264 ft (80m.) wide, which probably included a canal running across immediately in front of the house. The rather confusing sketch of the garden front by Edmund Prideaux in 1727 shows a large walled garden divided into four sections, the two near the house with parterres and fastigiate trees, probably yew, and the two farthest divided diagonally by paths. Beyond and outside are avenues radiating in several directions. The dovecote is also visible to the left of the house.

The family succession after the death of Sir William was not direct, but came eventually to Reginald, the great-grandson of Jane Carew, wife of Jonathan Rashleigh of Menabilly, who, as a grandson of Sir John Pole of Shute adopted the name of Pole Carew. Under Reginald Pole Carew (1753-1835) and his successors, Antony entered into its golden age. In 1788 he began to make changes in the garden, constructing a Cold Bath House, fed by sea-water, to designs by Thomas Parlby. Many trees were planted from seed brought back from America, and the (now decayed) figure-head of a ship, the *Jupiter*, was installed on the top of what became Jupiter Hill. The extensive and necessary shelter-belts were also formed at this time. Through the Rashleigh connection, Pole Carew became MP for Fowey, and a Privy Councillor under Pitt, who had consulted Repton over his estate at Holwood in Kent. On his recommendation Repton was invited to Antony, for which he prepared a Red Book. Pole Carew gained Repton's 'approbation' as a person 'whose judgement I much revere', and he became the channel for his introduction to other landowners. Repton considered this Red Book to be his *chef d'oeuvre*, an estimate confirmed at the present day by its being one of three selected for facsimile. All, however, was not left to Repton's discretion, but he was engaged in a lively discussion about 'convenience' in estate design, and Pole Carew collaborated in the carrying through and modification of his plans. Repton quoted from his experience at Antony in his *Sketches* of 1794 (pp. 53-5) and his *Observations* of 1803 (p. 94). In the National Trust guide it is recorded that:

> The lodge at Antony Passage and the lodge at the main gate bear a strong resemblance to Repton's drawings, but although his advice about planting seems to have been acted upon, his designs for embellishments to the house and terrace and its approaches were not adopted.

These would have obscured the eighteenth-century character of the site. It is not known whether the bold groupings of trees, and the central vista down to the water were actually designed by Repton himself, or simply followed his principles, but they have produced a most successful romantic landscape. The parterres to the garden front (as seen in the Prideaux sketch) were removed, and the walled garden relocated and rebuilt by Placido Columbani, which at present is occupied by a swimming pool and small greenhouse.

William Henry Pole Carew (1811-88) added the *porte-cochère* to the front of the house, built Maryfield Church, cut the first vista through the perimeter belt to give a view of Shillingham (belonging to the Bullers of Morval, to whom they were related), and began the yew walks which were extended in the next century, when the Burmese Bell Temple and granite lanterns were also erected. In 1901 an elaborate walled parterre was created to the north-west of the house, which ended with the *claire-voie*. This was returned to lawn in 1940, and the *claire-voie* moved to its present position.

During the whole of this period, although mentioned in the *Gardeners' Chronicle* of 1852, and listed in the *Hort. Direct.* from at least 1870 to 1924, Antony received no notice in the great horticultural journals. Its great reputation has grown up during this century under Sir Reginald Pole Carew (1849-1924), Sir John Carew Pole, (1902-93, who reversed the order of his names on succeeding to the Baronetcy of Pole of Shute in 1926), and his son, Sir Richard (b. 1938). In this they were encouraged and assisted by J.C. Williams of Caerhays and Lionel de Rothschild of Exbury, which led to the introduction of a great variety of azaleas, rhododendrons and magnolias. More recently an enclosed Summer Garden was begun in 1983 by the present Lady Carew Pole. Antony became one of Thurston's select gardens, and there is now a catalogue of 6,000 trees and shrubs on the estate. A specialist survey in 1990 concluded:

> Later 19th century developments [had] created a loosely formal layout which ignores Repton's advice but is successful in its own right, creating [an] interesting design which demonstrates the changing tastes in landscape over 250 years.

References: 17th, 18th, 19th (Hort. & Gen.) and 20th C; Illus; J. Harris, Artist and the Country House, *1979: 134; D. Jacques,* Georgian Gardens, *1983: 138; E. Malins,* Red Books of Humphry Repton, *a facsimile with introduction, 1976 i: 14-21.*

BAKE, near Trerulefoot

SX32 58 : EX108, GS348

English back = *ridge; the* Barton *and garden walls each listed grade II (the present* Bake House *is separate and not listed); small residual garden at 90m. altitude, on Upper Devonian slate, in an AGLV; rainfall 45-50", temperature zone D; private, the* Barton *is a farm.*

Gilbert, as was explained in our introduction, compared Catchfrench unfavourably with Bake, because it was not 'elevated' with a prospect. It is instructive to read, in one of his more purple passages, what he meant by 'sublime and beautiful, soft, luxuriant, and desolate':

> The surrounding dells, appear like the abodes of solitude and repose; while the distant view of Plymouth Sound, presents the sail of commerce, and the continual bustle of a warlike port. Beyond the varied windings of the Tamar, the bleak, far-stretching wilds of Dartmoor, meet the eye, whilst Hengston, rears its bold and gloomy eminence on the northern side, and Rough Tor, and Brownwilly, rise in conical forms, and throw a wild aspect on the western horizon. The mouldering walls of Trematon Castle, magnificent even in desolation, are also distinctly observed, and recal [*sic*] to the memory, the tales of age that have flown away; and while the spectator contemplates these interesting relics, - the memorials of departed greatness, he must be deeply impressed with the fleeting, fragile nature, of all sublunary things.

Here is the 'Picturesque' imagination in full spate. The old house at Bake had already burnt down in 1808, before this was written, but we are fortunate in possessing two sketches (which signify its importance in his eyes) drawn by Edmund Prideaux, in about 1727. The first shows a forecourt with central gateway and pillars, with an avenue of trees the whole width of the house (see Fig.7). The second is an oblique view, which is of particular interest. Two enclosed gardens can be seen: that along the end of the house and forecourt is relatively plain, but the adjoining enclosure to the rear of the house is elaborately laid out with parterres and cut trees, where two ladies walk in conversation.

93. Bake. Sketch by Edmund Prideaux, probably 1727. The garden where the ladies are walking is laid out as a parterre, which leads on into an orchard with trees planted in the quincunx pattern.

The area extending from this into the foreground is partially obscured by the frame, but on the right it appears to be an orchard planted in quincunx pattern, that is, with all the trees equidistant, so that they are in line when viewed either from the sides or the diagonals. In these sketches we have the rare benefit of seeing in some detail a late-seventeenth - early eighteenth-century Cornish garden. Nothing of this now survives: the detached acre-sized walled garden was built by Napoleonic prisoners.

References: 17th, 18th and 19th (Gen.).

CATCHFRENCH MANOR, St Germans

SX30 59 : EX108, GS348   OPEN

The name is probably from French, chasse franche = free warren, i.e. unrestricted game reserve (the field name 'Coney Yard' on the tithe map of c.1840 = rabbit warren); house listed grade II, ruins of manor house, and lodge, each II; garden 25 acres (10 ha) listed grade II, north facing slope 120-55m., with house at 87m., on Upper Devonian slates, with acid soil, in a SAGLV; rainfall 45-50", temperature zone D; private, open 1995-8 CGOG, 1995-6 NGS, daily (except Sundays), March through September.

Catchfrench was the principal house in the Duchy manor of Bonyalva, separated out of the Domesday manor of Pendrim and transferred to the Priory of Launceston. It passed by marriage from the Talverne family, of Talverne in Northill, to George Kekewich, from an Essex family, who came to Cornwall via Shropshire. Soon after, in 1580 as the date-stone reads, he rebuilt the house after a fire. Francis Fox, who had been cut off from his family in Wiltshire with £1,000 for becoming a Quaker, married Dorothy Kekewich in 1646 and came here. He later moved to Fowey, and from him stem the Fox families of Falmouth and Wadebridge. The property was briefly in the hands of Francis Robartes, Hugh Boscawen, and Hugh Fortescue Lord Clinton, before being sold in 1728 to Julius Glanville, of an old Devonshire family. In the late eighteenth century the house was remodelled, according to Sarah Gregor's (née Glanville) *Memoirs* (c. 1850), to designs of Rawlinson, a 'London' architect, but actually the Lostwithiel carpenter Charles Rawlinson. It was castellated

> by some thoroughly contemptible battlements which the wretched taste of the day was pleased to admire ... Altogether a worse specimen of building could hardly have been concocted by an ignorant pay-mistress and a very dull architect.

Gilbert had as little praise for the site of the house:

> The situation of Catchfrench House, appears to have been very injudiciously chosen, being placed under a hill, and thereby subject to considerable dampness; all its beauties being also hidden by its position, from the eye of the passenger. The choice of this spot, is also the more difficult to account for, as, had it been placed more south, it would have commanded, for many miles, the windings of the western road, and the variety of richly wooded vales, through which it passes.

Humphry Repton, working in the neighbourhood at Port Eliot, was invited by Francis Glanville in October 1792 to visit Catchfrench, and in the next year presented his Red Book. He wrote of the 'character and situation' of the place:

> The romantic situation of the house, its picturesque front, and the delightful scenery with which it is everywhere surrounded, leave little else to be done, but to give the whole place an air of extent and importance, by removing the appearance of a road so near its boundary, at the same time retaining the advantages of this public road which I have already hinted.

His chief work, which in great part still remains, was to re-route the approaches, to conceal the public highway (removed in about 1830), and to make 'the road for heavy carriages to the offices

... distinct from the coach roads or approaches to the house.' He designed a carriage ring with an oval centre at the entrance, which has now been tarmacked. On the western side of the house he proposed a 'view frame' looking from the house towards an 'eyecatcher' farm across the valley at Trebrownbridge, which he achieved by cutting a gentle bowl-shaped valley to the west of the house, using the spoil to raise the ground level by the dwelling. He also proposed a view to the north from a new, balustraded terrace, but this was never done. The quarry, probably the source of the building stone, he thought, if planted, would 'furnish an endless source of amusement, if conducted with the same taste and skill which are displayed in the rock scenery of Port Eliot' (q.v.). The description of the grounds by Gilbert, who was writing a quarter of a century after Repton's visit, shows how, with small expedients, he had been able to capitalize on the advantages of the site to improve its defects:

> The modern buildings, are in the castle style, and contain an excellent suit of apartments on the first floor. The whole of these, open into a terrace and shrubbery, tastefully laid out, with abundance of plants and flowers. A lawn gently unfolds itself from hence, through an easy descent, to the banks of the Seaton, surrounded with hills, which, through their different windings, let in many distant and interesting objects.

Gilbert, neither here nor elsewhere, ever mentions Repton, but his description shows that he was sensitive to, and aware of the objects of landscape design. Sarah Gregor's 'contemptible battlements' were removed in the nineteenth century, and the house reduced in size, with parts of the ruin, within which was an ice-house, retained as a romantic attachment. The Glanville family remained until 1930, after which the estate went into a decline, until in 1987 the present owners came with the intention of restoring the property from the neglect into which it had fallen. Catchfrench was one of Thurston's select gardens, but never listed in the *Hort. Direct.*, nor in the English Heritage *Register* until very recently. The Red Book is in the keeping of the Glanville family in Belper, Derbyshire, but typed extracts are lodged in the Cornwall Record Office, and at the house.

References: 17th, 18th, 19th (Hort. & Gen.) and 20th C; see Domesday (1086: 1.7), and Parl. (1649: 3).

COLDRENICK, Menheniot

SX29 61 : *EX107, GS348*

Cornish *kyl = nook, back + dreyn = thorny, pronounced colDRENick; *stable, now house, listed grade II, gate-piers II; medium to large estate, house at 90m., on Upper Devonian slates, with soil, 'acid overlying shillet'; rainfall 'around 40''', temperature zone E; private.*

Sir John Trelawny in 1592, at about the time he bought Trelawne (q.v.), also purchased Coldrenick, as *Hitchins* records, for a

> seat of a younger branch of the Trelawnys, which branch became extinct in 1764. Since that time it has passed successively into the families of Darell, Crabbe, and Stephens. This latter family took the name Trelawny, and Coldrinnick is now the property of his descendant Charles Trelawny, son of the late Edward Trelawny, Esq.

Gilbert adds that the mansion was

> erected ... in the beginning of the last century ... It stands on an agreeable elevation, surrounded with a park, which is now chiefly used as a pasture for sheep and cattle. It is pleasantly dotted over with clumps of firs, and various other trees.

A.C. Bartlett, when he visited Coldrenick in 1907, left with the impression that the principal planting of rare coniferous and other trees, had been by Edward John Trelawny (1792-1881), known as 'Greek Trelawny', because of his involvement in the Greek War of Independence. However, this is improbable since he neither lived here, nor is closely related. Trelawny had known Shelley and Byron in Italy in 1821, and prepared Shelley's tomb. He is described in the *Dictionary of National Biography* as a 'brilliant but inaccurate conversationalist' and inclined to 'romance'.

In 1876 the gardener, William Nanscawen, had sent to the *Garden* a list of twenty species of conifer, with their measurements. 'The newer kinds of Coniferae which we have planted,' he wrote, 'are making good specimens, and in a few years will equal, if not surpass, any in this country.' Bartlett later observed that:

> Contrary to the general custom in Cornwall, the mansion is built on high ground, and while it enjoys many fine views it is exposed to the fierce gales which periodically sweep the country. This has necessitated the planting of a broad belt of shelter trees to protect the rarer subjects. Attached to the mansion is a conservatory, and in front of this is a formal flower-garden.

The fierce gales in recent years, coupled with the age of the trees, has now made great inroads into this exceptional collection. The *Larix griffithii* figured in Bartlett's article was one such victim (see Fig.10), but I am informed that Hilliers have propagated material from it.

Thurston, who included Coldrenick among his select gardens, and commented on many of the conifers there in the 1930s, records that Charles Trelawny (recorded in the *Hort. Direct.* from 1870 to 1908), who developed the garden, 'had the trees labelled with name, date of planting, and country from which they came, but unfortunately the late owner [Maj.-Gen. John Jago Trelawny] had all the labels thrown away.' The garden remained listed until 1924.

The original house, which had been remodelled in the 1720s and is illustrated in Twycross (1846), was replaced in *c.* 1870 by a 'Half-timbered black and white Herefordshire- or Cheshire-looking Victorian mansion by C.F. Hayward,' (Pevsner). This was demolished in 1966 by the present owner, Mr Henry Sneyd, who inherited the estate from his grandmother in 1954, and now lives in the more convenient converted eighteenth-century stables. The surrounding gardens have been re-created in courtyards and shrubberies.

References: 17th, 18th, 19th (Hort. & Gen.) and 20th C; Illus.

COTEHELE, Calstock

SX42 68 : *EX108, GS337*   OPEN

Cornish cos = *wood* + *heyl = *estuary, pronounced* coTEEL; *house listed grade I, chapel, Prospect Tower, and dovecote each II*, garden walls, ice-house, and some other buildings and walls, each II; garden of 19 acres (7.6 ha) listed grade II, east sloping to river from 76m., on Upper Devonian slate to north, Culm Measures shale and grit to south, with acid soil, in a SAGLV, and in part an AGSV; rainfall 45-50", temperature zone F; given to the National Trust 'in 1947 by the Treasury ... in lieu of death duties from the 6th Earl of Mount Edgcumbe', open 1983-98 CGOG, 1987, 1991-8 NGS, daily, April through October, but without charge November through March. There are official guides in various editions.*

Cotehele, judged by Pevsner to be 'the most extensive and important Tudor house of Cornwall,' was until the reign of Edward III the seat of a family of that name, passing to the Edgcumbes by marriage to Hilaria de Cotehele. The old house, of which remnants remain in the lower walls, was remodelled for Sir Richard Edgcumbe (d. 1489) and his son Piers (d. 1539). Of the origin of the Chapel, Carew wrote:

> It is reported, and credited thereabouts, how Sir Richard Edgcumb the elder was driven to hide himself in those his thick woods, which overlook the river, what time being suspected of favouring the Earl of Richmond's party against King Richard the Third, he was hotly pursued, and narrowly searched for. Which extremity taught him a sudden policy, to put a stone in his cap, and tumble the same into the water, while these rangers were fast on his heels, who looking down

94. Cotehele, from the east. The first of four terraces 'laid out in old-fashioned flowers. No carpet bedding or any other monstrosities', and the house covered with 'plants to which no objection can apply.' (Garden 1893: ii. 21)

after the noise, and seeing the cap swimming thereon, supposed that he had desperately drowned himself, gave over their farther hunting, and left him his liberty to shift away, and ship over into Brittany: for a grateful remembrance of which delivery, he afterwards builded in the place of his lurking, a chapel, not yet utterly decayed.

There were in Carew's time two deer parks, which also appear on Norden's map, and a medieval dovecote, now restored. The oak and chestnut trees of great antiquity, although scarcely the thousand years suggested by Redding in 1842, regularly caused 'astonishment', and the yews were reckoned by Lipscombe in 1799 to be 'some of the largest ... in England'. The Edgcumbes transferred to Mount Edgcumbe in about 1553, after which Cotehele became no more than an occasional residence. The date of the Prospect Tower is debated, but is probably late eighteenth century, from the top of which, as late as 1870, it was said that Mount Edgcumbe itself could be distinctly seen. The house was remodelled about 1862, at about which time the terraces were laid out 'in old-fashioned beds and borders filled with hardy flowers', as seen in our illustration.

> The picturesque freedom of the planting and surroundings is delightful, especially to those who see so many stiff, trim gardens both in England and France.

The practice of covering the walls with 'plants to which no objection can apply' was also commended. Fitzherbert in 1902 felt that

> it is perhaps for its beds of simple flowers, its Cabbage Roses, Pinks, Carnations, Rockets, old Paeonies, and such like blossoms of a bygone day that its gardens are chiefly interesting.

In more recent years, since the grounds have been in the care of the National Trust, the gardens have been greatly developed. Below the terraces, and across the road in the upper valley garden are the dovecote, a nineteenth-century summerhouse, and a small lake which was probably the medieval stew-pond. There has been much planting in this area. Below, the lower valley becomes densely wooded, with clearings and pools with shrubs and water-loving plants. In the upper garden to the north-east of the house there is a square pond with lilies, and nearby an orchard. It was noted in 1893 that: 'This place' had been 'the centre of very extensive fruit gardens, hundreds of acres being devoted to Cherries, Strawberries, Raspberries, Plums, &c.', although not all of these, of course, were in the Cotehele estate itself. This was one of Thurston's select gardens, which had been listed in the *Hort. Direct.* from 1908 to 1924.

References: 17th, 18th, 19th (Hort. & Gen.) and 20th C; Illus; F.V.J. Arundell, Cothele, c. 1840-50; T. Garner, Domestic Architecture I, 1911: 49 (plan); Manpower Services Commission, 1982.

INCE CASTLE, Saltash

SX40 56 : *EX108, GS348*   OPEN*

Cornish probably enys = island or tongue of land, pronounced INS as in 'instant'; house documented as 1653, but in 1620 style, listed grade I, two archways each II; garden of 5 acres (2 ha), north and south-east sloping to river from 25m., on Upper Devonian slates, soil 'shale, acid', in a SAGLV, and in part an AGSV; rainfall 40-45", temperature zone D; private, open 1983-98 CGOG, 1987, 1991-8 NGS, one Sunday each month from March to August.

Although Ince is an ancient site which was once part of the Duchy manor of Trematon, the remarkable garden there has been created only since the Second World War. The property had been acquired, probably with the manor of Landrake, around 1578, by Sir Harry Killigrew of the Arwenack family. As a supporter of the Royalist cause, his son dug earth-works (there was no 'castle' here then) in an attempt to hold the peninsula for the King. But he was powerless against the Commonwealth garrison at Antony on the opposite shore. There is a legend that one

95. Ince Castle. Sketch by Edmund Prideaux, c. 1727. The house has now been refaced, the towers given hipped roofs, and there are other slight alterations.

96. Ince Castle, the south side. The parterre garden leads up to a lawn and paved area with crevice plants. The walled pond garden and shell house are to the left. (Country Life 1967)

of the Killigrews 'kept a wife in each tower' of the castle, 'neither of whom was aware of the existence of the others'. The improbability of this tale is compounded by the fact that a 'new house of brick', presumably the 'castle' as sketched by Edmund Prideaux in 1727, was built by Edward Nosworthy, a Truro tradesman, after he had purchased the estate from the Killigrews. However, Christopher Hussey still was of the opinion that stylistically it is more appropriate to the Killigrews than to a tradesman. The house was sequestered at the end of the Civil War, and passed through many changes of ownership before becoming a farmhouse and, in the nineteenth century, falling into decay.

After the First World War, Montague Eliot, later the eighth Earl of St Germans, bought Ince with the intention of restoring it, but he never lived there himself. It then changed hands several times, usually to those whose interests were maritime rather than horticultural. Then, in 1960, it was bought by Viscountess Boyd and her late husband, who are entirely responsible for the gardens around the house. On the south side a parterre has been laid out, with cobbled paths and a central fountain flanked by obelisks, as is seen in our illustration. The steps at the end lead up to a lawn, beyond which is a paved area or patio, in front of the house, with crevice plants, and a central basin. Leading out of the parterre garden at right angles is a walled garden with a canal pool, adorned at each end with stone cherubs riding on snails. The entrance piers, surmounted by lead urns, frame an octagonal shell house at the far end, built by Viscount Boyd himself.

To the south-west of the house the walls have been used to enclose a white garden, and from a lower terrace there is a dramatic panoramic view of the river and countryside beyond, with a toposcope to identify points of interest in the scenery. Nearby is a bathing area, with a summer-house, and a rectangular pool with semi-circular ends, where the obelisk theme from the parterre is continued, one being placed at each corner. There is a dovecote, among other features in the garden, many of which came from the courtyard of Lady Boyd's father, the Earl of Iveagh's house in St James's Square in London. A cherry walk leads away from the north-east corner of the lawn to the old woodland, now opened up and interspersed with many ornamental shrubs and trees.

Thurston had included Ince Castle among his select estates, presumably for its ancient trees, since the ornamental garden had not then been begun. Today Ince must certainly be numbered among the premier contemporary gardens in Cornwall, both for its planting and design. The house was damaged by fire in 1988, but has been restored.

References: 17th, 18th, 19th (Gen.), 20th C; Illus.

KEN CARO, St Ive

SX31 69 : *EX108, GS337*   OPEN*

Cornish [?*keyn = ridge] + carow = stag, pronounced KEN CARo as in arrow; 4 acre (1.6 ha) garden, east sloping, at 175m. altitude, on Upper Devonian slate, with 'very acid soil', in an AGLV; rainfall 45-50", temperature zone F; open 1983-98 CGOG, 1987, 1991-8 NGS, Sunday to Wednesday mid April through June, Tuesday and Wednesday July through August. There are plant sales.

Ken Caro is set high on the ground above Bicton Manor and Woods, whose former deer park is reflected in its name. Without protection, the garden would be windswept, but this has been guarded against by the planting of great conifer hedges along the eastern edge, which project north of the house to enclose island beds large enough to accommodate rhododendrons and small flowering trees. The bungalow lies in a depression on the south side of this enclosure, where the sloping banks on all four sides are planted with alpines, dwarf conifers and other appropriate plants, resulting in the dwelling almost disappearing from view. The northern side of the projection is devoted to vegetable and nursery beds. Along the western side of the garden are smaller beds, variously planted and protected here and there by specimen conifers, among which is a small Japanese garden. In one corner is a pond with water-fowl and aviary birds, and separately, a small dovecote on a pole.

The original garden, begun c. 1970 by Mr and Mrs Willcock, occupies some two acres (0.8 ha), but during the last five years it has been extended outwards to almost double this size, in a quite formal design. Artificial windbreaks are being used, until a natural shelter belt has grown up, but the exposure is only too evident, which increases one's admiration for the skilled cultivation that made it possible to create the earlier section so successfully. This is a plantsman's garden of great attraction and interest.

References: 20th C.

KLYMIARVEN HOTEL, see Waterloo Villa

MARY NEWMAN'S COTTAGE, Culver Road, Saltash

SX42 58 : EX108, GS348   OPEN*

Garden of 0.5 acre (0.2 ha), on Upper Devonian slates, in a SAGLV; rainfall 40-45", temperature zone E; open 1987-8, 1990-98 CGOG, 1987, 1991-6 NGS, Saturdays, Sundays, and Bank Holidays, May through September. There is an official leaflet.

Mary Newman was married to Francis Drake in 1569 when she was 17, at St Budeaux Church, Plymouth, where she lies buried. The tradition that she lived in this house had already become accepted by 1820, and there is no reason to disbelieve it. There have been dwellings on this spot since the twelfth century, although the house as it is at present would appear to date from the fifteenth or sixteenth century, perhaps incorporating earlier material. The site has been described as originally a 'burgage plot', in which a cow might be kept and vegetables grown. [Burgage plots in Salisbury, for example, were 3 by 7 perches, i.e. c. 50 by 115 feet.]

The present garden has been designed in a typically cottage style of a much later date. It is divided into three sections; that nearest the house is a herb garden, while the middle section is given over to a lawn, with borders, and an arbour from which there is a view of the river and its bridges. It has been romantically suggested that from an upper window-seat in the cottage, Mary herself could have seen her husband's ship rounding the headland into harbour. In the final section, paths wind through beds of roses, herbaceous and other plants. Among those worth mentioning are old-fashioned roses with the appropriate names, 'Sir Walter Raleigh', and 'William Shakespeare', and a green santolina brought from Sudeley Castle where it is said that Kathryn Parr used the plant from her herb garden to ease Henry VIII's legs. Other donations of plants have come from many sources. The Cottage has been restored and is maintained by the Tamar Protection Society.

References: 20th C.

MODITONHAM, Botus Fleming

SX41 61 : EX108, GS348

The derivation of the name is probably English, pronounced Muttenham *as spelt in the Parl.(1649); early 18th C. house listed grade II*, dovecote, pair of late 18th C. lodges and gate-piers, each II; medium to large estate, on south facing slope in a west-east valley, at 25m., on Upper Devonian slates and alluvium, with acid soil, in a SAGLV, an AGSV and in part a CNCS; rainfall 40-45", temperature zone E; private, divided into two residences as* Moditonham House, *and* Moditonham Park *(the former stables).*

Moditonham, wrote Moule in 1837,

> is the only manor in the parish, and was held in very early times by Philip de Valletort, under the Earl of Cornwall. It was afterwards possessed by the Dawney family, from which it passed to the Courtenays, and at a later period, was held by the Waddon family. In the year 1689, John Granville, Earl of Bath, and Governor of Plymouth [see also Stowe], held a meeting at this house, then the seat of John Waddon, Esq, with the commissioners of the Prince of Orange, about the surrender of Pendennis and Plymouth Castles, which were in consequence of a treaty delivered up.

It was, however, Charles Carpenter and his wife who, according to Gilbert, early in the nineteenth century, formed the garden,

> continually enriching and improving every department, by the introduction of rare plants, fruit trees, flowers, ornamental casts, &c. The entrance towards the house is at a neat lodge, in the form of two square towers, with Gothic windows; and passing through the lawn, a ridge of sloping grounds, facing the south, is seen, charmingly laid out in gardens, hot houses, and shrubberies. These are occasionally intermixed with neat walks, the edges of which are embellished with innumerable flowers; and in

97. Moditonham, south-west view. A road between the house and the dovecote, running down to a quay, has now divided the estate in two. (Gilbert 1820: ii. 439)

the sudden windings, are frequently discovered small rustic buildings, incrusted with moss, lighted with stained glass, and over-hung with clustering ivy.

It might be noted in passing that Repton deprecated the practice of twin lodges, for their 'forced symmetry' and because, as here, it made for cramped quarters. *Lake* added that Carpenter

> constructed an embankment across the bottom of the vale, and thereby not only increased the land of the estate, but also prevented the nauseous smell which arose from the mud, at the going out of the tide.

Moditonham House, which is now owned by the National Trust, has been let as a private residence, but since, prior to this, there had been no continuous ownership for many years, the handsome gardens described by Gilbert have become altered: by a division into two properties separated by a road to the quay; by the sale of one of the lodges and other parts of the estate; and also by their use, for a time, as a market garden. Nevertheless the original house, with its terrace, an old apple-house, one of the lodges, and the walled garden still survive as a unit. In the grounds surrounding the former stables, now known as Moditonham Park, there has been preserved a dovecote, described in the listing as 'unusually designed, ... and would have been viewed from Moditonham House, to the south, with the appearance of a Gothick folly.'

References: 17th, 18th, 19th (Gen.), 20th C; Illus.

MORVAL, CHURCHTOWN, near Looe*

SX25 56 : *EX107, GS348*

Garden of 7.5 acres (3 ha), at 40m. altitude, on Meadfoot Group slates and grit, with acid soil, in a SAGLV; rainfall 40-45", temperature zone D; opened 1984-97 CGOG.

'Churchtown' comprises a group of cottages, grounds and a 250-year-old walled kitchen garden, all originally part of the estate of Morval House, which is across the road. The formation of a new garden, by a former owner of the house, began in 1961. There has been foundation planting around the cottages, but the larger part of the ground has been kept as lawn, with one considerable area between the woodland (carpeted in spring with daffodils) and the walled garden, planted with ornamental shrubs. The walled garden itself is also of particular interest for the curved, south-facing end wall, intended to capture the maximum heat from the sun. The greenhouses, in which was found an old lead cistern - similar to another at Ince Castle, and both dated 1753 - became ruinous, and have been taken down, but this large area is still cultivated as a traditional kitchen garden, with vegetables grown in lines and a central area for fruit, all defined by neatly clipped box hedges.

References: see Morval House.

MORVAL HOUSE, Sandplace near Looe

SX25 56 : *EX107, GS348*

Named after a person or a manor, pronounced MOOR*val; house listed grade I, Steppes Lodge, gate-piers and garden* wall, each II; medium to large estate, house facing south-east at 40m. altitude, on Meadfoot Group slates and grit, with acid soil, in a SAGLV; rainfall 40-45", temperature zone D; private.

Morval House, which is Tudor in origin, was reckoned by Pevsner to be 'one of the best houses in Cornwall'. John Keast writes:

> The manor of Morval passed with one of the co-heiresses of the Glynns to the Coodes in the reign of Henry VIII and to the Bullers by marriage in 1637 ... [it] remained the seat of the Bullers until the late 19th century when it passed by marriage to the Tremaynes and later to the Kitsons, who recently sold the property.

However, they retained the area around the walled garden, now known as Morval Churchtown (q.v.). The house, wrote Gilbert,

> is situated at the head of an extensive lawn, dotted with large trees, through which is carried a coach road, afterwards continued through shady glens, bordering on an estuary of the Looe, whence the eye catches a pleasing glimpse across the water, and the beautifully wooded grounds of Trenant Park [q.v.]. The combination of scenery around Morval, is perhaps as picturesque and inviting as any in England.

More recently Betjeman wrote of the

> steep lane [which] plunges between ferny hedges and under huge beech trees to the landscaped park of Morval House ... turned comfortably towards its little park and green slopes with beech trees on top, winding woods and little lake in the middle distance.

This was one of Thurston's select gardens.

References: 17th, 18th, 19th (Gen.) and 20th C; Illus.

MOUNT EDGCUMBE, Cremyll, Torpoint

SX45 52 : EX108, GS348   OPEN

Formerly West Stonehouse, Devon; named after the family; house (restored after a fire during the Second World War) listed grade II, orangery, triumphal arch, shell seat, Temple of Milton, St Julian's Well, Rame Head Chapel, each II*, fountain, stairway [Italian Garden], Thomson's Seat, French House, Timothy Brett's monument, monument to Sophia [French Garden], English Garden house, Tudor Blockhouse, Garden Battery, Folly, Lady Emma's Cottage, Kennels, each II, and various ornaments, seats, lodges etc, in total over 50 listings; grounds and park 865 acres (350 ha), formal gardens 10 acres (4 ha) listed grade I, north-east sloping 116m. to sea, house at 45m., on Middle Devonian slates to north with limestone on shore and Staddon and Meadfoot Grits to south, with acid soil, in an AONB and HC, in part a CNCS, and an AGHV with AMs (Blockhouse and Round Barrow); rainfall 30-35", temperature zone D; Country Park, owned jointly by Plymouth City Council and Cornwall County Council, open daily all year. Official histories and guides.

Mount Edgcumbe, originally West Stonehouse, and part of the Valletort estate was, until 1844, in the county of Devon, although like Werrington ecclesiastically in Cornwall. This location, and the political and literary connections of the Edgcumbes up-country, have resulted in this being more an English than a typically Cornish garden. Sir Piers Edgcumbe of Cotehele, by his marriage to the wealthy heiress of the Durnfords, who owned the Valletort estates, came into possession of West Stonehouse, where in 1515 he received a licence from Henry VIII to impale deer. His son, Sir Richard (1499-1562) then decided to move from Cotehele to take up residence at the newly-named Mount Edgcumbe. Here, in 1547, he began to build a new house to the designs of Roger Palmer of North Buckland, which was completed in 1550.

This house is of particular interest in retaining the castellation of a fortified dwelling, yet being open and outward looking to 'the prospect', in the manner of a later age. As the generations succeeded, so too the estate began to be developed. Richard (1639-88), who was knighted at the Restoration, as so many other landowners at the time, improved his grounds by the replanting of woods, and the creation of vineyards and orchards. His successor, the first Lord Edgcumbe (1679-1758), is credited with uniting the deer park with the garden, and planting the terrace walk so that full advantage could be taken of the prospect. Professional landscapers were not engaged, but the head gardener, Thomas Hull, who was a subscriber to Switzer's *Practical Husbandman*, seems to have been capable enough on his own to carry through the designs. By this time Mount Edgcumbe was becoming, and was to remain, a popular destination for visitors on tour. Samuel Pepys called here in 1683, and Celia Fiennes on her side-saddle in 1695 mentioned the 'walks', 'a fine terrace', and 'esteemed' it 'the finest seat I have seen'.

Edmund Prideaux's sketches, made in 1716 or 1727, show the grounds as chiefly wooded, but with a broad avenue from the house. A few years later, in the aerial view by Badeslade in *Vitruvius Britannicus* (1739), the avenue extends to the shore, to the right the Cascade of Lakes, to the left an elaborate 'Wilderness' – a plantation of small trees with winding paths, which may be compared with the design at Prideaux Place (see Fig.113). On the extreme left of this view can be seen the Amphitheatre, a scooped vale, perhaps

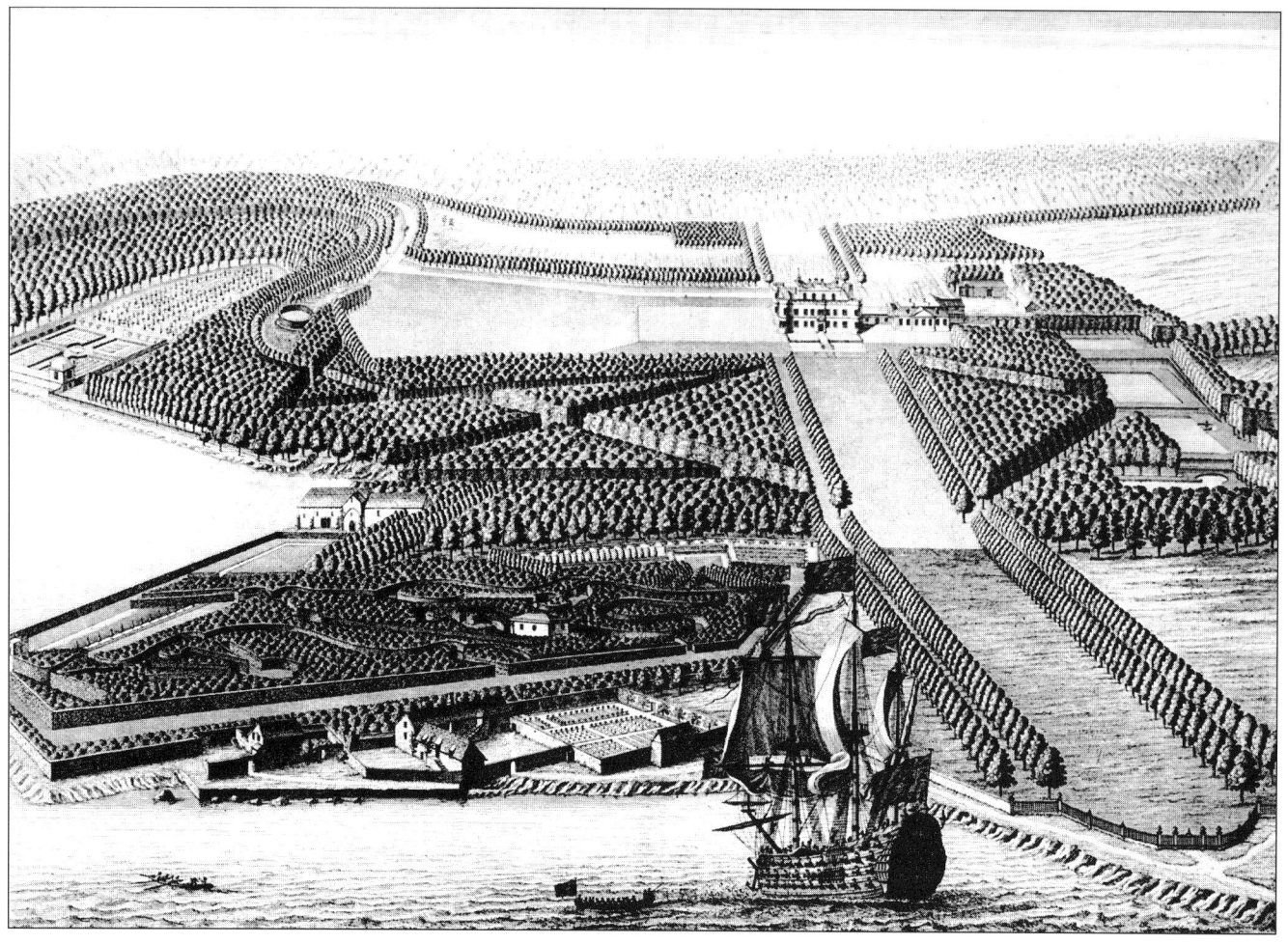

*98. Mount Edgcumbe. View by T. Badeslade, 1737. The destruction of the 'Wilderness' (bottom left) in the late eighteenth century afforded the opportunity to lay out the Italian and other gardens. The amphitheatre towards the top left of the picture became the site of the Temple of Milton and the 'Walls of Paradise'. (*Country Life *1960)*

assisted by quarrying, and, on the shoreline, a formal walled garden with two pavilions.

Lord Edgcumbe had been an MP and an intimate friend of Walpole. His son, George (1721-95) was a friend of the Royal Family, for which he received his Earldom in 1789 after a visit by King George III and Queen Charlotte. This was a period during which the family, who had a house in fashionable Richmond, became acquainted with many literary figures of the day and the writings of others, such as James Thomson, author of the *Seasons*, which were to influence directly the development of their estate in Cornwall. The first Earl was responsible for consciously designing the Amphitheatre to illustrate Milton's description of the 'Wall of Paradise', so effectively that some believed that the poet had actually written the lines, which were inscribed in his Temple, on the spot. The poet Thomson was commemorated with a seat in a Doric alcove. There was a ruined castle, grotto, and an arch on the cliff path. Walpole himself felt that it had 'the beauties of all other places added to beauties of its own,' which had been created by an intermix of wood and lawns. Pococke was taken around in 1750 by the Baron and his son to admire the view, with the help of a 'moveable camera obscura made in a centry box', which he thought 'by far the finest situation I ever saw, exceeding every thing in the beauty of the near prospects.' It was the upper terraces and the Amphitheatre which provided the broad panoramic views; the lower walks had picturesque 'hide and discover' glimpses.

In 1779 the American War of Independence alerted the government to the danger of invasion from France and Spain (see also Trewarthenick), so that many trees were felled which might hide lurking invaders. This was the signal for the first Earl's wife soon after to plan a flower garden, now the English Garden, in the position of the Wilderness on Badeslade's print. She wished the design to be similar to that described by William Mason at Nuneham:

> Irregular, yet not in patches quaint,
> But interspos'd between the wand'ring lines
> Of shaven turf ...

In 1783 he came himself from Yorkshire to supervise the planting. Lines from Cowper's poem *The Task* were inscribed on a seat at the entrance:

> Prospects, however lovely, may be seen
> Till half their beauties fade ...
> Then snug enclosures in some shelter'd spot,
> Where frequent hedges intercept the eye,
> Delight us ... .

The Orangery had already been rebuilt to the design of Thomas Pitt, second Lord Camelford, and became one of the main features of the Italian Garden laid out *c*. 1785 by Richard, the second Earl (1764-1839), and his wife Sophia. At the opposite side to the Orangery is a diagonal stairway. On its terrace is a bust of Ariosto and a quotation from his heroic romance. On the balustraded terrace stands the Apollo of Belvedere, between Venus de Medicii and Bacchus. In the centre is a fountain, the gift of the Earl of Bessborough, supported by marble figures resembling mermaids. A few years later, between about 1803 and 1806, another smaller enclosure was laid out in a formal parterre, with trellis arcades, and a basin of water, as a French Garden. An octagonal room with mirrors reflecting vistas from the garden, flanked by two conservatories, occupied one side. The Earl himself extended the Earl's Drive, and was responsible for much new planting.

Among other features were the Fernery in a small quarry, with classical relics, thought by Gilbert to have the appearance of a Roman (though now a dogs') cemetery, and the Shore Walk, with a restored late-sixteenth century blockhouse and a battery constructed in 1861. The 'romantic shrubbery' towards Picklecombe, and Mrs Damer's garden planted in the Zigzags probably in 1780, and visited by Beckford in 1781, formerly held the camellia collection. A survey in 1985 plotted over 6,000 trees. It is, however, impossible in a such a short note to do justice to a garden that is so rich in interest, but by way of summary the conclusion of the Garden History Society's report cannot be bettered:

> The unique importance of Mount Edgecumbe in situation, diversity of prospect, evolution from medieval deer park to sea-girt landscaped park, its layers of garden history and literary and historical associations, make it [an] outstanding national heritage. It has remained remarkably unspoiled and intact, a rare example of an early landscaped garden, where later additions have enhanced its essential character and historic interest.

References: 17th, 18th, 19th (Hort. & Gen.) and 20th C; *Illus:* E.D. Clarke, A tour through the south of England, *1793;* Duke of Rutland, Journal of a tour, *1805: 132-4,202-3;* W. Gilpin, Observations on the Western parts of England, *1808: 215-19;* A Walk around Mount Edgcumbe, *1808-41;* L. Simond, Journal of a Tour, *1815 vol.i. 7-9;* R. Havell, The tour, or select views on the south coast, *1827: pl. 18;* Britton & Brayley, Devonshire and Cornwall, *1832: 37-41;* J.L.P. Duprez, Visitors' Guide to Mount Edgcumbe, *1871;* W. Crossing, Mount Edgcumbe Park, *1899;* L. Melville, Life and Letters of William Beckford, *1910: 123;* H.S. Lewis (ed), Horace Walpole's Correspondence, *New Haven 1965, xxxiii: 211;* T. Gray, The Garden History of Devon, *Exeter 1995: 156-60.*

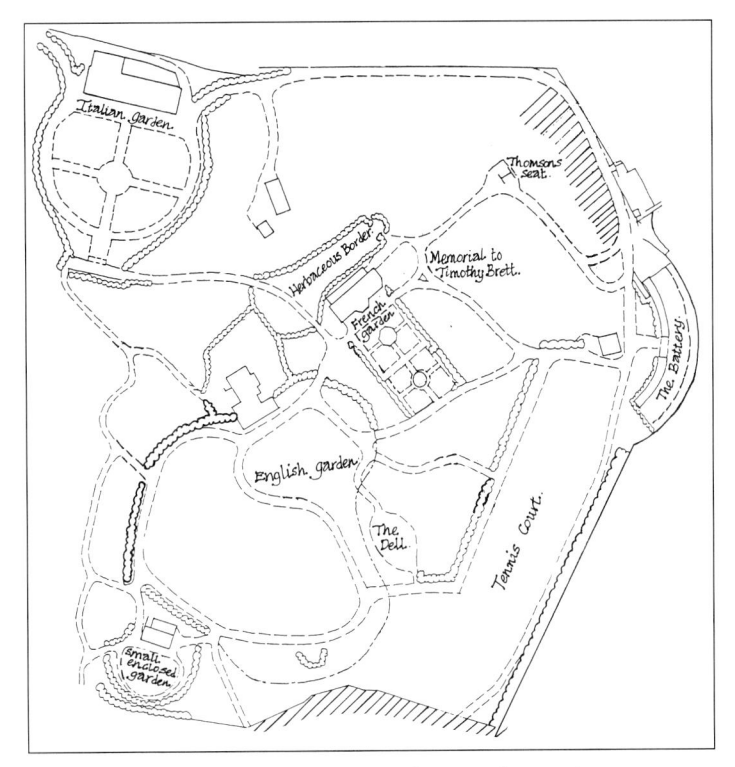

99. Mount Edgcumbe. Plan of the various gardens today.

MOYCLARE, Lodge Hill, Liskeard

SX24 63 : EX107, GS348   OPEN

Town garden of 1 acre (0.4 ha) at 100m., on Middle Devonian slates, with acid soil; rainfall 45-50", temperature zone E; open 1983-93 CGOG, 1986, 1998 NGS, holiday Mondays.

This is essentially a plantsman's garden, which was described in a series of articles in the *JRHS*, the last being entitled 'Cramming them in', which, Mrs Reid wrote ten years later, 'reflects my garden philosophy'. The garden began in 1927 from one-third of an acre (0.14 ha) of rough meadow, probably part of the Trevillis estate, which was extended ten years later to an acre (0.4 ha). The planting of trees all around, originally intended as wind-breaks, inadvertently turned the garden into a frost pocket. From the beginning it was decided, after visiting so many one-season Cornish gardens, that this would be planted for all-the-year-round flowering. Mrs Reid became a friend of Margery Fish, the gardening writer, who stayed here on several occasions, and shared with her a common interest in variegated plants, which they exchanged with each other. 'Most beds in this garden,' she wrote,

> are deliberately planted far too closely. I never want to see any bare earth at all. I am often surprised at the way many plants will flourish in close harmony ... Like most Cornish gardeners I try to grow plants that are really too tender and three times, in 1947, in 1963 and in 1979, the garden has been badly hit. Leptospermums, acacias, grevilleas, correas, callistemons, phormiums, mahonias, hebes and olearias were all destroyed.

From the outset the garden, which is on a flat site, was planned so that it could not be seen all at one glance, with the result that it appears to be larger than in fact it is. Moira Reid died recently, at an advanced age, and members of the Cornwall Garden Society miss her mellifluous Irish tones, distributing from huge trays 'crammed' with small packets, seed gathered from her own and other gardens. She claimed, with good reason, Moyclare to be the most televised garden in the county.

References: 20th C.

NEWTON FERRERS, near Callington

SX34 65 : *EX108, GS348*

Niweton Domesday 1086; English + family name; house and terrace listed grade I, terrace, three sets of gate piers, each I, stables dated 1688, store, 15th C. well-house, 17th C. bake-house, late 17th C. garden walls, each II; seven 18th C. garden artifacts, including a bust and statuary, each II; large grounds, south-east and west facing slope from house 75-40m., on Middle Culm Measure grits and shales, and Lower Culm Measure shales and cherts, with acid soil, in an AGLV, an AGSV and CNCS; rainfall 45-50", temperature zone E; private.

Newton is recorded in *Lake* as the property of the ancient family of

> De Ferrers, who resided here from a remote period until 1314, when Isolda, daughter and heiress of John de Ferrers, carried it in marriage to John Coryton, Esq., of Coryton in Lifton,

100. Newton Ferrers. The sketch of this large estate is not in essentials unlike that sketched by Prideaux in 1716, except that the top storey of the house had been removed. (Twycross 1846: 45)

Devon. The property continued in the Corytons until the family became extinct in the male line on the decease of Sir John Coryton in 1739.

Members of the Coryton family were also at Crocadon, and later at Pentillie Castle (q.v.). John Coryton's widow's family sold the property to Edward Collins, whose family are listed in the *Hort. Direct.* from at least 1870 until 1924. The dates on the gate-piers indicate that the mansion - to be seen illustrated among Prideaux's sketches - was built about 1686-95 for Sir William Coryton, and restored for Sir Digby Collins in 1880. It was described by Pevsner as:

> The earliest Cornish mansion of classical design, that is without any trace of Tudor survivals. Unfortunately two-thirds of the house were gutted by fire in 1940. Some of it has been rebuilt; the rest stands as a picturesque ruin. - Lead figures and a Nymph by one of the *Adam*, French C18, sculptors, on the lawn [some now stolen].

Gilbert described the grounds at some length:

> The lands, which stretch away from the house in different directions, to a great extent, have an uncommonly romantic appearance, and nature has thrown them into so many fanciful forms, as to render the whole particularly interesting to the spectator. Many of the eminences, are ornamented with large clusters of firs, between which, enormous rocks are seen rearing their shattered heads, beautifully contrasted by sloping declivities, clothed with lively verdure. The park is of great extent, and was formerly well stocked with deer; but is now used for the more useful purpose of grazing sheep, horses, and horned cattle: The greater part of the other lands is converted into tillage. The gardens at Newton are large, and produce excellent fruit, and a choice variety of shrubs and flowers. Here are also some excellent orchards, which in the autumn are loaded with fine apples; and in the adjoining grounds, are many open and extensive walks.

It is unaccountable that Gilbert does not mention the remarkable 'hard landscaping', especially the granite terraces, balustrades, gate-piers, and semi-circular steps, which so impressed a later age, since they date from before his time in the late seventeenth century. They were featured in *Country Life* in 1904, and again in 1938, and their photographs reprinted in Gertrude Jekyll's *Garden Ornaments* of 1918, although she felt that the ball finials were out of proportion. This was one of Thurston's select gardens, but he had little to say about it, and cited only the yew, mentioned in the 1904 article, and the two avenues of *Tilia platyphyllos* and *T. vulgaris*. There are lakes along the levels. The property has recently changed ownership, and it is possible that this impressive garden may again be open to the public.

References: 17th, 18th, 19th (Hort. & Gen.) and 20th C; Illus.

101. Newton Ferrers. The impressive seventeenth-century terraces, granite balustrades and steps, are the most celebrated feature of this estate. (Country Life 1904)

PELYNT VICARAGE, Pelynt

SX20 55 : EX107, GS348

Plunent *Domesday 1086, now* Pelynt House; *Cornish* plu = *parish* + St Nenna, *pronounced* PLINT *house listed grade II; garden of 3 acres (1.2 ha), at 125m. altitude, on Meadfoot Group slates and grits, with acid soil; rainfall 40-45", temperature zone D; private, open on occasions.*

The Vicarage was built for the Revd J.B. Kitson in 1841, in a Tudor style to the designs of the notable Cornish architect, George Wightwick. The late Geoffrey Grigson, whose father had been vicar here, informed Thurston (who included this among his select gardens) that the grounds had been laid out

> in the thirties or forties of the last century with chestnuts, oaks, conifers, etc., by Colonel Cox [Cocks] of the family still at Treverbyn Vean. Most of the rare shrubs have gradually gone.

Even so, the garden still has interest and some fine trees and shrubs, perhaps planted since these remarks in 1930. The lawn in front of the house was laid out in four terraces, with two flights of steps each flanked by two yews. The lower lawn had been levelled, first for croquet and then for tennis, but now has a pond at the south-east corner, while the land beyond rises with plantations of trees. At the south-west corner a path runs down into a dell, where a waterfall feeds a small pool. There is a small granite house, now set up for a generator or pump, which was formerly a privy. Anthony Bax, in his book *The English Parsonage* (1964), has a chapter on this 'necessary' subject of the 'Jericho', in which he wrote:

> The rectory drive might be 150 yards long, and wind impressively, but the rector retired after breakfast to read *The Times* in an earth closet under a spreading yew tree. (p.167.)

(And not only the rector, see Menabilly.) When the 'necessary house' is found entered in the Glebe Terriers of 1673 and 1735, this should not be regarded as a mere formality, but as an indication that these parsonages were considered superior and 'up-to-date'. The provision for sanitation, although rarely mentioned, is as much an essential part of estate design as other functional necessities such as water supplies, the provision for food in stew-ponds, dovecotes and kitchen gardens, and fuel from plantations.

Walking back towards the house, one meets what were once the walled kitchen gardens, one of which has now been planted as a formal rose garden, and the other less formally, with wall shrubs and climbers. An archway leads back to the terrace in front of the house. Geoffrey Grigson, who was born here in 1905, has described the parish and his life there in two books - *The Crest on the Silver* (1950) and *Freedom of the Parish* (1954). Perhaps of even more interest is a lesser-known volume entitled *Gardenage* (1952), where in the first chapter, he muses upon the inevitable decline of vicarage gardens in general, and of that at Pelynt in particular:

> They worry the vicars and the rectors who live each within his own wilderness. To enter and fight one's way about in them evokes sadness and even resentment if one happens to be a parson's child, old enough to remember a vicarage garden in due order, with the box edges clipped, the Gloire-de-Dijon nailed back to the wall above the drawing room window and the petals of the rose-scented peony falling on to a drive which was kept free of grass and plantain. (p.1.)

References: 17th, 19th (Gen.) and 20th C.

PENTILLIE CASTLE, St Mellion, near Callington
SX40 64 : *EX108, GS348*

102. Pentillie Castle, 'by nature, next' in Loudon's opinion, 'to Mount Edgcumbe'. The house had been recently remodelled by Wilkins father and son, the steep terracing, with its niches to the front providing many opportunities for planting. (Gilbert 1820: ii. 440)

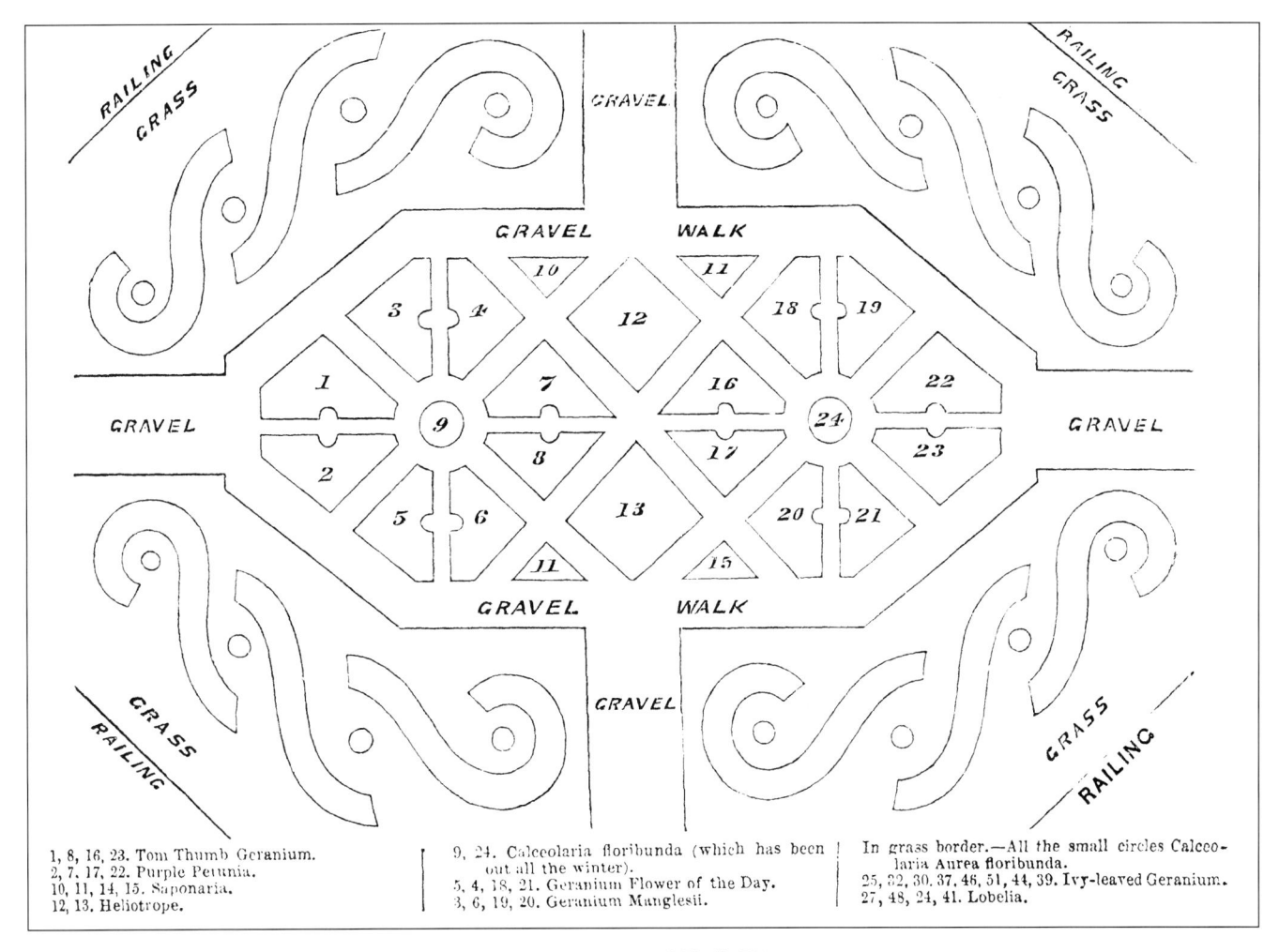

1, 8, 16, 23. Tom Thumb Geranium.	9, 24. Calceolaria floribunda (which has been out all the winter).	In grass border.—All the small circles Calceolaria Aurea floribunda.
2, 7, 17, 22. Purple Petunia.	5, 4, 18, 21. Geranium Flower of the Day.	25, 32, 30, 37, 46, 51, 44, 39. Ivy-leaved Geranium.
10, 11, 14, 15. Saponaria.	3, 6, 19, 20. Geranium Manglesii.	27, 48, 24, 41. Lobelia.
12, 13. Heliotrope.		

103. Pentille Castle. Plan of one of the flower gardens. (J. Hort. 1863: ii. 71)

Cornish pen + Tillie = family name, pronounced penTILLy; house dated 1698 with considerable remodelling, listed grade II*, mausoleum, and statue, each II*, service buildings, stables, terrace walls, kitchen garden walls, ice-house, well-house, folly lodge, gate-piers at entrance to avenue, walls + piers and railings at W entrance, keeper's cottage, gardener's cottage, Quay cottage, bathing house, and Quay steps, each II; large estate on east facing promontory and valley, 75m. to river, on Middle Culm Measures grit and shales ringed by Upper Devonian slates, with acid soil, in a SAGLV, an AGSV and CNCS; rainfall 45-50", temperature zone E; private.

James Tillie, who built Pentillie Castle in the seventeenth century (although in *Hitchins* it is said to have 'had nothing of the castellated character' as is confirmed in the Prideaux sketch), appears to have arisen from humble circumstances as a servant to the Coryton family. This provided the occasion for Hals to write one of his more scurrilous accounts, aggravated by the later unctuous moralizing of Whitaker, rector of Ruanlanihorne, who patronizingly classed him as

one of those persons whom we frequently see rising up in life: men born in a low situation, from their earliest years looking up to grandeur with a foolish feeling of admiration, and as they grow in manhood aspiring to procure, what they have so long envied.

All this was compounded by the legend that Tillie had impiously ordered that his body should not be interred, but propped up in his tower on Mount Ararat, in a chair, with a table before it, laid out with glasses, bottles and other convivial articles. Gilbert more generously gives the rumour the lie, by establishing that he was in fact buried in a vault, and that his will

so far from his principles being Atheistical, they breathe throughout, a disposition fraught with the utmost submission to the will of divine providence, and a perfect confidence in the wisdom and mercies of the creator.

He died childless in 1712, leaving his 'castle' to his nephew, whose daughter married John Coryton, by whom the estate passed to John

Tillie Coryton of Crocadon. The property by this time was run down, and the house dilapidated. Sir Reginald Pole Carew of Antony, who was in correspondence with Repton at the time, recommended him to Coryton, who had the means and desire to improve his new estate, which resulted in his advice being solicited, and a Red Book presented in 1810. Much of this was concerned with the house, but when Repton reflected on the distance of Pentillie Castle from his usual scene of action, he felt the impossibility of explaining all the improvements of which its picturesque features were capable.

William Wilkins senior, an associate of Repton, was engaged to remodel the building, which was completed after 1815 by the architect's son in a castellated style more suitable to its name, although berated by Moule for introducing ecclesiastical ornament into a secular building. In 1813 Irwin Kennedy of Hammersmith also submitted designs and proposals for the garden at Pentillie, which included a root house, and a Swiss bridge. Loudon included Pentillie among the ten Cornish gardens in his gazetteer of 1822, and visited it with his wife in 1842, shortly before his death, when he considered it 'a splendid place by nature, next in our opinion to Mount Edgcumbe.' He was most struck that

> the walks [were] covered with debris from the lead and copper mines, and those which have been laid with this material twenty years ago never bear a weed, not even moss.

The natural beauty of the scenery awakened the admiration of all writers who visited the garden, well expressed in the words of Redding:

> Coming round the land, and catching the house suddenly from the water, the effect is much heightened. The stranger unconsciously "suspends the dashing oar," that he may enjoy, to the fullest extent, a scene so charmingly picturesque.

It would appear from the 1896 article in the *Gardening World* that a large number of visitors would have first seen Pentillie from this viewpoint, coming 'by steamer from Plymouth and Devonport ... safely conveyed and landed on the quay in the very Castle grounds,' although Repton always advised that the comfort of those who inhabited a property ought not to be sacrificed to the public. The house, though high up, was sheltered in a hollow where the terrace is, wrote Luckhurst in 1877,

> of course, the most important feature of the gardens close by the Castle. It starts from a level expanse on the carriage front, and is continued along the south and east sides of the building ...

> The abrupt descent of the slopes from the south terrace renders its retaining wall a high one.

This, with its niches, was clothed with a wide variety of climbing and wall plants, and edged by a long 'ribbon border'. From the eastern terrace a lawn sloped gently to paths which wound down through plantations to the quay. The drive from a Regency Lodge, described by Pevsner as 'Palladio's villa plan *en miniature*', to the carriage ring, passed though undulating ground to a point from which paths radiated to various sections of the garden. One of these was to an American Garden where were planted Kalmias, Andromedas, Rhododendrons, Ghent and evergreen Azaleas and *Benthamidia fragifera* [*Cornus capitata*], in beds with irregularly curved outlines, opening up vistas to the river. 'It is true,' wrote Luckhurst, that

> the garden itself is a work of art, but this glimpse of rich natural scenery, lying far away beyond its boundaries, and yet apparently so near, imparts a charm and finish to it of which mere description can only serve to convey a faint idea.

Our selection of quotations from such varied sources, in the earliest years and throughout the nineteenth century, show this to have been regarded as among the greatest of Cornish gardens. The estate is still well kept, and the view from the river, or from Halton Quay is still remarkably fine. However, the house designed by the Wilkins was demolished in 1968, except for the seventeenth-century wing, and the grounds have not been open since the 1970s.

References: 17th, 18th, 19th (Hort. & Gen.) and 20th C. Illus.

POLVELLAN, West Looe

SX25 53 : *EX107, GS348*

Polvethan in Gilbert, who seems to have confused the name of this place with the manor of Polvethan (SX15 53) belonging to the Rashleighs; Cornish pol + melin = mill, pronounced polVELLan; north facing at river level, on Meadfoot Group slates and grits, and alluvium, in a SAGLV; rainfall 40-45", temperature zone D; until 1995 a local authority Residential Home. Came on the market in 1990.

The history of Polvellan, as Gilbert relates, shows that vandalism is no new phenomenon:

> [It is] a beautiful Gothic cottage, with delightful walks and plantations, which overlook the windings of the river Looe, and the opposite grounds of Trenant Park. The house was erected, and the grounds laid out, about thirty years ago [1786], by the late J. Lemon, esq. who lived to see the whole brought to a state of great

perfection; but since his decease, the neighbouring inhabitants, to whom the grounds were always open for recreation, have shamefully mutilated the ornamental buildings, by stripping their mossy linings, breaking down the wood work, and wantonly destroying whatever their mischievious hands could reach. It is indeed difficult to account for this outrage on so sweet a retirement, which is the chief ornament to the town of West Looe, and should be guarded by its inhabitants, as a most valuable appendage to the beauties of the surrounding scenery. Mr. Lemon, who died at this place, left it to his nephew John Buller, esq, the present proprietor.

John Lemon was son of William Lemon, junior, of Carclew, and had been MP for Saltash and Truro, later becoming a lord of the Admiralty. His sister, Anne, had married John Buller of Morval. Bond wrote:

> Below the house are a mill and pool, inclosed by a stone wall of about half a mile sweep, in a circular direction ... I apprehend the mill and pool-wall were built by one of the Arundells of Tremodart, in Duloe parish.

They had been granted the land in 1614. The house was later considerably enlarged by the Bullers, and in recent years has been a residential home. Part of the garden and some of the mill pool have been converted into a vast car-park.

References: 18th, 19th (Gen.) and 20th C.

PORT ELIOT, St Germans

SX35 57 : *EX108, GS348*

Formerly Porth Prior; Cornish porth + family name; early 18th C. house listed grade I, stables and gate-piers by Soane 1802-6, orangery, town lodge c. 1840, calf house at Lithiack by Soane, II*, fountain, ornamental battery, dairy, boat-house, and various lodges and artifacts, each II; estate of about 5,000 acres (2,023 ha), with ornamental grounds of 25 acres (10 ha) listed grade I, sloping north-east and east from 80m. to river, with house at 10m., on Upper Devonian slates with volcanic and diabase intrusions, and alluvium, with acid soil, in a SAGLV, a SSSI, an AGSV and CNCS; rainfall 40-45", temperature zone D; private, opened 1983 CGOG, and on other special occasions.

In 909 a diocese was established in Cornwall with a Saxon Cathedral at St Germans, but by 1050 this had become merged into the diocese of Exeter. The religious foundation then became a priory of Secular Canons, until in 1170 it was replaced by an Augustinian community, who built the present church. At the Dissolution their lands came into the possession of John Champernowne, in a curious manner, related by Carew:

> Now when the golden shower of the dissolved abbey lands rained wellnear into every gaper's mouth, some two or three gentlemen, ... waited at a door where the King was to pass forth, with purpose to beg such a matter at his hands: our gentleman became inquisitive to know their suit;

104. Port Eliot. Sketch by Edmund Prideaux, 1716, showing the river close to the buildings.

105. Port Eliot, with the foreground filled in to distance the house from the river. (Twycross 1846: 1)

they made strange to impart it. This while, out comes the King; they kneel down, so doth Mr. Champernowne; they prefer their petition; the King grants it: they render humble thanks, and so doth Mr. Champernowne: afterwards he requireth his share, they deny it.

However, after referring the matter to the King, the grant was confirmed. In 1553 Champernowne exchanged the Priory for John Eliot's house at Cotelands in Devon, the Eliots already having been lessees of the Bishop, and on occasion having resided at the Bishop's palace at Cuddenbeak. They were at this time wealthy merchants in Plymouth. Porth Prior, as up till then it had been known, 'at the general suppression' Carew reported, 'changing his note with his coat, is now named Port Eliot'. The Eliot family were early to achieve lasting distinction, Sir John Eliot (1592-1632) being imprisoned in the Tower for his defence of the people's rights against Charles I, thereafter being remembered as a champion of liberty. The house and grounds, nevertheless, were not impressive, so that in the early years of the eighteenth century, Edward Eliot 'much beautified the building', but, as Tonkin added, 'it was done in piecemeals, there was nothing very regular in it'. The river, he also wrote, quoting Browne Willis's *Notitia Parliamentaria*,

> opens into a large bason before the house, very pleasant when the tide is in, but something offensive when it is out, from the smell of the ooze and mud.

The situation can be observed in a print by S.& N. Buck of 1734 (which is usually on sale in the church), where the gate-posts below the house lead out on to what is shown in Edmund Prideaux's sketch of 1716, to have been a semi-circular quay. What is of equal historical interest in this print is the garden at the east end of the church, which is terraced, with two rising flights of steps. There is an avenue of round-topped trees along the lowest terrace; tall, pointed trees spaced along the edge of the middle terrace, and a lawn on the top terrace enclosed with fences, with a central plinth and statue. Edward Eliot (1683-1722) had intended to enclose the 'bason' with ramparts and a sluice gate to retain the water at all states of the tide, which would also, like Carew's 'fishful pond' at Antony, provide a source of sea fish, but 'he was suddenly cut off in his prime'. So it was left to his nephew, Edward (1727-1804) - created first Lord Eliot in 1784 - to drain and fill in the inlet, and build the Barrack Walk and embankment, thus opening up access to the parkland to the north. He also created the lake, with a rustic boat-house, and an ornamental dairy (possibly to a design of Soane), and was responsible for the woodlands, among them particularly the Craggs Wood with its 'sublime' rockwork and grotto. Maton, writing in 1797, however, was less deferential than some writers about another 'improvement'. 'There was formerly a burial ground around the church,' he wrote,

> but Lord Eliot a few years ago, took it into his lawn, and of course removed every sepulchral memorial, which occasioned no small murmur and complaint among the helpless inhabitants of the town. [See Werrington for a similar occurrence.]

Edward Eliot's heir had married the sister of William Pitt the Younger, who had consulted

Repton in 1791 about his grounds at Holwood Park, near Keston in Kent. As a consequence, the next year he was invited to submit a Red Book for Port Eliot, although, as we have seen, Lord Eliot himself had already begun improving his grounds, so that Repton tactfully conceded the owner's 'Judgement, Taste and persevering Energy', adding in respect of his work in the Craggs, 'Like the conquered magician I break my wand in the presence of superior skill' - words which were to prove prophetic, for his suggestions, in particular for joining the house to the Priory Church, and for the boat-house, were rejected. However, some of his ideas were to find a place in the designs proposed later, in 1804-6, by Soane for the remodelling of the buildings, and the grounds also show evidence of many characteristic Reptonian touches. Tucked into the Red Book, are later, though undated notes attributed to W.S. Gilpin on improvements to the landscape.

The house was further enlarged in 1829 by Henry Harrison for the second Lord Eliot (who was created Earl in 1815). The walled garden was constructed at about this time, divided into four quarters, and with an unusual open cistern beneath all four walls at the crossing. Adjoining the north-west corner of this garden is the Orangery, usually dated *c*. 1790, and thus before Repton, to which the Rose Garden has more recently been added. During the mid-nineteenth century an 'Azalea Garden' and a 'Rhododendron Garden' were laid out, and early in this century a formal enclosed garden, several summer-houses, and small temples have been introduced. A vignette in Redding (1842) depicted the house at that time with deer among the trees, although Repton had earlier warned that

> [the] difficulty of defending young plantations against Deer ... makes it almost impossible to introduce deer immediately into the grounds at Port Eliot.

There still survives in this vicinity a small pond with sloped ends believed to have been intended for deer. In recent years the parkland has been used for a pop festival, known as the 'Elephant Fair', organized by the present Earl, who was given a life-size wooden lattice-work elephant, which now inhabits the grounds. He is also responsible for the Leylandii maze, recently replanted with beech, which can be seen from the train when crossing the St Germans viaduct.

Port Eliot was one of Thurston's select gardens, and was listed in the *Hort. Direct.* from at least 1870 until 1916. More significantly it has, with Mount Edgcumbe, become one of only two gardens in Cornwall to be listed grade I in the English Heritage *Register*. Christopher Hussey's three-part article in *Country Life* (1948), as well as giving a history of the house, contains useful quotations and illustrations from Repton, whose Red Book is preserved by the family.

References: 17th, 18th, 19th (Hort. & Gen.) and 20th C; Illus.

RAME PLACE, near Millbrook

SX42 49 : *EX108, GS348*

English place = *mansion; house and gate-piers listed grade II; 1-2 acre (0.4 - 0.8 ha) grounds, at 85m. altitude, on Dartmouth Slate, in an AONB and HC, and an AGHV; now* Rame Barton Guest House, *with a residual garden.*

'The barton of Rame', Gilbert wrote,

> was, in the beginning of the seventeenth century, the property and dwelling of the Trevilles, who appear to have been considerable merchants here, and at Plymouth; ... In the early part of the eighteenth century, the barton was in the possession of the Edwardses, who rebuilt the mansion, and gave it the name of Place House. Thomas Edwards, esq. the present proprietor, has also improved the adjacent grounds, by planting, and forming some neat walks, with the addition of a respectable entrance to the same. It was the temporary residence of the earl St. Vincent, when he commanded the channel fleet.

Stephen Edwards was declared bankrupt in 1819, after which 'Place' was acquired by the Edgcumbes, gutted, and reduced again to a barton. The oak panelling, mahogany stairs and teak floors were removed to Wolsdon by the Bogers. Nothing of the garden remains today except a plain lawn, and curious gate-piers surmounted by ornamented bowl-like finials - presumably Gilbert's 'respectable entrance'.

References: 18th and 19th (Gen.) and 20th C.

ROSECRADDOCK MANOR, St Cleer

SX26 67 : *EX107, GS337*

Recharedoc, *Domesday 1086, Cornish* rid = *'ford' (which still survives as a place-name),* + Caradoc = *personal name (cf. the adjacent Caradon Hill), pronounced* roseCRADDock; *house listed grade II; originally large grounds, in south facing valley, 170-110m., on alluvium with calcareous metamorphosed slate on higher levels, soil generally acid, in an AGLV and CNCS; rainfall 45-50", temperature zone F; holiday accommodation, with relict grounds, the lodge and long drive are separately managed as two chalet parks.*

Although (unlike other hotels which have merely adopted the title) this is genuinely the site of a Domesday manor, which had been in the families of Bray, Dernford, Mayow and Langford.

Rosecraddock House is recorded in Allen (1856) as having been built in 1822 by the Revd George Poole Norris, rector of East Anstey in Devon, whose chief residence it was still in 1867. *Hitchins*, however, in 1824 stated that it was at that time owned by Ann Hodge. She was the daughter of a wealthy branch of a family from Stoke Damerel, in Devon, whose sister had married into the long-established Connock family of Treworgey (q.v.), to whom Norris's wife was related.

The river is a formative feature in the design of the grounds. The waterfall, or double cataract, rushing down at the northern end of the valley from hanging woods is a spectacular sight, descending into the stream that originally wound through a *potager*, or kitchen garden, broken up by ornamental box hedges, like a parterre. The valley at this point is narrow, so that the west-facing side was terraced, obviating the need for a walled garden. The house stands on a platform on the same side of the river, which runs under two bridges to feed into a large lake, surrounded by fine trees, the southern end of which, since it contains specimens grown from collected seed, is known as the 'American Garden'.

The drive enters below from a minor road, through the woodland along the western side of the grounds, until it turns to reveal the lake to the right, the bridge before, and the house set on slightly higher ground above. The designed effect is still impressive, especially when the old rhododendrons are in flower. The former kitchen garden and perimeter of the grounds are being developed, but the house, lake and ornamental plantations retain much of their original glory. A long drive, nearly half a mile (0.8km.) long and some 50 to 100 yards (46-91m.) wide, stretches from a once impressive lodge off the B3254 out of Liskeard, leading across the minor road into the main carriageway to the house. Despite being built over with holiday chalets, the surviving great arboreal rhododendrons create in the eye of imagination the effect of magnificence and spaciousness once intended to impress those who drove the long way up to the house.

References: 17th, 18th, 19th (Gen.) and 20th C; Illus.

SCAWNS HOUSE, Menheniot*

SX28 62 : EX107, GS348

Cornish scawen *= elder tree; garden of 3-4 acres (1.2 - 1.6 ha), west sloping from 105m., on Upper Devonian slate, with acid soil; rainfall 45-50", temperature zone E; opened 1983 CGOG, 1989 NGS.*

Scawns House was built in the mid-nineteenth century, in Menheniot Churchtown behind the rows of town houses. It is entered through an arch and gatehouse, with a plaque above representing Queen Victoria in relief, with the legend 'Empress of India' - well suited to the former residence of a tea importer.

The drive leads quite shortly to the house, which has a lawned area to the eastern garden front, and a tree-enclosed garden opposite the main entrance front. Between the two are recent office buildings relating to the business of the present owner. In another tree-enclosed area to the west of the drive there has recently been constructed a swimming pool, with a summer or bathing house, in character with the style of the dwelling, and perhaps incorporating earlier material. This circle of enclosures on one level constitutes the original garden, although at the extreme west of the grounds there is a lodge leading up into a tree-lined drive which ascends to the house along the northern edge of what originally must have been a paddock.

It is in this area, planted up by Mr T.J. Ford since the Second World War, that the great beauty of Scawns now lies. The western edge of the pool enclosure falls away precipitously, and in the centre this slope has been terraced, with two crescent-shaped beds. On the southern side, a path with steps winds down to the lawn below through a steep rock garden. The side adjacent to the long drive has been planted with ornamental conifers with coloured foliage which stand above a small pool in a glade below, in which there is a small hexagonal thatched summer-house. The edge of the drive has been planted with a variety of ornamental trees, as have both sides of the long lawn, which accentuates the perspective of length, since the site narrows towards the lodge. Looking back towards the house, the rock garden, central terrace, and tall conifers high above create an impressive effect. Scawns, which is little known and rarely open, is but one example of the many fine, but undiscovered gardens in the county.

SCONNER HOUSE, Sheviock

SX35 56 : EX108, GS348

Rosconern *1410; Cornish, Holmes suggests* ros + Conor *a personal name; house c. 1820 with additions, listed grade II; grounds of 7 acres (2.8 ha), north facing valley side, sloping from 90m. to river, with house at 25m., on Meadfoot Group slates and grits, and Meadfoot and Staddon grits above to the south, with acid soil, in a SAGLV, an AGSV and CNCS; rainfall 40-45", temperature zone D; until recently the* Cornwallis Country Manor Hotel.

Sconner House, built c. 1820, is described in Pevsner (1970), as 'Regency, stone-built and stuccoed. The design is attributed in part to Repton.' This may be because Repton worked at the adjoining Port Eliot (q.v.) and on the Antony estate (q.v.), to which Sconner once belonged. A Roger Skaner was mentioned as early as 1327, but the place passed through many hands, until by 1872 it had become the residence of the Dowager Countess of St Germans. *Lake* informs us that the Wallis family had once lived here, which, by association with one of the family names of the Eliot family, has led to the former hotel owner's misapprehension that the house was once occupied by General Cornwallis.

Perhaps Repton's influence may be detected in the prominent and effective siting of the house. This would have been more evident when, as the Ordnance Survey of 1809 shows, there was no road between Sconner and the river. The private drive, as can be seen from evidence in the lawn, entered lower down, to run along in front of the house before ascending on the opposite side to that used by the present, more direct route. This would have followed one of the axioms of Repton's design - namely, that an 'approach' should be indirect, opening at a certain point to reveal the whole house to view in a 'burst', to be admired by those entering.

References: 19th (Gen.) and 20th C.

STOKETON MANOR, near Notter Bridge

SX39 60 : *EX108, GS348*

Also found as Stocketon *or* Stokerton; *English derivation; house previously listed grade II; medium grounds, on steep north and west facing slope to the river, 65-10m., on Upper Devonian slates and alluvium, with acid soil, in a SAGLV, an AGSV and CNCS; rainfall 35-40", temperature zone E; now the* Crooked Inn.

Stoketon was recorded in the *Parliamentary Survey* of 1649 as the residence of Thomas Skelton. 'Stephen Drew, esq. having purchased the estate [in 1770] ... erected soon after a neat mansion, near the site of the old dwelling, and greatly beautified the grounds.' It was sold in 1809 to the Hon. Admiral De Courcy, later Lord Kincale, who remodelled the house in a style described by Pevsner as 'Gothic Revival'. In 1901 the property was bought by E.W. Rashleigh.

Unusually, the drive to the garden front runs along the inside edge of the ha-ha, with plantations to the right, eventually curving towards the house. This exposes on the left an open prospect, which, as Gilbert wrote,

> commands a fine view of lands, that rise in beautiful elevation over the eastern side of the Lynher, which is here crossed by Nottar Bridge [sic], shadowed by stupendous rocks, whose sides are clothed with foliage hanging over the stream in a variety of natural forms.

Unhappily the house was gutted by fire in 1984 and subsequently demolished. The walled garden, which had once been laid out with ornamental beds, was also removed to make way for an inn and holiday accommodation. When driving up the hill from Notter Bridge, where, until recently, this striking house stood out prominently, the surrounding fields still present a suggestion of former parkland.

References: 17th, 18th, 19th (Gen.) and 20th C.

THANCKES, Torpoint

SX43 55 : *EX108, GS348*

Originally Pengelly, *became* Thanckes *in the reign of Henry V, pronounced* THANKS; *house, now remodelled at Whitsand Bay, listed grade II; relict medium sized grounds, east sloping, 25m. to the estuary, on Upper Devonian slates; rainfall 35-40", temperature zone D; now a public park.*

Thanckes took its name from the family of Thonke, to whom it was enfranchised in the reign of Henry V. After passing through the families of Serles and Warne, it was brought by an heiress to Captain Thomas Graves, who in 1747 became Admiral in a family of Admirals, related by marriage to the Sawles of Penrice (q.v.). Gilbert, who provides an engraving of the house and grounds, added that:

> The present mansion of Thankes, was built by Mr. Warne, about the year 1713, since which time, it has received considerable additions and improvements, from the Graves family ... The gardens ... are sheltered on the north, by an extensive plantation of Norway firs, under whose deep shade, a walk about a mile in length, stretches over uneven grounds, the harbour [at Devonport, then known simply as Dock] discovering itself at intervals through the trees, with considerable effect ... The grounds which gently slope from the house into Hamoaze, are charmingly laid out. A beautiful promenade, which traverses the southern side of the hill, leads through a wicket gate, to a singular excavation or quarry, the sides of which, are over-run with luxurious vines, whose graceful tendrils, entwine themselves around the trunks and boughs of the trees, that hang over the surrounding precipices.

> ... "taper fingers catching at all things,
> To bind them all about with tiny rings."
>   KEATS

106. Thanckes. A view of activity on the river was considered a desirable feature at this time, not least by an Admiral. The quarry-vineyard is obscured by trees to the right of the house. The folly tower on the foreshore to the left, is in the grounds of Gravesend House. (Gilbert: 1820: ii. 394)

The leafage which surround this spot, thus beautifully intermixed with that of the vine, suspending in autumn its clusters of fruit, have an indescribable effect. There is also here, a happy variety of odorous plants, among which, the rose and the myrtle arrives to great perfection. The base of the quarry, is laid out in sections, and strewed with innumerable flowers, and blooming shrubs, whose beauty and fragrance delight the senses. The whole is protected from the prevalent western winds, by a quickset hedge, judiciously planted a few years since, for that purpose.

The grounds of Thanckes were acquired by the Torpoint Council in 1952, for a public park, the house having been 'translated' to Portwrinkle, where it was transformed into the Whitsand Bay Hotel, 'in a rather dull neo-Elizabethan style' (Pevsner). The old walled garden and the platform on which the house once stood still survive. The parkland around the house is recognizably that in the engraving, but the quarry, once well known as the 'Vineyard', has reverted to nature.

References: 17th, 18th, 19th (Gen.) and 20th C; Illus.

TRELAWNE MANOR, Pelynt

SX 22 53 : *EX107, GS348*

Trewellogen Domesday 1086, sometimes improperly spelt Trelawny; Cornish tre + lann, pronounced treLAWN; house listed grade II*, lodge, well-house, wall (?deer park), gate-piers, each II; originally an extensive estate, with house at 123m. altitude, on Meadfoot Group grits and shales, and Meadfoot and Staddon grits, with acid soil, in a SAGLV; rainfall 40-45", temperature zone D; now the Trelawne Manor Holiday Village.

The history of Trelawne and the Trelawnys is more than can be told in a short note. Leland wrote in 1535: 'Ther is a Maner Place caullid Trelaun about this Low Creke, sumtyme Bonville's, now the Marquise of Dorsete's.' Carew added in 1602 that it was 'lately purchased of her Highness by Sir Jonathan Trelawny, a knight well spoken, staid in his carriage, and of thrifty providence.' The Trelawnys, who had originated from Trelawny in Altarnun parish, were living, at the time of their move, at Pool in Menheniot, of which Carew wrote: 'Poole, for his low and moist seat, is not unaptly named, houseth Sir Jonathan Trelawny, far beneath his worth and calling.' Trelawne, then, was neither the ancestral home, nor the source of the Trelawny's name, since not only the spelling but also the pronunciation differs. The first castellated house had been built by Lord Bonville, which Sir Jonathan (1568-1604) virtually rebuilt after taking up residence. There had been a chapel here, but a new building was erected on the site by Sir Jonathan, Bishop of Winchester (1650-1721), who

> was committed to the tower in the reign of James II. for his strong attachment to the Protestant cause, ... [He] was so respected by the Cornish, that an insurrection in his favour might easily have been excited among them ... [as the chant goes]
>
> > "And shall Trelawny die?
> > Then thirty [twenty] thousand Cornishmen shall know the reason why."

Trelawne was again nearly rebuilt in about 1745 by Edward Trelawny (1699-1754), Governor of Jamaica, after it was destroyed by fire. It was remodelled for a third time, so *Lake* tells us:

> During the occupancy of the present proprietor, Sir John Salusbury-Trelawny, Bart. [1816-85], ... [who had] rebuilt, at immense cost, the greater part of the mansion from its foundations ... now in style and commodiousness fully adapted to the taste or requirements of the wealthiest and most fastidious of its ancient baronial owners.

But what of the grounds? Such ancient mansions of magnificence are usually adorned with deer parks, and indeed a wall is pointed out which may have impaled deer in the seventeenth century, although it now encloses the Warren Plantation, which suggests more lowly game. Originally, it may be surmised, the old house would have had several courtyards, with gardens laid out in the formal style so loved of the Elizabethans. 'However,' continues Carole Vivian,

> Sir Harry Trelawny 7th baronet [1756-1834] inherited the estate in 1772 [and] ordered his Steward ... to destroy all the old formal gardens including the Paradise Garden, pull down the fountains and fill in the fish ponds ... In the place of all these gardens Sir Harry had lawns laid right up to the house which were grazed by sheep and deer. He also had many hundred trees planted as we know from his notes.

This was the scene which won a place for Trelawne among Loudon's ten Cornish gardens in his gazetteer of 1822, and which was described by Gilbert as

> beautifully diversified by hill and dale, hanging woods, and open eminences. The scenery around Trelawny Mill wears an aspect of unusual tranquillity, and affords a rich variety for the pencil of the artist.

107. Trelawne Manor. This old house was destroyed by fire and remodelled in the nineteenth century in a style 'fully adapted to the taste and requirements of the wealthiest and most fastidious of its ancient baronial owners.' (Gilbert 1820: ii. 916)

Not so today. After a time as a retirement home for Church of England clergymen, the new owners had to be restrained from demolishing the old house, which is now the centre of a holiday village, humming, in season, with 'family fun'.

References: 17th, 18th, 19th (Hort. & Gen.) and 20th C; Illus; C. Vivian, The Trelawnys, Pelynt, *1990; A. Lanyon,* The Rooks of Trelawne, *London, 1976.*

TRELIDDEN, Liskeard*

SX23 63 : *EX107, GS348*

Cornish tre + [?]; pronounced treLIDDen; 1.5 acre (0.6 ha) garden, in a SAGLV; rainfall 45-50", temperature zone E; opened 1983, 1986-92 CGOG, 1989 NGS.

The house dates from *c.* 1970, but the garden at Trelidden was refurbished during 1981-2. The grounds are bisected by a stream with a series of natural waterfalls. There is a pond and bog garden, herbaceous borders, a herb garden and wooded area. By the terrace is a wisteria pergola and old-fashioned rose border. Throughout the garden are a number of specimen trees and shrubs, including maples, cherries, and camellias. The aim has been to provide 'colour and scent for as many months of the year as possible.' This was, until recently, the home of Marjorie Blamey, a notable botanical artist, and her husband.

References: 20th C.

TREMATON CASTLE, near Saltash

SX41 58 : *EX108, GS348*

Trematone *Domesday 1086; Cornish,* Dexter *suggests* tre + metin = complete, *or* matern = king's, *pronounced* TREMaton; *higher lodge 1807-8 listed grade II*, stables 1807-8, 3 Tudor archways probably 17th C or earlier, medieval doorway north-east of keep probably 14th C, crenellated wall north-east of keep probably early 19th C, links with former orangery, each II; grounds of about 7 acres (2.8 ha), at 73m. altitude, on a Diabase intrusion into slate, in a SAGLV, and an HS and AM (the Castle); rainfall 35-40", temperature zone D; private, Duchy property on lease.*

The Castle of Trematon has its own history, but we are here concerned with the house built in 1807, possibly to designs by D.A. Alexander (see *Country Life 104* 1948: 480), for which *Lake* informs us

> a grant for 90 years was made to Benjamin Tucker, Esq. surveyor-General of the Duchy, and for many years secretary to Admiral Earl St. Vincent. He built the modern mansion which occupies the bass-court of the ancient castle.

He was succeeded by his son, and brother. 'In one part' of the grounds, Stockdale adds, 'on a marble slab, is a bust of the late Admiral St. Vincent, with [an] inscription from the eclogues of Virgil.' Opinions about the house and its grounds were at variance. Stockdale considered it 'laid out with great taste.' Loudon, however,

108. Trematon Castle. In this view from the River Lynher, the house built by Benjamin Tucker in 1807 can be seen within the walls of the castle. (Lysons 1814: 288)

thought this 'might be a fine place, for there are some well defined portions of the castle still remaining; but it is ruined by indiscriminate planting.' Redding was even more blunt about what he considered the 'most perfect of all the remains of the ancient castles of Cornwall, until it was mutilated [in 1807-8] ... in an inexcusable manner, for the erection of a modern house.' Betjeman, rather characteristically, felt it to be 'all the more romantic for being still a private residence and unarchaeologized'. In the 1960s and 1970s, Trematon was leased from the Duchy by Hugh Foot, Lord Caradon.

Thurston included this among his select gardens in 1930, at which time there were box borders in the rose gardens 'in the shape of a Tudor fleur-de-lis'. It was listed in the *Hort. Direct.* from at least 1870 until 1924. Today the area around the house is principally lawned, although there are many fine trees and shrubs, There is also a sunken garden, an Italian garden, and an orchard.

References: 17th, 18th,19th (Hort. & Gen.) and 20th C; Illus.

TRENANT PARK, Duloe

SX24 55 : EX107, GS348

Trenand Domesday 1086; Cornish tre + nans, *pronounced* treNANT; *early 17th C. house remodelled early 18th and extended 19th C., listed grade II; very large grounds, the present farm 127 acres (51.4 ha), on a promontory east and south-east facing, 116m. to river level, house at 75m., on Meadfoot Group slates and grits, and Meadfoot and Staddon grits at southern point, with acid soil, in a SAGLV; rainfall 40-45"; temperature zone D; private, house in apartments, with residual grounds, estate now in agricultural use.*

Trenant, from an early period belonged to the Hewis family, but, after many changes, it was sold in 1806 to vice-Admiral Sir Edward Buller, who was created a baronet in 1808. On his death it was eventually sold to William Peel, a relative of Sir Robert Peel, the Prime Minister, who died in 1837. His son surviving him by only four years, Trenant passed to his grandson until his death in 1871. *Lake* describes it as

> an interesting and picturesque place, bounded on three sides by the rivers Dulo and Looe, which unite at the south-eastern point of the estate, commonly called Trenant point. The land stands high, and is diversified with plantation, lawn, and wood, and with extensive prospects ... On the headland above Trenant point stands a temple overlooking the entrance of Looe harbour.

This temple has now gone. Gilbert also informs us that:

> This park was formerly stocked with deer, but is now used for grazing cattle, and a sheep walk. It is several miles in circumference, and abounds with large timber, and extensive modern plantations. The house is unfortunately an ill-designed building, altogether at variance with the grandeur of the scenery by which it is surrounded.

The land is still in agricultural use.

References: 17th, 18th, 19th (Gen.) and 20th C.

TREWORGEY, St Cleer, near Liskeard

SX24 66 : EX107, GS348

Cornish tre + Wurci = *personal name, pronounced* treWORGie; *house, and former SW wing, each listed grade II; railings and gates, clock tower, railings and gate-piers, and retaining walls to main entrance drive, each II; small garden, north-west facing side of valley, 125-115m., on Middle Devonian slates and alluvium, soil 'stony'; rainfall 45-50", temperature zone F; private.*

Treworgey became the seat of the Connock family, who are believed to have originated as tanners in Wiltshire, in the time of Henry VIII. John Connock, who probably built the house, was receiver of the Duchy in 1532. Like so many Cornish houses, however, Treworgey suffered from a fire, and was refaced in the eighteenth century with a Tuscan porch. At about this time, Nicholas Connock married one of the co-heiresses of a Mr Hodge of Stoke Damarel over the border in Devon, who brought with her a large fortune. 'This lady,' wrote Gilbert,

> who survived her husband nearly forty years ... having no issue, bequeathed Treworgy, and other large estates to her sister, Mrs Arminel Inch, widow, and Miss Anne Hodge, spinster.

From them, the property passed to Mrs Inch's daughter, and thence to the Marshalls, her brother-in-law's family. His sister inherited the neighbouring manor of Rosecraddock (q.v.) where her husband, the Revd G.P. Norris, built a fine house and beautifully landscaped the grounds.

Gilbert wrote that Treworgey had been much neglected during the widowhood of Mrs Connock, but that the grounds were 'charmingly wooded, and inclose a small range for deer, and a sweep of pasturage, chiefly used as a sheep walk.' He has included a print which shows the weather-boarded clock-tower, dated 1733, with its 'Chinese roof', but there is also what appears to be a church tower in a hollow to the rear of the fenced enclosure, although the parish church of St Cleer is depicted far away on the horizon. The shrubs, perhaps yews, before

109. Treworgey, c. 1820. The clock tower at this date had a cupola. (Gilbert 1820: ii. 949)

the house, seem, from the angle of the peacock on the edge, to be growing on a level area raised above the parkland. Thurston described Treworgey in 1930 as: 'An old garden unlike any other in the county with old topiary yews and box hedge, sundials, statues and flower beds in the shape of the four suits in a pack of playing cards'.

Several splendid illustrations of this most interesting and elaborate garden appeared in the *Country Life* of 1904, one of which was reprinted in Gertrude Jekyll's *Garden Ornaments* of 1918. In a comparison with Gilbert's engraving of 1820, it should be noticed that the yews, though clearly venerable, are not in the same position as on the more recent print (that is if the drawing is accurate), where they must have been planted later, perhaps c. 1832 when the handsome railings were erected. The beds in the upper garden which were to occupy the fenced enclosure, in a photograph (not reproduced here) are seen with box edging surrounded by gravel paths after the fashion of the mid-century. Treworgey is one of the forgotten Cornish gardens, never opened to the public, but, although now showing the inevitable signs of advancing age, it is neither lost nor departed.

110. Treworgey. In this oblique view are seen the gates and topiary in the front court, the chinoiserie clock tower, and the steps leading to the upper garden, where the broderie parterres were in the shape of the four suits of a pack of cards. (Country Life 1904)

References: 17th, 18th, 19th (Gen.) and 20th C; Illus.

WATERLOO VILLA, now the Klymiarven (sic) Hotel, East Looe

SX25 53 : *EX107, GS348*

Named after the battle of Waterloo; Klymiarvan, in Cornish means 'culver field', pronounced klyMIARvan; grounds slope steeply west from c. 70m., on Meadfoot and Staddon grits, in a SAGLV and HS; rainfall 40-45", temperature zone D; Hotel with relict garden.

Gilbert wrote:

> Waterloo Villa [is] the seat of Nicholas Harris Nicolas, esq. The house was begun by the late Major Nicolas, who [dying before the completion] bequeathed it to his nephew, the present proprietor. It has since been finished with much taste, and contains a well-chosen library, and several good paintings. The entrance to the house is spacious, and the whole of the beautiful knoll stocked with a variety of flowering shrubs and evergreens. The most hardy of these hang in all their native wildness, over the jutting precipices, whilst others of a more tender description, fill the sheltered seclusions, or adorn the borders of the variety of walks which have been formed by the perservering hand of industry throughout this charming enclosure.

Although the garden is reduced in size, Gilbert's description is still apposite. Major Nicolas, who had been present at the taking of Bunker's Hill, though himself a native of East Looe, derived from a Huguenot family, who had moved there in the seventeenth century. His nephew was in the Inner Temple. Subsequently the name 'Waterloo' Villa' was changed to 'Klymiarvan', which, according to Twycross, was the Cornish name of the field on which it was built.

References: 18th, 19th (Gen.) C; Illus.

WESTBOURNE HOUSE, Dean Street, Liskeard

SX24 64 : *EX107, GS348*

House listed grade II, lodge II, monument II; relict, part extinct garden of 2-3 acres (0.8-1.2 ha), south facing slope at about 115m. altitude, on Upper Devonian slates, with acid soil; rainfall 45-50", temperature zone E; now a CCC Social Services Area Office.

Westbourne was built in 1816 (there is a dated rainwater head), possibly by J. Foulston for N. Wallis Penrose (d. 1822), a solicitor and descendant of the Penroses of Sennen. The front was altered by Henry Rice in the mid-late nineteenth century, when the home of Richard Hawke, who

> although of humble origin, was a banker, as well as having an income from land and business investments. Hawke was employing five servants in 1881, including a butler - the ultimate symbol of conspicuous consumption and a rarity in a small country town.

The grounds originally extended to Dean Street, where the 'Renaissance Gothic' style lodge added in the 1860s, probably also to the design of Rice, can be seen alongside the entrance to the Westbourne Gardens, now divided off from the house. They also at one time extended to occupy the present car-park, across Westbourne (or Bowden's) Lane, which was linked by a foot-bridge. The garden front of the house has a balustraded terrace, leading down central steps to a lawn still fringed with some good trees. There is a monument at the bottom of this garden, of a granite altar type, nine feet high, with an inscription which can be read from the Westbourne Gardens below: 'To Richard Hawke JP (died 1887)'. These lower public gardens are entirely lawned and surrounded by perimeter trees. Westbourne was listed in the *Hort. Direct.* from 1908 to 1924, in the name of W. Sargent, who was Borough Treasurer.

References: 19th (Gen.) and 20th C; B. Deacon, Liskeard and its People, 1989: 15, 29.

SUPPLEMENTARY LISTS

LESSER-KNOWN HISTORIC GARDENS

Bicton Manor, St Ive

SX31 69 : *EX108, GS337*

Devonian slate, with acid soil, in an AGLV; rainfall 45-50", temperature zone F; farmhouse with residual gardens.

Bicton, according to Norden (1590), was 'the howse of Willm Wraye, whervnto adioyneth a parke of fallow deare'. There are probably remains of this house incorporated in the central range of the present dwelling, built for Daniel Elliott c. 1660s-80s, with eighteenth-century extensions to the left. The right-hand extension, probably built for Lord Ashburton, has a date-stone 1850. Earlier in 1820, Gilbert described 'the approach towards the house on the northern side' as being 'through a long avenue of beech trees, and the adjoining vales' to be 'richly filled with wood'. The avenue has gone, but the Bicton Wood running down to the river still survives.

References: 17th, 18th and 19th (Gen.) C.

Bray House, Morval

SX27 57 : *EX107, GS348*

Cornish *bre = hill, probably a prominent hill; house listed grade II; grounds of 13 acres (5.25 ha), including 7 acres

(2.8 ha) of woodland, at 140m. altitude, to north on Meadfoot Group slates and grits, to south on Dartmouth Beds silts and slates, with felsite between, and acid soil, in a SAGLV; rainfall 40-50"; temperature zone D; private.

The house is late sixteenth- or early seventeenth-century in origin, built either for Philip Mayow (d. 1590), or his son, Philip (d. 1658), and remodelled in the nineteenth century. The Mayows were a family of some distinction. John Mayow (1645-79) - a physiologist and chemist - published a tract on respiration in 1668, and was described by Thomas Beddoes in the next century as 'one of the greatest chemists of any age or country.' The family lived at Bray until 1953, when the estate was divided. Gilbert describes it in his day as occupying

> an elevated situation on the eastern side of the river Looe, of which it commands most delightful views, and also of the country and sea beyond it. The house is ancient, and over the entrance, which opens to a lawn surrounded with plantations, is a tablet, bearing the family arms.

The approach is by a long drive through woodland. The view is seen over three brick-walled terraces with central steps, leading to lawns, with shrubs.

References: 17th, 18th and 19th (Gen., 20th C.

Burell House, Saltash

SX39 58 : EX108, GS348

Also Burrell, Cornish [?], pronounced buRELL; house listed grade II, two barns, each II; grounds at 85m., on Upper Devonian slates, surrounded by volcanic rocks, in a SAGLV; rainfall 35-40", temperature zone D; house derelict, garden extinct, now a farm.*

Burell was described by Gilbert as 'a neat mansion, rather ancient, with very pretty shrubberies, gardens, and pasture lands: it has been the family residence for several generations.' *Hitchins*, however, doubted that Arthur Burell, the owner in 1824, 'was descended from the ancient family, who formerly held the seat there.' Although described in the listing as 'an important house of the 17th century, probably on the site of a former house (see date stones 1621 and 1636)', with a re-modelled front, it has now been derelict for some time. The main drive survives as a farm lane, although the trees with which it may once have been lined have gone. A new farmhouse has been built in the walled garden, of which two of the original walls remain. It is difficult now to imagine what preceded the agricultural land.

References: 17th, 18th, 19th (Gen.) and 20th C.

Crocadon, St Mellion

SX39 66 : EX108, GS348

Pronounced CROCadon; house listed grade II; originally large estate with house at c. 110m., on Middle Culm Measures grits and shales, in a SAGLV and CNCS; rainfall 45-50", temperature zone E/F; now a farm, and agricultural land.

Crocadon is recorded by Norden as 'the howse of Thomas Tervise', and the Trevisa family, who were also mentioned by Carew, were resident there for many years. It was the birthplace of John Trevisa (1326-1412) who translated the Bible, and Ranulph Higden's *Polychronicon* into the English language. William Trevisa, the last of the family, sold the house to Sir William Coryton, whose descendant, John Tillie Coryton, inherited Pentillie Castle at the end of the eighteenth century. A great part of the mansion, which is depicted in the *Spoure Book* of c. 1690, was then demolished, and a steward installed. It eventually became a farmhouse. Gilbert, however, found

> the remains ... seated among beautiful undulations of grounds, on the western side of the Tamar. All the eminences are dotted over with clusters of stately firs, and the lower grounds are laid out into lawn, gardens, and shrubberies.

Reginald Pole Carew of Antony, writing to Repton in 1809, described Crocadon as 'a very inferior Place', but Betjeman, in 1964, was still conscious of 'the sense of a planted park in the valley below' - no doubt prompted by the woodlands on the perimeter, which is all that now survives.

References: 17th, 18th, and 19th (Gen.) C.

Doublebois House, Dobwalls

SX19 65 : EX107, GS347

Doublebois, Norman French = two woods, possibly referring to the two deer parks of Liskeard Castle, but with an Anglicized pronuciation Doubleboys; house listed grade II; grounds of 60 acres, north-west facing at c. 150m., sloping down to the River Fowey; on Middle Devonian slate, in an AGLV; rainfall 50-60", temperature zone E/F; now Doublebois Park holiday accommodation, grounds relict/extinct.

Doublebois House was built in 1883 to designs by Christopher White, but was extended for the Herman family, with a date-stone CMH 1896, in a High Victorian Gothic style. From 1908 to 1916 it was listed as open in the *Hort. Direct.* as the residence of the Revd George Edward Herman, vicar of St Neot, and later of his widow, with gardens described in Kelly's *Directory* as 'the greater part tastefully laid out'. The house, now divided into four residences, overlooks the wooded valley of the upper regions of the River Fowey. The grounds have been grassed over to form a nine-hole golf course, and a chalet park, which has invaded the former walled garden.

References: 19th (Hort.) and 20th C.

Duloe Vicarage and Churchyard, Duloe

SX23 58 : *EX107, GS348*

Cornish dew + *loch = *two pools; house listed grade II, in a SAGLV; now* Duloe Manor, *managed by* Holiday Property Bonds.

Thurston reported that:

> Fifty-nine lime trees [*Tilia vulgaris*] are recorded as having been in Vicarage Walk, Duloe, in 1727. It is noted by the Rev. John Wallis [in 1847] that "the two fine lime trees, at the entrance to Duloe churchyard, were planted by me on March 25th 1818." They no longer exist.

That is, the trees in the churchyard; there is still a walk between two lines of lime trees in the old vicarage garden.

References: 20th C.

Harewood House, Calstock

SX44 69 : *EX108, GS337*

Cornish *hyr-yarth = *long ridge; grounds of 50 acres (20 ha), sloping to the River Tamar from 50m., on Upper Devonian slate, valley gravel and head, in a SAGLV; rainfall 45-50", temperature zone F; divided occupation, with residual garden.*

Harewood House was built by John Pearson Foote, who had bought the site from the Duchy in 1798. In 1814 it was sold to Sir William Lewis Salusbury Trelawny, whose second son intended to sell it back to the Duke of Cornwall in 1866. However, the purchase was never completed. Instead, a school, founded in St Austell in 1840, moved there with the new title, Harewood House Collegiate School, 'intended to afford to the Sons of Gentlemen a First Class Education at a moderate expense.' Gilbert had described the house as

> nearly surrounded by a delightful lawn, skirted with a sunk fence [i.e. an ha-ha], over-hung with a rich variety of full grown trees. The whole is situated on a tongue of land, washed on three sides by the river Tamar; and from this beautiful seat, the waters are seen winding amidst the most diversified and enchanting scenery.

The headmaster in his prospectus to parents added that 'the situation [was] most healthy'. The house is now altered out of recognition, although the area cannot lose its natural beauty.

References: 17th, 18th, 19th (Gen.) and 20th C.

Hatt House, Hatt

SX39 62 : *EX108, GS348*

Late 16th, early 17th C. dwelling, with new house c. 1710 attached in front, listed grade II*, walls and gate-piers, and granary each II; small to medium grounds, with house at 70m. altitude, on Upper Devonian slates; rainfall 45-50", temperature zone E; private.

Hatt House was first recorded by Gascoyne (1699), and according to Gilbert had for nearly two centuries been the seat of the Symons. Their family tree is given in *Lake*, who also relates the tale of the curious disappearance of the grandfather of Nicholas Symons, the owner in 1867, subsequent to violent opposition to his marrying a woman of inferior standing. Gilbert thought the 'neat mansion' to be 'of a modern date. It is built of brick, and the shrubberies, gardens, and grounds, have altogether a very pretty appearance.' There are still good gardens.

References: 17th, 18th, 19th (Gen.) C.

Landulph Parsonage, Landulph

SX43 61 : *EX108, GS348*

Cornish lan + *proper name, pronounced* lanDULPH; *house dating from 16th C. listed grade II; small grounds in a SAGLV, an AGSV and CNCS in part; private.*

Francis Vyvyan Jago Arundell was rector of Landulph from 1805 to 1847. At first, since the high tide flowed to the hedge of the churchyard, he needed to be conveyed from his parsonage to church by boat. However, as Stockdale reported, he greatly improved his property, which commanded 'a beautiful prospect of the river and Saltash ... and raised an embankment round the house', converting the Gudlake into rich pasture and 'bringing the grounds and plantations into a high state of cultivation.' Arundell is also notable for his conversion of St Benet's into his occasional residence, and for a book on Cothele.

References: 17th, 18th and 19th (Gen.) C.

Luxstowe, Greenbank Road, Liskeard

SX25 64 : *EX107, GS348*

Lux = *Luke's; house by Wightwick, listed grade II; now* Caradon Council Offices, *grounds extinct.*

Luxstowe House was built in 1833-4 for William Glencross, Esq. (1784-1851), and was described by Twycross in 1846 as

> pleasantly situated on a slight elevation at the northern side of the town of Liskeard ... It is surrounded by thriving plantations, and was built in the Elizabethan style.

The family were merchants and bankers in Devonport, but William's eldest son was ordained, and followed his father at Luxstowe upon retiring as priest in charge of Tideford. He had married the eldest daughter of the Revd George Poole Norris of Rosecraddock (q.v.), and was succeeded by his wife and son. The present building is recognizably that in the illustration in the *Mansions of ... Cornwall*, but with considerable extensions. Such grounds as have escaped being over-run by the expansion of Liskeard, are now dedicated to car-parking.

References: 19th (Gen.) C; Illus.

111. Moorswater Lodge. Except for the trees and impressive rockwork by the pool, the house and parkland have retained their appearance. (Twycross 1846: 85)

Moorswater Lodge, Liskeard

SX23 64 : *EX107, GS348*

House possibly by Wightwick, extended late 19th C. listed grade II; medium grounds south-east sloping 75-50m., on Middle Devonian slates; rainfall 45-50", temperature zone E; private.

Moorswater Lodge was built in 1830, probably on the site of an earlier house, for John Lyne who was from a family believed to have come from Ringwood in Hampshire as early as 1300, to settle in Liskeard and Mevagissey. The father of John, Capt. Philip Lyne RN, had been in most of the celebrated engagements of Lord Nelson and Sir Thomas Troubridge. The house is described by Twycross as 'in the Gothic style, and in the construction of which great taste has been displayed', but his illustration concentrates attention more upon the lake, with its rock work, island, and rustic summer-house among the trees. This lake today appears much smaller, and is without these adornments, although the house and parkland when seen were still very well maintained. These grounds immediately adjoin the present Ladye Park, named after the second, or 'New' deer park of Liskeard Castle, known formerly also as 'Lodge Park'. It is from this historic association that the name 'Moorswater Lodge' is derived.

References: 19th (Gen.) C; Illus.

Pencrebar, near Callington

SX35 68 : *EX108, GS3337*

Cornish pen + name of old manor house, pronounced penCREEba; house, and stables each listed grade II; medium grounds, steeply sloping south, 135-80m., on Upper Devonian slate with diabase intrusions around house, in an AGLV; rainfall 45-50", temperature zone F; private.

Pencrebar - a 'charming Victorian house' - was built in 1849, in a Gothic style, for William David Horndon, Captain in the Royal Cornwall Militia and a county magistrate, on the site of the ancient mansion of Crebar. The entrance in the east has a granite surround to a possibly Tudor arch, and the coach-house and stables may also contain stonework from the demolished manor house. In 1927 this became the home of Isaac Foot MP, and his family, 'well known as the centre where eminent politicians were happy to be invited, to plant trees and to make speeches at Liberal garden parties.' A desirable hybrid daffodil discovered here is now in commerce with the name 'Pencrebar'.

References: 19th (Gen.) and 20th C.

Tor House, Torpoint

SX43 55 : *EX108, GS348*

Formerly Crinnis House, Cornish tor = belly or protuberance; house with terrace, walls and piers, listed grade II; dentist's surgery, with residual garden.*

The houses in Torpoint, Gilbert believed, were

> greatly eclipsed by a superb mansion, lately erected here, by Joshua Rowe, esq. with elegant pavilions, and beautiful gardens. Adjoining this mansion, there has lately been erected by subscription, a town chapel, or chapel of ease, to the church of Antony.

When built in 1792, the house was named Crinnis House after the rich mine near St Austell (see Pine Lodge) where Rowe had made his fortune. It had become Tor House by 1842, when visited by Loudon. The English Heritage report pays particular attention to the terrace with central steps which is all that is left of the 'beautiful gardens'. The erection of a 'town chapel' was but one stage in the growth of Torpoint, which has enveloped this house, and blotted out any of the virtues that might have attracted Loudon to be shown it.

References: 18th, 19th (Hort. & Gen.) and 20th C.

Trebrown, near Catchfrench

SX299 603 : *EX107, GS348*

Cornish tre + bron = *rounded hill, pronounced* treBROWN; *at 50m. altitude, on Upper Devonian slates and grits; rainfall 45-50", temperature zone D/E; farm, grounds extinct.*

Gilbert wrote that

> Trebrown, a neat house, with good lands, belonging to Francis Glanville, esq. [of Catchfrench q.v.] was formerly a seat of the Mayows [see Bray]: it is now the residence of Mr William Betenson, who has much improved and beautified the local scenery.

He was probably referring to the woods, now named Trebrownbridge Woods. The much reduced grounds of the house have been cut by the A38.

References: 18th and 19th (Gen.) C.

Trematon Hall, Saltash

SX39 59 : *EX108, GS348*

Trematone, Domesday 1086, Cornish tre + metin = *full i.e. complete* (*or* matern = *king's*), *pronounced* TREMaton; *house, boundary walls and barn are listed grade II; small garden, at 90m. altitude, on Upper Devonian slates with volcanic intrusions, in a SAGLV; rainfall 35-40", temperature zone E; private.*

Gilbert wrote:

> Trematon Hall, seated near a village of the same name, was lately a seat of the Bennetts, from which family it has been since purchased by Thomas Edwards, esq. the present proprietor and occupier. It is a neat modern building, with good shrubberies, paddock, and other highly cultivated grounds.

The well-maintained garden is confined within boundary walls with entrance gates, all contemporary with the house, built in the early nineteenth century.

References: 18th C.

Trethill House, Sheviock

SX37 54 : *EX108, GS348*

Cornish tre + [?], *pronounced* TRETHill, *to rhyme with 'Beth'; house by Wightwick, stables, linhay [lean-to open front shed], and bank barn each listed grade II; grounds of 7 acres (2.8 ha), at 55m. altitude, on Meadfoot Group slates and grits, in a SAGLV, and an AGSV; rainfall 35-40", temperature zone D; private.*

Trethill was the seat of the Wallis family [see also Sconner] from at least 1600. Gilbert wrote that although the house was in a decayed condition in his time, it was 'a very beautiful estate'. The present dwelling was built in about 1830, perhaps incorporating an earlier house of 1790. The family was related to Capt. Samuel Wallis (1728-95) of Camelford, who circumnavigated the world in the *Dolphin* between 1766 and 1768, during which voyage he discovered Tahiti and other islands in the Pacific. The property passed by marriage to the Roberts family, who remained there until 1945. The house and grounds, which are principally terraced lawns, with plantations, can be viewed from the Tregantle Fort - Antony road. There was a chapel, which is now a music room.

References: 18th, 19th (Gen.) and 20th C.

Trevillis House, Liskeard

SX247 634 : *EX107, GS348*

Trefilies, Domesday 1086, pronounced treVILLis; *small to medium grounds, at 100m. altitude, on Middle Devonian slates; rainfall 45-50", temperature zone E; NHS hospital, with relict grounds.*

Although named after a Domesday manor, Trevillis is a mid- to late-nineteenth-century house built for Lewis C. Foster, a banker and county magistrate, on the road south out of Liskeard. It was listed as open in the *Hort. Direct.* from 1908 to 1924. From the lawn in front of the house there is a panoramic view across the countryside to the east. To the west are plantations of varied and ornamental trees and shrubs. The housing estate to the north, with the name Trevillis Park, suggests that it was cut out of the original grounds. (See also Moyclare.)

References: 20th C.

Trewin, Sheviock

SX35 55 : *EX108, GS348*

Cornish tre + guyn = *white or fair, Pronounced* TRUIN; *house c. 1725 with later additions, stable, kitchen garden walls, each listed grade II; small to medium grounds, south-east sloping from 50m. altitude, on Staddon and Meadfoot grits, with acid soil, in a SAGLV; rainfall 35-40", temperature zone D; private.*

Gilbert wrote:

> Trewin, in Sheviock, the seat of John Littleton, esq. is situated near Polscove Mill, adjoining the great

western road. The house is modern, the grounds are finely wooded, and are washed by the waters of the river Lynher.

Today the entrance on the road from Sheviock winds through a striking curved avenue of copper beech. The house and sloping gardens, which are surrounded by a fine selection of boundary trees, are planted with rhododendrons and other shrubs. A walled kitchen garden adjoins the house.

References: 18th, 19th (Gen.) and 20th C.

Wivelscombe, Saltash

SX39 57 : *EX108, GS348*

House, remains of a medieval chapel (probably 14th century), barns, and cottage, each listed grade II; garden at 30m. altitude, on Upper Devonian slates in a SAGLV, and an AGSV; rainfall 40-45", temperature zone D; private.

Although in origin a seventeenth-century manor house, Wivelscombe has been altered and very heavily remodelled in modern times. The south is approached by steps 'with composition sphinxes and heraldic lions'. Gilbert had written that

> the ancient seat of the Wyvells, is pleasantly situated, near a creek of the Lynher: the grounds have been much improved, and ornamented with plantations, by its present owner and occupier [Robert Billing]. The house was built by the Wyvells, about the year 1600, and now bears the venerable features of antiquity.

The estate was purchased in the earlier nineteenth century by the Carews of Antony, who built there a cottage, 'probably' intended 'as an eyecatcher from Antony, later used as a shooting box (and a parish room)', with a small chapel. Today there is a walled kitchen garden, a courtyard garden, lawns with plantations, an avenue, and in the grounds a monument surmounted by a pyramid. Until recently this was a residence of the Lennox Boyd family, who also garden at Ince Castle.

References: 17th, 18th and 19th (Gen) C.

Wolsdon House, near St John

SX40 54 : *EX108, GS348*

Little Wolsden 1650, pronounced WOOLSdon; medium grounds, south-east sloping from 55m., on Staddon and Meadfoot grits, with acid soil, in an AGLV; rainfall 35-40", temperature zone D; private.

Gilbert wrote that this

> very agreeable seat ... occupies a most delightful situation [and] ... commands towards the east, many fine views: ... On the southern side, the grounds and plantations, fall rapidly into a solitary vale, which is washed by the waters of St John's Creek.

Originally in the Wolsdon family, in 1796 it passed by marriage to the Boger family. The place was formerly, for rather obvious reasons, known as 'Hill'. There is a good view of the house from St John's village.

References: 17th, 18th and 19th (Gen.) C; Illus.

ADDITIONAL CONTEMPORARY GARDENS

See also INCE CASTLE, KEN CARO, MARY NEWMAN'S COTTAGE, MORVAL CHURCHTOWN, SCAWNS HOUSE, and TRELIDDEN *in the main section.*

Crooked Park, Botus Fleming

SX40 61 : *EX108, GS348*

Opened 1988-90 CGOG, 1988 NGS.

Originally a market garden, this four-acre (1.6 ha) property began to be developed from a caravan in 1949. The area in front of the bungalow, which was built much later, was enclosed by high hedges pierced by arched openings, but the main garden, in which there is a swimming pool surrounded by flower beds, is informally planted with a variety of trees. A path leads out of this garden to a streamside which has been planted as a small arboretum. There is a modern dovecote on a pole near the vegetable garden to the rear of the house.

Jimmers, St Neot

SX18 67 : *PF1347, GS347*

Garden under 1 acre (0.4 ha), in an AGLV; opened 1991, 1993, 1994-6 NGS.

The garden at Jimmers was created by Mrs Bridget Okely in 1976 from a field, by forming a series of 'mini terraces ... There [was] a fruit cage for soft fruit', but planting 'concentrated mainly on shrubs, small trees and a variety of undercover.' Mrs Okely was, until her death in 1990, organizer of the NGS for Cornwall, and had arranged an innovative 'Gardener to Gardener Scheme' in the Cornwall Garden Society, through which garden owners could share their experiences. This attractive garden has been restored and developed by the present owners.

Loveny, Tremaddock Bridge, St Neot

SX18 68 : *EX109, GS335/336*

Pronounced loVENy; *small to medium garden in an AONB, and an AGSV; open 1991-3, 1995 NGS.*

Loveny, an interesting riverside garden developed in the 1960s, was laid out by the late Norman Nielsen and his wife, with many unusual trees and plants collected on holidays in Europe, particularly in the Alps and Pyrenees. It acquired a sufficient reputation to be televised on several occasions. After a period of neglect, it is now being restored by the present owner.

Miller's Meadow, St Neot

SX18 67 : *EX107, GS335/336*

Garden under 1 acre (0.4 ha), in a SAGLV; opened in 1991 NGS.

A rather more formal garden than the adjacent Old Barn, with conifers, fuchsias and roses. A well-kept lawn runs down to the river.

Northwood Farm, St Neot

SX20 69 : *EX109, GS337*

Garden of about 1 acre (0.4 ha), in an AONB, an AGSV and CNCS, and an AGHV; opened 1992-7 NGS.

The house - a barn conversion - and the garden are on the site of a china-clay 'dri' dating from 150 years ago. Natural springs have been used to create ponds, surrounded by herbaceous bedding, with a collection of water birds, all in all making this a most interesting garden.

The Old Barn, St Neot

SX18 67 : *EX107, GS335/336*

Garden under 1 acre (0.4 ha), in a SAGLV; opened 1991-6 NGS.

A riverside garden, at one time opened in conjunction with Miller's Meadow. It is less formal, with mature trees and shrubs, mixed perennials, roses, clematis and pelargoniums, and a pond with water lilies.

Peterdale, Millbrook, near Torpoint

SX40 53 : *EX108, GS348* OPEN*

Very small, but exceptionally well designed and planted garden, with a star rating in the Good Garden Guide, *in an AGLV; open 1988, and 1993-8 NGS, one Sunday in May, and by appointment.*

Pinetum, Calstock

SX44 69 : *EX108, GS323* OPEN*

A 2 acre (0.8 ha) pinetum in a SAGLV; open 1993-8 CGOG, and NGS, Wednesdays, May through August.

Reference: Pring (1996: -7-8).

Scawn Mill, St Keyne

SX21 62 : *EX107, GS348* OPEN*

Cornish scawen = *elder tree; in a SAGLV; open 1995-8 NGS, one Sunday each in June and July.*

Trago Mills, Glynn valley

SX18 64 : *EX107, GS347* OPEN*

Cornish tre + Jago = *personal name, pronounced* TRAYgo; *recently landscaped grounds of warehouse, in a SAGLV and CNCS; open to the public during business hours.*

Tremarkyn, Wenmouth Cross, St Neot

SX194 677 : *EX107 GS335/336*

2.5 acre (1 ha) garden, in a SAGLV, and an AGHV; opened 1996-7 NGS.

There are gardens arranged along the drive, and around granite out-buildings. The grounds surrounding the house, with a bog garden, are especially well planted.

Trethawle Farm, Menheniot

SX26 62 : *EX107, GS348*

Cornish tre + *tawel = *quiet, pronounced* treTHALL; *small garden in a SAGLV; opened 1988-9 NGS.*

A garden on several levels, incorporating water features, with a range of interesting shrubs and trees.

6
Deer Parks in Cornwall

Deer parks are not a subject that can be omitted from general garden history, for as Evelyn (1620-1706) - author of the forestry classic *Sylva* (1664) - believed, a park should be regarded as much an ornamental setting for the house as a place for hunting, a sentiment later echoed by Switzer (1682-1745). Deer had been impaled in England before the Conquest, but parks increased hugely in number with the arrival of the Normans, who brought with them traditions, not only from their own land dating back to the Roman occupation, but also from their more recent encounters with the hunting parks of the Arabs in 1060, during their campaign in Sicily.

Even though the Domesday survey of 1086 had recorded the existence of thirty-one parks, none of these was in Cornwall, where they must all have been created in the next century. However, with the exception of Boconnoc, none of the forty-one medieval parks has survived to the present day, and only four of them - the Priory at St Germans (later Port Eliot), Caerhays, Mount Edgcumbe and Newton Ferrers - became sites for eighteenth-century ornamental parkland.

This scene was to change radically as the country became more prosperous and peaceful under Queen Elizabeth. Many of the newly-formed sixteenth- and seventeenth-century parks were to survive for many years, until by the eighteenth and nineteenth centuries it became a fashion among the wealthy, not only to create a landscape setting for the growing number of newly-built mansions, but to populate their parks with deer. Recent researches, indeed, have established that such parks were always designed to graze animals of one sort or another, so that the origin of the ha-ha itself may be attributed to a change, probably for economic reasons, from the costly management of deer, to the rearing of bullocks, since deer are not usually intrusive upon habitations, and avoid human company, whereas bullocks are apt, not only to appear suddenly at windows to frighten the ladies, but to leave traces that would foul their shoes and dresses when they paraded on the lawns.

The following list, therefore, is intended to provide an opportunity to trace the social history of deer-parks from the earliest days up to the present.

At this stage little more can be done than to locate the sites with their ancient parishes and hundreds, and establish, so far as possible, their dates and the families responsible for them, backed up by references to the authorities consulted, thus laying a firm foundation for further investigation. The names of parks which, for the reasons already stated, do not appear in the foregoing topography of parks and gardens have been printed in italics, while Domesday manors where deer were later impaled have been asterisked. In the succeeding notes, when a source has stated, or by an illustration has shown that a park was in existence at that time, then this also has been signalled by an asterisk, other references being understood as referring to former or abandoned sites.

MEDIEVAL PARKS

The most ancient parks were a Royal prerogative, which was extended first to the Church, then to certain favoured individuals. In Cornwall there were originally nine Royal parks, eight of which became incorporated into the newly-formed Duchy in 1337, since Penlyne had already been disparked by that time. The Bishop of Exeter had been granted the right to impale deer on his manors from 1258, and had done so at Glasney (Penryn), Lanner (near Truro) and Pawton (near Wadebridge). The Priors of Bodmin, Plympton, St Germans and Tolcarne also had their own parks, but by about 1450 the Bishop's parks had been abandoned, and those of the Priors would not have survived any longer,

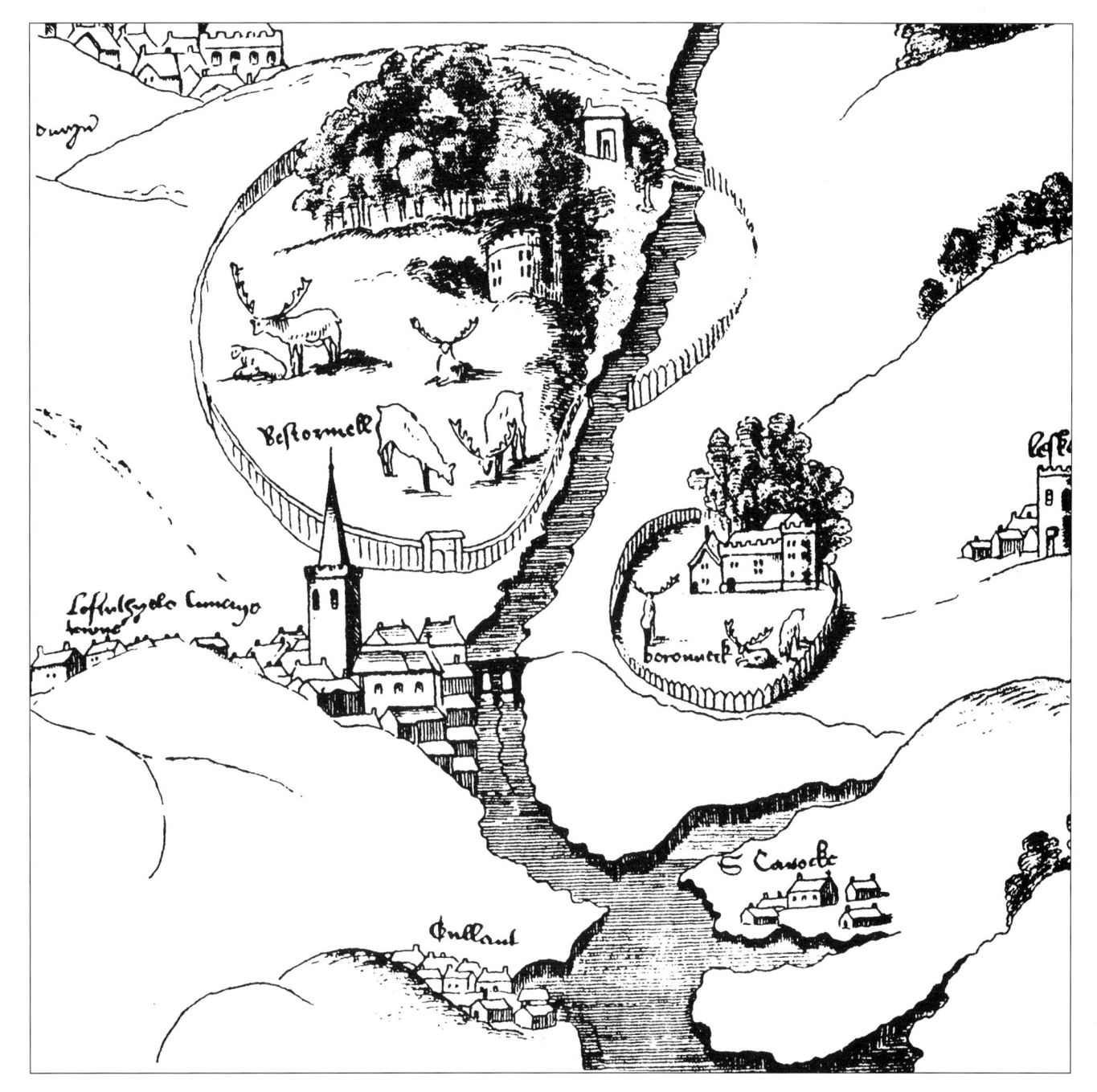

112. Deer parks at Restormel Castle and Boconnoc. Detail from the Henry VIII map of Fowey harbour. (Lysons 1814: 108)

some passing to laymen, as all would have done at the Dissolution. Indeed, in 1542 Henry VIII was himself persuaded by economic good sense to dispark the still surviving Duchy parks which were becoming a financial burden, even though they were already before this time being let out for pasturage.

In 1602 Carew wrote that 'most of the Cornish Gentlemen preferring gaine to delight, or making gaine their delight, shortly after followed the like practise, and made their Deere leape over the Pale to give the bullocks place,' probably intending thereby a pun on the name of the greatest of the Duchy deer parks, at Carrybullock. Norden indeed recorded in 1597 that the Arundells' park at Lanhadron, 'the most statelieste parke within the Shire, [was] now utterly decayde, and the woodes rooted vp, and the land sowed with corne.' But Carew had exercised his wit at the expense of strict accuracy. Of the eighteen or so private parks here recorded, Carn Brea, Merthen, Park, Trelawny (in Altarnun parish) and possibly Botelet had already gone before that time. Bicton, Boconnoc, Caerhays, Cotehele, Merther Uny, and Pool survived, a few even into the eighteenth century and beyond, and Bodrugan, Hornacott and Poldrode collapsed more from the decay of the families who owned them, than their avarice. Indeed, far from a decline within the next half century, there was to be a revival in the impaling of deer.

A. DUCHY PARKS

Carrybullock, Stoke Climsland : East

SX38 73 *(EX108)*

13th C : Duchy : Disparked 1542.

Caption* (1337: 115-16, 141), [*the park was 3 leagues (c. 9 miles) in circuit, and held 150 deer*]; Saxton* (1576), *although by this time disparked it was perhaps still impaled, but without deer*, Carew (1602: 273); *see especially* Kerrybullock, S. Pittman, Stoke Climsland 1990.

Helsbury, Michaelstow : Trigg

SX08 78 *(EX109)*

13th C : Duchy : Disparked 1542.

Caption* (1337: 24, 141), [*the 'new park' at Lanteglos was 3 leagues (c. 9 miles) in circuit, of 306 acres (124 ha), and capable of holding 200 deer.*]

Lanteglos, Lanteglos by Camelford : Lesnewth

SX08 81 *(EX109)*

13th C : Duchy : Disparked by 1337.

Caption* (1337: 24), [*the 'old park' in 1337 had become 102 English acres (41.3 ha) of arable land.*] *See also* Maclean (1876: ii.293-7).

Launceston*, St Mary Magdelene Launceston : East

SX33 64 *(EX108)*

13th C : Duchy : Disparked before 1534.

Caption* (1337: 2, 141), [*the park was 1 league (c. 3 miles) in circuit and could hold 40 deer*]; Leland (1534), [*mentions an 'old park', i.e. already disparked.*]

Liskeard*, Liskeard : West

SX25 64 *(EX107)*

13th C : Duchy : Disparked 1542.

Caption* (1337: 141), [*the 'new park' held 200 deer*]; Leland* (1534: 49); [*there were two parks: the Old, and Lodge, or sometimes Lady Park because there was a Chapel upon it. For a description see letter to Borlase 1573, O. Corn. vi 1961-7: 436.*]

Penlyne, St Winnow : Powder

c. SX11-12 59-63 *(EX107)*

Enlarged 1246-7 : Earl Edmund : Disparked by 1337.

Hatcher (1970: 179), 'It is noteworthy that the word Penlyne does not appear ever to have been a place-name within the manor ... [which] *formed the northern part of the parish of St Winnow*'; Parl. (1649: 101).

Restormel, Lanlivery : Powder

SX10 61 *(EX107)*

13th C : Duchy : Disparked 1542.

Caption* (1337: 42, 141), [*the park was capable of holding 300 deer*]; Leland* (1534: 44).

Trematon*, St Stephen by Saltash : East

SX41 58 *(EX108)*

13th C : Duchy : Disparked before 1540.

Caption* (1337: 122, 141); [*a small park on the North side, capable of holding 42 deer, had already been disparked before the time of Henry VIII.*]

B. ECCLESIASTICAL PARKS

Glasney, St Gluvias : Kerrier

SW78 34 *(EX104)*

c. 1320 : Bishop : Disparked c. 1450.

Leland (1534: 35).

Lanner, St Allen : Powder

SW82 48 *(EX104)*

13th C : Bishop : Disparked 1450.

Henderson (1928), '... the extensive Coppice known as Bishop's Wood remains as a vestige of this demesne.'

Lanow*, St Kew : Trigg

SX02 77 *(EX106)*

Pre-1500 : Priory of Plympton : Disparked before 1550.

Henderson (1928), 'There is a field [*called Deer Park*] on Treharrick and a Lodge Park on Little Hale both adjoining Lannowe.' [*the park passed from the Priory to the Giffard family.*]

*Pawton**, St Breock : Pydar

SW95 70 *(EX106)*

c. 1258 : Bishop : Disparked 1450.

Lysons (1814); Lake (1867: i.129). *Probably passed to the Prior of Bodmin.*

*Pendavey**, Egloshayle : Trigg

SX 00 69 *(EX106)*

Pre-1500 : Priory of Bodmin : Disparked before 1537.

Henderson (1928).

St Germans*, St Germans : East

SX36 57 *(EX108)*

Pre-15th C : Priory : Disparked 1539.

Henderson (1928), 'The Priory Deer Park afterwards called the Warren and now the Wooded Hill or Shrubbery [was] at the eastern side of Port Eliot house'; [*in 1541 the park was 12 acres (4.9 ha) in extent.*]

*Woolston**, Poundstock : Lesnewth

SX22 02 *(EX111)*

Pre-1500 : Prior of Tolcarne : Disparked before 1580.

Henderson (1928), [*passed from the Prior to the Beville family; there still remain fields named 'Deer Park'.*]

C. PRIVATE PARKS

Arallas, St Enoder : Pydar

SW88 54 *(EX106)*

Ancient : Trethurffe? : Disparked?

Henderson mss: 'On Resurrance are fields called the Deer Parks amounting to some 38 acres [15.4 ha]. These appear under this name in a survey of the Manor of Arallas dated 1810 at Trelowarren.'

Arwenack, Falmouth : Kerrier

SW81 32 *(EX105)*

Uncertain : Killigrew : Prob. c. 1660.

Burghley map* *c.* 1580 (*see Fig. 44*); Thurston (1930: 222, *quoting a 'History of Falmouth', 1827*).

*Bicton**, St Ive : East

SX31 69 *(EX108)*

Pre-1576 : Wrey : Disparked mid 17th C?

Saxton* (1576); Norden* (1597); [*the Wreys moved to Devon mid 17th C., see* Lake *1868: ii. 248.*]

*Boconnoc**, Boconnoc : West

SX14 60 *(EX107)*

15th C : Carminow : Surviving.

Saxton* (1576); Norden* (1597); etc. Henderson mss: 'The old park with its dike and ancient oaks remains but it has been greatly enlarged, and the deer now come much nearer the house. The first reference to it is to Le Dure-Park named in 1435.'

*Bodrugan**, Gorran : Powder

SX01 43 *(EX105)*

pre-1534 : Bodrigan : Disparked 16th C?

Leland* (1534: 39); [*Bodrigan was attainted for treason 1485.*]

Bonallack, Constantine : Kerrier

SW71 26 *(EX8)*

1300 : Bonallack : Disparked pre-1597.

Henderson mss: 'Granted by Roger de Carmenon Kt Lord of Merthyn.'

*Botelet**, Lanreath : West

SX18 60 *(EX107)*

Pre 1500 : Bottreaux : Disparked late 15th C?

Henderson (1928); [*the Bottreaux family died out in 1461; a field named Deer Park still remains.*]

Caerhays, St Michael Caerhays : Powder

SW97 41 *(EX105)*

15th C : Trevanion : Disparked c. 1853.

Saxton* (1576); Norden* (1597); Carew* (1602); etc. Henderson mss: 'Caerhays Park lay at Trevanion 1/2 mile up the Luney Valley from Caerhays House and extended across the river into Gorran. The Gorran portion known as Brown Berry was held by the Trevanions by chief rent under the Prior of Tywardreath as lords of Treveven.' [*probably the deer left with the Trevanions in 1853.*]

*Carn Brea**, Illogan : Penwith

SW68 40 *(EX104)*

Pre-1534 : Basset : Disparked by 1534.

Leland (1534: 21), 'now defacid' [*probably by mining*]; Tonkin (1736), 'the castle and park wall are still standing'; Henderson mss: 'In the middle ages Carn brea Hill seems to have been a Deer Park of the Bassets who had a chapel and castellated hunting box upon it.' [*A park was re-established at Tehidy in the 18th C.*]

Cothele, Calstock : East

SX42 68 *(EX108)*

Pre-1576 : Edgcumbe : Disparked 17th C.

Saxton* (1576); Norden* (1597), [*on map only*]; Carew (1602: 270), '... *appurtenanced with the necessaries of wood, water, fishing, parks, and mills ...*'; [there are two parks on Norden's map.]

Hornacott*, North Tamerton : Stratton

SX31 94 *(EX111)*

P.re-1500 : Courtenay : Disparked 15th C.?

Henderson (1928); [the Courtenay family died out; a field named Deer Park still remains.]

Lanhadron*, St Ewe : Powder

SW99 47 *(EX105)*

Pre-1500 : Arundell : Disparked before 1597.

Saxton* (1576); Norden (1597), '... *the most statlieste parke within the Shire, now utterly decayede, and the woodes rooted vp, and the land sowed with corne.*'

Lanherne*, Mawgan : Pydar

SW87 67 *(EX106)*

Pre-1500 : Arundell : Disparked before 1597.

Henderson (1928), '*Deer Park named as part of the Lanherne Demesne in 1659. This lies on top of the hill to the South of Lanherne.*'

Launcells*, Launcells : Stratton

SX24 05 *(EX111)*

1537 : Chamond : Disparked before 1736.

Saxton* (1576); Norden* (1597); Carew* (1602); Tonkin (1736), '*long since disparked*'; [the park came to the Chamonds on the dissolution of Hartland Abbey in 1537: the family died out in 1624.]

Lesnewth*, Lesnewth : Lesnewth

SX13 90 *(EX109)*

Norden* (1597), [*gives no details; not otherwise identified.*]

Merthen, Constantine : Kerrier

SW72 26 *(EX104)*

Pre-1500 : Reskymer : Disparked 16th C.

Leland (1534: 32), '*ruinus maner place and a fair park*'; Carew (1602), [who wrote Merthir, which was interpreted by Tonkin as Merthyn, but might equally have meant Merther Uni]; Tonkin (1736); '*long since disparked*'; Henderson (1928, 1937: 118). [Leland, Tonkin and Henderson seem definitely to be referring to 'Merthen'.]

Merther Uny, Wendron : Kerrier

SW70 29 *(EX8)*

Pre-1500 : Reskymer : Disparked pre-17th C.?

Norden* (1597), [who does not enter a park for Merthen, but both Gilbert (1820: ii. 770) and Hitchins (1824: ii. 671) each refer to former parks at 'Merther Uni', as well as at Merthen.]

Mount Edgcumbe, Maker : East

SX45 52 *(EX108)*

1539 : Edgcumbe : Disparked after 1928.

Carew* (1602: 240); etc. Henderson (1928); [this probably took the place of the parks at Cothele. The deer continue a feral existence around Rame Head.]

Newham, Kenwyn : Powder

SW82 44 *(EX104)*

Pre-1304 : Pridins : Disparked?

Henderson mss: notes an ancient indictment 34 EI 1304; '*Nich: Hogheles Willm Beaupre & Rbt Tryer de hoc quod fregerunt parcum Thome de Pridins de Nyweham & ibi ceperunt & aspartaverunt 4 damas*'.

Newton Ferrers*, St Mellion : East

SX34 65 *(EX108)*

c. 1550 : Coryton : Disparked by 19th C.

Saxton* (1576); Norden* (1597), [*on map only*]; Carew (1602), '*almost decayed*'; Tonkin* (1736); Henderson mss: '*c. 1710 Newton with new house, Park, Warren etc.*'

Norton, Launcells : Stratton

SX25 08 *(EX126)*

Pre-1602 : Arscott : Disparked.

Gilbert (1820: 543), '... *which is mentioned by Carew [1602: 279] as a seat of the Arscotts, who had a park there.*'

Park, Egloshayle : Trigg

SX03 71 *(EX109)*

Ancient : Peverell : Disparked 15th C.

Hals (1737: see Lake 1867: i. 310); [the Peverell family died out in the 15th C.]

Pengersick, Breage (St Breock) : Kerrier

SW58 28 *(EX7)*

? : Millaton : *Disparked late 16th C.*

There is no documentary evidence, but the Lanhydrock Map 1698 *mentions an 'Old Warren', also the* Estate Plan 1787 *and the* Tithe Map 1839 *both record 'The Park and Warren' of 26 1/2 acres. See P. Herring, et al.,* Pengersick, Breage, *Cornwall Archaeological Unit, Truro 1997: 26.*

Poldrode* (alias 'Polroad'), St Tudy : Trigg

SX05 78 *(EX109, marked as 'Manor House' unnamed)*

1357 : Carminow : *Disparked before 1550.*

Henderson (1928); [*the Carminow family died out in the 16th C.*]

Pool, Menheniot : East

SX28 61 *(EX107)*

Pre-1500 : Trelawny : *Disparked early 17th C.*

Norden* (1597); Carew* (1602), *'newly revived'*; Tonkin (1736), *'long since disparked'*; Henderson mss: *'This park lay on the South side of Poole Barton towards Chicken Tor. Below the Tor is a farm yet called Deer Park and a massive stone wall enclosing part of the Tor was probably part of the Park circuit. Poole decayed when the Trelawneys* [sic] *went to Trelawne about 1600.'*

Tregony, Cuby : Powder

SW92 46 *(EX105)*

Ancient : Pomeroy : *Disparked pre-1500.*

Henderson mss: *'A Park of the Pomeroy family ... of which Pomeroy Wood by the side of the Fal formed a part.'*

Trelawny, Altarnun : Lesnewth

SX21 82 *(EX111)*

Ancient : Trelawny : *Divided up 1449.*

Lysons (1814), *'Among the most ancient deer-parks ...'*; [*NB distinguish from Trelawne in Pelynt parish*].

Tymberthan alias Temple Park = Timbrelham ?, Lezant : East

SX36 80 *(EX112)*

Lake (1870: iii. 125); [*not otherwise identified*].

ELIZABETHAN and SEVENTEENTH-CENTURY PARKS

The revival of parks in the time of Elizabeth marked a rise in the fortunes of certain older families, and the entry into Cornwall of new ones. The Godolphins, and the Vyvyans at Trelowarren annexed deer parks to their newly-built mansions. Halton was inherited by Sir Anthony Rouse from Devon, as were Bicton and Trebigh by the Wreys, while Chamond had been granted Launcells - which formerly belonged to Hartland Abbey - by Henry VIII at the Dissolution in 1537. The Edgcumbes, who had moved from Cotehele to Mount Edgcumbe about the turn of the century, began to impale deer there, probably eventually abandoning the parks at their former residence.

The troubled days of the Civil War were no time for personal aggrandisement, but, as Polwhele observed (iv. 118), 'At the Restoration, most of the seats of gentlemen in Cornwall, were either newly built or materially repaired.' All of the new parks in the mid seventeenth century were a direct consequence of rewards received on the return of the monarchy. The first Lord Robartes was restored to rebuild Lanhydrock, and to create a park there and at Pinchley (now Pinsla). Hugh Boscawen built a new house at Tregothnan and annexed a deer-park which has survived to this present day. Morice improved his grounds at Werrington, and Grylls enclosed a paddock at Court Barton, Launcells - both having been knighted for their services to the Crown.

Clowance, Crowan : Penwith

SW63 34 *(EX104)*

Pre 1667 : St Aubyn : *Disparked before 1736.*

St Aubyn document 1667*; Hals* (Lake 1867: i. 263); [*not in Tonkin (1736).*]

Court Barton, Lanreath : West

SX18 56 *(EX107)*

c. 1650 : Grylls : *Disparked?*

Henderson (1928).

Ethy, St Winnow : West

SX13 57 *(EX107)*

Elizabethan : Courtenay : *Disparked?*

Norden* (1597); [*on map only; Carew does not mention parks at either Ethy or St Winnow. It is not clear whether there were two separate parks, or one described under two names.*]

Godolphin, Breage (St Breock) : Kerrier
SW60 31 *(EX7)*

c. 1560 : Godolphin : Disparked after 1820.

Tonkin* (1736); Borlase* (1758); etc. Henderson (1928), *'The fields called the Deer Park remain behind the old mansion sloping up the side of Godolphin Hill.'* See P. Herring, Godolphin, Breage, Cornwall Archaeological Unit, Truro 1997: 70-2, 105, 123, 238-54.

Halton, St Dominic : East
SX41 65 *(EX108)*

c. 1580 : Rouse : Disparked before 1700.

Norden* (1597); Carew* (1602), *'lately impaled'*; Tonkin (1736), *'long since disparked'*.

Lanhydrock, Lanhydrock : Pydar
SX08 63 *(EX107)*

1657 : Robartes : Disparked c. 1780.

Tonkin* (1730); Borlase* (1758); JRIC (1988: 221); [*see also* PINSLA]

Pinsla also **Pinchley** or **Pinsley, Cardinham** : West
SX12 66 *(EX107)*

1657 : Robartes : Disparked 1780.

Tonkin* (1736); Borlase* (1758); JRIC (1988: 221); [*possibly this had been a park of the Cardinhams before 1600.*]

St Winnow*, St Winnow : West
SX11 57 *(EX107)*

Elizabethan : Lower : Disparked?

Henderson (1928); [Carew (1602: 209), *does not mention that the Lowers had a park. There seems some confusion whether there were parks at both Ethy and St Winnow, or both names were used for a single park.*]

Stowe, Kilkhampton : Stratton
SX21 11 *(EX126)*

Pre-1597. Grenville. Demolished 1739.

Norden* (1597).

Trebigh, St Ive : East
SX30 67 *(EX108)*

After 1600? : Wrey : Disparked mid 17th C.

Gilbert (1820: ii. 458), *'A range of rising lands ... displays the remains of the deer park'*; [*the Wreys removed to Devon mid 17th C. see* Lake 1868: ii. 248.]

Tregothnan, St Michael Penkevil : Powder
SW85 41 *(EX105)*

c. 1660 : Boscawen : Surviving.

Tonkin* (1736); Borlase* (1758); etc.

Trelowarren*, Mawgan in Meneage : Kerrier
SW72 23 *(EX8)*

Elizabethan : Vyvyan : Disparked before 1736.

Norden* (1597); Carew* (1602); Tonkin (1736), *'long since disparked'*; Henderson mss: *'The site is not known but there is a part of the demesne called the Warren.'*

Treluddra, Kenwyn : Powder
SW76 46 *(EX104,* 'Deerpark' only, not named*)*

Elizabethan : Borlase : Disparked by 1730.

Tonkin (1730), *'now left to ruin, though a park by patent'*; Lysons (1814); Henderson mss: *'The name of Deer Park still clings to the site.'*

Werrington*, Werrington : East
SX32 87 *(EX112)*

c. 1680 : Morice : Disparked after 1928.

Tonkin* (1736); Borlase* (1758); Henderson (1928); [*the park was 179 acres (72.5 ha) in extent.*]

EIGHTEENTH- and NINETEENTH-CENTURY PARKS

Charles Gilbert, looking back to the prosperous years of the eighteenth century, wrote that 'fallow deer, in the same manner as in other counties, may be seen in the parks of most gentlemen of fortune.' (1817: i. 313). Besides those which had survived from the previous centuries, some twenty-one new deer parks were impaled after 1700. It was also a time when others, equally fortunate, but with no interest in, and some without sufficient means to pursue venery, felt nevertheless a need similarly to surround their houses with vast parklands, though naked of deer, or sometimes even of cattle or sheep.

Bradridge, Boyton : Stratton
SW31 93 *(EX112)*

pre-1730 : Coster : Disparked by 1814.

Tonkin* (1730); Lysons (1814); Henderson mss: *'This place had previously been a favorite hunting seat of Sir William Pendarves'*.

Carclew, Mylor : Kerrier

SW77 38 *(EX104)*

1770 : Lemon : Disparked after 1928.

Lysons* (1814); Henderson (1928); [*no deer park was shown on the estate map of 1764.*]

Lavethan, Blisland : Trigg

SX09 73 *(EX109)*

c. 1760 : Treise : Disparked before 1800.

Henderson (1928).

Pencarrow*, Egloshayle : Trigg

SX03 71 *(EX109)*

Pre-1758 : Molesworth : Disparked by 1814.

Borlase* (1758); Lysons (1814); Henderson mss: 'The old stone palings of the Park can be seen sticking out of the top of the earth bank or hedge, west of the present drive'. See also Maclean (1873: i. 446).

Pendarves, Camborne : Penwith

SW64 37 *(EX104)*

Pre-1780 : Stackhouse : Disparked by 1814.

Documents from Tehidy record re-stocking deer in 1782 from Pendarves Park, and repairing fences there; see M. Tangye, Tehidy and the Bassets, Redruth 1984: 40-41. Neither Lysons (1814), nor Gilbert (1820) mention deer at Pendarves.

Penrice, St Austell : Powder

SX02 49 *(EX107)*

c. 1770 : Sawle : Disparked after 1928.

Lysons* (1814); Gilbert* (II: 1820); etc. Henderson (1928).

Penrose, Sithney : Kerrier

SW64 25 *(EX8)*

1785 : Rogers : Disparked before 1820.

Lysons* (1814), 'a small paddock ...'.

Port Eliot, St Germans : East

SX35 57 *(EX108)*

19th C? : Eliot : Disparked?

Redding* (1842: 89 illus.) [*not otherwise identified, except for a pool reputed to be a watering place for deer.*] See also St Germans Priory above.

Prideaux Place*, Padstow : Pydar

SW91 75 *(EX106)*

Pre-1758 : Prideaux-Brune : Surviving.

Borlase* (1758: 51 illus.); Polwhele* (1806), 'a small park'.

Rosteague, St Gerrans : Powder

SW87 33 *(EX105)*

? : Hartley : Deer sold 1844.

See Life in Cornwall in the mid 19th C. *1971:111*, quoting the West Briton, *11 Oct.1844.*

Samson, Isles of Scilly

SV87 12 *(EX101)*

1860 : Smith : 1860s.

[*Unsuccessfully attempted c.1860 by Augustus Smith, after evacuating the island. It was then used as a warren, with black rabbits which still survive. See E.Berry The Samson Buildings, Cornish Archaeological Unit, 1994: 15, 73.*]

Tehidy*, Illogan : Penwith

SW64 43 *(EX104)*

Pre-1758 : Basset : Disparked by 1814.

Borlase* (1758); Lysons (1814).

Trefusis, Mylor : Kerrier

SW81 34 *(EX105)*

c. 1760 : Trefusis : Disparked before 1790.

Henderson (1928); 'Two maps of the estate 1764 & 1767 show the fields known as the Creggoes enclosed as a Deer Paddock. The two pillars of the gate giving access to the Paddock from Mylor Church yet remain but the grove of trees and the palisades have quite disappeared. [Since not otherwise mentioned] it was presumably short-lived.'

Tregrehan, St Blazey : Powder

SX05 53 *(EX107)*

19th C : Carlyon : Disparked?

Twycross (1846: 47, illustration); [*not otherwise identified*].

Trelawne*, Pelynt : West

SX22 53 *(EX107)*

? : Trelawny : Disparked?

Henderson mss: 'A field ... bears the name 'Deer Park' though no Park of Deer is recorded at this place by old writers.' [*the wall enclosing the Warren Plantation has been listed by English Heritage as possibly the relict of a deer-park ...*].

Tremough, Mabe : Kerrier

SW76 34 *(EX104)*

After 1703 : Worth : Disparked before 1820.

Tonkin* (1742, see *Lake* iii. 197), *'Mr Worth ... hath enclosed a small park of deer'.*

Trenant, Duloe : West

SX24 55 *(EX107)*

After 1760 : Morshead : Disparked before 1820.

Lysons* (1814).

Trengoffe, Warleggan : West

SX15 67 *(EX107)*

c. 1700 : Nance : Disparked before 1780.

Henderson mss.

Trevaunance, St Agnes : Pydar

SW72 51 *(EX104)*

Pre-1736 : Tonkin : Disparked by 1814.

Tonkin* (1736); Lysons (1814).

Trevethoe, Lelant : Penwith

SW53 37 *(EX7)*

Pre-1736 : Praed : Disparked by 1814.

Tonkin* (1736); Borlase* (1758); Lysons (1814).

Trewan, St Columb Major : Pydar

SW91 64 *(EX106)*

18th C? : Vivian : Disparked?

Stockdale* (1824: 100-01, illus.); [*not otherwise identified*].

Trewithen, Probus : Powder

SW91 47 *(EX105)*

Pre-1758 : Hawkins : Disparked before 1820.

Borlase* (1758: 228 illus.); Lysons* (1814), *'a paddock ...'.*

Treworgey, St Cleer : West

SW24 66 *(EX107)*

18th C : Connock : Disparked?

Gilbert* (1820: ii. 948); *'The grounds ... inclose a small range for deer', (with illus.);* Henderson mss: *'This Park or Paddock lay in front of Treworgey House and remains of the dike and groves of trees can be seen. The fields yet bear the name of Deer Park ...'.*

In conclusion, it must be emphasized once again that this can be but a first step towards a more complete survey. When it is realized that so far the only records found for the presence of deer at Port Eliot, Tregrehan and Trewan are illustrations, and at Rosteague, an advertisement in the *West Briton*, it may be expected that further research will turn up even more parks belonging to 'gentlemen of fortune.' A beginning may be made by following up the hints of Charles Henderson in his manuscript notes on deer parks, preserved at the Royal Institution of Cornwall. He has included the names of Catchfrench, Colquite, Nanswhyden, Penheale, Reterth in St Columb Major, and Rialton in St Columb Minor parishes, but without further comment. Several map references, however, offer more definite clues - such as 'Durfold' in Blisland, which was spelt 'Deer-fold' in 1600. Erisey has a 'Deer Stile' listed by English Heritage; Lansallos at Treweers there is a 'Deers Hill', and in Northill at Castick there is a 'Deer Slade'. A 'Park Lodge' was recorded at Place, Anthony, in 1543; there is another 'Deer Hill' at St Breward, and a 'Deer Park' at Maders in Southill. A more intensive scrutiny of ancient documents and field-names will surely reveal many more.

REFERENCES

The general abbreviations are explained in the various *Bibliographies*. In addition, 'Saxton' refers to his *Map of Cornwall*, 1576, 'Tonkin (1736)' to the Tonkin MSS, printed on page 76 of de Dunstanville's edition of Carew (1811), and 'Henderson (1928)' to his article on deer parks in the *Western Morning News*, reprinted in *Essays in Cornish History* (1935:179). His valuable preliminary notes, from which quotations have been made, are preserved in the library of the Royal Institution of Cornwall. Individual references to deer parks will be found in Borlase (1758: 288), Polwhele (1806: iv. 130), and Lysons (1814: clxxix, clxxx) - who also quotes from Carew, Tonkin and Borlase. In his *Rural Economy ... in the Duchy of Cornwall, 1300-1500* (Cambridge 1970), J. Hatcher has dealt in detail with the Duchy deer parks.

The Bibliographies

An explanation

A straightforward catalogue of book titles is always unrevealing, offering a reader no more than raw material. Yet an adequate, unabbreviated garden-by-garden bibliography of over 400 sites, though desirable - and indeed in the course of preparation, - would occupy a disproportionate space in an appendix, and if dispersed through the main text, would defeat its prime object, which was to provide an unencumbered and readable account of the sites in their localities. An alternative presented itself in a series of chronological bibliographies, with synoptic and other tables, which, as well as listing the sources, would provide both an historical overview of the whole subject and an opportunity for comparative studies. It must be emphasized that this expedient did not grow out of either arbitrary necessity or subjective choice, but, as will presently be shown, from the inherent nature of the material itself.

Chronological bibliographies

Cornwall is fortunate in possessing a rich supply of topographies, parochial histories and other sources of reference, which chart the history of the various sites over a long tract of time. They fall naturally into four quite distinctive types, characteristic of four periods, viz., the pre-seventeenth, and the eighteenth, nineteenth and twentieth centuries. Up to the *seventeenth century* they consist for the most part of official surveys and map making, culminating in Richard Carew's masterly *Survey*, and the maps of Norden and Gascoyne. The *eighteenth century*, however, saw the first attempts at systematic parochial history and topography, reaching its climax in the topographical section of Charles Gilbert's *Historical Survey*, which, though published in 1820, essentially represents the state of affairs in the previous century. By the *nineteenth century* there gradually emerged a more specifically horticultural interest, reflected in the many new gardening journals. Even though itineraries, topographies and parochial histories continued - that of *Lake* being among the greatest - they nonetheless are, for our purposes, secondary since gardening references in them are incidental. In the *twentieth century*, Thurston's *Trees and Shrubs of Cornwall*, published in 1930, may be considered the crowning point of the more specialized horticultural trends of the preceding century. Since the Second World War this has been followed by more general and colourful descriptive books and guides.

A series of chronological bibliographies, therefore, does no more than follow the natural divisions of the subject matter. An added advantage of this arrangement is that, by recording the tokens *17th, 18th, 19th (Horticultural and/or General), 20th Century*, and *Illustrations*, under the individual entries in the topography, the period, and any sequence in the growth of a particular garden, may be seen at a glance, and readily substantiated by reference to the appropriate bibliography.

In a minority of cases, single and specific references or monographs are treated as exceptions, and printed in full after the token references.

Subject bibliographies

At the end of the topography, a gazetteer of *Deer Parks* has been added, which concludes with a number of related references. Similarly the sections on *Plant Records, Garden Types and Features*, and the *Biographical Notes*, contain references and lists of specialist books and articles, which have not been recorded elsewhere. Here again, it was considered more convenient to document a subject in the section where the references are most needed.

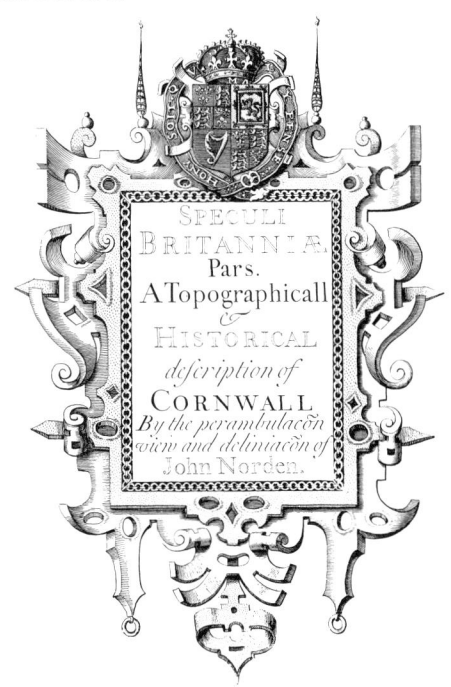

Pre-Seventeenth Century: Early Site References, 1086–1699

The purpose of this table is to establish the antiquity of those sites which *later* received horticultural recognition. It must be emphasized that, with quite minor exceptions, the references are to sites only, and not to ornamental parks or gardens. The exceptions are a few deer parks - mostly disparked, - and the passing mention of the Arwenack and Enys estates as rewards to the Creator's assistants in a fifteenth-century Cornish Creation play, presumably because they were regarded by contemporaries as paradisial. A further mention of the fine gardens at Enys is found in the 1709 edition of Camden's *Magna Britannica*, while a lively description of Hall Walk was given by Carew in 1602.

Norden's *Speculi Britanniae* has been used here as the central point of reference since, although not published until 1728, it represents the state of affairs at the time of his survey around 1597. He indicated houses on his maps by a symbol, usually with the name of the resident, supplemented by alphabetical tables, hundred by hundred, as well as a summary list of 'gentlemen's seats'.

The references to the left of the Norden list are to citations in the earlier centuries, and to the right, in the seventeenth century.

Pre-Norden

While Norden was gathering information at the end of the sixteenth century, Richard Carew was preparing his *Survey* (1602), which also included a topography, less comprehensive than Norden's, but valuable for comparison. The keen observations of Leland, in his earlier *Itineraries* of 1535-43, which included Cornwall, were inevitably limited to what he saw along his chosen routes, but these two sources, taken together with Norden's more complete gazetteer, present a representative picture of the social scene during the sixteenth century.

For the fifteenth century, we must rely upon the *Itineraries* of William of Worcester made between 1478 and 1480 which, in Cornwall, did little more than list the ancient castles, many of which find a place in our topography.

From the fourteenth century, the *Caption of Seisen* (1337), or instrument of tenancies, supplies us with supplementary information of quite a different nature. This survey was made at the formation of the Duchy of Cornwall which, though extensive, covered less that half the county. The tenancies were sometimes at sites mentioned in Norden, but often at other places, which have been entered in the following table. Those who held the tenancies characteristically added their place of origin after their Christian name - such as 'Ralph de Charyhays' [Caerhays]. This provides valuable information on the occurrence of place-names at other than Duchy properties. These also have been included in the following table in round brackets.

The earliest of the entries in this section are taken from the *Domesday* survey of 1086.

Post-Norden

Almost exactly a century after Norden, Joel Gascoyne surveyed and mapped the county. He similarly indicated gentlemen's seats with symbols, although with far fewer names of residents, possibly only those who were his sponsors. Nevertheless, his detailed and accurate mapping, as well as adding many further seats - presumably those which had become established, or at least grown in importance during the seventeenth century - more precisely defines the entries in Norden,

The *Parliamentary Survey* of the Duchy made for the Commonwealth in 1649 is an exact parallel to the *Caption* of 1337, and offers the opportunity for direct comparison at a distance of some three centuries.

Finally, references to the sketches of Edmund Prideaux, although made during his visits to the residences of his relatives and friends during 1716 and 1727, have been included, since in many cases they represent the maturity of grounds planted at an earlier period.

Explanatory notes

Names of sites not in Norden are printed alongside their earliest source. Page references are given, to de Dunstanville's edition of Carew to the edition of Leland in *Early Tours* (1967), and to that of Worcester's *Itinerary*, in the 'Supplementary Papers' at the end of volume iv of *Lake's Parochial History*. The other works contain excellent indexes for those who wish to pursue the subject further.

The names of places and persons have all been normalized to conform to those usually found in later sources. The identifications of sites in *Domesday*, the *Caption* and the *Parliamentary Survey*, are those suggested in the editions listed on page 265

Early Site References, 1086-1699

References

Camden (1586) *Magna Britannica*, William Camden 1586. [The garden at Enys is mentioned in the edition of 1709.]

Caption (1337) *The Caption of Seisen of the Duchy of Cornwall*, ed. P.L. Hull, Devon and Cornwall Record Society, vol.17, Torquay 1971.

Carew (1602) *The Survey of Cornwall*, Richard Carew, 1602. Lord de Dunstanville's edition of 1811 has been used. F.E. Halliday's edition of 1953 is not complete.

Domesday (1086) *Domesday Book: 10. Cornwall*, repr. Chichester 1979.

Early Tours (1967) *Early Tours in Devon and Cornwall*, ed. R. Pearse Chope, 1918, reprinted Newton Abbott, 1967; contains Leland (1535) and Fiennes (1695).

Fiennes (1695) *Through England on a Side Saddle*, Celia Fiennes, 1695. See *Early Tours* (1967). The gardens at Mount Edgcumbe, Stowe and Tregothnan are mentioned, and also Hall, Launceston Castle and St Michael's Mount.

Gascoyne (1699) *A Map of the County of Cornwall*, Joel Gascoyne, 1699, reprinted Devon and Cornwall Record Society, vol.34, 1991.

Leland (1535) *Leland's Itinerary ... 1535-43*, ed. L. Toulmin Smith, Fontwell, Sussex 1964, is the standard edition. See also Davies Gilbert, *Parochial History*, vol. iv 1838, *Lake's Parochial History*, vol.iv 1872, and *Early Tours* (1967), to which references here are made.

Norden (1597) *Speculi Britanniae*, 1728. [survey c. 1597]. Reprinted Newcastle upon Tyne 1966. See also *John Norden's Manuscript Maps of Cornwall ...* introduced by W. Ravenhill, Exeter 1972.

Parl. (1649) *The Parliamentary Survey of the Duchy of Cornwall*, 2 vols, ed. N.J.G. Pounds, Devon and Cornwall Record Society, vols. 25, 27, Torquay 1982 and 1984.

Prideaux (1716-27) 'Collection of Topographical Drawings', ed. J. Harris, *Architectural History*, vol.7: 1964.

Spoure (1690) *The Spoure Book*, manuscript copy in the Cornwall Record Office FS3/93/3/125-135; with sketches of Bochym, Crocadon, Penheale and Trebartha; also Anderton (Launcells), Battens (Northill), Froxton (Whitstone), Holwood (Quethiock), and William Hooper's house in Linkinhorne.

Terriers (1974) *A Calendar of Cornish Glebe Terriers 1673-1735*, ed. R. Potts, Devon and Cornwall Record Society, vol. 19, Torquay 1974. [See Lamorran 70-71, and Ludgvan 93-5.]

Worcester (1478) *Itineraries, 1478-80*, William of Worcester, ed. J.H. Harvey, Oxford 1969, is the standard edition. See also Davies Gilbert, *Parochial History*, vol. iv 1838, and the 'Supplementary Papers' in *Lake's Parochial History*, vol.iv 1872, to which the references here are made.

The following books are of general interest in the study of the topography of Cornwall:

Barker, K., and Kain, R., *Maps and History in South-West England*, Exeter 1991.

Brayshay, M., ed. *Topographical Writers in South-West England*, Exeter 1996.

Quixley, R.C.E., *Antique Maps of Cornwall and the Isles of Scilly*, Penzance 1966.

Domesday: 1086	Caption: 1337	Worcester: 1478	Leland: 1535	Carew: 1602	NORDEN 1597	Parl: 1649	Gascoyne: 1699	Prideaux 1716-27
				38 ANTHONY, Place			G	
D				244	**Antony E.** Richard Carew	P	G	
			33	363	**Arwenack** John Killigrew		G	
				261	**Bake** - Moyle		G	
D					**Bicton** William Wraye		G	
D					**Bochym** Francis Bellot (or Billet)		G	
D			94 ['Blekennok']		**Boconnoc** Sir Reginald Mohun		G	
	(C) BODREAN							
					Bonython Reskymer Bonithon		G	
					Boskenna Walter Carthew		G	
							G BRAY	
							G BURELL	
	(C)			332	**Caerhays** Trevanion heir		G	
				365	**Carclew** John Bonithon			
			94 [C. Fust]		**Carnanton** Edward Noye	P	G	
D CASTLE								
					Castle Horneck ['a ruin']			
D [Bonyalva]				257	**Catchfrench** George Kekewich	P	G	
						P CLEAVE		
				368	**Clowance** Thomas St Aubyn		G	
							G COLDRENICK	
D	C				**Colquite** Lord Marney	P [Kilquite]	G	
	(C)			269	**Cotehele** Peter Edgcumbe		G	
							G CROAN	
				269	**Crocadon** John Trevisa		G	
	C DARLEY					P		
	C DOUBLEBOYS					P	G	
	C DUPORTH					P		
						P EASTAWAY		
					Enys Thomas Enys	P	G	

Domesday: 1086	Caption: 1337	Worcester: 1478	Leland: 1535	Carew: 1602	NORDEN 1597	Parl: 1649	Gascoyne: 1699	Prideaux 1716-27
	(C)			368	**Erisey** Erisey heir		G	
	(C)		46		**Ethy** - Courtenay			
			42	314	**Fowey, Place** Treffry heir			
	C GARLENICK					P	G	
D				310	**Glynn** [*William Glynn*]		G	Pr
		94	29	371	**Godolphin** Sir Francis Godolphin		G	
D [Lanisley]					**Gulval**			
			47	310	**Hall** Sir Reginald Mohun		G	
D				268	**Halton** Anthony Rouse	P	G	
D HAMATETHY								
	C HAREWOOD					P	G	
							G HARLYN	
							G HATT	
	C HELIGAN					P	G	
							G HENGAR	
							G HEXWORTHY	Pr
	C INCE					P	G	Pr
					Kenegie Mr Tripconey		G	
						P KILLAGORDEN		
					Killiow Mr Tredenham		G	
	C LAMBESSO					P	G	
D LAMELLEN								
				36 LAMORRAN			G	
							G LANARTH	
D LANCARFFE							G	
					Landue Thomas Trefusis		G	
	C [Nansladron]			327	**Lanhadron** Arundell	P		
	(C)				**Lanhydrock** Mr Trenance	P	G	Pr
D LANDULPH	C							
	C				**Lanteglos** [Camelford]	P		
D	C	94	9	275	**Launceston**	P		Pr
					Lavethan Humphry Kempe		G	
D LAWHITTON						P		
D	C	94	49	303	**Liskeard**	P		
D LUDGVAN								
	(C)			278	**Manaton** Edward Manaton	P	G	
				317	**Menabilly** [*John Rashleigh*]		G	
	C MICHAELSTOW					P		
	C MODITONHAM					P	G	
D MORESK						P		
			49		**Morval** William Coode		G	
			52	239	**Mount Edgcumbe** [*map only*]	P	G	Pr
	C NANSLOE							
							G NANSWHYDEN	
D				276	**Newton Ferrers** Peter Coryton		G	Pr
	(C)				**Ogbeare** William Lovice			
D				340	**Padstow, Place** Nicholas Prideaux		G	Pr
	(C) PARK		12				G	
			49	323	**Pelyn** [*Kendall*]	P	G	
D PELYNT								
	C PENAIR [= Penarth]					P		
	C PENCALENICK [= Penarth]					P [= Penair]		
D PENCARROW								
	C		29	370	**Pengersick** Nicholas Hale		G	
D	C			275	**Penheale** George Grenville		G	
						P PENHELLICK [= Penmount]		
							G PENNANS	
	(C) PENRICE					P	G	
				368		P PENROSE	G	
					Pentillie		G	Pr
	C				**Penvose** Humphry Nicholl			
					Penwarne Richard Penwarne		G	
	C	94		338	**Polwhele** - Polwhele	P	G	
				258	**PortEliot** Richard Eliot		G	Pr
	(C) PRIDEAUX						G	

Domesday: 1086	Caption: 1337	Worcester: 1478	Leland: 1535	Carew: 1602	NORDEN 1597	Parl: 1649	Gascoyne: 1699	Prideaux 1716-27
	C	94, 106	44	323	**Restormel** Samuel	P		Pr
D ROSECRADDOCK			21.RIVIERE					
						P ROSEMUNDY G		
							G ROSEWARNE	
	(C)				**Roskrow** John Roscrow		G	
					St Benet's Henry Courtenay			
			46 ST CADIX		**St Michael's Mount**	P		
	C	96, 101	28	376		P		
D			46	309 ST WINNOW				
	C STOKETON							
							G ROSTEAGUE	
				280	**Stowe** Bernard Grenville		G	Pr
D		93 [Carnbrea]	21	373	**Tehidy** George Basset		G	
						P THANCKES G		
	C		94	13	284	**Tintagel**	P	G
				280	**Tonacombe** John Kempthorne		G	
D				[278]	**Trebartha** Henry Spoure	P	G	
							G TREBURSYE	
							G TREDETHY	
							G TREDIDON	
							G TREDINNICK	
							G	
			34	363	**Trefusis** John Trefusis		G TREGEMBO	
					Tregenna Thomas Tregenna	P		
	(C) TREGOLLS					P		
	C TREGREHAN			336	**Tregothnan** Nicholas Boscawen		G	
							G TREGYE	
					Trehane		G	
D				[278, 338]	**Trelaske** Thomas Lower			
D			48	178	**Trelawne** Sir John Trelawny	P	G	
D				368	**Trelowarren** Hanibal Vyvyan		G	
							G TRELUDICK	
D	C	94	52	264	**Trematon**	P	G	
					Tremeer Edward Lower	P		
D TRENANT								
	C TRENARREN					P		
							G TRENEERE	
					Trengwainton William Cowlins			
D	C				**Trenowth** —		G	
D			19	347	**Trerice** John Arundell		G	
					Tresillian —	P	G	
						P TREVARNO G		
	(C) TREVARRICK					P		
							G TREVAYLOR	
							G TREVETHOE	
D TREVILLIS								
					Trevince William Beauchamp		G	
	(C) TREWAN					P	G	
							G TREWANE [=Trewarne]	
					Trewarthenick —		G	Pr
	(C) TREWHIDDLE					P		
					Trewince George Courtenay		G	
				20	**Trewinnard** Richard Mannering	P	G	
	C TREWITHEN						G	
				26	[386]	**Trewoofe** Arthur Levelis		G
					Treworgey John Connock		G	
							G TRUTHAN	
D					**Werrington** [map only]			Pr
						P WHITEFORD		
							G WIVELSCOMBE	
						P WOLSDON		

Eighteenth Century: Topographical References, 1716-1824

As was stated in the opening note, Charles Gilbert, in his *Historical Survey of Cornwall* (1820), was the first, and indeed the only topographer, systematically to include descriptions of the grounds of the seats he noticed. For this reason his topography has been chosen here as the centre of reference even though it was published in the early years of the nineteenth century, since he may be taken as largely representing the state of affairs during, and especially at the end of, the previous century. Hitchins and Drew's *History* and Stockdale's *Excursions*, both published in 1824 so closely after Gilbert, often provide useful supplementary information. The earlier surveys of Polwhele (1803-6) and the Lysons (1814), however, have not been collated here since, whatever their other virtues, the material relevant for our purposes has been sufficiently incorporated into these later histories.

There remain three other important sources during the eighteenth century itself. The 'Parochial History' of William Hals was published in 1750, and here, amidst much gossip and fanciful etymology, some threads of gold are to be found; Tonkin's more reliable essay into this field remained in manuscript. Both authors are well represented in *Lake's Parochial History* (1867-72), where they are arranged under parishes, there being no general index. William Borlase in his *Natural History* (1758) included engravings of eleven great houses, which contain considerably more detailed information about the gardens than might appear at first sight. Prideaux's sketches have also been included again here, to illustrate the changing trends in the early years of the century.

Together, these sources introduce some sixty-seven new sites, the great majority of which, in contrast to the primarily agricultural settlements of the earlier centuries, were developed by mine-owners, industrialists, merchants, attorneys and others, some of them incomers to the county, in situations often unsuitable for farming, and not infrequently selected for their 'prospect' or view.

This synopsis represents the horticultural evidence in topographies justifying the inclusion of these locations in our review of parks and gardens.

Explanatory notes

The central list contains page references to all those sites in our topography which are to be found in the second volume of Gilbert's *Survey*. Where he has not commented on the grounds, the place-names have been printed in italics.

To the right are the page references in *Hitchins* (whose index is neither complete, nor wholly alphabetical), and in Stockdale (which has no index). They are asterisked if there is any horticultural notice. Only the first page of a reference has been noted.

To the left are the eighteenth century references. Those for Hals and Tonkin are to the volumes of *Lake's Parochial History*, except for a few references to de Dunstanville's transcript of the Tonkin manuscript in his edition of Carew's *Survey*, where this contains additional information. The references to Prideaux and Borlase are, unless otherwise stated, to the plate- and not the page-numbers in the editions cited. Here, as before, an asterisk indicates an horticultural reference. [*pr*] signifies 'proprietor'; [*res*], 'resident'.

References

Detailed site references are supplied for those sources not included in the following table:

Borlase (1758) *The Natural History of Cornwall*, W. Borlase, Oxford 1758. See also *Topographical Sketches ... to elucidate the ... Parochial History of Cornwall*, 1748; manuscript Z19/16/1 in the Devon Record Office; sketches of Godolphin, Mt. Edgcumbe, Prideaux Place, Tehidy, Trelawne, Trevethoe, and Werrington.

Defoe (1724) *A Tour through Great Britain, by a Gentleman* [D. Defoe], 1724. See *Early Tours* (1967). The seats at Godolphin 165, Lanhydrock 167, Prideaux Place 168, Trefusis 167, and Trerice 167-8 are mentioned.

Early Tours (1967) *Early Tours in Devon and Cornwall*, ed. R. Pearse Chope, 1918 repr. Newton Abbot 1967; contains Defoe (1724), Pococke (1750), Shaw (1788), and Maton (1797).

Forbes (1794) 'Tour into Cornwall to the Land's End: (on a visit to Glynn) ...', J. Forbes, *JRIC* 1981: 146-206, mentions in this order Mt Edgcumbe 152-5, Thanckes 158, Coldrenick 160, Glynn 160 etc., Lanhydrock 162,

195, Bocconoc 165-7, Calenick 170, Carclew 170, St Michael's Mt 173, Clowance 173, 187, Pendarves 187, Trelawne 193-5, Pencarrow 195, Restormel Castle and House 196, Priory, Bodmin 200, Launceston Castle 203.

Fraser (1794) *General View of the County of Cornwall*, R. Fraser, 1794. Clowance 25, 61, Godolphin 61, Tregothnan 26, Trelowarren, 26, and Trevethoe 24-5, 60-61, are mentioned.

Gilbert (1817, 1820) *Historical Survey of Cornwall*, C.S. Gilbert, 2 vols, I: 1817; II: 1820.

Hals (1737) *Parochial History of Cornwall*, W. Hals, 1750 [1737 is the year of his death.]. See *Lake* (1867-72). See also Davies Gilbert, *Parochial History*, 1838.

Hitchins (1824) *The History of Cornwall*, F. Hitchins and S. Drew, 2 vols, Helston 1824. The *History*, though planned by Hitchins, was entirely written by Samuel Drew. 'Hitchins' therefore is always italicized.

Lake (1867-72) *Lake's Parochial History ... of Cornwall*, J. Polsue, Truro, 4 vols, I: 1867; II: 1868; III: 1870; IV: 1872. 'Lake', as publisher and not author, is italicized.

Lipscombe (1799) *A Journey into Cornwall*, G. Lipscombe, Warwick 1799. In addition to grounds at Boconnoc 239, Cotehele 306, and Mt Edgcumbe 219-23, the buildings etc. at Trematon Castle 204-7, Antony 208, and Port Eliot 279-89, are noticed.

Maton (1797) *Observations on the Western Counties of England*, W.G. Maton, 2 vols 1797. See *Early Tours* (1967). Mentions features at Menabilly 250, Pengersick 255, Penrose 255, Pentillie 268, Place, Fowey 249-50, Port Eliot 246, and St Michael's Mount 256.

Pococke (1750) *Travels through England*, R. Pococke, 1750. See *Early Tours* (1967). Mentions features at Hall 190, Mount Edgcumbe 188-9, Nanswhyden 200, Port Eliot 189, Prideaux Place 201, Restormel 202-3, St Michael's Mount 195-6, Tehidy 190, Trelawne 190, and especially Werrington 201, 207-8; also Arwenack 198, Boconnoc 203, Cothele 205, Godolphin 196, and Pencarrow 201.

Prideaux (1716-27) 'Collection of Topographical Drawings', ed. J.Harris, *Architectural History*, vol. 7:1964.

Shaw (1788) *A Tour to the West of England*, S. Shaw, 1788. See *Early Tours* (1967). Mentions features at Boconnoc 228, Restormel Castle and House 227-8, and Mount Edgcumbe.

Staniforth (1800) *The Staniforth Diary a visit to Cornwall in 1800*, ed. J. Hext, Truro 1965. Observes Boconnoc 18, Glynn 29, Menabilly 67, Restormel House where he lodged, and St Winnow 38-9. [See also in 19th C. General Notices.]

Stockdale (1824) *Excursions through ... Cornwall*, F.W.L. Stockdale, 1824.

Swete (1780) 'A Tour in Cornwall in 1780', the Revd J. Swete, *JRIC*.1971: 185-219, mentions Werrington 194, Trevethoe 199, Tregenna 203, Castle Horneck 207, St Michael's Mt 208, Arwenack 213, Trewithen, Pennans 216, Catchfrench, Trematon Castle, Antony, Ince Castle 217, and Mt Edgcumbe 218.

— *Travels in Georgian Devon*, J. Swete, ed. T.Gray, Devon 1997, Mt Edgcumbe 140-45, Pentillie 137-8, Werrington 124-6.

Tonkin (1742) 'Parochial History of Cornwall', unpublished [1742 is the year of his death.] See *Lake* (1867-72). See also Davies Gilbert, *Parochial History*, 1838, and R. Carew, *Survey of Cornwall*, ed. Lord de Dunstanville, 1811, with notes from the Tonkin manuscript, some of which are not in *Lake*.

Warner (1800) *A Walk through some Western Counties of England*, R. Warner, Bath 1800, Werrington, see pp. 145-7.

— (1809) *A Tour through Cornwall ... 1808*, R. Warner, Bath 1809, mentions Grove Hill 120, Scorrier 240-41, Tregenna Castle 137-8. [See also in 19th C. General Notices.]

Wynne (1755) 'A Visit to Cornwall in 1755', William Wynne, *JRIC*. 1981: 338-49, mentions Trehane where he lodged, Pendarves 338, 346, Castle Horneck 344, and St Michael's Mt 345.

The title page of Gilbert's Survey of the County of Cornwall.

270 The Bibliographies

Prideaux: 1716-27	Hals: 1737	Tonkin: 1742	Borlase: 1758	GILBERT 1820		Hitchins: 1820	Stockdale 1824
				Acton Castle Buckley Praed	756	540	
1-3		*i.23	*9	**Antony** Rt Hon. Reginald Pole Carew	391	*38	34
	i.388	i.392		**Arwenack** Lord Wodehouse [pr] [*a ruin*]	799	258	65
4,5	ii.38	[Carew:261]		**Bake** Sir Joseph Copley [pr] [*burnt down 1808*]	412	283	36
				Behan Park Rev. Jeremiah Trist	838	*665	
				Bicton Hon. William Eliot [pr] [*old mansion demolished*]	458	341	
	i.286	i.287		*Bochym* Thomas Hartley	772	204	
	i.70	i.71	p.219,288	*Boconnoc* Lord Camelford	908	*84	*45
				Bodrean Henry Prynn Andrews	370	158	
	i.286	i.287		**Bonython** Thomas Hartley	772	204	
				Bosahan Thomas Grylls	777	*32	
		*i.160		**Boskenna** -Paynter	727	132	
				Bosvigo Sir William Lemon [pr]	810	364	
				Bray Philip Wynhall Mayow	933	499	
				Budock Vean *late* Benjamin Pender	784		
				Burell John Burell	433	620	
				John Williams BURNCOOSE		304	
	iii.337	*iii.337	p.288	**Caerhays** J.T.P.B. Trevanion	845	*480	*51
				[*Calenick*]	820	357	[59]
		*iii.388	*11	**Carclew** Sir William Lemon	802	*488	*60
	iii.288			**Carnanton** James Willyams	661	458	*100
				Castle Horneck Samuel Borlase	734	437	
	ii.39			**Catchfrench** Francis Glanville	411	284	145
		iv.51		**Chyverton** John Thomas	683	*544	
				Cleave Rev. John Rouse [pr]	559	502	
	*i.263		*22	**Clowance** Sir John St Aubyn	697	*189	*72
	ii.38			**Coldrenick** Charles Trelawny	413	283	*145
	iii.200			**Colquite** Deeble Peter [pr]	616	434	
				Comprigney William Michel [res]	810		
	i.208			**Condurra** Vivian family [pr] Mr Sholl [res]	823	157	
24	i.173			**Cotehele** Earl of Mt Edgcumbe	449	*135	*128
	i.311	i.312		*Croan* Rev. H.H. Tremayne	618	215	
	iii.305	[Carew:269]		**Crocadon** John Tillie Coryton [pr] [*old mansion demolished: steward resident*]	444	462	
				Duporth Charles Rashleigh	370	*59	
				Eastaway Miss C. Manning	558	501	
	ii.78	*ii.79	*7	**Enys** Francis Enys	789	*293	*63
	iv.129			**Erisey** Lord Falmouth [pr]	774	*299,593	
	iv.323			**Ethy** Adml. Sir S.V. Penrose	906	*680	
				Flexbury Rev .Charles Dayman	561	563	
	i.258			*Garlenick* Rev. George Moore	860	187	*54
44,45	*i.194			*Glynn* E.J. Glynn	907	148	*155
	*i.132		*12,p.288	**Godolphin** [*forsaken mansion*]	758	*110	72
				Gonvena Edward Fox	843	*217	
				Greatwood Joseph Fox [= WOOD COTTAGE]	803		
				Grove Hill George Croker Fox	799		
		*iii.45		**Hall** Samuel Kekewich [pr]	901	*405	
	i.296	i.297		**Halton** Rev. Peter Blewett [pr]	454	208	
				Hamatethy [*divided ownership*]	620		
				Harewood Salusbury Trelawny	452	*138	130
	iii.318			*Harlyn* Henry Peter	653	*466	
				Hatt Rev. Charles Tucker	439	104	
	i.376	i.377		**Heligan** Rev. Henry Hawkins Tremayne	853	*240	*49

Prideaux: 1716-27	Hals: 1737	Tonkin: 1742	Borlase: 1758	GILBERT 1820		Hitchins: 1820	Stockdale 1824
	iv.263			**Hengar** Mrs Michel	614	652	
48		iii.93		**Hexworthy** Edmund Prideaux	499	414	
51				**Ince** Edward Smith	434	619	139
		ii.115	*5	**Kenegie** William Arundell Harris	738	301	*80
				Killiganoon Admiral Spry	808	263	
	ii.316	ii.317		**Killiow** Robert Lovell Gwatkins [pr] [unoccupied]	809	360	
				Kilmarth William Rashleigh [pr] [unoccupied]	876	657	
	i.208	i.209		*Lambesso* ['much decayed']	824	157	
	ii.339			**Lanarth** Lt.-Col. William Sandys	776	*366	
	i.79			*Lancarffe* Capt. William Hext	632	102	
		iii.118		**Landue** William Bant	497	419	
				Landulph Rev. F.V.J. Arundell	446		*131
	i.375	i.377	p.219	**Lanhadron** Rev. H.H. Tremayne [pr]	853	*238	
56		*iii.4	p.288	**Lanhydrock** Hon. Mrs Agar	636	*388	*155
				Laregan Thomas Pascoe	735		
52-5		*iii.64		**Launceston** C.	508	*410	123
	i.66			**Lavethan** General Moorhead	622	80	
		iii.133		**Liskeard** C.	949	*425	
		i.377		**Luney** Earl of Mt Edgcumbe [pr] [gardens etc. destroyed]	854	241	
	iv.155	iv.155		**Manaton** John Kinsman [pr]	467	608	
	iv.271		p.228	**Menabilly** William Rashleigh	874	*656	*40
				Menacuddle Joseph Sawle Sawle [pr]	866	57	*49
				Gregor [pr] MEUDON Mr Fox [res]		460	
				Mevagissey Rectory Rev. Dr Lyne	850		
	i.111			**Moditonham** Charles Carpenter	438	103	*132
				Henry Prynn Andrew MORESK			157
				Morval John Buller	932	498	
60-2	iii.245			**Mt Edgcumbe** Earl of Mt Edgcumbe	374	*444	*34
				Nancealverne John Scobell	735		80
				Richard Fox NANSIDWELL		460	
				Nansloe Philip Vyvyan Robinson	769	672	69
				Nansough Charles Andrews	828		
	i.229		*8	**Nanswhyden** Rev. Robert Hoblyn [burnt down 1803]	668	169	98
				Newham Ralph Allen Daniell	810	363	
68	iii.305	iii.306		**Newton Ferrers** Weston Helyar	444	*461	
				Ogbeare Sir William Pratt Call	533		
	*i.310			*Park* Sir A.O. Molesworth [pr] [farmhouse]	618	*214	
				Pelyn Rev. Nicholas Kendall	878	394	
	i.209			**Penair** Capt. Barrington Reynolds	823	*158	
				Pencalenick Mrs Vivian	823	*158	
	*i.310	*i.312	p.288	**Pencarrow** Sir A.O. Molesworth	618	215	*106
	i.182		*14	**Pendarves** Edward Wynne Pendarves	694	*145	*92
	*i.134			*Pengersick* C.	759	113	73
				Pengreep Joseph Beauchamp	806	304	
	i.322	i.322		**Penheale** [divided ownership]	527	218	
		i.209 [= Penhellick]		**Penmount** Mr Williams [pr]	824	158	
	i.257	i.258	p.228	*Pennans* Thomas Carlyon	860	*185	
				Penpoll Richard Oke Millet	371	557	
	i.42			**Penrice** Joseph Sawle Sawle	868	*59	49
		iv.150		**Penrose** John Rogers	761	602	*69
77	iii.305			**Pentillie** John Tillie Coryton	440	*559	*130

272 The Bibliographies

Prideaux: 1716-27	Hals: 1737	Tonkin: 1742	Borlase: 1758	GILBERT 1820		Hitchins: 1820	Stockdale 1824
	iv.263			**Penvose** Samuel Kekewich [pr]	614	651	
	iii.300	iii.300		*Penwarne* Stephen Usticke	791	460	
	ii.15			**Place**, Fowey, J.T. Austen	894	*274	39
	i.37			*Place*, St Anthony, Admiral Spry	842	34	
				Poltair George Scobell D.D.	735		80
				Polvellan [= Polvethan] John Buller	924	*628	37
	i.209	i.209		*Polwhele* Rev. Richard Polwhele	823	159	
86	ii.38	ii.40,* [Carew:258]		**Port Eliot** Earl of St Germans	409	*280	*143
		iii.185		**Prideaux House** John Colman Rashleigh	871	431	*46
69-75			*4, p.288	**Prideaux Place**. Rev. Chas Prideaux Brune	650	*526	105
	i.77			**Priory**, Bodmin Walter Raleigh Gilbert	629	89,102	
				Rame Place Thomas Edwards	386	574	
91				**Restormel** C.	879	394	*43
				Restormel House Earl of Mt Edgcumbe [pr]	881	394	44
				John Hext [res]			
				Joseph Carne *RIVIERE*		*556	
				Roscadgehill John Tremenheere	735		
				R.W. Fox [res]			
				[Miss] Ann Hodge *ROSECRADDOCK* 155			
				Rosehill Pz. *late* Richard Oxnam	734		
				Rosemorran George John	738	*301	
				Rosemundy John James	684	*22	
	i.182			**Rosewarne** Mrs Harris	695	*145	
	ii.78	ii.79		*Roskrow* Lord De Dunstanville [pr]	789	292	
	ii.71	ii.72		**Rosteague** Henry Harris	843	289	
				Ruanlanihorne parsonage	854		
				St Benet's Rev. F.V.J. Arundell	639	391	*166
	iv.283			**St Cadix** Mrs Wymond	903	*659	
				St Just in Penwith	721		
				St Just in Roseland	838	*352	
		*ii.184	p.221	**St Michael's Mount** Sir John St Aubyn	756	*321	74
	iv.323			**St Winnow** Rev. Robert Walker	904	679	
				Sanders Hill Thomas Rawlings [demolished]	652	*527	105
				Saveock Michael Allen	809	360	
				Scorrier John Williams	806	*306	95
				Skisdon Lodge Mrs Braddon	610	371	
				Stoketon Hon. Adml. de Courcy	435	*620	139
101-2	ii.364			**Stowe** [*demolished 1739*]	552	372	*120
	ii.218	*ii.219	*10, p288	**Tehidy** Lord De Dunstanville	690	*334	*92
		i.23		**Thanckes** Lord Graves	393	*38	34
				Tolcarne Thomas Tinney	673		
				Tonacombe William Waddon Martin	558	502	
				Tor House Joshua Rowe	395		
				Torfrey - Sleemans	878	596	
	iv.5			**Trebartha** Francis Hearle Rodd	485	*519	*126
				Trebrown William Betenson	415		
				Trebursye Hon. William Eliot	492	540	126
				Tredethy Francis John Hext	616	435	
				Tredidon Henry Spry	520	634	
				Tredinnick James Buller [pr]	838		
				Mr W.P.C. Hugoe [res]			
				[*Tredrea*] George Fox	803	*539	
				Tredudwell Canon Howell	902		
		*iii.389		**Trefusis** Lord Clinton	801	489	67
				Tregeare William Baron	528	219,387	
	ii.183			*Tregembo* Rev. Humphry Willyams	740	321	

Topographical References, 1716-1824   273

Prideaux: 1716-27	Hals: 1737	Tonkin: 1742	Borlase: 1758	GILBERT 1820		Hitchins: 1820	Stockdale 1824
				Tregenna C. Samuel Stephens	719	346	90
				Tregolls Admiral Spry	824	159	
	iii.344	iii.345	p.288	**Tregothnan** Lord Falmouth	834	*358,483	*56
		*i.60		**Tregrehan** Thomas Carlyon	872	*76	
		ii.3		*Tregye* [= TREGEW] Ralph A. Daniell [pr]	808	263	
		i.346		**Trehane** William Stackhouse	830	570	
		iii.111		**Trelaske** Samuel Archer	488	417	
				Trelawne Rev. Sir Harry Trelawny	916	*534	37
				Trelissick Ralph Allen Daniell	807	263	
	iii.277		*6	**Trelowarren** Sir Richard Vyvyan	779	*455	*71
	i.322 [=Tre-lyn-ike]			**Treludick** Peter Hurden	528	219	
	iv.170			**Trematon** C. Benjamin Tucker	423	614	*135
				Trematon Hall Thomas Edwards	435		
				Tremeal Samuel Archer	493	548	
				Tremeer Mrs Reed	614	651	166
	iii.196	*iii.197		**Tremough** [*deserted, in ruins*]	785	*433	
	i.303	i.303		**Trenant** Vice-Adml. Sir Edward Buller	936	212	
	*i.43	i.43		**Trenarren** Thomas Hext	869	57	
				Treneere H.P. Tremenheere	734	437	
				Trengwainton Sir Rose Price	733	437	*80
				[*Trenowth under family only*]	300	570	
				Trereife Rev. Charles V. Le Grice	735	438	
		iii.415		**Trerice** Sir Thomas Dyke Acland	678	515	*97
		iii.415		**Tresillian** J. Gully Bennet	679	517	
				Trethill Wallis family [*in a state of decay*]	402		
				Trevarno Christopher Wallis	762	604	
				Trevarrick Henry Lakes	868	*59	
				Trevaylor William Veale	735	301	
			p.288	**Trevethoe** William Praed	710	379	*91
				Trevillet J.S. Wortley	586	636	
	ii.129			**Trevince** Joseph Beauchamp [pr] Michael Williams [res]	806	304	
	i.228			**Trewan** Richard Vyvyan	668	168	100
				Trewardale Mrs Elizabeth Collins	622	80	
				Trewarne Rev. Richard Gerveys Grylls [also TREWANE]	611	370	
106	i.248	i.248		**Trewarthenick** Mrs Gregor	831	*180	52
				Trewhiddle Francis Polkinhorne	868	*59	
				Trewin John Littleton	402		
	ii.71			**Trewince** Richard Johns	843	289	
	i.356	i.358		**Trewinnard** Sir Christopher Hawkins [*occasional residence*]	709	232	91
		*iv.92	*23	**Trewithen** Sir Christopher Hawkins	830	*570	*55
	i.159			*Trewoofe* [*demolished*]	727	131	
	i.202			**Treworgey** Miss Arminel Inch	948	155	*151
	i.345	i.346		**Truthan** Edward Collins	827	229	
				Waterloo Villa Nicholas Harris Nicolas	928		
108			p.288	**Werrington** Duke of Northumberland	521		*121
				Whiteford Sir William Pratt Call	477	623	*127
	iv.171			**Wivelscombe** Robert Billing	432	619	
				Wolsdon John Boger	396		

Nineteenth Century:
Horticultural and General References, 1792-1899

The early nineteenth century saw, particularly in the works of the indefatigable Loudon, a rise in the number of publications devoted exclusively to horticulture. They were addressed to a rising and prosperous middle class, rather than to the landed gentry, who sought the advice of such as Brown and Repton. Loudon's *Encyclopedia* of 1822, followed in 1830 by his *Gardener's Magazine*, paved the way in mid-century for the *Gardeners' Chronicle* (1841) and the *Cottage Gardener* (1848) – later the *Journal of Horticulture*. These and many other such journals are our primary source of garden information throughout the nineteenth century. The topographies and histories now take second place, filling in essential background detail, but without contributing greatly to our knowledge of the gardens themselves, except on the rare occasions when they mention one which has otherwise escaped notice. They are collated in a GENERAL table which follows after the present list of references to periodicals.

A. HORTICULTURAL RECOGNITION

The ensuing catalogue opens from the date of the first *Red Book* of Repton, and the gazetteer in Loudon's *Encyclopaedia*, since together they establish from the outset the most celebrated gardens at the turn of the century. The locations have been arranged alphabetically, with their journal references listed chronologically into the next century. The sequence in which gardens came to the notice of the horticultural journals has been found illuminating, so that a chronological table of first notices has been compiled to present more clearly information which it would otherwise be tedious to extract from the main list. Even though this may not provide absolute evidence for their age, it does chart the rise in interest in particular gardens, at least among horticultural writers.

It is not practicable in the following abbreviated references to distinguish between major articles, plant records, and mere passing notices, although the contributions by the leading authors are listed under their names in the 'Biographical Notes' below. A great majority of articles upon examination will be found to be principally concerned with cultivation, where indeed they are not simply bald lists of plants. In part, this reflects the current enthusiasm for the introduction and nurture of new species, but it also illustrates a more general shift in emphasis away from the eighteenth-century preoccupation with landscape design.

A key to the abbreviated titles of the various journals follows this section.

DECEMBER

THE

Gardeners' Chronicle.

SATURDAY, DECEMBER 28, 1889.

CORNISH GARDENS AND THEIR LESSONS.*

Horticultural and General References, 1792-1899   275

CHRONOLOGICAL TABLE

1792	ANTONY		TREMATON CASTLE		TREBAH		LAREGAN
	PORT ELIOT	1846	PENVENTON		TREBURSYE		MARLBOROUGH HOUSE
1793	CATCHFRENCH		TRUTHAN		TREDREA		MORRAB GARDENS
	TREWARTHENICK	1848	TRELASKE		TREGOLLS		OGBEARE HALL
1809	TREGOTHNAN	1852	PORTHGWIDDEN		TREGREHAN		PENLEE PARK
1810	PENTILLIE CASTLE		TREHANE		TREMORVAH		PENMERE
1822	CARCLEW	1855	PENDREA		TREMOUGH		POLWITHEN
	CLOWANCE	1861	PENROSE		YORK HOUSE		TOLVEAN
	COTEHELE		TREGULLOW	1872	GULVAL		TREDARVAH
	MENABILLY	1864	PENJERRICK	1873	PENLEE HOUSE		TRENGWAINTON
	PENDARVES		TRESCO	1875	LAMORRAN		TULLIMAAR
	TEHIDY	1866	TREVINCE	1877	KIMBERLEY PARK	1890	CARNANTON
	TREBARTHA	1870	ALVERTON		ROSEMUNDY		CHYMORVAH
	TRELAWNE		COLDRENICK	1879	GLANMOR		COMPRIGNEY
1830	TRELOWARREN		DUPORTH	1880	ROSEHILL		PENMARE
	TREWITHEN		GLYNN		TREVARRICK		PRIDEAUX HOUSE
1831	WHITEFORD		GOONVREA		TREWIDDEN		TREWARDALE
1833	ST MICHAEL'S MOUNT		KENEGIE	1881	PENALVERNE	1891	POLTAIR
1834	GROVE HILL		KILLIOW	1883	PRIDEAUX PLACE	1893	DOUBLEBOIS
1835	TRELISSICK		LANHYDROCK		TREVARNO		PENHELLIS
1836	HELIGAN		LANTEGLOS	1887	DOWNES	1894	BOSCAWEN PARK
1837	BOCCONOC		NEWTON FERRERS		ARWENACK	1895	BOSAHAN
	ENYS		PENAIR	1888	ROSEMORRAN	1897	BURNCOOSE
	TREVETHOE		POLWHELE	1889	BOCHYM		PENCALENICK
	WERRINGTON		PONSANDANE		CARMINO	1898	CARNE = Boskenwyn
1842	PENCARROW		SCORRIER		CASTLE HORNECK		Manor
	TOR HOUSE		SOUTHLEIGH		HEXWORTHY	1899	ACTON CASTLE

Acton Castle   G.Ch. 1899: ii 237.
Alverton   H.D. 1870; C.G. 1993: 93.
Antony   Repton 1792, 1794: 53-5, 1803: 94; G.Ch. 1852: 374; H.D. 1870-1924; C.L. 74 1933: 172, 202, 134 1963: 978, G.Ch. 1963: ii 244; Arch. Hist. 1964: 1-3.
Arwenack   JRIC. 1887: 160; G.Ch. 1889: ii 749.
Bocconoc   G. Mag. 1837: 121; G.Ch. 1856: 230, 1869: 363; H.D. 1870-1924; G.Ch. 1888: i 339; JRHS. 1892: 486, 568 etc.; G.Ch. 1897: i 260; Con. Conf. 1932: 320 etc., 384; Arch. Rev. 73 1933: 156.
Bochym   H.D. 1889-1916; JRHS. 1943: 303, 1947: 33; C.G. 1987: 44.
Bosahan   G.Ch. 1895: ii 214; G.Ch.1896: i 364, 1902: i 245; G.W. 1904: 649; G.Ch. 1906: ii 159; H.D. 1908-24; G.Ch. 1909: i 60; G.M. 1909: 125; G. 1914: ii 566; Rh.N. 1926: 139; Con .Conf. 1932: 384; G. Illus. 1938: 86; JRHS. 1943: 297; G.Ch. 1968: ii 13.
Boscawen Park   G.Ch. 1894: ii 730; G. Illus. 1934: 297.
Boskenwyn   see Carne.
Burncoose   JRIC. 1897: 328; G. 1898: ii 252; G. Illus. 1907: 6; Con. Conf. 1932 :385; JRHS. 1943: 298, 1948: 210.
Carclew   Loudon 1822: 1247; G. Mag. 1831: 225, 1832: 746; Trans. Hort. Soc. 1833: 509; G. Mag. 1836: 28, 412, 1837: 43, 87, 1838: 29, 396; RHS Corn. 1838: 8; G. Mag. 1839: 630, 1840: 16, 23, 475, 549, 593; G. Ch. 1841: 55, 72, 119, 263; G. Mag. 1843: 35, 446; G.Ch. 1846: 693, 803, 1851: 821, 1852: 86, 1854: 710; H.D. 1870-1924; G.Ch. 1874: i 838; J.Hort. 1874: ii 383, 403; JRHS. 1892: 488, 568 etc; K.B. 1893: 355; JRIC. 1897: 326; G.Ch. 1898: ii 399;
G.W. 1904: 649; JRHS. 1907: 189; G.M. 1908: 201; G.Ch. 1911: i 252, 1912: i 321, 1913: i 339; JRHS. 1914: 79; C.L. 39 1916: 590; G. Illus. 29th May 1925; Con. Conf. 1932: 320 etc., 385; C.L. 75 1934: 378; JRHS. 1943: 262, 1947: 33, 1948: 203; C.L. 132 1962: 774.
Carmino   G.Ch. 1889: ii 749; JRHS. 1912: 65.
Carnanton   H.D. 1890-1924.
Carne = Boskenwyn Manor   G.Ch. 1898: i 298.
Castle Horneck   H.D. 1889-1924; Con. Conf. 1932: 386.
Catchfrench   Repton 1793, 1794: 18n., 1803: 10; JRIC. 1969: 16; C.G. 1996: 26.
Chymorvah   G.Ch. 1890: ii 507; 1896: ii. 763; H.D. 1908-24.
Clowance   Loudon 1822: 1247; G. Mag. 1830: 229, 1833: 379, 529, 582, 584, 1835: 694; 1836: 413, 1837: 121, 521, 1838: 271; H.D. 1870-1919.
Coldrenick   H.D. 1870-1924; G. 1876: ii 492, 1877: i 20; G.Ch. 1907: i 130; Con. Conf. 1932: 319 etc., 386; JRHS. 1943: 267.
Comprigney   H.D. 1890-1924.
Cotehele   Loudon 1822: 1247; G. 1893: ii 21, 117; C.L. 11 1902: 364, 485; G. 1902: ii 44, 364; C.L. 17 1905: 822; H.D. 1908-24; C.L. 56 1924: 324; Con. Conf. 1932: 387; JRHS. 1960: 345; G.Ch. 1961: ii 102; Arch. Hist. 1964: 24; JRHS .1971: 219; C.L. 1990: 5/52, 6/68.
Doublebois House   Kelly's 1893: 1171; H.D. 1908-16.
Downes   Br. Arch. 1887: 282, 480; G.Ch 1898: i 219; C.G. 1994: 66; CGT: 1996: 19.
Duporth   H.D. 1870-1924.
Enys   G. Mag. 1837: 496; G.Ch. 1869: 816, 1870: 531; H.D. 1870-1924; G. 1875: ii 447; J. Hort. 1879: i 78;

G.Ch. 1889: ii 747, 756; K.B. 1893: 357; JRIC. 1897: 322; G. 1901: ii 45; G.Ch. 1901: i 417, 1902: ii 31, 1906: ii 185; G.M. 1908: 203; G.Ch. 1912: i 320, 1913: i 339; Con. Conf. 1932: 321 etc.,387; JRHS. 1943: 268; JRIC. 1996: 30.

Glanmor J. Hort. 1879: i 77.

Glynn H.D. 1870-1908; G.Ch. 1870: 1704; Arch. Rev. 73 1933: 154; Arch. Hist. 1964: 44, 45; JRIC. 1980: 173.

Goonvrea H.D. 1870-1916; J. Hort. 1879: i 78.

Grove Hill G. Mag. 1834: 87, 1835: 694, 1836: 370; RHS Corn. 1838: 9; G. Mag.1840: 475; JRIC. 1864: 71; G.Ch. 1889: ii 748; JRIC. 1897: 321; H.D. 1908-16; JRHS. 1943: 267.

Gulval G. 1872: i 580; J. Hort. 1880: i 293; G. 1881: i 314; C.G. 1992: 95.

Heligan G. Mag. 1836: 28, 62; G.Ch. 1841: 119, 1843: 524; H.D. 1870-1924; G. 1877: i 515; G.Ch. 1896: ii 747; JRIC. 1897: 340; G.Ch. 1909: i 29; Con. Conf. 1932: 321 etc., 388; JRHS. 1943: 263, 1948: 205; Rh.Y. 1982/3: 1; C.G. 1983: 41, 1985: 19; O. Corn. 1985-91: x 376; C.G. 1987: 70, 1993: 39; C.L. 1992: 13/50; CGT. 1993: 16; C.G. 1994: 82, 1997: 9.

Hexworthy H.D. 1889-1916; Arch. Hist. 1964: 48.

Kenegie H.D. 1870-91; O. Corn. iv 1943-50: 224, 303, vii 1967-73: 31-3; JRIC. 1972: 320, 1980: 250; C.G. 1995: 96.

Killiow H.D. 1870-1916; J. Hort. 1879: i 77; G.Ch. 1894: ii 434; JRIC. 1897: 334; Con. Conf. 1932: 327, 389; JRHS. 1943: 262.

Kimberley Park G.Ch. 1877: i 692; Times 26 May 1877: 8; G. 1880: i 345; G.Ch. 1889: ii 749; G. 1907: ii 599.

Lamorran G.Ch. 1875: i 593; G. 1876: i 48, ii 446, 1877: i 540, ii 352; J. Hort. 1877: ii 177, 217; G.Ch. 1878: i 377; G. 1880: i 284; J. Hort. 1880: ii 182; G.Ch. 1881: i 751, 1882: i 57; J. Hort. 1884: i 384; G. 1886: i 61; G.Ch. 1886: i 365, 1889: ii 749, 1902: i 245; Con. Conf. 1932: 320 etc., 390; JRHS. 1943: 265; C.G. 1992: 93.

Lanhydrock H.D. 1870-1924; C.L. 14 1903: 890; Con. Conf. 1932: 390; Arch. Hist. 1864: 56; C.L. 147 1970: 542; JRHS. 1971: 220; JRIC. 1988: 221; C.G. 1993: 16, 1994: 64.

Laregan H.D. 1889-1916.

Marlborough House G.Ch. 1889: ii 749.

Menabilly Loudon 1822: 1247; H.D. 1870-1924; G.Ch. 1886: i 817; JRHS. 1892: 487, 569 etc., 575; K.B. 1893: 358; G.Ch. 1896: i 700, 1897: i 205; JRIC. 1897: 337; G.Ch. 1903: i 234, 416; G.W. 1904: 287; JRHS. 1943: 264, 1948: 202.

Morrab Gardens G.Ch. 1889: ii 163, 750; R Poly SC. 1889: 42; G. 1895: i 322; G.W. 1904: 409; G. 1907: ii 599; JRHS. 1907: 190; G. Illus. 1934: 297; G.Ch. 1962: ii 282; C.G. 1982: 28.

Mt Edgcumbe The World 1789; Loudon 1822: 1247; G. Mag. 1836: 411; G.Ch. 1841: 38, 312; G. Mag. 1842: 547; J. Hort. 1858: 147; G. 1872: i 552; G.Ch. 1873: 814; J. Hort. 1877: ii 402, 419; Pall Mall, May 1877: 4; G.Ch. 1882: ii 7, 39; G.M. 1887: 432; Illus. Lond. News 1894: cv. 110; C.L. 2 1897: 238, 11 1902: 317; G.W. 1904: 287; H.D. 1908-16; Con. Conf. 1932: 391; C.L. 116 1953: 794, 119 1956: 746, 128 1960: 1550, 1598, 129 1961: 188; Arch. Hist. 1964: 60-2; G.Ch. 1975: ii 22; C.G. 1976: 25; O. Corn. viii 1976: 332; G. Hist. 1996: 24(1) 9.

Newton Ferrers H.D. 1870-1924; C.L. 15 1904: 54; C.L. 84 1938: 604, 628; Arch. Hist. 1964: 68.

Ogbeare Hall H.D. 1889-1916; O. Corn. viii 1973: 41; C.G. 1995: 103.

Penair H.D. 1870-1916.

Penalverne G. 1881: i 204; J. Hort. 1884: i 384; H.D. 1891-1916.

Pencalenick JRIC. 1897: 336; H.D. 1908-24; JRHS. 1943: 302; R Poly SC 1952: 35; JRIC. 1974: 165.

Pencarrow G. Mag. 1842: 471; G.Ch. 1842: 560; H.D. 1870-1916; J. Hort. 1878: i 69; JRHS. 1892: 575; G.Ch. 1899: i 234, 236, ii 35, 264, 362, 421, 489, 1900: i 234, 236, 1902: i 392; Gdn. Life Oct. 1903; C.L. 11 1902: 457; G. Ch. 1903: i 10, 1905: ii 380, 395, 1907: i 93, 141, 1908: i 277; G.M. 1909: 103; G.Ch. 1910: i 294; Con. Conf. 1932: 316 etc., 391; JRHS. 1943: 262, 364, 1946: 364; C.L. 116 1954: 118, 200.

Pendarves Loudon 1822: 1247; G. Mag. 1827: 174, 1832: 576, 1835: 359, 634, 1836: 412, 1837: 122, 354, 1838: 418; H.D. 1889-1924; C.G. 1995: 98.

Pendrea G.Ch. 1855: 317; J. Hort. 1880: i 293; G. 1881: i 111, 204; J. Hort. 1884: i 384; H.D. 1889-91; C.G. 1986: 48.

Penhellis Kelly's 1893: 1124.

Penjerrick JRIC. 1864: 71; G.Ch. 1871: 1490, 1874: i 308, 375, i 370, 1889: ii 749; H.D. 1889-1924; JRIC. 1897: 317; G.Ch. 1898: ii 399; Corn. Mag. 1899: 275; G. 1899: i 31, ii 413, 424; G.Ch. 1901: i 309, 386, 1902: ii 31; G.W. 1904: 648; G.M. 1908: 183; G. 1915: i 162; Rh. N. 1928: 252; Con. Conf. 1932: 314, 318 etc, 393; G. Illus. 1932: 137; JRHS. 1943: 267, 1948: 206; Rh. Y. 1965: 15, 1980/81: 26, 40; C.G. 1980: 17, 1982: 47; Gdn. 1986: 30, 143; C.G. 1989: 49.

Penlee House G.Ch. 1873: 951; G. 1875: i 104, 148; G.Ch. 1889: ii 639; C.G. 1987: 134.

Penlee Park H.D. 1889-1924; G.Ch. 1962: ii 283; C.G. 1984: 16.

Penmare H.D. 1890-91.

Penmere G.Ch. 1889: ii 748.

Penrose G.Ch. 1861: 314, 1136; JRIC. 1876: 282; G. 1877: ii 44, 289; JRIC. 1879: 281, 282; H.D. 1908-24; Con. Conf. 1932: 394.

Pentillie Castle Repton 1810; Loudon 1822: 1247; G. Mag. 1842: 548; J. Hort. 1863: ii 71; H.D. 1870-1924; J. Hort. 1877: ii 346; G.Ch. 1895: ii 650, 1896: i 23; G.W. 1896: 231; G.Ch. 1901: i 329; JRHS. 1948: 208; Arch. Hist. 1964: 77; Arch. Rev. June 1968: 469.

Poltair H.D. 1891.

Polwhele H.D. 1870-1916.

Polwithen H.D. 1889-1916; G.Ch. 1889: ii 748.

Ponsandane H.D. 1870-1924.

Port Eliot Repton 1793, 1794: 18n., 1803: 16, 192-4; Loudon, 1822: 1247; G. Mag 1836: 28; G Ch. 1852: 118; J. Hort. 1860: 208; H.D. 1870-1916; G.Ch. 1885: ii 85; Con. Conf. 1932: 395; C.L. 104 1948: 778, 828, 882; Arch. Hist. 1964: 86.

Porthgwidden JRHS. 1852: 24; G.Ch. 1861: 577, 1863: 656; H.D. 1870-91; G.Ch. 1879: i 686; JRIC. 1897: 333; JRHS. 1943: 262; JRIC. 1974: 165; C.G. 1992: 90.

Prideaux House H.D. 1890-1916.

Prideaux Place G. 1883: i 28, 150, 238; H.D. 1889-1924; J. Hort. 1900: i 289; G.M. 1909: 104; G.Ch. 1911: ii 219; C.L. 131 1962: 226, 274; Arch. Hist. 1964: 69-75; C.G. 1991: 33.

Rosehill G.Ch. 1880: i 345; G.Ch. 1889: ii 749, 1894: ii 697,756; G. 1895: 406; G.Ch. 1896: i 176; JRIC. 1897: 318; G. 1898: i 32; G.W. 1904: 478; G.Ch. 1905: ii 103, 1906: ii 159; G. Illus. 1906: 101, 595; G.M. 1908: 182; H.D. 1908-24; G.Ch. 1909: i 61, 1911: i 252, 1912: i 321; R Poly SC. 1939: 38; JRHS. 1943: 267; C.G. 1992: 50, 1993: 3; CGT. 1996: 23.

Rosemorran G. 1888: i 138, 1918: i 11, 29.

Rosemundy J. Hort. 1877: ii 476; G.Ch. 1889: ii 749; H.D. 1916-19.

St Michael's Mt G. Mag. 1833: 543; G. Mag. 1834: 351; J. Hort. 1884: i 425; G. 1896: i 235; JRHS. 1907: 190; H.D. 1908-24; C.L. 56 1924: 672, 714; G. 1924: 823.

Scorrier H.D. 1870-1916; G. 1881: i 204; J. Hort. 1884: i 384; JRHS. 1892: 486, 575; Rh. N. 1927: 204; Con. Conf. 1932: 319 etc., 395; JRHS. 1942: 48, 1943: 266, 1948: 203.

Southleigh H.D. 1870; G. Illus. 1906: 20, 61.

Tehidy Loudon 1822: 1247; G. Mag. 1837: 122; H.D. 1870-1924; J. Hort. 1878: i 109.

Tolvean H.D. 1889-1924; G.W. 1904: 409.

Tor House G. Mag. 1842: 547.

Trebah H.D. 1870-1924; F&S. 1904: 353; G.M. 1908: 202; G.Ch. 1912: i 321; G. 1913: 277; Con. Conf. 1932: 326 etc., 397; JRHS. 1943: 300; C.G.1983: 56; Gdn. 1986: 30, 254; C.G. 1989: 79; C.L. 1990: 8/110; CGT.1991: 9; 1994: 6; Gdn. 1998: 100.

Trebartha Loudon 1822: 1247; H.D. 1870-1924.

Trebursye H.D. 1870-1916.

Tredarvah G.Ch. 1889: ii 748.

Tredrea H.D. 1870-90; J. Hort. 1874: ii 361; G.Ch. 1876: i 372, 1879: i 212.

Tregolls H.D. 1870-91.

Tregothnan Repton 1809; G. Mag. 1837:121; H.D. 1870-1924; G.Ch. 1874: i 252; J. Hort. 1877: ii 269, 288; JRIC. 1897: 329; G.Ch. 1898: ii 400, 1902: ii. 31; G.W. 1904: 648; G.Ch. 1906: ii 159, 1909: i 289, 1912: i 320; G. 1913: 397; Con. Conf. 1932: 318 etc., 397; JRHS. 1943: 265, 1948: 204; C.L. 119 1956: 1051, 1112; Rh. Y. 1968: 1, 1976: 7, C.G. 1986: 83, 1994: 41.

Tregrehan H.D. 1870-1924; K.B. 1916: 140; Con. Conf. 1932: 321 etc., 398; G.Ch. 1939: ii 120; JRHS. 1943: 297, 1948: 202; Rh.Y. 1976/40, 1983/4: 25, 1984/5: 51; Field 24 Aug.1985: 50; C.G. 1985: 34, 1986: 22; Rh. Y. 1985/6: 46; Gdn. 1986: 143; Rh. Y. 1987/8: 70; C.G. 1992: 83, 1994: 63.

Tregullow G.Ch. 1861: 340; H.D. 1870-1891; G. 1891: ii 237, 310; G.W. 1891: 52; Con. Conf. 1932: 319, 401.

Trehane G.Ch. 1852: 374; G.Ch. 1874: ii 784, 1913: i 339, 1914: ii 372; G. Illus. 27 May 1922; JRHS. 1943: 298, 1948: 203, 1950: 326; C.G. 1971: 7, 1979: 28, 1986: 16; Gdn. 1986: 141; C.L. 1989: 7/86.

Trelaske G.Ch. 1848: 374.

Trelawne Loudon 1822: 1247; H.D. 1919-24.

Trelissick G. Mag. 1835: 266; H.D. 1870-1924; G. 1893: i 433; G.Ch. 1894: ii 500, 1895: i 76, 1896: i 485; G. 1897: i 257, ii 151; W. Morn. News 1897 [see C.G. 1988: 24]; JRIC. 1897: 330; G.Ch. 1898: ii 400, 1901: i 342; G. 1901: ii 45; G.W. 1904: 648; G.M. 1908: 182; JRHS. 1943: 262, 1948: 202, 1960: 353; C.L. 131 1962: 54; G.Ch. 1964: ii 96; JRHS. 1971: 219; Rh. Y. 1980/81: 40; C.G. 1985: 37; C.L. 1992: 13/42; C.G. 1993: 103.

Trelowarren G. Mag. 1830: 420; G. Mag. 1837: 121; H.D. 1870-1924; C.L. 39 1916: 450; Con. Conf. 1932: 401.

Trematon Castle G. Mag. 1842: 548; H.D. 1870-1924; C.L. 104 1948: 428, 478.

Tremorvah H.D. 1870-1916.

Tremough H.D. 1870-1916; G.Ch. 1876: ii 719; J. Hort. 1879: i 78; K.B. 1893: 355; JRIC. 1897: 325; G.Ch. 1899: i 4, 1900: ii 439, 440, 1901: i 246; G. 1901: ii 45; G.Ch. 1902: ii 31; G.W. 1904: 648; G.M. 1908: 181; G.Ch. 1909: i 267, 1913: i 339; JRHS. 1943: 264.

Trengwainton H.D. 1889-1924; G.Ch. 1894: ii 732; G.W. 1904: 477; G. Illus. 1938: 89; JRHS. 1943: 302, 1948: 205; Rh. Y. 1957: 29; G.Ch. 1962: ii 26; Rh. Y. 1964: 75, 1965: 14, 149; JRHS. 1971: 220; C.G. 1978: 24; Rh. Y. 1980/81: 40; C.G. 1985: 37; C.L. 1998: 13/64, 21/94.

Tresco Abbey JRIC. 1864: 71; G.Ch. 1872: 1102, 1129; G. 1875: ii 324; G.Ch. 1875: ii 810; 1876: i 80, ii 464, 1878: i 663, ii 19; G. 1879: ii 433; G.Ch. 1879: ii 659, 680, 1881: i 84; G. 1884: ii 333; G.M. 1885: 356; G.Ch. 1886: i 7, 40, ii 558; G.M. 1887: 466; G.Ch. 1891: ii 737; Trans. Penzance Nat. Hist. Soc. 1891: 157; G. 1898: ii 473; G.W. 1898: 757; G. 1902: i 227; G.M. 1902: 246; G.W. 1904: 477; G.M. 1908: 7; K.B. 1920: 170; G. 1925: 658; G. Illus. 1934: 591; G. 1935: ii 102; JRHS. 1943: 268, 1947: 177, 221; G.Ch. 1947: i 43, 189, ii 118, 1949: i 28; Endeavour 1949: 125; G. Illus. 1951: 240; G.Ch. 1960: 494; JRHS. 1961: 41; G.Ch. 1961: ii 274, 299, 1964: ii 354, 366; N. Wales Gdnr. 1964: 11; JRHS 1966: 512, 1968: 319; C.G. 1975: 15; C.L. 167 1980: 1094, 1190; JRHS. 1982: 87; C.L. 173 1983: 612; C.G. 1986: 62, 1991: 40, 1994: 93.

Trevarno Kelly's 1883: 1017; H.D 1889-1924; Field 31 Aug. 1985: 54.

Trevarrick G.M. 1880: 373; G.M. 1883: 729; G.Ch. 1885: ii 115; JRHS. 1892: 575; G. 1894: i 17, 542, 1896: i 204, 1897: i 179; G.M. 1909: 105; Con. Conf. 1932: 320 etc., 401.

Trevethoe G. Mag. 1837: 122; H.D. 1870-1924; JRHS. 1943: 302.

Trevince G.Ch. 1866: 9; H.D. 1870-1924; G.W. 1904: 409; G.Ch. 1905: ii 205, 435, 1906: i 173, 1907: i 77, 223, ii 228; Con. Conf. 1932: 327, 402.

Trewardale H.D. 1890-91.

Trewarthenick Repton 1793, 1794: 24n.; Arch. Hist. 1964: 106; JC Fam HS. 1990: Dec. 34.

Trewidden J. Hort. 1880: i 293; J. Hort. 1884: i 384, 425; H.D. 1889-1924; G.Ch. 1889: ii 748, 1894: i 346, 1904: i 156; G.W. 1904: 409; Corn. Notes & Queries 1906: 248; G.Ch. 1906: i 307; G. Illus. 1906: 558; G. 1907: 611; JRHS. 1907: 189; G.Ch. 1908: ii 451; G.M. 1909: 126; G.Ch. 1912: i 321; G.M. 1913: 266; G.Ch. 1920: ii 109; Rh. N. 1927: 199; Con. Conf. 1932: 327, 402; G. Illus. 1938: 89; JRHS. 1943: 298, 1948: 204; Rh. Y. 1980/81: 40.

Trewithen G. Mag. 1830: 575; G. 1876: ii 446; H.D. 1919-24; NF&S. 1931: 154; JRHS. 1937: 93, 1943: 301, 1948: 206; Rh. Y. 1950: 20; C.L. 113 1953: 990, 1072, 1512; Rh. Y. 1965: 15, 150; IDSY. 1973: 6; Rh. Y. 1980/81: 40; Conoisseur 1981: 183; C.G. 1985: 37; Gdn. 1998:100.

Tullimaar H.D. 1889-1924.

278 The Bibliographies

Werrington G. Mag. 1837: 121; H.D. 1908-24; Con. Conf. 1932: 402; JRHS. 1943: 301, 1948: 208; Arch. Hist. 1964: 108; Daff. Y. 1964: 185, 1965: 178; Rh. Y. 1966: 9; O. Corn. viii 1973-9: 520, 572, ix 1982: 321; C.G. 1994: 54.

Whiteford G. Mag. 1831: 280; G. Mag. 1842: 549; H.D. 1870; GGT. 1996: 25.

York House H.D 1870.

Periodicals consulted

Arch. Hist.	*Architectural History*, 1958-.
Arch. Rev.	*Architectural Review*, 1896-.
Br. Arch.	*The British Architect*, 1874-1919, when it was incorporated in *The Builder*.
C.G.	*The Cornish Garden*, 1958-.
C.G.T.	*The Journal of the Cornwall Garden Trust*, 1990-.
C.L.	*Country Life*, 1897- : references to December 1986 are to the year, volume and page; from January 1987 to the year, week and page.
Con. Conf.	*Conifers in Cultivation*, Report of the Conifer Conference 1931, RHS 1932.
Daff. Y.	*Daffodil Year-Book* 1913-15, 1933-42; *Daffodil & Tulip Year Book* 1946-71; and *Daffodils* 1971-.
F&S.	*Flora and Sylva*, 1903-5.
NF&S.	*New Flora and Sylva*, 1928-40.
G.	*The Garden*, 1871-1927. There were two volumes each year; i January - June, ii July - December, until 1907.
Gdn.	*The Garden*, 1976-, successor to the *JRHS* (see below).
G.Ch.	*The Gardeners' Chronicle*, 1841-1986, when it became *The Horticultural Weekly*. From 1874 there were two volumes each year; i January - June, ii July - December.
GCOG.	*Gardens of Cornwall Open Guide*, annually.
G. Hist.	*Garden History*, 1973-.
G. Illus.	*Gardening Illustrated*, 1880-1956.
G. Mag.	*The Gardener's Magazine*, 1826-44.
G.M.	*The Gardeners' Magazine*, 1856-1916.
G.W.	*Gardening World*, 1885-1908.
H.D.	*The Horticultural Directory*, from 1860 to 1915 published by the *J. Hort.*, thereafter by the *G.Ch.*. The years 1870, 1889, 1890, 1891, 1908, 1916, 1919 and 1924 only have been found available. The qualification for entry at first was a recommendation from two nurserymen; later by the employment of at least two full-time gardeners.
IDSY	*The International Dendrological Society Yearbook*.
JC Fam HS.	*Journal of the Cornwall Family History Society*, July 1976-.
J. Hort.	*Journal of Horticulture, and Cottage Gardener. Cottage Gardener* 1848-61; *Journal of Horticulture* 1861-1915. In 1861 there were two volumes, i April - September, ii October 1861 - March 1862; in 1862 one volume from April - December; thereafter two volumes, i January - June, ii July - December.
JRHS.	*Journal of the Royal Horticultural Society*, 1845-1975, continued as *The Garden*.
JRIC.	*Journal of the Royal Institution of Cornwall*, 1864-.
K.B.	*The Kew Bulletin*, 1912-.
Kelly's	*Kelly's Directory ...*, published irregularly from 1853, sometimes in combination with Devon.
My Gd.	*My Garden*, 1934-1951.
NGS.	*National Garden Scheme*, annually.
O. Corn.	*Old Cornwall*, bi-annual. In vols i 1925-31 and ii 1931-6, each issue is paginated separately; from vol. iii 1937-42, the volumes are paginated consecutively.
Rh. N.	*Rhododendron Society Notes*, 1916, 1929-31.
Rh. Y.	*The Rhododendron Year Book* 1946-53; *The Rhododendron & Camelia Year Book* 1954-71; *Rhododendrons with Magnolias & Camellias* 1972-.
R. Hort SC.	*Annual Report of the Royal Horticultural Society of Cornwall*, 1833-1860.
R. Poly SC.	*Annual Report of the Royal Polytechnic Society of Cornwall*, 1833-.

B. GENERAL NOTICES

The nineteenth century was not short of itineraries, guides, surveys, topographies and parochial histories, but in view of the considerable rise in specific horticultural information they play a secondary, though not necessarily an unimportant role. They often are able to fill in essential background detail, even when they contribute little to our knowledge of the gardens themselves. For this reason, the two categories of reference have been separated; first so as not to confuse the clear evidence of horticultural recognition in journals, and second to gather together this secondary material where it can be examined in its own light. For clarity, citations which contain some, even though small horticultural content are marked with an asterisk.

Moule's *Counties Delineated* (1837), Murray's *Handbook* (1859), and Lake's *Parochial History* (1867-72) have been systematically collated, which in the case of Moule and *Lake* compensate for their lack of an index. Several other sources with a more circumscribed coverage have also been included. In the last quarter of the century the most comprehensive source of general information is to be found in the various issues of Kelly's *Directory*, horticultural notices from which have been cited in the previous section.

In a few exceptional cases the first (or only) horticultural recognition occurs in these secondary sources. Such are Lanwithan, Luxstowe, Moor Cottage, Moorswater Lodge, Penventon and Rosecraddock, which were noticed or illustrated in Twycross (1846); Lamellen, Lanteglos by

Camelford Rectory, Point Neptune, Ruan Lanihorne Rectory, Tregembo, Tregenna (Michaelstow) House, Trewinnard and Westerham in Lake; and Trewoofe in Paris (1824). In addition, Bodrean, Harlyn, Newham, Sandhill Manor and Trenowth have been included for their special features or associations.

Acton Castle Paris (1824: 216*); Moule (1837: 295); *Murray* (1859: 194, 261*); *Lake* (1872: iv. 46-7).
Alverton House *Lake* (1867: i. 217).
Antony Polwhele (1806: 118); Moule (1837: 284-5*); Twycross (1846: 34-8*); Burke (1855: 2nd ser. i. 96-8); *Murray* (1859: 232*, 274); *Lake* (1867: i. 29*).
Arwenack Lysons (1814: 99-100, 102-3); Moule (1837: 287); Redding (1842: 133*); *Murray* (1859: 269); *Lake* (1867: i. 408-9*).
Bake Moule (1837: 285); *Murray* (1859: 275); *Lake* (1868: ii. 53).
Behan Park Moule (1837: 303); *Lake* (1872: iv. 296).
Bicton Manor *Lake* (1868: ii. 248).
Bochym Moule (1837: 287), *Lake* (1867: i. 288-9*).
Boconnoc Staniforth (1800: 18*); Polwhele (1806: 117); Moule (1833: 309-10*); Redding (1842: 101-2*); Twycross (1846: 19-23*); Burke (1853: ii. 11); *Murray* (1859: 240*); *Lake* (1867: i. 72-5*).
Bodrean *Lake* (1867: i. 216).
Bonython Moule (1837: 287), *Lake* (1867: i. 289*).
Bosahan *Murray* (1859: 258), *Lake* (1867: i.36*).
Boskenna Paris (1824: 112*); Burke (1854: 2nd ser. i. 196); *Murray* (1859: 197*); *Lake* (1867: i. 165*); Bottrell (1873: 36-58).
Bosvigo *Lake* (1868: ii. 334).
Bray Twycross (1846: 88-9*); *Lake* (1870: iii. 378*); Bond (1823: 370).
Budock Vean *Lake* (1867: i. 247).
Burell *Lake* (1872: iv. 178).
Burncoose Twycross (1846: 89*); *Murray* (1859: 176*); *Lake* (1868: ii. 141).
Caerhays Castle Polwhele (1806: 118); Moule (1837: 297-8*); Twycross (1846: 51-2*); *Murray* (1859: 245-6); *Lake* (1870: iii. 341-3).
Carclew Polwhele (1806: 119); Moule (1837: 289*); Twycross (1846: 29-30*); *Murray* 1859: 249*, 271); *Lake* (1870: iii. 395*).
Carnanton Moule (1837: 305); Twycross (1846: 61-2*); *Murray* (1859: 228); *Lake* (1870: iii. 297-8*).
Carwinion *Lake* (1870: iii. 303).
Castle *Lake* (1870: iii. 31).
Castle Horneck Paris (1824: 75*); Moule (1837: 294); Courtney (1845: 61-2*); *Murray* (1859: 187, 188); *Lake* (1870: iii. 221*).
Catchfrench Moule (1837: 285); Twycross (1846: 71-2*); *Murray* (1859: 232*); *Lake* (1868: ii. 54-5*).
Chyverton Moule (1837: 306); *Lake* (1872: iv. 57*).
Cleave House *Lake* (1870: iii. 384).
Clowance Paris (1824: 198); Moule (1837: 293*); Twycross (1846: 65-7); *Murray* (1859: 178*); *Lake* (1867: i. 268*, 272).
Coldrenick Moule (1837: 285); Twycross (1846: 72-3*); *Murray* (1859: 232*); *Lake* (1868: ii. 54*).
Colquite Moule (1837: 309); Twycross (1846: 80-81); *Lake* (1870: iii. 205, 207*); Maclean (1876: ii. 475-84, 509).
Comprigney *Lake* (1868: ii. 333-4).

Cothele Polwhele (1803: 117); Moule (1837: 282*); Redding (1842: 68-70); Twycross (1846: 5-7*); *Murray* (1859: 275-6*); *Lake* (1867: i. 176-8*).
Croan Manor (1867: i. 318); Maclean (1873: i. 440-1).
Crocadon Moule (1837: 282); Redding (1842: 78); *Murray* (1859: 275); *Lake* (1870: iii. 309).
Darley *Lake* (1870: iii.131).
Dinham Maclean (1879: iii. 66).
Duporth Moule (1837: 297); *Murray* (1859: 243); *Lake* (1867: i. 53).
Eastaway Manor *Lake* (1870: iii. 383).
Enys Moule (1837: 289); Twycross (1846: 64*); *Murray* (1859: 268*); *Lake* (1868: ii. 86-7*).
Erisey Moule (1837: 287, 289); *Murray* (1859: 257); *Lake* (1868: ii. 110-111*).
Ethy *Lake* (1872: iv. 329*).
Flexbury Hall Moule (1837: 307); *Lake* (1872: iv. 87).
Garlenick Moule (1837: 301); *Lake* (1867: i. 260).
Glendurgan *Lake* (1870: iii. 303).
Glynn Staniforth (1800: 29*); Polwhele (1806: 119); Twycross (1846: 16-18*); Burke (1852: i. 241); *Murray* (1839: 168); *Lake* (1867: i. 198-9).
Godolphin Polwhele (1806: 117); Moule (1837: 286); *Murray* (1859: 259-60); *Lake* (1867: i. 137-8*).
Gonvena *Lake* (1867: i. 319*); Maclean (1873: i. 451-2).
Goonvrea *Lake* (1872: iv .43).
Grove Hill Warner (1809: 120*); Twycross (1846: 68-9*); *Murray* (1859: 270*); *Lake* (1867: i. 411*).
Gulval Blight (1861: 200-02*).
Gwithian Churchyard Lysons (1814: cxcix*); Kilvert (1870: 99*).
Gyllyngdune *Murray* (1859: 270); *Lake* (1867: i. 397, 411).
Hall *Murray* (1859: 267*); *Lake* (1870: iii. 49-50).
Hamatethy *Lake* (1867: i. 143).
Harewood House Twycross (1846: 23-4*); *Murray* (1859: 104, 120*); *Lake* (1867: i. 178).
Harlyn Moule (1837: 305); *Lake* (1870: iii. 322).
Hatt *Lake* (1867: i. 114).
Heligan Moule (1837: 298*); Twycross (1846: 42-4); *Murray* (1859: 243); *Lake* (1867: i. 383).
Hengar Moule (1837: 309); Twycross (1846: 82); *Murray* (1859: 224); *Lake* (1872: iv. 269); Maclean (1879: iii. 347-9).
Hexworthy *Murray* (1859: 278); *Lake* (1870: iii. 96).
Ince Castle *Murray* (1859: 274); *Lake* (1872: iv. 178).
Kenegie Paris (1824: 143*); Moule (1837: 293*); *Murray* (1859: 187*, 207*); *Lake* (1868: ii. 121); Bottrell (1880: 21-47).
Killiganoon Moule (1837: 301); *Murray* (1859: 170, 248); *Lake* (1868: ii. 7*).
Killiow *Murray* (1859: 170, 248); *Lake* (1868: ii. 322*).
Kilmarth Moule (1837: 300); *Lake* (1872: iv. 280).
Klymiarvan see Waterloo Villa
Lambesso *Lake* (1867: i. 215).
Lamellen *Lake* (1872: iv. 269*); Maclean (1879: iii. 355).
Lamorran *Lake* (1868: ii. 389); Hole (1892: 216-221*, 1899: 230-31*).
Lanarth *Lake* (1868: ii. 348-50*).
Lancarffe Twycross (1846: 79); *Lake* (1867: i. 99); Maclean (1873: i. 260-2).
Landue Twycross (1846: 75*); *Lake* (1870: iii. 122-3).
Landulph Parsonage *Lake* (1869: ii. 408-9*).

Lanhadron Moule (1837: 298*); *Lake* (1867: i. 380*).
Lanhydrock Polwhele (1806: 118); Moule (1837: 305*); Twycross (1846: 44-5*); Burke (1855: ii. 174); *Murray* (1859: 239-40*); *Lake* (1870: iii. 7*, 10).
Lanteglos by Camelford **Rectory** *Lake* (1870: iii. 56*).
Lanwithan Twycross (1846:84*); *Lake* (1872: iv. 330).
Laregan Moule (1837; 294); Courtney (1845: 61); *Murray* (1859: 187); *Lake* (1870: iii. 243*).
Launceston Castle Moule (1837: 283); *Murray* (1839: 159-61*); *Lake* (1870: iii. 81-7*).
Lavethan Moule (1837: 309); Twycross (1846: 82*); *Lake* (1867: i. 68-9*); Maclean (1873; i. 74-8).
Lawhitton Rectory *Lake* (1870: iii. 94).
Luney *Lake* (1867: i. 381).
Luxstowe Twycross (1846: 85*); Allen (1856: 452, 523).
Manaccan Churchyard *Lake* (1870: iii. 259*).
Manaton Moule (1837: 283); *Lake* (1872: iv. 158).
Marlborough House Twycross (1846: 89*); *Lake* (1867: i. 410).
Mellingey *Lake* (1872: iv. 43).
Menabilly Staniforth (1800: 67*); Paris (1824: 203-6*); Moule (1837: 300*); Twycross (1846: 40-2*), Burke (1855: 2nd ser. ii. 149); *Murray* (1859: 267-8*); *Lake* (1872: iv. 279-80).
Menacuddle Moule (1837: 297*); *Murray* (1859: 243*); *Lake* (1867: i. 50).
Meudon *Lake* (1870: iii. 302-3).
Michaelstow House see Tregenna House.
Moditonham Moule (1837: 285*); *Murray* (1839: 120*); *Lake* (1867: i. 113-14*).
Moor Cottage Twycross (1846: 84*); *Lake* (1867: i. 53).
Moorswater Lodge Twycross (1846: 85*); Allen (1856: 452, 511).
Moresk Moule (1837: 300).
Morval House Moule (1837: 311); Twycross (1846: 38-40*); *Murray* (1859: 262*); *Lake* (1867: i.45, 1870: iii. 378*).
Mt Edgcumbe Warner (1809: 73-81*); Moule (1837: 286); Burke (1853: ii. 27); *Murray* (1859: 119*); *Lake* (1870: iii. 256-8*).
Nancealverne Paris (1824: 119); *Murray* (1859: 187); *Lake* (1870: iii. 224*).
Nansidwell *Lake* (1870: iii. 302).
Nansloe *Murray* (1859: 252); *Lake* (1872: iv. 312).
Nansough *Lake* (1868: ii. 385).
Nanswhyden Polwhele (1806: 118, 121); Moule (1837: 304); *Murray* (1859: 228); *Lake* (1867: i. 233-4).
Newham *Lake* (1868: ii. 333*).
Newton Ferrers Polwhele (1806: 118); Moule (1837: 282); Twycross (1846: 45*); *Murray* (1859: 275); *Lake* (1870: iii. 309).
Ogbeare Hall *Lake* (1872: iv. 208-9).
Park Lysons (1814: 81-2); *Murray* (1879: 168); *Lake* (1867: i. 318); Maclean (1873: i. 447-8).
Pelyn Twycross (1846: 55-6*); *Murray* (1859: 240); *Lake* (1870: iii. 31*).
Pelynt Vicarage *Lake* (1872: iv. 33).
Penair Moule (1837: 301); Twycross (1846: 55*); *Murray* (1859: 170); *Lake* (1867: i. 215).
Pencalenick Moule (1837: 301); Twycross (1846: 67-8*); *Murray* (1859: 248); *Lake* (1867: i. 216*).
Pencarrow Polwhele (1806: 118); Moule (1837: 309); Twycross (1846: 27-9*); Burke (1853: ii. 59); *Murray* (1859: 168); *Lake* (1867: i. 319*); Maclean (1873: i. 442-7*, 463-72).

Pencrebar *Lake* (1867: i. 172).
Pendarves Paris (1824: 198); D. Gilbert (1838: iv. 181*); Twycross (1846: 33-4*); *Murray* (1859: 177*); Lake (1867: i. 187*).
Pendrea Courtney (1845: 98*); *Murray* (1859: 187); *Lake* (1868: ii. 122*).
Pengersick Castle Polwhele (1806: 117); Paris (1824: 216); *Murray* (1859: 195, 260); *Lake* (1867: i. 136-7).
Pengreep Moule (1837: 287); *Murray* (1859: 176); *Lake* (1868: ii. 141*).
Penheale Manor Twycross (1846: 56-7*); Burke (1853: ii. 148); *Lake* (1867: i. 325-7*).
Penjerrick *Murray* (1859: 270); Hole (1892: 227-9*).
Penmere *Lake* (1867: i. 157).
Penmount Moule (1837: 301); *Lake* (1867: i. 215*).
Pennans Twycross (1846: 47-8*); *Murray* (1859: 246*); *Lake* (1867: i. 260)
Penpol *Lake* (1872: iv. 70).
Penrice Moule (1837: 297*); Twycross (1846: 32-3*); *Murray* (1859: 243); *Lake* (1867: i. 53*).
Penrose Paris (1824: 223*); Moule (1837: 288, 290*); Redding (1842: 151); Twycross (1846: 64-5*); Burke (1852: i. 59); *Murray* (1859: 252*); *Lake* (1872: iv. 152).
Pentillie Castle Moule (1837: 282-3*); Redding (1842: 75-6*); Twycross (1846: 46-7*); Burke (1854: 2nd ser. i. 151); *Murray* (1859: 275*); *Lake* (1872: iv. 81*).
Penventon Twycross (1846: 87-8*).
Penvose *Lake* (1872: iv. 268); Maclean (1879: iii. 349-52*, 366-72).
Penwarne Moule (1837: 289); Redding (1842: 137); *Lake* (1870: iii. 302).
Place, Fowey Polwhele (1806: 117); Lysons (1814: xxvi); Moule (1837: 298); Twycross (1846: 57-9*); *Murray* (1859: 266-7); *Lake* (1868: ii. 30*).
Place Manor Moule (1837: 300); Twycross (1846: 59-61*); *Murray* (1859: 272); *Lake* (1867: i. 41).
Point Neptune *Lake* (1868: ii. 32*).
Polapit Tamar *Lake* (Additions. p.iii.).
Polcarne *Lake* (1867: i. 53).
Poltair Paris (1824: 119); Moule (1837: 194); *Murray* (1859: 187); *Lake* (1870: iii. 243).
Polvellan Bond (1823: 70-2, 74); D. Gilbert (1838: iv. 33-4).
Polwhele Moule (1837: 301); *Murray* (1859: 170); *Lake* (1867: i. 216-17),
Polwithen Bottrell (1870: 157-8*).
Ponsandane *Murray* (1859: 187*), Blight (1861: 200); *Lake* (1868: ii. 122).
Porthgwidden Twycross (1846: 87*); *Lake* (1868: ii. 7); Hole (1892: 221-7*).
Port Eliot Moule (1837: 285); Redding (1842: 89*); Twycross (1846: 1-4*); Burke (1853: ii. 232, 1855: 2nd ser. ii. 136); *Murray* (1859: 274*); *Lake* (1868: ii. 49-52*).
Prideaux House Moule (1837: 299); Twycross (1846: 31-2*); *Murray* (1859: 240); *Lake* (1870: iii. 192*).
Prideaux Place Polwhele (1806: 117); Moule (1837: 306); Twycross (1846: 62-3*); Burke (1855: 2nd ser. ii. 170); *Murray* (1859: 225); *Lake* (1872: iv. 19).
Priory, Bodmin Polwhele (1806: 121); Moule (1837: 308), *Lake* (1867: i. 94*); Maclean (1873: i. 141-2, 301-3).
Rame Place Moule (1837: 286); *Lake* (1872: iv. 110).
Restormel Castle Moule (1837: 299); Twycross (1846: 7-8*); *Murray* (1859: 239); *Lake* (1870: iii. 24-8*).

Restormel House Staniforth* (*passim*); Moule (1827: 299); Twycross (1846: 8-9*); *Murray* (1859: 239); *Lake* (1870: iii. 28).
Riviere House Paris (1824: 31); Kilvert (1870: 33-4*).
Roscadghill *Murray* (1859: 187); *Lake* (1870: iii. 243).
Rosecraddock Manor Twycross (1846: 86*); Allen (1856: 452, 449); *Lake* (1867: i. 206).
Rosehill, Penzance Paris (1824: 75*); Moule (1837: 294); Courtney (1845: 62); *Murray* (1859: 186-7); Lake (1870: iii. 243).
Rosemorran Paris (1824: 143*); Courtney (1845: 97*); *Murray* (1859: 187); *Lake* (1868: ii. 122*).
Rosemundy Moule (1837: 304); *Lake* (1867: i. 8).
Rosewarne *Lake* (1867: i. 187); Kilvert (1870: 101*).
Roskrow *Lake* (1868: ii. 85-6).
Rosteague *Lake* (1868: ii. 75).
Ruan Lanihorne Rectory *Lake* (1872: iv. 127*).
St Benet's Moule (1837: 305); Redding (1842: 49*); *Murray* (1859: 168*); *Lake* (1870: iii. 18).
St Cadix House Moule (1837: 312); *Murray* (1859: 266); *Lake* (1872: iv. 287).
St Columb Major Rectory Moule (1837: 304*).
St Just in Penwith Vicarage *Lake* (1868: ii. 293*).
St Just in Roseland Churchyard *Murray* (1859: 271).
St Winnow Staniforth (1800: 38-9*); *Lake* (1872: iv. 324 *et seq.*).
Sanders Hill Polwhele (1806: 121); Moule (1837: 306*); *Lake* (1872: iv. 20-1).
Sandhill Manor *Lake* (1867: i.178-80).
Saveock House Moule (1837: 301); *Lake* (1868: ii. 322).
Sconner House *Lake* (1872: iv. 148).
Scorrier House Warner (1809: 240-1*); Paris (1824: 206-7); Moule (1837: 287); *Murray* (1859: 174); *Lake* (1868: ii. 141).
Skisdon Lodge Moule (1837: 309); *Lake* (1868: ii. 362); Maclean (1876: ii. 143-4).
Stoketon Moule (1837: 286*); Twycross (1846: 83-4*); *Lake* (1872: iv. 178).
Stowe Polwhele (1806: 118, 121*); Moule (1837: 307); *Murray* (1859: 281); *Lake* (1868: ii. 376-7*).
Tehidy Polwhele (1806: 116); Paris (1824: 198); Moule (1837: 293); Redding (1842: 191, 194); Twycross (1846: 13-16*); Burke (1855: 2nd ser. ii. 157); *Murray* (1859: 177); *Lake* (1868: ii. 227-230*).
Thanckes Moule (1837: 284-5*); Twycross (1846: 18-19*); *Murray* (1859: 232); *Lake* (1867: i. 30-31*).
Tonacombe *Lake* (1870: iii. 383); Maclean (1873: i. 314).
Torfrey Moule (1837: 300); *Lake* (1868: ii. 98).
Tor House *Lake* (1867: i. 31, 32).
Trebartha Hall Twycross (1846: 48-9*); *Murray* (1859: 161*); *Lake* (1872: iv. 9*).
Trebrown *Lake* (1868: ii. 57*).
Trebursye Moule (1837: 284); Twycross (1846: 63-4); *Lake* (1872: iv. 65).
Tredethy Moule (1837: 309); Twycross (1846: 79); *Lake* (1870: iii. 205-6*); Maclean (1875: ii. 497*).
Tredidon *Lake* (1872: iv. 222).
Tredinnick *Lake* (1872: iv. 295).
Tredrea *Lake* (1872: iv. 43).
Tredudwell Manor *Lake* (1870: iii. 51*).
Trefusis House Lysons (1814: 235-6); Moule (1837: 289); Burke (1855: 2nd ser. ii. 83); *Murray* (1859: 270-71*); *Lake* (1870: iii. 395).
Tregeare Moule (1837: 283); Twycross (1846: 69-70); *Lake* (1867: i. 327, 1870: iii. 2).

Tregembo *Lake* (1868: ii. 195*).
Tregenna Castle Warner (1809: 137-8); Paris (1824: 157); Moule (1837: 294); Courtney (1845: 170); Twycross (1846: 75-6); Burke (1852: i. 210); *Murray* (1859: 181); *Lake* (1868: ii. 262-3).
Tregenna (Michaelstow) **House** *Lake* (1870: iii. 357-8*); Maclean (1876: ii. 572*).
Tregolls House Moule (1837: 303); Twycross (1846: 61); *Murray* (1859: 170); *Lake* (1867: i. 215).
Tregothnan Staniforth (1800: 35*, 67*); Polwhele (1806: 118); Moule (1837: 302*); Twycross (1846: 10-12*); Burke (1855: 2nd ser. ii. 7); *Murray* (1859: 170, 171*), *Lake* (1870: iii. 328*, 346-7, 354*).
Tregrehan Moule (1837: 297); Twycross (1846: 47*); Burke (1855: 2nd ser. ii. 87); *Murray* (1859: 242*); *Lake* (1867: i. 62).
Tregullow Twycross (1846: 84*); *Lake* (1868: ii. 141).
Trehane Moule (1837: 303); *Murray* (1859: 248); Twycross (1846: 74-5*); *Lake* (1867: i. 349, 351, 1872: iv. 98*).
Trelaske Twycross (1846: 77-9*); *Lake* (1870: iii. 114-16*).
Trelawne Manor Bond (1823, see *Lake* 1872: iv. 32*); Moule (1837: 311-12); Twycross (1846: 77); Burke (1855: 2nd ser. ii. 148); *Murray* (1859: 264); *Lake* (1872: iv. 40*).
Treliske Moule (1837: 303).
Trelissick Polwhele (1806: 119*); Moule (1837: 301); Twycross (1846: 86-7*); *Murray* (1859: 171*); *Lake* (1868: ii. 6-7*).
Trelowarren Polwhele (1806: 117*); Moule (1837: 288); Twycross (1846: 25-6); Burke (1855: 2nd ser. ii. 149); *Murray* (1859: 258-9); *Lake* (1870: iii. 280-81).
Treludick Moule (1837: 283); *Lake* (1867: i. 327-8).
Trematon Castle Moule (1837: 286); Redding (1842: 81); Twycross (1946: 53-5*); Burke (1855: 2nd ser. ii. 171); *Murray* (1859: 273*); *Lake* (1872: iv. 176-7).
Tremeal Farm *Lake* (1872: iv .65).
Tremeer Twycross (1846: 79); *Lake* (1872: iv. 269); Maclean (1879: iii. 352-4, 373-4).
Tremough Moule (1837: 288*); *Lake* (1870: iii. 199*).
Tremorvah *Lake* (1867: i. 217).
Trenant Park Twycross (1846: 70-1*); *Murray* (1859: 264); *Lake* (1867: i. 307*).
Trenarren Burke (1854: 2nd ser. i. 86); *Lake* (1867: i. 53).
Treneere Courtney (1845: 88*); *Lake* (1870: iii. 243).
Trengwainton Paris (1824: 119*); Twycross (1846: 76); *Murray* (1859: 187*); *Lake* (1870: iii. 219-20*).
Trenowth *Lake* (1872: iv. 99).
Trenython *Lake* (1872: iv. 281).
Trereife Paris (1924: 76*); Moule (1837: 294); Courtney (1845: 64-5*); Burke (1853: ii. 178); *Murray* (1859: 187*); Blight (1861: 65-6); *Lake* (1870: iii. 219*).
Trerice Moule (1837: 306); *Murray* (1859: 169, 229); *Lake* (1867: i. 15).
Tresillian House Moule (1837: 306); Twycross (1846: 83); *Lake* (1872: iv.3-4*).
Trethill House *Murray* (1839: 232), Redding (1842: 88), *Lake* (1872: iv. 148); Maclean (1876 :ii. 370-3).
Trevarno Moule (1837: 290); Twycross (1846: 76*); Burke (1852: i. 46); *Lake* (1872: iv. 153*); Maclean (1873: i. 322).
Trevarrick Hall Moule (1837: 297); *Lake* (1867: i. 53).
Trevaylor Burke (1853: ii. 203); *Murray* (1859: 187); Blight (1861: 207*); *Lake* (1868: ii. 121-2*).

Trevethoe Paris (1824: 171*); Moule (1837: 294); Redding (1842: 184-5); Courtney (1845: 165-6); Twycross (1846: 73-4*); *Murray* (1859: 182*); *Lake* (1870: iii. 101-2*).

Trevillet *Murray* (1859: 219*); *Lake* (1872: iv. 236*); Maclean (1879: iii. 247-8, 261-3).

Trevince Moule (1837: 287); *Murray* (1859: 176*); *Lake* (1868: ii. 140-41).

Trevissome House *Lake* (1870: iii. 396).

Trewan Hall Moule (1837: 304*); Redding (1842: 223*); *Murray* (1959: 228*); *Lake* (1867: i. 234*).

Trewardale Twycross (1846: 70*); *Lake* (1867: i .69*); Maclean (1873: i. 45-6*).

Trewarne *Lake* (1868: ii. 361); Maclean (1876: ii. 138-9, 164-6).

Trewarthenick Staniforth (1800: 35-6*); Twycross (1846: 50-1*); Burke (1854: 2nd ser .i. 178); *Murray* (1859: 247); *Lake* (1867: i. 250-51*).

Trewhiddle Moule (1837: 297); *Lake* (1867: i. 53).

Trewidden *Murray* (1859: 187).

Trewin *Lake* (1872: iv. 148).

Trewince *Lake* (1868: ii. 75).

Trewinnard Lysons (1814: 93); Moule (1837: 293); *Murray* (1859: 182); *Lake* (1867: i. 363*).

Trewithen Moule (1837: 302*); Twycross (1846: 49-50*); *Murray* (1859: 247*); *Lake* (1872: iv. 98*).

Trewoofe Paris (1824: 113*); Moule (1837: 292*); Courtney (1845: 203); *Murray* (1859: 195*); Blight (1861: 52-3); *Lake* (1867; i. 165); Bottrell (1870: 245-87*).

Treworder Mill *Lake* (1868: ii. 335).

Treworgey Moule (1837: 310); *Lake* (1867: i. 206).

Truthan Moule (1837: 301); Twycross (1846: 45-6*); *Lake* (1867: i. 351).

Tullimaar Twycross (1846: 85); Kilvert (1870: 25*,etc.) *Lake* (1872: iv. 43).

Waterloo Villa Twycross (1846: 86* as 'Klymiarvan'); Bond (1823: 191).

Werrington Warner (1800: 145-7*); Redding (1842: 20*); *Murray* (1859: 161, 278).

Westbourne House Allen (1856: 452, 487).

Wetherham *Lake* (1872: iv. 264*); Maclean (1879: iii. 307, 310-12).

Whiteford Moule (1837: 284*); Twycross (1846: 30-1*); *Murray* (1859: 277); *Lake* (1872: iv. 187*).

Wivelscombe *Lake* (1872: iv. 178).

Wolsdon House Moule (1837: 285); Twycross (1846: 85); *Lake* (1867: i. 31).

York House Courtney (1845: 61); *Murray* (1859: 187-8); *Lake* (1870: iii. 243-4).

References

Amherst (1895) *A History of Gardens in England*, Alicia Amherst, 1895. (Penjerrick, Menabilly, Heligan, Tregothnan and Carclew are mentioned as 'among the finest of [the] Cornish gardens'.)

Bond (1823) *Topographical and Historical Sketches of the Borough of East and West Looe*, T. Bond, 1823.

Bottrell (1870, 1873) *Traditions and Hearthside Stories of West Cornwall*, William Bottrell, Penzance first series, 1870; second series, 1873.

— (1880) *Stories and Folk-lore of West Cornwall*, William Bottrell, Penzance 1880.

Blight (1861) *A Week at the Land's End*, J.T. Blight, 1861.

Burke (1852-50) *A Visitation of the seats and arms of the noblemen and gentlemen of Great Britain*, J.B. Burke, 4 vols 1852-5, i. 1852, ii. 1853; 2nd series i. 1854, ii. 1855.

Courtney (1845) *Guide to Penzance*, L. Courtney, Penzance 1845.

D. Gilbert (1838) *The Parochial History of Cornwall*, Davies Gilbert, 4 vols, 1838.

Hole (1892) *A Book about the Garden and the Gardener*, Dean S.R. Hole, 1892.

— (1899) *Our Gardens*, Dean S.R. Hole, 1899.

Kilvert (1870) *Kilvert's Cornish Diary*, ed. R. Maber & A. Tregoning, Penzance 1989.

Lake (1867-72) *Lake's Parochial History ... of Cornwall*, J. Polsue, Truro, I: 1867, II: 1868, III: 1870, IV: 1872. 'Lake', as a title, is italicized.

Loudon (1822) *Encyclopaedia of Horticulture*, J.C. Loudon, 1822.

Lysons (1814) *Magna Britannia ... volume the third Cornwall*, D.& S. Lysons, 1814.

Maclean (1868) *The Deanery of Trigg Minor*, 3 vols, Sir John Maclean, 1868-79.

Moule (1837) *The Counties Delineated ...*, Thomas Moule, 1837, Cornwall pp. 281-312.

Murray (1859) *Murray's Handbook for Travellers in Devon & Cornwall*, pub. Murray, 4th edition 1859. 'Murray' as a title, is italicized. The Cornish and Scillonian sections of the first four editions are known to have been written by T.C. Paris, son of J.A. Paris (see below).

Polwhele (1806) *History of Cornwall*, R. Polwhele, vol. 3 (1806) was used (of 7 vols 1803-16).

Paris (1824) *A Guide to the Mount's Bay and the Land's End ... by a Physician*, [J.A. Paris], 1816, the 2nd ed. of 1824 was used.

Redding (1842) *Illustrated Itinerary of ... Cornwall*, Cyrus Redding, 1842.

Repton (1792, 1793, 1809, 1810) *Red Books*, unpublished. (Antony 1792, Port Eliot, Catchfrench and Trewarthenick 1793, Tregothnan 1809, and Pentillie 1810.)

— (1794) *Sketches and Hints on Landscape Gardening*, Humphry Repton, 1794.

— (1803) *Observations on the Theory & Practice of Landscape Gardening*, H. Repton, 1803.

Staniforth (1800) *The Staniforth Diary a visit to Cornwall in 1800*, ed. J. Hext, Truro 1965.

Twycross (1846) *The Mansions of England ... Cornwall*, E. Twycross, 1846.

Warner (1800) *A Walk through some Western Counties of England*, R. Warner, Bath 1800.

— (1809) *A Tour through Cornwall ... 1808*, R. Warner, Bath 1809.

Twentieth-Century References

The early twentieth century saw the maturing of late nineteenth-century gardens and the establishment of many new ones. Their names occur particularly in the pages of the *Horticultural Directory* up to the beginning of the First World War, after which there was a significant decline. Thurston's survey in the late 1920s, for his book *Trees and Shrubs in Cornwall* (1930), nevertheless introduced many substantial gardens which had escaped notice in print up to that time. The Second World War dealt another, often mortal blow to the economics of garden maintenance. But in recent years there has been an increasing interest in reading about and visiting large gardens, which has led to a spate of colourful descriptive books and guides. A comprehensive selection has been made from among these, together with local histories and a few standard works which refer to the houses alone.

Journal notices for gardens which received their first horticultural recognition in the nineteenth-century section, were cited through into the twentieth century, and are not repeated here, for the pattern of horticultural recognition in nineteenth-century periodicals through to the next century forms a discrete entity.

Many gardens, however, did not receive their first horticultural recognition (as distinct from topographical reference) until the twentieth century, even when they existed before. To distinguish these from the ongoing entries for gardens first noticed in the previous century, their initial citation is italicized. As in the last section, a chronological table of first notices has been compiled for the twentieth century. The key to references used in this section follows the garden listings.

CHRONOLOGICAL TABLE

Year	Garden	Year	Garden	Year	Garden	Year	Garden
1900	TREVILLIS		TREVISSOME HOUSE		TOLCARNE HOUSE		TRELEAN
1902	TREGYE	1924	FLEXBURY HALL		TREVERVEN	1987	HEADLAND
1904	LUDGVAN	1925	PENHEALE MANOR		WODEHOUSE PLACE		KEN CARO
1905	TRELOYHAN	1926	QUEEN MARY GARDENS	1931	EAGLE'S NEST		MAIDENWELL
1906	CAERHAYS CASTLE	1928	ROSKROW	1934	MERKJASTEINN		PENPOL
1908	BASSET VILLA		ST WINNOW		TRENANCE PARK	1988	MORESK
	DOUBLEBOIS HOUSE		STOWE	1937	CALAMANSAC		PENGERSICK Castle
	LANARTH		TONACOMBE		RIVIERE		POLGWYNNE
	MELLINGEY	1930	BOSKENNA		TREVIADES BARTON	1989	TREWYN Studio
	PENARWYN		BOSLOWICK	1943	KILLAGORDEN	1990	BOSVIGO
	PENMORVAH		CARWINION	1948	ROSEWARNE		CALENICK
	POLAPIT TAMAR		CASTLE		LIS ESCOP		LAMORRAN HOUSE
	POLGWIN		CHYVERTON	1962	ROSEWARNE	1991	The HOLLIES
	POLSTRONG		DARLEY		Horticultural Station		LANCARFFE
	ROCKY HILL, Scilly		DULOE VICARAGE	1964	BAKE		PINE LODGE
	TOLROY		GARLENICK		CROAN		POLDOWRIAN
	TREDETHY		GLENDURGAN		PLACE MANOR	1992	LONG CROSS
	TRELISKE		GWITHIAN C/Y		POLCARNE		MARY NEWMAN'S Cott.
	TRENYTHON		LAMBESSO		ST COLUMB RECTORY		MEUDON
	TREVARTHIAN		LANHADRON		TREGENNA CASTLE		TREVEGEAN
	WEATH		LAUNCESTON CASTLE	1965	LORAINE	1993	ESTRAY PARK
	WESTBOURNE HOUSE		LAWHITTON RECTORY	1969	PROBUS Gdns	1995	LANTERNS
1910	VICTORIA GARDENS		LOSTWITHIEL (Rudge)	1970	MOYCLARE		ROSECRADDOCK
	WATERFALL GARDENS		MANACCAN C/Y	1979	GREATWOOD		ROSTEAGUE
1911	TRERICE		NEWLYN E. C/Y	1980	TRIST HOUSE	1996	CREED HOUSE
1916	TORFREY		NEWLYN W.	1981	GYLLYNGDUNE GDNS		FURZEBALL COTTAGE
1919	FOWEY HALL		PENBERTH	1982	OLD RECTORY		TREWORDER MILL
	MENEHAY		PENCREBAR		TRELIDDEN	1997	BOSAVERN MILL
	NANSIDWELL		PELYNT VICARAGE	1983	CHURCHTOWN FARM		LADOCK HOUSE
	TRELAWNEY		PENWARNE	1985	EDEN VALLEY		NEWTON HOUSE
	TREVEDDO		ST JUST in ROSELAND	1986	PORTHPEAN		

Acton Castle Pevsner (1970: 35); Desmond (1988).
Alverton House Pevsner (1970: 235); Truro (1988: 16, 18, 27, 34, 26)
Antony House Thurston (1930: 51); Stroud (1962: 69, 70, 77); Betjeman (1964: 13); Nicholson (1965: 190); Pevsner (1970: 37); Hyams (1971: 154, 231); Napier (1972: 131); Evans (1974: 9-10); Harris (1976: 38n. 19, 110-12, 124, etc); Hellyer (1977: 77); Synge (1977: 85-7); Thomas (1979: 95-6); Carter (1982: 150); Norwich (1985: 126); Holmes (1986); Mitchell (1986); Pearson (1986: 77); Desmond (1988); Rose (1991 etc.); Taylor (1995: 98-9); Lacey (1996: 18-20); McCabe (1996: 33-5); Pring (1996: 51-3); Harris (1998: 28-37).
Arwenack Gay (1903: 31, 76); Thurston (1930: 222-3); Dunstan (1968: 45-50); Pevsner (1970: 68); Barham (1981: 32-3, 35); Bird (1985: 6); McCabe (1996: 103-4).
Bake Arch. Hist. 1964: 4, 5; Desmond (1988); C.G. 1995: 95.
Basset Villa H.D. 1908.
Behan Park JRIC. 1980: 191; C.G. 1992: 88.
Bochym Manor Thurston (1930: 97, 109, 156-7, 252); Hunkin (1943: 303); Pevsner (1970: 82).
Boconnoc Henderson (1928: 152); Arch. Rev. 1933: 156; Betjeman (1964: 16-17); Thurston (1930: 51); Delderfield (1968: 14-17); Pevsner (1970: 39-40); Napier (1972: 131-2); Holmes (1986); Mitchell (1986); Rix (1987: 44); Desmond (1988); McCabe (1996: 50-53); Pring (1996: 54).
Bodrean Barratt (1980: 10).
Bonython Manor Norwich (1995: 129).
Bosahan Millais (1913: 216, 1927: 30); Thurston (1930: 51-2); Henderson (1937: 82-7, 238); Hunkin (1943: 297-8); Desmond (1988); Rose (1991 etc.); Pring (1996: 54).
Bosavern Mill Rose (1997).
Boscawen Park Thurston (1930: 52); Truro (1988: 69-70); Pring (1996: 121-2).
Boskenna Thurston (1930: 52); C.G. 1985: 22; Holmes (1986); McCabe (1996: 139).
Boskenwyn Manor see Carne.
Boslowick Thurston (1930: 52); Budock (1993: 44).
Bosvigo Barratt (1980: 32); C.G. 1990: 27; Rose (1992 etc.); Gdn. 1994: 298; C.L. 1995: 9/80; Taylor (1995: 104); Pring (1996: 55-6); Truro (1996: 54).
Bray Keast (1987: 23, 141).
Budock Vean Henderson (1937: 201-6, 239).
Burell Pevsner (1970: 48).
Burncoose Thurston (1930: 52); James (n.d: 99, 145); Hunkin (1943: 298); Townsend (1990: 8); Taylor (1995: 105-6); Pring (1996: 56-7).
Caerhays Castle Corn. Notes & Queries 1906: 248; H.D. 1908-24; Millais (1917: 8, 31, 1924: 57, 1927: 30); G. 1925: 616; Henderson (1928: 155-66); Thurston (1930: 52); NFGS. 1939: 13; JRHS. 1943: 9, 43; Hunkin (1943: 298); JRHS. 1948: 208, 209, 210; Rh. Y. 1949: 142; G.Ch. 1956: i 364; Rh. Y. 1960: 107, 1961: 94; Stroud (1962: 77); Betjeman (1964: 83); Hyams (1964: 212-4); Rh. Y. 1965: 13, 120, 151; JRHS. 1966: 279; Pevsner (1970: 192); J. Scot. Rock Gdns. 1973: 175; JRHS. 1974: 364; Rh. Y. 1976: 22; Synge (1977: 88-90); Barratt (1980: 17); Rh. Y. 1980/81: 40; C.G. 1979: 17, 1985: 37; Field 27 July 1985: 86; Norwich (1985: 128); Holmes (1986); Mitchell (1986); Pearson (1986: 78); Desmond (1988); Hollis (1989: 77-8); Townsend (1990: 9-10); Rose (1991 etc.); Gdn. 1992: 62; Wright (1993: 18-9); Taylor (1992/5: 106); (1995: 174-5); McCabe (1996: 100-2); Pring (1996: 57-8); C.G. 1997: 15; Harris (1998: 64-73).
Calenick C.G. 1990: 27.
Calamansac Henderson (1937: 198-201, 240).
Carclew Olivey (1907: 184-216); Henderson (1928: 154); Thurston (1930: 52-3); Hunkin (1943: 262-3); Betjeman (1964: 37); Pevsner (1970: 125); Synge (1977: 91-2); Barratt (1980: 27); Holmes (1986); Mitchell (1986); Rix (1987: 44); Desmond (1988); McCabe (1996: 104-6); Pring (1996: 58-9).
Carmino Thurston (1930: 91, 93, 119, 122, 140, 144, 160).
Carnanton Delderfield (1968: 21-3); Pevsner (1970: 116); Rabey (1979: 44-5, 46); Norwich (1985: 143); Holmes (1986); Desmond (1988).
Carne (Boskenwyn Manor) Desmond (1988).
Carwinion Thurston (1930: 53); Townsend (1990: 1); Rose (1994 etc.); McCabe (1996: 112); Pring (1996: 59-60).
Castle Thurston (1930: 53); Con. Conf. 1932: 386; Betjeman (1964: 74).
Castle Horneck Thurston (1930: 53); Pevsner (1970: 139); Pool (1974: 184).
Catchfrench Henderson (1928: 155); Thurston (1930: 53); Stroud (1964: 69, 77); Hyams (1971: 154, 156); Carter (1982: 150); Desmond (1988); Pring (1996: 60-1); Rose (1997).
Churchtown Farm C.G. 1983: 50; Harpur (1985: 70-3).
Chyverton Thurston (1930: 148, 200, 267); Hunkin (1943: 262); JRHS. 1948: 205; Pevsner (1970: 140); Rh. Y. 1973: 67, 1974: 63; Synge (1977: 93-5); Barratt (1980: 13-14); Rh. Y. 1880/81: 40; JRHS. 1985: 95; Plumptre (1985: 235-7); C.G. 1985: 38, 1987: 75 ; Rix (1987: 45); Desmond (1988); Hollis (1989: 96); C.G. 1990: 46 [from Hortus II]; Gdn. 1991: 538; Johnson (1991: 22-5); Rose (1991 etc.); Wheeler (1991: 150-53); Gdn. 1994: 99; Pring (1996: 62-3); Harris (1998: 84-95).
Clowance Thurston (1930: 53); Pevsner (1970: 54); Desmond (1988).
Coldrenick Thurston (1930: 53-4); Hunkin (1943: 267-8); Betjeman (1964: 79); Pevsner (1970: 54); Napier (1972: 132).
Colquite Pevsner (1970: 55).
Comprigney Barratt (1980: 32-5); Truro (1996: 7, 8, 45).
Condurra Truro (1991: 12-13).
Cotehele Thurston (1930: 54); Hellyer (1956: 47); Betjeman (1964: 37-8); Allan (1970: 119-20); Pevsner (1970: 57); O. Corn. viii 1974: 59; Evans (1974: 11-12); Hellyer (1977: 116); Synge (1977: 96-7); Thomas (1979: 124-6); Saville (1982: 42); Read. Dig. (1984: 54-5); Norwich (1985: 128); Holmes (1986); Pearson (1986: 80); Lennox-Boyd (1987: 53); Rix (1987: 45); Desmond (1988); Hollis (1989: 105-6); Keen (1989: 171); Gapper (1991: 84-6); Rose (1991 etc.); Taylor (1995: 111-12); Lacey (1996: 89-91); McCabe (1996: 22-7); Pring (1996: 62-4); Harris (1998: 16-27).
Creed House Pring (1996: 64-6); Rose (1997).
Croan Manor Betjeman (1964: 38); Pevsner (1970: 59).
Crocadon Betjeman (1964: 79).
Darley Thurston (1930: 191-2).
Doublebois House Pevsner (1970: 105).
Downes, The Thurston (1930: 139-40); Noall (1985: 128-9, 134); Elliott (1986: 164, Desmond (1986).

Duloe Vicarage & Churchyard *Thurston (1930: 215)*.
Eagle's Nest *G. Illus. 1931: 544, 593, 657*; NF&S. 1938: 199, 1939: 196; Hunkin (1943: 262, 302); JRHS. 1948: 204; G.Ch. 1968: ii 14.
Eden Valley C.G. 1985: 48, 1986: 41.
Enys Millais (1917: 70); Henderson (1928: 155); Thurston (1930: 54); Hunkin (1943: 268); Desmond (1988); Townsend (1990: 4); McCabe (1996: 108-10); Pring (1996: 65-6).
Erisey Henderson (1928: 153-4); JRIC. 1946: 61; Oates (1951: 128-36) C.G. 1995: 91.
Estray Park *Budock (1993: 49)*; Pring (1996: 66-7).
Ethy Thurston (1930: 54); Hunkin (1943: 268); Betjeman (1964: 128); Pevsner (1970: 66).
Flexbury Hall *H.D. 1924*.
Fowey Hall *H.D. 1919-24*; Keast (1950: 121-2).
Furzeball Cottage *Pring (1996: 68-9)*; C.G. 1998: 70-80.
Garlenick *Thurston (1930: 78)*.
Glanmor Thurston (1930: 215); Barratt (1980: 36).
Glendurgan *Thurston (1930: 54-5)*; Con. Conf. 1932: 320 etc., 388, JRHS. 1963: 197; G.Ch. 1963: i 404; Allan (1970: 125-6); JRHS. 1971: 220; JRIC. 1972: 320; Napier (1972: 132); Evans (1974: 7-8); Hellyer (1977: 141); Synge (1977: 99-101); Thomas (1979: 138-9); JRIC. 1980: 250; Rh. Y. 1980/81: 40; Trinick (1981); Saville (1982: 43); Elliott (1986: 43-4); Mitchell (1986); Pearson (1986: 83); Desmond (1988); Hollis (1989: 134-5); Keen (1989: 11, 146, 154); Townsend (1990: 5); Gapper (1991: 87-9); Rose (1991 etc.); C.L. 1992: 10/54; Taylor (1995: 118); Lacey (1996: 120-2); McCabe (196: 110); Pring (1996: 69-71); Harris (1998: 108-17).
Glynn Thurston (1930: 55); Betjeman (1964: 28); Pevsner (1970: 52); Holmes (1986); Desmond (1988); McCabe (1996: 48-50).
Godolphin House C.L. 38 1915: 868; Henderson (1928: 154); Thurston (1930: 85); Oates (1951: 5-16); Betjeman (1964: 47); Delderfield (1968: 60-63); Pevsner (1970: 73); Norwich (1985: 129); Holmes (1986); Desmond (1988); C.L. 1994: 5/76; CGT. 1995: 16; McCabe (1996: 115-17); Pring (1996: 71-2).
Gonvena House Pevsner (1970: 238).
Goonvrea Barratt (1980: 22).
Greatwood *O. Corn. ix 1979*: 19; JRIC. 1980: 250.
Grove Hill Thurston (1930: 55); Bird (1985: 39); Gilson (1990: 59).
Gulval Churchyard Thurston (1930: 109); Wood (1956); Betjeman (1964: 49).
Gwithian Churchyard *Thurston (1930: 125)*.
Gyllyngdune Gardens *Barham (1981: 42-3)*; Gilson (1990: 73-6); Rose (1994 etc.); Pring (1996: 68).
Hall Henderson (1928: 153); Keast (1987: 30); C.G. 1995: 90; Pring (1996: 73).
Harewood House Pevsner (1970: 49).
Headland *Rix (1987: 45)*; Saville (1988: 167-71); Rose (1991 etc.); CGT. 1994: 9; Taylor (1995: 122); Pring (1996: 73-4).
Heligan Millais (1917: 70); Thurston (1930: 55-6); Hunkin (1943: 263-4); Betjeman (1964: 43); Pevsner (1970: 80); Desmond (1988); Rose (1992 etc.); Wright (1993: 34-5); Taylor (1992/5: 123); (1995: 152-3); McCabe (1996: 89-90); Pring (1996: 74-6); Harris (1998: 52-63).
Hengar O. Corn. i. Apr. 1927: 2; Betjeman (1964: 122).
Hexworthy Thurston (1930: 56); Desmond (1988).
Hollies, The *Rose (1991 etc.)*; Pring (1996: 77-8).

Ince Castle Porter (1905: 266-71); Thurston (1930: 56); Arch. Hist.1964: 51; Betjeman (1964: 109); C.L. 141 1967: 592, 648; Pevsner (1970: 83); Synge (1977: 102-4); Lees-Milne (1980: 41-4); Norwich (1985: 130); C.G. 1986: 58; Hobhouse (1986: 24-30); Desmond (1988); Plumptre (1988: 101-2, 162); Pring (1996: 78).
Ken Caro *Rix (1987: 45)*; Hollis (1989: 176); Johnson (1991: 38-41); Pring (1996: 78-9).
Kenegie Wood (1956: 75-7); Desmond (1988).
Killagorden *Hunkin (1943: 262)*; Pevsner (1970: 165); Barratt (1980: 6); Truro (1993: 31-4).
Killiganoon Thurston (1930: 56); Barratt (1980: 21-2); O'Toole (1980: 36).
Killiow Millais (1917: 70, 1924: 54); Thurston (1930: 56); Hunkin (1943: 262); Barratt (1980: 20-21); Truro (1988: 50).
Kimberley Park Thurston (1930: 56); Betjeman (1964: 44).
Klymiarvan see Waterloo Villa.
Ladock House *Rose (1997)*.
Lambesso *Thurston (1930: 214)*; Con. Conf. 1932: 389; Barratt (1980: 9-10); Truro (1991: 79-81).
Lamellen G.Ch. 1911: i 59; Rh.N. 1916: 23; Millais (1917: 70); H.D. 1919-24; Millais (1924: 54); Thurston (1930: 56-7); Con. Conf. 1932: 320, 389; Hunkin (1943: 300-301); JRHS. 1948: 206; G. Illus. 1929-38 (articles by 'Peter the Hermit' = E.J.P. Magor of Lamellen); Rh. Y. 1964: 63, 75, 1965: 16, 29; Napier (1972: 132-3); Synge (1977: 105-7); Rh. Y. 1979/80: 44; C.G. 1985: 14; Desmond (1988).
Lamorran House C.G. 1990: 31; Rose (1991 etc.); Pring (1996: 79).
Lamorran Rectory Henderson (1928: 156); Thurston (1930: 57); Hunkin (1943: 265-6); Desmond (1988); Read (1988: 19-24).
Lanarth *H.D. 1908-24*; Daff. Y. 1914: 14, 84; Rh. Y. 1916: 39; Millais (1917: 222), G.Ch. 1927: i 223; Millais (1927: 30); JRHS. 1928: 115; Thurston (1930: 57); G. Illus. 1931: 290; Con. Conf. 1932: 390; G. Illus: 1936: 2; G.Ch. 1939: ii 45; NF&S. 1939: 43; Hunkin (1943: 299); JRHS. 1945: 63, 104, 132, 1948: 206, 210; Daff. Y. 1986/7: 45; Desmond (1988); Townsend (1990: 7).
Lancarffe Pevsner (1970: 44); *Rose (1991 etc.)*; Pring (1996: 81).
Landue H.D. 1924; Thurston (1930: 57).
Lanhadron *Thurston (1930: 186)*.
Lanhydrock Thurston (1930: 57); Rockley (1938: 162-3); Betjeman (1964: 61); Delderfield (1968: 89-92); Allan (1970: 130-31); Pevsner (1970: 89-90); Napier (1972: 133); Evans (1974: 5-6); Synge (1977: 107-110); Thomas (1979: 164-5); Hellyer (1980: 110-114); Saville (1982: 44); Read. Dig. (1984; 89-90); Harpur (1985: 26-9); Norwich (1985: 130); Holmes (1986); Pearson (1986: 84); Rix (1987: 45); Hollis (1989: 183); Desmond (1988); Gapper (1991: 89-92); Rose (1991 etc.); Taylor (1995: 126); Lacey (1996: 164-7); Titchmarsh (1995: 110-15); McCabe (1996: 77-82); Pring (1996: 82-3); Harris (1998: 38-51).
Lanterns Gdn. 1995: 210; Pring (1996: 83).
Lanwithan Fraser (1983: 54).
Laregan Pool (1974: 205).
Launceston Castle *Thurston (1930: 73)*; Arch. Hist. 1964: 52-5; Pevsner (1970: 98); McCabe (1996: 16-18).
Lawhitton Rectory *Thurston (1930: 149)*.
Lis Escop, Kenwyn *JRHS. 1948: 204*; Read (1988:

110-13); Barratt (1980: 36-9); C.G. 1993: 91; Truro (1996: 26, 31).

Long Cross O. Corn. ii Winter 1933: 17; *Rose (1992 etc.)*; Pring (1996: 83-4).

Loraine G.Ch. 1965: ii 540; Desmond (1988).

Lostwithiel (Dr Rudge) Thurston (1930: 57); Con. Conf. 1932: 391).

Ludgvan Rectory G.Ch. 1904: i 156; G.W. 1904: 477; G.Ch. 1912: i 321, 1916: ii 1; JRHS. 1923: 1; G.Ch. 1929: i 183; Thurston (1930: 57); G.Ch. 1939: ii 71; K.B. 1939: 329; JRIC. 1942: 1; Hunkin (1943: 299-300); JRHS. 1948: 203; G.Ch. 1962: ii 297; JRIC. 1972: 273; IDSY. 1981: 99; C.G. 1981: 28, Desmond (1988); Read (1988: 75-80); C.G. 1992: 99; JRIC. 1994: 28.

Maidenwell *Chivers (1987: 96-101)*.

Manaccan Churchyard Thurston (1930: 126).

Marlborough House Thurston (1930: 87, 222); Dunstan (1968: 67-72).

Mary Newman's Cott. *Rose (1992 etc.)*; Pring (1996: 83).

Mellingey H.D. 1908-24; Henderson (1937: 246); Barratt (1980: 27).

Menabilly Millais (1917: 70); Thurston (1930: 57-8); Hunkin (1943: 264-5); Pevsner (1970: 116-17); Holmes (1986); Desmond (1988); Townsend (1990: 12); McCabe (1996: 88-9).

Menacuddle Pevsner (1970: 158); Desmond (1988); Pring (1996: 85).

Menehay H.D. 1919-24; Thurston (1930: 58).

Merkjasteinn *My Gd. 1934*.

Meudon CGT. 1992: 4.

Mevagissey Vicarage Thurston (1930: 144).

Moditonham Porter (1905: 280-81); Betjeman (1964: 21); Pevsner (1970: 121); Holmes (1986); Desmond (1988).

Moresk Truro (1988: 50-51).

Morrab Gardens Thurston (1930: 58); Pool (1974: 191); Desmond (1988); Rose (1994 etc.): Pring (1996: 29, 95-6).

Morval House 1904: 90; Thurston (1930: 58); Pevsner (1970: 122); Betjeman (1964: 86); Keast (1987: 20, 32-3, 61-2, 143); Desmond (1988); McCabe (1996: 53-4); Pring (1996: 61).

Mt Edgcumbe Malan (1902: 147); Henderson (1928: 155); Thurston (1930: 58-9); Betjeman (1964: 76); Pevsner (1970: 123-4); Napier (1972: 133); O. Corn. 1975: 332; Fleming (1979: 142-3, 145, 162-4); Carne (1985: 81-2); Holmes (1986); Mitchell (1986); Pearson (1986: 86); Desmond (1988); Hollis (1989: 202); Thacker (1989: 90-91); Batey (1990: 236-41); Gapper (1991: 92); *Rose (1991 etc.)*; Taylor (1992/5: 132); (1995: 74-5); McCabe (1996: 27-31); Pring (1996: 86-7).

Moyclare *Allan (1970: 132-3)*; JRHS 1972: 13, 294, 1974: 77; Gdn. 1975: 422, Lees-Milne (1980. 111-12); C.G. 1984: 27; Desmond (1988).

Nancealverne Pevsner (1970: 139); Pool (1974: 183-4).

Nansidwell H.D. 1919-24.

Nanswhyden Henderson (1928: 155); C.L. 132 1962: 775; Rabey (1979: 46, 48); Desmond (1988).

Newham House Barratt (1980: 36).

Newlyn East Churchyard Thurston (1930: 126).

Newlyn West Thurston (1930: 160).

Newton Ferrers Thurston (1930: 59); Pevsner (1970: 127); Desmond (1988).

Newton House *Rose (1997)*.

Ogbeare Hall Pevsner (1970: 128).

Old Rectory *C.G. 1982: 58*.

Pelyn Pevsner (1970: 132); Fraser (1993: 50-51).

Pelynt Vicarage Thurston (1930: 59); C.L. 179 1986: 1208; Read (1988: 151-54).

Penair Barratt (1980: 9); Truro (1991: 69-71).

Penalverne Pool (1974: 201).

Penarwyn H.D. 1908-16.

Penberth Thurston (1930: 59); C.G. 1988: 53; Rose (1991 etc.); McCabe (1996: 137); Pring (1996: 88-9).

Pencalenick Thurston (1930: 59); Hunkin (1943: 302-3); Betjeman (1964: 41); Pevsner (1970: 133); Barratt (1980: 6-7); Truro (1991: 71-7).

Pencarrow Thurston (1930: 59-60); Hunkin (1943: 262); Betjeman (1964: 38); Pevsner (1970: 133); Napier (1972: 133-5); Synge (1977: 110-13); Norwich (1985: 133); Plumptre (1985: 237-9); Elliott (1986: 95, 99); Mitchell (1986); Desmond (1988); Gapper (1991: 95); Rose (1991 etc.); Taylor (1995: 134); McCabe (1996: 64-7); Pring (1996: 89-90).

Pencrebar Thurston (1930: 276); Lightbody (1982: 58-61, 121-5).

Pendarves Thurston (1930: 200); Betjeman (1964: 27, 115); Pevsner (1970: 228); Desmond (1988).

Pendrea Thurston (1930: 60); Wood (1956: 79).

Pengersick Castle JRIC. 1924: 285; O. Corn. v 1951-60: 89; Pevsner (1970: 134); *McCabe (1988: 116-18, 2nd ed. 1996: 117-20)*.

Pengreep G.Ch. 1906: i 173; Thurston (1930: 60); James (n.d: 103, 146, 239-40); Betjeman (1964: 49); Pevsner (1970: 135); Barratt (1980: 28).

Penheale Manor C.L. 57 1925: 484, 524; Thurston (1930: 60); Betjeman (1964: 39); Pevsner (1970: 135); Hobhouse (1986: 30-6); Holmes (1986); Desmond (1988); JRIC. 1989: 267; Pring (1996: 90-91).

Penjerrick Millais (1917: 30, 1924: 4, 8, 63, 1927: 30); Thurston (1930: 60-61); Hunkin (1943: 267); Betjeman (1964: 25); Allan (1970: 133-4); Napier (1972: 175); Synge (1977: 113-15); Mitchell (1986); Desmond (1988); Keen (1989: 145): Townsend (1990: 3); Budock (1993: 49-50); Taylor (1995: 135); McCabe (1996: 110-11); Pring (1996: 91-2).

Penlee Park Pool (1974: 193); Pring (1996: 96).

Penmere Thurston 1930: 61.

Penmorvah G.M. 1908: 204.

Penmount Thurston (1930: 183); Barratt (1980: 6).

Penpol House *Noall (1985: 23-4, 27, 138)*; Rix (1987: 45); C.G. 1988: 32; Saville (1988: 39); Hollis (1989: 221); *Rose (1991 etc.)*; Pring (1996: 93).

Penrice H.D. 1908-24; Thurston (1930: 61); Con. Conf. 1932: 394; Pevsner (1970: 135).

Penrose Thurston (1930: 61); Pevsner (1970: 136); Holmes (1986); Mitchell (1986); Pring (1996: 93-4).

Pentillie Castle Holme (1907: pl.110, 111), Henderson (1928: 154); Thurston (1930: 61); Stroud (1962: 77); Betjeman (1964: 99-100); Pevsner (1970: 137); Carter (1982: 150); Holmes (1986); Desmond (1988).

Penwarne Thurston (1930: 61); Rh. Y. 1980/81: 40; C.G. 1984: 66; Rose (1991 etc.); Pring (1996: 94-5).

Peterdale *Rose (1996 etc.)*.

Pine Lodge *Rose (1991 etc.)*; Pring (1996: 96-7).

Pinetum *Rose (1996 etc.)*.

Place House, Fowey H.D. 1908-16; C.L. 131 1962: 1510, 1568; Betjeman (1964: 44, 46); Pevsner (1970: 70-71); Norwich (1985); Holmes (1986); Desmond (1988); C.G. 1994: 66; McCabe (1996: 86-7).

Place Manor *Betjeman (1964: 12-13)*; Pevsner (1970: 156); O'Toole (1978: 53-4, 1980).
Polapit Tamar H.D. 1908-24; O. Corn. viii 1972-9: 575.
Polcarne *Betjeman (1964: 14)*.
Poldowrian CGT. 1991: 3-4; Rose (1997).
Polgwin H.D. 1908-24.
Polgwynne *Read (1988: 94-5)*; Rose (1991 etc.); Pring (1996: 98-9).
Polstrong H.D. 1908-16.
Polvellen Keast (1981: 87).
Polwhele Pevsner (1970: 143); Barratt (1980: 5).
Polwithen Pool (1974: 194, 198).
Ponsandane Wood (1956: 78); Noall (1983: 63).
Port Eliot Henderson (1928: 155); Thurston (1930: 61-2); Stroud (1962: 69); Betjeman (1964: 46); Pevsner (1970: 143-4); Hyams (1971: 154-5); Carter (1982: 150); Norwich (1985: 136); Holmes (1986); Desmond (1988); Thacker (1989: 100-101,150-51); McCabe (1996: 35-8).
Porthgwidden Thurston (1930: 62); Hunkin (1943: 262); Barratt (1980: 21); Elliott (1986: 62); Read (1988: 94-8); Truro (1985: 13).
Porthpean C.G. 1986: 82; C.L. 1989: 1/96; Rh. Y. 1990: 52; Rose (1991 etc.); Pring (1996: 99-100).
Prideaux House Pevsner (1970: 146); McCabe (1988: 88).
Prideaux Place Henderson (1928: 154); Thurston (1930: 62); Betjeman (1964: 92); Delderfield (1968: 120-4); Pevsner (1970: 130); Rawe (1984;43-8, 95); Norwich (1985: 133); Holmes (1986); Desmond (1988); Whittingstall (1990: 123-4); McCabe (1996: 70-72); Pring (1996: 100-101).
Probus Gardens C.G. 1969: 16, 1971: 4; Synge (1977: 98-9); Gdn. 1978: 265, 1979: 141, 1980: 187; Pearson (1986: 81); Hollis (1989: 231); Rose (1991 etc.); C.G. 1994: 110; Taylor (1995: 135); Pring (1996: 101-2).
Q. Mary Gardens *Kelly's (1926: 112)*; Gilson (1990: 87); Rose (1994 etc.); C.G. 1996: 67-70; Pring (1996: 68).
Rame Place Carne (1985: 81-2).
Restormel Castle Thurston (1930: 148, 237); Arch. Hist. 1964: 91; Betjeman (1964: 74); Pevsner (1970: 151-2); McCabe (1996: 83-4).
Restormel House Betjeman (1964: 74); Pevsner (1970: 152).
Riviere House F&S. 1937: 86, 163, 260; Hunkin (1943: 303); O. Corn. ix 1979-85: 118.
Rocky Hill, Scilly G.M. 1908: 27.
Roscadghill Chesher (1968: 101, 127); Pevsner (1970: 139); Pool (1974: 183); McCabe (1996: 127).
Rosecraddock Manor C.G. 1995: 101.
Rosehill, Penzance Pevsner (1970: 138); Pool (1974: 183, 185).
Rosehill, Falmouth Millais (1917: 70); Thurston (1930: 62); Betjeman (1964: 44); Pearson (1986: 82); Desmond (1988); Hollis (1989: 129-130); Pring (1996: 67).
Rosemorran Thurston (1930: 87); Wood (1956: 77-8).
Rosemundy Gay (1903: 148); Bizley (1955: 180-81); Desmond (1988).
Rosewarne JRHS. 1948: 205; JC Fam HS. 1990: June 28.
Rosewarne Hort. Station C.G. 1962: 7, 1987: 99, 1991: 56, 1994: 36.
Roskrow *Henderson (1928: 153)*; G. Illus. 1930: 501; McCabe (1996: 106-8).
Rosteague O'Toole (1978: 50, 53, 56-8); Thompson (1994: 25-8); *C.G. 1995: 94*; CGT. 1995: 18.

St Benet's Pevsner (1970: 158-9); McCabe (1996: 72-4).
St Columb Rectory *Betjeman (1964: 30)*; Pevsner (1971: 165); Rabey (1979: 48).
St Just in Roseland *Thurston (1930: 216)*; Betjeman (1964: 55); Pevsner (1970: 183); O'Toole (1978: 29-31); Pring (1996: 102).
St Michael's Mount Malan (1902: 297); Thurston (1930: 62); Betjeman (1964: 83); Nicholson (1965: 10); Delderfield (1968: 128-32); Pevsner (1970: 193-5); Synge (1977: 115-17); Thomas (1979: 206); Norwich (1985: 138); Holmes (1986); Rix (1987: 45); Desmond (1988); Rose (1991 etc.); Lacey (1996: 228-30); McCabe (1996: 122-6); Pring (1996: 102-4).
St Winnow *Henderson (1928: 152)*; Read (1988: 138-42).
Sanders Hill Rawe (1984: 25-6, 56, 63); Desmond (1988).
Sconner House Pevsner (1970: 213); Kempthorne (n.d: 61).
Scorrier House Thurston (1930: 63); Hunkin (1943: 266-7); Delderfield (1968: 133); Pevsner (1970: 211); Napier (1972: 135); Barratt (1980: 28); Holmes (1986); Mitchell (1986); Desmond (1988).
Skisdon Lodge Desmond (1988).
Southleigh Barratt (1980: 28-32).
Stoketon Manor Porter (1905: 274); Pevsner (1970: 206).
Stowe *Henderson (1928: 155)*; C.L. 131 1962: 528; Arch. Hist. 1964: 101, 102; Pevsner (1970: 216-17); JRIC. 1979: 90, 1986/7: 58; Desmond (1988); McCabe (1988: 5-8); Corn. Arch. 1993: 112; C.G. 1995: 92.
Tehidy Park Thurston (1930: 92); Betjeman (1964: 52, 94); Pevsner (1970: 218); Holmes (1986); Desmond (1988); McCabe (1996: 131-5); Pring (1996: 105-6).
Thanckes Thurston (1930: 231); Pevsner (1970: 145, 221); Harris (1976: 124, 172, 179); Desmond (1988).
Tolcarne House *Thurston (1930: 218)*.
Tolroy H.D. 1908-16.
Tonacombe *Henderson (1928: 154)*; Thurston (1930: 63); C.L. 74 1933: 500; Rockley (1938: 92-3); Pevsner (1970: 221); Desmond (1988); C.G. 1995: 89.
Torfrey H.D. 1916; Thurston (1930: 138); Fenwick (1986: 21-2).
Tor House Betjeman (1964: 115); Pevsner (1970: 221); Harris (1976: 79, 80, 129).
Trebah Millais (1917: 30, 1924: frontispiece); Thurston (1930: 63); Henderson (1937: 206-9, 250); Hunkin (1943: 300); Mitchell (1986); Rix (1987: 45); Hollis (1989: 276); C.L. 1990: 8/110; Townsend (1990: 6); Gapper (1991: 97-100); Rose (1991 etc.); Wright (1993: 56-7); Taylor (1992/5: 139); (1995: 144-5); Lloyd (1995: 93-8); Titchmarsh (1995: 46-9); McCabe (1996: 111-12); Pring (1996: 106-7); Harris (1998: 118-31).
Trebartha Thurston (1930: 63); Betjeman (1964: 92); Mitchell (1986); Rix (1987: 45); Desmond (1988).
Trebursye Thurston (1930: 63); Betjeman (1964: 106); Pevsner (1970: 222).
Tredarvah Pool (1974: 183).
Tredethy H.D. 1908-24; Thurston (1930: 63-4).
Tredrea Barratt (1980: 22); Desmond (1988).
Trefusis House Olivey (1907: 216-21); Holmes (1986).
Tregeare C.G. 1995: 100.
Tregenna Castle *Betjeman (1964: 53)*; Pevsner (1970: 181); Noall (1979: 9, 61); Holmes (1986).

Tregolls House Barratt (1980: 36); O'Toole (1980: 25-6); Truro (1988: 6, 16, 23, 28, 34, 42).

Tregothnan Millais (1827: 30); Henderson (1928: 156); Thurston (1930: 64); Hunkin (1943: 265-6); Stroud (1962: 77); Betjeman (1964: 41,83-4); Pevsner (1970: 224); Napier (1972: 135-6); Barratt (1980: 17-20); Carter (1982: 150); Holmes (1986); Desmond (1988); McCabe (1996: 96-7).

Tregrehan Millais (1917: 70); Thurston (1930: 64); Hunkin (1943: 297); Betjeman (1964: 92-3); Pevsner (1970: 224); Napier (1972: 136-7); Holmes (1986); Mitchell (1986); Desmond (1988); Hollis (1989: 276-7); Townsend (1990: 13); Rose (1991 etc.); McCabe (1996: 94-5); Pring (1996: 107-8).

Tregullow Thurston (1930: 64); James (n.d: 104); Barratt (1980: 28); Pring (1996: 108).

Tregye *G.Ch. 1902: i 311*; G.M. 1909: 126; Thurston (1930: 64); Hunkin (1943: 300); Rh. Y. 1975: 23; Barratt (1980: 22).

Trehane Thurston (1930: 131); Hunkin (1943: 298); Pevsner (1970: 148); Rix (1987: 45); Rose (1991 etc.); Pring (1996: 108-9).

Trelaske Betjeman (1964: 68); Thurston (1930: 64); Desmond (1988).

Trelawne Manor Thurston (1930: 171); Betjeman (1964: 94); Pevsner (1970: 224); Holmes (1986); Keast (1987: 17, 143); Desmond (1988); McCabe (1996: 55-6).

Trelawney *H.D. 1919-24.*

Trelean *Rh. Y. 1986/7: 1*; C.G. 1992: 13; Rix (1987: 45); Rose (1992 etc.); McCabe (1996: 112).

Trelidden *C.G. 1982: 36*; Rose (1992-3).

Treliske *H.D. 1908-24*; Barratt (1980: 32).

Trelissick Thurston (1930: 64); Hunkin (1943: 262); Betjeman (1964: 44); Allan (1970: 137); Pevsner (1970: 225); Hellyer (1977: 223); Synge (1977: 118-19); Thomas (1979: 227-9); Barratt (1980: 21); Trinick (1981); Saville (1982: 45); Read.Dig. (1984: 144); Norwich (1985: 143); Holmes (1986); Mitchell (1986); Pearson (1986: 88); Rix (1987: 45); Desmond (1988); Hollis (1989: 277); Gapper (1991: 100-103); Rose (1991 etc.); Taylor (1995: 140); Lacey (1996: 271-3); McCabe (1996: 97-100); Pring (1996: 109-10); Harris (1998: 96-107).

Trelowarren Thurston (1930: 64-5); Betjeman (1964: 77-8); Pevsner (1970: 225); Norwich (1985: 140); Holmes (1986); Desmond (1988); McCabe (1996: 112-15); Pring (1996: 110-12).

Treloyhan Manor *G.Ch. 1905: i 84*; H.D. 1908-24; Desmond (1988); C.G. 1994: 66; Rose (1997).

Trematon Castle Porter (1905: 246-52); Thurston (1930: 65); Betjeman (1964: 109); Pevsner (1970: 225-6); Norwich (1985: 141); Holmes (1986); McCabe (1996: 18-22).

Tremeer Henderson (1928: 154); C.L. 128 1960: 1018; G.Ch. 1965: i 504; Rh. Y. 1965: 15, 153, 1966: 13, 1970: 37; Pevsner (1970: 203); Synge (1977: 120-23); C.L. 168 1980: 1548; Pearson (1986: 89); Rix (1987: 45); Desmond (1988); Plumptre (1988: 133-5,169); Hollis (1989: 277-8); Rose (1991 etc.); McCabe (1996: 62-4).

Tremorvah Barratt (1980: 35); Truro (1988: 6, 17, 18, 36).

Tremough Millais (1917: 30, 1924: 51); Thurston (1930: 65); Hunkin (1943: 264); Pevsner (1970: 226); Desmond (1988).

Trenance Park *G. Illus. 1934: 298.*

Trenant Park Betjeman (1964: 38); Keast (1987: 17, 142).

Trenarren C.G. 1981: 10; Holmes (1986); Chivers (1987: 40-43); Fraser (1993: 54).

Treneere Manor Pool (1974: 184-5,203).

Trengwainton Thurston (1930: 65); Hunkin (1943: 302); Allan (1970: 138-9); Hellyer (1977: 224); Synge (1977: 123-34); Boase (1976: 34-5, 84-9); Thomas (1979: 229-31); Trinick (1981); Saville (1982: 45); Plumptre (1985: 239-42); Mitchell (1986); Desmond (1988); Hollis (1989: 278); Keen (1989: 147, 173, 226); Gapper (1991: 103-6); Rose (1991 etc.); Taylor (1995: 140); Lacey (1996: 274-6); McCabe (1996: 126-7); Pring (1996: 113); Harris (1998: 132-41).

Trenowth Pevsner (1970: 227).

Trenython *H.D. 1908-24*; C.G. 1981: 23, 1986: 50, Fenwick (1986: 20-21); C.G. 1987: 134, 1993: 94.

Trereife H.D. 1908-24; Thurston (1930: 273-4); Pevsner (1970: 227); Pool (1974: 183); Boase (1976: 62-7); Holmes (1986); McCabe (1996: 127-9).

Trerice C.L. 30 1911: 206; Betjeman (1964: 91); Delderfield (1968: 142-4); Pevsner (1970: 227); JRHS. 1971: 220; Synge (1977: 147); Thomas (1979: 231); Barratt (1980: 14-15); C.G. 1986: 26; Norwich (1985: 141); Holmes (1986); Rix (1987: 45); Desmond (1988); Hollis (1989: 280); Rose (1991 etc.); C.L. 1992: 44/62; Taylor (1992: 142); Lacey (1996: 276-8); McCabe (1996: 74-7); Pring (1996: 113-14).

Tresco Abbey Millais (1917: 70); Hunkin (1943: 268); Hellyer (1956: 150-51); Hyams (1964: 218-23); Allan (1970: 139-41); Napier (1972: 138); Coats (1977: 94-7); Hellyer (1977: 226); Fleming (1979: 207); Synge (1977: 134-41); Hellyer (1980: 47-9); Forsyth (1983: 44); Read.Dig.(1984: 147-50); Hobhouse (1986: 18-23); Pearson (1986: 90); Rix (1987: 44); Desmond (1988); Hollis (1989: 280-81); Thacker (1989: 123); Evans (1991: 146); Rose (1991 etc.); Wright (1993: 58-9); Taylor (1992/5: 141); (1995: 204-5); Titchmarsh (1995: 150-3); McCabe (1996: 139-40); Pring (1996: 114-16); Harris (1998: 142-55).

Trethill House Kempthorne (n.d: 63).

Trevarno Thurston (1930: 90); Betjeman (1964: 106); Holmes (1986); Rose (1991 etc.); Pring (1996: 116-17).

Trevarrick Hall Thurston (1930: 65); Napier (1972: 138).

Trevarthian *H.D. 1908-16.*

Trevaylor Thurston (1930: 65); Holmes (1986); Wood (1956: 72-5).

Treveddo *H.D. 1919-24.*

Trevegean *Rose (1992 etc.).*

Treverven *Thurston (1930: 65).*

Trevethoe Thurston (1930: 263); Hunkin (1943: 302); Betjeman (1964: 67).

Treviades Barton *Henderson (1937: 182-7, 236, 254).*

Trevillis G. 1900; ii 379; H.D. 1908.

Trevince Thurston (1930: 65); James (n.d. 59-64, 105), Betjeman (1964: 49); Barratt (1980: 27).

Trevissome House *H.D. 1919-24.*

Trevorick (Carclew) *Mitchell (1986).*

Trewan Thurston (1930: 181, 214, 215); Pevsner (1970: 166); Rabey (1979: 47, 49); Holmes (1986); Desmond (1988).

Trewarne (Trewane) C.L. 132 1962: 576; Pevsner (1970: 230); Holmes (1986).

Trewarthenick Henderson (1928: 156); Stroud (1962: 69, 77); Pevsner (1970: 230); Hyams (1971: 154, 156); Carter (1982: 150); Holmes (1986); Desmond (1988).

Trewhiddle H.D. 1919-24; Thurston (1930: 65-6).
Trewidden Millais (1917: 70); *Thurston* (1930: 66); Hunkin (1943: 298); *Rose* (1992 etc.); Pring (1996: 117).
Trewin Kempthorne (n.d: 59-60).
Trewince Pevsner (1970: 230); O'Toole (1978: 54-6); Thompson (1994: 28-30).
Trewinnard Pevsner (1970: 172).
Trewithen Thurston (1930: 66); Hunkin (1943: 301); Daff. Y. 1960: 9; Betjeman (1964: 101); Allan (1970: 141-2); Pevsner (1970: 231); Hellyer (1977: 227); Synge (1977: 142-5); Barratt (1980: 13); Saville (1982: 46); Plumptre (1985: 242-5); Hobhouse (1986: 12-17); Norwich (1985: 145); Holmes (1986); Mitchell (1986); Pearson (1986: 91); Desmond (1988); Saville (1988: 91, 159); Hollis (1989: 281-2); Evans (1991: 146-7); Gapper (1991: 106-8); Rose (1991 etc.); Wright (1993: 60-61); Taylor (1995: 141-2); McCabe (1996: 90-94); Pring (1996: 121); Harris (1998: 74-83).
Trewoofe O. Corn. ii Summer 1932: 5; Pevsner (1970: 231); McCabe (1996: 135); Pring (1996: 121); Rose (1997).
Treworder Mill *Truro (1996: 7)*; Rose (1997).
Treworgey C.L. 15 1904: 378; Thurston (1930: 66); Betjeman (1964: 69); Pevsner (1970: 231); Desmond (1988).
Trewyn Studio *Hollis (1989: 47-8)*; Rose (1994 etc.); Pring (1996: 53); Rose (1997).
Trist House JRIC. 1980: 191; C.G. 1992: 88.
Truthan Pevsner (1970: 236); Barratt (1980: 10-11); Truro (1993: 6-8).
Tullimaar Barratt (1980: 22-7).
Victoria & Waterfall Gardens *Kelly's 1910: 345*; Truro (1985: 35-6); Rose (1992 etc.); Pring (1996: 121).
Waterloo Villa (Klymiarvan) Keast (1987: 66).
Weath H.D. 1908.
Werrington Park Hunkin (1943: 301-2); Napier (1972: 138); Pevsner (1991: 896); Holmes (1986); Mitchell (1986); Desmond (1988).
Westbourne House H.D. 1908-24.
Whiteford House Betjeman (1964: 109); Pevsner (1970: 240); Lightbody (1982: 61-3); Desmond (1988).
Wodehouse Place *Thurston (1930: 66)*.
York House Pool (1974: 191, 202).

References

The abbreviations used for periodicals are listed at the end of the previous horticultural synopsis. Books dealing with specific subjects, such as follies, dovecotes, sundials etc. will be found under the Index of *Garden Types and Features*. Similarly, family histories appear in the *Biographical Notes*.

Allan (1970) *Fisons Guide to Gardens*, M. Allan, 1970.
Barham (1981) *Yesterday and Today around Falmouth*, F. Barham, Falmouth 1981.
Barratt (1980) *Stately Homes in and around Truro*, R. Barratt, Redruth [1980].
Batey (1990) *The English Garden Tour*, M. Batey and D. Lambert, 1990.
Betjeman (1964) *Cornwall, A Shell Guide*, John Betjeman, 1964.
Bird (1985) *Bygone Falmouth*, S. Bird, Chichester 1985.
Bizley (1955) *Friendly Retreat*, Truro 1955.
Boase (1976) *Reminiscences of Penzance*, G.C. Boase, Penzance 1976.
Budock (1993) *St Budock*, vol.ii, Budock Parish History Group, 1993.
Carne (1985) *Cornwall's Forgotten Corner*, T .Carne, Plymouth 1985.
Carter (1982) *Humphry Repton ...*, G. Carter, 1982.
Chesher (1968) *The Cornishman's House*, V.M. & F.J. Chesher, Truro 1968.
Chivers (1987) *Gardens of the Heart*, S. Chivers & S. Woloszynska, 1987.
Coats (1977) *Great Gardens of Britain*, P. Coats, 1977.
Delderfield (1968) *West Country Houses I, Cornwall, ...*, E.R. Delderfield, 1968.
Desmond (1988) *Bibliography of British Gardens*, R. Desmond, reprint, Winchester 1988.
Dunstan (1968) *Falmouth's Famous Past*, B. Dunstan, Falmouth 1968.
Elliott (1986) *Victorian Gardens*, B. Elliott, 1986.
Evans (1974) *The Beautiful Gardens of Britain*, Humphrey Evans, 1968, new ed. 1974.
Evans (1991) *Gardens*, Hazel Evans, 1991.
Fenwick (1986) *The Parish of Sampson*, J. Fenwick, Redruth 1986.
Fleming (1979) *The English Garden*, L. Fleming & A. Gore, 1979.
Forsyth (1983) *Yesterday's Gardens*, A. Forsyth, 1983.
Fraser (1993) *The Book of Lostwithiel*, B. Fraser, 1993.
Gapper (1991) *Blue Guide to Gardens*, F.& P. Gapper, 1991.
Gay (1903) *Old Falmouth*, S. Gay, 1903.
Gilson (1990) *Falmouth in Old Photographs*, P. Gilson, Stroud 1990.
Harpur (1985) *The Gardener's Garden*, J. Harpur, 1985.
Harris (1998) *Cornwall's Great Gardens*, D. Harris photographer, text T. Russell, Oakham Leicestershire 1998.
Harris (1976) *The Making of a Cornish Town. Torpoint and Neighbourhood*, G. and F.L. Harris, 1976.
Hellyer (1956) *English Gardens Open to the Public*, A.G.L. Hellyer, 1956.
— (1977) *The Shell Guide to Gardens*, A.G.L. Hellyer, 1977.
— (1980) *Gardens of Genius*, A.G.L. Hellyer, 1980.
Henderson (1928) 'Cornish Gardens', *Essays in Cornish History*, C. Henderson, Oxford 1935: 152-6. [The essay was first published in 1928.]
— (1937) *A History of the Parish of Constantine ...*, C. Henderson, ed. G.H. Doble, Long Compton 1937.
Hobhouse (1986) *Private Gardens of England*, P. Hobhouse, 1986.
Hollis (1989) *The Shell Guide to ... Gardens ...*, S. Hollis & D. Moore, 1989.
Holme (1907) *The Gardens of England in the Southern and Western Counties*, C. Holme, 1907.
Holmes (1985) *The Country House Described*, St Paul's Bibliographies, M. Holmes, Winchester 1986.
Hunkin (1943) 'A Hundred years of Cornish Gardening', J.W .Hunkin, JRHS, 1943: 260-68; 296-304.
Hunt/Pett (1991) *Historic Gardens in Cornwall*, D. Hunt & D.E. Pett, 1991.
Hyams (1964) *The English Garden*, E. Hyams, 1964.
— (1971) *Capability Brown & Humphry Repton*, E. Hyams, 1971.
James (n.d.) *A History of the Parish of Gwennap*, C.C. James, Penzance n.d.

Johnson (1991) *English Private Gardens*, J. Johnson & S. Berry, 1991.
Keast (1987) *A History of East and West Looe*, J. Keast, Chichester 1987.
Keen (1989) *The Glory of the English Garden*, M. Keen, 1989.
Kempthorne (n.d.) *A History of the Parish of Sheviock*, G.A. Kempthorne. Glasgow n.d.
Lacey (1996) *Gardens of the National Trust*, S. Lacey, 1996.
Lees-Milne (1980) *The Englishwoman's Garden*, A. Lees-Milne & R. Verey, 1980.
Lennox-Boyd (1987) *Traditional English Gardens*, A. Lennox-Boyd, 1987.
Lightbody (1982) *Callington. A Cornish Community*, S. Lightbody, Buckingham 1982.
Lloyd (1995) *Other People's Gardens*, C. Lloyd, 1995.
McCabe (1988) *Houses and Gardens in Cornwall*, ... H. McCabe, Padstow 1988, 2nd ed. 1996 used.
Malan (1902) *More Famous Houses*, A.H. Malan, 1902.
Millais (1917) *Rhododendrons and the various hybrids*, J.G. Millais, 1917.
— (1924) *Rhododendrons and the various hybrids*, second series, J.G. Millais, 1924. Only the references to the text and illustrations are noted, which signify the principal early rhododendron gardens. There are also many further references in the long plant lists.
— (1927) Magnolias, J.G. Millais, 1927.
Mitchell (1986) *Champion Trees in the British Isles*, A.F. Mitchell & V.E. Hallett, Farnham 1986. [The Cornish trees are conveniently listed, with some others, in a review by Walter Magor in *C.G.* 1986: 90-2.]
Napier (1972) *Conifers in the British Isles*, Proceedings of the third Conifer Conference, 1970, ed. E. Napier, RHS 1972. [see also references to *JRHS*. 1892, and Con. Conf. 1932 above under 'Nineteenth Century', for the first and second conferences.]
Nicholson (1965) *Great Houses of Britain*, N. Nicholson, 1965.
Noall (1979) *Yesterday's Town, St Ives*, C. Noall, Buckingham 1979.
— (1983) *The Book of Penzance*, C. Noall, Buckingham 1983.
— (1985) *The Book of Hayle*, C. Noall, Buckingham 1985.
Norwich (1985) *The Architecture of Southern Britain*, J.J. Norwich, 1985.
Oates (1951) *Around Helston in the Old Days*, A.S. Oates, Truro 1951, repr. 1953.
Olivey (1907) *Notes on the Parish of Mylor*, H.P. Olivey, Taunton 1907.
O'Toole (1978) *The Roseland between River and Sea*, L. O'Toole, Padstow 1978.
— (1980) *Place and the Sprys*, L. O'Toole, St Anthony in Roseland 1980.
Pearson (1986) *The Ordnance Survey Guide to Gardens in Britain*, R. Pearson, et al., 1986.
Pevsner (1970) *The Buildings of England. Cornwall*, N. Pevsner, 2nd ed. revised E. Radcliffe, 1970.
— (1991) *The Buildings of England. Devon*, B. Cherry and N. Pevsner, 2nd ed. 1991.
Plumptre (1985) *Collins Book of British Gardens*, G. Plumptre, 1985.
— (1988) *The Latest Country Gardens*, G. Plumptre, 1988.

Pool (1974) *The History of Penzance*, P. Pool, 1974, chap. iv, 'The Architecture of Penzance', by P. Laws.
Porter (1905) *Around and about Saltash*, P.E.B. Porter, Saltash 1905.
Pring (1996) *Glorious Gardens of Cornwall*, ed. S. Pring, CGT 1996.
Rabey (1979) *The Book of St Columb and St Mawgan*, J. Rabey, Buckingham 1979.
Rawe (1984) *Padstow and District*, D.R. Rawe and J. Ingrey, Padstow 1984.
Read (1988) *The English Vicarage Garden*, Miss Read, text by P. Dudgeon, 1988.
Read. Dig. (1984) *Great Gardens*, Readers' Digest, 1984.
Rix (1987) *Gardens Open Today*, M.& A. Rix, 1987.
Rockley (1938) *Historic Gardens of England*, Lady Alicia Rockley [née Amherst], 1938.
Rose (1991 etc.) *The Good Garden Guide*, G. Rose & P. King, 1991, and annually thereafter. [Note that the gardens marked ** as 'amongst the finest gardens in the world', and * as 'of very high quality', do not correspond with those graded as 'of national significance' by English Heritage.]
Saville (1982) *The Observers' Book of Gardens*, D. Saville, 1982.
— (1988) *Gardens for Small Country Houses*, D. Saville, 1988.
Stroud (1962) *Humphry Repton*, D. Stroud, 1962.
Synge (1977) *The Gardens of Britain I. Devon and Cornwall*, P. Synge, 1977.
Taylor (1992/5) *The Gardeners' Guide*, P. Taylor, 1992, new ed. 1995.
— (1995) *One Hundred English Gardens*, P. Taylor, 1995.
Thacker (1989) *England's Historic Gardens*, C. Thacker, 1989.
Thomas (1979) *The Gardens of the National Trust*, G.S. Thomas, 1979.
Thompson (1994) *A History of the Parish of Gerrans 1800-1914*, part 1. Farms and Farmers, H. Thompson, Portscatho 1994
Thurston (1930) *British & Foreign Trees and Shrubs in Cornwall*, E. Thurston, Cambridge 1930.
Titchmarsh (1995) *Favorite Gardens*, A. Titchmarsh, 1995.
Townsend (1990) *Study Tour of Cornish Gardens Growing Bamboos*, May 14th-19th, R.F. Townsend, Royal Botanic Gardens Kew 1990.
Toy (1936) *The History of Helston*, H.S. Toy, 1936.
Trinick (1981) *The National Trust's Cornish Gardens*, G.M. Trinick, 1981.
Truro (1985-96) Truro Buildings Research Group
— (1985) *River Street and its Neighbourhood*.
— (1988) *From Moresk Road to Malpas*.
— (1991) *In and around St Clement Churchtown*.
— (1993) *Idless and the River Allen*.
— (1996) *Kenwyn ...*
Wheeler (1991) *Panoramas of English Gardens*, D. Wheeler, 1991.
Whittingstall (1990) *Historic Gardens*, J. Fearnley-Whittingstall, 1990.
Wood (1956) *The Parish of Gulval Past and Present*, W. Wood, Penzance 1956.
Wright (1993) *Explore Britain's Country Gardens*, M. Wright, AA 1993.

Historic Illustrations

Synopsis and index

The following list provides a chronological synopsis of the earliest illustrations of sites in the topography. It must be borne in mind, however, that the various sources differ both in their origin and purpose. The choice of illustrations in Borlase and Gilbert, for example, depended on patronage from the owners of the house, whereas those in Stockdale were inspired by his own eye for the picturesque. The *Mansions* of Twycross, however, although published by subscription, was clearly intended as a comprehensive coverage of the county. By way of contrast, most of the other collections ranged over the whole country, so their examples from Cornwall would have been highly selective. Nevertheless, where comparisons can be made between prints from different periods they may be expected to provide valuable evidence for garden history.

Those illustrations which have been reproduced in the text are indicated by the addition of their numbers in bold print, in square brackets. The references to the sources follow directly after the synopsis. A complete *Index of Illustrations and Figures* reproduced in this book follows as the second part of this section, concluding with acknowledgement to those who have made their reproduction possible.

Synopsis of illustrations

Antony	Prideaux 1727: 1, 2 [**91**], 3; Buck 1734 (see Trematon Castle); Twycross 1846: 34, 36 [**92**].
Bake	Prideaux 1727: 4 [**7**], 5 [**93**].
Bochym	Spoure (1690).
Boconnoc	Lysons 1814: Pl. xxxiii [**112**]; Gilbert 1820: ii. 910, [**59**]; Stockdale 1824: 45.
Burncoose	Twycross 1846: 89.
Caerhays	Gilbert 1820: ii. 845, [**52**]; Stockdale 1824: 61.
Carclew	Borlase 1758: Pl. xi, [**36**]; Stockdale 1824: 61.
Carnanton	Morris 1866-80: iv. 25 [**69**].
Clowance	Borlase 1758: Pl .xxii, [**23**]; Akermann 1827: ix. Pl. 2; Gendall 1830: ii. 72; Twycross 1846: 65, [**24**].
Coldrenick	Twycross 1846: 72.
Colquite	Twycross 1846: 80.
Cotehele	Prideaux 1716-27: 24; Swete 1792: 138; Stockdale 1824: 129; Allom 1831: 24; Jewitt 1874: 76, 77.
Enys	Borlase 1758: Pl. vii, [**45**].
Glynn	Prideaux 1727: 44 [**77**], 45.
Godolphin	Borlase sketch in Morrab Library [**6**], 1748, 1758: Pl. xii, [**27**]
Grove Hill	Twycross 1846: 68, [**46**]
Hengar	Twycross 1846: 82.
Hexworthy	Prideaux 1716: 48 [**85**].
Ince Castle	Prideaux 1727: 51 [**95**]
Kenegie	Borlase 1758: Pl. v, [**16**].
Klymiarvan	see Waterloo Villa.
Lancarffe	Twycross 1846: 79.
Lanhydrock	Prideaux 1727: 56; Akermann 1827: x. Pl. 8; Stockdale 1824: 155; Gendall 1830: i. 19; Allom 1831: 38; Morris 1866-80: v. 39, *Lake* 1870: iii. frontispiece.
Lanwithan	Twycross 1846: 84.
Launceston Castle	Prideaux 1716-27: 52-5; Buck 1734: i; Lysons 1814: Pl. xxxvi; Gilbert 1820: ii. 514; *Hitchins* 1824: i. 631; Stockdale 1824: 121, 124, 125; Allom 1831: 12; *Lake* 1870: iii. 66.
Lavethan	Twycross 1846: 82.
Luxstowe	Twcross 1846: 85.
Marlborough House	Twycross 1846: 89, two plates, [**47**].
Menabilly	Stockdale 1824: 41.
Menacuddle	Gilbert 1820: ii. 866, [**62**].
Moditonham	Neale 1818: i.; Gilbert 1820: ii. 439, [**97**]; Jones 1829.
Moor Cottage	Twycross 1846: 84 [**68**].
Moorswater Lodge	Twycross 1846: 85, [**111**].
Morval House	Allom 1831: 68
Mt Edgcumbe	Prideaux 1716 or 27: 60-62; Badeslade 1739: Pls 94-5, [**98**]; Borlase 1748; Swete 1792: 141, 142, 145; Britton 1803: iv. 189-90; Akermann 1826: vii. Pl. 19; Clarke 1820; Payne 1826: Pls 10, 12.; Gendall 1830: i. 81-6; Britton 1832: 37-41; Morris 1866-80: ii. 57; Jewitt 1874: 54-72.
Nanswhyden	Borlase 1758: Pl. viii, [**70**].
Newton Ferrers	Prideaux 1716: 68; Twycross (1846: 45) [**100**].
Penair	Twycross 1846: 55.
Pencarrow	Akermann 1826: vii. Pl. 14; Gendall 1830: i. 105; Twycross 1846: 27. [**79**].
Pendarves	Borlase 1758: Pl. xiv. [**31**].
Pengersick Castle	Borlase (sketch in Morrab Library, Penzance); Gilbert 1820: ii. 759.
Penheale	Twycross 1846: 56, [**86**].

292 The Bibliographies

Pennans	Twycross 1846: 47, [54].
Penrice	Twycross 1846: 32, two plates, [63].
Penrose	Allom 1831: 46; Twycross 1846: 64, [29]
Pentillie	Prideaux 1716-34: 77; Gilbert 1820: ii. 440, [102]; Lewis 1823; Stockdale 1824: 130; Gendall 1830: i. 73; Allom 1831: 24.
Penventon	Twycross 1846: 87.
Place, Antony	Twycross 1846: 59.
Place, Fowey	Lysons 1814: Pl. xxxiii [64]; Stockdale 1824: 40; Allom 1831: 49; Twycross 1846: 57 [65].
Port Eliot	Prideaux 1716: 86 [104]; Buck 1734: i; Polwhele 1816: ii. 163; Akermann 1826: vii. Pl. 32; Gendall 1830: i. 110; Allom 1831: 32; Twycross 1846: 1, [105].
Porthgwidden	Twycross 1846: 87, [40].
Prideaux House	Twycross 1846: 31.
Prideaux Place	Prideaux 1816-34: 70 [71], 71, 72 [8], 73, 74 (dated 1734) [118], 75; Borlase 1848, 1858: iv, [72]; Allom 1831: 43.
Priory, Bodmin	Gilbert 1820: ii. 629, [82].
Restormel Castle	Prideaux 1827: 91; Buck 1734: i; Lysons 1814: Pl. xxxiii [112]; Stockdale 1824: 43, 44; Allom 1831: 52; *Lake 1872*: iv. 1.
Rosecraddock	Twycross 1846: 86.
St Benet's	Lysons 1814: Pl. xxi; Stockdale 1824: 167.
St Michael's Mount	Buck 1734: iii. two views; Borlase 1769: Pl. lxxxiv; Lysons 1814: Pls xxxiv, xxxv; *Hitchins* 1824: i. 17; Stockdale 1824: 76; Allom 1931: 46; etc.
St Nectan's Kieve	see Trevillet
Sanders Hill	Neale 1825: ii.; Gilbert 1820: ii. 652, [73]; Jones 1829.
Skisdon Lodge	Gilbert 1820: ii. 610.
Stowe	Prideaux 1716: 101 [84], 102.
Tehidy	Borlase 1748, 1758: Pl. x; Watts [32]; Gilbert 1820: ii. 691; Allom 1831: 57.
Thanckes	Gilbert 1820; ii. 394, [106]; Twycross 1846: 18.
Tintagel	Norden 1697 [74]
Trebartha	Spoure *c.* 1690 [87]; Twycross 1846: 48.
Trebursey	Twycross 1846: 63.
Tredethy	Twycross 1846: 79.
Tregeare	Twycross 1846: 69.
Tregenna Castle	Twycross 1846: 75, [20].
Tregothnan	Neale 1818: i.; Stockdale 1824: 56; Allom 1831: 35; Twycross 1846: 10 two plates, [41]; Morris 1866-80: v. 29; Lake 1872: iv. frontispiece.
Tregrehan	Twycross 1846: 47 two plates, [67].
Tregullow	Twycross 1846: 84, [33].
Trelaske	Twycross 1846: 77, [88].
Trelawne	Borlase 1748; Gilbert 1820: ii. 916, [107].
Trelissick	Akermann 1927: ix. Pl. 8; Gilbert 1820: ii. 808, [42]; Gendall 1830: i. 35; Allom 1831: 61.
Trelowarren	Borlase 1858: Pl. vi; Polwhele 1806: iv. 116, [30]; Stockdale 1824: 71; Allom 1831: 58.
Trematon Castle	Buck 1734 (with Antony in the distance); Lysons 1814: Pl. xxiv, xxxviii [108]; Gilbert 1817: i. 76; Hitchins 1824: i. 211; Stockdale 1824: 136; Allom 1831: 32.
Tremeer	Twycross 1846: 79, [81].
Trerice	Stockdale 1924: 98.
Tresillian House	Twycross 1846: 83.
Trevethoe	Borlase 1748, [22]
Trevillet	(St Nectan's Kieve) Gilbert 1820: ii. 586, [75]; Allom 1831: 21.
Trewan	Gilbert 1820: ii. 668, [76]; Stockdale 1824: 100.
Trewardale	Twycross 1846: 70.
Trewarthenick	Prideaux 1727: 106, [56]; Allom 1831: 64, [57].
Trewithen	Borlase 1758: Pl. xxiii, [58]; Twycross 1846: 49.
Treworgey	Gilbert 1820: ii. 949, [109].
Truthan	Twycross 1846: 45, [43].
Tullimaar	Twycross 1846: 85, [51].
Waterloo Villa	Twycross 1846: 86, (as Klymiarvan).
Werrington	Prideaux 1716: 18, [89]; Borlase 1748; Swete 1792: 125, 126; Gilbert 1820: ii. frontispiece, & 522, [Frontis. & 90]; Lewis 1823: three sketches; Allom 1829.
Whiteford House	Stockdale 1824: 128.
Wolsdon	Twycross 1846: 85.

References

Akermann (1809-28) *The Repository of arts ...*, R. Akermann, 40 vols, 1809-28.

Allom (1831) *Cornwall Illustrated*, T. Allom, with Historical and Descriptive Accounts by J. Britton & E.W. Brayley, 1831. See also Britton (1832) for Mt Edgcumbe, and Werrington.

Badeslade (1739) *Vitruvius Brittanicus*, vol. 4, T. Badeslade & J. Rocque, 1739.

Borlase (1748) Topographical Sketches, W. Borlase, in manuscript, Devon Record Office Z19/16/1. See also sketches in the Morrab Library, Penzance.

— (1758) *The Natural History of Cornwall*, W. Borlase, Oxford 1758.

— (1769) *Antiquities ... of Cornwall*, W. Borlase, 1869.

Britton (1803) *Beauties of England and Wales*, vol. 4, J. Britton & E.W. Brayley, 1803.

— (1832) *Devonshire and Cornwall*, J. Britton & E.W. Brayley, 1832 [the counties were also issued separately, that for Cornwall being here listed under Allom, the artist].

Buck (1734) *Antiquities ...*, S. and N. Buck, vol. i Cornish views, vol. iii two views of St Michael's Mount, 1734.

Clarke (1820) *Eight Views of Mount Edgcumbe*, W. Clarke, 1820.

Gendall (1830) *Views of the country seats of the royal family, nobility and gentry of England*, 2 vols, W.W.J. Gendall, 1830.

Gilbert (1820) *An Historical Survey of Cornwall*, vol. 2 C.S. Gilbert, Plymouth 1820.

Historic Illustrations   293

Hitchins (1824) *The History of Cornwall*, F. Hitchins &
S. Drew, 2 vols, Helston 1824.
Jewitt (1874) *The Stately Homes of England*, L. Jewitt
& S.C. Hall, 2nd series 1874.
Jones (1829) *Jones's Views of the seats ... etc. of
noblemen and gentlemen in England, Wales, Scotland
and Ireland ...*, etc, 1829.
Lake (1867-72) *Lake's Parochial History ... of Cornwall*,
J. Polsue, Truro 4 vols 1867-1872.
Lewis (1823) *The Scenery of the River Tamar and
Tavy*, F.C. Lewis, 1823.
Lysons (1814) *Magna Britannia ... volume the third,
Cornwall*, D. and S. Lysons, 1814.
Morris (1866-80) *A Series of picturesque views of seats
of the noblemen and gentlemen of Great Britain and
Ireland*, F.O. Morris, 6 vols, 1866-80.
Neale (1818-23) *Views of the seats of noblemen and
gentlemen in England, Wales, Scotland and Ireland*,
6 vols, J.P .Neale, 1818-23, vols.1 and 2.
Norden (1597) *Speculi Britanniae*, 1728. [survey
c. 1597]. Reprinted Newcastle upon Tyne 1966.
Payne (1826) *Picturesque Views in Devonshire,
Cornwall etc.*, W. Payne, 1826.
Polwhele (1803-16) *History of Cornwall*, R. Polwhele,
7 vols 1703-16.
Prideaux (1716-27) 'Collection of Topographical
Drawings', Edmund Prideaux, ed. J. Harris, *Arch.
Hist.* vol.7. 1964. [The dates cited are either from the
sketches or have been suggested by the editor; the
numbers are of the reproductions in Harris (1964).]
Spoure (*c.* 1690) 'The Spoure Book', manuscript *c.*
1690 [copy in Cornwall Record Office
F53/93/3/125-135] with sketches of Bochym,
Crocadon, Penheale and Trebartha; also Anderton
(Launcells), Battens (Northill), Froxton (Whitstone),
Holwood (Quethiock), and William Hooper's house in
Linkinhorne.
Stockdale (1824) *Excursions in Cornwall*, F.W.L.
Stockdale, 1824.
Swete (1792) 'Picturesque Sketches of Devon', 1792,
J. Swete, in manuscript, published as *Travels in
Georgian Devon*, ed. T. Gray, vol.i. 1997.
Twycross (1846) *The Mansions of England and Wales,
County of Cornwall*, E. Twycross, engravings by H.
Moreland, 1846.
Watts (1779) *The Seats of the Nobility and Gentry ...*,
W. Watts, 1779.

Index of illustrations and figures

The source references are given in the captions to
the illustrations themselves.

Frontispiece **Werrington** with Triumphal Arch, 1820.
1. Geology of Cornwall.
2. Annual average rainfall, 1881-1915.
3. Average maximum and minimum temperature, 1941-1970.
4. Average days frost 1961-1980.
5. Mean daily minimum temperature in February, 1941-1970.
6. **Godolphin** in the sixteenth century.
7. **Bake**, the avenue *c*. 1716-27.
8. **Prideaux Place**, south front, *c*. 1716-27.
9. **Antony**, prospect, 1721.
10. **Coldrenick**, *Larix griffithii*, 1907.
11. **Scilly**, narcissus, *c*. 1890s.
12. **Abbey Gardens**, Tresco, plan in 1940s.
13. **Tresco**, Neptune Steps, Abbey Gardens, *c*. 1900.
14. **Scilly**,'Armorel's Cottage', *c*. 1900.
15. **Scilly**, the Trevellick family, *c*. 1900.
16. **Kenegie**, prospect over Penzance, 1758.
17. **Ludgvan Rectory**, 1942.
18. **Morrab Gardens**, Penzance, plan *c*. 1910.
19. **St Michael's Mount**, 1833.
20. **Tregenna Castle**, 1846.
21. **Trengwainton**, 1866.
22. **Trevethoe**, drawing by W .Borlase 1748.
23. **Clowance**, before rebuilding, in the 1770s.
24. **Clowance**, 1846.
25. **The Downes**, perspective by J.D. Sedding, 1891.
26. **The Downes**, sketch by T. Raffles Davison, 1887.
27. **Godolphin**, 1758.
28. **Pengersick Castle** and **Godolphin**, drawings by W. Borlase.
29. **Penrose** and Loe Pool, 1846.
30. **Trelowarren**, 1806.
31. **Pendarves**, 1758.
32. **Tehidy**, 1781.
33. **Tregullow**, with parkland, 1846.
34. **Tregullow**, the Yew Walk, 1891.
35. **Boscawen Park**, Truro, original plan, 1894.
36. **Carclew**, the house, 1758.
37. **Carclew**, terrace garden, 1874.
38. **Lamorran Rectory**, 1881.
39. **Pencalenick**, and Italian garden, 1888.
40. **Porthgwidden**, the terrace, 1846.
41. **Tregothnan**, from the river, 1846.
42. **Trelissick**, and parkland, 1820
43. **Truthan**, 1846.
44. **Arwenack**, Falmouth, map *c*. 1580.
45. **Enys** and gardens, 1758.
46. **Grove Hill**, 1846.
47. **Marlborough House**, 1846.
48. **Penjerrick**, 1874.
49. **Rosehill**, *Musa ensete*, 1894.
50. **Roskrow**, sketch in 1690.
51. **Tullimaar** and terraces, 1846.
52. **Caerhays Castle**, 1820.
53. **Heligan**, formal garden, 1735.
54. **Pennans** and avenue, 1846.
55. **Rosteague**, plan of *c.* seventeenth-century parterres.
56. **Trewarthenick**, sketch by Prideaux, 1727.
57. **Trewarthenick**, 1831
58. **Trewithen** and grounds, 1758.
59. **Boconnoc** and parkland, 1820.
60. **Menabilly**, the Grotto.
61. **Menabilly**, the lawn, 1886.
62. **Menacuddle** Chapel, 1820
63. **Penrice**, 1846
64. **Place**, Fowey, in the time of Henry VIII.
65. **Place House**, Fowey, 1846.
66. **Tregrehan**, plan of Nesfield's parterres, 1843.
67. **Tregrehan**, house and terrace, 1846.
68. **Moor Cottage** and grounds, 1846.
69. **Carnanton** in the 1870s.
70. **Nanswhyden**, 1758.
71. **Prideaux Place**, sketch by Prideaux in 1830s.
72. **Prideaux Place**, as re-designed, 1758.
73. **Sanders Hill**, 1820.
74. **Tintagel Castle**, 1728.

75. **St Nectan's Kieve**, 1820.
76. **Trewan Hall**, 1820.
77. **Glynn**, sketch by Prideaux, 1727.
78. **Lanhydrock**, parterres, 1903.
79. **Pencarrow**, and rockery, 1846.
80. **Pencarrow**, the rockery, 1878.
81. **Tremeer** and terraces, 1846.
82. **The Priory**, Bodmin, 1820.
83. **Merkjasteinn**, Flexbury, 1936.
84. **Stowe**, sketch by Prideaux, 1716.
85. **Hexworthy**, sketch by Prideaux, 1716.
86. **Penheale**, and gardens 1846
87. **Trebartha**, terraced garden, c. 1690.
88. **Trelaske** and parkland, 1846.
89. **Werrington**, sketch by Prideaux, 1716.
90. **Werrington**, from same direction as Fig. 83, 1820.
91. **Antony**, sketch of garden by Prideaux, 1727.
92. **Antony**, entrance front, 1846.
93. **Bake**, sketch by Prideaux, 1827.
94. **Cotehele**, the terraces, 1893.
95. **Ince Castle**, sketch by Prideaux, c. 1727.
96. **Ince Castle**, parterre garden, 1967.
97. **Moditonham**, south-west view, 1820.
98. **Mount Edgcumbe**, view by Badeslade, 1737.
99. **Mount Edgcumbe**, plan of gardens.
100. **Newton Ferrers**, 1846.
101. **Newton Ferrers**, terraces, 1904.
102. **Pentillie Castle**, 1820.
103. **Pentillie Castle**, plan of flower garden, 1863.
104. **Port Eliot**, sketch by Prideaux, 1716.
105. **Port Eliot**, 1846.
106. **Thanckes**, from the river, 1820.
107. **Trelawne Manor**, 1820.
108. **Trematon Castle**, 1814.
109. **Treworgey**, 1820.
110. **Treworgey**, 1904.
111. **Moorswater Lodge** and garden, 1846.
112. **Deer Parks**, Restormel Castle, and Boconnoc, in the time of Henry VIII.
113. **Speculi Britanniae**, title page 1728.
114. **Topography**, title page, C.S. Gilbert, 1820.
115. **Gardeners' Chronicle**, editorial, 1889.
116. **Thurston**, *Trees and Shrubs ... in Cornwall*, 1930, title page.
117. **Carclew**, *Picea lemonii*, 1833.
118. **The Wilderness**, Prideaux Place, 1734.
119. **Richard Carew**, 1586.

Acknowledgements

Acknowlegment is made to the following for permission to reproduce maps, tables, and illustrations in their possession, or of which they hold the copyright.

Prof. W.G.V. Balchin, 1; Col. E.T. Bolitho, 21; Cornwall County Council, 2; Cornwall Garden Society, 53; Country Life, 9, 78, 96, 98, 101, 110; Frank Gibson, 11, 14, 15; Gay Lush, 87, 99; Meteorological Office, 3, 4, 5; Ordnance Survey, 18; P.J.N. Prideaux-Brune, 7, 8, 56, 71, 77, 84, 85, 89, 91, 93, 95, 104, 118; Sue Pring, 55, 66; Royal Institution of Cornwall, 17, 32, 39, 44, 50, 60, 69, 87; Rose Tempest, 22; the late Mrs Michael Trinick, 20, 24, 29, 33, 40, 41, 43, 46, 47, 51, 54, 63, 65, 67, 68, 69, 79, 81, 86, 88, 92, 100, 105, 111. I am especially grateful to Ian Lewis for preparing transparencies from Borlase (1758), Lysons (1814), Gilbert (1820) and Twycross (1846).

Plant Records

Plant records

Planting in Cornwall, especially since the beginning of the nineteenth century, reflects the unique climate of the county, which, by comparison with the rest of the country, is milder and more equable. However, the *Guide to the Mount's Bay and the Land's End*, published in 1816 by a local physician, J.A. Paris, is representative in at first considering that it was the medical benefits of the climate, rather than any horticultural potential, which were its greatest recommendation. Nevertheless, with the introduction of new varieties of plants towards the end of the eighteenth and the beginning of the nineteenth centuries, the 'acclimatisation of exotics' came more and more to excite the attention of horticulturists, until in 1841 it formed the subject of an opening editorial in the recently published *Gardeners' Chronicle* (i. 275).

Thomas Rutger, brought up in Longleat, where his father had been gardener, and himself working at Clowance and St Michael's Mount from 1800 to the first years of the 1830s, had already been experimenting with South African heathers when he wrote to the *Gardener's Magazine* in 1830 'to solicit.a list or lists of such exotics indigenous to warmer climes than our own, as upon trial have been found to endure our most severe winters without protection' (p. 229). By 1833 he had left Cornwall for Shortgrove, the Earl of Thomond's estate near Saffron Walden in Essex, but the colder climate did not dampen his enthusiasm, for he wrote complaining that 'nothing of the kind had appeared'. He went on to outline the type of list he had in mind, concluding:

> I shall be happy to become a contributor, by sending you a list of such acclimatised plants as have come under my observation in the western part of England, which might be incorporated with those you may receive from other persons. (1833: 583)

There was little response, and certainly nothing as systematic as he was hoping for.

Not so, however, in Cornwall. At the third exhibition of the newly-formed Royal Horticultural Society of Cornwall, Sir Charles Lemon, the Chairman, was reported as saying that:

> our climate is particularly favourable for making experiments on the comparative hardiness of exotic plants. There are few, he supposed, who had not at one time or another had the curiosity to enter on this interesting subject. He had himself pursued it to some extent, and, he might add, with tolerable success ... He hoped the matter might not be lost sight of by the Horticultural Society and that it might receive an additional impulse from the members communicating, at some of their future meetings, the results of their several experiments. (*G. Mag.* 1832: 746)

It was not to be left to chance. The RHSC was given by the Horticultural Society of London a silver Banksian Medal which it could present locally to the winner of a competition of its own choosing. In the Society's fifth Report of 1837, the committee begged to suggest that:

> the Medal should this year be offered *for an account of the largest number of new and hitherto undescribed plants, which shall have flowered in the possession of the Competitor, with a description of their character, habits, and treatment.*

In the event, the medal was won by George Croker Fox of Grove Hill House, Falmouth, for a list of 223 plants. They were carefully arranged in three sections: Stove, Green-House and Frame Plants. The Latin name, number of years' exposure, soil, situation, height in feet and remarks were entered for each. It was long years before the reputation gained by Croker Fox in this competition was forgotten.

In the same year the Committee also suggested that a Silver Medal

> be offered for the Master or Commander of H.M. Packets of Falmouth, who shall introduce to the County the larger number of plants or roots from Foreign Countries.

No winner was announced in the subsequent Reports, but Sir Charles Lemon himself submitted from Carclew a list of twenty-four new plants that he had received from five different seamen. This provides interesting evidence for an important source for many of the exotic plants which began appearing at this time, and goes some way to explaining why Falmouth was moving faster ahead than Penzance, which enjoyed a marginally better climate.

Rutger's earlier appeal, nevertheless, did not go entirely unheeded, for in 1836 James Mitchinson, who was head gardener at Pendarves, a near neighbour of Clowance, sent to the *Gardener's Magazine* a 'List of [74] Plants which have stood in the open Air ...' (1837: 354). A year later, in the third appendix to Davies Gilbert's *Parochial History of Cornwall*, 1838 (iv: 181), there appeared a longer list of ninety-five species under a similar title. Even though the two lists do not exactly correspond, there seems little doubt but that they are from the same hand. In addition to the named species and varieties, in some cases 'several' or 'many', unnamed varieties were claimed to have been grown. If the two lists are taken together the total now rises to 130 named plants, to which several more unspecified varieties can be added.

It must be remembered that these, the earliest Cornish lists, come from a period lasting from about 1760 to 1860, which has been called the 'Little Ice Age'. The winter of 1837-8 was particularly harsh, which prompted John Lindley to read a detailed paper to the London Horticultural Society that same year, on his 'Observations upon the Effects produced ... by the Frost ...' (*G. Mag.* 1840: 475-513). This consisted of an analysis of plants continent by continent, with the effect of the frost in different areas of Britain. He was assisted in this by information sent by Beattie Booth, gardener at Carclew, drawn from his own experience and that of Croker Fox in Falmouth, showing how much more favoured they had been. Nevertheless, despite such setbacks, the exceptional nature of the climate in Cornwall was sufficient to arouse disbelief in the minds of some readers of journals, so that it became a recurring topic in the horticultural literature, generating an increasing number of plant lists exhibiting the achievements of 'acclimatization'.

Garden records

It is perhaps natural, as a primary source of information, to seek out the original planting records kept by the gardeners of individual estates, but, as Rutger himself found, this is not always easy, and unfortunately it is still not an area that has so far attracted serious research in Cornwall. Indeed, except in a few cases, there is scarcely any hint of their existence. Two are known to be held in the Record Office: 'The Rashleigh Collection 1790-1880', relating to Menabilly, which contains notes on cultivation and dates of planting, and the 'Johnstone Papers (Hawkins family of Trewithen, Grampound), 1745', which contain 'a few papers relating to ... horticulture and a book of notes on tree cultivation'.

Records have been kept of the important historic plantings at Caerhays Castle, where in 1917 J.C. Williams allowed a list of 258 species to be published for the information of members of the Rhododendron Society. His planting books were reviewed by his grandson, Julian, in his year-book for 1960. The records of J.C., and of P.D. Williams at Lanarth formed the subject of articles in the *Journal of the Royal Horticultural Society* by Bishop Hunkin (1943: 9-18, 43-8; 1945: 63-72, 104-10, 132-5), who did a similar service for the 'Garden Book' 1833-1853 of Sir William Molesworth of Pencarrow (*JRHS* 1946: 364-9). Recently, the 'Index of Plants, Trehane 1888', which continues until 1900, has surfaced with over 5,000 entries. Of these, nearly 4,000 have full species names and sources. The surprising and important feature of this list is that the great majority of the plants, unusually for Cornwall, are herbaceous. Plant recording is also known to have been taking place at Lamellen, Porthpean, Tremeer and Trengwainton, but the nearest to a methodical recording of planting to have been discovered so far, is that at Tresco, where a comprehensive inventory was entered on a card index in 1935. This, the richest mine of information in the county, will be discussed under a separate heading.

Until there has been a thorough search for the primary sources, the only alternative upon which we can rely must be published material, which, since the benefits of the county's unusual climate aroused so much interest in the horticultural public, is not perhaps as unrewarding as at first it might appear.

Published records

It should be remembered that the introduction and cultivation of exotic species in these early days was undertaken not so much to enhance garden ornament, as for botanical research. The course of lectures delivered at Torquay by Charles Daubeny, Professor of Botany at Cambridge, later published with the title *Climate: an Inquiry into the Causes of its differences, and into its Influences on Vegetable Life*, (1863) is just such an example, for it included a list of more than 166 plants, not found hardy at Cambridge, growing at Falmouth and on the Isles of Scilly, which aroused so much local interest that it was reprinted as the opening article in the first issue of the scholarly *Journal of the Royal Institution of Cornwall*, (1864-5: 71).

This same *Journal* published towards the end of the century a much more comprehensive article on the 'Acclimatisation of Exotics in Cornwall. The Falmouth Truro District' (1897: 313-42), showing that the subject was still very much alive. It was written by F. Hamilton Davey, a gifted botanist, who was to publish a *Flora* of Cornwall in 1909. Curiously his article, even at this late date, still began with a survey of medical opinion on the 'health-restoring qualities of the Cornish climate', almost as if to gain some scientific respectability for what was to follow! He reviewed fourteen of the most prominent gardens in the district, following his introductory notes with lists of plants.

This article was described as a 'First Paper', concluding with the words, 'On a future occasion the Penzance district will be called upon to contribute its quota, and from the two papers the public will be able to view the dominating idea [i.e. acclimatization] in its true bearing'. Either because lists were not forthcoming, or because Davey never completed the article, a 'Second Paper' never appeared, thereby truncating what was intended to be a comprehensive and authoritative coverage of the subject.

Two of the gardens which were prominent in Davey's survey were later to contribute their own much more substantial lists. In 1909 J.D. Enys, who had been enriching his own, and other gardens with seeds and plants sent home from his foreign travels - mostly from the Antipodes - privately published an inventory of around 1,100 plants in his garden, many in variety.

Over the turn of the century, Rosehill began to supplant Penjerrick as the most celebrated of the Fox gardens. Howard Fox died in 1922, but in 1939 William Jenkin, his gardener, prepared a 'List of Plants in the Garden of Rosehill, Falmouth' for the *Annual Report of the Royal Polytechnic Society of Cornwall*, a society founded by Anna and Caroline Fox to promote scientific research. Evidently by this time it was not considered inappropriate to publish such a list in this context. Over 330 plants were listed, although the unsystematic, and sometimes repetitive nature of the recording affirms that it owed its origin to the notes of a working gardener.

Thurston's *Trees and Shrubs in Cornwall*

The zenith of plant recording in Cornwall arrived with the publication by the Royal Institution of Cornwall in 1930 of Edgar Thurston's *British & Foreign Trees and Shrubs in Cornwall*. Thurston, who had retired from a working life in India where he had written on ethnology and numismatics, turned his interests to the native and exotic flora of Cornwall. The book has introductory chapters on woodlands by Charles Henderson, on hedges by R.L. Clowes, and plant-names in the Cornish language by Morton Nance. The plant lists themselves are separated into two sections - non-coniferous and coniferous - in which the species are arranged alphabetically with notes identifying the sites where they were to be found. Thurston had visited eighty-three prominent gardens which he briefly described in his fifth chapter, but citations of lesser numbers of plants were made from other significant gardens, as well as from parsonages and churchyards.

In preparing his lists, Thurston used some of the sources already mentioned, supplemented by the *Trees of Great Britain ... 1906-13*, by Elwes and Henry, who had visited Cornwall and made measurements which Thurston was able to update, and by the works of W. Dallimore on *Coniferae* and of W.J. Bean, which contained specific information on Cornish specimens. The survey was a massive undertaking which took several years, and the volume still holds its place as an authority on the subject. For our purposes, however, it does suffer from two deficiencies. The first was inevitable, arising from its very object - namely to provide a survey of all the significant trees and shrubs growing at a particular point in time. It did not aim to be historical. Second, for reasons of space and complexity, rhododendrons and camellias - genera for which Cornwall is famous - were omitted.

Periodical publications

In contrast to most of the sources so far discussed, the great nineteenth-century horticultural journals were essentially ephemeral, which, from the historical point of view, may be considered one of their strengths. They recorded week by week the observations of owners, professional gardeners, and journalists who worked in or had visited the gardens they described. In general the journals were more concerned with plants and their cultivation, than with garden design - at least this is true of the Cornish gardens, which tended to attract the interest of their readers for their range of exotic plants, and the vagaries of an exceptional climate. They provide therefore a rich source of contemporary information.

It is, however, only when the great variety and diversity of the articles in the whole range of periodicals has been systematically worked over, that their full value becomes evident. When test inventories were extracted for eight gardens in the Penzance, Camborne and Falmouth districts, the results exceeded all expectations. Rosehill, for example, as might be foreseen, since it already had

---

BRITISH & FOREIGN TREES
AND SHRUBS IN CORNWALL

by

EDGAR THURSTON, C.I.E.

CAMBRIDGE
PUBLISHED FOR THE
ROYAL INSTITUTION OF CORNWALL BY THE
CAMBRIDGE UNIVERSITY PRESS
1930

the benefit of a long list from a former gardener, came out with the greatest number of recorded plants, exceeding 560 varieties. Trewidden in Penzance, which has perhaps never quite achieved the widespread reputation of the Fox gardens in Falmouth, produced the surprising total of 450

A variety of Pinus pinaster *named after Sir Charles Lemon, based on a drawing by his gardener, W. Beattie Booth. (Trans. Hort. Soc. 1833: 509)*

varieties mentioned in print. In contrast, Thurston himself had cited only eighty-six plants from Rosehill, and fifty-one from Trewidden, although this still placed them in the upper range of his selected gardens.

When these inventories are examined more critically, it soon becomes apparent that a wider variety of plants was being noticed by the observers than appear in Thurston. In the first place, since the sources are dated, the lists in them are authentically historical. Some, indeed, such as that from Pendarves in 1836 or Grove Hill in 1837, were very early, so that it now becomes possible to examine the succession of plant introductions into the coun-

ty in a longer perspective. Perhaps of equal interest is the varying character of the lists themselves, which reflect not only the local climates in the different parts of the county, but also the tastes and interests of the owners.

As has been remarked, although the absence of manuscript records may force a reliance upon printed rather than documentary sources, this may have its own advantages, and such has proved to be the case. Even though there is still a great deal of work to be done, it cannot be said that Cornwall lacks the necessary material to compile an adequate historical Flora of hardy and exotic plants.

The Abbey Gardens, Tresco

If there are very few gardens in mainland Cornwall which can boast sufficient documentation for a continuous assessment of their development, this is fortunately not the case with Tresco, which therefore deserves separate treatment.

The garden began to be laid out soon after Augustus Smith had completed his house in about 1840, but none of the primary records for this period has survived intact. There remain, however, three important secondary sources. Although his correspondence has not been preserved, Lady Sophia Tower, a friend and distant relative, in 1873, shortly after his death, published his letters to her, with the title *Scilly and its Emperor*, and which provide a running commentary on the creation of the garden. Augustus Smith's sister, Fanny Le Marchant, an artist of great talent, towards the end of his life and for several years after, painted a series of watercolours depicting sheaths of flowers from the garden, usually annotated with their names. These form a valuable supplement to the scattered remarks in the correspondence. Third, the card index of 1935 contains information clearly drawn from invoices and other papers of which, regrettably, very few remain. Together these three sources make it possible to form a reasonably complete picture of the original construction and foundation planting of the Abbey Gardens.

Augustus was unmarried and arranged that his nephew should succeed him. After a career in the army, Algernon Dorrien, who had adopted the name of Smith, had no specific horticultural training or experience, but he entered upon his inheritance with enthusiasm. The first task to present itself to him as Proprietor was to encourage and promote the trade in narcissus, to offset the economic difficulties of the island. He at once set about daffodil trials, which he conducted with military precision, at first importing some 250 bulbs from the Continent. He has left from these times a stock-book, *Narcissus List 1882,* and an untitled planting list for 1884-7 which record, in meticulous detail, the planting, flowering dates, descriptions and quality of around 350 bulbs. This same attention to detail he applied to the garden itself, recording in a ledger all, it would seem, of the invoices for plant deliveries to the estate, which is exceedingly valuable for dating introductions, and as evidence of their origin.

During this period articles were beginning to appear in the horticultural journals, but among them one stands out as of the greatest importance. After an excursion from the Penzance Natural History Society to the Abbey Gardens in 1889, A. Henwood Teague contributed to their *Transactions* in 1891 a list of 'Plants growing in Tresco Abbey Gardens', in number 837. It is virtually certain that this inventory, compiled with the cooperation of Dorrien Smith himself, was intended at that juncture to be a definitive list. However, in 1906, towards the end of his life, Dorrien Smith decided to publish privately his own catalogue. A copy of this small book, containing the names of more than 1 670 plants, thereafter was always left in the billiard room of the Abbey so that he, or any of his friends or relations, could add their comments, of which there are several on every page. This invaluable version now resides in the archives.

Unlike his father, Major Arthur Dorrien Smith, who succeeded to the estate in 1918, was already an amateur botanist of ability, and it was during his tenancy that a complete inventory of the plants at Tresco was drawn up, which, by 1935 had been entered into a card index. This recorded the name of every plant that was known to have been brought into the garden, together with its date and source of introduction. Since that time the index has been regularly updated, acquisitions entered, and the names revised, until, in accordance with current practice, it was recently transferred to a computer database.

Major Dorrien Smith died in 1955. A few years later, there appeared a duplicated inventory with the title *Tresco Abbey Gardens, ... Lists of Trees, Shrubs and Plants. October, 1959*. It comprises three lists: I. Trees and Shrubs [974 plants], II. Cacti & Succulents, and other Xerophytic plants, including Bromeliacaea [507], and III. Herbaceous Plants and Ferns, bulbous & tuberous plants [385]. This was the first comprehensive printed list (outside of the card index), to cover adequately succulent and herbaceous plants. Other than that certain symbols indicate that it might have emanated from Kew, the origin of this valuable document is not known. The only complete copies that I was able to locate were those in the libraries of Kew and the Royal Horticultural Society.

In conclusion, a brief mention must be made of the typescript 'Catalogue of Plants' drawn up in 1985 by Peter Clough, the then head gardener, with the assistance of K. Spencer. This was an advance on all previous lists since, as well as entering the names, families, and dates of introduction, it was the first time that the actual locations of the plants in the garden were given. This catalogue was printed in full at the end of Ronald King's book, *Tresco: England's Island of Flowers*, 1985 (although regrettably without due acknowledgement), where it is now easily accessible. Unfortunately the storms of 1987 and 1988 caused so much havoc that this estimable catalogue has now been reduced to the level of an historic account of what once was.

Present-day plant recording

As the half century since the publication of Thurston's classic survey drew near, the Cornwall Garden Society felt that it was time for the book to be updated. At first the late Major Walter Magor took this in hand, but during the 1980s he was joined by Dr David Hunt, a taxonomist from Kew, and Chairman of the International Dendrological Society, who began the systematic mapping, labelling and recording of trees in major collections, such as those at Bosahan, Lanarth, Pencarrow and Trebah. During this same period Michael Lear was engaged by the National Trust and the Tresco Abbey Gardens to compile similar records, and comprehensive plant lists were also undertaken at Antony and Mount Edgcumbe. Some individual garden owners, such as Peter Bickford-Smith at Trevarno, had indeed already been inspired to begin keeping their own records, but in 1989 a meeting was held by the IDS at Tregothnan, with the express object of encouraging other owners of collections to follow suit, by using their well tried and standard methods of recording. At three major Shows of the Cornwall Garden Society, in 1987, 1988 and 1989, exhibitions of Cornish daffodils, rhododendrons, and magnolias were mounted, the fruit of their preliminary research being preserved in their archives.

Following upon all this activity, the Cornwall Biological Record Unit at Pool (an extension of Exeter University) agreed in principal to set aside space on their computer for the creation of a database of cultivated trees and shrubs in the county, to supplement their already uniquely extensive coverage of indigenous plants. These scattered projects should, however, be interpreted rather as pointers to the future, than as a record of solid achievement. Even so, David Hunt, now retired from Kew, has already set up his own personal database containing the names and locations of several thousand trees, which together with the increasing interest in the county for the recording of gardens and their plants, augurs well for the future.

Garden Types and Features

The purpose of this index is to provide a representative selection of the more prominent or unusual features in the gardens recorded in the topography. A brief identification of the nature of the items is supplied where it seems necessary, as well as their date and period; the names of designers are also added, where known, together with the English Heritage gradings. In a few cases references have been made to monographs or articles on specific subjects, chiefly those referring to Cornwall, but also more generally, for any who seek further information. Sections on public cemeteries and parks, not listed in the topography, have been included, since they are currently arousing interest among garden historians. In most cases the terminology used is that found in Symes (1993). Discretion, and the wishes of owners, has necessitated the omission, or withholding the location of certain important, though transportable artifacts, in consequence of the prevalence of garden theft. Only items mentioned in published works, or publicly on view in open gardens, have been included. The page numbers of the various sites will be found in the *Index of Places*.

A

ALCOVE
Gyllyngdune, grotto seat
Lis Escop, former summer-house
Mount Edgcumbe, Thomson's Seat II
Trewan, now empty

AMERICAN GARDEN, *plantations of conifers, rhododendrons etc.*
Glynn
Pencarrow
Pentillie
Rosecraddock
Trebartha

AMPHITHEATRE
Acton Castle, sunken garden
Mount Edgcumbe, 'Walls of Paradise'
Pine Lodge, pinetum

APPROACH (Repton), see DRIVE

AQUARIUM
Victoria Park, Truro, 1898

ARBORETUM, *collection of trees,* see also AMERICAN GARDENS and PINETUM.
Bosahan
Carclew
Coldrenick, relict
Enys
Heligan
Menabilly, eucalyptus etc.
Penjerrick

Pine Lodge, 1980s
Tregrehan
Trewithen

ARBOUR
Hall Walk, summer-houses 17C
Mary Newman's Cottage
St Michael's Mount, 'bower house', 18-19C

AVENUE, *a selection.*
Behan Park, May trees, now gone
Bicton, beech, now gone
Heligan, of *Cornus capitata, c.* 1830s, being replanted
Lancarffe, Japanese maple, 1936
Landue, oak 1820-7
Lanhydrock, 3 rows each side, planted originally in 1648
Lavethan, oak
Marlborough House, Bull's Avenue, Cornish Elm
Newton Ferrers, *Tilia platyphyllos* and *T.x europaea*
Pencarrow, *Auracaria*
Peheale, lime
Pennans, 18C extinct
Penpol, cut down 1980
Rosehill, Falmouth, of '*Dracaenas*'
Scorrier, *Sequoiadendron giganteum*, later 19C, now gone
Trelowarren, 'Ilex Avenue'

Tremough, lime
Trewin, Copper Beech.
[See *Banks* (1991: 192)]

AVIARY
Ken Caro, also water fowl
Paradise Park, bird sanctuary
Tremayne Cottage

B

BALUSTRADE
Newton Ferrers, 17C I [see *Jekyll* (1918)]
Porthgwidden, on terrace
Tregrehan, in parterre
Tregullow, north of house
Westbourne House, garden terrace

BAMBOO COLLECTION
Bosahan, early 19C
Burncoose, Mrs Powys Rogers, 1890s
Caerhays Castle, 1890s
Carwinion, late 20C
Heligan, late 19C
Lanarth, 1890s
Menabilly, late 1890s
Penjerrick, 19C
Trevethoe, Bamboo Walk
[See *Townsend* (1990)]

BANANA HOUSE
Heligan
Torfrey

BANDSTAND see PUBLIC PARKS

BANQUETING HOUSE, *usually for light meals;* see also GAZEBO

Enys
Kenegie
Pelyn

BARBICAN, *a gatehouse with an upper room, intended for defensive purposes;* see GATEHOUSE

BARK HOUSE, see also LOG, MOSS and ROOT HOUSES
Lismore House, mid 19C.

BATH HOUSE, *either with a bath, or as a dressing room*

Antony, by Parlby 18C II
Boconnoc, 19C II
Mount Edgcumbe, II
Penrose, *c.* 1837 II
Pentillie Castle, *c.* 1850 II
Porthgwidden, late 19C
Scawns, late 20C incorporating earlier material

BATTERY, *a terrace with cannon.*

Bosahan
Mount Edgcumbe, II
Port Eliot, c. mid 19C II
Prideaux Place, 18C II
St Michael's Mount

BEE BOLES
Godolphin
Heligan, 19C
Trewoofe
[See *Foster* (1988);
Robertson (1979)]

BELL TOWER
Torfrey
Trevarno, boathouse
with bell-cote spire

BOATHOUSE
Chymorvah, boat-pen
Clowance
Port Eliot, mid-late 19C
II
Porthgwidden, Swiss
style
Tehidy
Trebartha, with grotto
Tregothnan
Trevarno, neo-Gothic,
late 19C

BOG GARDEN, see also
WATER GARDEN
Lower Hamatethy, along
stream
Trelidden, along stream
Trengwainton, 'Stream
Garden'
Trevarno, end of lake,
1920s
Trewoofe, mill stream

BOTANIC GARDEN
Churchtown Farm,
Lanlivery
Trelowarren, [see
G. Mag. (1830: 420)]

BOTHY, *gardeners'
lodgings.*
Bosloe
Lismore House, as
eye-catcher, dated
1839 II
Trengwainton II

BOWLING GREEN,
common in the 17C.
Behan Park, ancient
Calstock Parsonage, 17C
[see p. 18]
Clowance
Cotehele
Erisey, 17C
Hall Walk, 17C
Port Eliot, mid 19C
Werrington Park, on site
of churchyard

BRIDGE
Caerhays, late 19C II
Chyverton, c. 1780 II*
Lamellen, c. mid 19C II
Penjerrick, footbridge to
lower garden, 19C
Penrose, c. 1847
Pentillie, Swiss Bridge,
1813, designed by
Irwin Kennedy,
Hammersmith
Prideaux Place,
footbridge, c. 19C II*
footbridge with
fortifications, 19C II*
Rosecraddock, mid-late
19C II
St Columb Old Rectory,
over moat, with walls
and gate, II*
Trebartha, two, II
Trelissick, to Carcaddon
gardens, in reinforced
concrete
Trelowarren, Ton
Bridge, 1840s
Werrington, wooden
'White Bridge', 18C,
burnt and rebuilt II
'Duchess's Bridge',
19C

BRODERIE or 'Parterre de
Broderie', *with paths of
coloured stones.*
Lanhydrock, by Gilbert
Scott, 1857
Tregothnan, by
Vulliamy, 1845-8
Tregrehan, by Nesfield,
1843
[See *Banks* (1991)]

C
CACTUS HOUSE
Old Rectory, Marazion

CANAL, *a long, parallel-
sided lake.*
Ince Castle, canal pool,
post-1960
Penheale Manor, long
straight-sided lake
Trevethoe, serpentine
Whiteford

CANNON, see BATTERY

CARRIAGE RIDE, *a scenic
tour of an estate.*
Boconnoc, 6-mile circuit
Clowance, 'Green Drive'
Pelyn, through woods
Tregothnan, 4 miles
along river
Trelissick, through
woods with vistas of
the river

CARRIAGE RING, *for
turning vehicles at the
house entrance.*
Carwinion, late 18C
Castle, with central
pond and fountain
Catchfrench, by Repton,
1793
Tregrehan, by Nesfield,
c. 1843

CARRIAGE WASH
Stowe, late 17C II

CASCADE, *water falling
by steps.*
Heligan, in Ravine
Tehidy, 18C
Trelidden, natural
Trevarno, into lake
Trevillet, natural; St
Nectan's Kieve

CASTELLATED HOUSES
Acton Castle, by Wood,
c. 1775 II*
Arwenack, 16C
Boconnoc, 16C
Bosahan Castle,
(demolished)
Castle, c. 1840 II
Catchfrench, by
Rawlinson, c. 1780 II
Cotehele, 14C I
Godolphin, from 16C I
Lanhydrock, 17C I
Lavethan, 17C
gatehouse II
Mount Edgcumbe,
Roger Palmer, 1554
Pentillie Castle, by
Wilkins senr and jnr,
1810-15 II*
Place, Fowey, I
Port Eliot, by Soane, and
Harrison 18C I
Prideaux Place, by
Edmund Prideaux,
17C I
Restormel House, late
18C II
St Michael's Mount, I
Tregenna Castle, by
Wood, 1774
Tregothnan, by Wilkins
jnr, 1816-18 I
Trelowarren, 17C I
Treworgan, 19C
entrance tower

CASTLES, *real and
pseudo.*
Acton Castle, by Wood,
1773
Bosahan Castle, 19C,
demolished 1950s
Carn Brea, see Tehidy
Castle, on ancient site

Castle Horneck, named
after ancient earthwork
Ince Castle
Launceston Castle, ruin
Liskeard Castle, extinct
Pengersick Castle,
fortified house, 16C
Pentillie Castle,
1810-15
Restormel Castle, ruin
Riviere Castle, an
ancient site
Tintagel Castle, ruin
Tregenna Castle, by
Wood, 1774
Trematon Castle, ruin

CATARACT *i.e. with a
sheer drop.*
Boconnoc, high, but
small
Lamorran House, small
Pengreep, between
lakes
Rosecraddock, twin,
from high ground

CEMETERIES: *those laid
out by the Burial Boards,
with their dates, as
recorded in the Kelly's
Directories are listed
below, but are not
included in the
topography.*
Bodmin, New Cemetery
1893
Callington, 1877
Charlestown, 1901
Egloshayle, 1857,
enlarged 1894
Falmouth, 1857 [see
Brooks (1989: 134)]
Fowey, 1873, enlarged
1890 and 1919
Launceston, 1855
Lostwithiel, Burial
Ground, 1857
Madron, 1880
Mevagissey, 1882
Newquay, 1874, New
Cemetery, 1896
Padstow, 1881
Paul, 1879
Polperro, 1897
Pool, 1880
Redruth, 1878 [see
Brooks (1989: 173)]
St Austell, 1878
St Blazey, 1862
St Columb, 1856,
enlarged 1878 and
1924
St Columb Minor, 1874,
enlarged 1909
St Gluvias, Burial
Ground, 1871

St Hilary, New
Cemetery, 1893
St Ives, 1855
St Minver, enlarged
1878
St Stephen in Brannel,
1876
Treslothan, 1885
Truro, Burial Ground,
1878 [see *Brooks*
(1989: 173)]
[See *Brooks* (1989)]

CHAPELS or **CHURCHES**,
*associated with the
houses of parks and
gardens in the
topography.*
Alverton, Edmund
Sedding, 1910, II*
Bake, in house, 20C
Boconnoc, church I
Budock Vean, former
Celtic chapel
Carclew, now a
dwelling, II*
Clowance, now gone
Colquite, in ruins
Cotehele, *c.* 1490 II*
Downes, Convent
chapel, 20C
Erisey, ruin
Gyllyngdune,
oratory/gazebo, mid
19C
Hall, ruin
Hexworthy, in house,
c. 1700 II
Lanhydrock, parish
church I
Lis Escop, now
Copeland Court,
Convent, formerly
Bishop's residence
Mount Edgcumbe, Rame
Head Chapel of St
Michael II*
Menacuddle, II*
Place, Anthony, 16C
Port Eliot, 12C
Priory, Bodmin, on site of
Restormel House, on
site of extinct Trinity
Chapel
St Benet's Priory
St Cadix, Priory ruins
11C
St Michael's Mount
Tehidy, 'Lady Mary's
Retreat'
Trelowarren,
Strawberry Hill Gothic
Trenython, post 1891
when Bishop's
residence
Trethill House, now a
music room

Trewarne, over holy
well 11C, relict
Trewinnard, now gone
Trist House Lodge,
masonry from St Nun's
Chapel
Wivelscombe, medieval
ruins, 14C?
Werrington, parish
church of St Martin,
1742 I

CHURCHYARD, *several of
the churchyards cited in
Thurston (1930) are
listed in the topography;
the remainder, with
those noticed by Gilbert
have been included
below, with their
references.*
Duloe (*Thurston* 215)
Gulval, exotic planting
Gwithian, fig tree
Kea (*Thurston* 103)
Lanhydrock (*Thurston*
183)
Lawhitton, with trees
Manaccan, fig tree
Mylor (*Thurston* 273,
275)
Newlyn East, fig tree
Newlyn West, olive tree,
extinct
Perranzabuloe
(*Thurston* 101)
St Austell Old
Churchyard (*Thurston*
201)
St Breock (*Gilbert* 1820:
ii. 643)
St Just in Roseland
South Petherwin
(*Gilbert* 1820: ii. 490)
[see *Bailey* (1994)]

CISTERN, *rectangular lead
containers for rainwater.*
Churchtown, Morval,
dated 1753
Ince Castle, similar to
Morval, with same date

CLAIREVOIE, *gate
through which a view
can be seen.*
Antony, late 19C II

CLOCK TOWER
Alverton, entrance
tower by Ninian
Comper, 1898 II*
Bochym, probably 1887
II
Calenick, dated 1752 II*
Enys, Italian 1840 II
Porthgwidden, *c.* 1855
II

Tregothnan, by Wilkins
1816-18 II*
Trelowarren, on stables,
18C
Trewithen, coach-house
1840 by Edwards I
Treworgey, dated 1733
II

COACH HOUSE, see also
STABLES
Killagorden, late 18C II
Killiow II*
Trewinnard, early 18C
II*
Trewithen, by Edwards
1840 I
Werrington, probably
18C II

COADE STONE, *artificial
stone from the Coade
factory.*
Mount Edgcumbe,
Timothy Brett
monument, 1791 II
Tehidy, statue of
Farnese (or Antonine)
Flora
two tigers, 1799, now
gone
Trelowarren, two urns,
1813, damaged
Whiteford, relief on
Temple
[see *Kelly* (1990)]

COCK PIT
Pencarrow
Trewithen, now a
rockery
Werrington, two with
terraces

COLONNADE see LOGGIA

COMPARTMENT or
ROOMS, *a garden with
separate sections.*
Penheale Manor II
Penpol House
Trehane

CONSERVATORY
Bosvigo, 19C now
detached
Downes, by J.D.
Sedding *c.* 1868, now
gone
Gyllyngdune, post 1840,
demolished
Killiow, demolished
Lismore, 19C II
Penlee House, 19C II
Polstrong, two-storey,
with aisles II
Raffles, mid-19C
Rosehill, Penzance
Scorrier
Tregullow, Victorian II

Trevarno, cottage folly
etc, 1840s

COTTAGE GARDEN,
*informal with mixed
plantings.*
Mary Newman's Cottage
Penpol House, 'Grey
Garden'

COTTAGE ORNÉE, *rustic,
usually assymetric
buildings, often with
decorated
weatherboarding; see
also* LODGES.
Penjerrick, 'Guest
House' II
Rosemorran, thatched
with Gothic features
II*

COURTYARD, *within or
attached to the house.*
Boconnoc II
Bosahan, courtyard
garden
Erisey, relict II
Godolphin, relict
Lavethan II
Penheale, inner and
around the house II
Porthgwidden, *c.*1855 II
Tonacombe, with three
inner courts, and a
'Pleasaunce' I
Tredinnick II
Trewarne, *c.*1645 II*
Trewinnard, early 18C
II*

CREMATORIUM GARDEN
Penmount, Memorial
rose garden

CRINKLE CRANKLE, *see*
SERPENTINE

CROSS, *ancient, listed or
Ancient Monuments.*
Boconnoc AM
Clowance, 3 medieval II
Heligan, pre-Conquest
II
Lancarffe, *c.* 15C AM
Lanhydrock, in
church-yard II
Treffry Cross II
Lanteglos by Camelford
Lavethan, three, one
medieval? II
Lis Escop, on sundial,
from pinnacle of St
Mary's Church, Truro
Menabilly, II
Morrab Gardens, II
Old Vicarage,
Perranarworthal,
incised, removed from
Glebe II

Penberth, pre-Conquest II
Penlee Gardens, AM II
Rosemorran, wheel-head II
St Benet's, on pinnacle, 15C II
St Just in Penwith, two
Scorrier, two medieval AM
Tonacombe, 'Red Cross Stone', II*
Trebartha, four by well
Trewarne, 15C lantern cross, now in St Neot's churchyard

CULVER HOUSE, *the usual name for a Dovecote in Cornwall.*

D
DAIRY
Port Eliot, ornamental, early 19C (now house) II
Prideaux Place, grotto, early 19C II*
Scorrier, 'Folly Dairy'

DEER HOUSE
Mount Edgcumbe, Upper and Lower II

DEER PARKS, *surviving.*
Boconnoc, 15C
Prideaux Place, c.1770
Tregothnan, pre-1730
Trelawne, walls, perhaps of 17C deer park II
[see section on Deer Parks, for former parks]

DEER SLADE, *'slade' is a term current chiefly in western counties for a 'breadth of green-sward in plough'd land or in plantations', or between banks.*
Castick, in Northhill, [see p. 262]
Godolphin
Newton Ferrers, shown alongside the house on sketch by Prideaux (1716: 68)?

DEER STILE, *allowing deer in, but not out.*
Erisey, *c.* 18C II

DEMONSTRATION GARDEN
Probus

DIPPING POOL, *for cleaning pots, and watering.*
Castle, in walled garden
Heligan, in walled garden

DOG or **PET'S CEMETERY**, *see also* KENNELS
Clowance
Lanteglos by Camelford, headstone
Mount Edgcumbe
Point Neptune, on St Catherine's Point
St Michael's Mount, in Civil War redoubt
Tehidy
Tredethy
Trevarno, 1920s

DOVECOTE, or **CULVER HOUSE**

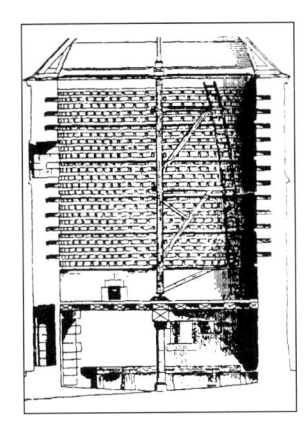

Antony 1. Elizabethan II* 2. remains 1700-20 II
Bochym
Boconnoc, early 18C II
Carclew
Cotehele, late 16C early 17C reconstructed, II*
Croan, remains II
Crooked Park, modern on pole
Garlenick, 18C, demolished 1940
Glynn, [see Prideaux sketch 1727]
Harlyn, unusual ornamental type c.18C II*
Heligan, modern on pole
Ince Castle
Ken Caro, modern on pole
Lamorran Rectory, medieval (now gone)
Long Cross, medieval reproduction 20C
Meudon
Moditonham, folly II
Nanswhyden, ruin
Penheale, 18C II
Penwarne
Place, Anthony, ruin 13C?
Prideaux Place
Rosteague, ruin, perhaps 13C II
Tregeare, gazebo, originally a dovecote, II
Trelowarren, William and Mary
Trematon Castle
Trenarren
Trenowth
Trewoofe, Tudor, also a gazebo

in addition, the following have place or field names on their estates which include the word 'Culver':-
Castle
Caerhays Castle
St Cadix
Trewin
Trethill
Waterloo Villa, now Klymiarvan = 'culver field'
[see *Hansell* (1988); *Henderson* (1928); *Penhallurick* (1978); *Robertson* (1979)]

DOVE or **PIGEON HOLES**
Bosloe, in eaves of Bothy
Clowance, in kitchen garden II
Croan, II
Penwarne
St Michael's Mount, built into rock crevices
Sandhill, late 18C II
Tredinnick, in wall of house II
Trevethoe

DRIVE, or **APPROACH** (Repton), *selected examples of a common feature.*
Carclew
Lanhydrock, through an impressive avenue
Mount Edgcumbe, with bridge II
Pencarrow, with fine trees
Place, Fowey, with tunnel
Rosecraddock
Stoketon, along ha-ha
Tonacombe, 'The Street'
Trewidden, between stone 'hedges'

E
EMBANKMENT
Landulph Parsonage, to reclaim land
Moditonham, to reclaim land
Port Eliot, to reclaim land
Price's Folly, see Trengwainton

ENGLISH GARDEN
Mount Edgcumbe

ENTRANCE PILLARS, *see also* GATE-PIERS.
Arwenack, early 18C, now detached II
Bochym, c.1699
Erisey, with ball finials dated 1640 II
Newton Ferrers, with ball finials 17C I [see *Jekyll* (1918)]
Rame Place, with unusual finials, II
Trebursye, pyramidal finials, 1840-50 II
Tregenna (Michaelstow) House, 1876 II
Tregullow, and walls c.1830 II
Trewince, with eagles, early 19C II

ESTRADE, *'trees trained or clipped to form successive tiers surrounding the trunk', e.g. see:-*
Hexworthy
Prideaux Place

ESTRAY, *'any beast not wild, found within any Lordship, and not owned by any man.'* Legal term.
Estray Park, originally the pound for Kerrier Hundred

EXEDRA, *essentially a permeable structure, usually semicircular, through which a prospect may be viewed; but in England often a semicircle of statues backed by a hedge or stone work.*
Pendarves, on ha-ha

EXOTIC PLANTING, *the 'acclimatisation of exotics' was widely practised in Cornwall, especially in the Falmouth, Truro and Penzance areas; see also* SUB-TROPICAL GARDENS

304 Garden Types and Features

EYE-CATCHER, *to create a point of interest in the landscape.*
   Carnanton, schoolhouse, 1845 II
   Chyverton, 'Hunters' Tower', late 18C
   Lismore, garden house dated 1839 II
   Tregothnan, ruined Church at Kea
   Wivelscombe, cottage, eye-catcher to Antony, mid 19C II

F

FERME ORNÉE, *'mixing the useful and profitable Parts of Gard'ning with the Pleasurable ...'* Switzer 1715.
   Killiow
   Trewarthenick

FERNERY
   Bosahan, tree ferns
   Ferny Park, Bossiney
   Furzball Cottage
   Heligan, in Ravine
   Penjerrick, adjoining the original house
   Tremough, in rockery
   Trewidden, Fern Pit

FISH POND, *ornamental, see also STEW POND.*
   Menacuddle, with gold and silver fish, 1889
   Morrab Gardens, with goldfish c.1895
   Old Vicarage, Perranarworthal
   Trebah, with Koi Carp
   Tremayne Cottage
   Tremough, with gold and silver fish
   Victoria Park, Truro, 1898

FOLLY, *the eccentric, excessive, expensive, or useless.*
   Arwenack, pyramid 1773 II
   Boconnoc, Obelisk 1771 II
   Caerhays Castle, by Nash 1808 I [see *Jones* (1974: 298)]
   Caerhays, Folly Tower by Nash 1808 I
   Carwinion, 'The Rogers' Tower', late 18C, collapsed 1930
   Chyverton, 'Hunters' Tower' late 18C
   Clowance, classical style gazebo II
   'folly in the wood' Cotehele, Prospect Tower, 18C II*
   Lismore, rock arch
   Long Cross, small tower, Victorian
   Marlborough House, Oriental Summer-house, extinct
   Moditonham, Folly Dovecote II
   Mount Edgcumbe, Monument to Timothy Brett 18C II
   Ruin c.1750 II
   Thomson's Seat II
   Pentillie Castle, SW lodge, 18C II
   Tillie Mausoleum Tower, early 18C II*
   Port Eliot, wooden lattice-work elephant, late 20C.
   Price's Folly, see Trengwainton
   Scorrier, Folly Dairy
   Thanckes, mock medieval tower [see *Pevsner* 1970: 221]
   Trelissick, Water Tower c. 1860
   Trelowarren, Folly Turret Gothic 'Folly' windows in Lady Vyvyan's Garden
   Trenant Park, Temple (demolished)
   Tresco, Valhalla
   Trevarno, cottage folly on outside of walled garden, with conservatory inside, c. 1840
   Trewarne, possibly the gatehouse, 19C II
   Treworgey, 'Chinese' clock tower 1733 II
   Werrington, Terrace House = 'Hermitage' mid 18C II
   'Tomb of the Horatii', early-mid 18C. II
   [see *Headley* (1986); *Jones* (1974); *Whitelaw* (1990)]

FOUNTAIN, *selected examples.*
   Lancarffe
   Maidenwell, memorial
   Morrab Gardens
   Mount Edgcumbe, in Italian Garden, and two others II
   Pencarrow, Italian copy, late 19C II
   Port Eliot, 1913 II
   Tregenna House, c. 1869 now dismantled, [see *Lake* (1870: iii. 358)]
   Tregrehan, in parterre Dolphin fountain in walled garden, both by Nesfield, 1843
   Trevarno, cast-iron Victoria Park, Truro, 1898

FRENCH GARDEN
   Mount Edgcumbe, 'The French House' and Orangery II
   Rosteague, 'French Garden', late 17C

FRUIT STORE
   Enys, apple store
   Tregeare, apple-loft converted from dovecote II

G

GAME LARDER
   Trebah, mid-late 19C II
   Tregeare, converted from Dovecote II

GARDEN, *an area cultivated, usually in a formal manner, and often enclosed, which Gilbert (and others) distinguish from parks, plantations and shrubberies.*

GATEHOUSE, see also BARBICAN and LODGE.
   Lanhydrock, mid 17C I
   Lavethan, c. 17C II
   Penberth, by Drewitt of Penzance, c. 1912 II
   Penheale, for Paul Specott, c. 1636 I
   Place, Fowey
   Port Eliot, c. 1840 II*
   Scawns, with arch
   Tregothnan, by Vulliamy, 1845-8 II [see *Mowl* (1985)]
   Trewan, part of house II*
   Trewarne, to courtyard garden, 19C? II

GATE-PIERS, *listed examples.*
   Bonython, and walls II
   Croan, c. 18C II
   Garlenick, dated 1685 II
   Hengar, II
   Kenegie, with obelisk finials II
   Lambesso, detached, late 17C. II
   Manaton, at gate II at entrance to grounds surmounted by hounds
   Newton Ferrers, with ball finials, 17C I [see *Jekyll* (1918)]
   Penheale, and walls, 16C reused, II*
   with walls and gate c. 18C I
   Rame, with finials II
   Sandhill II
   Skisdon Lodge II
   Tonacombe, with eagles, perhaps from Stowe, II
   Trebursye, with pyramidal finials, 1840-50 II
   Tredinnick II
   Tregeare II
   Tregenna (Michaelstow) House, 1872 II
   Tregullow, 'linked by unusual stone railings' II
   Trelaske, removed from Lydcott II
   Trewince, with eagles II
   Truthan II
   Werrington, to north and south lodges II

GATES, *see under*, RAILINGS and GATES

GATEWAY
   Caerhays, by Nash, 1808 I
   Prideaux Place, mock fortification pre-1758 I
   South entrance, pre-1758 II*
   St Columb Old Rectory, over moat II*
   Trevose, dated 'A.N. 1646'
   Tregeare, reconstruction with date-stone, 1582
   Trewardale, ruin with date-stone, 1680

GAZEBO, *summer, or banqueting house, with a view from the upper floor, typically with a store beneath, often attached to a wall.*
   Chymorvah, a pair, c. 1860 II
   Clowance, gardener's office II
   Garlenick, early 18C II
   Gyllyngdune, gazebo/ oratory, post-1840
   Kenegie, mid 18C II
   Marlborough House, now a residence
   Pelyn, extinct

Prideaux House, with screen wall II
Stowe, 1679, demolished
Tehidy, formerly 'Lady Basset's Retreat', 19C
Trefusis, 'pleasure house' with 'prospect' early 18C
Tregeare, thatched, converted from dovecote II
Trehane, 'temple or pleasure house', to watch trains, 1861
Trewoofe, Tudor dovecote/gazebo

GEOMETRICAL GARDEN, *using squares, rectangles or circles.*
Downes, by J.D. Sedding, *c.* 1868
Penheale, 1920s
Trenowth, 1920s

GOTHICK, *used to distinguish revivals or imitations, but not used with any consistency among writers; see* LODGES *etc.*

GREENHOUSE, *selected examples of an almost universal feature.*
Churchtown Farm, training greenhouse, 1974
Gyllyngdune, on terrace, demolished
Heligan, various
Port Eliot, in walled garden
Porthgwidden, [see *JRHS* (1852: 24)]
Tremough, eight specialized

GROTTO
Clowance, from a former fireplace, 18C
Gyllyngdune, grotto/seat
Heligan, in rockery
Lamorran House, in Japanese Garden
Luxulyan Vicarage (see Water Meadow), three grottoes II
Menabilly, late 18C II [see *Jones*, 1974: 298-9]
Mount Edgcumbe, 18C II
Pencarrow, *c.* 1840 II
Pendarves, or 'fossilary' *c.* 1747

Penjerrick, alongside lake, 1837 relict 'fern grotto', extinct
Port Eliot, in Craggs Wood, 18C
Prideaux Place, Grotto-dairy early 19C II*
Grotto niche in terrace *c.* 1740 II*
— by horse trough, 19C II
St Michael's Mount, 'St Michael's Cave'
Scorrier, 'Quartz Grotto Garden'
Stowe, *c.* 1679 demolished
Trebartha, boathouse
Tregye, in Happy Valley
Tremorvah, early 19C, demolished
Tremough, like Lourdes, 1943
Trevarno, in rockery, 19C

GROVE, *a group of trees, usually of a single species; often an early feature.*
Menabilly, 'Hooker Grove'
Morrab Gardens 'palm grove'
Trefusis, early 18C.
Trenython, of maples, late 1940s

H
HA-HA, *listed and notable examples.*

Behan Park, 19C
Bosloe
Clowance, around 'Horse Field', 17C
Gonvena, *c.* 1790 II
Pendarves, pre-1758 in form of an 'exedra'
Lavethan, *c.* 18C II
Mount Edgcumbe, II
Scorrier, later 18C II
Tregothnan, 1816-18, Wilkins, improved 1845-8 by Vulliamy, II
Trewardale, *c.* 18C II
Trewarthenick, now with mature yews

Werrington II [See *Banks* (1991: 194)]

HANGING WOOD, *trees on a steep slope, obscuring the summit; there are many examples in Cornwall, e.g.*
Meudon
Penrose
Rosecraddock
Trebartha
Trelawne
Trelissick

HEATHER GARDEN
Eden Valley, 1930s
Maidenwell, recent
Tremeer, post-1960s

HEDGES, *notable examples.*
Antony, yew hedge
Godolphin, old box hedge
Ken Caro, windbreak
Penheale, yew 'parterre'

HERB GARDEN
Chymorvah
Colquite, recent
Mary Newman's Cottage, recent
The Old Herbary, nursery
Trelidden, 1980s

HERMITAGE
Menacuddle, 'rustic' building
Tremorvah, early 19C extinct
Werrington, 'Terrace House' mid 18C possibly = Hermitage II

HORTUS CONCLUSUS, *a medieval enclosed garden, often associated with the BV Mary.*
Ladies Garden, Star Castle, Scilly
Tintagel Castle, medieval, relict
Tonacombe, the 'Pleasaunce'

HUNTING LODGE or **BOX**
Mount Edgcumbe
Tehidy, Carn Brea
Wivelscombe, also an 'eye-catcher'

I
ICE-HOUSE

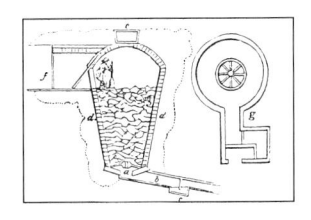

Catchfrench, in the ruins
Chyverton [see *Old Cornwall* (1965)]
Cotehele, 18C II
Mount Edgcumbe, II
Pelyn, near extinct summer-house
Pencarrow, *c.* late 18C II
Penjerrick [see *Notes and Queries* 22.1. 1941: 137]
Pentillie, late 18C II
Polwhele
St Michael's Mount, 18-19C
Tehidy, by lake, now gone, 1781
Trebartha
Tregullow, in a tunnel
Trengwainton, 1814
Werrington, a 'good example' II
[see *Beaman* (1990); *Buxbaum* (1992); *Robertson* (1988)]

ITALIAN GARDEN
Glynn, 19C relict
Heligan, modelled on those in Pompeii, 19C
Lamorran House, 1980s
Mount Edgcumbe, late 18C II*
Pencalenick, late 19C, relict
Pencarrow, 1840s
Tremough, 19C relict
Trevarno, 19C, re-designed 20C

J
JAPANESE GARDEN
Heligan, former name of lower garden
'The Japanese Garden', St Mawgan
Ken Caro, small, 1980s
Lamorran House, 1980s
Pine Lodge, under construction

K
KENNELS, *notable examples*
Carnanton II
Mount Edgcumbe II
Tehidy

KITCHEN GARDEN, *walled gardens (q.v.) used for vegetables etc., as distinct from other purposes: principally listed examples.*
Clowance, with gazebo, boiler house etc. II
Croan, with two pavilions, gates etc. II

Garden Types and Features 305

Heligan, early 19C II
Killiow, with 'crinkle-crankle' wall, 18C II
Lamellen, mid-19C II
Lanhydrock, 1694 II
Lismore, mid-19C II
Morval Churchtown, with curved end to conserve the heat of the sun
Nanswhyden, late 18C early 19C II
Pencarrow, late 18C II
Pennans, early-mid 18C II
Pentillie, early 19C II
Port Eliot, quartered by walls
Porthgwidden, c. 1855 II
Rosecraddock, terraced without walls, relict
Sandhill, late 18C with reset date-stone 1637 II
Trefusis, II
Trelissick, c. mid 19C II
Trelowarren, former Botanic Garden
Melon Garden
Treneere, late 18C 'with ramp coping' II
Trengwainton, with ramped beds 1814 II
Trereife, 18C II
Trevaylor II
Trevethoe, with intact boiler-house
Trewidden, with ramped beds, mid 19C II
Trewin, late 18C early 19C II
Werrington, 18C early 19C II

KNOT GARDEN, see PARTERRE, 'knot garden' became a generic term for any elaborately patterned garden.

L

LADIES GARDEN, usually signifies 'Our Lady's Garden', a medieval hortus conclusus (q.v.).
Enys, 'Ladies Garden', origin uncertain

LAKE, a 'sheet of water' usually of irregular shape with natural edges.
Bonython, 'Lake Joy', in three parts
Carclew, 'Higher Pond', and 'Wheel Pond'
Chyverton, serpentine
Clowance
Enys, two
Killiganoon, seven in succession down valley
Lamorran Rectory, dammed river
Lanteglos by Camelford
Manaton, probably from stew-ponds
Newton Ferrers
Ogbeare Hall, 2 acres with islands
Pencarrow
Pendarves
Pengreep, three linked by cascades
Penheale, two, probably from stew ponds
Penjerrick, in lower garden
Penwarne, near house, and pool in valley
Pine Lodge, two
Port Eliot
Priory, Bodmin, possibly from stew-ponds
Rosecraddock
Saveock, now gone
Tehidy
Trebartha, the 'Swan Pond'
Trago Mills, from damming the river
Tregye, two pools
Trenance Gardens, boating lake
Trevarno, 1840, enlarged after 1870s
Trevethoe, made from canal
Werrington, serpentine

LAWN, term used for 'well-maintained fields used not for grazing cattle, but as a setting for ornamental trees and shrubs', e.g. see:

Boconnoc [Gilbert, 1820: 910]
Lanwithan
Menabilly [see Fig. 61]

LODGE, principally listed examples; see also GATEHOUSE and ENTRANCE PILLARS.
Antony, by Repton II
Bosahan, cottage ornée, late 19C II
Caerhays, Gothic, Nash 1808 II [see Mowl (1985)]
Catchfrench, near Hessenford road
Glynn, with railings, c. 1830 II
Killagorden, early 19C Gothic II
Killiow, detached cottage ornée
Landue, dated 1816, 'Picturesque Gothic' II
Lanhydrock, a pair II*
Mellingey, 'Bay Tree Lodge', now detached II
Moditonham, twin, late 18C II
Morval, 'Steppes Lodge' II
Mount Edgcumbe, four lodges II
Pencalenick, early 19C thatched cottage ornée II
Pencarrow, pair c. 1840, II
Pendarves, 'Boteto', and 'Ramsgate' Lodges II
Penrose, Helston Lodge, 'Victorian Tudor', mid 19C
'Bar Lodge' by Prynne, 1895-8
Pentillie, 'Folly Lodge', c. 18C II
Polstrong, twin, recently demolished
Port Eliot, 'Town Lodge' c. 1840 II*, [see Mowl (1985)]
Rosecraddock, dated '1845', asymmetrical Gothic, II
Tehidy, two thatched cottages ornées II
Trebursye, c. 1840-50, thatched, now cut off from drive, II
Tregenna (Michaelstow) House, dated 1876 II
Tregeare, with date-stone 'TCBL 1868'
Tregolls, surviving lodge to demolished house
Tregrehan, mid 19C. II
Tregullow, c. 1830 II
Trelissick, neo-Greek c. 1825 II [see Mowl (1985)]
Trelowarren, Double Lodges, etc.
Tremorvah, cottage ornée, c.1849
Trengwainton
Trevaylor, on opposite side of road, II
Trist House, incorporating Gothic remains, c. 1834 II
Werrington, north and south lodges II
Westbourne House, by Rice, mid 19C II
[See Mowl (1985)]

LOGGIA or **COLONNADE**
Carclew, colonnades c. 1750 II*
Godolphin I
Penheale, gatehouse with loggia for Specott I
Torfrey, granite c. 1886
Tregembo, c. early-mid 17C Doric colonnade, II*

LOG HOUSE, see also BARK and ROOT HOUSES.
Trelissick, summer-house
[See Banks (1991: 201)]

M

MARKET GARDEN, in commercial use
Bonython, growing asparagus
Gulval 'Golden Mile'
Loraine, site of
Pencarrow, in walled garden

MAUSOLEUM, containing mortal remains.
Pentillie, for Tillie early 18C II*
Point Neptune, for Rashleighs on St Catherine's Point
Tredidon, for James Bucknell, c. 1865 II

MAZE

Clowance, semi-circular box maze, now gone
Glendurgan, laurel, c. 1833 or later

Port Eliot, Leylandii 1976, replanted with beech
Trewithen, 'pleasing labyrinth', mid 18C
[See *Fisher* (1990 and 1991); *Pennick* (1990)]

MEDIEVAL GARDEN
Scilly, possibly the Ladies' (Our Lady's?) Garden, St Mary's
Tintagel Castle

MEDITERRANEAN GARDEN
Rosehill
Tresco

MILL
Enys, horse-mill c. 1840 II

MILLPOOL and LEAT
Mellingey, Cornish for 'mill-house'
Old Mill Herbary
Polvellan, Cornish for 'millpool'
Scawn Mill
Trago Mills
Tremeer, former leat made into lakes
Trewoofe
Treworder Mill
Trist House, with mill leat

MOAT
St Columb Old Rectory, ancient

MONUMENT
Arwenack, Killigrew Monument II
Boconnoc, Obelisk to Sir Richard Lyttleton, 1771 II
Mount Edgcumbe, to Timothy Brett 18C; to Sophia, Countess of Mt Edgecumbe, in French Garden II
Roman funerary monument II
Port Eliot, to former Earl
Tredidon, to James Bucknell, c. 1865 II
Werrington, Tomb of Horatii, early-mid 18C II
Westbourne House, to Richard Hawke, 1887 II

MOSS HOUSE, *a rustic building with moss pressed between the wall slats, popular in the 19C. See also BARK, LOG and*

ROOT HOUSES.
Greatwood, 'moss-house'
Menacuddle, 'moss seats'
Moditonham, 'rustic buildings, encrusted with moss'
Polvellan, 'ornamental buildings [with] mossy linings'
[See *Banks* (1991: 201)]

MOUNT, *an artificial hill, from which to obtain a better view of the garden or countryside.*
Godolphin, in early relict garden[?] 17-18C
Heligan, possibly a tumulus or beacon
Long Cross, Victorian, to view countryside
Trebartha, over grotto, to view the lake
Trelowarren, 'Three Seas Point'
Trevarno, in rockery

MUSEUM
Menabilly, former mineralogical collection
Morrab Gardens, house now a library
Penhellis, former ornithological
Penlee Gardens, house a museum and gallery
Scorrier, former mineralogical collection
Trewyn Studios, Barbara Hepworth Museum

N

NECESSARY HOUSE or **OFFICES**, see PRIVY.

NURSERIES, *associated or in connection with places listed in the topography.*
Bosvigo, 1980s
Burncoose and Southdown, 1984
Gills, see Tremough, late 19-20C
Loraine, on site of pre-1950 nursery
Mitchinson, see Glanmor and Pendarves
Moresk, Treseders, 1840
Old Mill Herbary
Penlee House, Tregony, Tyerman 1870s

Roseland House, Chacewater
St Just in Roseland, Treseder, 19C
Southleigh, former nursery, early 19C
Trebah, 1980s
Trelowarren, recent
Treseders, see Moresk and St Just in Roseland
Trewidden, post-war
Trewithen, post-war
Trewollack
Woodland Gardens

NYMPHAEUM, *grotto with pool where nymphs may bathe.*
Trevarno, 19C

O

OBELISK
Boconnoc, 1771 II
Ince Castle, in parterre, and by swimming pool
Lanhydrock, ornamenting gate-house and walls
Pencalenick, 19C, without inscription
Prideaux Place, removed in 18C

OBSERVATORY
Carwinion, 'The Rogers' Tower' [see *Lake* (1870: iii. 302)]

ORANGERY
Bray, now gone
Chymorvah, c. 1860, now gone
Clowance, c. late 18C II
Glynn, relict
Mount Edgcumbe in Italian garden II* in French Garden II
Port Eliot, with urn and busts, c. 1790 II*
Trelaske
Trematon Castle II
[See also Grove Hill and Rosehill for oranges grown in the open.]

ORCHARDS, *commonly found; see also* QUINCUNX
Killiow [see *G.Ch.* 1894: ii. 434]
Trerice, reproduced qincunx pattern

ORCHID HOUSE
Missenden, two
Porthgwidden
Tredrea, a speciality in 19C [see *G.Ch.* (1876: i 372)]

P

PALM HOUSE, *usually glasshouses.*
Morrab Gardens
Pencarrow, uncharacteristic wooden shelter

PARADISE GARDEN, *expressing the perfection of the Garden of Eden; an Islamic term, but derived from the same source.*
Enys
Trelawne

PARKLAND, *as marked on Ordnance Survey maps, with EH garden grades.*
Antony, EH II
Boconnoc, EH II*
Caerhays, EH II*
Carnanton
Enys, EH II
Lanhydrock, EH II*
Menabilly, EH II
Morval
Mount Edgcumbe, EH I
Pentillie Castle
Polapit Tamar
Port Eliot, EH I
Prideaux House
Tregeare
Tregothnan, EH II*
Trelaske
Trelissick, EH II
Trewarthenick, EH II
Trewithen, EH II*
Werrington, EH II
[See *Landun* (1991).]

PARSONAGES, *several parsonages were numbered among the great gardens of Cornwall, and many more were cited in* Gilbert (1820), Thurston (1930), *etc. References are added below for those not in the topography.*
Behan Parc, 1802 II
Blisland (*Thurston* 79; *Gilbert* ii. 621)
Boconnoc, (*Gilbert* ii. 911)
Bradock, (*Thurston* 144)
Calstock. (*Gilbert* ii. 448) II
Creed House
Duloe House, with lime walk II
Goran (*Thurston* 244) II
Gulval
Ladock House II
Lamorran Rectory, demolished

Landulph II
Lanreath (*Gilbert* ii. 918) II
Lanteglos by Camelford
Lawhitton II
Lewannick (*Gilbert* ii. 487) II
Lis Escop (Copeland Court), 18C II
Ludgvan Rectory, 18C. II*
Luxulyan Vicarage, 18C now King's Acre, and Water Meadow II
Mabyn (*Thurston* 124, 231, 242)
Mevagissey II
Nansawsan House
Newlyn East II
Newlyn West
Old Rectory, Marazion
Old Vicarage, Perranarworthal
Otterham (*Thurston* 101, 123) II
Porthgwidden
Redruth (*Thurston* 125) II
Roche (*Hitchins* ii. 587) II
Ruan Lanihorne Old Rectory II
St Breock (*Gilbert* ii. 645) II*
St Columb Old Rectory, 1857, II*
St Dominick (*Gilbert* ii. 454) II
St Hilary (*Thurston* 92) II
St Just in Penwith II
St Just in Roseland II*
St Martins (*Gilbert* ii. 930) II
St Minver (*Gilbert* ii. 605) II
St Winnow, *c.* 1740, II
South Petherwin (*Gilbert* ii. 491) II
Stoke Climsland (*Gilbert* ii. 476) II
Stratton Old Vicarage (*Thurston* 130, 193)
Trenython, Bishop's residence
Trist House (Veryan Vicarage), 1834 II
Week St Mary (*Gilbert* ii. 537)
Withiel (*Hitchins* ii. 683) II
[See *Bax* (1964).]

PARTERRE, see also BRODERIE.

Antony, 17C, and 19C both removed
Arwenack, reproduction 20C.
Dinham, modern
Downes, geometrical garden by J.D. Sedding *c.* 1868
Ethy, with box hedging, 19C.
Ince Castle, post-1960
Lanhydrock, by Gilbert Scott, mid 19C
Mount Edgcumbe, various
Penheale, by Lutyens 1920s
Rosteague, 17C designs II
Scorrier, modern quatrefoil knot garden
Tehidy, designs by Nesfield, implemented?
Tregothnan, broderie, mid 19C now removed, attributed to Vulliamy, but designs extant by Nesfield
Tregrehan, Nesfield broderie, 1843
Trewithen, designs by Nesfield, implemented?
Treworgey, in form of the suits of playing cards, 19C
[See *Banks* (1991).]

PAVILION, *a building separate from the house with one or more rooms; originally meant a tent.*
Antony, each side of house I
Carclew, now a ruin
Croan, attached to garden walls, *c.* early 18C II
Enys, two attached to walled garden
Glynn, two [see Prideaux sketch, 1727]
Godolphin, two (now gone) [illustrated

Borlase (1758)]
Penheale, two on garden walls, 18C II*
Pentillie, at each end of house, II*
Tehidy, attached to house, 1734 II
Tor House, 'elegant pavilions' (*Gilbert*), now gone
Trewithen, as coach-houses, 1740 I

PERGOLA
Bosahan, rustic arches
Churchtown Farm, Lanlivery, 1974
Ethy, 41 feet long, with *Ficus carica*, [*Thurston* (1930: 126)], extinct
Loraine
Pentillie [see *Holme* (1907) for illustration]
Place House, Fowey, relict possibly with Mawson influence
Torfrey, now derelict
Trelidden, wisteria, 1980s
Tresillian, 1930s
Trevarno, as Yew tunnel, *c.* 1840
Trevethoe, relict

PHEASANTRY
Clowance, Pheasant Cottage
Killiow
Lanhydrock, 1694

PIGEON HOLES or **LOFT** see DOVE HOLES

PINETUM
Boconnoc, *c.* 1840
Menehay, early 20C
Pine Lodge, 1980s
Pinetum, 1975
Scorrier, mid 19C
Tregrehan, 19C
Trevarno, late 19C

PLANTATION, *usually distinguished from natural woodland.*

PLAYING PLACE, *Cornish for an open air stage.*
Rosemundy, 1954

PLEASAUNCE, *equivalent to* PLEASURE GARDENS.
Tonacombe, so named

PLEASURE GARDENS or GROUNDS.
Trelowarren, so named, late 18C, early 19C

POND, *formal, or with constructed edges,*

usually thought of as smaller than a lake.
Acton Castle, seaweed tanks
Clowance, the King's Pond, and lily pond
Glensilva, lily pond
Godolphin, 'Pond Garden', on 1786 map
Greatwood
Heligan, formal in Italian Garden
Ince Castle, formal
Lamorran House, various
Lancarffe, in formal walled garden
Ogbeare, lily pond
Penpol, formal in walled garden
Polgwynne, formal with waterfall
Port Eliot, formal
Porthgwidden
Scawns
Trebah, three ponds
Tregothnan
Tregrehan, two with fountains, by Nesfield, 1843
Trenowth, formal
Trewithen, formal in walled garden

PRIVY, *Jericho or Necessary House,* see:
Menabilly
Pelynt House
Restormel Castle

PROSPECT, *a panoramic view much sought after by the 18C and 19C designers;* see also VISTA.

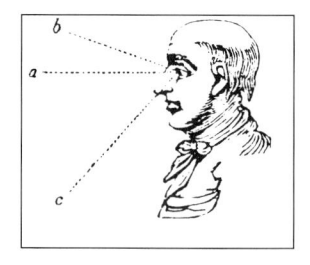

PUBLIC PARKS, *the principal parks in Cornwall are listed; those in italics have not been described in the topography.*
Bedford Bolitho Gardens, Penzance, *c.* 1914
Boscawen Park, Truro, by Meyer, late 1880s

Castle Park, Liskeard,
  enlarged 1893
Foster Bolitho Gardens,
  Penzance, *c.* 1914
George V Walk, Hayle,
  see Riviere House
Gyllyngdune Gardens,
  and Princess Pavilion,
  Falmouth, with band-
  stand, prior to 1910
Kimberley Park,
  Falmouth, by Tyerman,
  1877
Morrab Gardens,
  Penzance, with
  bandstand, by Upcher,
  1889
Penlee Memorial
  Gardens, Penzance, 1945
Priory Park, Bodmin,
  post-1926 [?]
Queen Mary's Garden,
  Falmouth, 1913
*St Anthony Gardens,
  Penzance*, 1933
Thanckes Park, Torpoint,
  1952
Trelawney Park, Penryn,
  1910-24 [?]
Trenance Gardens,
  Newquay, with
  bandstand, 1906
Trewyn Garden, St Ives
  [see *Rose* (1997)]
*Victoria Jubilee Park,
  Redruth*, 1898
Victoria Park, Saltash,
  c. 1898
Victoria Park, Truro,
  with bandstand, 1898
Waterfall Gardens,
  Truro, 1893 by
  Mitchinson
Westbourne Gardens,
  Liskeard
[See *Conway* (1991) and
  Landun (1991) for
  public parks generally]

PYRAMID
  Arwenack, 1773 II
  Trevethoe, Knill
  Monument

Q
QUARRY GARDEN,
  notable examples
  Catchfrench, Repton,
    1793, relict
  Gyllyngdune, public
    gardens
  Thanckes, extinct
  Port Eliot, in 'Craggs
    Wood', Repton, 1792,
    relict
  Trewarthenick, *c.* 1820,
    relict

QUAY
  Budock Vean, ferry
  Pentillie, steps 18C, and
    cottage, 1854 II
  Trelowarren, Tremayne
    Quay
  Trevissome, marina
  Trewince, early 19C

QUINCUNX *pattern
  orchard, where the trees
  are in line when viewed
  in any direction.*
  Bake [see Prideaux sketch]
  Trerice, reproduction
  [See *Banks* (1991: 192).]

R
RAILINGS and GATES,
  see also GATE-PIERS
  Glynn, two lodges II
  Marlborough House,
    early 19C II*
  Nanswhyden, II
  Tehidy, gates, now
    removed
  Tregenna (Michael-
    stow) House II
  Tregothnan, 1845-8 by
    Vulliamy, II
  Tregullow, around park
  Treludick, early 18C II*
  Treworgey, 1832 II

RAISED WALK,
  *investigation might
  uncover several more.*
  Carnanton, with
    yews,near Elizabethan
    house [?]
  Godolphin
  Hall Walk
  Penheale, extension of
    terrace along house
  Trelowarren, along edge
    of 'Pleasure Gardens'

RAVINE GARDEN, *or
  rockery.*
  Heligan

REAL TENNIS COURT
  Stowe, late 17C, part
    used as shippon, II

RIBBON BEDDING, *'a long
  narrow bed arranged in
  continuous lines of single
  colours.'*
  Pentillie Castle, mid 19C

RIDING HALL, *for
  exercising horses.*
  Clowance, *c.* 1670

RIDING TRACK, *for
  exercising horses.*
  Clowance, 'Green
    Drive', 18C
  Prideaux House, post
    Second World War

RILLS, *narrow stream in
  constructed channel.*
  Polgwynne
  St Just in Roseland
    Churchyard, 1980s

ROCK GARDEN, *and*
ROCK WORK
  Boskenna
  Burncoose, alpine
    collection in 1890s
  Churchtown Farm,
    Lanlivery, 1974
  Eagle's Nest, 1930s
  Glensilva
  Gyllyngdune, in quarry,
    mid 19C
  Headland, on cliff, 1974
  Heligan, separate from
    Ravine
  Lower Hamatethy, post-
    World War II
  Ludgvan Rectory
  Moorswater Lodge,
    rockwork by pool, 19C
    extinct
  Penberth, valley side,
    1920s
  Pencarrow, early
    pioneering example by
    Corbett, *c.* 1840 II
  Thanckes, in quarry,
    relict
  Torfrey, with pool, relict
  Tredarvah, by Meyer,
    extinct
  Treloyhan, by Meyer,
    c. 1892
  Tremough, with ferns,
    late 19C
  Trenython, with waterfall
  Tresco, extensive
  Trevarno, with pool,
    grotto and mount
  Trevarrick, late 19C,
    extinct
  Trewidden, with pond
    and waterfall
  Trewithen, cock pit
  Trist House, with pool,
    relict

ROOKERY, *a feature
  recorded in* c. 75
  *gardens. They have been
  marked in the 'Index of
  Places'.*[See *Penhallurick*
  (1978)]

ROOT HOUSE, *garden
  building made, or
  ornamented with roots,
  stumps or branches of
  trees.*
  Pentillie, 1813,
    designed by Irwin
    Kennedy,
    Hammersmith

ROSE GARDEN
  Comprigney, walled
  Lis Escop, late 19C,
    relict
  Lismore House, now
    gone
  Loraine, 1950s
  Penheale, 1920s
    designed by Lutyens
  Penmount Crematorium,
    Memorial garden, 20C
  Penpol, post-World
    War II
  Place House, Fowey,
    possibly with Mawson
    influence
  Trematon Castle, 'in
    shape of a 'Tudor
    fleur-de-lis'
  Treworgan, recent

ROTUNDA
  Carclew, *c.* 1965
  Porthgwidden, in former
    grounds

RUINS, see also under
  FOLLY
  Carclew, burnt house II*
  Catchfrench, 16C house
    II
  Mount Edgcumbe, Folly
    c. 1750 II
  St Cadix Priory,
    dissolved 1536
  Trehane, burnt house
    dated 1703 II
  Werrington, ruined
    castle 18C, now gone

RUSTIC WORK, see also
  COTTAGE ORNÉE
  Lismore House, Bark
    House, and Rock arch
  Menacuddle, 'rustic'
    Hermitage and seats
  Moditonham, 'rustic'
    moss-houses
  Moorswater Lodge,
    rustic summer-house,
    extinct
  Polvellan, moss houses
  Port Eliot, 'rustic'
    boathouse
  Werrington, hermitage,
    rustic seat. etc.

S
SCULPTURE GARDEN
  Trewyn Studio, by
    Barbara Hepworth

SEAT
  Bosloe, settle, *c.* 1903 II
  Erisey, two hooded
    seats, now at
    Tregothnan
  Gyllyngdune,
    grotto/seat

Menacuddle, 'moss seats'
Mount Edgcumbe, 'Shell Seat' II*, and four others II
Prideaux Place, date-stone 1740 II*
Trewan, alcove possibly once with a seat
Werrington, wooden lattice seat by Kent? now gone.
[See Banks (1991: 200).]

SERPENTINE, a 'waving line of beauty', (Hogarth). Serpentine walls gave added strength, and were built E-W to reflect the heat of the sun on fruit trees.
Chyverton, lake c. 1780
Killiow, 'crinkle crankle', i.e. serpentine wall
Lismore House, small lake or pond
Penrose, Loe Pool
Werrington, lake, 18C

SHADING, i.e. blending colours imperceptibly one into another.
Pine Lodge, herbaceous beds planted to follow the sequence of colours in the rainbow

SHELL HOUSE
Ince Castle, 1960s
Prideaux Place, remains c. mid 19C II

SHRUBBERY, collections of shrubs, such as camellias, or rhododendrons, for ornamental effect were extremely common in Cornwall; Gilbert distinguishes plantations (i.e. trees), shrubberies (in 19C often laurel), and gardens.

STABLES, principally listed examples; see also COACH HOUSES.
Carnanton, a particularly complete example II
Lancarffe II*
Lanhydrock II
Penheale, 1620 for Specott I
Penrose, with clock turret II
Port Eliot, by Soane, 1802-6 II*
Prideaux Place, 'The Rink', 18C II*
Tregothnan, yard 1816-18 by Wilkins, II*
Trelowarren, 1697, with clock 18C
Trewardale, with wall sundial II

STATUARY, a selection limited by the prevalence of theft.
Downes, St Michael, 1934 II
Glendurgan, two 'Arundell' lions
Godolphin, now lost
Ince Castle, cherubs riding on snails
Menacuddle, bust of the Earl of Mt Edgcumbe, now gone
Mount Edgcumbe, statue of Hermes, and bust, II
Nansidwell, Mercury
Newton Ferrers, various II and II*
Pendarves, statues on 'exedra', extinct or not executed
Pentillie, of Tillie, late 17C II*
Prideaux Place, various II and II*
Tehidy, two lions and Bacchus on temple 18C, later demolished Antonine Flora, formerly over house entrance
Trebartha, 17C now gone
Trago Mills, statues late 20C
Tregrehan, 'The Four Seasons' in Nesfield's parterre, 1843
Trematon, bust of Adm. St Vincent
Trerice, two 'Arundell' lions
Trevarno, two lions, and relict statues from Italian garden
Trewithen, 'Statue of Pomona', 18C extinct
Trewyn Studios, Barbara Hepworth Museum
Wivelscombe, 'composition sphinxes and heraldic lions'
[Also three private gardens are noted for their statuary; (see Jekyll 1918).]

STEPS
Godolphin, in relict of old garden
Gyllyngdune, to terrace and greenhouses
Headland, 100 down to sea
Lavethan, to terrace II
Mount Edgcumbe, stairway in Italian Garden, II
Newton Ferrers, 17C I [see Jekyll (1918).]
Pencarrow, in Italian garden
Stowe, c. 1679 now gone
Tor House, 1792 II*
Trelowarren, steps to Pleasure Gardens, 19C
Tresco, Neptune Steps
Trewarne, to gate-house, from old masonry
Treworgan
Wivelscombe, with statuary

STEW POND, medieval fish ponds, for food; 'stew' from Old French, meaning 'stored'.
Antony, Carew's 'fishful pond' (sea-water)
Cotehele, medieval
Manaton
Penheale, two, now lakes
Priory, Bodmin, now lake
Stowe
Tonacombe, medieval
Trelawne, filled in late 18C
Trewarne, medieval, probably altered

SUB-TROPICAL GARDEN, with exotic plantings.
Grove Hill, c. 1800
Lamorran House, since 1982
Morrab Gardens, 1889
Old Rectory, Marazion, since 1960s
Rocky Valley, 'Little Tresco', St Mary's, Isles of Scilly, 1880s
Rosehill, Falmouth, since 1820s
Tresco, Abbey Gardens, begun 1840

SUMMER-HOUSE, see also BARK, LOG, MOSS and ROOT HOUSES.
Carclew
Downes, by J.D. Sedding, c. 1868 II*
Marlborough House,
Oriental summer-house now gone
Moorswater Lodge, by lake, now gone
Mount Edgcumbe, on Cedar Lawn
Pelyn, now gone
Place House, Fowey, possibly with Mawson influence
Polgwynne
Port Eliot, various
Rosteague, thatched, mid 19C II
St Michael's Mount, two
Scawns, hexagonal thatched
Trelissick, in memory of Jack Lilley
Trevarno, Edwardian
Trewithen, in walled garden

SUNDIALS, a selection limited by the prevalence of theft.

Horizontal:
Antony, 19C
Boconnoc Church, 1716
Bosahan
Boskenna, M.E. Melvin, Sydenham, early-mid 19C
Burncoose
Carwinion
Enys, with toposcope (not on show), 1865
Glendurgan
Lanhydrock
Mount Edgcumbe
Pencrebar, 1722
Pengreep, with Beauchamp arms, Will Petherick, Truro, 18C II
Penwarne, in walled garden
Pine Lodge, slave
Polgwynne, 20C

Port Eliot, 1925
Port Eliot, W.S. Jones, London
Prideaux Place
Queen Mary Gardens, 20C
St Michael's Mount
Scorrier
Tehidy
Tregrehan, Nesfield, 1846
Trelissick, 1987
Trelowarren, Martin, London
Trengwainton, Newton, Camborne, 1909
Trerice, L.E. Dubois, 1858
Trevarno, Newton, Camborne, 1898
'Made by Heath and Wing in the Strand', a firm which flourished from 1730 to 1770. (Site withheld.)
Vertical: on walls
Cotehele
Lavethan, 20C
Trevarno, 1982
Trewardale, 1688
Pillar:
Carclew, 4-sided
Equinoctial, or Equatorial Armillary:
(in private gardens)
Cross
Lis Escop (constructed from pinnacle of old St Mary's, Truro), but wrongly orientated
Heliochronometer, by Negretti and Zambra
Tregothnan
[See *Daniel* (1986); *Martin* (1994).]

SUNKEN GARDEN
Hengar, in walled garden
Ogbeare, with lily pond
Prideaux Place, mid 19C, restored 1989 II
Polwithen, *c.* 1970

SWIMMING POOL
Acton Castle, rock bathing pool on beach, *c.* 1795
Boconnoc (Bathing Pool), 19C
Ince Castle, 1960s
Penheale, 1920s
Penwarne, late 20C in walled garden
Scawns, with bathing house
Tregrehan, in Nesfield parterre

SWISS COTTAGE
Grove Hill, lodge
Porthgwidden, former boat-house

T
TEA HOUSE
'The Japanese Garden', St Mawgan
Penrose, Bar Lodge with balcony, 1895-8
Tregothnan, summer-house

TEMPLE
Boconnoc, two shrines, 1771 II
Clowance, demolished, but roundel preserved
Downes, 'St Germoe's Chair' by J.D. Sedding II*
Garlenick
Lamorran House
Mount Edgcumbe, 'Thomson's Seat' II Temple of Milton II*
Penrose, formerly in Temple Plantation?
Port Eliot, various
Prideaux Place, 1738-9 II*
Tehidy, 'Temple of Bacchus and social mirth', 18C, demolished early 19C
Trehane, 'temple or pleasure house'
Trenant Park, on point, demolished
Trevillet, 'Picturesque', at St Nectan's Kieve
Trewan, alcove
Whiteford, now house, 1799 II
Werrington, of the Sun 18C (demolished)

TERRACE
Bochym, 17C II*
Bosloe, 1903 II
Bray, of brick
Carclew II
Crag, terraced garden
Downes, by J.D. Sedding, *c.* 1868 II*
Glensilva, with twin curved steps, 20C
Glynn, with steps, *c.* 1830 II
Gyllyngdune, with greenhouses
Killiow, *c.* early 19C II
Lancarffe, *c.* 1936
Lavethan, stone terrace II
Lismore House, on eye-catcher
Mellingey, terraced garden
Mount Edgcumbe, with ornaments II
Nansidwell, terraced garden
Newton Ferrers, 17C I, [see *Jekyll* (1918)]
Pentillie, walls and steps II
Place House, Fowey, with pergola
Polapit Tamar, and steps II
Polgwynne, terraced garden
Porthgwidden, [illustrated *Twycross* (1846: 87)]
Tor House, 1792, II*
Trelowarren, lawn terrace to Pleasure Gardens, 19C
Tremeer, possibly 17C origins II
Trenython, terraced garden, *c.* 1870s
Trerice, 'nearly unique in Cornwall'
Tresco, 'Grecian Rock Terrace', 1920s
Trevarno, 'Lakeside Terraces', late 19C
Trist House, 1834 II
Tullimaar, *c.* 1828 [illustrated *Twycross* (1846), see Fig. 51]

TOPIARY, *seen in sketches in the Spoure Book (1698) and by Prideaux 1717 and 1727: other examples are:*
Carnanton, 18C
Lanhydrock, yews
Penheale, yew hedges
Trewinnard, extinct
Treworgey, yews

TOPOSCOPE, *which points to the direction of local sites.*
Enys, on sundial (not on show), 1865
Ince Castle, on swimming pool terrace, 20C

TORRENT, *i.e. flooding down from moorland.*
Trebartha

TOWER, *'tower houses' were prevalent in the 16C, see Introduction, pages 17-18.*
Alverton, Entrance Tower by Ninian Comper, 1898 II*
Caerhays, Gateway and Folly Tower, Nash I
Ornamental Tower, Nash II
Carwinion, 'The Rogers' Tower', late 18C, collapsed 1930
Cotehele, Prospect Tower, 18C. II*
Ogbeare, Entrance Tower, *c.* 1880 II*
Park, 'tower house', now gone
Pentillie, Tillie Mausoleum Tower, early 18C. II*
St Benet's, 19C II*
Trelissick, Water Tower II

TOWN GARDENS, see URBAN GARDENS

TRIUMPHAL ARCH
Mount Edgcumbe, 18C II
Werrington, 18C (demolished)

TUNNEL
Acton Castle, down to shore
Burncoose, for cattle
Place House, Fowey, in drive
Trevarno, Yew tunnel
Werrington, ash house or larder II

U
URBAN GARDEN, *the most significant historic examples from the topography.*
Alverton House, Truro
Basset Villa, Camborne
Carmino, Falmouth
Glanmor, Truro
The Hollies, Grampound
Lismore House, Helston II
Penhellis, Helston
Polcarne, St Austell
Polgwin, Bodmin
Southleigh, Truro
Tolvean, Redruth
Tor House, Torpoint
Trelawney House, St Austell
Tremorvah House, Truro
Trevarthian House, St Austell
Treveddo, Newquay
Westbourne House, Liskeard
Wodehouse Place, Falmouth

Garden Types and Features

URN, *some notable examples, limited by vulnerability to theft.*
  Lanhydrock, bronze from France II
  Lismore House, on walls of eye-catcher
  Mount Edgcumbe, various
  Pencarrow, in Italian garden
  Porthgwidden, on terrace
  Scorrier, classical, on front lawn
  Tregrehan, in Nesfield's parterre, 1846
  Trelowarren, on steps, and before house, 19C
  Trist House, on terraces, 1834 II

V
VALLEY GARDEN, *a characteristic type of Cornish garden, of which notable examples (with their EH garden grades) are:*
  Bosahan
  Boskenna
  Carwinion
  Glendurgan, EH II
  Heligan, EH II
  Meudon and Treworgan
  Penberth
  Penjerrick, EH II
  Penwarne
  Trebah, EH II
  Tregye, Happy Valley, 1890s, rejuvenated since 1971
  Trelean, created since 1979
  Treverven, relict

VINERY
  Penpol, in greenhouse
  Ruanlanihorne Old Rectory, extinct
  Steward's House, St Mary's Isles of Scilly, extinct
  Thanckes, in Quarry, extinct

VISTA, *a designed narrow and framed view to create a centre of attention; some examples are:*
  Antony, over river
  Bonython, around Lake Joy
  Catchfrench, by Repton, 1793
  Clowance, to Temple etc, 18C
  Downes, axial views by J.D. Sedding, c. 1868
  Greatwood, on to river
  Mount Edgcumbe, reflected in mirrors in French garden, and various others
  Penjerrick
  Penrose, over Loe Pool
  Pentillie, over the Tamar
  Prideaux Place
  Rosehill, along avenue of Dracaenas
  St Just in Roseland Churchyard
  Trebah, to Helford river
  Tregothnan, to the Fal, by Repton, 1809
  Trelissick, to Tregothnan, and to Carrick Roads
  Trewan, to alcove temple
  Trewithen, from glades onto lawn

W
WALKS, *were an important feature of early gardens from the 16th to 18th centuries, and are regularly mentioned*, see Introduction pages 18-19.
  Bosahan, 'Lapageria Walk'
  Duloe, 'Vicarage Walk'
  Ince Castle, 'Cherry Walk'
  Godolphin, on 1786 map
  Hall Walk, 17C
  Marlborough House, 'The Captain's Walk'
  Thanckes, with views of Devonport
  Tregullow, 'Yew Walks'
  Tresco, the 'Long Walk'

WALL
  Antony, various II
  Clowance, perimeter wall, 1670
  Lanhydrock, garden walls by Gilbert Scott, 1857 I
  Pendarves, perimeter wall, 18C
  Penheale, camellia wall
  Prideaux Place, garden walls II*
  Scorrier, camellia wall
  Tregothnan, camellia wall
  Tremough, camellia wall II

WALLED GARDEN, *i.e. enclosed ornamental gardens;* see also KITCHEN GARDEN
  Antony, various
  Bake, barton walls II
  Bonython, Pleasure Gardens, planted by Treseders, 1950
  Cotehele, c. 16C II
  Croan, with dovecote (remains), early 18C II
  Downes, with heated wall
  Enys, 17C
  Garlenick, with Gazebo, early 18C II
  Hengar, terrace, and sunken garden
  Killiganoon, 18C II
  Lanarth, herbaceous garden, c. 1900
  Lancarffe, formal with pond
  Lanhydrock, by Gilbert Scott II*
  Morrab Gardens, by Upcher, 1889
  Mount Edgcumbe, various
  Penheale, with pavilions, c. 18C II*, and Lutyens parterre
  Penlee Memorial Garden
  Pennans, early 18C II, relict
  Penpol, formal with pool
  Place, Anthony
  Polgwynne, formal with pond and waterfall
  Port Eliot, and Orangery II*
  Rosteague, with parterres II
  St Michael's Mount, walled garden, 18C or earlier
  Scilly, 'Ladies' Garden' on Garrison, derelict
  Scorrier, Pinetum
  Stowe, c. 1679 demolished
  Tehidy, c. 1777-82 II
  Tintagel, medieval walled garden
  Tonacombe, walled 'Pleasance'
  Tredinnick, garden walls II
  Tregeare, used for flowers II
  Tregullow, two, one elliptical
  Trelowarren, Lady Vyvyan's Garden, proposed Botanic Garden, etc
  Treneere II
  Trerice II
  Trevarno, with conservatories etc, c. 1840
  Trewarne, courtyard garden walls
  Trewinnard, early 18C II*
  Trewithen, formal gardens with pond II
  Trewoofe, re-erected 1887 II
  Tullimaar, early 19C II
  Whiteford, c. 1775 II

WARREN, *a game reserve with Royal prerogatives, where the hunting of game, water birds, and smaller animals such as rabbits and hare, were restricted with severe penalties; a 'free warren' was without such restrictions.*
  Catchfrench, the name probably is derived from the Norman French for a 'free warren'
  Trelawne, the walls of the 'Warren Plantation' may perhaps have formerly enclosed a 17C deer park, II

WATERFALL, *a general term*, see also CASCADE, CATARACT, and TORRENT *which have more specific meanings.*
  Boconnoc, small cataract form
  Heligan, cascade in rockery
  Lamorran House, small cataract type
  Pine Lodge, ornamental
  Polgwynne, into formal pond
  Rosecraddock, cataract
  Scawns, into pond
  Trebartha, torrent
  Trenython, in rockery
  Trevarno, cascade type
  Trewidden, in rockery

WATER GARDEN, *for other water features see:* CANAL, FISHPOND, FOUNTAIN, LAKE, POND, SWIMMING POOL, *and the various waterfalls.*
  Carclew Mill, sunken water garden
  Furzeball Cottage
  Grignan

Lanterns
Missenden
Northwood Farm, on former clay workings
Pine Lodge
Piper's Barn
Springfield Farm
Tremayne Cottage
Trenowth, formal architectural
Trewithen, in shape of an eagle, c. 1745
Treworder Mill
Watergate
Water Meadow

WATERMILL
Castle, early 19C II

WATER PUMP
Lismore, dated 1844, II
Penpol II

WATER TOWER
Trelissick II

WATERWHEEL, *used to raise water to the house.*
Carclew
Enys, *c.* 1840

WELL or **WELL HOUSE**
Killiow II
Lanhydrock, holy well II
Lavethan, medieval holy (?) well house, II
well house, 19C II
Manaton, 17C II
Menacuddle, holy well, 15C II*

Mount Edgcumbe, two wells II; St Julian's Well II
Penpol, well in wall II
Pentillie, 19C II
Trebartha
Trelawne, 1840 II
Trewarne, holy well with chapel, 11C
Truthan, 18C or 19C II

WILDERNESS, *not a 'Wild Garden', but essentially a designed plantation, sometimes of low hedges, with irregular walks.*
Lanhydrock
Mount Edgcumbe [see Fig.98 above]
Prideaux Place [see Fig. below right]

WOOD, WOODLAND GARDENS and **PLANTATIONS**

Antony and Woodland Garden, Wilderness and Jupiter Plantation
Bicton, Bicton Wood
Boconnoc
Calamansack, ancient coppice from 13C
Carnanton, Carnanton Woods, and Vale of Lanherne
Clowance, Fox and Crenver Groves, etc.
Colquite, ancient, mentioned in Domesday
Enys, with bluebells
Ethy
Glynn, clothing the Glynn valley
Lavethan, Lavethan Woods
Menabilly
Pelyn
Pendarves, Pendarves Woods
Pentillie Castle, Bittleford Wood, and Ball Plantation
Port Eliot, Craggs Wood, etc.
Prideaux House, Warren Wood and Pengall Plantation
Rosecraddock, Rosecraddock Wood, with bluebells
Tehidy, Oak Wood, and North Cliff Plantation
Trebartha, Castic Plantation and Woods
Tredethy
Tregothnan
Trelissick, 'Woodland Walks', South, and Carcaddon Woods
Trelowarren, 'Pleasure Grounds' and Tremayne Woods
Trenowth, ancient, mentioned in Domesday
Trevarno, with bluebells
Trevince, with bluebells
[See *Banks* (1991: 192).]

X Y Z

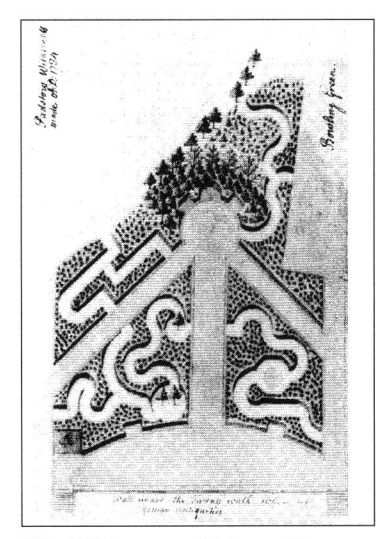

The Wilderness, Prideaux Place. (Sketch by Prideaux, 1734)

References

Bailey (1994) *Churchyards of England and Wales*, B. Bailey, new edition, Leicester 1994.
Banks (1991) *Creating Period Gardens*, E. Banks, Oxford 1991.
Bax (1964) *The English Parsonage*, A. Bax, 1964.
Beaman (1990) *The Ice Houses of Britain*, S.P. Beaman and S. Roof, 1990.
Brooks (1989) *Mortal Remains*, C. Brooks, Exeter 1989.
Buxbaum (1992) *Ice-houses*, T. Buxbaum, Shire 278, 1992.
Conway (1991) *The Design and Development of Victorian Parks in Britain*, H. Conway, 1991.
Daniel (1986) *Sundials*, C. St J.H. Daniel, Shire 176, 1986.
Fisher (1990) *The Art of the Maze*, A. Fisher and G. Gerster, 1990.
Fisher (1991) *Mazes*, A. Fisher and D. Kingham, Shire 264, 1991.
Foster (1988) *Bee Boles and Bee Houses*, A.M. Foster, Shire 204, 1988.
Hansell (1988) *Dovecots*, P .and J. Hansell, Shire 213, 1988.
Headley (1986) *Follies*, G .Headley and W. Meulenkamp, 1986, revised 1990.
Henderson (1928) 'Cornish Culver-Houses' (1928), *Essays in Cornish History*, C. Henderson, 1935: 211.
Jekyll (1918) *Garden Ornament*, Gertrude Jekyll, 1918.
Kelly (1990) *Mrs Coade's Stone*, A. Kelly, 1990.
Jones (1974) *Follies and Grottoes*, B. Jones, 2nd ed. 1974.
Landun (1991) *The English Park*, S. Landun, 1991.
Martin (1994) *A Celebration of Cornish Sun Dials*, C. Martin, Trewirgie, Cornwall 1994.
Mowl (1985) *Trumpet at a Distant Gate, the Lodge as Prelude to the Country House*, T. Mowl and B. Earnshaw, 1985.
Penhallurick (1978) 'The Rookeries of Cornwall (1975-6)' and 'The Dovecots of Cornwall', *The Birds of Cornwall*, R.D. Penhallurick, Penzance 1978: 385, 367.
Pennick (1990) *Mazes and Labyrinths*, Nigel Pennick, 1990.
Robertson (1979) 'Some Aspects of Domestic Archaeology in Cornwall', *CCRA*, 1979.
Symes (1993) *A Glossary of Garden History*, Michael Symes, Shire, 1993.
Townsend (1990) *Study Tour of Cornish Gardens Growing Bamboos*, R.F. Townsend, RBG Kew 1990.

Biographical Notes

This index is not designed to provide the page numbers for every person mentioned in the text, which would be both impractical, and in many instances of little consequence. Instead it is the result of a careful selection from among those who have made a significant contribution to horticulture in the county of Cornwall. It includes architects (since buildings are an integral part of the landscape), designers, horticulturists, botanists and writers, as well as owners or residents who built houses, created and opened gardens, or laid out and improved grounds. The information is in many cases supplementary to that in the main entries and bibliographies. However, page numbers are not usually given, since the relevant garden can be readily located in the *Index of Places*. Similarly, references to books and journal articles have been reduced to the minimum (often only the year of publication) necessary for further details to be looked up in the *Bibliographies*. A number of local and more general sources for biographical information are listed at the end, where they will be more fully explained. The pedigrees of the three gardening dynasties - the Bolithos of Penzance, the Foxes of Falmouth, and the Williams of Scorrier - who each occupied more than twelve sites in the topography - and a few others such as the Hexts, Rashleighs and St Aubyns are given in detail.

A

Alexander Daniel Asher (1768-1846), architect, of London, possibly designed the house in TREMATON CASTLE 1807. See *DNB*.

Allanson Robert (1735-1773) of York, architect, partly rebuilt PENCARROW 1760-75.

Andrew Charles, rebuilt NANSOUGH with plantations, early 19C.

Archer family, see under TRELASKE and TREMEAL; pedigrees *Lake* (1870: iii. 114 for Trelaske, and 115 for Archer families), *Collect*: 40, and *Maclean* (1876: ii. 180 etc.).

Arnold-Foster William (1885-1951), politician, artist, horticulturist and author of *Shrubs for the Milder Counties* 1948, created garden at EAGLE'S NEST. Obits *G.Ch.* 1951: ii 153, *G. Illus*. Dec. 1951: 336.

Arundell family, see under TRERICE, Gill (1995: 1), and *O. Corn*. vii 1967-73: 350-6.

Arundell The Revd Francis Vyvyan Jago (1780-1846), improved LANDULPH PARSONAGE and ST BENET'S, wrote a history of Cotehele (*c*. 1840-50). See *Biblio*.

Austen George (d. 1876), gardener PORTHGWIDDEN *c*. 1850-70, and TRESCO 1870-6; raised 'Austen's Incomparable' melon. Obit. *G.Ch.* 1876: ii 597.

B

Backhouse Edmund, married Juliet, daughter of Charles Fox of TREBAH, which he inherited in 1878 and developed.

Barnes James (1806-77), gardener at Bicton, Devon, reported on Mt Edgcumbe in the *Garden* (1872).

Baron family, built TREGEARE 1790-1820, developed by John Christopher Baron Lethbridge (1839-80). Pedigree *Lake* (1870: iii .2). See also under TRELUDICK, and *Collect*: 496.

Bartlett Aubrey Cecil (d. 1950), trained at Kew, gardener PENCARROW, correspondent to the *G.Ch.*, reported on Pencarrow (1900), Treloyhan (1905), Coldrenick (1907), Prideaux Place (1911), and on the weather in N. Cornwall (1900-1908). Obit. *G.Ch.* 1950: i 69; see also *Garden Life* Oct. 1903.

Basset Francis, Lord De Dunstanville (1757-1835), laid out the park at TEHIDY late 18th early 19C Pedigree *Lake* (1868: ii. 227-9), see also *DNB*, Gill (1995: 7) and Tregellas (1884: i. 107) for family.

Basset John Pendarves, built and laid out TEHIDY 1734-9.

Bean William Jackson (1863-1947), reported on Tregrehan in the *K.B.* (1916); visited Cornwall, and included references in the 3rd volume of his *Trees and Shrubs*, 1933. See Hadfield (1980: 30).

Beauchamp family, see under PENGREEP and TREVINCE. They were distantly related to the Williams of Scorrier by the marriage of Michael Williams I, whose wife's grandmother was a Beauchamp. See pedigree *Lake* (1968: ii. 140).

Beckford William (1759-1844), writer and exponent of the 'Picturesque' at Fonthill, visited and commented on Mt Edgumbe 1781, and Pengreep and Trefusis in 1787. See *DNB* and Hadfield (1980: 33).

Bennet family inherited TRESILLIAN HOUSE from Richard Gully in 1792, and built a new house in 1846. See *Collect*: 69.

Bickford Mrs, opened BASSET VILLA 1908.

Bickford-Smith family, descended from William Bickford (1744-1834, see *Biblio*: 1060), inventor of a safety fuse. See TREVARNO, and *Collect*: 906-7.

Billet (or **Bellot**) family laid out a fine 17C garden at BOCHYM, illustrated in the manuscript 'Spoure Book' *c*. 1600.

Bird The Revd Roger, built and laid out LANTEGLOS by CAMELFORD RECTORY 1847.

Blake Peter, Horticultural Advisor to the county 1961-90, designed the County Demonstration Gardens in 1971, now PROBUS GARDENS.

Blamey Marjorie, celebrated flower painter, and her husband, created valley garden at TRELIDDEN 1981.

Boger family, see under WOLSDON; pedigree *Lake* (1870: iii. 252 etc.), and *Collect*: 86.

Bolitho family, see page 315.

Bolitho Family

Thomas (1742-1807), 3rd son of Simon of Penryn, moved from Wendron to COOMBE in Madron parish *c.* 1765. He had two sons: **A** Thomas II who founded the Madron line, and **B** William who founded the Gulval line.

A. Madron

Thomas II (1765-1858) of COOMBE had three sons: 1 Edward (Trewidden), 2 Thomas Simon (Trengwainton), and 3 William (Polwithen).

1. Trewidden

Edward (1804-90) built TREWIDDEN, probably *c.* 1830, enlarged in 1848.
Thomas Bedford (1835-1915), 3nd and only surviving son of Edward, created the garden at TREWIDDEN.
Mary Frances (d. 1977), only child of Thomas Bedford, m. Charles Williams (Caerhays); returned as widow to TREWIDDEN in 1955. Obit. *C.G.* 1977: 8.

2. Trengwainton

Thomas Simon (1808-87) purchased PENALVERNE *c.* 1838, KENEGIE in 1866 and TRENGWAINTON in 1867. He had four sons: i. Thomas Robins, ii. Edward Alverne, iii. Otho Glynn, iv. John Borlase.
(i) Thomas Robins (1840-1925), agriculturalist, succeeded to PENALVERNE *c.* 1870, and to TRENGWAINTON in 1887, which he bequeathed to his nephew, son of Edward Alverne.
Lt-Col., later Sir Edward Hoblyn Warren (1882-1969), inherited TRENGWAINTON 1925. He sponsored Kingdon Ward's expedition from which he received and planted seeds. VMH 1961. Obit. *C.G.* 1970: 4.
Maj. Simon (1916-91), his son, succeeded to the estate, followed by his son, Edward (b. 1955).
(ii) Edward Alverne (1842-1908) took over LAREGAN from his aunt's husband, Walter Borlase, *c.* 1881, which he enlarged, mid-late 19C.
William Alverne (son of Edward Alverne) inherited PENDREA from Richard Foster II (see Ponsandane below) in 1932 and lived there until it was sold to Penzance Corporation 1954.
(iii) Otho Glynn (1844-1911) resided at POLTAIR, but retired to KENEGIE early 1890s, which he rebuilt.
(iv) John Borlase (1845-76) resided at TREVAYLOR from *c.* 1867; m. Elizabeth d. of J.M. Williams (Caerhays). He had two sons; the elder, John Williams Horton (b. 1873), resided at PENMERE, sometime with his brother Thomas Robins Evelyn (b. 1875), who also lived with his mother at TREGOLLS.

3. Polwithen

William (1815-95) built and laid out POLWITHEN 1870, his son:
William Edward Thomas (1862-1919) resided at PENDREA from *c.* 1889, and from 1910 at YORK HOUSE. He had no male descendants. (Polwithen was then sold, and Pendrea leased from 1915 to 1932 to Miss Sybil Wingfield (q.v.).

B. Gulval

Ponsandane

William I (1773-1856) began to reside at PONSANDANE, probably on his marriage in 1798.
Richard Foster (1799-1882) built present PONSANDANE 1857; had two sons: William II and Richard Foster II.
William II (1830-94) inherited PONSANDANE in 1882.
Richard Foster II (1840-1932) inherited PONSANDANE from his brother in 1894.

[See Gill (1995: 11), and *C.G.* 1996: 71-84 for family.]

Bonithon family, see under BONYTHON and CARCLEW.
Booth William Beattie (*c.* 1804-74), botanist and gardener CARCLEW 1830-53; active in RHS of Cornwall and wrote *Cottager's Manual* 1834; contributor to *Gdn's Mag.*, the *Botanical Mag.* and *Register*; later Asst Sec. to the London Horticultural Society, 1858-9. Obit. *G.Ch.* 1874: i 838, *J. Hort.* 1874: i 511, *Proc. Linn. Soc.* 1874-5: xxxvii, see also Hadfield (1980: 41).
Borlase The Revd Walter (1694-1776), built and laid out CASTLE HORNECK late 18C. See pedigree *Lake* (1868: ii. 297, 1870: iii. 222), *DNB*, and Tregellas (1884: i. 167) for Borlase family. See also under ROSCADGHILL.
Borlase The Revd Dr William (1695-1772), author of the *Antiquities* (1754), and *Natural History of Cornwall* (1758) etc., gardened at LUDGVAN Rectory, (see *JRIC.* 1994: 28). See also P.A.S. Pool, *William Borlase*, Truro 1986, and *Biblio*.
Boscawen family, Viscounts Falmouth since 1720, see under TREGOTHNAN; pedigree *Lake* (1870: iii. 346), Tregellas (1884: i. 189), and Gill (1995: 16).

Boscawen Canon Arthur Townshend (1862-1939), son of the Revd J.T. Boscawen, horticulturist, created garden at LUDGVAN RECTORY; VMH 1922. Obits *G.Ch.* 1939: ii 71, *K.B.* 1939: 329, *JRIC.* 1942: 1.

Boscawen The Hon. John R. de C. (d. 1915), built and laid out TREGYE; Obit. *Garden* 1915: 632, *G.M.* 1915: 582

Boscawen The Hon. and Revd John Townshend (1820-89), horticulturist, built LAMORRAN RECTORY and created garden. Obits *G.Ch.* 1889: ii 46, *J. Hort.* 1889: ii 17, *Proc. Linn. Soc.* 1889-90: 94.

Bowen Humphry, of Lambeth, designed a garden in front of ANTONY 1713.

Boyd Viscountess, with her late husband created garden at INCE CASTLE since 1960.

Branwell J.R. (b. 1824), miller, of a Penzance family related to the mother of the Brontë sisters (see *Collect*: 103-4), built and laid out PENLEE c. 1865-6.

Bull Capt. John (1772-1851), of the Falmouth Packets, altered MARLBOROUGH HOUSE, and created garden after 1805.

Buller family, see under MORVAL, TREDINNICK, TRENANT PARK, and WATERLOO VILLA (Klymiarvan); pedigree *Lake* (1970: iii. 379).

Buller Charles D., opened TREVISSOME 1916-19.

Bullock Capt., of the Falmouth Packets, built and laid out PENMERE, later occupied by Alfred Lloyd Fox, and Horton Bolitho.

Burn William (1782-1870), architect, of Edinburgh and London, altered and enlarged TEHIDY 1861. See *DNB*.

C

Call Sir John (1732-1801), built and laid out WHITEFORD 1775, now demolished; the family also owned, and sometime resided at OGBEARE HALL. See pedigree *Lake* (1872: iv. 188), also *DNB*, and Baring-Gould (1908: i. 154).

Carew family, see under ANTONY, also Gill (1995: 21); pedigree *Lake* (1867: i. 23, 28-30).

Carew Richard (1555-1620), wrote *Survey of Cornwall*, 1602, and developed ANTONY. See *DNB*.

Carew Reginald Pole, name adopted by Reginald Pole (1753-1835) on succeeding to ANTONY; the order of names was reversed by Sir John Carew Pole on succeeding to the Baronetcy of Pole of Shute in 1926.

Carew Pole Sir John (1902–83), new surname adopted on succeeding to the Baronetcy of Pole of Shute in 1926. He and his son Sir Richard (b. 1938) developed garden at ANTONY.

Carlyon family, see under TREGREHAN; pedigree Gilbert (1820: ii. 51-2), *Lake* (1967: i. 65, and at front).

Carlyon Olga Gillian (1924-87), camellia hybridizer at TREGREHAN. Obit. *Rh. Y.* 1987/8: 69.

Carne William Naylor, 'one of Cornwall's "gardeners"' at ROSEMUNDY (Gay) c. 1900.

Carpenter Charles, lawyer returning from London, 'enriched' and 'improved' MODITONHAM early 19C

Carveth, built NANCEALVERNE 18C.

Chapman Douglas and Irene, created plantsman's garden at LANTERNS since 1966.

Clemo Raymond and Shirley, have created a fine large garden at PINE LODGE since 1948.

Coad Richard (b. 1825), of Liskeard and London, pupil of Gilbert Scott, assisted him in 1857 at, and in 1881 rebuilt LANHYDROCK after fire; see *Collect*: 149.

Cock Ernie, plantsman, head gardener PENLEE MEMORIAL PARK 1946-86; received RHS Long Service Medal.

Cock Francis Hearle, solicitor and Town Clerk of Truro, opened TULLIMAAR 1889. See *Collect*: 150.

Cocks Lt.-Col. Charles Lygon (1821-85), of Treverbyn Vean, planted out the garden at Pelynt Vicarage 1830-40. See *Collect*: 151.

Cole John, JP, built TREWORGAN latter 19C, opened 1916.

Collins of TRUTHAN, see also under NEWTON FERRERS, LANWITHAN, PENMOUNT (Penhellick) and TREWARDALE; pedigree *Lake* (1867: i. 353).

Collins family 'tastefully and judiciously laid out' TREWARDALE, early to mid 19C and still reside there; see Maclean (1873: i. 325).

Columbani Placido (c. 1744-?) of Milan, designed walled garden 1793, and made working drawings for Repton's Lodge at ANTONY.

Colville Norman, engaged Lutyens to restore and extend PENHEALE, and Jekyll to advise on his planning of the garden, after purchasing the Manor in 1920.

Comper Sir John Ninian (1864-1960), architect, designed entrance clock tower at ALVERTON in 1898.

Connock, and CONNOCK MARSHALL family, see under TREWORGEY. Related by marriage to the Revd G.P. Norris at ROSECRADDOCK. (q.v.).

Coode family, of bankers and solicitors, see MOOR COTTAGE, MORVAL, POLAPIT TAMAR, POLCARNE, and TREVARTHIAN. They were also at Pond Dhu, St Austell, not included in our topography, and leased LAUNCESTON CASTLE. (q.v.) Pedigree *Lake* (1867: i 45, 52), and *Collect*: 159.

Coode Edward, built and laid out POLAPIT TAMAR 1866, extended 1901-3 by R.C. Coode, opened 1908.

Coope The Revd W.J. (1809-70), vicar of Falmouth, created the garden at GYLLYNGDUNE c. 1840. See *Collect*: 160.

Copeland Mrs Ida, inherited TRELISSICK in 1937 and with her husband Ronald, director of Spode, created the garden, which she donated to the National Trust in 1955.

Corbett Mr., gardener to Sir William Molesworth of PENCARROW, created rockery c. 1840. See *G.Ch.* 1842: 560.

Cornelius Alfred J. (fl. early 20th C), FRIBA, architect, of Truro, successor to Sylvanus Trevail, altered CATCHFRENCH 1913 with designs for a formal garden to replace the ruined house, never implemented, and also possibly designed TRENOWTH 1928.

Coryton family, see under CROCADON, NEWTON FERRERS and PENTILLIE; pedigree *Lake* (1872: iv. 82), See also Baring Gould (1908: ii. 14).

Coryton John Tillie (1773-1843), inherited PENTILLIE CASTLE, and engaged Wilkins senr. and jun. to remodel the house, and Repton to advise on the grounds, 1809-15.

Coryton Sir William, built and laid out NEWTON FERRERS 1686-95.

Coulson William (1801-77), surgeon, of Penzance family, resided at KENEGIE 1863-4, sold 1866; *Biblio*: 95, Collect: 171.

Cowell, Drewitt and Wheatley, architects of Newquay, Penzance and Truro, enlarged COMPRIGNEY in 1922.

Croggon Mrs N.B. 'Jill', created garden at the HOLLIES since Second World War.

Curtis Charles Henry (1869-1958), editor *G.M.* 1892-1917 (see Hadfield 1980: 86), visited and reported in 1908, on Tremough, Trelissick, Rosehill, Penjerrick, and Carclew; and Trebah, Enys, and Penmorvah; and in 1909, on Pencarrow, Prideaux Place, and Trevarrick; and Bosahan, Tregye and Trewidden.

D

Dallimore William (1871-1959), foreman of Kew arboretum and author (see Hadfield 1980: 90), visited and reported (in this order) on Mt Edgcumbe and Menabilly; Trevince, Tolvean, Gauntlett's Nursery, Morrab Gardens and Trewidden; Tresco, Trengwainton, Ludgvan and Rosehill; Trelissick, Tregothnan, Tremough, Bosahan, Carclew and Gill's Nursery in *G.W.* 1904.

Dance S.W., from 1930 head gardener at TRENYTHON, wrote reminiscences *C.G.* 1981: 23, 1986: 50; Obit. 1987: 134.

Daniell J.R., opened POLSTRONG 1908; followed in 1916 by Capt. R.A. Thomas.

Daniell Ralph Allen (1762-1823) of Truro, mine owner, built NEWHAM, and in 1800 purchased TRELISSICK.

Daniell Thomas (d. 1866), son of Ralph Allen, remodelled TRELISSICK after 1825.

Daubeny Charles G.B. (1795-1867), FRS, and Professor of Botany, Oxford (see *DNB*) in his lectures at Torquay in 1863, published as *Climate an Inquiry into the Causes ... and Influence on Vegetable Life*, included a list of plants, from Grove Hill, Penjerrick and Tresco Abbey, reprinted in *JRIC*. 1864-5: 71.

Daubuz family, see under KILLIOW, and *Collect*: 188-9.

Davey Frederick Hamilton (1868-1915), FLS, Cornish botanist, wrote on 'Aclimatisation' at (in this order) Penjerrick, Rosehill, Grove Hill, Enys, Tremough, Carclew, Burncoose, Tregothnan, Trelissick, Porthgwidden, Killiow, Pencalenick, Menabilly, and Heligan, in the *JRIC*. 1897: 313.

Davey Stephen (1785-1864), whose daughters Elizabeth Maria married J.M. Williams of Burncoose in 1852, and Charlotte Mary Horton, George Williams of Scorrier in 1859, in mid 1860s for three years employed William Lobb from Veitch's Nursery to 'improve' his grounds; opened by his son, Joshua Sydney (b. 1842) 1889-1916. See *Collect*: 191.

Davison Thomas Raffles (1853-1937), architect and editor of *Br. Arch.*, sketched DOWNES etc. in 1887. See *Collect*: 1491.

Davy Edmund (*fl.* 1750), grandfather of Sir Humphry Davy, designed TRELISSICK *c.* 1750.

Dayman Charles (1786-1844), sometime curate of Poughill, 'improved' FLEXBURY HALL the family seat, early 19C. See *Collect*: 199.

De Courcy The Hon. Adm., later Lord Kincale, purchased STOKETON 1809, and erected Regency Gothic house, burnt down in 1980s.

Dorrien Smith, NB is **not** hyphenated, see under **Smith**.

Dowman Capt. W.H., developed the garden at TREVISSOME after 1920, where he brought the 'Cutty Sark' in 1922 for renovation.

Drew Stephen (d. 1826), barrister in Jamaica, purchased STOKETON in 1770, erected a mansion (rebuilt 1809) and 'beautified the grounds'. See *Biblio*.

Drewitt Frederick George (1877-1958), Penzance architect, designed gatehouse at PENBERTH 1912; and Col. Geoffrey Drewitt reduced TREVARNO in 1980.

Druery Charles Thomas (1843-1917), FLS, VMH, pteridologist, visited and reported generally on gardens in Cornwall, in *G.Ch.* 1906: ii 159.

Dudley-Cooke Robert, has been creating an exotic garden at LAMORRAN HOUSE since 1982; see *C.G.* 1990: 31.

Duncan William, gardener at TRELOWARREN described proposals for a botanic garden there in the *G. Mag.* 1830.

E

Edgcumbe family, see under COTEHELE and MT EDGCUMBE; pedigree *Lake* (1867: i. 181), *DNB*, and Gill (1995: 26).

Edgcumbe Sir Richard (d. 1489) and Sir Piers (1469-1539), built COTEHELE.

Edgcumbe Sir Richard (1499-1562), built MOUNT EDGCUMBE 1547-54.

Edridge Tom, contributed. articles on Tremeer (1960), Trelissick (1962), and Antony (1963) to *C.L.* and on Trengwainton (1962) and Tremeer (1965) to *G.Ch.*

Edwards John (*c.* 1729-1807), manager of the Cornish Copper Co., built RIVIERE 1791; see *Collect*: 230.

Edwards Thomas (d. 1775) of Greenwich, architect, designed CARCLEW 1735; probably NANSWHYDEN; TEHIDY 1734-9; TREWITHEN 1738-40; and TRELOWARREN 1753-60. (See *C.L.* 132 1962: 774).

Eliot family, Earls of St Germans, see under PORT ELIOT, INCE CASTLE, SCONNER and TREBURSYE; pedigree *Lake* (1868: ii. 62-4), *DNB*, Gill (1995: 32).

Eliot William (1767-1845), built and laid out TREBURSYE in 1810 before inheriting the Earldom in 1823.

Ellis family of brewers, leased PENPOL 1890, purchased by Col. John Ellis in 1921, garden developed by Maj. and Mrs T.F. Ellis since World War II.

Elwes Henry John (1846-1922), with A. Henry (q.v.), wrote *Trees of Great Britain* in 7 vols 1906-13, which included many measured trees in Cornwall, quoted in Thurston (1930). See Hadfield (1980: 115).

Enys family, see under ENYS; pedigree *Lake* (1868: ii. 86).

Enys John Davies (1837-1912), collected plants in New Zealand Alps and Chatham Islands 1861-91, which he sent back to ENYS, and other gardens. He privately published a list of plants at Enys in 1907. *Biblio*: 1176, Obit. *K.B.* 1912: 393, see also *JRIC*. 1996: 30.

Erisey Richard (d. 1668), remodelled ERISEY 1620; gardens planted by his son James (1616-92) in 1671. Pedigree *Lake* (1868: ii. 110).

F

Farrer Reginald John (1880-1920), collected plants in China 1914-16, and Upper Burma 1919, with sponsorship from J.C. Williams of CAERHAYS.

Favell Dr R. Vernon, built and laid out PENBERTH 1912.

Field family probably built *c.* 1840, and Col. T.W. opened CHYMORVAH 1908.

Fish Margery (d. 1969), horticulturist and writer, of East Lambrook, was often a guest and exchanged plants at MOYCLARE.

Fish R. (1808-73), contributor to *G.Ch.*, *G. Mag.*, visited and described Mt Edgcumbe in the *J. Hort.* 1858.

Fitch John (1642-1706), architect, who built Citadel at Plymouth, probably designed STOWE 1679.

Fitzherbert S. Wyndham (d. 1916) of Devon; contributor on the West Country to *G.Ch.* and other journals, visited and reported on Tremough (1900, and *Garden* 1901), Penjerrick (1901: i 309), Pentillie (1901), Trelissick (1901), Enys (1901), Cotehele (*G.* 1902: ii 44), Menabilly (1903), Trebah (*F&S.* 1904), Ludgvan (1904 and 1912), Trewidden (1904 and 1906), Rosehill (1905), and Tregothnan (1909). Obit *G.Ch.* 1916: i 54.

Foote John, attorney and Town Clerk of Truro, grandfather of dramatist Samuel Foote (see *DNB* and Baring-Gould 1908: i. 280) rebuilt LAMBESSO 17C. See PENCALENICK and *Collect*: 253 for Foote family.

Foote John Pearson (*c.* 1767-1809), purchased and built HAREWOOD 1798, formerly leased by his father. See *Collect*: 253.

Ford Mrs Mary, sister of Sir William Molesworth, inherited PENCARROW and continued to develop the garden there, until 1909.

Ford T.J. created a new garden at SCAWNS since the Second World War.

Forrest George (1873-1932), FLS, VMH, made 7 plant expeditions 1904-32, chiefly sponsored by J.C. Williams of CAERHAYS, supported by Col. Edward Bolitho of TRENGWAINTON, and George Johnstone of TREWITHEN.

Fortescue The Hon. George Matthew (1791-1877), inherited BOCONNOC 1864. See *Collect*: 256, also *G.Ch.* 1856: 230.

Foster Lewis Charles (b. 1844), son of Richard, banker, built and laid out TREVILLIS late 19C. See *Garden* 1900: ii 379.

Foster Richard (1808-69), son of William, banker, built and laid out CASTLE early-mid 19C. For family see *Collect*: 258-9.

Foster William (1775-1849), banker, built and laid out LANWITHAN 1827.

Foster-Melliar Robert Aubrey, son of a noted rose specialist, the Revd Andrew Foster-Melliar (d. 1904) of Suffolk, built and laid out MERKJASTEINN early 20C, which he described in articles in *My Gd*, shortly after published as *My Garden by the Sea*, 1936.

Foulston John (1772-1842), architect, of Plymouth, possibly designed WESTBOURNE HOUSE 1816. George Wightwick (q.v.) took over his practice *c.* 1830.

Fox Family

George I of Par (d. 1781), a descendant of a Wiltshire branch, had three sons: **A** Edward I, by his first wife, **B** George Croker I, and **C** Joseph I by his second wife, who became heads of three family lines.

A. Wadebridge/Perran

Edward II (d. 1817), third son of Edward I, purchased and rebuilt GONVENA, Wadebridge, in 1790: sold 1829.

George II (d. 1816), eldest son of Edward I, built TREDREA 1770.

George III (1782-1858) succeeded to TREDREA, but departed to Lake District 1825, leaving house occupied by Charles (Trebah) until sold to Michael Henry Williams (q.v.) in 1848.

B. George Croker I moved to Falmouth, built BANK HOUSE in 1759, and died at PENJERRICK in 1781. He had two sons: 1 George Croker II (Grove Hill), and 2 Robert Were I (Penjerrick).

1. Grove Hill

George Croker II (1752-1807), built GROVE HILL 1788.

George Croker III (1784-1850), inherited GROVE HILL, rented TREFUSIS and part of PENJERRICK, and built GOONVREA early 19C. His wife died 1859, but he left no descendants, Grove Hill passing to his nephew, Robert Barclay, and then to his son, Robert Barclay II.

2. Penjerrick

Robert Were Fox I (1768-1848) of Bank House and PENJERRICK (where his sister Mary (d. 1839) lived), also leased ROSKROW and established the Perran Foundry. Four of his seven sons were (i) Robert Were II (Rosehill), (ii) Joshua (Tregedna), (iii) Alfred (Glendurgan), and (iv) Charles (Trebah).

i. ROSEHILL/PENJERRICK

Robert Were Fox II (1789-1877), FRS, built ROSEHILL in *c.* 1820, became owner of PENJERRICK 1839 and retired there in 1872. His three children were Anna Maria, Robert Barclay and Caroline (1819-71). See *DNB*.

Robert Barclay (1817-55), m. Jane Backhouse; farmed PENJERRICK 1837, but retired to GROVE HILL, and then ROSKROW as his health deteriorated. His son, Robert, inherited GROVE HILL. Anna Maria (1815-97) succeeded to PENJERRICK until 1897.

Robert Barclay II (1845-1934), son of Robert Barclay, succeeded to PENJERRICK, after the death of his aunt Anna Maria.

Waldo Trench succeeded in 1934, who was followed by his wife, and then by Rachel [Morin].

Fox Family *(cont'd)*

(b) Howard (1836-1922), bought ROSEHILL from Robert Were II in 1872, presented garden to Falmouth Council, and the house after the death of his daughters.

(c) George Henry (1845-1931) succeeded to WODEHOUSE PLACE and GLENDURGAN 1891 after his mother's death. BOSLOE was built on Glendurgan land *c.* 1880.

Cuthbert Lloyd (1885-1972), son of George Henry, inherited GLENDURGAN in 1936, gave garden to NT in 1962.

Philip succeeded in 1972.

(d) Wilson Lloyd (b. 1847) of CARMINO corresponded with Edgar Thurston about the Fox family etc.

iv. TREBAH

Charles (1797-1878) resided at TREDREA 1825-48, and occupied TREBAH from *c.* 1826, which was given him by his father in 1842.

Juliet, daughter of Charles, m. Edmund Backhouse, inherited TREBAH in 1878, which was sold to Charles Hawkins Hext (q.v.) in 1906.

C. Wood Cottage (later GREATWOOD)

Joseph II (1759-1832), grandson of George (of Par), a physician, retired to WOOD COTTAGE in 1800.

Richard (1764-1841), brother to Joseph II and also a physician, occupied NANSIDWELL.

ii. TREGEDNA

Joshua (1792-1877) farmed TREGEDNA (at southern end of Penjerrick). His eldest daughter m. Capt. James Bull jun. of MARLBOROUGH HOUSE (q.v.).

iii. GLENDURGAN/WODEHOUSE PLACE

Alfred (1794-1874), occupied GLENDURGAN from *c.* 1820, built WODEHOUSE PLACE 1821: four of his six sons were:- (a) Alfred Lloyd, (b) Howard, (c) George Henry, (d) Wilson Lloyd.

(a) Alfred Lloyd (b. 1829) resided at PENMERE from *c.* 1863, which eventually passed to Horton Bolitho (q.v.)

[See *Barclay Fox's Journal*, 1979; Gill (1995: 26), *C.G.* 1998: 87.]

Freeman Daniel, of Penryn, master-builder, built TREGENNA CASTLE 1774, but see also John Wood.

G

Gauntlett Victor Norman (d. 1954), founded 'Japanese Nursery', Chiddingford, Surrey; branch in Redruth.

Gibbs James (1682-1754), architect, said in Lysons (1814) to have designed ANTONY 1718-29. See *DNB*.

Gilbert (né GIDDY) John Davies (1811-54), agriculturalist, son of the compiler of the *History of Cornwall* (1838), purchased TRELISSICK in 1840. He was followed by his son Carew (1852-1913). See *Collect*: 276.

Gilbert Richard, has developed garden at LANCARFFE since 1950s.

Gilbert Sir Walter Raleigh (1785-1853), purchased and developed PRIORY Bodmin early 19C. Pedigree *Lake* (1867: i. 110), *DNB*.

Gill Herbert, son of Richard, collected in India, and was head of Indian Royal Gardens.

Gill Norman (*c.* 1878-1924), son of Richard, collected in India; superintended botanic gardens. Obit. *G.Ch.* 1924: i 246.

Gill Richard, gardener, rhododendron hybridizer and nurseryman at TREMOUGH (pre-1875 to 1925), and at PENJERRICK after 1925, later joined son in Kernick nursery. See Millais (1917: 30; 1924: 51).

Gill Richard Ernest (1875-1942), eldest son of Richard, nurseryman at Treluswell (1907), and later at Kernick; specialized in rhododendrons.

Glanville Francis (1762-1846), remodelled CATCHFRENCH and engaged Repton to improve the grounds, 1792. He also owned TREBROWN. The family was related to the Boscawens and the Gregors of Trewarthenick. Pedigree *Lake* (1868: ii. 54).

Glencross William (1784-1851), built LUXSTOWE 1833-4. See *Collect*.

Glynn family, see under GLYNN; pedigree *Lake* (1867: i. 200), Maclean (1876: ii. 58-74), and Gill (1995: 96). For Sergeant John Glynn (1722-79) see *DNB* and *Biblio*: 176.

Godolphin family, see under GODOLPHIN; pedigree *Lake* (1867: i. 137), *DNB*, Gill (1995: 41) and Tregellas (1884: i. 337).

Gott John, Bishop of Truro (1891-1906) built chapel, gardened at, and 1908-16 opened TRENYTHON.

Graves Adm. Thomas (1680-1755), inherited THANCKES. The family were related by marriage to the Sawles of Penrice. Pedigree *Lake* (1867: i. 44).

Gray Thomas, an associate of Lancelot Brown, drew up a plan of HELIGAN (*c.* 1780-90).

Gregor Francis (1760-1815), engaged Repton to remodel house and grounds at TREWARTHENICK *c.* 1793. See *Collect*: 291-2, and JC Fam HS. 1990: Dec. 34-9.

Gregor Sarah (née Glanville, 1792-1864), niece of Francis, extended TREWARTHENICK and renovated grounds 1840s. See *JRIC*. 1969: 16.

Grenville Sir John (1628-1701), 1st Earl of Bath (1661), built and laid out STOWE 1679. See *DNB*, Gill (1995: 46), Tregellas (1884: ii. 1). See also MODITONHAM.

Grigson Geoffrey, author and poet, son of vicar of PELYNT, wrote of the garden and his life there.

Grylls Glynn (*c.* 1800-1866), son of Thomas, built and laid out LISMORE HOUSE; see *Collect*: 301.

Grylls Thomas (1760-1813), attorney, built and laid out BOSAHAN early 19C., sold by representatives of his son Humphry Millett (1789-1834), banker, in 1882; see *Collect*: 299-300, and Toy (1936: 593) for Grylls family.

Gully family, see under TRESILLIAN.

Gundry William (d. 1950), architect, who took over the practice of Sylvanus Trevail, designed TORFREY 1886-8 as his residence.

Gurney The Revd Richard (1749-1825), vicar of Cuby with Tregony 1815-25, built and laid out PENLEE HOUSE, *c.* 1820; see *Collect*: 305.

Gwatkin Robert Lovell (1757-1843), whose wife was niece and co-heiress of Sir Joshua Reynolds, rebuilt KILLIOW and improved the grounds. His son John (1786-1855) married the eldest daughter of Jeremiah Trist. (q.v.) See *Collect*: 307.

H

Hain Sir Edward, ship owner, built and laid out TRELOYHAN 1892. See *O. Corn.* viii 1973-9: 131.

Hamilton Charles (1704-86), who, after 1738, landscaped Painshill in Surrey, was MP for Truro 1741-7, and may have influenced local landowners who were 'improving' their estates. See Hadfield (1980: 141)

Hanson Sir Charles A., of Fowey, Alderman and Lord Mayor of London, built and laid out FOWEY HALL early 20C, opened 1919-24.

Harris, later Arundell Harris family, resided at KENEGIE. See *Collect*: 43, *O. Corn.* iv 1943-50: 224.

Harris G.H. engineering manufacturer, built CRAG late 19C.

Harrison Maj.-Gen. Eric G.W. (1893-1987), rhododendron hybridizer at TREMEER. Obits *Rh. Y.* 1988/9: 76, *C.G.* 1988: 87.

Harrison Henry (*c.* 1785- *c.* 1865), architect, of London, designed entrance hall and porch at PORT ELIOT 1829; altered CARCLEW, HELIGAN, and PRIDEAUX HOUSE, and designed the East Lodge PENROSE in 1830s; altered and added wings to TREWARTHENICK and probably also designed TRIST HOUSE and Lodge 1831; designed PENDARVES in 1832, and ENYS Mansion with garden in 1833.

Hawke Richard (d. 1887), banker of Liskeard, altered WESTBOURNE HOUSE 1860s, developed the garden.

Hawkins family, see under PENNANS, TREWINNARD and TREWITHEN; pedigree *Lake* (1867: i 262, 1872: iv. 103), D. Gilbert (1838: i. 356-8), *Collect*: 340-3, Baring-Gould (1908: ii. 141), J.H.B. Irving, *The Hawkins of Trewithen* [obtainable from the nursery], and Toy (1936: 594).

Hayward Charles Foster (1830-1905), architect, designed COLDRENICK *c.* 1870. (demolished 1965).

Hellyer Arthur G.L. (1902-93), horticultural writer, visited and reported in *C.L.* and other journals on Trewithen (1953), Caerhays (*G.Ch.* 1956), Lanhydrock (1970), South Down Nurseries (*Gdn.* 1979), Tremeer (1980), Porthpean (1989), and Trehane (1989).

Henderson Charles (1900-33), of PENMOUNT, Cornish historian; first to write on gardens, deer parks, and culver-houses; contributed to Thurston (1930). See *Essays in Cornish History* 1935: xv-xxiv.

Henry Augustine (1857-1930), co-author with H.J. Elwes. (q.v.) See also Hadfield (1980: 147).

Hensley The Revd Ed., rector of Parkham, Devon, built and laid out PENMORVAH.

Hepworth Barbara (1903-75), sculptor, created sculpture garden at TREWYN.

Herbert Henry, 9th Earl of Pembroke (*c.* 1693-1751), architect, designed south front at CLOWANCE *c.* 1750. See *DNB*.

Herle Edward (d. 1721), inherited LANDUE and built the present façade to the 15C. house.

Herman The Revd George Edward, vicar of St Neot, opened DOUBLEBOIS 1908.

Hext Family

Connected with nine gardens, and six other gardening families; pedigree *Lake* (1870: iii. 29, 206), Maclean (1876: ii. 526-9).

Trenarren (see Parl. 1649).

The senior line, originated with Samuel I (d. 1680), grandson of John of Kingstone, Devon.

Samuel II (b. 1639), son of Samuel I, entailed the estate to Thomas, his great-nephew (d. 1767), who in 1725 married Gertrude, granddaughter of Henry Hawkins of Ponnans. The estate eventually passed to Arthur Staniforth Hext (b. 1847), until at least the late 1920s, and was leased to the late Dr A.L. Rowse in 1953.

Capt. John (1766-1838), grandson of Thomas, leased RESTORMEL HOUSE on his marriage in 1799. His two sisters:

Barbara, married Richard Foster of Lostwithiel in 1805 (see CASTLE and TREVILLIS), and

Lucy, married John Boger of WOLSDON (q.v.).

Frances Margery, his daughter, created a garden at LOSTWITHIEL (see Thurston 1930: 57), and his grandson:

Charles Hawkins (1851-1917), at first gardened at POLGWIN Bodmin, and then from 1910 at TREBAH, being succeeded by his wife until her death in 1939.

Hext Family (cont'd)

Lancarffe and Tredethy line
Francis John (1703-70), brother of Thomas (who inherited Trenarren), married Catherine Mounsteven of LANCARFFE.
Francis John II (1731-1803), purchased Lancarffe in 1787, and married Margaret Lang heiress of TREDETHY.
Adm. William (1780-1866), second son of Francis John II, inherited TREDETHY, married Barbara Reed (or Read), heiress of TREMEER (see below).
Francis John IV (1817-90), his eldest son, who married the daughter of J. Sawle Graves Sawle of Penrice (q.v.), thus inherited TREDETHY, which passed to:
Francis John V (b. 1854),). Tredethy then passed to:
Arthur Charles (see Thurston 1930: 63).

Tremeer
The Revd George Hext (b. 1819), vicar of St Veep, third son of Adm. William, resided at Tremeer, and was married to Elizabeth Magor of LAMELLEN (q.v.). Tremeer was occupied late 19C by John Oliver Marwood, and in the early 1920s by Inspector Gen. William May, RN, and later in 1939 by Maj.-Gen. E.G.W. Harrison. (q.v.).

Hichens Richard (d. 1815), merchant of St Ives, rebuilt and laid out POLTAIR, a property of the Veales (q.v.), in the early 19C. See *Collect*: 355.

Hicks James (b. 1846), architect of Redruth, rebuilt KILLIGANOON 1874-5, built TRELISKE, TOLVEAN, made additions to TREVARNO late 1870s, and MELLINGEY *c.* 1883, and designed TREFUSIS 1891. See *Collect*: 362.

Hicks Capt.J.N., RN, (d. 1973), Chairman of the *CGS* 1969, created valley garden at WATERGATE. Obit. *C.G.* 1974: 33.

Hill Frederick (1807-74)), solicitor and Town Clerk of Helston, built and laid out PENHELLIS mid 19C See *Collect*: 365.

Hill John and Jean, created an unusual garden at HEADLAND from 1974.

Hillier Harold (b. 1905), nurseryman, advised Treve Holman on planting at CHYVERTON.

Hoblyn Edward (d. 1706), of the Nanswhyden family, rebuilt CROAN *c.* 1696, later passed to the Tremaynes (q.v.) by marriage.

Hoblyn Robert (1710-56), FRS (1745), MP for Bristol (1742-54), began to rebuild NANSWHYDEN 1740s, which was burnt down 1803. See *DNB*.

Hocken William, of Michaelstowe, a retired merchant from Manchester, built and laid out TREGENNA (later Michaelstowe) HOUSE 1869.

Hole Dean Samuel Reynolds (1819-1904), horticultural writer, visited and described Lamorran, Penjerrick, and Porthgwidden in *A Book about the Garden*, 1892: 216-19, and Lamorran in *Our Gardens*, 1899: 230-31.

Holman J.F., built and laid out LORAINE in the 1950s.

Holman Nigel, son of Treve, and plantsman, took over CHYVERTON 1959; continues Cornish tradition of growing new introductions.

Holman Treve (d. 1959) purchased CHYVERTON 1924 from Peter family, planted magnolias and rhododendrons, and subscribed to Kingdon Ward's expeditions. Obit. *C.G.* 1960: 15.

Holt Maj., of Farnborough Grange, Devon, restored, laid out the grounds, and opened OGBEARE 1889-1924.

Hooker Sir Joseph Dalton (1817-1911), sponsored by Sir Charles Lemon of CARCLEW in his Himalayan expeditions, from which seed was distributed in Cornwall (Introduction p. 17).Hadfield (1980: 154).

Hooker Sir William Jackson (1785-1865), father of Joseph, corresponded, among others, with Smith at TRESCO, and Lemon at CARCLEW, and was made honorary member of the RHS of Cornwall in 1836. See Hadfield (1980: 155).

Horndon William David (1803-80), built and laid out PENCREBAR 1848, succeeded by his brother. See S. Lightbody, *Callington ...*, 1982: 59-61, for family.

Hosken W., opened PENMARE 1890.

Hovell William, gardener at GLYNN, wrote a note on a Wellingtonia there, *G.Ch.* 1870.

Hull Thomas (fl. early 18C), gardener, carried through the designs of the 1st Lord Mount Edgcumbe.

Hunkin Bishop Joseph Wellington (1887-1950), gardener and foremost among Cornish horticultural writers, developed and planted LIS ESCOP after 1935; wrote on Ludgvan and A.T. Boscawen in the *JRIC*. 1942, and in the *JRHS*. on the Lobbs (1942: 48 and 1947: 33), Caerhays and J.C. Williams (1943), *100 years of Cornish Gardens* (1943), Lanarth (1945), Pencarrow (1946), Tresco (1947; and also in E.A. Belcher, *The Isles of Scilly* 1947: 33-59; *G.Ch.* 1947; and *Endeavour* 1949), Capt Pinwill of Trehane (1950), on 'notable plants in Cornish gardens' (1948), and various notes. He published a booklet, *Trees and Shrubs for Cornwall*, and on 'Shrubs of Scilly' in the *Scillonian* Mar. 1948: 51-4. He also contributed 40 gardening articles (39 published) to the *Guardian* 1942 until his death. Obits *G.Ch.* 1950: i 123, (memoir) and ii. 194, *JRHS*. 1951: 265. See also *C.G.* 1991: 100.

Hussey Christopher E.C. (1899-1970), contributor to *C.L.*, described houses and gardens at St Michael's Mount (1924), Antony (1933, 1953), Tonacombe (1933), Newton Ferrers (1938), Port Eliot (1948), Trewithen (1953), Pencarrow (1954), Tregothnan (1956), Ince Castle (1967). See Hadfield (1980: 158).

Hussey Richard (1713-70), MP, Attorney General to Queen Charlotte etc, built KILLIGANOON *c.* 1750. See *DNB*.

Hutchens Charles, designed greenhouses at SCORRIER early 19C.

Hyams Edward (1910-75), garden historian, described Ludgvan Rectory, *G.Ch.* 1962. See Hadfield (1980: 159).

I

J

Jackson John Reader (1837-1920), Keeper Kew Museums 1858-1901, visited and reported on the Morrab Gardens, Kimberley Park and Trewidden in the *Garden* 1907: ii 599, 611.

Jekyll Miss Gertrude (1843-1932), advised on planting at PENHEALE in 1920s. See Hadfield (1980: 163).

Jenkin William, head gardener ROSEHILL, Falmouth. A plant list by him was published in R Poly SC. 1939: 38.

John George (1759-1847), solicitor and Town Clerk of Penzance, improved ROSEMORRAN; see *Collect*: 429.

Johns family, see under TREWINCE, and *Collect*: 433.

Johnstone George Horace (1882-1960), VMH 1951, created TREWITHEN garden 1904, sponsored Forrest and Kingdon Ward's expeditions, and was notable breeder of daffodils. Obits *Daff. Y.* 1960: 9, *C.G.* 1960: 15, *JRHS.* 1960: 267, see also *Daff. Y.* 1984/5: 27.

Jose John, miner who made a fortune in S. America, built and laid out MELLINGEY mid 19C.

K

Kekewich Dorothy, of CATCHFRENCH married Francis Fox in 1640, who moved to Fowey founding the Falmouth line of Foxes. Catchfrench was sold to Julius Glanville in 1728. Kekewich pedigree *Lake* (1968: ii. 54).

Kempe Nicholas, son of John who settled at ROSTEAGUE *c.* 1619, remodelled house *c.* 1700.

Kempe Richard, from Kent settled at LAVETHAN in 16C; Humphry remodelled the house 1653. Pedigree Lake (1868: ii. 75), Maclean (1873: i. 74-8).

Kempe Samuel (1669-1728), of Penryn came into CARCLEW by marriage to Jane Bonithon, which he rebuilt and began to lay out, later completed by the Lemons (q.v.). He was not of the Lavethan family. See *Collect*: 90.

Kendall family, see under PELYN; pedigree *Lake* (1870: iii. 28-31).

Kent William (*c.* 1685-1748), architect of the Palladian school, and landscape designer, influenced or designed WERRINGTON. See DNB and Hadfield (1980: 167).

Killigrew family, see under ARWENACK; the Killigrew line became extinct in 1704, the estate passing by a sequence of marriages to the Wodehouse family, who were created Earls of Kimberley (Norfolk) in 1866. See *Collect*: 1281, *DNB*, *Lake* (1867: i. 407-9), Gill (1995: 53), and Tregellas (1884: ii. 113).

Kimber Phyllis, horticultural writer, visited and reported to G Ch on Morrab Gardens (1962), Antony (1963), and on Loraine (1965).

Kimberley John Lord Wodehouse, Earl of, donated land for and opened KIMBERLEY PARK in 1877, and for the QUEEN MARY GARDENS 1913.

King John, gardener, drew up plans to 'alter' ENYS garden in 1748.

Knight Francis Philip (*c.* 1903-85), gardener at WERRINGTON, became Director of Nottcutt's nursery 1944-54, and later of Wisley 1955-69. Obits *Gdn.* 1985: 478, *Rh. Y.* 1985/6: 52.

Knowles Ivens, gardened at KILLAGORDEN.

L

Lakes Henry, built TREVARRICK, early 19C.

Lakes Robert Gould (b. 1813), 2nd son of Henry Lakes, developed garden and planted conifers at TREVARRICK. Corresponded and sent boxes of flowers to the *G. Mag.* 1880, 1883, and to the *Garden* 1894.

Lanyon Alfred (b. 1836), from a family of ironmongers in Redruth, resided at TOLVEAN, opened 1889-1916.

Le Grice The Revd Charles Valentine (1773-1858), priest in charge of St Mary's, Penzance, inherited TREREIFE, which has remained in his family. See *DNB*, and *Collect*: 485-7 for family

Lemon Sir Charles (*c.* 1784-1868), 3rd son of Sir William Lemon, cultivated foreign plants at CARCLEW; founder member 1832, and President 1833 of the RHS of Cornwall.

Lemon Col. John (1754-1814), 2nd son of William Lemon jnr, MP and Lord of the Admiralty, built and laid out POLVELLEN *c.* 1786.

Lemon William (1696-1760), of Germoe, made fortune in mining, to become 'the great Mr. Lemon' of Truro. He purchased CARCLEW in 1749, and also owned BOSVIGO. Pedigree *Lake* (1868: ii. 67, 69), *Collect*: 488-90, see also Polwhele (1831: i. 7-9), and Baring-Gould (1908: i. 342).

Lemon William (1724-57), jun., married Anne Willyams of Carnanton, predeceasing his father.

Lemon Sir William (1748-1824), of CARCLEW, son of William Lemon jun., MP for Penryn and Cornwall, married Jane Buller of Morval (his sister Anne marrying John Buller of Morval).

Levelis family, see under TREWOOFE, and W. Bottrell, *Traditions ... of W. Cornwall*, 2nd series, Penzance 1873: 271-3.

Lilly Jack (1914-94), BEM, gardener TRELISSICK from 1931, head gardener 1955-82. See J. Stone and L Brodie, *Tales of the Old Gardeners*, Newton Abbot 1994: 97-108, and Obit. *C.G.* 1994: 108.

Lindley John (1799-1865), botanist, was made an honorary member of the RHS of Cornwall in 1835; reviewed the effects of the frost of 1837-8, citing Carclew and Grove Hill in detail, from information from W.B. Booth. (*G. Mag.* 1840: 475).

Lobb Thomas (1820-94), plant collector for Veitch of Exeter in India, Burma, Malaya, Java, Borneo, and Philippines from 1840s. His plants are listed in *London J. Botany* 1847-8. See *JRHS.* 1942: 48, 1947: 33, *C.G.* 1981: 13-21, 1982: 17-18, 1987: 44, Hadfield (1980: 185) and especially *History around the Fal* part V, Fal Local History Group 1990: 55-77.

Lobb William (1809-63), brother of Thomas, plant collector for Veitch of Exeter in Brazil, Chile, Patagonia, Peru, Ecuador, and Columbia 1840-48, and in California and Oregon 1849-57. See op.cit. above, and *C.G.* 1980: 17-20, 1995: 44-9, 1996: 55-7.

Loudon John Claudius (1783-1843), horticulturist and writer, visited with his wife and commented upon Mt Edgcumbe, Pentillie, Tor House, Trematon Castle, and Whiteford in 1842. Included Carclew, Clowance, Cothele, *Menabilly, Pendarves, *Pentillie Castle, Tehidy Park, Trebartha Hall and Trelawne House in the Gazetteer of his *Encyclopaedia* 1822: 1247, the * signifying 'showplaces'. In 1837 Boconnoc, Tregothnan, Trelowarren, Trevethoe and Werrington were added, and Clowance, Pendarves, and Tehidy amended. See *DNB*, Hadfield (1980: 189), and *C.G.* 1994: 61.

Lovice family, see under OGBEARE, and pedigree Lake (1872: iv. 208).

Lower family, see under TREMEER, and pedigree *Lake* (1872: iv. 332) and Maclean (1879: iii. 384 etc.). See also *DNB* (Richard Lower 1631-91), and Baring-Gould (1908: i. 126, Sir William Lower, born *c.* 1600).

Luckhurst Henry (*c.* 1836-1906), horticultural lecturer and writer; visited and wrote 'Notes from Cornish Gardens' in the *J. Hort.* on Lamorran, Tregothnan, Pentillie Castle, Mt Edgcumbe, and Rosemundy in 1877; and Pencarrow and Tehidy in 1878. Obits *G.Ch.* 1906: ii 168, *G.M.* 1906: ii 590.

Lutyens Sir Edwin Landseer (1869-1944), architect, designed cottages, entrance wing and parterre at PENHEALE 1920s. See Hadfield (1980: 193).

Lyne John, built MOORSWATER LODGE in 1830. See *Collect*: 519 for family.

M

Macarmick Gen. William (1742-1815), purchased Penhellick in 1775, rebuilt as PENMOUNT, see *Collect*: 520.

Macers J., gardener at CHYMORVAH; wrote notes to *G.Ch.* 1890, 1896.

Maddern George (*c.* 1828-94), gardener TREWIDDEN for 45 years; Obit. *G.Ch.* 1894: i 346.

Magor John Penberthy (1796-1862), banker, gardened at PENVENTON *c.* 1846, rebuilt and laid out LAMELLEN after 1849. See *Collect*: 526.

Magor E.J.P. (1874-1941), barrister, grandson of J.P. Magor, created garden at LAMELLEN; he cultivated seeds from Wilson's and later expeditions, providing material for the *Botanical Magazine*; joined Farrer in his collection in the Alps 1909; was notable rhododendron hybridizer; contributed to *Rh. Y.*; and 1929-38 wrote regularly in *G. Illus.* as 'Peter the Hermit'.

Magor Maj. E.W.M 'Walter' (1911-95), son of E.J.P. Magor, botanist, restored LAMELLEN after 1961; received Veitch Memorial Medal 1966; edited *Rh. Y.* 1974-82, and was chairman of the Rhododendron and Camellia Group. Obits *Times* 24.5.1995, *C.G.* 1996: 93-4.

Malone family, see under TREVAYLOR and ROSEMORRAN.

Manaton Francis, rebuilt MANATON 1697; pedigree Gilbert (1820: ii. 195).

Mangles James Henry (*c.* 1832-84), contributor to journals, collected rhododendrons which he described at LAMORRAN (*G.Ch.* 1881: i 751).

Marney family, of Essex, owned COLQUITE; see Maclean (1876: ii. 504-8, 592).

Mason The Revd William (1725-97), writer and garden designer, advised on and visited the 'English Garden' at MOUNT EDGCUMBE, 1783; also visited BOCONNOC. See *DNB*, Hadfield (1980: 200).

Matthews John (d. 1871), borough surveyor at Penzance, may have designed MORRAB HOUSE 1865-6.

Mawson Thomas Hayton (1861-1933), landscape architect, visited and may have advised on PLACE, FOWEY. See Hadfield (1980: 201).

Mayow family, see under BRAY and TREBROWN, *Collect*: 547-9, and *O. Corn.* iv 1943-50: 89-93.

Meyer F.W. (*fl.* 1880-1906), trained at Proskau in Silesia, became designer for Veitch, Exeter; designed grounds at TREDARVAH, and TRELOYHAN *c.* 1892, and BOSCAWEN PARK *c.* 1894; described Penjerrick (*Garden* 1899: i 31) and Bosahan (*G.Ch.* 1902), and wrote *Rock and Water Gardens* 1910. Obit. *G.Ch.* ii 1906: 120, see also *C.G.* 1994: 66.

Michell Richard Ferris (b. 1832), alderman of Truro, timber importer and merchant, built GLANMOR 1870s. See *Collect*: 557; for garden see Mitchinson.

Millais John Guille, (1865-1931), reviewed Cornish gardens in his *Rhododendrons ...* 1917, and 2nd series 1924.

Mills Mrs A.E., opened TORFREY 1916.

Mills Henry, gardener at ENYS, described in the *G.Ch.*, the climate in Cornwall (1869-70), Penjerrick (1871), and Tremough (1876).

Mitchell A.H., opened WEATH garden 1908.

Mitchinson James, gardener at PENDARVES and correspondent to *G. Mag.* 1827-8.

Mitchinson John (d. 1901), relative of James Mitchinson?, nurseryman at Truro, St Austell (where he took over his grandfather's nursery) and Penzance; designed GLANMOR (1872), and WATERFALL GARDENS (1891) in Truro; listed plants at Tresco in *G.Ch.* 1881: i 84.

Mohun family, see under BOCHYM, BOCONNOC, HALL, LUNEY and TREWINNARD; also *DNB*, *Biblio.*, Gilbert (1817: i. 534), and Baring-Gould (1908: i. 298).

Molesworth Sir John (1705-66), began rebuilding PENCARROW 1760-75.

Molesworth Sir William (1810-55), inherited PENCARROW 1831 and created garden. Pedigree *Lake* 1867: i. 321), and Maclean (1873: i. 463-72); see also Collect: 584-6, *DNB*, and Gill (1995: 58).

Molesworth-St Aubyn Lt.-Col. Sir Arscott (1926-98), restored PENCARROW gardens since 1970s.

Moore The Revd George (1761-1832), Rector of Ladock 1814-32, rebuilt GARLENICK 1812 with 'beautiful gardens' (Stockdale 1824). See *Collect*: 588.

Morice Sir William (1602-76), Knt., purchased WERRINGTON after the Restoration, and with his son, Sir William (d. 1690), 1st Bt., began improvements.

Morice Sir Nicholas (d. 1726), son of his second marriage, succeeded Sir William, Bt., and married Catherine Herbert, d. of the Earl of Pembroke. He enlarged the house and continued to improve the grounds at WERRINGTON in the style of (or with assistance by) William Kent.

Morice Sir William (d. 1750), 3rd Bt., continued developments at WERRINGTON, rebuilding the church. He died without issue.

Moyle family, see BAKE, pedigree *Lake* (1868: ii. 63).

Murton J, gardener at TREDREA, listed orchids there in *G.Ch.* 1876.

Mylne Robert (1733-1811), architect of Edinburgh, advised on rebuilding front at CLOWANCE 1775-6. See *DNB*.

N

Nanscawen W. gardener at COLDRENICK reported size of conifers in the *Garden* 1876 and 1877.

Napper W., of Chelsea reported on Trevarrick (*G.Ch.* 1885), and Tregullow (*G.W.* 1891).

Nash John (1752-1835), architect, one-time associate of Repton, designed CAERHAYS *c.* 1808. See *DNB*.

Neale Jack, built TREVORICK (in grounds of Carclew) 1960.
Neale Mr and Mrs H.K., built and laid out POLGWYNNE 1923-30.
Needham Edward, has 'rejuvenated', and developed TREGYE since 1970. See *Rh. Y.* 1975: 23.
Nesfield William Andrews (1793-1881), designed parterre etc. at TREGREHAN 1843. See *DNB*, Hadfield (1980: 212), *C.G.* 1994: 63. There also survive designs for Tehidy, Tregothnan and Trewithen.
Newton Ernest (1865-1922), architect, of London, modernized interior of PENCARROW 1919.
Nicholl (or Nicholls) family, see PENVOSE, TREWARNE, and Maclean (1876: ii. 164 etc.).
Nicholls family, see under TREREIFE, and *Collect*: 621-2.
Nichols John, a follower of Brown, re-landscaped CLOWANCE pre-1824.
Nicolas Maj. Nicholas Harris (1755-1816), built and laid out WATERLOO VILLA (later Klymiarvan) early 19C.; see *Biblio*: 390.
Norris The Revd George Poole (d. 1869), built house at ROSECRADDOCK 1822, which had been inherited by his wife, related on female side to the Connocks of Treworgey. See *Collect*: 628.
Northumberland, 1st Duke of (1715-86), purchased WERRINGTON in 1783 for the political influence from his 'pocket' MPs. The 2nd Duke (1742-1817) was interested in the estate, and the 3rd and 4th Dukes improved the grounds of LAUNCESTON CASTLE, but after the Reform Bills, the family departed.

O

Oliver family, see TRENEERE, TREVARNO, and *Biblio*: 412-13, 1297.
Oliver William (d. 1716), MD, FRS, 'of the family of Trevarnoe' (*Biblio*: 411), came to England 1688 in the army of William III.
Oliver William (d. 1764), MD, FRS purchased TREVARNO 1746, corresponded with Pope etc., *Biblio*: 412-13, 1297.
Onslow Sir William Wallace Rhoderick (b. 1845), rebuilt HENGAR 1905 after fire. See *Collect*: 641.
Oxnam Richard (1768-1844), banker, ship owner and general merchant, built and laid out ROSEHILL Penzance 1814; see *Collect*: 647.

P

Palmer Roger, of N. Buckland, Devon, designed MOUNT EDGCUMBE 1554.
Parlby Thomas, designed the Cold Bath House at ANTONY *c.* 1788.
Pascoe Thomas (1744-1818), JP and DL for Cornwall, built and laid out LAREGAN 1814; see *Collect*: 655.
Paull John Richards (1793-1882), solicitor, resident at BOSVIGO; *Collect*: 664.
Paxton Sir Joseph (1801-65), gardener and architect, reputed to have remodelled KILLIOW *c.* 1850. See *DNB* and Hadfield (1980: 223).
Paynter family, see under BOSKENNA and *Collect*: 671-3, etc.
Peard Col. John Whitehead (1811-80), fought with Garibaldi, who later visited him at Penquite. On his advice, built and laid out TRENYTHON in retirement 1869-70; see *DNB*, and *Collect*: 690.

Pembroke Earl of, see Henry HERBERT.
Pendarves Alexander (1662-1725/6), MP, and the Pendarves family, see under ROSKROW and PENDARVES.
Pendarves Edward Wynne (d. 1853), changed his name from Stackhouse to Wynne with an inheritance, to which he added the name of PENDARVES on also inheriting that estate, which he 'improved' early 19C. See *Collect*: 702.
Pendarves William Cole (b. 1841), son of E.W. Pendarves' sister, changed his name from Wood to Pendarves in 1860 after inheriting the estate. See *Collect*: 702.
Penneck Charles (d. 1801), son of John, 'considerably improved' TREGEMBO (*Lake*), mid to late 17C., which was sold 1802. See *Collect*: 706.
Penneck John (1633-1710), steward of the Godolphin estates, purchased TREGEMBO 1684. See *Collect*: 705.
Pennington William (d. 1789), Mayor of Bodmin, built and laid out PRIORY *c.* 1768. See Baring Gould (1908: i. 222).
Penrose vice-Adm. Sir Charles Vinicombe (1759-1830), improved ETHY, contributed an account of his system of farming to Worgan's *General view of the Agriculture of ... Cornwall*, 1811: 27-30, 75-83. See *Collect*: 713, and Baring-Gould (1908: ii. 126).
Penrose William, built a new house at TREGYE 1809.
Perry Michael and Wendy, restored and have been creating a new garden at BOSVIGO since 1983.
Peter family of HARLYN were related by marriage to Thomas of CHYVERTON, see William Peter, *Collect*: 724.
Petherick Maurice (1894-1985), nephew of Mrs Charles Hext of Trebah, MP for St Austell, created camellia garden at PORTHPEAN in mid-1950s. Obit. *C.G.* 1986: 82.
Pettigrew Andrew (*c.* 1830-1903), gardener Cardiff Castle, visited and reported (in this order) on Treseder's Nursery, Glanmor, Killiow, Goonvrea, Carclew, Enys, and Tremough, in the *J. Hort.* 1879: i 77.
Phillips Charles, manager of the West Cornwall Bank, Penryn, developed the garden at MENEHAY, opened 1919-24.
Phillpotts Canon Thomas (1807-90), horticulturist active in the RHS of Cornwall, and agriculturalist active in the Bath and West Society, resided at PORTHGWIDDEN from 1844. See *Collect*: 733.
Pidwell Samuel (1808-54), brewer, built and laid out MORRAB HOUSE 1841. See *Collect*: 737.
Pinwill Capt. William Stackhouse Church (1831-1926), VMH 1915, collected sedges in India, and plants in Malacca. Created garden at TREHANE. Wrote 'Index of Plants' at Trehane 1888. Obit. *G.Ch.* 1926: i 430, see also *JRHS*. 1950: 326.
Pitt family, see under BOCONNOC, and Gilbert (1817: i. 540-41).
Pitt Thomas (1653-1726), purchased BOCONNOC from the Mohuns with the proceeds of the 'Pitt Diamond'; see *Biblio*: 499.
Pitt Thomas, 1st Baron Camelford, (1737-93), landscaped, raised obelisk and designed south wing of BOCONNOC *c.* 1771 (mostly demolished 1975), and engaged Soane (q.v.) for repairs in 1786. See *DNB*.
Pitt Thomas, 2nd Baron Camelford (1775-1804),

exponent of the 'Picturesque' style, designed Orangery at MOUNT EDGCUMBE. See *DNB*, and Baring-Gould (1908: i. 318).

Pococke Richard, bishop of Ossory (1704-65), visited and described Werrington in his *Travels through England,* 1750.

Polkinghorne Francis (1758-1837), built and laid out TREWHIDDLE *c.* 1820, 'at vast expense' (*Hitchins*).

Polwhele The Revd Richard (1760-1838), of POLWHELE, author of *History of Cornwall*, 7 vols 1803-16, and *Biographical sketches in Cornwall*, 3 vols 1831. Pedigree *Lake* (1867: i. 210), *DNB* and *Biblio*.

Pope Alexander (1688-1744), poet and landscaper, corresponded with Dr William Borlase of LUDGVAN, and perhaps also visited William Oliver at TREVARNO. See *Biblio*: 519, *DNB*, and Hadfield (1980: 228).

Pope John (1751-1827), of Camelford, after gaining a fortune in the United States, built and laid out YORK HOUSE 1825. See *Collect*: 750.

Potter John, carpenter and owner of the Little Theatre, Haymarket, reputed to have designed NANSWHYDEN, but known to have assisted Thomas Edwards (q.v.) in Cornwall.

Praed Humphrey Mackworth (*c.* 1719-1803) MP, rebuilt TREVETHOE in 1761 and laid out the grounds, introducing the *Pinus pinaster* into Cornwall. Pedigree *Lake* (1870: iii. 101-2), *Collect*: 758 and *Biblio*.

Price Sir Rose (1768-1834), remodelled house and grounds at TRENGWAINTON 1817, after previously occupying TREVAYLOR and KENEGIE. Pedigree *Lake* (1870: iii. 219) and *Collect*: 762-5.

Prideaux family, see PRIDEAUX PLACE, and HEXWORTHY. Pedigrees Maclean (1876: 207-9, 214-17, 226-9, 237-9); see also Gill (1995: 63).

Prideaux Edmund (1693-1745), son of The Revd Dr Humphrey (1648-1724), Dean of Norwich, in 1730s extended and partly remodelled the house and garden at PRIDEAUX PLACE, which had been rebuilt *c.* 1592 by Sir Nicholas Prideaux (1550-1628). He also sketched many houses of relatives in Cornwall and other places, 1716-27. See *Arch. Hist.* (1964).

Prideaux Humphrey (1719-93), son of Edmund, redesigned the garden at PRIDEAUX PLACE.

Prideaux-Brune The Revd Charles (1760-1833), son of Humphrey, considerably remodelled PRIDEAUX PLACE and gardens 1810-33. The 'Brune' was added in response to the will of his maternal uncle.

Prynne George Halford Fellowes (b. 1853), architect, of Plymouth, designed Bar Lodge at PENROSE 1895. See *Collect*: 770.

Q

R

Rashleigh Family

From Chumleigh in Devon, began trading in Fowey in 1529. By 1596 they had settled at MENABILLY, where their descendants still live today. The significant stages in that descent are plotted below: the numbers apply to the sequence of names in the complete succession. See pedigree *Lake* (1870: iii. 189), *Biblio*: 545-8, *Collect*: 782-3, and Gill (1995: 67).

John II (1552-1624), of the third generation in Fowey, began to build MENABILLY in 1596. It was completed by his grandson, Jonathan I (1591-1675). See *O. Corn.* vii 1967-73: 113-20.

Jonathan III (1690-1764), of the seventh generation, inherited MENABILLY, and was followed by his sons who founded three family lines: 1 Philip III (Menabilly); 2 John III (Penquite/Prideaux), and 3 Charles (Duporth).

1. Menabilly

Philip III (1729-1811), eldest son of Jonathan III above, inherited MENABILLY and built the Grotto. See *DNB*.

William I (1777-1855), FRS (1814), nephew of Philip III, an algologist, who made a notable collection of exotic plants at KILMARTH, inherited MENABILLY. See *Biblio*: 547.

William II (*c.* 1817-71), the eldest son of William I, built POINT NEPTUNE in preference to Menabilly.

Jonathan V (1820-1905), younger son of William I, greatly developed the garden at MENABILLY, specializing in bamboos, conifers and eucalypts. Obit. *G.Ch.* 1905: i 248. The estate then passed to his son Jonathan VI (b. 1845) and then, by way of a Stoketon line, to the Prideaux line (see below).

2. Penquite/Prideaux House

John Colman (1772-1847), son of John (1742-1803) of Penquite (son of Jonathan III above), built PRIDEAUX HOUSE *c.* 1808. His descendant, the 6th baronet, Sir Richard (b. 1958), is the present owner of MENABILLY.

3. Duporth

Charles (1747-1823), youngest son of Jonathan III above, probably planted up PRIDEAUX, established Charlestown harbour, and built and laid out DUPORTH. He had no male descendants.

Rawlings Thomas (1757-1820), merchant and banker of Padstow, built SANDERS HILL *c*. 1803; demolished soon after his death; see *Collect*: 787.

Rawlings William John (1815-90), Associate British Archaeol. Assoc., built and created garden at DOWNES 1868. See *Collect*: 789, and *Biblio*.

Rawlings family, laid out LANCARFFE *c*. 1936, later sold by Adm. Sir Bernard Rawlings in 1956.

Rawlinson Charles (1729-86), carpenter of Lostwithiel, employed by Pitt (q.v.) at BOCONNOC, rebuilt front at CLOWANCE 1775-6 (see Mylne), and partly rebuilt CATCHFRENCH *c*. 1780; also designed Long Gallery at PORT ELIOT (demolished 1824).

Reid Mrs Moira Rose (d. 1993), created garden at MOYCLARE 1927, and contributed articles on the garden to various journals. Obit. *C.G.* 1993: 109.

Repton Humphry (1752-1818), produced Red Books for ANTONY 1792, PORT ELIOT, CATCHFRENCH, and TREWARTHENICK 1793, TREGOTHNAN 1809, and PENTILLIE 1810; reputed to have designed SCONNER HOUSE (see also BEHAN PARK, TREBURSYE and TRIST HOUSE). See *DNB*, Carter (1982: 150), Hadfield (1980: 237), Hyams (1971: 154-6), Pevsner (1971: 37, 137, 144, 213), and Stroud (1962: 69-78).

Reynolds Adm. Robert Carthew (1745-1811), inherited PENAIR, where his son, Sir Barrington (1785-1861) built a new house late 18C, early 19C; see *Collect*: 797.

Richards William (d. *c*. 1827), architect, designed SANDERS HILL, and possibly remodelled GLYNN (see *Arch. Rev.* 73 1933: 154).

Rice Henry, architect, of Liskeard, refronted WESTBOURNE HOUSE, and built lodge in 1860s.

Robartes family, see under LANHYDROCK; pedigree *Lake* (1870: iii. 10), see also Baring-Gould (1908: ii. 344), and Gill (1995: 70).

Roberts Harry (1871-1946), teacher, physician, and writer, contributed a series describing his 'little garden' at Redruth to the *G.Ch*. 1898, later published as *The Chronicle of a Cornish Garden*, 1901; also reported to the *G.Ch*. on Downes and Carne (now Boskenwyn Manor) in 1898.

Roberts Joseph (1815-77), solicitor, opened SOUTHLEIGH 1870; see *Collect*: 814, also 662.

Roberts William (1862-1940), born Madron, contributed 'Notes from Cornwall' to the *Garden* 1881: i 111, 204, 314, 1888: i 138, and reported on camellias etc. at Trewidden (*J. Hort*. 1880), and on Heligan (*G.Ch*. 1896). Reviewed 'Exotic plants in Cornwall' at Pendrea, Penalverne, Scorrier, Lamorran, Trewidden, and Mitchinson's garden (Parc Clies, Penzance) in *J. Hort*.(1884: i 384). Obit. *Times* 11.4.1940, see also *Collect*: 817.

Robinson family, from Bochym, built and laid out NANSLOE *c*. 1734. See Toy (1936: 597-8).

Robinson Peter Frederick (1776-1858), architect, of Leamington, rebuilt TRELISSICK and added portico 1825.

Robson John (d. 1886), gardener Linton Park, Kent, reported in *J. Hort*. on Port Eliot (1860: 208), Tredrea (1874), and Carclew (1874: ii 383, 403); Obit. *G.Ch*. 1886: i 183.

Robyns Thomas, built TRENEERE late 1758; see *Collect*: 822.

Rodd family, see under TREBARTHA and St JUST in ROSELAND, pedigree *Lake* (1872: iv. 11), and *Collect*: 823.

Rogers Mrs Charlotte Powys, (née Williams), re-created garden at BURNCOOSE *c*. 1890, and developed TREGYE and 'Happy Valley' after 1916.

Rogers Hugh (1719-68), purchased PENROSE in 1770 from Grace Cumming, niece of John Penrose (d. 1744). See *Collect*: 710.

Rogers John (1750-1832), son of Hugh, re-landscaped PENROSE, adding a deer paddock in 1785. See *Lake* (1872: iv. 152), *Collect*., *Biblio*. and Toy (1936: 598-601) for Rogers family.

Rogers The Revd John (1778-1856), succeeded his father John at PENROSE.

Rogers John Jope (1816-80), eldest son of the Revd John, barrister, developed PENROSE; wrote in various journals on conifers and the effect of weather on plants. See *Biblio*.

Rogers Reginald (b. 1819), third son of the Revd John, built CARWINION and laid out grounds, which were developed by his son Reginald (b. 1854).

Rosewarne Henry (d. 1783), MP, vice-Warden of the Stannaries and Recorder of Truro, enlarged BOSVIGO 1780.

Ross Charles Campbell (b. 1849), MP and banker, built and laid out CARNE (now Boskenwyn Manor) *c*. 1880. See *Collect*: 841.

Rowe Joshua (1771-1827), built and laid out Crinnis, now TOR HOUSE, 1792; visited by Loudon in 1842. See *Biblio*.

Rowlatt Sir Sidney, a Judge, built and laid out NANSIDWELL 1905.

Rowse Dr A.L., CH (1903-97), distinguished Cornish historian resided at TRENARREN.

Rutger Thomas (fl. 1800-50s), brought up at Longleat, gardener at CLOWANCE and ST MICHAEL'S MOUNT *c*. 1800-33; pioneer of acclimatization; contributed articles and garden designs to *G. Mag*., and the *Floral Cabinet*.

S

St Aubyn Family

Clowance

The succession of the baronets, all named John, is: 1st (1645-79); 2nd (1669-1714); 3rd (1696-1744), who planted Clowance from 1723, and introduced *Platanus orientalis*; 4th (1726-72); 5th (1758-1839), who rebuilt the house and remodelled the garden. Clowance then passed to the Revd John Molesworth, a younger son of the Pencarrow family (who took the St Aubyn name). His descendant, the Revd Sir St Aubyn Hender Molesworth St Aubyn (1833-1913) inherited the Pencarrow title as 12th baronet. The Clowance St Aubyns thereafter moved to PENCARROW in 1921.

St Aubyn Family *(cont'd)*

St Michael's Mount

John St Aubyn purchased the Mount from Sir Arthur Basset in 1648, which then continued in the Clowance family. James (1783-1862), natural son of the 5th baronet, inherited the Mount, followed by Edward (1799-1872), who was knighted in 1866, and Sir John (1829-1908), who was created Lord St Levan. The family donated the Mount to the National Trust in 1956, but are still in residence.

[Pedigree *Lake* (1867: i. 272), *Collect*: 854-9, *The St Aubyns of Cornwall 1200-1977*, D. Hartley, Chesham 1977, see also *DNB*, Gill (1995: 76), and Tregellas (1884: ii. 279)].

St Aubyn James Piers (1815-95), architect, rebuilt CLOWANCE after fire in 1843, altered ST MICHAEL'S MOUNT mid and later 19C, designed PENCALENICK 1881. See *Biblio*, and *Collect*: 856.

Sampson Benjamin (1770-1840), iron founder, who established the Powder Mills at Kennal Vale, built and laid out TULLIMAAR *c.* 1828. See *Collect*: 861-2.

Sandys Lt.-Col. William (1759-1829), rebuilt LANARTH *c.* 1820. Pedigree *Lake* (1868: ii. 348-50), *Collect*: 864-70, and Toy (1936: 601-2).

Sargent W., Borough Treasurer of Liskeard, opened WESTBOURNE HOUSE 1908.

Sawle family, see under PENRICE; related to the Graves family of Thanckes. (q.v.) Pedigree *Lake* (1867: i. 44).

Scobell John (1779-1866), married Susannah Usticke, through whom his family inherited NANCEALVERNE; see *Collect*: 879.

Scott Sir George Gilbert (1811-78), architect, designed formal gardens at LANHYDROCK mid 19C., and extensions to POLWHELE *c.* 1870 (Pevsner). See *DNB*.

Sedding Edmund (1836-68), architect, of Penzance, designed the house at DOWNES *c.* 1867. See *DNB*.

Sedding E.H. (d. 1921), son of Edmund, architect, extended LIS ESCOP *c.* 1906, designed chapel at ALVERTON 1910.

Sedding John Dando (1838-91), brother of Edmund, architect and founder member of the Art Workers' Guild, author of *Garden Craft Old and New* (1891), designed garden, conservatory etc. at DOWNES *c.* 1867. See *DNB* and Hadfield (1980: 258).

Senior Dr Robert E., has created a garden of exotic and tender plants at the OLD RECTORY, Marazion since 1960s.

Shepherd Frederick (1910-91), VMH, first director of the ROSEWARNE Horticulture Experimental Station 1951, President of the Cornwall Garden Society 1988, and gardened at BOSBIGAL. Obit *C.G.* 1992: 108-10.

Shilson Daniel, solicitor, son of William, 'well laid out the gardens' (Thurston) at TREWHIDDLE, known for its rhododendrons, and opened 1919-24.

Shilson William (1806-75), solicitor, developed garden at TREMOUGH 1870, specialized in rhododendrons; see *Collect*: 895.

Sholl family, see under CONDURRA, BOSVIGO, and *Biblio*.

Simmons James (*c.* 1852-1914), gardener at CARCLEW for 35 years, raised many Himalayan rhododendrons. Obit. G.Ch. 1914: i 426.

Smith Augustus (1804-72) designed TRESCO ABBEY, and laid out garden *c.* 1840-70. See *DNB*, Hadfield (1980: 265), E. Inglis-Jones, *Augustus Smith of Scilly*, 1969.

Smith Arthur Algernon Dorrien (1876-1955), son of T.A. Dorrien Smith; botanist, VMH 1943, collected plants in S. Africa, Australia, New Zealand and Chatham Islands 1910, developed TRESCO from 1918. Obits *G.Gh.* 1955: i 234, *G. Illus.* 1955: 195.

Smith Thomas Algernon Dorrien (*c.* 1845-1918), nephew of Augustus Smith, inherited and developed TRESCO; pioneered the narcissus trade on Scilly. Obits *G.Ch.* 1918: ii 64, *K.B.* 1918: 242.

Smith Sir George, of the firm of Bickford Smith and Co, opened TRELISKE 1908-24.

Smith Sir Philip Prothero (1810-82), vice-Warden of the Stannaries, built and laid out TREMORVAH 1841. See *Collect*: 909.

Smith Samuel, gardener at PENJERRICK 1889-1935, was an expert rhododendron hybridizer.

Soane Sir John (1753-1837), architect, repaired BOCONNOC for Thomas Pitt 1786-8, and refaced PORT ELIOT 1804-6. See *DNB*.

Specott Sir John, of Somerset, inherited PENHEALE and built the fine stables 1620.

Specott Paul (d. 1644), 2nd son of John, improved PENHEALE, building the gatehouse.

Spoure family, see under TREBARTHA, also at BOCHYM, CROCADON, PENHEALE and several other houses not in our topography, which are illustrated in the manuscript Spoure Book, *c.* 1690. See *Collect*: 916.

Spring Howard, and his wife moved from Hoopers Hill, Mylor to The Cottage (renamed White Cottage), Falmouth, now RAFFLES, in 1947, where they created a garden described by Marion Howard Spring in *Memories and Gardens*, 1964.

Spry Sir Samuel (1804-68), MP, 'improved' PLACE, Anthony 1840. See *Biblio*.

Spry Adm. Thomas Davy (1752-1828), 'considerably enlarged the house and improved the grounds' at KILLIGANOON; also, through his wife, owned TREGOLLS. See *Biblio*.

Stackhouse John (1742-1819), born at TREHANE, botanist and algologist, FLS 1795, inherited and resided at PENDARVES 1763-1804, built ACTON CASTLE *c.* 1775 with tanks to study seaweed, published *Nereis Britannica* 1795; see *Collect*: 923. Obit. *Gent. Mag.* 1819: ii 569, see also Polwhele (1831: 12-17).

Stephens Samuel (d. 1794), built and laid out TREGENNA CASTLE 1773 to designs of John Wood, jun. Pedigree *Lake* (1868: ii. 262) and *Collect*: 927-8.

Stevens Mrs, created garden at ELIM COTTAGE in 1920s, planting many Gill hybrid rhododendrons.

Stocker Thomas Medland, one of the first Directors of English China Clay, built and laid out TRELAWNEY *c.* 1900.

Stokes Leonard A.S. (1858-1925), architect, designed NANSIDWELL 1905, for Judge Rowlatt.

Stubbs Charles William, Bishop of Truro (1906-12), extended LIS ESCOP and developed garden.

Swan W., gardener at Bystock, described PENTILLIE in *G.Ch.* and *G.W* 1896.

Symons family, see under HATT; pedigree *Lake* (supplementary papers p. 113), and *Collect*: 951-2.

Symons T. succeeded Rutger (q.v.) as gardener at CLOWANCE, *c.* 1833; wrote to *G. Mag.* 1836, 1838.

Synge Patrick Millington (1910-82), plant collector, wrote *Gardens of Britain I ... Cornwall*, 1977, describing 19 Cornish gardens, noted in 20C synopsis above. See Hadfield (1980: 274).

T

Tallack John C., gardener at PRIDEAUX PLACE, sent flowers to the *Garden*, January, February and March 1883.

Taylor Sir Robert (1714-88), architect, of London, made additions to TREWITHEN *c.* 1763-4. See *DNB*.

Teague William (1821-86), mine owner, built and laid out TRELISKE mid-late 19C. See *Collect*: 972-3.

Tenison Marika Hanbury (deceased), laid out the garden at MAIDENWELL since *c.* 1960.

Thomas Graham Stuart (1909-), OBE, VMH, notable horticulturist and author, included Cotehele, and Trelissick in his *JRHS* article on National Trust gardens in 1960, and Glendurgan in 1963; also these and others in *The Gardens of the National Trust*, 1979. See Hadfield (1980: 280).

Thomas John (1740-1825), attorney and vice-Warden of the Stannary, extended and laid out CHYVERTON early-mid 18C. See *Biblio*.

Tillie Sir James (d. 1712), built and laid out PENTILLIE 1698-9. See *Biblio* and Baring-Gould (1908: ii. 25).

Tilly Harry (b. 1839), solicitor, son of Tobias Tilly (1808-66) of TREMOUGH, created garden at BOSLOWICK late 19C. See *Collect*: 991-2.

Tom Philip Sandy (1795-1885), remodelled KILLAGORDEN (Rosedale) mid-late 19C. See *Collect*: 1003.

Tonkin The Revd John, curate locally and at St Buryan 1856-64, created garden at TREVERVEN: married Mary Usticke Peters of PENWARNE in 1881, which he later developed; see *Collect*: 1013.

Treffry family, see PLACE FOWEY, and Gill (1995: 82).

Treffry J.de Cressy (b. 1859), general merchant, built and laid out PENARWYN *c.* 1900, opened 1908-16.

Trefusis family, see under TREFUSIS, pedigree *Lake* (1870: iii. 397): also LANDUE, pedigree *Lake* (1870: iii. 125).

Trehane David (b. 1909), horticulturist, and camellia specialist, Veitch Memorial Medal 1987, President of the Cornwall Garden Society 1985-7, restored TREHANE since 1903.

Trelawny family, originally of Trelawny in Altarnon, and Pool in Menheniot; see under TRELAWNE, COLDRENICK, HAREWOOD and BAKE. Pedigree *Lake* (1872: iv. 37-40), see also *Biblio*: 1492-3, *DNB*, Gill (1995: 88) and Baring-Gould (1908: ii. 67).

Trelawny family of COLDRENICK, pedigree *Lake* (1868: ii. 64), *Collect*: 1034.

Trelawny Edward (d. 1630), attorney, probably built BAKE 1610, before his marriage in 1611.

Trelawny Edward (1699-1754), rebuilt TRELAWNE after fire 1745 and remodelled the garden. See *DNB*.

Trelawny Sir Jonathan (1650-1721), rebuilt and laid out TRELAWNE. See *DNB*.

Tremayne family, see under HELIGAN, CARCLEW, and CROAN; pedigree *Lake* (1867: i. 383), *Collect*: 1047-9, and *O. Corn.* x 1985-91: 376-84.

Tremayne Arthur (*c.* 1827-1905), 5th son of John Hearle Tremayne of Heligan, inherited CARCLEW in 1868, through his wife, Sir Charles Lemon's sister. He considerably improved the gardens. Obit. *G.Ch.* 1905: ii 400.

Tremayne John (1825-1901), 4th son of J.H. Tremayne planted valley at HELIGAN.

Tremayne John Hearle (1780-1851), son of the Revd H.H. Tremayne planted drive at HELIGAN.

Tremayne The Revd Henry Hawkins (1735-1829), inherited CROAN, HELIGAN, and Sydenham in Devon, 1766.

Treseder family, nurserymen, ST JUST in Roseland, and MORESK, Truro. See *Truro* (1988: 50-51).

Tresilian Sir Robert, Lord Chief Justice, of TRESILLIAN HOUSE, was hanged at Tyburn in 1388. See *DNB*, *Biblio*, and Baring-Gould (1908: ii. 58).

Trevanion John Trevanion Purnell Bettesworth (1780-1840), who had adopted the name of Trevanion, built and laid out CAERHAYS CASTLE to designs of Nash, 1808. Pedigree *Lake* (Supplementary papers p. 116, 1870: iii. 341), *Collect*: 1078-80, and Gill (1995: 92).

Trevellick William, with Augustus Smith initiated the narcissus trade on Scilly in the 1870s. He had an exotic garden at ROCKY HILL described as a 'little Tresco'.

Trevithick John Harvey (1806-77), of Harveys of Hayle owned TOLROY, where house and grounds were improved by Henry Harvey (b. 1848), probably his son, and opened 1908-16. See *Collect*: 1091.

Trevithick William Edward Roberts (1858-1929), of Helston, gardener at TREVARNO and then other estates; Obit. *G.Ch.* 1929: i 151.

Trist The Revd Jeremiah (1755-1829), built and laid out BEHAN PARC *c.* 1802-10. Revised, and contributed chapter on the management of woods, plantations and willows to Worgan's *General View of Agriculture in Cornwall*, 1811: 99-100, 101-3, 171-7; see *Biblio*: 803, *Collect*: 1103-6, and *JRIC*. 1980: 191, for Trist family, also Polwhele (1831: 104-10).

Trist The Revd Samuel (1791-1869), 2nd son of Jeremiah, built and laid out Veryan Vicarage, now TRIST HOUSE 1831.

Tucker Benjamin (*c.* 1762-1829), Surveyor General to the Duchy, built house in TREMATON CASTLE 1807. See *Collect*: 1110.

Tucker E. Beauchamp (b. 1833), who changed his surname to Beauchamp, remodelled TREVINCE *c.* 1870. See *Collect*: 63.

Tupper E. St J. (m. Wilhelmina Bolitho, d.of William B. of Polwithen), developed CARNE (now Boskenwyn Manor) late 1890s.

Tweedy Robert (b. 1806), banker, active in RHS of Cornwall, opened TREGOLLS 1870.

Tweedy William Mansell (1796-1859), banker, treasurer of RHS of Cornwall, built and created garden at ALVERTON.

Tyerman John Simpson (*c.* 1830-89), a Kew gardener, later Curator and designer of the Palm House at the Liverpool Botanic Gardens, retired to PENLEE HOUSE,

Tregony, with a small nursery. Designed KIMBERLEY PARK, 1877. He was also a notable pteridologist and conchologist. Obit. *G.Ch.* 1889: ii 639.

U

Upcher Reginald, of London, designed MORRAB GARDENS 1889; may have been related to the Upchers of Sherringham, Norfolk, otherwise unknown.

V

Vallance G.D. (d. 1889), for 14 years gardener at TRESCO, where he was succeeded by his son. Obits *G.W.* 1889: 825, *J. Hort.* 1889: ii 157.

Veale The Revd William (1783-1867), rebuilt and laid out TREVAYLOR; see also under POLTAIR; pedigree *Lake* (1868: ii. 121), and *Collect*: 1135-6.

Vivian family, see under, COMPRIGNEY, GLYNN, PENCALENICK and TREWAN; also *Collect*: 1153-69.

Vivian Arthur Pendarves (b. 1834), 6th son of John Henry Vivian, brother of Sir Richard Hussey V., purchased chief part of BOSAHAN 1882. See *Collect*: 1161.

Vivian John (c. 1582-1647), restored and altered TREWAN c. 1633.

Vivian John (1784-1854), of PENCALENICK, who had changed his name from Tippett, banker, was founder in 1832 and first president of the Royal Horticultural Society of Cornwall. See *Collect*: 994.

Vivian Sir Richard Hussey (1775-1842), restored GLYNN 1833. Pedigree *Lake* (1867: i. 201), *Collect*: 1166, Gill (1995: 96), and Tregellas (1884: ii. 343).

Vulliamy Lewis (1791-1871), architect, enlarged TREGOTHNAN 1842-8, and also designed the railings to the forecourt, and Nansawn Lodge, and probably also LAMORRAN RECTORY. See *DNB*.

Vyvyan family, see under TRELOWARREN, pedigree *Lake* (1867: i. 167), *Collect*: 1174-80, and Gill (1995: 101); see also under TREWAN.

Vyvyan Lady Clara (c. 1886-1976), daughter of Mrs Powys Rogers (q.v.), and 2nd wife of Sir Courtenay Vyvyan (1858-1941), author, restored the 'Pleasure Gardens' at TRELOWARREN which she described in *Letters from a Cornish Garden*, 1972, and other books. Obit. *Times* 4.3.1976.

W

Waddon John (1648-95), son of Thomas, resided at MODITONHAM. See *Collect*: 1182-3.

Waddon Thomas (1615-84), by marriage to the daughter of John Kempthorne inherited TONACOMBE in 1646; see *Collect*: 1182. See also CLEAVE HOUSE.

Walker The Revd Robert (1754-1834), agriculturalist, revised and contributed to Worgan's *General View of the Agriculture ... of Cornwall*, 1811: 155-7; remodelled ST WINNOW RECTORY in the 1800s. See *Biblio*: 845.

Walker The Revd Dr Samuel Edmund (c. 1811-69), restored and laid out ST COLUMB RECTORY 1851 as a residence for a prospective bishop; see *Biblio*: 848.

Wallace P.B., opened TREVEDDO 1919.

Wallis Christopher (1744-1826), 'greatly improved the grounds' at TREVARNO late 18C early 19C, followed by his grandson Christopher Wallis Popham (1803-72). See *Collect*: 1191 and 751.

Wallis family, see under SCONNER and TRETHILL.

Walpole Horace, 4th Earl of Orford (1717-97), garden and landscape dilettante, associated with, advised, and visited the Edgcumbes of Mt Edgcumbe, who also had a house at Richmond. See *DNB*, Hadfield (1980: 298).

Ward Francis Kingdon (1885-1958), plant collector in China, Burma, Tibet, and Thailand, 1909-56, supported financially by J.C. Williams (Caerhays), Col. Bolitho (Trengwainton) and George Johnstone (Trewithen), visited and described LUDGVAN RECTORY (*G.Ch.* 1916). See Hadfield (1980: 169).

Waterer Miss Gertrude (1882-1974), botanist, remotely related to the nurserymen, lived and gardened at EDEN VALLEY; see *C.G.* 1986: 41.

Watson William (1858-1925), horticulturist, wrote on horticulture in Cornwall in the *K.B.* 1893, citing Carclew, Enys, Grove Hill, Menabilly, Penjerrick and Tremough. See Hadfield (1980: 300).

Whellock Robert Phillips (1834-1905), architect, extended POLAPIT TAMAR 1901-3.

White Christopher, architect, designed DOUBLEBOYS HOUSE 1883.

White William (1825-1900), architect, who had worked for Gilbert Scott, designed ST COLUMB RECTORY 1850, restored and altered TREWAN c. 1860-70.

Wightwick George (1802-72) of Plymouth, architect who had worked in the office of Sir John Soane, possibly designed MOORSWATER LODGE, designed TRETHILL, and LUXSTOWE 1829-31, TREVARNO and GYLLYNGDUNE 1837, and PENHELLIS 1839, altered and extended MT EDGCUMBE 1840-44, designed PELYNT VICARAGE 1841, altered PENDARVES 1841 (demolished 1955), remodelled TREGREHAN c. 1840-45, and PENCARROW 1844, enlarged TREGENNA CASTLE 1845. See *DNB* and *O. Corn.* vii 1967-83: 338-50, 402-14, 556-7.

Wilkins William (1751-1815), architect and associate of REPTON, added to PENTILLIE 1810.

Wilkins William jun. (1778-1839), architect, added to PENTILLIE 1815 (demolished 1968), and remodelled TREGOTHNAN 1816-18. See *DNB*.

Wilks Robert [?*fl.* 1790-1831], architect, remodelled ST WINNOW VICARAGE c. 1800.

Willcock Mr and Mrs K.R., created garden at KEN CARO since 1970s.

Williams family, see page 330 below.

Willyams family, see under CARNANTON; pedigree *Lake* (1870: iii. 299), and *Collect*: 1271-5.

Wilson Ernest Henry (1876-1930), plant collector in China, Japan and Far East; sponsored by J.C. Williams (Caerhays), and distributed seeds to many Cornish gardens. See Hadfield (1980: 208).

Wingfield Miss Sybil, niece of The Revd W.W. Wingfield, gardened at PENDREA c. 1919-32.

Wingfield The Revd William Wriothesley (1814-1912), planted the churchyard, and caused an enquiry into market gardening at GULVAL 1872. See *Biblio*: 895.

Winter E.L., opened FLEXBURY HALL 1924.

Witherwick Sqn.Ldr. George (d. 1996), retired dentist, created a new valley garden at TRELEAN 1979. See *Rh. Y.* 1986/7: 1.

Wodehouse, see KIMBERLEY, and *Collect*: 1281.

Wood John, jun. (1728-81) of Bath, architect, designed TREGENNA CASTLE in 1774, and probably ACTON CASTLE c. 1775. See *DNB*.

Williams Family

James (*fl.* 1650-73) emigrated from Wales to Stithians before the birth in *c.* 1654 of his son Richard W. The family succession is here arranged under houses.

Burncoose, *built 1715*

John I (*c.* 1685-1761), son of Richard, built BURNCOOSE 1715.

Michael I (1730-75), youngest son of John I, inherited BURNCOOSE.

John II (1753-1841), eldest son of Michael I, inherited BURNCOOSE, 'built and planted' SCORRIER in 1778, purchased Manor of Calstock 1809, retired to SANDHILL *c.* 1832. Three of his sons were John III (Burncoose), Michael II (Scorrier), and William (Tregullow).

John III (1777-1849) inherited and 'improved' BURNCOOSE.

John Michael (1813-89,) nephew of John III, son of Michael II, further improved BURNCOOSE which then passed to the Caerhays line.

Charlotte, d. of John Michael, m. E. Powys Rogers, 'recreated' garden at BURNCOOSE, moved to TREGYE in 1916 and developed the garden there.

Charlotte II, d. of Charlotte I, m. James Malcolm Maclaren who lived at BURNCOOSE.

Peter Michael, third son of John Charles of CAERHAYS, resided at BURNCOOSE.

Charles, son of Julian of CAERHAYS, now at BURNCOOSE.

Scorrier, *built 1778 by John Williams II of Burncoose*

Michael II (1785-1858), second son of John II, inherited SCORRIER, purchased CAERHAYS 1854, but lived at TREVINCE, leased from the Beauchamps.

George (1827-90), 3rd son of Michael II, built new house 1862 and improved SCORRIER; he purchased LANARTH in late 1860s.

John IV (b. 1861), elder son of George, inherited SCORRIER.

George Percival, second son of John IV, lived at SCORRIER, moved to TREGULLOW *c.* 1930.

John Gage (b. 1893), eldest son of John IV, lived at SCORRIER from 1930.

Tregullow, *built 1826*

Sir William (1791-1870), fourth son of John II, built TREGULLOW 1826. Pedigree *Lake* (1868: ii. 141).

Sir Frederick Martin (1830-78), second son of Sir William, inherited TREGULLOW, but before this had been living at GOONVREA.

Sir William Robert (1860-1903) inherited TREGULLOW.

George Percival, second son of John IV of SCORRIER, was resident from *c.* 1930.

Tredrea, *built 1776 by George Fox (q.v.)*

Michael Henry (1823-1902), second son of Michael II, occupied TREDREA from *c.* 1848. In 1880 he purchased PENCALENICK, rebuilt 1883.

Henry Harcourt (1869-1927), elder son of Michael Henry, occupied PENCALENICK and later PENAIR.

Godfrey Trevelyan (b. 1870), younger son of Michael Henry, succeeded to TREDREA.

Caerhays, *purchased 1854 by Michael Williams II of Scorrier*

John Michael (1813-80), eldest son of Michael II, inherited CAERHAYS and BURNCOOSE. (His daughter, Elizabeth, m. J.B. Bolitho of TREVAYLOR).

John Charles (1861-1939), second son of John Michael, lived early life at PENGREEP, inherited CAERHAYS, and purchased WERRINGTON. He received and planted seed from collectors whom he he had sponsored. Obits *G.Ch*. 1939: i 223, *K.B.* 1939: 252, *JRHS*. 1943: 9. 43.

Charles (1886-1952), eldest son of John Charles, inherited CAERHAYS, m. his cousin, Mary Bolitho of TREWIDDEN, but died childless.

Julian (1927-), his nephew, son of Alfred Martin succeeded to CAERHAYS.

Lanarth, *purchased mid 1860s by George Williams of Scorrier*

Percival Dacres (1865-1935), younger son of George, inherited LANARTH. Horticulturist and daffodil breeder; VMH 1927, obit. *G.Ch*. 1935: ii 361, *Daff. YB.* 1936: 1.

Michael, son of P.D., succeeded, the estate passing to his godson, Paul Tylor, on his death in 1963.

Werrington, *purchased 1882 by John Charles Williams of Caerhays*

Alfred Martin (1897-1985), second son of John Charles of CAERHAYS, succeeded to WERRINGTON 1920.

Robert, son of Alfred Martin, inherited.

[Pedigree, Maclean (1876: ii. 432-7, 443-4), *Collect*: 1239-67, Gill (1995: 105), James (n.d. 90-97), and *C.G.* 1997: 85.]

Wood William, pupil of Thomas Edwards of Greenwich, may have designed the front of BONYTHON in the 1780s.

Worth John (1672-1731), Sheriff 1711, purchased TREMOUGH 1703, built a large house, and improved the grounds. See *Collect*: 1294.

Worsley Arthington (1861-1930), collected and grew American plants, visited and commented on Trewidden, Carclew, and also St Michael's Mt, and Morrab Gardens, in the *JRHS*. 1907.

Wyatville Sir Jeffry (1766-1840), architect, said to have designed TREBURSYE *c.* 1810. See *DNB*.

X Y Z

References

The histories of the Lysons (1814), Gilbert (1817, 1820), *Hitchins* (1824), Davies Gilbert (1838), *Lake* (1867-72), and Maclean (1868-79); the *Mansions* of Twycross (1846), and the volumes of the *Horticultural* (1870-1924) and *Kelly's Directories*, each indicate the family successions in their descriptions of the various sites, in greater or lesser detail. In addition, the section on Heraldry in the first volume of Gilbert (1817: 409-592) provides extensive family histories of the titled classes, and in his second volume (1820: 1-350) of the gentry. Pedigrees of many prominent families are also scattered through the four volumes of *Lake*, to which, since they are not conveniently indexed, references have been given above. The following books have also been used:

Baring-Gould (1908) *Cornish Characters and Strange Events*, S. Baring Gould, 2 series, 1908.
Biblio: *Bibliotheca Cornubiensis*, G.C. Boase and W.P. Courtney, 3 vols, 1874-82.
Collect: *Collectanea Cornubiensia*, G.C. Boase, Truro 1890.
  Although these two items are a mine of information, only selected references have been given above. The *Collectanea* contains references to the family histories in Maclean (1868-79), and other sources.
Colvin (1995) *A Biographical Dictionary of British Architects, 1600-1840*, H. Colvin, 3rd ed. 1995.

Richard Carew, author of the Survey of Cornwall, *in 1586. (De Dunstanville's edition, 1811)*

Desmond (1994) *Dictionary of British and Irish Botanists and Horticulturists*, R. Desmond, revised ed. 1994.
DNB *Dictionary of National Biography*.
Gill (1995) *The Great Cornish Families*, C. Gill, Tiverton 1995.
Hadfield (1980) *British Gardeners, a biographical dictionary*, M. Hadfield, et al. 1980.
Polwhele (1831) *Biographical Sketches in Cornwall*, R. Polwhele, 3 vols 1831.
Tregellas (1884) *Cornish Worthies*, W.H. Tregellas, 2 vols 1884.

Index of Places

This index is arranged alphabetically, with the page numbers of the major entries in bold print, and the figure numbers of the illustrations in italics. The opportunity has also been taken to convey a great deal of additional information:

(a) by the use of different type styles for the names of sites, and by preliminary symbols, viz.:

- **Bold** = historic gardens or sites.
- *Italic* = contemporary, i.e. post-Second World War gardens.
- * = deer parks, or gardens with deer parks or paddocks.
- † = rookeries listed in the 1975 census (Penhallurick 1978: 366-79).

(b) by supplementary notes in the order:

1. ancient parishes and hundreds, which have not been entered in the topography but are necessary to locate references in such older books as *Lake*, which is arranged by parishes, and *Moule*, which is grouped under hundreds, both being without indexes.

2. garden grades as listed in the English Heritage (EH) *Register of Historic Parks and Gardens,* in bold print.

3. designations indicated summarily by the letters (L) landscape; (H) history, and (S) science. National designations, as distinct from those in the County Plan, are indicated by an asterisk (see page 28 above).

A

Acton Castle, Perranuthnoe, Penwith, (L*) **58**
Alverton House, St Clement, Powder, 86, **87**
Antony House, Antony, East, **EH.II** (L.S) 22, **218-21**, 299; *9, 91, 92*
***Arallas**, St Enoder, Pydar, **257**
***Arwenack**, Falmouth, Kerrier, (H) 18, 109, **110-11**, 257; *44*

B

Bake, St Germans, East, (L) 20, 22, **221-2**; *7, 93*
Bank House, Falmouth, Kerrier, 109
Basset Villa, Camborne, Penwith, 75, **85**
Bedford Bolitho Gardens, Penzance, Penwith, 36
Behan Park, Veryan, Powder, (L*) 134, **135**
Benbol, Lostwithiel, Powder, **169**
Berriow Bridge & Middlewood Gardens, Northill, East, (S) 205, **217**
*†**Bicton Manor**, St Ive, East, (L) 247, **257**
†**Bochym Manor**, Cury, Kerrier, (L*.S) 12, 20, 57, **58**
Boconnoc**, Boconnoc, West, **EH.II (L.H*.S*) 18, 22, 25, **151-3**, 257; *59, 112*
Bodellan Farm, St Levan, Penwith, 56
Bodrean, St Clement, Powder, (L) **103**
***Bodrugan**, Gorran, Powder, **257**
Bodwannick Manor Farm, Lanivet, Pydar, **199**
***Bonallack**, Constantine, Kerrier, **257**
Bonython Manor, Cury, Kerrier, (L*.S) 12, 57, **58-9**
†**Bosahan**, Anthony, Kerrier, (L*.S) 13, 57, **59-60**, 299
Bosavern Mill, St Just, Penwith, **56**
Bosbigal, Feock, Powder, **107**
Boscawen Park, St Clement, Powder, **87-8**; *35*
Boskenna, St Buryan, Penwith, (L*.H.S*) 13, 36, **37**
†**Boskenwyn Manor** (alias Carne), Madron, Penwith, (H) **37**
Bosloe, Mawnan, Kerrier, (L*.S) **111**
Boslowick, Falmouth, Kerrier, 110, **111-12**
Bosvigo House, Kenwyn, Powder, **88**
***Botelet**, Lanreath, West, **257**
***Bradridge**, Boyton, Stratton, **260**
Bray House, Morval, West, (L) 218, **247-8**
Budock Vean, Constantine, Kerrier, (L*.S) **131**
Burell House, Saltash, East, (L) **248**
†**Burncoose**, Gwennap, Kerrier, 12, 75, **76**
Butts Parc, St Tudy, Trigg, **199**

C

*†**Caerhays Castle**, St Michael Caerhays, Powder, **EH.II*** (L*.S) 24, 75, 134, **135-7**, 257, 296; *52*
Calamansac House, Constantine, Kerrier, (L*.S) **132**
Calenick House, Kea, Powder, **107**
***Carclew**, Mylor, Kerrier, **EH.II** (L*.H*) 12, 13, 23, 25, 86, **88-90**, 261, 295, 296; *36, 37, 116*
Carclew Mill, Mylor, Kerrier, (L*.H) **107**
Carmino, Falmouth, Kerrier, **131**
Carnanton, St Mawgan, Pydar, (L) **171-3**; *69*
***Carn Brea**, Illogan, Penwith, 75, **257**
Carne (see Boskenwyn Manor)
Carnowell, Crowan, Penwith, **74**
***Carrybullock**, Stoke Climsland, East, **256**
Carwinion, Mawnan, Kerrier, (L*.S) **112**
Castle, Lanlivery, Powder, (L) 150, **153**
Castle Horneck, Madron, Penwith, (H*) **37-8**
Catchfrench Manor, St Germans, East, **EH.II** (L) 22, 25, 109, **222-3**
†*Churchtown Farm*, Lanlivery, Powder, **169**
Churchtown Morval (see Morval)
Chymorvah, Marazion, Penwith, (L) **38**
Chyverton, Perranzabuloe, Powder, 25, 171, **173**
Cleave House, Morwenstow, Stratton, (L*.S) **204**
*†**Clowance**, Crowan, Penwith, (H*) 22, 25, 45-6, 57, **60-2**, 259, 295; *23, 24*
†**Coldrenick**, St Germans, East, **223-4**; *10*
Coleraine, St Austell, Powder, **170**
Colquite, St Mabyn, Trigg, (L.S) 185, **197-8**
Comprigney, Kenwyn, Powder, **103-4**
Condurra, St Clement, Powder, (L*.S) **104**
Coombe, Madron, Penwith, 36

Copeland Court (see Lis Escop)
*Cotehele, Calstock, East, EH.II (L.S) 13, 19, 25, 219, 224-5, 258; *94*
County Demonstration Garden, The (see Probus Gardens)
*Court Barton, Lanreath, West, 259
Crag, The, St Breock, Pydar, 171, 182-3
†*Creed House* (formerly Rectory), St Creed, Powder, 134, 149
Crinnis House (see Tor House)
†Croan Manor, Egloshayle, Trigg, 185-6
Crocadon, St Mellion, East, (L.S) 22, 248
Crooked Park, Botus Fleming, East, 252

D

Darley, Linkinhorne, East, (L) 216
Dinham House, St Minver, Trigg, (L*.S) 171, 183
†Doublebois House, St Neot, West, (L) 218, 248
Downes, The, Hayle, Penwith, EH.II 57, 62-3; *25, 26*
Duloe Churchyard, Duloe, West, (L) 249
Duporth House, St Austell, Powder, 150, 153

E

Eagle's Nest, Zennor, Penwith, (L*.H.S*) 36, 38-9
Eastaway Manor, Morwenstow, Stratton, (L*.S) 204
Eden Valley, Ludgvan, Penwith, 53-4
Elim Cottage, St Gluvias, Kerrier, 132
Enys, St Gluvias, Kerrier, EH.II (L.H*) 13, 22, 86, 110, 112-14, 297; *45*
†Erisey, Grade, Kerrier, (L.H.S) 12, 63, 262
Estray Park, Mawnan, Kerrier, (L*) 132
Ethy, St Winnow, West, (L) 151, 153-4, 259

F

Ferny Park, Tintagel, Lesnewth, (L*.S) 184
Flambards, Helston, Kerrier, 74
Flexbury Hall, Poughill, Stratton, 204
†Fowey Hall, Fowey, Pydar, (L*) 166
Fox Rosehill Gardens (see Rosehill)
Foxstones (see Penberth)
Furzeball Cottage, Lanteglos by Fowey, West, (L*) 170

G

Garlenick, St Creed, Powder, (L) 134, 137

Garvinick Farm, Kenwyn, Powder, 108
Gladys Holman House (see Rosewarne)
Glanmor, Kenwyn, Powder, 86, 104
*Glasney, St Gluvias, Kerrier, 109, 256
Glendurgan, Mawnan, Kerrier, EH.II (L*.S) 13, 24, 109, 114-15
Glensilva, Mylor, Kerrier, 132
Glynn, Cardinham. West, (L.H*.S) 185, 186-7; *77*
*†Godolphin House, St Breock (Breage), Kerrier, (L) 18, 19, 57, 64-5, 260; *6, 27, 28*
Gonvena House, Egloshayle, Trigg, 171, 173-4
Goonvrea, Perran-ar-worthal, Kerrier, (L) 75, 109, 115
Greatwood, Mylor, Kerrier, (L*) 115-16
Grignan, Perranzabuloe, Powder, 184
Grove Hill House, Falmouth, Kerrier, 23, 109, 116-17, 295, 296, 298; *46*
Gulval Vicarage & Churchyard, Gulval, Penwith, 39
†Gwithian Churchyard, Gwithian, Penwith, 73
Gyllyngdune Gardens, Falmouth, Kerrier, 117-18

H

Hall, Lanteglos by Fowey, West, (L*) 18, 151, 154-5
Hallowarren, St Anthony in Meneage, Kerrier, (L*.S) 74
*Halton, St Dominic, East, 219, 260
Harewood House, Calstock, East, (L) 219, 249
†Harlyn House, St Merran, or Merryn, Pydar, (L*.H.S) 183
†Hatt House, Botus Fleming, East 249
Headland, Lanteglos by Fowey, West, (L*) 151, 155
Heligan, St Ewe, Powder, EH.II (L*.H*) 21, 134, 137-9; *53*
*Helsbury, Michaelstow, Trigg, 256
Hengar House, St Tudy, Trigg, 187
Hexworthy, Lawhitton, East, 20, 205-6; *85*
Higher Truscott, St Stephen by Launceston, East, 217
High Noon, Ladock, Powder, 108
Hogus House (see Ludgvan Rectory)
The Hollies, Grampound, Powder, (L.H) 134, 139
*Hornacott, North Tamerton, Stratton, 258

I

†Ince Castle, St Stephen by Saltash, East, (L.S) 19, 219, 225-6; *95, 96*

J

Japanese Garden, The, St Mawgan, Pydar, 184
Jarn Syvy, Lanteglos by Fowey, West, 170
Jimmers, St Neot, West, (L), 252

K

Ken Caro, St Ive, East, (L) 226-7
Kenegie, Gulval, Penwith, (L*.H) 22, 39-40, *16*
Ker Vean, St Just in Roseland, Powder, (L*) 149
Killagorden, Kenwyn, Powder, 104
†Killiganoon, Feock, Powder, 90-91
Killiow, Kea, Powder, 86, 91
†Kilmarth, Tywardreath, Powder, (L*) 151, 155
Kimberley Park, Falmouth, Kerrier 118
Kingberry, Bodmin, Trigg 199
Klymiarvan (see Waterloo Villa)

L

Ladock House, Ladock, Powder 108
Lambesso, St Clement, Powder, (L*) 104-5
Lamellen, St Tudy, Trigg, EH.II (L) 24, 185, 187-8, 296
Lamorran House, St Just in Roseland, Powder, (L*) 134, 139-40
Lamorran Rectory, Lamorran, Powder, (L*.S) 16, 92; *38*
†Lanarth, St Keverne, Kerrier, (L*.S) 12, 24, 65, 75, 296, 299
Lancarffe, Bodmin, Trigg, (L.H*) 185, 188-9
†Landue, Lezant, East, 206-7
†Landulph Parsonage, Landulph, East, (L.S) 219, 249
Lanhadron, St Ewe, Powder, (H) 148, 258
*Lanherne, St Mawgan, Pydar, 258
**†Lanhydrock, Lanhydrock, Pydar, EH.II* (L.S) 20, 185, 189-90, 260; *78*
*Lanner, St Allen, Powder, 256
*Lanow, St Kew, Trigg, 256
*Lanteglos by Camelford, 256
†Lanteglos by Camelford Rectory, Lanteglos, Lesnewth, (L) 183
Lanterns, Mylor, Kerrier, (L*) 118
Lanwithen, St Winnow, West, (L) 166
†Laregan, Penzance, Penwith, 54
*Launcells, Launcells, Stratton, 258
Launceston Castle, St Mary Magdalen Launceston, East, (H) 205, 207, 256
Lavethan, Blisland, Trigg, (L.S) 185, 190-91, 261
Lawhitton Rectory, Lawhitton, East, 205, 216
*Lesnewth, Lesnewth, Lesnewth, 258

Index of Places 333

Index of Places

Lis Escop (now Copeland Court), Kenwyn, Powder, **93**
*****Liskeard**, Liskeard, West, 218, **256**
Lismore House, Helston, Kerrier, EH.II 57, **65-6**
Long Cross, St Endellion, Trigg, (L*) 171, **174**
Loraine, St Ives, Penwith, **40-41**
Lostwithiel (Dr Rudge), Lostwithiel, Powder, **166**
Loveny, St Neot, West, (L*.S) **252**
Lower Hamatethy, Breward, Trigg, (L.H.S) **199**
Lower Treneague, St Breock, Pydar, (L.S) **184**
†**Ludgvan Rectory** (now Hogus House), Ludgvan, Penwith, 13, 15, 16, 22, 37, **41-2**; *17*
Luney, St Ewe, Powder, 19, **149**
Luxstowe, Liskeard, West, 218, **249**

M

Maen Anneth, Roche, Powder, **184**
Maidenwell, Cardinham, West, (L*.S) **191**
Manaccan Churchyard, Manaccan, Kerrier, (L*.S) **73-4**
Manaton House, Southill, East, **216**
Marlborough House, Falmouth, Kerrier, 109, **118-19**; *47*
Mary Newman's Cottage, Saltash, East, (L) 219, **227**
Mellingey, Perran-ar-worthal, Kerrier, **119-20**
†**Menabilly**, Tywardreath, Powder, EH.II (L*.H*.S) 25, 151, **155-8**, 296; *60, 61*
Menacuddle, St Austell, Powder, (H*) 150, **158**; *62*
Menehay, Budock, Kerrier, **120**
†**Merkjasteinn**, Poughill, Stratton, **201**; *83*
*****Merthen**, Constantine, Kerrier, **258**
*****Merther Uny**, Wendron, Kerrier, **258**
†**Meudon**, Mawnan, Kerrier, (L*.S) **120**
Mevagissey Vicarage, Mevagissey, Powder, (L*) **140**
Michaelstow House (see Tregenna House)
Miller's Meadow, St Neot, West, (L) **253**
Missendon, Mylor, Kerrier, (L*) **132**
Moditonham, Botus Fleming, East, (L.S) 219, **227-8**; *97*
Moor Cottage, St Austell, Powder, 150, **166-7**; *68*
Moorswater Lodge, Liskeard, West, **250**; *111*
Moresk, St Clements, Powder, 86, **105**
Morrab Gardens, Penzance, Penwith, 36, **42-3**; *18*
Morval House, & Churchtown Morval, Morval, West, (L) 218, **228-9**

*****Mount Edgcumbe**, Maker, East, EH.I (L*.H*.S) 19, 20, 23, 218, 229-31, 258, 299; *98, 99*
Moyclare, Liskeard, West, 218, **231-2**

N

Nancealverne, Madron, Penwith, **54**
Nansawsan House, Ladock, Powder, **108**
Nansidwell, Mawnan, Kerrier, (L*.S) **120-21**
Nansloe, Wendron or Gwendron, Kerrier, 57, **66**
Nansough, Ladock, Powder, **183**
Nanswhyden, St Columb Major, Pydar, 171, **174-5**; *70*
*****Newham**, Kenwyn, Powder, **258**
Newham House, Kenwyn, Powder, 86, **105**
†**Newlyn East Churchyard**, Newlyn East, Pydar, **184**
Newlyn West Churchyard & Vicarage, Newlyn West, Penwith, **54**
*****Newton Ferrers**, St Mellion, East, (L.S) **232-3**, 258; *100, 101*
Newton House, Lanhydrock, Pydar, (L) **199**
Northwood Farm, St Neot, West, (L*.H.S) **253**
*****Norton**, Launcells, Stratton, **258**

O

Oak Lodge, Lanivet, Pydar, (L) **199**
Oak Tree House, Perran-ar-worthal, Kerrier, **133**
Ogbeare Hall, North Tamerton, Stratton, 200, **201-2**
Old Barn, The, St Neot, West, (L) **253**
Old Mill Herbary, The, St Mabyn, Trigg, (L) **199**
Old Rectory, The, Marazion, Penwith, **43**
Old Vicarage, The, Perran-ar-worthal, Kerrier, **133**

P

Paradise Park, Hayle, Penwith, **74**
*****Park**, Egloshayle, Trigg, 18, 25, 105, 198, 258
*****Pawton**, St Breock, Pydar, **257**
Pelyn, Lanlivery, Powder, (L.S) 150, **158-9**
Pelynt Vicarage (now Pelynt House), Pelynt, West, **233-4**
Penair, St Clement, Powder, (L) **105**
Penalverne, Penzance, Penwith, 39, **54**
Penarwyn, Tywardreath, Powder, 150, **167**
Penberth (alias Foxstones), St Buryan, Penwith, (L*.H.S) 13, 36, **43**

†**Pencalenick**, St Clement, Powder, (L*.S) 25, 75, **93-5**; *39*
*†**Pencarrow**, Egloshayle, Trigg, EH.II (H*) 23, 185, **191-4**, 261, 296, 299; *79, 80*
†**Pencrebar**, Callington, East, (L) **250**
Pendarves, Camborne, Penwith, (L.H*) 25, 75, **76-7**, 261, 295-6, 298; *31*
*****Pendavey**, Egloshayle, Trigg, **257**
Pendrea, Gulval, Penwith, 39, **43-4**
*†**Pengersick Castle**, St Breock (Breage), Kerrier, (L*.H*) 17, 18, **66-7**, 259; *28*
Pengreep, Gwennap, Kerrier, (S) 75, **78**
Penheale Barton, Egloskerry, East, **209**
Penheale Manor, Egloskerry, East, EH.II 19, 200, 205, **207-9**; *86*
†**Penhellis**, Helston, Kerrier, 57, **74**
Penjerrick, Budock, Kerrier, EH.II (L*) 13, 23, 24, 109, **121-3**; *48*
Penlee House, Tregony, Powder, (L.H) 134, **140-41**
Penlee Memorial Park, Penzance, Penwith, (H*) **44**
*****Penlyne**, St Winnow, Powder, **256**
Penmare, Hayle, Penwith, **74**
Penmere, Budock, Kerrier, 109, **123**
Penmorvah, Budock, Kerrier, (L*) **123**
Penmount, St Clement, Powder, (L) **95**
Pennans, St Creed, Powder, 134, **141-2**; *54*
Penpol House, Phillack, Penwith, 57, **67**
*****Penrice**, St Austell, Powder, (L*.S) 150, **159-60**, 261; *63*
*†**Penrose**, Sithney, Kerrier, (L*.S*) 57, **68-9**, 261; *29*
Pentillie Castle, Pillaton, East, (L.S) 13, 23, 25, 219, **234-6**; *102, 103*
†**Penventon**, Redruth, Penwith, **85**
Penvose, St Tudy, Trigg, (L.S) **198**
Penwarne, Mawnan, Kerrier, (L*) 110, **123-4**
Peterdale, St Johns, East, (L) **253**
Pine Lodge, St Blazey, Powder, 150, **160**
†*Pinetum*, Callington, East, (L) **253**
*****Pinsla**, Cardinham, West, **260**
Pipers Barn, Feock, Powder, (L*) **108**
†**Place House**, Fowey, Powder, (L*.H) 18, 150-51, **160-61**; *64, 65*
Place Manor, St Anthony in Roseland, Powder, (L*.S) 86, 134, **142**
Point Neptune, Fowey, Powder, (L*) 151, **167-8**
Polapit Tamar, Boyton, Stratton, 200, 205, **209**
Polcarne, St Austell, Powder, 150, **168**

Index of Places 335

Poldowrian, Grade-Ruan, Kerrier, (L*.H.S) 74
*Poldrode, St Tudy, Trigg, **259**
Polgwin, Bodmin, Trigg, 185, **198**
Polgwynne, Feock, Powder, (L*) 95-6
†**Polstrong**, Camborne, Penwith, **85**
†**Poltair**, Madron, Penwith, 39, **54-5**
Polvellan (alias Polvethan), Talland, West, (L) 218, **236-7**
Polwhele, St Clement, Powder, (L) 105-6
Polwithen, Penzance, Penwith, **44**
Ponsandane, Gulval, Penwith, **44-5**
*Pool, Menheniot, East, **259**
Port Eliot, St Germans, East, EH.I (L.S) 22, 25, 218, 219, **237-9**, 261; *104, 105*
Porthgwidden (see also Polgwynne), Feock, Powder, (L*.S) **96-7**; *40*
Porthpean House, St Austell, Powder, 150, **162**, 296
Prideaux House, Luxulyan, Powder, (L.H*) 150, **162**
*†**Prideaux Place**, Padstow, Pydar, EH.II (L*.H*) 20, 21, 171, **175-6**, 261; *8, 71, 72, 118*
Priory Bodmin, The, Bodmin, Trigg, (H) 185, **198-9**; *82*
Probus Gardens, Probus, Powder, **142**

Q

Queen Mary Gardens, Falmouth, Kerrier, **124**

R

Raffles (alias White Cottage), Falmouth, Kerrier, **124**
†**Rame Place**, Rame, East, (L*.H) **239**
Restormel Castle, Lanlivery, Powder, (H) 150, **162-3**, **256**; *112*
Restormel House, Lanlivery, Powder, (L) 150, **168**
Richard Foster Bolitho Gardens, Penzance, Penwith, 36
Riviera Gardens (now in Lamorran House), St Just in Roseland, Powder, (L*) **149**
Riviere House, Phillack, Penwith, 57, **69**
Roscadghill, Madron, Penwith, **55**
†**Rosecraddock**, St Cleer, West, (L.S) 218, **239-40**
Rosehill, Falmouth, Kerrier, 24, 109, **125**, 297-8; *49*
Rosehill, Madron, Penwith, **55**
Roseland House, Chacewater, Powder, **108**
Rosemary Cottage, Mylor, Kerrier, **133**
Rosemorran, Gulval, Penwith, (L.H*) **55**
†**Rosemundy**, St Agnes, Pydar, 171, **177**
Rosewarne (now Gladys Holman House), Camborne, Penwith, 75, **78-9**
Rosewarne Horticulture Station, Camborne, Penwith, **79**
Roskrow, St Gluvias, Kerrier, **125-6**; *50*
Rosteague, St Gerrans, Powder, (L.S) 20, 134, **143**, **261**; *55*
Ruanlanihorne Old Rectory, Ruanlanihorne, Powder, (L*.S) **106**

S

St Benet's, Lanivet, Pydar, **199**
St Cadix House, St Veep, West, 151, 168
St Columb Major Rectory, St Columb Major, Pydar, 171, **177**
*St Germans, St Germans, East, 218, **257**
St Just in Penwith Vicarage, St Just, Penwith, (L*.H) **55**
†St Just in Roseland Churchyard, St Just, Powder, (L*.S) 134, **143-4**
St Michael's Mount, St Hilary (Marazion), Penwith, EH.II (L*.H*) **45-6**, 57, 295; *19*
*St Winnow, St Winnow, West, 151, 163, 260
Sanders Hill, Padstow, Pydar, 171, **177-8**; *73*
Sandhill Manor, Calstock, East, 75, 205, **216-17**
Saveock House, Kea, Powder, 106
Scawn Mill, St Keyne, West, (L) 253
Scawns House, Menheniot, East, 240
Scilly, 'Armorel's Cottage', Samson, 33; *14*
Scilly, 'Ladies' Garden', St Mary's, 17, **34**
Scilly, Master Gunner's House, St Mary's, **34-5**
Scilly, Rocky Hill, St Mary's, 29, **35**; *15*
*Scilly, Samson, 261; *14*
Scilly, Steward's House, St Mary's, 29, **35**
Scilly, Tresco Abbey, EH.I, 24, **30-33**, 298-9; *12, 13*
Sconner House, Sheviock, East, (L.S) 219, **240-41**
Scorrier House, Gwennap, Kerrier, (H*) 12, 75, **79-80**
†Skisdon Lodge, St Kew, Trigg, **194**
Southleigh, Kenwyn, St John's, Truro, Powder, 106
Springfield Farm, St Allen, Powder, 108
Stoketon Manor, St Stephen by Saltash, East, (L.S) **241**
Stowe, Kilkampton, Stratton, (L.S) 20, 200, **202-3**, 260; *84*

T

*†**Tehidy Park**, Illogan, Penwith, (L*.S) 22, 25, 75, **80-82**, 261; *32*

Thanckes, Antony, East, 218, 241-2,; *106*
Tintagel Castle, Tintagel, Lesnewth, 17, 34, **179**; *74*
Tolcarne House, St Columb Minor, Pydar, 184
†**Tolroy**, St Erth, Penwith, **69**
Tolvean, Redruth, Penwith, 75, **85**
†**Tonacombe**, Morwenstow, Stratton, (L*.H*.S) 18, 200, **203-4**
Tor House (formerly Crinnis House), Antony, East, 23, 218, **250-51**
Torfrey, Golant (St Sampson), Powder, (L*) 151, **168-9**
Torwalla, Falmouth, Kerrier, **133**
Towan Camellias, Feock, Powder, (L*) **108**
Trago Mills, St Pinnock, West, (L.S) **253**
Trannack House, Madron, Penwith, (H) 37
Trebah, Mawnan, Kerrier, EH.II (L*.S) 13, 109, **126-7**, 299
†**Trebartha Hall**, Northill, East, (L*.H*.S) 21, 25, 134, 205, **209-10**; *87*
*Trebigh, St Ive, East, **260**
Trebrown, St Germans, East, **251**
†**Trebursye**, South Petherwin, East, 205, **210-11**
Tredarvah, Penzance, Penwith, **55-6**
†**Tredethy**, St Mabyn, Trigg, (L) 185, **194**
Tredidon Barton, St Thomas, Launceston, East, (L) 205, **217**
Tredinnick, Veryan, Powder, **149**
†**Tredrea**, Perran-ar-worthal, Kerrier, 75, **127-8**
Tredudwell Manor, Lanteglos by Fowey, West, **169**
Trefusis House, Mylor, Kerrier, (L) **128**, 261
†**Tregeare House**, Egloskerry & Laneast, Trigg, (L) 205, **211**
Tregedna, Budock, Kerrier, **109**
Tregembo, St Hilary, Penwith, **56**
†**Tregenna Castle**, St Ives, Penwith, 36, **46-7**; *20*
Tregenna House (later Michaelstow House), Michaelstow, Trigg, **194-5**
Tregilliowe Farm, Ludgvan, Penwith, **56**
Tregolls House, St Clement, Powder, 86, **97**
Tregonan, St Ewe, Powder, 137
*Tregony, Cuby, Powder, 134, **259**
*†**Tregothnan**, St Michael Penkevil, Powder, EH.II* (L*.S), 22, 23, 25, 86, **97-9**, 260, 299; *41*
Tregrehan, St Blazey, Powder, EH.II 24, 150, **163-4**, 261; *66, 67*
Tregullow, Gwennap, Kerrier, 75, **82-4**; *33, 34*
Tregye, Feock, Powder, **99-100**
Trehane, St Erme, Powder, (S) 24, **100-101**, 296

Trelan, Madron, Penwith, (L*.H) 56
Trelaske, Lewannick, East, (H*) 22, 205, **211-12**; *88*
*†**Trelawne Manor**, Pelynt, West, (L) 21, 25, 218, **242-4**, **261**; *107*
Trelawney, St Austell, Powder, 150, **169**
*****Trelawny**, Altarnun, Lesnewth, 259
Trelean, St Martin in Meneage, Kerrier, (L*.S) 13, **70**
Trelidden, Liskeard, West, (L) 218, **244**
†**Treliske**, Kenwyn, Powder, **106**
Trelissick, Feock, Powder, EH.II (L*.H*.S) 24, 86, **101-2**; *42*
*****Trelowarren**, Mawgan in Meneage, Kerrier, EH.II (L*.S) 25, 57, **70-72**, **260**; *30*
Treloyhan Manor, St Ives, Penwith, 13, **47-8**
*****Treluddra**, Kenwyn, Powder, **260**
Treludick, Egloskerry, Trigg, 200, 205, **217**
Tremarken, St Neot, West, (L.H) 253
*****Trematon Castle**, St Stephen by Saltash, East, (L.H*) 19, 23, 219, **244-5**, **256**; *108*
Trematon Hall, St Stephen by Saltash, East, (L) **251**
Tremayne Cottage, St Tudy, Trigg, 185, **199**
Tremeal Farm, South Petherwin, East, **217**
Tremeer, St Tudy, Trigg, 24, 185, **195-6**, **296**; *81*
Tremorvah, St Clement, Powder, 86, **102-3**
*†**Tremough**, Mabe, Kerrier, 23, **109-10**, **128-9**, **262**
Trenance, Launceston, East, **217**
†**Trenance Gardens**, Newquay, Pydar, 171, **179**
*†**Trenant Park**, Duloe, West, (L) 218, **245**, **262**
Trenarren, St Austell, Powder, (L*) 150, **169**
Trenarth, Constantine, Kerrier, (L*.S) **133**
Treneere Manor, Madron, Penwith, **56**
*****Trengoffe**, Warleggan, West, **262**
†**Trengwainton**, Madron, Penwith, EH.II (L*.H.S) 13, 24, 37, 39, **48-9**, **296**; *21*
Trenowth, Probus, Powder, (L.S*) 134, **149**
Trenython, Tywardreath, Powder, (H*) 150, **164-5**
Trereife, Madron, Penwith, **49**
Trerice, St Allen, Powder, 171, **180**
Tresco Abbey (see under Scilly)
Treskewes Cottage, Stithians, Kerrier, **85**
†**Tresillian House**, Newlyn East, Pydar, 171, **180-81**
Trethawle Farm, Menheniot, East, (L) **253**

Trethill House, Sheviock, East, (L.S) 219, **251**
†*Trevarno*, Sithney, Kerrier, 22, 57, **72-3**, **299**
Trevarrick Hall, St Austell, Powder, 150, **165**
Trevarthian, St Austell, Powder, 150, **169**
*****Trevaunance**, St Agnes, Pydar, **262**
Trevaylor, Gulval, Penwith, (H) **50**
Treveddo, St Columb Minor, Pydar, 171, **184**
Trevegean, Madron, Penwith, **56**
Treverven, St Buryan, Penwith, (L*.H) **50**
*****Trevethoe**, Lelant, Penwith, 25, **50-51**, **262**; *22*
Treviades Gardens, Constantine, Kerrier, (L*.S) **133**
Trevillet, Tintagel, Lesnewth, (L*.S) **181-2**; *75*
Trevillis House, St Pinnock, West, 218, **251**
Trevince, Gwennap, Kerrier, 75, **84**
Trevissome House, Mylor, Kerrier, (L*) **131-2**
Trevorick (part of Carclew), Mylor, Kerrier, (L*.H*) **103**
*†**Trewan Hall**, St Columb Major, Pydar, 171, **182**, **262**; *76*
Trewardale, Blisland, Trigg, (L.H*) **196**
Trewarne (alias Trewane), St Kew, Trigg, (L) 19, 185, **197**
Trewarthenick, Cornelly, Powder, EH.II (L*.S) 22, 134, **144-6**; *56, 57*
Trewhiddle, St Austell, Powder, 150, **165-6**
Trewidden, Madron, Penwith, (L) 13, 36, 37, **51-2**, **298**
Trewin, Sheviock, East, (L) **251-2**
Trewince House, St Gerrans, Powder, (L*) 134, **146**
Trewinnard Manor, St Erth, Penwith, 57, **73**
*****Trewithen**, Probus, Powder, EH.II* 22, 24, 134, **146-8**, **262**, **296**; *58*
Trewollack, St Just in Roseland, Powder, (L*.S) **149**
†**Trewoofe House**, St Buryan, Penwith, (L*.H.S) 25, **52-3**
Treworder Mill, Kenwyn, Powder, (S) **108**
Treworgan, Mawnan, Kerrier, (L*.S) **132**
*†**Treworgey**, St Cleer, West, 218, **245-6**, **262**; *109, 110*
Trewyn Studio, St Ives, Penwith, **53**
†**Trist House** (formerly Veryan Vicarage), Veryan, Powder, (L*) **148**
†**Truthan**, St Erme, Powder, **106-7**; *43*
Tullimaar, Perran-ar-worthal, Kerrier, **130**; *51*
*****Tymberthan** or Temple Park, Lezant, East, **259**

V

Veryan Vicarage (see Trist House)
Victoria Park & Waterfall Gardens, Kenwyn, St George's Truro, Powder, **103**

W

Watergate, St Tudy, Trigg, (L) **197**
Waterloo Villa (later Klymiarvan), St Martin's by Looe, West, (L.H) 218, **247**
Water Meadow, Luxulyan, Powder, **170**
Weath Garden, Helston, Kerrier, **74**
*****Werrington Park**, Werrington, East, EH.II (L.H*) 22, 25, 75, 200, 205, **212-15**, **260**; *Frontispiece, 89, 90*
Westbourne House, Liskeard, West, 218, **247**
Wetherham, St Tudy, Trigg, 185, **199**
White Cottage (see Raffles)
†**Whiteford House**, Stoke Climsland, East, 205, **215-16**
Wivelscombe, St Stephen by Saltash, East, (L.S) **252**
Wodehouse Place, Falmouth, Kerrier, 109, **131**
*†**Wolsdon House**, Antony, East, (L) 218, **252**
Woodland Nursery, Mawgan in Meneage, Kerrier, (L*.S) **74**
*****Woolston**, Poundstock, Lesnewth, **257**
Wynlands, Manaccan, Kerrier, (L*.S) **74**

Y

York House, Penzance, Penwith, **53**

Z

Zoar, Mylor, Kerrier, (L*) **133**

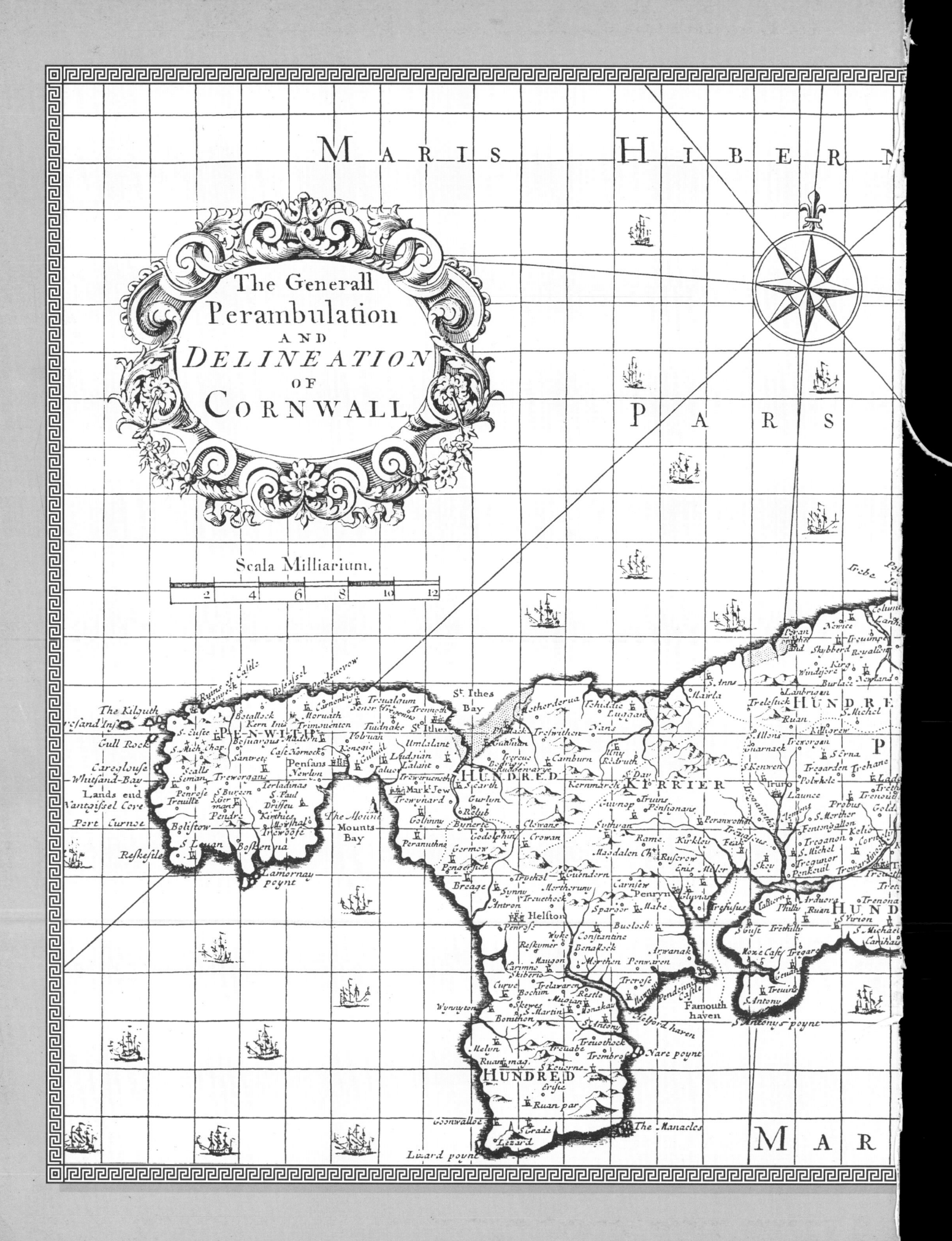

The Generall Perambulation AND *DELINEATION* OF CORNWALL

MARIS HIBERN... PARS

Scala Milliarium.
2 4 6 8 10 12

MAR...

The Kilquth / 'sand Inf / Gull Rock / Careglouse / Whitsand-Bay / Lands end / Vantaissel Cove / Port Curnoe / Reskestle

Ruines of Castle / Bossalsl / Dendenevow / Botallack / S. Euste / Kern Inis / Bessavarus Madron / S. Mich. Chap / Santrete / Scalls / S. Senan / Treworgans / S. Buren / Penrose / Treuille / Sber mans / Pendre / Bolistow / S. Leuan / Bossenua

PEN-WITH

Carnonbigh / Morvath / Trimounten / Tuidnake / Senor Gr. / Trennoch / Pensans / Newlun / Terladinas / S. Paul / Driseu / Kirthies / Morshal / Trewoose / Lamornay poynt

S. Ithes Bay / Tobuan / Renegie / Conhuil / Lelant / Talvec / Treweruenoth / Mark Jew / Trewynard / Gulvn / The Mount / Mounts Bay / Golhinu / Bynerte / Peranuthno / Gormon / Pengerfick / Breage

Lether derua / Phillack Treswithen / Pans / S. Ithes / Guthian / Tegrens Bojethian Rusternary / Camburn R. truth / S. Earth / Kenmarch / Cuvnop / Sythuan / Godolphin / Crowan / Trevthol / Guendern / Synny / Treuethock / Sparger / Mausan / Antron / Helston / Penrose / Wyke / Constantine / Reskymer / Benasieck / Carimno Ibério / Curve / Bochim / Trelavaren / S. Kewne / Wynnyton / Skewes / Bonithon / S. Martin / Melun / Ruan mag / Treuabe / Treuothock / Trembros / HUNDRED / Erisie / Ruan par / Goonwallce / Grade / Lezard / Lizard poynt

Tchidtic Luggan / Mairla / Ruan / S. Michel / Allons Killigrew / Guarnack Treworgan / S. Kenwen Scrna / Truro Polwhele / Launce Probus / Amet S. Morther Fentongallon / Rame Kirkley / Rusbrow / Magdalen Ch / Carnier / Penryn / Mabe / Peranrothan / Enis Miler / Skeu / Buslock / Arwanak / Morthen Penwren / Restle / Harmer / Pendenny Castle / Famouth haven / S. Antonv / Helford haven / S. Antony / Nare poynt / The Manacles

HUNDRED KIRRIER
HUNDRED
HUNDRE... / HUND...